D1083651

Film Noir

Film Noir

*A Comprehensive,
Illustrated Reference
to Movies, Terms
and Persons*

by
MICHAEL L. STEPHENS

McFarland & Company, Inc., Publishers
Jefferson, North Carolina, and London

Frontispiece: Veronica Lake and Alan Ladd in *This Gun for Hire* (Paramount, 1942)

British Library Cataloguing-in-Publication data are available

Library of Congress Cataloguing-in-Publication Data

Stephens, Michael L., 1961–
    Film noir : a comprehensive, illustrated reference to movies,
terms and persons / by Michael L. Stephens.
        p.   cm.
    Includes bibliographical references and index. ∞
    ISBN 0-89950-802-2 (lib. bdg. : 50# alk. paper)
    1. Film noir — United States — Encyclopedias.   I. Title.
PN1995.9.F54S74   1995
791.43'655 — dc20   94-16585
                                                       CIP

Manufactured in the United States of America

McFarland & Company, Inc., Publishers
  Box 611, Jefferson, North Carolina 28640

For my parents,
Ron and Betty Stephens

Introduction

Periodically, the debate arises anew: Is *film noir* truly a genre or merely a style? There should, however, be no question: *Film noir* is a genre in which style plays an important part.

To understand the genre, one must have a sense of its history and the various elements of which it is formed. The term *film noir* seems to have originated in the 1930's. It was used by certain French critics to describe individual films, particularly one or two directed by Marcel Carné, but it was not until the late 1950's that the term was applied (also by the French) to a group of films. These critics were then describing a specific group of American crime movies with contemporary characters that, thematically, had links to "*roman noir*," or the group of hard-boiled crime novels of the thirties and forties.

As the term evolved and was adapted by certain American critics, it came to mean, for some, a particular style: always black and white and "expressionist." Important thematic links were ignored by these critics as was, oddly, the very difficult problem of expressionist elements in other genres. In style, for example, *Son of Frankenstein* (Universal, 1939) is indistinguishable from *Stranger on the Third Floor* (RKO, 1940). In addition, the style of the early *films noirs* is radically different from that of the later *noirs*. The early, extravagant expressionism gave way to a flatter, more "realistic" style in the 1950's.

Thus, as a genre, *film noir* had historical links, stylistically, to German expressionist cinema of the 1920's and, thematically, to the new breed of hard-boiled crime fiction that emerged in the early thirties. The existential themes and character types familiar to *film noir* first appeared in the pulp literature of James M. Cain, Raymond Chandler, Cornell Woolrich, Dashiell Hammet, and others.

Film noir might be described as follows. First, it is a contemporary crime movie in which the characters are corrupt or corruptible. Generally the milieu is urban and middle class. The overall feel is one of repression and fatalism. Finally, style, whether expressed in black and white or color, reinforces these themes. The use of black and white is merely coincidental — nearly all films before 1959 were shot in black and white.

The combined elements of expressionist style and pulp literature themes began to creep into popular American cinema as early as 1927 via Joseph Von Sternberg's *Underworld* (Paramount, 1927). There were early *noir*-like films throughout the thirties, but it took World War II to help kick off the genre. Political and social elements (particularly the general post-war malaise and the beginnings of the collapse of the social structure) found a home in the metaphors of the emerging genre.

Perhaps the problem of defining *film noir* arises in the fact that it emerged gradually and unconsciously — there was no *noir* manifesto. Thus, while certain filmmakers were predisposed to the style and themes of the genre (Fritz Lang, Curtis Bernhardt, Robert Siodmak, Alfred Hitchcock, Henry Hathaway), the majority of *films noirs* were made by studio hacks who appropriated the characteristics of the genre for one or two films. The massive success of the *noirs* released in 1944 (*Double Indemnity* [Paramount, 1944], *Murder, My Sweet* [RKO, 1944], *The Woman in the Window* [RKO, 1944], etc.) kicked off a rash of imitators, both good and bad, that did not begin to subside for well over a decade. An earlier, similar phenomenon occurred with the popularity of a number of Gothic horror films that launched a group of movies in the early thirties. This cycle too lasted a little over a decade.

However one defines the term, there is little question about *film noir's* influence beyond its peak years. *Film noir* has never really gone away, but evolved into new subgenres. And, of course, there is the new breed of self-conscious modern *noirs* that crop up from time to time.

This book is a reference to the genre as a whole — from its beginning to its post-genre classics. One might quibble with certain omissions and inclusions; but the book covers all the agreed-upon classics and most of the lesser known and "B" titles, as well as the related personalities, filmmakers and terms.

Originally, *film noir* was espoused as one of the strongest arguments for the auteur theory by the New Wave/*Cahiers du Cinéma* crowd and their American counterparts in the late fifties; but for many modern critics, the genre had come to symbolize the "genius of the system": that is, emerging from the classic Hollywood studio system, and reaching its creative peak at the height of that system, the genre's artistic success proves that the environment of the system was a nurturing one that encouraged artistic experimentation. Critical data for this book are derived from sources of both theories: the earliest studies of the genre and its creators by Andre Bazin and others, and recent studies of the studio system and the genre by Thomas Schatz and other contemporary Hollywood studio historians. This encyclopedia covers the genre's feature releases, and includes all of the major, many of the minor, and assorted related/off-genre titles. Filmographies, biographical data, credits, and synopses are derived from numerous sources including studio histories, catalogs of releases from the individual studios, and university archives including those of the Southern Methodist University, the University of Texas, and UCLA, and miscellaneous other sources including the Americam Film Institute Library in Los Angeles, California. For sociological/historical background, *Time, Life,* and other periodicals from the era were consulted, along with several book-length studies of Los Angeles, San Francisco, and New York in the 1940s and 1950s, and numerous Hollywood/political histories (particularly those pertaining to the McCarthy Witchhunt which had such a profound impact on many of the genre's creators) of the same era.

The Encyclopedia

Abandoned (Universal, 1949). 78 min.

Producer: Jerry Bresler. Director: Joseph M. Newman. Screenplay: Irwin Gielgud, with additional dialog by William Bowers; based on articles published in the *Los Angeles Mirror*. Director of Photography: William Daniels. Music: Walter Schaff. Art Direction: Bernard Herzbrun and Robert Boyle. Editor: Edward Curtiss.

Cast: Dennis O'Keefe (Mark Sitko); Gale Storm (Paula Considine); Jeff Chandler (Chief McRae); Meg Randall (Dottie Jensen); Raymond Burr (Kerrie); Jeanette Nolan (Major Ross). With: William Page, Sid Tomak, Clifton Young, Bert Conway, Billy Gray.

A young woman, Paula Considine, comes to Los Angeles to find her missing sister. Assisted by friendly newspaperman Mark Sitko, she discovers her sister apparently committed suicide after giving birth to her illegitimate child. Their investigation uncovers a sinister baby stealing racket run by a man named Kerrie.

Abandoned is not a major *film noir*. Its contrived plot relies too heavily on cliches and functions as little more than an exposé of criminal activity and a corrupt city. It is notable chiefly for the excellent cinematography of the great William Daniels. His low-key vision of rain-slick streets creates a surrealistic vision of the city and Los Angeles has rarely appeared more sinister or malevolent. The film is also notable for Raymond Burr's performance in one of his most chilling roles.

Academy Awards

The Academy of Motion Picture Arts and Sciences has always favored dramatic films (particularly those in which the main characters are morally transformed) and epics. Genre films and comedies are rarely awarded Oscars. A survey of the peak years of *film noir* (1944–1956) demonstrates this fact explicitly. In its initial phase, a few of the key films were nominated, but few actually won. Only the most financially successful films were nominated, while equally or more important titles were ignored by the Academy. In 1944 for example, *Double Indemnity* and *Laura* were nominated for several awards while Fritz Lang's *Woman in the Window* and Edward Dmytryk's *Murder, My Sweet*, although box-office hits, were completely ignored. By the fifties, nominations for *films noirs* were rare indeed, with no nominations in 1955 or 1956, the last years of the *noir* cycle.

The following is a list of the nominations and awards given by the Academy to *films noirs* during the genre's peak decade. *Academy Award Winner. **1944:** *Double Indemnity* (Paramount) for Best Picture. Barbara Stanwyck — Best Actress for *Double Indemnity*. Billy Wilder — Best Director for *Double Indemnity*. Raymond Chandler and Billy Wilder — Best Screenplay for *Double Indemnity*. Jay Dratler, Samuel

1

Barbara Stanwyck, Fred MacMurray in *Double Indemnity* (Paramount, 1944).

Hoffenstein and Betty Reinhardt—Best Screenplay for *Laura* (20th Century-Fox). Joseph LaShelle*—Cinematography for *Laura*. Lyle Wheeler and Leonard Fuller—Art Direction for *Laura*. Miklos Rozsa—Best Score for *Double Indemnity*. **1945:** *Mildred Pierce* (Warner Bros.)—Best Picture. Gene Tierney—Best Actress for *Leave Her to Heaven* (20th Century-Fox). Eve Arden—Best Supporting Actress for *Mildred Pierce*. Ann Blyth—Best Supporting Actress for *Mildred Pierce*. Charles G. Booth*—Best Original Screenplay for *House on 92nd Street* (20th Century-Fox). Ronald MacDougall—Best Screenplay for *Mildred Pierce*. Ernest Haller—Cinematography for *Mildred Pierce*. Leon Shamroy*—Best Color Cinematography for *Leave Her to Heaven*. **1946:** Claude Rains—Best Supporting Actor for *Notorious* (RKO). Ethel Barrymore—Best Supporting Actress for *Spiral Staircase* (RKO). Robert Siodmak—Best Director for *The Killers* (Universal). Vladimir Rozner—Best Original Story for *The Dark Mirror* (Universal). Raymond Chandler—Best Original Screenplay for *The Blue Dahlia* (Paramount). Anthony Veillor—Best Screenplay for *The Killers*. Miklos Rozsa—Best Score for *The Killers*. **1947:** *Crossfire* (RKO)—Best Picture. Ronald Colman*—Best Actor for *A Double Life* (Universal). John Garfield—Best Actor for *Body and Soul* (United Artists). Joan Crawford—Best Actress for *Possessed* (Warner Bros.). Thomas Gomez—Best Supporting Actor for *Ride the Pink Horse* (Universal). Gloria Grahame—Best Supporting Actress for *Crossfire*. George Cukor—Best Director for *A Double Life*. Elezar Lipsky—Best Original Story for *Kiss of Death* (20th Century-Fox). Ruth Gordon and Garson Kanin—Best Original Story for *A Double Life*. Richard Murphy—Best Screenplay for *Boomerang!* (20th

Marilyn Maxwell, Kirk Douglas in publicity still for *Champion* (United Artists, 1949).

Century-Fox). John Paxton — Best Screenplay for *Crossfire*. Francis Lyon and Robert Parrish — Editing for *Body and Soul*. Miklos Rozsa* — Best Score for *A Double Life*. **1948:** Barbara Stanwyck — Best Actress for *Sorry, Wrong Number* (Paramount). Claire Trevor* — Best Supporting Actress for *Key Largo* (Warner Bros.). William Daniels — Best Cinematography for *The Naked City* (Universal). Marvin Wald — Best Original Story for *The Naked City*. **1949:** Kirk Douglas — Best Actor for *Champion* (United Artists). Arthur Kennedy — Best Supporting Actor for *Champion*. Virginia Kellogg — Best Original Story for *White Heat* (Warner Bros.). Carl Foreman — Best Screenplay for *Champion*. Franz Planer — Best Cinematography for *Champion*. Dimitri Tiomkin — Best Score for *Champion*. **1950:** *Sunset Boulevard*

(Paramount) — Best Picture. William Holden — Best Actor for *Sunset Boulevard*. Eleanor Parker — Best Actress for *Caged* (Warner Bros.). Gloria Swanson — Best Actress for *Sunset Boulevard*. Sam Jaffe — Best Supporting Actor for *The Asphalt Jungle* (MGM). Erich Von Stroheim — Best Supporting Actor for *Sunset Boulevard*. John Huston — Best Director for *The Asphalt Jungle*. Billy Wilder — Best Director for *Sunset Boulevard*. Billy Wilder*, Charles Brackett and D. M. Marshman, Jr. — Best Story and Screenplay for *Sunset Boulevard*. Ben Maddow and John Huston — Best Screenplay for *The Asphalt Jungle*. Virginia Kellogg and Bernard C. Shoenfeld — Best Screenplay for *Caged*. Harold Rosson — Best Cinematography for *The Asphalt Jungle*. John F. Seitz — Best Cinematography for *Sunset Boulevard*. Hans Dreier*, John Meehan, Sam Comet and Ray Moyer — Best Art Direction for *Sunset Boulevard*. Franz Waxman* — Best Score for *Sunset Boulevard* **1951:** Eleanor Parker — Best Actress for *Detective Story* (Paramount). Lee Grant — Best Supporting Actress for *Detective Story*. Philip Yordan and Robert Wyler — Best Screenplay for *Detective Story*. Billy Wilder, Lesser Samuels and Walter Newman — Best Story and Screenplay for *The Big Carnival* (Paramount). Lyle Wheeler and Leland Fuller — Best Art Direction for *Fourteen Hours* (20th Century-Fox). Lyle Wheeler and John Decuir — Best Art Direction for *The House on Telegraph Hill* (20th Century-Fox). **1952:** Joan Crawford — Best Actress for *Sudden Fear* (RKO). Jack Palance — Best Supporting Actor for *Sudden Fear*. Martin Goldsmith and Jack Leonard — Best Story for *The Narrow Margin* (RKO). Charles B. Lang, Jr. — Best Cinematography for *Sudden Fear*. Herschel Burke Golbert — Best Score for *The Thief* (United Artists). **1953:** Thelma Ritter — Best Supporting Actress for *Pickup on South Street*

(20th Century-Fox). **1954:** Alfred Hitchcock — Best Director for *Rear Window* (Paramount). John Michael Hayes — Best Screenplay for *Rear Window*. Robert Burks — Best Color Cinematography for *Rear Window*.

The Accused (Paramount, 1949). 101 min.

Producer: Hal B. Wallis. Director: William Dieterle. Screenplay: Ketti Frings, based on the novel *Be Still, My Love* by June Truesdell. Director of Photography: Milton Krasner. Sound: Don McKay and Walter Oberst. Music: Victor Young. Art Direction: Hans Dreier and Earl Hedrick. Editor: Warren Low.

Cast: Loretta Young (Wilma Tuttle). Robert Cummings (Warren Ford), Wendell Corey (Lt. Ted Dorgan), Douglas Dick (Bill Perry), Sam Jaffe (Dr. Romley), Suzanne Dalbert (Susan Duval). With: Sara Allgood, Ann Doran, George Armstrong, Bill Perrott, Carol Mathews.

A tale of psychological torment and sexual guilt, *The Accused* gave Loretta Young her best *film noir* role. She stars as a spinsterish young professor of psychology who accidentally kills one of her students, Bill Perry, when he attempts to seduce her. She makes the homicide look like an accidental drowning, but two men, Warren Ford, a lawyer who was also a guardian of the victim, and Ted Dorgan, an investigating detective, become suspicious because of her bizarre behavior. They are both romantically attracted to her and eventually, through their machinations, prove her "innocence."

William Dieterle, the director of *The Accused*, is a sadly neglected master, perhaps because he never developed a series of personal themes in the manner of an *auteur*. Yet, he was a great pictorial stylist and capable of enormous psychological insight. This is true of *The Accused*, a slow, almost lethargic film in which most of the action is internalized. Dieterle makes particularly

Humphrey Bogart, Lizabeth Scott in *Dead Reckoning* (Columbia, 1947).

effective use of dream sequences which are overloaded with Freudian symbolism, but not nearly as surreal as Hitchcock's dream sequences.

While *The Accused* is certainly not a classic, it remains one of the most compelling and consistently entertaining of the late forties' *films noirs*.

Ace in the Hole *see* The Big Carnival

Act of Violence (MGM, 1949). 81 min.
Producer: William H. Wright. Director: Fred F. Zinnemann. Screenplay: Robert L Richards, story by Collier Young. Director of Photography: Robert Surtees. Music: Bronislau Kaper, conducted by Andre Previn. Art Directors: Cedric Gibbons and Hans Peters. Editor: Conrad A. Nervig.
Cast: Van Heflin (Frank R. Enley), Robert Ryan (Joe Parkson), Janet Leigh (Edith Enley), Mary Astor (Pat), Phyllis Thaxter (Ann Sturges), Barry

Kroeger (Johnny). With: Tom Hanlan, Phil Tead, Eddie Waglin, Irene Seidner.

Joe Parkson, a disabled war vet, has traveled to California in search of a man named Frank Enley. Enley, a respected contractor, had betrayed his fellow prison camp inmates in World War II, resulting in their death. Actually, Enley had betrayed their escape plans believing they were futile and would result in their deaths, but the Germans allowed them to go through with it and then shot them as they tried to escape. Parkson was the only survivor and, mentally and physically, scarred by his experiences, he desperately wants revenge. Terrorized by Parkson, Enley confesses to his wife and then flees into the night. He takes refuge with a woman of the evening, Pat, who helps arrange a hired killer to "take care" of Parkson. Enley, however, is overcome with guilt and remorse, intervenes at the last moment, saving

Parkson and resulting in his own death and redemption.

Act of Violence is a neglected classic, a dark and moody film with few redeeming characters. Enley, of course, is a corrupt figure actually guilty of treason, and Parkson is mentally unbalanced, obsessed by his desire for revenge. The female characters are equally corrupt and unnurturing. This madness is rendered, typically, in a cool, detached manner. This was the style of the director Fred F. Zinnemann, a neglected master who specialized in violent, realist, drama. Like Billy Wilder and Robert Siodmak, Zinnemann's roots were in German cinema of the 1920's and, although more commercially oriented than Wilder or Siodmak, he could also be unrelentingly pessimistic. *Act of Violence* is certainly one of his most bitter, cynical films, beautifully photographed and acted, and it deserves renewed interest.

Adams, Gerald Drayson (1904–)

Canadian born screenwriter, Drayson, for many years a literary agent, began writing screenplays in the late forties. His best work dates from this early period and includes several *films noirs*. Among these is one of the toughest Humphrey Bogart *noirs*, *Dead Reckoning*, and Don Siegel's highly entertaining *The Big Steal*.

Adams' style was tough and direct, and his screenplays (almost all written in collaboration) sparkle with brilliant dialog. In the late sixties he co-wrote several Elvis Presley vehicles before retiring.

Filmography: *Dead Reckoning* (Columbia, 1947). *The Big Steal* (RKO, 1949). *Armored Car Robbery* (RKO, 1950). *His Kind of Woman* (RKO, 1951). *Between Midnight and Dawn* (RKO, 1952).

Adler, Jay (1899–1978)

Character actor. Like his younger brother Luther, Jay Adler was a chisel-faced actor who specialized in tough guys of various sorts. His roles were mostly very small and included policemen as well as bad guys. He appeared in some good *films noirs*, generally as a crooked sideman.

Filmography: *Cry Danger* (RKO, 1951). *The Mob* (Columbia, 1951). *Scandal Sheet* (Columbia, 1952). *99 River Street* (United Artists, 1953). *The Long Wait* (United Artists, 1954). *The Big Combo* (Allied Artists, 1955). *Murder Is My Beat* (Allied Artists, 1955). *Crime of Passion* (United Artists, 1957). *Sweet Smell of Success* (United Artists, 1957).

Adler, Luther (1903–1984)

Character actor. Luther Adler, with his brother Jay and sister Stella, was a member of a successful Yiddish stage family. Luther and Stella spent most of their careers on stage. His heavy features made him a natural to play villains, his main character type in the two dozen films he acted in. He appeared in five excellent *films noirs*, always in villainous roles.

Filmography: *Cornered* (RKO, 1945). *House of Strangers* (20th Century-Fox, 1949). *D.O.A.* (United Artists. 1950). *Kiss Tomorrow Goodbye* (Warner Bros., 1950). *M* (Columbia, 1951).

Affair in Trinidad (Columbia, 1952). 98 min.

Producer and Director: Vincent Sherman. Screenplay: Oscar Saul and James Gunn; based on a story by Virginia Upp and Berne Giler. Director of Photography: Joseph Waller. Music: George Duning. Editor: Gene Havlick.

Cast: Rita Hayworth (Chris Emery); Glenn Ford (Steve Emery); Alexander Scourby (Max Fabian); Valerie Bettis (Veronica); Torin Thatcher (Inspector Smythe); Howard Wendell (Anderson).

A failed attempt to recapture the magic of *Gilda* (Columbia, 1946), an *Affair in Trinidad*, is, nevertheless, an

Torin Thatcher (left) and Rita Hayworth from *Affair in Trinidad* (Columbia, 1952).

enjoyable little film. The story is simple: Steve Emery arrives in Trinidad in search of the killer of his brother. He suspects his brother's widow, Chris Emery, a beautiful nightclub entertainer, had a hand in the murder, but, in fact, she is working undercover for the local police. Despite their mutual distrust, they eventually solve the crime.

In many ways, *Affair in Trinidad* was an attempt to remake *Gilda*, but with more palatable characters. The same thing was done earlier when the stars of *Out of the Past* (RKO, 1947), Robert Mitchum and Jane Greer, were reteamed in *The Big Steal* (RKO, 1949). Indeed, Greer's character in the latter and Hayworth's in this film are similar. At first, to the male character in each film, both women seem to be guilty, but, in the end, turn out to be innocent.

Affair in Trinidad was a moderate success on its initial release, perhaps because of the exotic locations and the popularity of its two stars. It has since been remembered as little more than a pale imitation of a classic.

Agar, John T. (1921–)
Rugged leading man, once married to Shirley Temple. A big star of B-movies in the late forties and early fifties. He starred mainly in action pictures. Agar co-starred in one minor *film noir*, playing a variation of his good-guy character.

Filmography: *Woman on Pier 13* (RKO, 1949).

Ahern, Lloyd (1909–)
Staff cinematographer for 20th Century-Fox. Ahern was an adaptable cinematographer who worked on a number of important films. He had an agreeable, if not particularly, distinguishable style. He was the director of

photography for two interesting *films noirs*, both of which were directed by two strong-willed artists whose own style dominated the films.

Filmography: *The Brasher Doubloon* (20th Century–Fox, 1947). *Cry of the City* (20th Century–Fox, 1948).

Alda, Robert (Alfonso Giuseppe Giovanni Roberto D'Abruzzo) (1914–1986)

Actor. Robert Alda is probably best known as the father of actor Alan Alda and for his role as George Gershwin in the bioptic *Rhapsody in Blue* (Warner Bros., 1945). Although he was a very good actor, Alda never became a full-fledged star. He co-starred in two minor *films noirs*, but his easygoing personality was ill-suited to the genre.

Filmography: *The Man I Love* (Warner Bros., 1946). *Nora Prentiss* (Warner Bros., 1947).

Aldrich, Robert (1918–1983)

Director. A larger than life character, Robert Aldrich was a Hollywood maverick. He had a special affection for larger than life characters, both male and female, in his movies. He was not embarrassed by strong emotions or excessive violence and his films could be both crass and vulgar. A strong believer in an all-American style of punchy, dramatic entertainment, he was at his best with thrillers and action films like his late *noir* masterpiece *Kiss Me Deadly*, the great war film *The Dirty Dozen* (MGM, 1969), and *Ulzana's Raid* (Universal, 1970), a superior western.

Aldrich came from a family of bankers. He studied economics at university before deciding on a career in motion pictures. Beginning in the early forties, he worked his way up through the industry, eventually becoming an assistant director to a diverse group of filmmakers including Jean Renoir, Joseph Losey and William Wellman. His career as a director began in television and success in that medium lead naturally back to film, where in 1955,

he completed his first *film noir*, *World for Ransom*. He made use of many of his television collaborators including cameraman Joseph Biroc, an important talent. A lively, fast-moving and very entertaining little *noir*, the film has a visceral effect and despite its tiny budget, it demonstrated Aldrich's qualities as a film director. It was a box-office hit and lead directly to Aldrich's masterpiece, the *film noir* classic *Kiss Me Deadly*.

Kiss Me Deadly is certainly one of the great *noir* films, although it was not a success on its initial release. Loosely based on the Mickey Spillane novel of the same title, the film is crisply photographed by the brilliant cinematographer Ernest Laszlo. The film is rich in visual and aural textures and contains excellent performances by Ralph Meeker (as Mike Hammer) and the rest of its cast. The film mixes eroticism with violence in a way that was shocking and new in the mid fifties. Furthermore, the film gradually takes on a nightmarish quality as the gritty California reality is left behind and emerges as a metaphor of the pervasive paranoia, even managing to make a statement about the dangers of the Cold War.

The Big Knife followed *Kiss Me Deadly*. Although not as great a film as its predecessor, it remains one of the most powerful evocations of Hollywood corruption. The film is based on a play by Clifford Odets and like so many of the films based on his plays, it is a bit static and too talky.

Unfortunately, like its predecessor, *The Big Knife* was also a box-office failure and Aldrich was fired from his next film *The Garment Jungle* before it was finished. It proved to be his last *film noir*. Later in his career he returned to some of the same themes. *Hustle*, for example, is generally considered an admirable, if failed, attempt to return to the themes he had explored in his *films noirs*.

Robert Aldrich was a richly varied

George Montgomery in *The Brasher Doubloon* (20th Century — Fox, 1947).

talent, a kind of later version of Howard Hawks. Like Hawks, he moved easily and successfully through various genres. He excelled at westerns and action films of various types and he created one of the most unique of all *films noirs*. At least for that one film, *Kiss Me Deadly*, Robert Aldrich deserves his reputation as one of late *noir's* greatest talents.

Filmography: *World for Ransom* (Allied Artists, 1954). *Kiss Me Deadly* (United Artists, 1955). *The Big Knife* (United Artists, 1956). *The Garment Jungle* (uncredited co-direction) (Columbia, 1957). *Hustle* (Paramount, 1975).

All the King's Men (Columbia, 1949). 109 min.

Producer and Director: Robert Rossen. Screenplay: Robert Rossen, based on the novel by Robert Penn Warren. Director of Photography: Burnett Guffey. Music: Louis Gruenberg. Art Director: Sturges Carne. Editor: Viola Lawrence.

Cast: Broderick Crawford (Willie Stark), John Derek (Tom Stark), Jo-anne Dru (Ann Stanton), John Ireland (Jack Burchem), Sheppard Strudnick (Adam Stanton). With: Ralph Dumke, Anne Seymour, Katherine Warren, Raymond Greenleaf.

Willie Stark, an honest man from a small town, works his way up through various political offices until he becomes governor, but power corrupts him, and he ruins his life and the lives of those around him before he is assassinated.

Robert Rossen's version of Robert Penn Warren's novel is a classic — an archetypal American political melodrama based on the real life of Louisiana governor Huey Long. Its style is strongly *noir*, yet, like Elia Kazan's *On the Waterfront* (Columbia, 1954), its concentration on political themes is

Cornel Wilde, Ted DeCorsia in *The Big Combo* **(Allied Artists Corporation, 1955).**

alien to the genre. It proves, as does Kazan's movie, that mere style does not determine whether a picture is *film noir* or not, but rather an integration of style and themes.

Allen, Lewis (1905–1976)

Director. A once promising director, Lewis Allen never lived up to his early reputation. His best known film is *The Uninvited* (Paramount, 1944), a great ghost story. The film is an excellent example of Allen's melancholy lighting and graciously fluid camera work. These are also technical characteristics of his three *film noir* titles. Unfortunately, the screenplays are not up to the standard of this great film, but they have their moments. *Appointment with Danger* and *Chicago Deadline* are two of the lesser known Alan Ladd *noirs*. *Suddenly* was made with a low budget and starred Frank Sinatra as a psychotic assassin. It holds up well today

and remains, with *The Uninvited*, one of Lewis Allen's best films.

Filmography: *Chicago Deadline* (Paramount, 1949). *Appointment with Danger* (Paramount, 1951). *Suddenly* (United Artists, 1954).

Allied Artists Corporation

A second-features production and releasing company, Allied Artists was one of several such companies that competed with the "Big Seven" (MGM, Paramount, Columbia, Universal, 20th Century–Fox, RKO, Warner Bros.) in the thirties and forties. Its policy was to put out "second rate" material through its subsidiary Monogram Pictures Corporation, although it is difficult to tell the difference between the product quality of the two companies. Budgets were minimal and production values poor, but the studio provided a home for talent on their way up or down, or talent that was too individualistic to survive the big studios. Talented directors like Joseph H. Lewis, Sam Fuller, Robert Aldrich, Phil Karlson, and Edgar Ulmer all made important *films noirs* for the studio.

Releases: *Southside 1-1000* (1950). *Cry Vengeance* (1954). *World for Ransom* (1954). *Loophole* (1954). *The Big Combo* (1955). *The Gangster* (1955). *Murder Is My Beat* (1955). *The Phenix City Story* (1955). *The Naked Kiss* (1964).

Alonzo, John (1934–)

Cinematographer. Alonzo is one of the great contemporary cinematographers. His work on *Vanishing Point* (Columbia, 1971), *Lady Sings the Blues* (United Artists, 1972), and *Close Encounters of the Third Kind* (Universal, 1977) are among the outstanding and innovative examples of color cinematography in modern American cinema. His cinematography for Roman Polansky's *Chinatown* is a provocative interpretation of black and white *noir* photography in color.

Filmography: *Chinatown* (Paramount, 1974). *Farewell, My Lovely* (Avco-Embassy, 1975).

Alton, John (1901–)

Hungarian born cinematographer, in Hollywood from 1924. The author of a number of books on cinematography, Alton was equally at home working in color or black and white, but he excelled in the latter. One of the most prolific *noir* cinematographers, his highly stylized photography showed an unambiguous debt to German expressionism, which he had absorbed as a young man. Alton was equally at home in the studio or on location, and he is one of the few *noir* cinematographers whose exterior work can be compared favorably with his studio work: his location photography exploits contrasts between sunlit scenes and dark shadows. Like the best *noir* photograph, Alton's work can often be seen as a metaphor. This is particularly true in the low budget masterpiece *The Big Combo* (directed by Joseph H. Lewis) where Alton's photography starkly counterpoints the film's perverse, violent sexuality. John Alton is clearly a major figure in *film noir*.

Filmography: *The Pretender* (Republic, 1947). *Canon City* (Eagle-Lion, 1948). *Hollow Triumph* (Eagle-Lion, 1948). *Raw Deal* (Eagle-Lion, 1948). *T-Men* (Eagle-Lion, 1948). *Border Incident* (MGM, 1949). *The Crooked Way* (United Artists, 1949) *Mystery Street* (MGM, 1950). *He Walked By Night* (Eagle-Lion, 1951). *Talk About a Stranger* (MGM, 1952). *I, the Jury* (United Artists, 1953). *Witness to Murder* (United Artists, 1954). *The Big Combo* (Allied Artists, 1955).

Ambler, Eric (1909–)

British novelist and screenwriter. Although he is not as well known as his contemporary Grahame Greene, Eric Ambler is one of the great British espionage and adventure novelists of his generation. Like Greene, Ambler's work can stand on its own as literature. Many of his novels have been adapted for the screen and television including two unique *films noirs*. Both are important in the early development of the genre, although his style of exoticism was quickly abandoned in favor of the realist style of American novelists.

Filmography: *Journey into Fear* (RKO, 1943). *The Mask of Dimitrios* (Warner Bros., 1944).

Ames, Leon (Leon Wycoff) (1903–)

Character actor. Ames had a long and successful career in motion pictures and television, generally playing variations of the kindly man next door. He appeared in small roles in several good *films noirs* including the classic version of James M. Cain's *The Postman Always Rings Twice*.

Filmography: *The Postman Always Rings Twice* (MGM, 1946). *Lady in the Lake* (MGM, 1946). *Scene of the Crime* (MGM, 1949). *Angel Face* (RKO, 1953).

Joseph Cotten sets off on the *Journey into Fear* (RKO, 1943).

Ames, Preston (1905–1983)

Production designer. Ames is associated mainly with the glossy, color musicals of MGM's golden age. Among his more famous production designs were those for *An American in Paris* (MGM, 1951) and *Gigi* (MGM, 1958). Although he specialized in the pseudo-impressionist style of the two films above, he also contributed set designs for several important black and white films including Robert Montgomery's *Lady in the Lake*, which demonstrates a more restrained, realist style. It is his only *noir* title.

Filmography: *Lady in the Lake*. (MGM, 1947)

Amfitheotrof, Daniele (1901–1983)

Russian born composer, in Hollywood from 1938. Daniele Amfitheotrof contributed scores for many films. He was prolific and adaptable, but seemed to specialize in mysteries and suspense films. He had a rather dour, Russian romantic quality to his music. Few of the films he worked on, however, are outstanding.

Filmography: *Suspense* (Monogram, 1946). *House of Stranger* (20th Century-Fox, 1949). *Backfire* (Warner Bros., 1950). *The Capture* (RKO, 1950). *The Damned Don't Cry* (Warner Bros., 1950). *Side Street* (MGM, 1950). *The Big Heat* (Columbia, 1954) *Human Desire* (Columbia, 1954).

Amnesia

Surprisingly, amnesia is a recurrent theme in *film noir*. It was a convenient plot device initially, but it became a way to create an "innocent" character without a past of corruption: the victim of amnesia uncovers a world of corruption as he/she regains memory. The first *film noir* to exploit this theme was

Robert Montgomery, Claire Trevor in *Lady in the Lake* (MGM, 1947).

Street of Chance (Paramount, 1942), based on a story by Cornell Woolrich. The story concerns a man who has an accident at work, returns home and is told by his wife that he has been missing for a year. Over the course of the film he uncovers a series of events that could endanger his and his family's lives. *Fear in the Night* (Paramount, 1947), is also based on a Woolrich story. It concerns a man who discovers his dream of committing murder might, in fact, be a reality. The element of a hidden psychological perversion is common

Robert Mitchum, Jean Simmons in *Angel Face* (RKO, 1953).

almost operatic extreme. Diane Tremayne, as portrayed by Jean Simmons (here cast against type) is the ultimate *femme-fatale*: spoiled and beautiful, she will stop at nothing to get her way. Her hatred of her stepmother and her overwhelming greed have turned her into a self-destructive monster, and ultimately she destroys all those who stand in her way. Robert Mitchum, once again, portrays the victim of the predatory female; his own uncontrollable lust for her traps him in an inescapable web of madness and murder. Yet, although guilty of no crime himself, he is powerless to escape. Indeed, one might say that Jessup is a willing victim.

While not as well known as *Laura* (20th Century–Fox, 1944), this Preminger *film noir* is more typical of the genre. It is directed with a visual flair, and its sets, designed by the brilliant art director, Caroll Clarke, are cluttered and claustrophobic, echoing Diane Tremayne's own confusion and mental instability. Frank Nugent's screenplay, in collaboration with Oscar Millar, which marked a distinct departure for the great screenwriter (who is best known for his screenplays for John Ford), is one of the best studies of psychological perversion in American commercial film. Altogether, *Angel Face* is a classic of the genre and one of Otto Preminger's best films.

Anhalt, Edna (1914–) and **Edward** (1914–)

Husband and wife screenwriters. The Anhalts co-wrote a number of intellectually ambitious screenplays which generally fall short of their intentions. Nevertheless, they did write one of the more unique *films noirs*, *Panic in the Streets*, the story of the attempt to stop a potentially devastating virus before it enters the general population. They also wrote *The Sniper*, the last *film noir* directed by Edward Dmytryk.

Filmography: *Panic in the Streets* (20th Century–Fox, 1950). *The Sniper* (Columbia, 1952).

Another Man's Poison (United Artists, 1952). 88 min.

Producer: Daniel M. Angel. Executive Producer: Douglas Fairbanks, Jr. Director: Irving Rapper. Screenplay: Val Guest, based on the play *Deadlock* by Leslie Sands. Director of Photography: Robert Krasner. Music: Paul Sawtell. Editor: Gordon Hales.

Cast: Bette Davis (Janet Frobischer), Gary Merrill (George Bates), Anthony Steel (Larry Stevens), Emylyn Williams (Dr. Henderson). With: Barbara Murray and Reginald Beckwith.

A female mystery writer kills her husband and is then blackmailed by a criminal on the run.

A British *film noir*? Well, yes and no. In fact, *Another Man's Poison* is set entirely in Great Britain and Bette Davis speaks with a thick, rather unconvincing English accent. Yet the screenplay by the brilliant British screenwriter Val Guest is moody and imbued with a sense of inevitable tragedy. Director Irving Rapper gives the film an appropriate sense of gloom and manages to convey the character's sense of mental alienation. Yet, the source material, a West End play, is thoroughly in the tradition of British mystery genre and the film balances uneasily between *film noir* and conventional theatrical tragedy.

Nevertheless, despite its European source and setting, the film is very much in the *noir* tradition . It is similar in some ways to *Night and the City* (20th Century–Fox, 1950), the classic *film noir* also set in London. The same sense of fatalism pervades both films. *Another Man's Poison* is unexpectedly unreserved for a British film, with a strong performance by Davis and her off-screen husband Gary Merrill as the blackmailer.

However, despite some favorable critical notice, the film was not a box-office hit. It remains a curiosity, an example of the influence and impact *film noir* had on European cinema in the fifties.

Anthiel, George (1900–1959)

Composer. Anthiel is an interesting, if all but forgotten, composer and concert pianist from the first half of the twentieth century. In the 1920's, he was one of the most active and famous American ex-patriots in Paris, where he was associated with the surrealists. His most famous concert piece, the *Concerto for Two Typewriters and Orchestra*, dates from this period. His film scores are slightly modernist and polytonal and rooted in American folk music and jazz. He worked mainly on minor films, including three *films noirs*.

Filmography: *Knock on Any Door* (Columbia, 1949). *House by the River* (Republic, 1950). *The Sniper* (Columbia, 1952).

Appointment with a Shadow (Universal, 1958). 73 min.

Producer: Howie Horwitz. Director: Richard Carlson. Screenplay: Alec Coppel and Norman Jolley, story by Hugh Pentecost. Director of Photography: William E. Snyder. Music: Joseph Gershenson. Editor: Darrell Duning.

Cast: George Nader (Paul Baxter), Joanna Moore (Penny), Brian Keith (Lt. Spencer), Virginia Field (Florence Knapp), Frank Dekova (Dutch Hayden), Stephen Chase (Sam Crewe).

Appointment with a Shadow is a very minor *film noir*. The story, which takes place in a single day, concerns an alcoholic reporter, Paul Baxter, who puts his alcoholism behind him and makes a professional comeback when he is present when a notorious criminal is apprehended, and he realizes that the wrong man has been shot by the police when the real fugitive that he was mistaken for engineers an escape.

The film is essentially a character

Left to right: Joanna Moore, Brian Keith, George Nader from *Appointment with a Shadow* **(Universal, 1958).**

study, a story of personal redemption. The crime element is played down, and the story is rather stagnant and unconvincing. It is not a particularly memorable film, although its female lead, Joanna Moore (a star of "B" movies in the late fifties), is always good to watch.

Appointment with Danger (Paramount, 1951). 89 min.

Producer: Robert Fellows. Director: Lewis Allen. Screenplay: John F. Seitz. Music: Victor Young. Art Directors: Hans Dreier and Albert Nozaki. Editor: Leroy Stone.

Cast: Alan Ladd (Al Goddard), Phyllis Calvert (Sister Augustine), Paul Stewart (Earl Boettiger), Jan Sterling (Dodie), Jack Webb (Joe Regas), Henry Morgan (George Soderquist). With: David Wolfe, Dan Ross, Paul Lees, Geraldine Wall, Leo Cronin.

An unsuccessful attempt to recapture the success of the earlier *Chicago Deadline* (Paramount, 1949). Like this earlier film directed by Lewis Allen, *Appointment with Danger* was the last *film noir* to star Alan Ladd. He plays a postal detective sent to investigate the murder of another detective and, in the process of his investigation, uncovers a scheme to defraud the post office of millions of dollars.

A rather conventional mystery/thriller, the film lacks the corrosiveness of *The Glass Key* (Paramount, 1941), and *The Blue Dahlia* (Paramount, 1946), the two most important Ladd *noirs*. The problem here is with an inadequate script which relies on cliche dialog and scenes. Yet, the director, Lewis Allen, was capable of brilliant work, and even here manages to rise above the mediocrity of the script with a few good scenes. Sadly, while Alan Ladd made several more excellent films, Lewis Allen's career went into a rapid decline despite his unquestionable talent.

Armored Car Robbery (RKO, 1950). 67 min.

Producer: Harold Schlom. Director: Richard Fleischer. Screenplay: Earl Felton and Gerald Drayson Adams, story by Robert Angus and Robert Leeds. Director of Photography: Guy Roe. Music: Roy Webb. Music Director: Constantin Bakaleinikoff. Art Directors: Albert S. D'Agostino and Ralph Berger. Editor: Desmond Marquette.

Cast: Charles McGraw (Cordell), Adele Jergens (Yvonne), William Talman (Dave Purvis), Steve Brodie (Al Mapes), Gene Evans (Ace Foster). With: Annie O'Neal, Barry Brooks, Linda Johnson, Carl Saxe.

An unpretentious caper film, *Armored Car Robbery* is one of the best "B" noirs. As the title suggests, the story is simple and direct. A group of criminals plan and execute an armored car robbery while a police detective, against all odds, brings the criminals to justice. Like *The Asphalt Jungle* (MGM, 1950) and *The Killing* (United Artists, 1956), much of the plot is devoted to the planning of the crime, although here the aftermath of the crime and its rather predictable disastrous consequences for the criminals are explored in some detail.

While *Armored Car Robbery* is a less pretentious film than *The Asphalt Jungle* and *The Killing*, it does have the visual style of *film noir*: enormous contrasts between shadows and light and extravagant camera angles. Director Richard Fleischer, one of the best "B" directors, keeps the action moving and the screenplay rarely resorts to cliches. The performances are tough, hardboiled and generally excellent. And the score, by Roy Webb, is better than average.

Armstrong, Charlotte (1909–)

Novelist and short-story writer. Armstrong was a popular novelist whose work was occasionally adapted for the screen. Both of the *films noirs* based on her work are unique contributions to the genre.

Filmography: *The Unsuspected* (based on her novel), (Warner Bros., 1947). *Talk About a Stranger* (based on her short story) (MGM, 1952).

The Asphalt Jungle (MGM, 1950). 112 min.

Producer: Arthur Hornblow, Jr. Director: John Huston. Screenplay: Ben Maddow and John Huston, based on the novel by W. R. Burnett. Director of Photography: Harold Rosson. Music: Miklos Rozsa. Art Directors: Cedric Gibbons and Randall Duell. Editor: George Bremler.

Cast: Sterling Hayden (Dix Handley), Louis Calhern (Alonzo D. Emmerich), Jean Hagen (Doll Conovan), James Whitmore (Gus Minissi), Sam Jaffe (Doc Riedenschneider), Marilyn Monroe (Angela Phinlay). With: John McIntyre, Marc Lawrence, Barry Kelly, Anthony Caruso.

John Huston's brooding tale of a jewelry heist gone wrong is one of *film noir's* enduring classics and one of cinema's outstanding caper films. Huston managed to assimilate seemingly disparate styles to create a moody meditation that remains a cynical masterpiece about the underbelly of American society.

An ingenious jewel robbery is planned by ex-con Doc Riedenschneider. A gentle, vulnerable and brilliant criminal, he hooks up with a crooked lawyer, Alonzo D. Emmerich, to give him financial backing. The robbery team he brings together includes an expert safecracker (Anthony Caruso), a tough strong arm (Sterling Hayden), and a getaway driver (James Whitmore). Unanticipated difficulties arise partially caused by the crooked lawyer and by each individual's own greed and corruption.

Sam Jaffe (center) sells the caper in *The Asphalt Jungle* (MGM, 1950).

Sterling Hayden, Anthony Caruso, Sam Jaffe in *The Asphalt Jungle*.

Eventually, after the caper has been pulled, the whole operation collapses resulting in everyone's capture or death.

Huston combined documentary style with controlled studio techniques to create a bleak, cold portrait of the criminal underworld. Harold Rossen's clever cinematography recalls the work of depression-era still photographs. In fact, the plot, which is quite standard, is secondary to the overall atmosphere and cinematic techniques.

The performances are superb all around. Each character has a real identity and is not merely a "type." Jaffe, as the mastermind, for example, has a weakness for young girls. This turns out to be a fatal flaw. Toward the end of the film while hiding out in a roadhouse he gives a handful of nickels to a teenage girl so that she can play the juke box and he can watch her dance. He is entranced, unable to move, an easy capture for the cops who are closing in on him.

In fact, sexuality, as in all true *film noir*, plays an important, subversive role in the plot. This is particularly true of Louis Calhern's scenes with Marilyn Monroe as his mistress. The luscious Monroe is a voluptuous tease, always promising but never delivering the goods. Her all too brief time on camera is some of the most memorable in the film.

Finally, one cannot overlook the extraordinary performances of Sterling Hayden and Jean Hagen as Doll. The couple is the moral center of this corrupt universe, which should demonstrate further how truly corrupt and immoral the characters in this film are. Hayden's performance is typically stoic, a plus for the character he plays.

The Asphalt Jungle is a portrait of a savage and cruel destiny. The characters are doomed. They all sense it, but they also know there is no way out.

Astor, Mary (Lucille Langehanke) (1906–1987)

Actress. Deceptively quiet spoken and demure on screen, Astor was one of the "wild women" of Hollywood's golden age, known for her passionate affairs with men like the playwright George S. Kaufman.

Astor's film career began in the twenties. She was a major star of the late silent era, and with the coming of sound, took on character roles. She played a variety of good girls and working women in dozens of films in the thirties and forties, but is probably best known for her wicked portrait of feminine evil in the early *film noir* classic *The Maltese Falcon*. The role is a seminal *femme-fatale*. She played a variation of the *femme-fatale* in her other *noir*, *Act of Violence*, an equally compelling, but less well known performance.

Filmography: *The Maltese Falcon* (Warner Bros., 1941). *Act of Violence* (MGM, 1949).

Auer, John H. (1909–1975)

Director. Auer is one of the important "B" movie directors, making the majority of his films for Republic studios. Unlike most of Republic's directors, Auer did not make westerns, but concentrated on contemporary themes. Of his two *film noir* titles, *The City That Never Sleeps* is the best. It is a peculiar, dark film with an assortment of downtrodden, corrupt characters.

Filmography: *The City That Never Sleeps* (Republic, 1953). *Hell's Half Acre* (Republic, 1954).

Baby Face Nelson (United Artists, 1957). 85 min.

Producer: Al Zimbalist. Director: Don Siegel. Screenplay: Daniel Mainwaring, story by Robert Adler. Director of Photography: Hal Mohr. Music: Van Alexander. Art Director: David Milton. Editor: Leon Barsche.

Cast: Mickey Rooney (Lester "Baby Face Nelson" Gillis), Carolyn Jones (Sue), Sir Cedric Hardewick (Don Saunders), Leo Gordon (John Dillinger), Ted DeCorsia (Rocco), Jack Elam

(Fatso). With: Emile Meyer, Debbs Greer, Bob Osterloh, Dick Crockett.

After his release from prison, a two-bit hood, Lester Gillis (known to his friends as "Baby Face Nelson"), begins a violent, murderous career with his girlfriend (and later wife) Sue at his side.

Ferocious and crude, the low-budget *Baby Face Nelson* has little to do with the real life criminal on whom it is based, but is a heightened portrait of the imagined criminal underworld. Despite its low budget, the film has an undeniable artistry. Like all of Don Siegel's films, the movie has a visceral power and kinetic energy. Siegel substitutes violence for subtlety, making him a strikingly modern filmmaker. *Baby Face Nelson* is his most violent film of the 1950's and it points the way to such later Siegel-directed classics as *Dirty Harry* (Warner Bros.. 1970), which continued the *noir* tradition into the contemporary age.

Style, however, is not the only element which separates *Baby Face Nelson* from the run-of-the-mill gangster film. The film's treatment of the characters (indeed of society as a whole) is less than generous: no one is innocent. This, of course, is one of *noir*'s major themes.

The screen writer, Daniel Mainwaring, under the pseudonym Geoffrey Homes, was the author of *Out of the Past* (RKO, 1947), one of the most significant *films noirs*. While *Baby Face Nelson* is not on the level of that important film, it is very well written.

Finally, the performance of Mickey Rooney in the title role cannot be overlooked. He is surprisingly intense, even vicious and brings an almost palpable cruelty to his portrayal of the notorious criminal.

Of course, *Baby Face Nelson* is not a major film; but in lieu of what its director would achieve, it is an important one.

Bacall, Lauren (Betty Jane Perskey) (1924–)

Bacall was a nineteen-year-old model when director Howard Hawks saw her photograph on the cover of *Harper's Bazaar* and signed her to a contract. She made her screen debut in Hawk's *To Have and Have Not* (Warner Bros., 1944), making an impression on both the public and her costar Humphrey Bogart, who fell in love with her and married her shortly thereafter. The chemistry of Bogart-Bacall was magic at the box-office and they co-starred in three consecutive hits, all major *films noirs*. All of Bacall's roles were modeled on the character she played in her debut: gutsy, tough and independent.

Filmography: *The Big Sleep* (Warner Bros., 1946). *Dark Passage* (Warner Bros., 1947). *Key Largo* (Warner Bros., 1948).

Backfire (Warner Bros., 1950). 91 min. Producer and Director: Vincent Sherman. Screenplay: Larry Marcus, Ivan Guff and Ben Roberts, story by Larry Marcus. Director of Photography: Carl Guthrie. Music: Daniele Amfitheotrof. Editor: Folmer Blangsted. Cast: Virginia Mayo (Julie Benson), Gordon MacRae (Bob Corey), Edmond O'Brien (Steve Connolly), Ed Begley (Captain Garcia), Viveca Linfors (Lysa Randolph), Dane Clark (Ben Arno).

One of two *films noirs* directed by Vincent Sherman, a good director of "B" movies, *Backfire* is probably the best. Gordon MacRae stars as a war veteran who, while searching for a missing friend, finds a twisting path of violence and uncovers a world of official corruption.

One of several *films noirs* in which the main character is a war veteran, *Backfire* is more typical of "B" movies: violence and action are substituted for metaphor and subtlety. Still, it is a surprisingly good film, reasonably well directed (although, not particularly inventive), and well acted by a second-string cast. Virginia Mayo, whose star

Left to right: Lauren Bacall, John Ridgeley and Humphrey Bogart from *The Big Sleep* **(Warner Bros., 1946).**

had dimmed considerably, is particularly notable as the girl who helps the veteran.

Backfire is a minor film, but it is well made and watchable, more than can be said for many similar productions.

Backus, Jim (1913–)

Burly character actor and comedian, Backus is best known as the voice of cartoon character Mr. Magoo and as the millionaire castaway on television's *Gilligan's Island*. He also played in small roles in a couple of *films noirs*, generally in a variation of his surly character.

Filmography: *His Kind of Woman* (RKO, 1951). *Angel Face* (RKO, 1953).

Bakaleinikoff, Constantin (1898–1966)

Composer and music director, with RKO 1941–1952. Bakaleinikoff was one

of the finest film composers and music arrangers of his time. His association with RKO was distinguished by many excellent scores, particularly for *films noirs*. His younger brother Mischa, was also a busy film composer.

Filmography: *Notorious* (RKO, 1946). *Born to Kill* (RKO, 1947). *The Set-Up* (RKO, 1949). *The Racket* (RKO, 1951). *Angel Face* (RKO, 1953).

Ball, Lucille (1910–1991)

Before her success as a television comedienne, Lucille Ball was a contract actress for RKO. Her career at the studio began in the thirties but, despite many attempts, she never became a full-fledged star. Except as the lead in some minor comedies, Ball mainly played second female lead in musicals and melodramas. She also played in two *films noirs* in the mid-forties including

Vincent Price, Gene Tierney in *Laura* (20th Century-Fox, 1951).

the minor classic, *The Dark Corner*, but she did not develop into a *noir* icon.

Filmography: *The Dark Corner* (20th Century-Fox, 1946). *Lured* (United Artists, 1947).

Ballard, Lucien (1908–)

Cinematographer. A distinguished cinematographer, Ballard's career began in the thirties and stretches over four decades. His filmography includes many fine films of various genres. Many of these were directed by filmmakers with a strong visual style and it is debatable how important Ballard's contributions were to these films. Nevertheless, he worked on several of the most important *films noirs* and his dreamy, almost surreal style had a profound influence on the look of the genre.

Filmography: *Berlin Express* (RKO, 1948). *Laura* (co-photographed) (20th Century-Fox, 1951). *House on Telegraph Hill* (20th Century-Fox, 1951).

The Killer Is Loose (United Artists, 1956). *The Killing* (United Artists, 1956). *City of Fear* (Columbia, 1959).

Bancroft, Anne (1931–)

Anne Bancroft worked in Hollywood for many years with little success until the sixties. At the same time, however, she was a major Broadway star. Her tenacity paid off when she was cast as Annie Sullivan in *The Miracle Worker* (Warner Bros., 1962). Much of her film career was devoted to "B" movies and includes two late, minor *films noirs*.

Filmography: *New York Confidential* (Warner Bros., 1955). *Nightfall* (Columbia, 1957).

Bancroft, George (1881-1956)

Actor. Bancroft is one of the forgotten stars from the late twenties and early thirties. Burly and menacing, Bancroft was a natural for villainous roles, often starring as a gangster or criminal. In the late twenties, Bancroft starred in two silent films, both directed by Josef Von Sternberg and considered important influences, thematically and stylistically, on the subsequent gangster and *noir* genres.

Filmography: *Underworld* (Paramount, 1927). *Thunderbolt* (Paramount, 1929).

Bari, Lynn (Marjorie Fisher) (1915–)

Former showgirl, Bari began her film career as a dancer in the early thirties. She graduated to leads and supporting roles and in the late thirties and early forties, she was acting in over a half-dozen titles a year. She was a mainstay in "B" movies, playing a variety of parts including working girls. She starred in one *film noir*, Alfred Werker's *Shock*, as a woman who witnesses a murder, goes into shock and is "treated" by a psychiatrist (Vincent Price) who actually committed the crime. It is an excellent performance and unfortunately Bari's only *noir* appearance.

Filmography: *Shock* (20th Century-Fox, 1946).

Barry, Gene (Eugene Klass) (1921–)

Handsome and debonair, but with limited talent, Barry starred in a number of action films in the fifties. He later became a big television star. He appeared in two minor *films noirs*, typically in a variation of his heroic screen personality.

Filmography: *The Naked Alibi* (Universal, 1954). *Thunder Road* (United Artists, 1958).

Barrymore, John, Jr. (1932–)

Ruggedly handsome and very talented, Barrymore is the son of notorious alcoholic actor John Barrymore. Barrymore, Jr., like his father, also suffered from chemical dependency and his career was cut short by his various addictions. His brief film career was devoted to playing mainly rugged, heroic leads and he might have developed into a modern film hero in the style of Clint

Eastwood. Nevertheless, before his career came to an end, he starred in two very good, if minor, *films noirs*.

Filmography: *The Big Night* (United Artists, 1951). *While the City Sleeps* (RKO, 1956)

Basehart, Richard (1914–1984)

Basehart, an excellent actor and leading man somewhat in the style of Gregory Peck, appeared in many popular films but never quite achieved the stardom expected for him. He played both heroes and villains in a handful of minor *films noirs* in the early fifties.

Filmography: *He Walked By Night* (Eagle-Lion, 1949). *Tension* (MGM, 1950). *Fourteen Hours* (20th Century-Fox, 1951). *House on Telegraph Hill* (20th Century-Fox, 1951).

Basevi, James (1890–1979)

Art director. Basevi, an English architect and World War I hero, came to Hollywood as a draftsman in the late twenties and quickly established himself as an inventive production designer. He specialized in special effects, working on many Twentieth Century Fox epics including John Ford's *Hurricane* (1937). He worked on production designs for glossy entertainments, but was easily adaptable and worked on several interesting *films noirs*. The budgets he was forced to work with were modest, but his work is never less than very good, occasionally even excellent.

Filmography: *The Dark Corner* (20th Century-Fox, 1946). *Somewhere in the Night* (20th Century-Fox, 1947). *The Brasher Doubloon* (20th Century-Fox, 1947). *The People Against O'Hara* (MGM, 1951).

Bazin, Andre (1918–1958)

An influential French critic, Bazin was the founder of *Cahiers du Cinéma*, one of the first film magazines to take the medium serious as an art form. Bazin wrote books on American film and, through his magazine articles, helped establish the *auteur* theory and the growing cult of *film noir*. Many of his disciples, including film critics-turned-directors Jean-Luc Godard, François Truffaut and Claude Lelouch, were devotees of the American genre and helped build the critical foundation in the mid fifties for later *noir* critics and historians.

Beast of the City (MGM, 1932). 74 min.
Producer: Hunt Stromberg. Director: Charles Brabin. Screenplay: John Lee Mahin, based on a story by W. R. Burnett. Director of Photography: Norbett Brodine. Editor: Anne Bauchens.

Cast: Walter Huston (Captain Jim Fitzpatrick), Jean Harlow (Daisey Stevens), Wallace Ford (Ed Fitzpatrick), Jean Hersholt (Sam Bellmonte), Dorothy Peterson (Mary Fitzpatrick). With: Tully Marshall, Mickey Rooney, John Milijan, Emmett Corrigan.

A conscientious police captain is elevated to heroic status when he prevents a bank robbery, despite a corrupt city administration that would rather not encourage the promotion of an honest cop. Unfortunately, the police captain's brother gets involved in the gang and, in the end, his relentless pursuit of the criminals leads to a climactic shootout that leaves all the major characters dead.

Beast of the City is unique among the thirties gangster films. It is not merely an exposé of the criminal underworld, or a moral tale, but rather a biting critique of modern city life, a city's inhabitants, and official corruption. Unlike *Little Caeser* (Warner Bros., 1930), the archetypal gangster film, this is not a "bad guys get their comeuppance" tale, nor is it a typical "good guys vs. bad guys" movie. On the contrary, no individual or element of society is left unscathed in its attack. The police are just as corrupt as the mob. More importantly, it is the overwhelming sense of helplessness and inevitable doom that makes this an important, seminal *film noir*.

The Beat Generation (MGM, 1959). 93 min.
Producer: Albert Zugsmith. Director Charles Haas. Screenplay: Richard Matheson and Lewis Meltzer. Director of Photography: Walter H. Castle. Music: Lewis Meltzer and Albert Glasser. Songs: "Someday You'll Be Sorry" by Louis Armstrong, and "The Beat Generation" by Tom Walter and Walter Kent. Art Directors: William A. Horning and Addison Hehr. Editor: Ben Lewis.

Cast: Steve Cochran (Dave Culloran), Mamie Van Doren (Georgia Altera), Ray Danton (Sten Hess), Fay Spain (Frances Culloran), Jim Mitchum (Art Jester). With: Louis Armstrong and His All Stars, Maggie Hayes, Jackie Coogan, Cathy Crosby.

Promoted at the time as a quasi-satire, *The Beat Generation* is actually a compelling character study of indifferent cops and callous youth. The plot, which concerns the hunt for a robber-rapist known as the Aspirin Kid, serves mainly as a convenient device for the cops to explore the "youth underground" of jazz clubs and tea rooms. In the process they discover a world of corruption and malaise. The cops are no better. They are obsessively misogynist. They are very reluctantly assigned to the case, reasoning that the Aspirin Kid's victims "deserve what they get" and only solve the case through the carelessness of the main suspect, Art Jester.

A late *noir*, *The Beat Generation* has some quality and it remains only a marginal film in the genre. Interestingly, Jim Mitchum, who plays Art Jester, the Aspirin Kid, is the son of Robert Mitchum, one of *film noir*'s greatest icons. Jim Mitchum acted in a number of films but never caught on.

Begley, Ed (1901–1970)
Character actor. After a stint in the United States Navy in the late twenties, Begley worked as a popular radio personality before making his Broadway

Barbara Stanwyck, Burt Lancaster in *Sorry, Wrong Number* **(Paramount, 1948).**

debut in 1943. His film career began four years later with a supporting role in *Boomerang*, a popular success. Over the course of the next several years, Begley became one of the busiest *film noir* character actors, appearing in over a half-dozen *noirs*. His roles were varied, encompassing everything from a garish, snarling gambler in *Dark City*, a murderous and corrupt politician in *The Turning Point* and a police captain in *On Dangerous Ground*.

Filmography: *Boomerang* (20th Century-Fox, 1947). *Sorry, Wrong Number* (Paramount, 1948). *Street with No Name* (20th Century-Fox,

1948). *Convicted* (Columbia, 1950). *Dark City* (Paramount, 1950). *On Dangerous Ground* (RKO, 1952). *The Turning Point* (Paramount, 1952). *Odds Against Tomorrow* (United Artists, 1959).

Behind Locked Doors (Eagle-Lion, 1948). 62 min.

Producer: Eugene Ling. Director: Budd Boetticher. Screenplay: Marvin Wald and Eugene Ling, story by Marvin Wald. Director of Photography: Guy Roe. Music: Irving Friedman. Art Director: Edward L. Ilou. Editor: Norman Colbert.

Cast: Lucille Bremer (Kathy Lawrence), Richard Carlson (Ross Stewart), Douglas Fowley (Larson), Thomas Brown Henry (Dr. Clifford Porter). With: Ralf Harolde, Gaven Donavan, Morgan Farley, Trevor Bardette.

Behind Locked Doors is a predictable thriller with a good premise. An ambitious reporter, eager to find a missing judge accused of various crimes, follows the judge's daughter, Kathy Lawrence, to a mental hospital where the judge is apparently hiding out. The reporter gets himself committed to the institution, only to discover a neverending nightmare of fear and paranoia. Eventually, he discovers that the judge is being held by a group of criminals who have framed him and are using the hospital as a front.

As one might expect from an Eagle-Lion release, the production values are minimal, the screenplay inferior at best and the direction poor. A very minor film, it demonstrates how *noir* aesthetics even influenced low-budget studios in the late forties.

Bel Geddes, Barbara (1922–1991)

Actress. Bel Geddes is a familiar face from television. As an actress, her career began on Broadway in the early forties. Her film career began in the late forties. She quickly established herself as one of the best character actresses of

her generation. Her most important *noir* role is as Leonora Eames in Max Ophul's *Caught*. Her other two *noir* performances are equally effective, despite the relatively short time she is on screen.

Filmography: *Panic in the Streets* (20th Century–Fox, 1950). *Caught* (MGM, 1951). *Vertigo* (Universal, 1958).

Belita (Gladys Jepson-Turner) (1924–)

A former ice-skating champion from Great Britain, Belita came to Hollywood in the late forties to try her hand at film acting, but she never caught on and retired after starring in several minor, insignificant films including one *film noir*.

Filmography: *The Gangster* (Allied Artists, 1947).

Bendix, William (1906–1964)

William Bendix began his career as a stage actor in New York in the 1930's. He specialized in stereotypical New York toughs: hulking, dimwitted, brazen. His gruff, burly presence cast dangerous shadows over a number of *films noirs* in which he played mainly hired guns and mob henchmen. He co-starred with his real life off screen friend Alan Ladd in several important, early *noirs* including *The Blue Dahlia*. Buzz Wanchek, the desensitized veteran he played in *The Blue Dahlia* remains one of *film noir's* most indelible characters.

Filmography: *The Glass Key* (Paramount, 1942). *The Blue Dahlia* (Paramount, 1946). *The Dark Corner* (20th Century–Fox, 1946). *Calcutta* (Paramount, 1947). *The Web* (Universal, 1947). *Race Street* (RKO, 1948). *Detective Story* (Paramount, 1951). *Gambling House* (RKO, 1951).

Bennett, Bruce (Herman Brix) (1909–)

Under his real name, the former Olympic shot-putter starred in several serials in the thirties, most famously as Tarzan. In 1940, Brix changed his name to Bruce Bennett and played leads and

Alan Ladd, Veronica Lake in *The Blue Dahlia* **(Paramount, 1946).**

supporting roles as a granite-jawed soldier in several World War II action films. He also played small roles in other films including John Huston's classic western *Treasure of the Sierra Madre* (Warner Bros., 1949) and William Castle's minor *film noir, Undertow.*

Filmography: *Undertow* (Universal), 1949).

Bennett, Joan (1910–)

One of the biggest stars of the 1940's, Joan Bennett's film career actually stretched back to her mid teens. While her older sister Constance was a major star of the twenties and thirties, Joan struggled as a minor star of mostly indifferent films. Like Constance, Joan was a vivacious blonde; but in 1940 she dyed her hair black, took on a more sultry on-screen character, and her fame increased enormously. Part of the increased popularity of the actress can

be attributed to the quality of her film roles, which had grown better as she matured. She was, in fact, one of the most sensual and alluring stars of the forties and remains one of *film noir*'s greatest female icons.

Joan Bennett took an important, active role in the development of *film noir*, thanks to her friendship with the great director Fritz Lang. Lang had cast her in *Manhunt* (Universal, 1941), a Hitchcock type thriller that firmly established Lang as a viable commercial director and Bennett as a box-office draw. Bennett and Lang became close, platonic friends and Bennett worshipped the director, quite rightly, as one of cinema's greatest talents. Together, with Bennett's husband Walter Wanger, they formed the short-lived Diana Productions, an independent production company that made *The Woman in the Window* and *Secret Beyond the Door*.

Edward G. Robinson (left) in *Scarlet Street* (Universal, 1945).

Bennett's dark, voluptuous beauty was put to good use by Fritz Lang in *Scarlet Street* and *Woman in the Window* and both epitomize the *femme-fatale* character. Interestingly, these are Bennett's only performances as a true villainess. She is also memorable in Max Ophul's masterpiece *The Reckless Moment* and the minor *Hollow Triumph* as victims of circumstance.

Although she starred in only five *films noirs*, Joan Bennett's impact was such that she remains, for many, the ultimate *femme-fatale* in all of cinema.

Filmography: *Scarlet Street* (Universal, 1945). *Woman in the Window* (RKO, 1945). *Hollow Triumph* (Eagle-Lion, 1948). *Secret Beyond the Door* (Universal, 1948). *The Reckless Moment* (Columbia, 1949).

Bercovici, Leonardo ( )

Screenwriter and scenarist. Bercovici is the perfect example of the Hollywood golden age screenwriter: as the consummate professional, he contributed dialog, scenarios and worked on all aspects of a screenplay with little more than screen credit. He worked on two *noir* screenplays, contributing to one minor classic, *Dark City* and co-writing another minor, but interesting *film noir*.

Filmography: *Kiss the Blood Off My Hands* (Universal, 1948). *Dark City* (Paramount, 1950).

Berger, Ralph (1904–)

Art director. Chiefly employed at RKO, Berger collaborated on the art direction for many of the routine action and genre pictures. Some of his most memorable work was for *films noirs*. *Macao*'s sets are appropriately exotic, as are the somewhat more interesting set designs for *The Big Steal*, much of which is set in Mexico. *Where Danger Lives*, one of John Farrow's neglected classics, has sets which are both claustrophobic and darkly moody, mirroring the film's tragic tale of erotic obsession and self-destruction.

Filmography: *The Big Steal* (RKO, 1949). *Where Danger Lives* (RKO, 1950). *Macao* (RKO, 1952).

Bergman, Ingrid (1915–1982)

At first, Ingrid Bergman's cool, mysterious beauty might seem perfectly suited for *film noir*, but in fact her on-screen personality was too delicate and exotic for a hard-boiled, American genre. Nevertheless, her single *noir* performance, in Alfred Hitchcock's superior thriller *Notorious*, is one of the most memorable and vulnerable female characters in early *film noir*.

Filmography: *Notorious* (RKO, 1946).

Berlin Express (RKO, 1948). 86 min.

Executive Producer: Dore Schary. Producer: Bert Granet. Director: Jacques Tourneur. Screenplay: Harold Medford, story by Curt Siodmak. Director of Photography: Lucien Ballard. Music: Frederick Hollander. Music Director: Constantin Bakaleinikoff. Art Directors: Albert S. D'Agostino and Alfred Hermann. Editor: Sherman Todd

Cast: Merle Oberon (Lucienne), Robert Ryan (Robert Lindley), Charles Korvin (Perrot), Paul Lukas (Dr. H. Bernhardt), Robert Coote (Sterling). With: Reinhold Schunzel, Roman Toporow, Peter Von Zerneck, Otto Waldis.

Berlin Express is a superior *noir* espionage thriller, similar to Eric Ambler's tales. Set and shot entirely in Germany, the story concerns the search for a brilliant humanist, Dr. H. Bernhardt, who has been kidnapped by a fanatical neo–Nazi organization. Lucienne, Bernhardt's secretary, is accompanied by an American scientist, Robert Lindly, in the search for her boss. Although they do not entirely trust one another, they work together and eventually, by sheer accident, stumble on the hideout of the gang and rescue Bernhardt.

The film echoes the alienating qualities of Franz Kafka's fiction. This is not surprising considering the author of this scenario was Curt Siodmak, the younger brother of director Robert Siodmak. Curt was a specialist of horror and suspense stories of a decidedly modern type. Furthermore, the film was photographed in Frankfurt, Germany, a once bustling city that had been reduced to rubble by allied bombing during the second world war.

A sense of imminent danger pervades the film and is brilliantly rendered by director Jacques Tourneur and cinematographer Lucien Ballard. Tourneur was a master of atmospheric techniques — as can be seen in his *noir* classic *Out of the Past* (RKO, 1947) — and he creates a haunting, spooky film told in dark shadows and rubble-strewn streets.

In some ways, *Berlin Express* resembles the famous *noir* like mystery *The Third Man* (United Artists, 1948), with its story and technique. On the surface, both films are romantic trifles, but they both had a serious anti-war message, and they both remain relevant today.

Berman, Pandro S. (1905–)

The legendary Pandro Berman is one of Hollywood's most significant, neglected figures. In his late twenties, after a decade in the industry and a brief stint as one of David O. Selznick's assistants, Berman was promoted to production chief of RKO in 1934. Berman managed that studio's important mid to late thirties productions and promoted the careers of Fred Astaire, Ginger Rogers, Katherine Hepburn, and directors Howard Hawks and George Stevens among others. His career as producer at MGM in the forties was equally distinguished, marked by good taste. He managed, more than any other producer of his time, to engineer a relatively high standard of product. Interestingly, the two *films noirs* he produced were not among his best films, although both are interesting and notable for a number of reasons.

Filmography: *Undercurrent* (MGM, 1946). *The Bribe* (MGM, 1949).

Bernhard, Jack (1913–)

A minor director of a few Monogram films, Bernhard directed an interesting low-budget *film noir* for that studio. Like all of Monogram's films, it is rather cheap, literally and figuratively, and is poorly written and acted. Yet, it is appropriately gloomy and surprisingly effective, despite its flaws and it is also Bernhard's only film of note.

Filmography: *Decoy* (Monogram, 1946).

Bernhardt, Curtis (1899–1981)

Director. Bernhardt was a distinguished commercial filmmaker whose career began in Germany in the silent era. Like so many European directors, Bernhardt borrowed expressionist techniques and applied them to commercial cinema. In the 1940's he came to the United States where he joined Warner Bros. and helped define the pseudo-expressionist, Warner's style of the period that has become so familiar in films like *Casablanca* (Warner Bros., 1942), directed by another important emigree, Michael Curtiz. The 1940's were Bernhardt's strongest period and he created several interesting films including two important *films noirs*. If neither is quite a classic, they have much to demonstrate about cinematic technique. *Conflict*, the standout of the two films, is a stylish melodrama starring Humphrey Bogart in one of his most sinister roles as a psychotic wife-murderer.

Filmography: *Conflict* (Warner Bros., 1945). *The High Wall* (MGM, 1947).

Bernstein, Elmer (1922–)

Composer. The only surviving film composer from the golden age of American film still active, Elmer Bernstein continues the tradition of great film music in the movies of contemporary directors like Martin Scorsese. In the fifties and sixties, Bernstein composed the scores for many well known films, winning two Academy Awards. He is particularly adept at capturing the paranoid world of *film noir* and he has done some of his best work for films of the genre. His attachment to the genre has continued with his excellent, hauntingly, beautiful score for *The Grifters*, one of the best contemporary *noirs*.

Filmography: *Sudden Fear* (RKO, 1952). *Storm Fear* (United Artists, 1956). *Sweet Smell of Success* (United Artists, 1957). *The Grifters* (Miramax, 1991).

Berry, John (1917–)

Director. Berry began in New York in the 1930's as an actor and was briefly a member of Orson Welles' Mercury Theatre. His first association with film came as Billy Wilder's assistant director on the *film noir* classic *Double Indemnity* (Paramount, 1944). As a director, Berry specialized in mild dramas and adventures including the semi-legendary *Casbah* (Universal, 1948). He also directed a few scenes for Max Ophuls' *Caught*, when the great director fell ill. *He Ran All the Way* is generally considered Berry's best film. A grim and powerful tale of a wanted man trying desperately to stay free, it was John Garfield's last film. Unfortunately, Berry's career went into rapid decline immediately after and he never again reached the heights of his late forties films.

Filmography: *Caught* (uncredited co-director) (MGM, 1945). *Tension* (MGM, 1949). *He Ran All the Way* (United Artists, 1951).

Bettis, Valerie (1929–)

Character actress. Valarie Bettis appeared in a few minor films in the late forties and early fifties including a supporting role in one minor *noir*.

Filmography: *Affair in Trinidad* (Columbia, 1952).

Robert Ryan, Barbara Bel Geddes in *Caught* (MGM, 1945).

Between Midnight and Dawn (Columbia, 1950). 89 min.

Producer: Hunt Stromberg. Director of Photography: Gordon Douglas. Screenplay: Eugene Ling, story by Gerald Drayson Adams and Leo Katcher. Director of Photography: George

E. Diskant. Music: George Duning. Art Director: George Brooks. Editor: Gene Havlick.

Cast: Mark Stevens (Rocky Barnes), Edmond O'Brien (Dan Purvis), Gale Storm (Kate Mallory), Donald Buka (Richie Garris), Gale Robbins (Terry

Romaine). With: Anthony Ross, Roland Winters, Tito Vuolo, Madge Blake.

Two childhood friends, now both police officers, are torn apart by big city corruption.

That, in a nutshell, is the plot to one of the best "B" *films noirs*. Uncompromising and unsentimental, the admittedly weak story is held together by director Gordon Douglas and splendid hard-boiled performances by its leads, Mark Stevens and Edmond O'Brien. The film is heavy on action and violence and is less a character study than a critique of big city corruption and its effects on its citizens. The opening credits, over a long-shot of Los Angeles, firmly establishes the theme of alienation and desperation in an overwhelming large city.

Unjustly overlooked, *Between Midnight and Dawn* is one of the strongest "B" *films noirs*.

Beware, My Lovely (RKO, 1952). 76 min.

Producer: Collier Young Director: Harry Horner. Screenplay: Mel Dinelli, based on his short story and play *The Man*. Director of Photography: George E. Diskant. Music: Leith Stevens. Art Directors: Albert S. D'Agostino and Alfred Herman. Editor: Paul Weatherwas.

Cast: Ida Lupino (Mrs. Gordon), Robert Ryan (Howard), Taylor Holmes (Mr. Armstrong), Barbara Whiting (Ruth Williams), James Williams (Mr. Stevens), O.Z. Whitehead (Mr. Francs).

Beware, My Lovely is the story of madness vs. stability in a chaotic world. Howard, an itinerant handyman, flees in terror when he finds his employer strangled, not realizing he has killed her in a moment of blind rage. He flees to another town where he finds work and temporary refuge at the home of an unsuspecting war widow, Mrs. Gordon. The tranquility, however, is short lived. When he comes to believe Mrs. Gordon is spying on him,

he holds her hostage in her home. His mood swings between calm and rage, but eventually he quietly surrenders to a telephone repairman who has unknowingly stumbled onto the situation.

Despite its potentially compelling set up, the film ultimately fails to rise above mediocre. The screenwriter, Mel Dinelli, specialized in suspenseful *films noirs*, but his screenplay for this film is rather static and lacks suspense. This is an inherent problem with adaptions of stage plays. Although the performances are excellent, the film is , ultimately, a minor one.

Bewitched (MGM, 1945). 65 min.

Producer and Director: Arch Obler. Screenplay: Arch Obler, based on his short story "Alter Ego". Director of Photography: Charles Salerno, Jr. Music: Bronislau Kaper. Art Directors: Cedric Gibbons and Stan Rogers. Editor: Albert Akst.

Cast: Phyllis Thaxter (Joan/Karen), Horace McNally (Eric), Edmond Gwenn (Dr. Bergson), Henry H. Daniels (Bob), Addison Richards (Mr. Ellis), Kathleen Lockhart (Mrs. Ellis).

Joan, a young pretty girl, has an alternate personality that is quite evil—she murders her fiancé on the eve of her wedding. A spiritualist manages to "exorcise" the evil personality, thus saving her from a long prison term.

Bewitched is a silly MGM, "B" *noir* that, nevertheless, is interesting for its expressionist style and early treatment in the genre of the *doppelganger* (mirror image) theme.

Beyond a Reasonable Doubt (RKO, 1956). 80 min.

Producer: Bert Friedlob. Director: Fritz Lang. Screenplay: Douglas Morrow. Director of Photography: William Snyder. Music: Herschel Burke Gilbert. Art Director: Carroll Clark. Editor: Gene Fowler, Jr.

Cast: Dana Andrews (Tom Garrett), Joan Fontaine (Susan Spencer), Sidney

Blackmer (Austin Spencer), Philip Bourneur (Thompson), Sheppard Strudwick (Wilson). With: Arthur Franz, Edward Binns, Robin Raymond, Barbara Nichols.

Fritz Lang's last American film is a character study of a psychotic murderer. It has elements of Hitchcockian duplicity in its tale of a seemingly innocent man who is charged with a murder and who, in fact, turns out to be guilty of the crime, although evidence points elsewhere.

Despite its low budget and comparatively poor production values, *Beyond a Reasonable Doubt* is compelling and suspenseful. It is not particularly well written, but Lang was incapable of making a bad film. And while undeniably not a classic, the film is filled with typical Lang themes of corruption, psychosis and the nature of guilt. It is also very well acted, with Dana Andrews being particularly notable as the murderer.

Beyond the Forest (Warner Bros., 1949). 97 min.

Producer: Henry Blanke. Director: King Vidor. Screenplay: Leonore Coffee, based on the novel by Stuart Engstrand. Director of Photography: Robert Burks. Music: Max Steiner. Art Director: Robert Haas. Editor: Rudi Fehr.

Cast: Bette Davis (Rosa Moline), Joseph Cotten (Dr. Lewis Moline), David Brian (Neil Latimer), Ruth Roman (Carol), Minor Watson (Moose), Dona Drake (Jenny). With Regis Toomey, Sarah Selby, Ann Doran.

A notable exception to the general rule in *film noir* which views rural life as sedate, safe and nurturing, *Beyond the Forest* is, more than anything, an attack against the narrow-mindedness of small town America.

On the surface, the film is the tale of sexual infidelity and its consequences. Rosa Moline, a middle-aged housewife, is having an affair with Neil Latimer. When the affair is threatened with exposure, she resorts to murder and, in typical Hollywood fashion, in the end must pay with her own life.

Essentially a tragic melodrama with *noir* like elements, *Beyond the Forest* was the most cynical of King Vidor's movies. Big city and corporate corruption were his usual themes, but he was, generally speaking, an optimist. But there is little optimistic or reassuring about this film. Vidor seems to be saying that the very environment of small town America is repressive and destructive and he uses the relationship between Rosa and her husband Dr. Lewis Moline as a metaphor for this theme. Expressionist style, repeated close ups, claustrophobic, densely forested and dark exteriors, all combine to enhance the depressing "hemmed-in" mood.

Although *Beyond the Forest* is not a major film, it is an important one in the *oeuvre* of King Vidor and an interesting example of the influence of *film noir* aesthetics in the late forties.

Bezzerides, A. I. (Albert Issac) (1908–)

Screenwriter. Bezzerides was a hardboiled novelist who also was an active screenwriter. He specialized in crime and action films. He wrote several excellent *films noirs*. *Thieves' Highway* and *On Dangerous Ground* were directed by Nicholas Ray and are typically tough-minded and uncompromising in their view of the exploited working class. *Kiss Me Deadly*, an adaption of Mickey Spillane's novel, is a spirited departure from the clichés inherent in Spillane's work, while also retaining the violent, independent spirit of the author's novels.

Filmography: *Thieves' Highway* (wrote screenplay based on his novel, *Thieves Market*) (20th Century-Fox, 1949). *On Dangerous Ground* (RKO, 1952). *Kiss Me Deadly* (United Artists, 1955).

Bickford, Charles (1889–1967)

Character actor. A graduate of MIT, Bickford turned to the stage relatively late in life, at thirty, making his

Ralph Meeker, Gaby Rodgers in *Kiss Me Deadly* (United Artists, 1955).

Broadway debut in 1919. His dashing good looks made him instantly popular. Like so many Broadway stars, he was recruited by Hollywood in the early days of sound and was quickly established as a favored leading man. He shot to stardom as Greta Garbo's lover in *Anna Christie* (MGM, 1930), but Bickford moved to character roles as younger actors became more popular.

His craggy, intense features made him a natural as bad guys of various types, but an occasional good guy and he always commanded attention on screen. He appeared in two *films noirs* including the classic *Brute Force* in which he had a small but effective role as Gallagher, the convict leader who joins a doomed prison breakout.

Filmography: *Fallen Angel* (20th

Century-Fox, 1946). *Brute Force* (Universal, 1947).

The Big Carnival (aka *Ace in the Hole*) (Paramount, 1951). 112 min.

Producer and Director: Billy Wilder. Screenplay: Billy Wilder, Lesser Samuels and Walter Newman. Director of Photography: Charles B. Lang. Music: Hugo Friedhofer. Art Directors: Hal Pereira and Earl Hedrick. Editor: Arthur Schmidt.

Cast Kirk Douglas (Charles Tatum), Jan Sterling (Lorraine), Robert Arthur (Herbie Cook), Richard Benedict (Leo Minosa), Porter Hale (Jacob Q. Boot), Ray Teal (Sheriff). With Frances Dominquez, Gene Evans, Frank Jacquet, Geraldine Hall.

In Albuquerque, New Mexico, Charles Tatum, a once ambitious reporter who has fallen on bad times and alcoholism, is looking for a way back into the big time. He stumbles onto a seemingly minor story of Leo Minosa, a concession-operator trapped in a cave-in. Realizing this may be his lucky break, Tatum exploits the situation, even going so far as to convince the rescuers to dig a longer, supposedly safer route to the victim. Leo's faithless wife, Lorraine, sides with Tatum, pretending to be the grieving wife, while in reality only interested in her own publicity and how many concessions she can sell to her husband's rescuers. Reporters pour in from all over to cover the story. But Tatum's plan has backfired. He is overshadowed by the publicity and intense interest in the story. In frustration, he verbally attacks Lorainne and she stabs him. He stumbles back to his newspaper and dies while, at the same time, Minosa dies awaiting his rescuers.

The Big Carnival is one of the most grimly cynical motion-pictures ever to emerge from Hollywood. Indeed, many reporters were so offended by Wilder's film that they threatened to sue for slander; but, of course, they missed the point of the film. It is not merely an attack against their profession, but a criticism of the evils of post-war America and its repressive atmosphere. In an era of the McCarthy witch-hunt, this was a brave, bitter, unflinching attack against those who would sell out their fellow men for personal gain. Of course, it proved too strong for audiences of the time and the film was not a box-office success.

As Charles Tatum, Kirk Douglas is superb as a bundle of desperation and cold calculation. But it is Jan Sterling, as Lorraine, who is the film's dark center. Her performance is ferocious and unforgettable. The character is a unique *femme-fatale*, one who exploits her femininity without resorting to overt, cheap sexuality. There is a memorable scene when she is asked to pose for pictures praying on her knees for her husband. She snarls angrily at the reporters, "I don't pray! Kneeling bags my nylons."

The characters' arid personalities are further enhanced by the bleak, desert location and by Wilder's detached technique. All of the major characters can be seen as typical *film noir* anti-heroes, but Leo Minosa is the most alienated and desperate of them all. When he dies of pneumonia waiting for his rescuers, the viewer can almost feel the chill that has taken his life. Such is the impact of this extraordinary film.

The Big Clock (Paramount, 1948). 95 min.

Producer: Richard Maibaum. Director: John Farrow. Screenplay: Johnathan Latimer, adapted by Harold Goldman from the novel by Kenneth Fearing. Director of Photography: John F. Seitz. Music: Victor Young. Song: "The Big Clock" by Jay Livingston and Ray Evans. Art Directors: Hans Dreier, Roland Anderson and Albert Nozaki. Editor: Gene Ruggiero.

Cast: Ray Milland (George Stroud), Charles Laughton (Earl Janoth), Maureen O'Sullivan (Georgette Stroud), George Macready (Steve Hagen), Rita

Ray Milland, Maureen O'Sullivan, Rita Johnson in *The Big Clock* (Paramount, 1948).

Johnson (Pauline Delos), Elsa Lanchester (Louise Patterson). With Harold Vermilyea, Dan Tobin, Henry Morgan.

John Farrow is one of the neglected masters of *film noir* and *The Big Clock* is one of his best films. Farrow was a devout Roman Catholic and he found, in these crime films, the perfect genre to explore the nature of man and his moral destiny. While these are the underlying themes of all of Farrow's work, it does not overwhelm the entertainment value of his movies.

The Big Clock is another disparaging view of the publishing business and reporters—a minor theme in *film noir*. George Stroud, a star reporter for a crime magazine, on the eve of his long overdue honeymoon with his wife of five years, misses the train that would have taken him to the vacation resort where she is waiting for him. Depressed, he goes to a bar. There, he

meets Pauline Delos, unaware that she is the mistress of his magazine's tyrannical publisher, Earl Janoth. They hit it off and after a wild, but innocent, night on the town, he leaves her at her apartment. Unfortunately, Janoth arrives at the building just as Stroud is leaving. Janoth cannot make out the man in the shadow, but sure that his mistress is seeing another man, he becomes overwhelmed by jealousy. In a violent rage, he murders Pauline.

Stroud, meanwhile, has at last joined his wife. But the honeymoon has barely begun when he is called back to the city by Janoth to help "solve" the murder of his lover. Realizing he could be implicated, Stroud returns and begins investigating the crime, managing to stay just ahead of the police and his own staff, all of whom are working on the case. At last, he realizes that Janoth is the murderer and in the ensuing confrontation, Janoth is killed when he

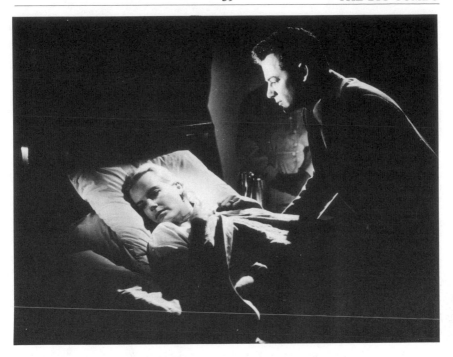

Jean Wallace, Cornel Wilde in *The Big Combo* **(Allied Artists, 1955).**

falls down an elevator shaft. Stroud is reunited with his wife and they finally leave for their honeymoon.

The film opens with a classic *noir* element, a pan across a dark city scape, into a darkened corridor where a mysterious, shadowy figure (George Stroud) bemoans his fate in a voice over. Much of the story is then told in flashback.

Farrow was a master of cinematic technique and his films are filled with technical innovations. This is certainly true of *The Big Clock*, which is made up of low-key lighting, asymmetric compositions and dramatic camera angles.

The film's overall mood is dark and melancholy, but there are lighter moments. Charles Laughton's real-life spouse, Elsa Lanchester, stands out as an eccentric artist, a perfect contrast to Laughton's decidedly more dark version of madness.

The film was remade as *No Way Out* (Paramount, 1987), which made a star of Kevin Costner, but lost much of its bite and artistic value. The original version is a masterpiece and one of *film noir*'s most satisfying films.

The Big Combo (Allied Artists, 1955). 89 min.
Producer: Sidney Harmon. Director: Joseph H. Lewis. Screenplay: Philip Yordan. Director of Photography: John Alton. Music: David Raksin. Production/Art Design: Ruchi Feld. Editor: Robert Eisen
Cast: Cornel Wilde (Leonard Diamond), Richard Conte (Mr. Brown), Brian Donlevy (McClure), Jean Wallace (Susan Lowell), Robert Middleton (Peterson), Lee Van Cleef (Fante), Earl Holliman (Mingo). With: Helen Walker, Jay Adler, Ted DeCorsia, Whit Bissell.

The head of a local mob, Mr. Brown, is captivated by the sensual Susan Lowell, a young society woman.

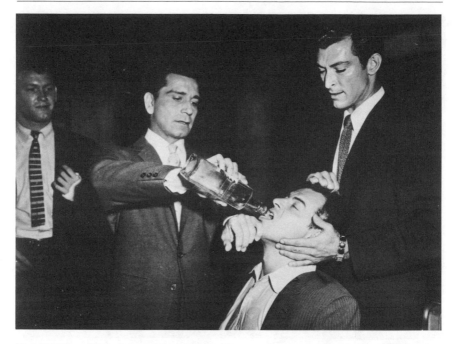

Earl Holliman, Richard Conte, Cornel Wilde, Lee Van Cleef in *The Big Combo* **(Allied Artists, 1955).**

Meanwhile, Leonard Diamond, a zealous police detective, closes in on the crime boss and wants Susan for himself. Brown puts out a contract on Diamond. Two sadistic thugs, Mingo and Fante, kidnap and torture Diamond as a "warning" to lay off his investigation; but after Diamond recovers, he is more determined than ever to get Brown. When Diamond convinces Brown's associates that Brown had double-crossed them in order to gain power, Brown finds the tables turned on him and decides to flee the city. At the hanger where he keeps a private plane, he is cornered by Diamond and in the subsequent shootout, Brown is killed.

The Big Combo is Joseph H. Lewis' masterpiece. A violent melodrama, with more action than one usually associates with *film noir*, it is a visceral, exciting film, at times even breathtakingly brilliant. It also has an excep-

tional sense of fatalism and perverse sexuality. Jean Wallace was a genuinely sensual actress mostly in "B" productions and she seems to revel in her role as Susan. Lewis dwells on her voluptuous sensuality, making the most of her time on screen. This is one of the most overtly sexual films of the fifties.

John Alton's cinematography is extravagant and extraordinarily inventive. There are striking contrasts between light and dark areas which, at times, seems to isolate the characters in a dark insular universe of unspoken repression. *The Big Combo* was made on a small budget, yet it looks more lush than many "A" productions.

The Big Combo might well be the best "B" movie of all time. It is, unquestionably, John H. Lewis' best film, and it remains one of the finest of the *film noir* classics.

Gloria Grahame, Glenn Ford in *The Big Heat* **(Columbia, 1953).**

The Big Heat (Columbia, 1953). 90 min.

Producer: Robert Arthur. Director: Fritz Lang. Screenplay: Sydney Boehm, based on the novel by William P. McGivern. Director of Photography: Charles Lang. Music: Daniele Amfitheotrof. Music Director: Mischa Bakaleinikoff. Art Director: Robert Peterson. Editor: Charles Nelson.

Cast: Glenn Ford (Dave Bannion), Gloria Grahame (Debby Marsh), Jocelyn Brando (Katie Bannion), Alexander Scourby (Mike Lagana), Lee Marvin (Vince Stone). With Peter Whitney, Willis Bouchey, Carolyn Jones.

Fritz Lang's story of a crusading cop and the mobsters he attempts to bring to justice, is one of the great *films noirs*. It set the standard for all cop films to follow — *noir* and otherwise — and it remains one of the genre's most well known and respected films.

The story is simple: a tough, independent cop, Dave Bannion, fights against all odds, including his own department's corruption, to bring down a mobster, Mike Lagana. What distinguishes the story is the way the characters are represented. Lagana, for example is particularly cruel, resorting to the murder of innocent bystanders if they get in the way. He has his vulnerable side as well, and it is this duplicity of character which interests Lang the most. Bannion is equally compassionate and violent and, likewise, will let no one stand is his way in his single minded fight against Lagana.

The most sympathetic character in the film is Debby Marsh, splendidly portrayed by Gloria Grahame. Marsh is the promiscuous girlfriend of Lagana who is also having an affair with his sadistic sidekick, Vince Stone. Grahame gives the character a palpable sensuality and understated masochism. Her relationships with both Lagana and Stone is masochistic, leading to tragic results in the latter case. During an argument, Stone throws scalding coffee into Debby's face, permanently disfiguring her. Later, however, she gets revenge by doing the same to him, before he kills her.

Although Bannion ultimately triumphs, he leaves behind him a wake of death and destruction. The character is the ultimate modern anti-hero, pointing the way to "Dirty Harry" and other such characters to come.

The film is directed with exceptional style by Fritz Lang. It is also one of the most violent and sadistic of all the major *films noirs*. Debby Marsh, for example, positively revels in her debasement and both Dave Bannion and Mike Lagana seem to enjoy killing.

Uncompromising and bleak, *The Big Heat* is a nihilistic vision of crime and punishment in the modern world.

The Big Knife (United Artists, 1955). 111 min.

Producer and Director: Robert Aldrich. Screenplay: James Poe, based on the play by Clifford Odets. Director of Photography: Ernest Laszlo. Music: Frank DeVol. Art Director: William Glascow. Editor: Michael Luciano.

Cast: Jack Palance (Charlie Castle), Ida Lupino (Marion Castle), Wendell Corey (Smiley Coy), Jean Hagen (Connie Bliss), Rod Steiger (Stanley Hoff), Shelley Winters (Dixie Evans). With: Everett Sloane, Wesley Addy, Paul Langton.

Robert Aldrich's Hollywood exposé, adapted from a play by Clifford Odets, is at least as bitter as Billy Wilder's *Sunset Boulevard*, although not nearly as good a film. The plot is typical *noir*: Charlie Castle, a former Broadway actor, now a major film star, does not want to renew his contract with the studio. Many years before, he had accidentally killed a woman in a hit-and-run for which his friend Buddy Bliss, took the blame. Dixie Evans, a bit player who witnessed the crime, is blackmailing the actor. He agrees to renew his contract, but only if producer Smiley Coy "takes care" of Dixie. Coy arranges an elaborate "accident" that kills her, but Castle's problems have not diminished. His wife leaves him, pushing him further into despair. Eventually, although, she agrees to return to him, but Castle cannot live with the burden of his deeds and commits suicide.

Obviously, Charlie Castle is a metaphor for the corruption of the film business: he is the ultimate sell-out so despised in Hollywood and yet embraced and championed by those very same people. This invective against Hollywood does not make for pleasant viewing and the film suffers from its overwhelming bitterness. James Poe's screenplay stays close to Odet's play (his angriest), which accounts for its somewhat static nature. Nevertheless, the film contains several excellent performances and gave Jack Palance one of his most unique roles as a villain.

The Big Night (United Artists, 1951). 75 min.

Producer: Philip A. Wasman. Director: Joseph Losey. Screenplay: Stanley Ellin and Joseph Losey, based on the novel *Dreadful Summit* by Stanley Ellin. Director of Photography: Hal Mohr. Music: Lynn Murray. Art Director: Nicholas Remisoff. Editor: Edward Mann.

Cast: John Barrymore, Jr. (George LaMain), Preston Foster (Andy LaMain), Joan Lorring (Marion Rostina), Howard St. John (Al Judge), Dorothy Comingore (Julie Rostina). With: Philip Bourneuf, Howland Chamberlin, Emil Meyer, Robert Aldrich.

In many ways typical of director Joseph Losey's mature films *The Big Night* is a moral tale, self-righteously allegorical. When a teenager, George LaMain, sees his father submitting to a beating by the town bully, Al Judge, he becomes obsessed with getting revenge. Eventually, he shoots Judge, a moral, psychological and physical cripple, but he only wounds him, in the end leaving events unresolved.

All of Losey's work was about the existential nature of man and his place in the increasingly desensitized modern world. This is certainly true of *The Big Night*, which is somewhat more explicit in its exploration of these themes than his later films.

Although a very minor film, *The Big Night* has some compelling performances (particularly by John Barrymore, Jr.) and is reasonably well directed, in typically heavy-handed expressionist style, by Joseph Losey. He would explore similar themes in better films a decade or so later.

The Big Sleep (Warner Bros., 1946). 118 min.

Producer and Director: Howard Hawks. Screenplay: William Faulkner, Leigh Brackett and Jules Furtham, based on the novel by Raymond Chandler. Director of Photography: Sid Hickox. Music: Max Steiner. Art Director: Carl Jules Weyl. Editor: Christian Nybo.

Cast: Humphrey Bogart (Philip Marlowe), Lauren Bacall (Vivian Sternwood), John Ridgeley (Eddie Mars), Martha Vickers (Carmen Sternwood), Dorothy Malone (book store proprietress). With: Patricia Clarke, Regis Toomey, Louis Jean Heydt, Elisha Cook Jr., Joy Barlowe.

Essentially a faithful adaption of Raymond Chandler's novel, the story centers around private investigator Philip Marlowe's entanglement with the wealthy, spoiled Sternwood daughters and the search for the blackmailer of the younger daughter, Carmen. As his investigation progresses, it grows increasingly complicated, involving the elder sister (with whom he becomes romantically involved), gamblers, drug dealers and murder. His own life is endangered, but eventually he discovers that a local gambler, Eddie Mars, is the culprit behind the blackmailing scheme. The inevitable confrontation occurs in an abandoned house as Marlowe outwits Mars, who is then killed by his own henchmen.

The film version differs from the novel in several ways. In Chandler's novels, Philip Marlowe is the ultimate misogynist, avoiding sexual or romantic contact with all women. In this film, however, there is a surprising playful attitude toward sex. Women are often the initiators. It is established quite early in the film that Vivian (Lauren Bacall) is not "innocent" and she is far more interested in him than he is in her. Wherever Marlowe goes, he seems to attract sexually voracious women— from a book store proprietress (a stunning Dorothy Malone) to a taxi driver who, although he is in the cab for less than a minute, flirts with him and even manages to set up a date!

All of this can be attributed to director Howard Hawks who preferred strong-willed women characters in his films and who treated even the darkest material with wit. Indeed, in this film Hawk's touch is a tad too light.

In fact, *The Big Sleep* is one of the lightest *films noirs*. Neither Vivian or Carmen is a *femme-fatale* in the classic sense. But there are other elements which strongly confirm the film's place in the genre — Philip Marlowe as the lone knight fighting against an impossible corrupt villain is a typical *noir* protagonist and the film's style, which is strongly influenced by expressionism both in terms of its lighting and design of its sets, is *film noir* at its glossiest best. And the film is populated with *noir* icons: Humphrey Bogart, Lauren Bacall, Dorothy Malone, Elisha Cook, Jr. and Regis Toomey.

The Big Sleep remains the best film adaption of a Raymond Chandler novel. Perhaps most important, as a huge box-office success, it firmly established Bogart's on screen image, providing the genre with one of its most endurable male leads.

A remake of *The Big Sleep* was made in 1977. Written and directed by Michael Winner, it stars Robert Mitchum as Philip Marlowe. The action remains essentially the same, but the British setting and uninspired direction are annoying. Still, Robert Mitchum's performance is very good.

The Big Steal (RKO, 1949). 72 min.
Executive Producer: Sid Rogell. Producer: Jack L. Gross. Director: Don Siegel. Screenwriter: Gerald Drayson Adams and Geoffrey Homes, based on the story "The Road to Carmichaels" by Richard Wormser. Director of Photography: Harry J. Wild. Music: Leigh Harline. Art Directors: Albert S. D'Agostino and Jack Okey. Editor: Samuel E. Beetly.
Cast: Robert Mitchum (Duke), Jane Greer (Joan), William Bendix (Blake), Patric Knowles (Fiske), Ramon Novarro (Col. Ortega).

One of Don Siegel's first features as a director (he was an established editor), *The Big Steal* is an action-oriented *film noir*. It was designed to cash in on the charisma and popularity of Jane Greer and Robert Mitchum who had starred together two years earlier in the phenomenally successful *Out of the Past* (RKO, 1947). Although the film does not live up to the greatness of its predecessor, it is an entertaining dynamo, one of the finest chase films ever.

The plot is simple. Duke, suspected of stealing an Army payroll, chases the real crooks through Mexico while he, in turn, is pursued by his army superior, Blake, who suspects him of being in with the thieves. Meanwhile, Joan is chasing the same group of criminals, headed by Fiske, because he hustled her for a thousand dollars. Of course, Duke and Joan meet and team up, although they do not trust one another. Unlike *Out of the Past*, the general mood here is lighthearted.

Don Siegel keeps the pace quick, building it around the theme of the chase. The dialog is equally thrifty and often quite funny. Interestingly, the screenplay, by *noir* veterans Gerald Drayson Adams and Geoffrey Homes, is by two of the genre's most fatalistic writers. Homes is Daniel Mainwaring's pseudonym, the same name he used when he wrote the *noir* classic *Out of the Past*. While this film does not retain the classic's sense of fatalism, it is still filled with the *noir* themes of corruption, mindless violence and dangerous sexuality, all reinforced by Siegel's direction.

Biroc, Joseph (1903–)
Cinematographer. A reliable professional, Biroc's career began in the mid-forties and he was still going strong in the early eighties. He photographed a number of minor *films noirs* and at least one moderately important *noir*, *The Glass Key*. He brought a sense of studio polish to all of his films.

Ronald Colman, Signe Hasso in *A Double Life* **(Universal, 1948).**

Filmography: *The Glass Key* (Paramount, 1942). *The Killer That Stalked New York* (Columbia, 1950). *Cry Danger* (RKO, 1951). *Loan Shark* (Lippert, 1952). *World for Ransom* (Allied Artists, 1954). *Nightmare* (United Artists, 1956). *The Garment Jungle* (Columbia, 1957). *Hustle* (Paramount, 1975).

Bischoff, Samuel (1890–1975)

Producer. Bischoff's long, generally distinguished career began at Warner Bros. where he produced a variety of successful films. In the early forties he moved to Columbia before becoming an independent producer in the latter part of the decade. It was then that he produced all of his *noirs*. Probably the most important of these is Phil Karlson's *The Phenix City Story*, a low-budget, violent melodrama based on real events.

Filmography: *The Pitfall* (United Artists, 1948). *Macao* (Executive Producer) (RKO, 1952). *The Phenix City Story* (Allied Artists, 1955).

Bissell, Whit (1919–1981)

Character actor. Bissell is the ultimate small parts actor, playing everything from big city lawyers to dimwitted gas station attendants. His most famous role was as the mad doctor in *I Was a Teenage Frankenstein* (American-International, 1957). He appeared in a dozen *films noirs*, always in very small parts and rarely appearing on screen for more than a few minutes per film.

Filmography: *Somewhere in the Night* (20th Century–Fox, 1946). *Canon City* (Eagle-Lion, 1948). *A Double Life* (Universal, 1948). *Raw Deal* (Eagle-Lion, 1948). *He Walked By Night* (Eagle-Lion, 1949). *Convicted* (Columbia, 1950). *Side Street* (MGM, 1950). *The Killer That Stalked New York*

(Columbia, 1951). *The Turning Point* (Paramount, 1952). *The Big Combo* (United Artists, 1955). *The Naked Street* (United Artists, 1955). *The Manchurian Candidate* (United Artists, 1962).

Black Angel (Universal, 1946). 83 min.

Producers: Tom McKnight and Roy William Neill. Director: Roy William Neill. Screenplay: Roy Chanslor, based on the novel by Cornell Woolrich. Director of Photography: Paul Ivano. Music: Frank Skinner. Songs "Heartbreak," "I Wanted to Talk About," "Time Will Tell" and "Continental Gentleman" by Edgar Fairchild and Jack Brooks. Art Directors : Jack Otterson and Martin Obzina. Editor: Saul A. Goodkind.

Cast: Dan Duryea (Martin Blair), June Vincent (Catherine), Peter Lorre (Marko), Broderick Crawford (Captain Flood), Constance Dowling (Marvis Marlowe), Wallace Ford (Joe). With: Freddie Steele, Hobart Cavanaugh, Pat Sterling.

Black Angel is a modest but imaginative film with an ingenious script. Dan Duryea, so often type cast as a pathological villain, here plays a comparatively sympathetic part. He stars as an alcoholic composer who helps search for the killer of his estranged, promiscuous wife. After another man is convicted of the crime, he falls in love with the wife of the accused man, but when she spurns his entreaties, he realizes he committed the crime in an act of blind rage and turns himself into the police shortly before the accused man is to be executed.

Interestingly, although the part Duryea plays, Martin Blair, is in fact, the murderer, he remains the most sympathetic character in the film. The female characters are shrewish and incapable of real emotional attachment.

Black Angel is well directed with several innovative techniques including a complicated opening boom shot. There are also some interesting expressionist techniques used in the scenes where Martin begins to remember how, he, in a drunken state, murdered his wife.

Although one of the least known "B" *noirs*, it is one of the most intriguing and well made minor films of the genre.

Black Mask

A monthly pulp magazine that was popular from the 1920's to the 1950's. *Black Mask* was the predominant detective and crime fiction magazine, with an editorial policy which encouraged literary pretensions and experimentation. *Black Mask* proved to be the starting point for the careers of many important American crime writers and through the magazine a place where they could develop themes and styles. It is here that the mythological American private detective first appeared, mainly in the stories of Dashiell Hammett and Raymond Chandler. Cornell Woolrich and David Goodis, among others, also published stories in the magazine. As a breeding ground for the ideas that would appear later in *film noir*, *Black Mask* had an indirect but profound influence on the genre.

Black Tuesday (United Artists, 1954). 80 min.

Producer and Director: Hugo Fregonese. Screenplay: Sydney Boehm. Director of Photography: Stanley Cortez. Music: Paul Dunlap. Editor: Robert Golden.

Cast: Edward G. Robinson (Vincent Canelli), Peter Graves (Peter Manning), Jean Parker (Hatti Combest), Milburn Stone (Father Slocum), Warren Stevens (Joey Stewart), Jack Kelly (Frank Carson).

On the day of his scheduled execution, Vincent Canelli, a vicious gangster, engineers an elaborate escape, and hides out with a group of hostages in an unused warehouse.

Black Tuesday is a minor *film noir* that works mainly as a character study. Except for some action at the beginning and a violent climax, it is a surprisingly static film. The screenplay, by *noir* writer Sydney Boehm, is obviously patterned after *Key Largo* (Warner Bros., 1949) and the gangster classic *Petrified Forest* (Warner Bros.,) both originally stage plays in which much of the action takes place in a single location. *Black Tuesday* has some tension in its interplay between the characters, but generally the film is rather slow.

This was also one of Edward G. Robinson's last starring vehicles, a disappointing reprise of the roles he had made famous in much better films in the past.

Blanke, Henry (1901–1981)

Producer. The German born Blanke was, for many years, an employee of Warner Bros. Blanke's long career at the studio saw him produce many of their most important films. Among these are *The Maltese Falcon* and *The Mask of Dimitrios*, two important, seminal *films noirs*.

Filmography: *The Maltese Falcon* (Warner Bros., 1941). *The Mask of Dimitrios* (Warner Bros., 1944). *Beyond the Forest* (Warner Bros., 1949).

Blast of Silence (Universal, 1961). 83 min.

Producer: Merrill Brody. Director: Allen Baron. Screenplay: Allen Brody. Director of Photography: Merrill Brody. Music: Meyer Kuperman. Art Director: Charles Rosen. Editor: Merrill Brody.

Cast: Allen Baron (Frank Bono), Molly McCarthy (Lorrie), Larry Tucker (Big Ralph), Peter Clume (Troina). With: Canny Meeham, Milda Memonas, Dean Sheldon.

Frank Bono, a hired killer, arrives in Manhattan with the assignment to kill Big Ralph. A cautious professional, Bono investigates the background of his victims, a perverse ritual before he assassinates them. In the process he rekindles a relationship with an old girlfriend, even contemplating retiring from his profession and starting a new

life with her. Eventually, however, he carries out his assignment. When he goes to the assigned place to pick up his pay, he is, in turn, gunned down by assassins.

Blast of Silence is an obscure, late *noir* that looks and feels almost like an art film. It was a family affair, written, produced and edited by the Brody brothers, Merrill and Allen, which as their only major production.

Coming at the tail end of *films noirs* initial phase, *Blast of Silence* is one of the darkest, most fatalistic of all *noirs*. The film opens with a famous shot of a commuter train hurtling out of a tunnel, a shot which establishes the theme of the film: the characters are rushing toward their tragic destinies, unquestioning and yet determined to get there against all odds.

Blondell, Joan (1909–1979)

Actress. A wide-eyed blonde, Blondell was a popular comic heroine of musicals and comedies in the 1930's. In the forties she varied her dizzy screen personality with dramatic parts. She co-starred in *Nightmare Alley* as the assistant of a fake spiritualist. (Tyrone Power), her only *film noir*.

Filmography: *Nightmare Alley* (20th Century–Fox, 1947).

The Blue Dahlia (Paramount, 1946). 98 min.

Producer: John Houseman. Director: George Marshall. Screenplay: Raymond Chandler. Director of Photography: Lionel Lindon. Music: Victor Young. Art Directors: Hans Dreier and Walter Tyler. Editor: Arthur Schmidt.

Cast: Alan Ladd (Johnny Morrison), Veronica Lake (Joyce Harwood), William Bendix (Buzz Wanchek), Howard DaSilva (Eddie Harwood), Doris Dowling (Helen Morrison), Tom Powers (Captain Hendrickson), Will Wright (Dad Newell), Hugh Beaumont (George Copeland). With: Frank Faylen, Vera Marshe, Mae Marsh, Milton Kibbee.

When Johnny Morrison, a war veteran and hero, returns to Los Angeles with his friends Buzz and George, he discovers his wife, Helen, has been unfaithful. Disgusted, he leaves her, but she is discovered murdered the following morning. Johnny is the only suspect and the police issue a warrant for his arrest. While fleeing the police, he befriends Joyce Harwood, a mysterious, beautiful young woman. He later discovers that she is the wife of Eddie Harwood, the owner of The Blue Dahlia, a nightclub. Harwood was having an affair with Helen Morrison, Johnny's wife and Johnny believes Eddie is the murderer.

Meanwhile, Buzz and George are trying to help prove Johnny's innocence, but it appears that Buzz actually committed the crime while suffering from a black-out caused by a war injury.

Johnny, kidnapped by Harwood's henchmen is taken to an abandoned house. But in an ensuing fight, Harwood is killed and Johnny escapes.

Buzz and George arrive at The Blue Dahlia to confront Harwood. Upset by the jazz being played, Buzz confesses to the murder and the police are called. Johnny arrives and convinces the police that Buzz is innocent. Dad Newell, a cheap hotel detective who was a "witness" of Helen Morrison's murder confesses that, in fact, he murdered Mrs. Morrison when she had refused to cooperate with his blackmail scheme. He tries to grab a policeman's gun, but is shot and killed by Captain Hendrickson.

Raymond Chandler's only original screenplay, *The Blue Dahlia*, is one of the most important early post-war *films noirs*. It is brimming with a number of important *noir* themes: the disillusions of returning war veterans, amnesia, destructive sexuality and the corruption of big cities. The latter was an important theme in all of Chandler's works, with Los Angeles often appearing as a dangerous, corrupt city.

There are certain improbabilities and continuity problems with the script. Most importantly, in the original screenplay, Buzz in fact, was the real killer. He was desensitized to violence after his experiences during the war and the injury to his head. The Navy Department, however, objected to such a portrayal and Chandler had to rewrite the screenplay accordingly. Also, the final sequence in an office at The Blue Dahlia, is a little too conventional, reminding one of the concluding drawing room sequences in Victoria mystery novels.

The Blue Dahlia was the third of five films featuring Alan Ladd and Veronica Lake and was the last of their really big hits. Although Lake was not a very good actress, she had a certain screen presence and together, they had a powerful sexual chemistry.

The film is stylishly directed by George Marshall, one of the most prolific directors of Hollywood's golden age. Even though he specialized in glossy, color comedies, he was very adaptable and with collaborators Lionel Lindon, Hans Dreier and Walter Tyler, created a near perfect example of studio craftsmanship at its best.

With Chandler's sparkling, brazen dialog and the overwhelming sense of corruption hidden just below the surface of the characters, *The Blue Dahlia* remains one of the most fascinating illustrations of early post-war *noir*.

The Blue Gardenia (Warner Bros., 1953). 90 min.

Producer: Alex Gottlieb. Director: Fritz Lang. Screenplay: Charles Hoffman, based on the short story "Gardenia" by Vera Caspary. Director of Photography: Nicholas Musuraca. Music: Raoul Kraushaar. Song: "The Blue Gardenia" by Bob Russell and Lester Cole, sung by Nat "King" Cole. Art Director: Daniel Hall. Editor: Edward Mann.

Cast: Anne Baxter (Norah Larkin),

Anne Baxter, Richard Conte in *The Blue Gardenia* (Warner Bros., 1953).

Richard Conte (Casey Mayo), Ann Sothern (Crystal Carpenter), Raymond Burr (Harry Prebble), Jeff Donnell (Sally Ellis), George Reeves (Captain Haynes). With: Ruth Storey, Ray Walker, Nat "King" Cole, Alex Gottlieb.

After receiving a "Dear Jane" letter from her fiancé in Korea, Norah Larkin impulsively accepts a blind date with a man calling for her roommate, Crystal. They meet at the Blue Gardenia, a popular Hollywood restaurant. The beautiful, vulnerable Norah is easy prey for suave playboy Harry Prebble. He gets her drunk and takes her back to his place where he tries to seduce her. She hits him over the head with a fireplace poker and flees. She wakes up the following morning with a bad hangover and not much memory about the night before, until she reads in the paper that Prebble has been beaten to death.

Casey Mayo, a newspaper reporter, puts a "Letter to an Unknown Murderess" in his paper, in a desperate attempt to help catch the criminal. Norah responds, pretending to be a friend of the murderess. She falls in love with Mayo. Although she eventually confesses to him, he has discovered that another girl, Rose, Prebble's pregnant girlfriend had been in his apartment the night he was murdered. When confronted with this evidence by Mayo, Rose admits she killed Prebble after he refused to marry her.

Of the four major Fritz Lang directed *films noirs* made in the 1950's — *Clash by Night* (RKO, 1952), *The Big Heat* (Columbia, 1953), *Human Desire* (Columbia, 1954) and *The Blue Gardenia* — the latter is probably the weakest. Its plot is rather conventional and only moderately suspenseful. Yet, being a Lang film it is better than average.

The lighting is surprisingly flat (obviously influenced by the new medium of television). Even so, the cinema-

Anne Baxter being fingerprinted in *The Blue Gardenia.*

tographer, Nicholas Musuraca, had helped define the influential RKO/expressionist style in the late forties. Perhaps the film's most interesting aspect is that much of it was shot on location, giving it a less artificial, studio bound look. Otherwise, it is a somewhat disappointing film for talents as great as Lang and Musuraca.

Blue Velvet (D.E.G./Lorimar, 1986). 120 min.

Producer: Richard Roth. Director: David Lynch. Screenplay: David Lynch. Director of Photography: Frederick Elmes. Art Director: Patricia Norris. Editor: Duwayne Dunham.

Cast: Isabella Rossilini (Miranda), Kyle Maclachlan (Jeffrey), Dennis Hopper (Floyd), Laura Dern (Sonia), Hope Lang (Mrs. Williams), Dean Stockwell (Ben). With: George Dickerson, Priscilla Pointer, Frances Bay.

David Lynch's story of a small town's corruption has generated more praise and controversy than any recent film. Through all the hyperbole surrounding the film, critics seemed to have missed the fact that the film is one of the most effective attempts to recapture the spirit of *film noir*: the deceptive tranquility of "normality," destructive sexuality, layers of corruption that includes the police and criminals, etc.

Interestingly, in its use of cinematography and coordination of colors (muted and dark), combined with music, the film is also technically close to the great forties *films noirs*.

Blythe, Ann (1928–)

Actress. A juvenile singer, Blythe made a striking first appearance at sixteen in the *film noir* classic *Mildred Pierce*. As the precocious and vindictive Veda Pierce, she is one of the genre's unique *femme-fatale*. It remains her most memorable role, although she continued to act in movies for over two

John Garfield, polishing off his opponent in *Body and Soul* (United Artists, 1947).

decades. Her part in *Brute Force* is small and insignificant.

Filmography: *Mildred Pierce* (Warner Bros., 1945). *Brute Force* (Universal, 1947).

Body and Soul (United Artists, 1947). 105 min.

Producer: Bob Roberts. Director: Robert Rossen. Screenplay: Abraham Polonsky. Director of Photography: James Wong Howe. Music: Hugo Friedhofer. Song: "Body and Soul" by Johnny Green, Edward Newman, Robert Sour and Frank Eyton. Art Director: Nathan Juran. Editor: Robert Parrish.

Cast: John Garfield (Charlie Davis), Lilli Palmer (Peg Bron), Hazel Brooks (Alice), Anne Revere (Anna Davis), William Conrad (Quinn), Joseph Pevney (Shorty Polaski), Lloyd Guff (Roberts). With: Canada Lee, Art Smith, James Burke.

Arguably the best of the *noir* boxing films, *Body and Soul* is certainly the most famous. Its tale of a boxer from the ghettos who triumphs over his own greed is something of a cliche today, but it had a powerful impact at the time and the film still has a power to move the viewer.

Charlie Davis, a young man from the slums, is determined to escape poverty. He decides to exploit his skill as a street fighter, teams with his friend Roberts (who works as his manager) and starts his rise to fame as a professional boxer. His never ending search for money and fame alienates him from his family and friends. He rejects his childhood sweetheart, for a more "sophisticated" woman. Finally, as the ultimate act of corruption, Roberts wants him to throw a fight for a large sum of money. But when he sees Roberts kill a man, Charlie has a change of heart and he decides to try to win the fight.

William Hurt, Kathleen Turner in *Body Heat* (Warner Bros., 1981).

Basically an attack against corruption and greed, *Body and Soul* was the last cry of overt liberalism before the House Unamerican Activities Committee ruined the careers of a number of prominent Hollywood figures including screenwriter Abraham Polonsky.

Robert Rossen, formally a top editor (and protégé of producer Val Lewton), directed with great skill but not much imagination. Visually, the film is surprisingly restrained except for the extraordinary fight scenes which used the then new technique of hand held cameras. It had a profound influence on later filmmakers.

Body Heat (Warner Bros., 1981). 113 min.
Producer: Fred T. Gallo. Director: Lawrence Kasdan. Screenplay: Lawrence Kasdan. Director of Photography: Richard H. Kline. Music: John Barry. Art Director: Bill Kenney. Editor: Carol Littleton.

Cast: William Hurt (Ned Racine), Kathleen Turner (Matty Walker), Richard Crenna (Edmund Walker), Ted Danson (Peter Lowenstein), J. A. Preston (Oscar Grace), Mickey Rourke (Teddy Lewis). With Kim Zimmer, Jane Hallaran, Lanna Saunders, Michael Ryan.

Ned Racine is a casual, likable, unambitious Florida lawyer whose life is coasting along in neutral, just the way he likes it, until he meets Matty Walker. From the moment of their "chance" meeting at an outdoor jazz concert, Racine is entranced by her sexual magnetism. She entraps him with lust and convinces him to murder her husband for insurance money. But he soon finds himself doublecrossed and in prison, while his ex-lover has disappeared somewhere in the South Pacific with the insurance funds.

Body Heat is a sexy, sordid, haunting story that resembles the James M. Cain inspired *film noir* classic *Double Indemnity* (Paramount, 1944) and *The Postman Always Rings Twice* (MGM, 1946); but writer/director Lawrence Kasdan brought a sense of energy, irony and sexual explicitness that is only possible today.

Hurt and then-newcomer Turner ignite the screen with a feverish intensity. Their steamy love scenes were considered daring even at the time. Turner's character is the archetypal *femme-fatale* and Hurt's character, the archetypal male victim. Like his predecessors in *Double Indemnity* and *The Postman Always Rings Twice*, he finds himself a subconsciously willing participant in his own degradation.

Kasdan and cinematographer Richard H. Kline bring a sense of 1940's *noir* ambience to the film, aided by a dreamy, jazz laden score. Those who do not believe that *films noirs* can be made in color, or that the genre still has a powerful impact on contemporary cinema should see *Body Heat*. The film is, without a doubt, within the tradition of the genre and one of the most extraordinary, modern *films noirs*.

Bodyguard (RKO, 1948). 62 min.
Producer: Lewis J. Rachmil. Director: Richard Fleischer. Screenplay: Fred Niblo and Harry Essex, story by George W. George and Robert B. Altman. Director of Photography: Robert de Grasse. Music: Paul Sawtell. Art Directors: Albert S. D'Agostino and Howard Hall. Editor: Robert Golden.

Cast: Lawrence Tierney (Mike Carter), Priscilla Lane (Doris Brewster), Philip Reed (Freddie Dysen), Steve Brodie (Fenton), Frank Fenton (Lt. Borden). With: June Clayworth and Elizabeth Wisdom.

Bodyguard gave Lawrence Tierney one of his few good guy roles. He plays a plainclothes officer who resigns from the force and takes a job as a bodyguard for a wealthy widow, Elizabeth Risdon. He soon finds himself hunted by his police buddies when accused of murder. His efforts to avoid arrest and catch the real killer are aided by his fiancee Doris Brewster, a clerk who has access to public files which he needs to prove his innocence. Eventually, he discovers that it is a group of crooked cops in his former precinct who are guilty.

Bodyguard clocks in at just over an hour. The emphasis is on violence and action and the film is appropriately fast and zippy.

Richard Fleischer was one of the best "B" movie directors and *Bodyguard*, although not one of his best films, is a fine example of cheap movie making at its best. He exploits the sparse sets with innovative camera work and dark lighting to hide the empty spaces. In addition, the screenplay, co-written by silent film director turned screenwriter Fred Niblo, manages to avoid the usual cliches of "B" movies.

Boehm, Sydney (1908–)
Screenwriter. Boehm was a journeyman writer who worked on a variety of films for all the major studios. However, he specialized in hard-boiled crime stories and is a major figure of *film noir*. Not all of Boehm's *noir* titles are major films, but he worked on a number of outstanding films which are important contributions to the genre.

Filmography: *The High Wall* (MGM, 1947). *The Undercover Man* (Columbia, 1949). *Mystery Street* (MGM, 1950). *Side Street* (MGM, 1950). *Union Station* (Paramount, 1950). *The Big Heat* (Columbia, 1953). *Black Tuesday* (United Artists, 1954). *Rogue Cop* (MGM, 1954).

Boetticher, Budd (1916–)
Director. An ex-bullfighter and adventurer, Boetticher was a talented director of "B" movies, especially action films. He directed an excellent, low-budget gangster bioptic, *The Rise*

is aware of the real killer). Shocking for its time, it was also very innovative. It was Elia Kazan's third feature and his most important at that point, showing the way to his later films. Its documentary style was also very influential, predating *The Naked City* (Universal, 1948) by a year.

Boone, Richard (1917–1981)

Actor. Boone, one of the fifties's most memorable tough guys, was a graduate of New York's Actor's Studio, whose other students included Marlon Brando and Marilyn Monroe among many others. Although craggy and commanding, he was also articulate and intelligent and often played heroes or smart anti-heroes.

Richard Boone acted in four minor, but interesting *films noirs*. In *Vicki* he played police Lt. Cornell, the ironic catalyst of the tragedy. He also had an important role in *The Garment Jungle*, as a particularly memorable villain. His most unique *noir* role, however, was the off screen narrator of Robert Aldrich's *The Big Knife*.

Filmography: *Vicki* (20th Century–Fox, 1953). *The Big Knife* (United Artists. 1955). *The Garment Jungle* (Columbia, 1957). *The Kremlin Letter* (20th Century–Fox 1970).

Border Incident (MGM, 1949). 96 min.

Producer: Nicholas Mayfack. Director: Anthony Mann. Screenplay: John C. Higgins, story by John C. Higgins and George Zuckerman. Director of Photography: John Alton. Music Director: Andre Previn. Art Directors: Cedric Gibbons and Hans Peters. Editor: Conrad A. Nervig.

Cast: Richardo Montalban (Pablo Rodriguez), George Murphy (Jack Bearnes), Howard da Silva (Owen Parkson), James Mitchell (Juan Garcia), Arnold Moss (Zopilote). With: Alfonso Bedoya, Teresa Celli, Charles McGraw, Jose Torvay.

Border Incident was the first "A" picture directed by Anthony Mann and one of his last *films noirs* before teaming with actor James Stewart for a series of brilliant westerns in the 1950's.

An American immigration agent, Jack Bearnes, teams with a Mexican agent, Pablo Rodriquez, to infiltrate an illegal immigration ring run by a crooked rancher, Owen Parkson. Parkson runs his organization by terror, even resorting to murder when necessary. When Jack's true identity is discovered, Parkson's henchmen torture and murder him while the helpless Pablo watches. Eventually, however, Pablo, with the help of American authorities, breaks up the gang and Parkson is sent to prison.

Border Incident has much in common with Mann's Eagle-Lion productions and is a variation on the plot of *T-Men*, (Eagle-Lion, 1948). Indeed, several scenes from the early film are repeated virtually intact in this film, most notably the torture/murder of the federal agent.

While the story is a fairly conventional undercover cop type, Mann and his cinematographer John Alton (one of his chief collaborators from Eagle-Lion), imbue it with a great sense of "B" aesthetics. The film is fast paced and Alton's beautifully photographed film is excellent consisting primarily of deep focus compositions with high contrast lighting. Landscapes are photographed in a pseudo-impressionist style, at least as much as black and white photography can resemble the style.

Except for the access to a higher budget and better production facilities, there is little to distinguish *Border Incident* from Mann's low-budget *films noirs*.

Borgnine, Ernest (1915–)

Character actor. Borgnine's good natured humor did not make him a very convincing villain or, for that matter, hero. He has always imbued his gruff character roles with a comic sensibility. In *The Mob*, one of his early film appearances, he played a small role as a mob henchman. He had bigger parts in two important post-*noirs*, but most of his career after 1960 was devoted to comic roles on television.

Filmography: *The Mob* (Columbia, 1951). *The Split* (MGM, 1968). *Hustle* (Paramount, 1975).

Born to Kill (RKO, 1947). 92 min.

Producer: Herman Schlom. Director: Robert Wise. Screenplay: Eve Greene and Richard Macaulay, based on the novel *Deadlier Than the Male* by James Gunn. Director of Photography: Robert de Grasse. Music: Paul Sawtell. Music Director: Constantin Bakaleinikoff. Art Directors: Albert S. D'Agostino and Walter Keller. Editor: Les Milbrook.

Cast: Claire Trevor (Helen Trent), Lawrence Tierney (Sam Wild), Walter Slezak (Arnold Arnett), Phillip Terry (Fred Grover), Audrey Long (Georgia Staples), Elisha Cook, Jr. (Marty Veaterman), Isabel Jewell (Laury Palmer). With Esther Howard, Kathryn Card, Tony Barrett.

Sam Wild, a former boxer and rancher, lives in Reno, Nevada. He suffers from a violent temper. When he sees an ex-girlfriend Laury Palmer out with another man, he becomes enraged by jealousy killing them both and flees to San Francisco.

Later that evening, the bodies are discovered in a boarding house by a tenant, Helen Trent, who does not report the murders because she is leaving town that night to return home, by coincidence to San Francisco.

Meeting on the train to San Francisco, Helen is attracted to the rugged and handsome Wild, but she refuses a date—the adopted sister of Georgia Staples, a newspaper heiress, Helen is engaged to a young heir of an industrial fortune, Fred Grover. Later, when Sam visits Helen at the Staples mansion, he meets and begins to court Georgia Staples simply because of her wealth and the impressionable young heiress falls in love with him. They are soon married.

Sam's friend Marty who had remained in Reno to follow the murder investigation arrives in San Francisco, followed by a crooked private detective, setting off a series of complicated twists which results in Sam killing Marty, whom he believes is having an affair with Helen.

Although she knows of Sam's murderous passions, Helen is perversely attracted to him and her hatred of Georgia causes her to seduce Sam in front of her adopted sister. However, she has also called the police, hoping to extricate herself from suspicion of involvement in Sam's crimes. The police arrive, but when Sam finds out Helen called them, he shoots her and in turn, is shot and killed by the police.

For a low budget feature, the Robert Wise directed *Born to Kill* was a relatively star studded production. Wise, like Jacques Tourneur, was a veteran of the RKO/Val Lewton group. Like his Lewton contemporaries, Wise specialized in gothic thrillers, but Wise did not have the inventive flair of Tourneur. Still, Wise was an adequate technician and *Born to Kill* is a perfect example of his simple, unobtrusive style.

Despite an improbable plot, Wise somehow managed to hold the film together. Events unfold rapidly and the tension is palpable and menacing. Claire Trevor is excellent as the fidgety, sexually frustrated Helen Trent. But it is Tierney's fierce performance as the psychotic Sam Wild that really makes the film such a striking vision of paranoia and madness.

Born to Kill is a minor classic, worthy of all the praise lavished on it in recent years.

Bowers, William (1916–1987)

Screenwriter. Bowers was a major screenwriter whose career spanned over three decades beginning in the mid-forties. During this long and generally distinguished career, he wrote or co-wrote a variety of excellent films including comedies and several interesting westerns. His *films noirs* are not really as distinguished as his other films but have much to recommend them including a surprisingly adult approach to the themes and a tendency toward violence.

Filmography: *The Web* (Universal, 1947). *Larceny* (Universal, 1948). *Abandoned* (Universal, 1949). *Convicted* (Columbia, 1950). *Cry Danger* (RKO, 1951). *The Mob* (Columbia, 1951).

Boxers

Perhaps because of the inherently existential nature of their profession and lives, boxers are central characters in several important *films noirs*. The cycle of boxing *noirs* began with Robert Rossen's classic *Body and Soul* (United Artists, 1947). With *The Set-Up* (RKO, 1949), *Body and Soul* is both a character study and an exposé of the corrupt, violent world of boxing; and in both, the protagonists triumph over greedy gamblers and gangsters by deciding not to give in to the temptation of throwing a fight for money. Both films are distinguished by a visceral, inventive style, particularly in the fight scenes and strong performances by John Garfield in the former and Robert Ryan in the latter.

Perhaps the greatest of all boxing films, until Martin Scorsese's *Raging Bull* (Universal, 1980), was *Champion* (United Artists, 1949), directed by Mark Robson. A vicious film, *Champion* starred Kirk Douglas as a boxer who claws his way to the top, spurred on by a vision of possessing a blonde sexpot played by the sensual Marilyn Maxwell. In the end, however, he discovers that, despite his achievements and hard-headed fight for fame, he is still only a pawn in the mobsters' game and as helpless as ever: the ultimate *film noir* theme of quiet desperation.

For a change of pace, the central character in *99 River Street* (United Artists, 1953) is a boxer in a non-boxing *film noir*. John Payne stars in Phil

Karlson's violent *noir* as an embittered ex-boxer framed for his wife's murder. And in *Second Chance* (RKO, 1951), a boxer who has accidentally killed an opponent in the ring finds redemption while battling a vicious gangster in South America.

Boyle, Robert (1910–)

Art director. After a long apprenticeship at RKO and Paramount, Boyle became one of the busiest independent art directors in the American film industry. Mainly associated with Alfred Hitchcock, he also worked on a number of important *films noirs*. Boyle had a luxuriant style, working mainly with big sets, and had an imaginative use of space.

Filmography: *Shadow of a Doubt* (Universal, 1943). *Nocturne* (RKO, 1946). *Ride the Pink Horse* (Universal, 1947). *They Won't Believe Me* (RKO, 1947). *Abandoned* (Universal, 1949). *Undertow* (Universal, 1949). *Forbidden* (Universal, 1954). *The Brothers Rico* (Columbia, 1957). *The Crimson Kimono* (Columbia, 1959). *Cape Fear* (Universal, 1962).

Brackett, Charles (1892–1969)

Screenwriter and producer. While his name is not as well known as it should be, there is little question about Charles Brackett's importance to American film. With Billy Wilder, his collaborator from the mid-thirties to the late-forties, he was part of one of the most important collaborations in cinematic history. Indeed, most of the films written and produced/directed by the two are considered masterpieces today.

Brackett was born into wealth and was a popular novelist in the mid-twenties. Several of his novels were made into popular films and Brackett was lured to Hollywood by the glamour and the work. Brackett was always puritanical when it came to his career and was a prolific screenwriter. But it was only when he teamed with Wilder that he achieved real success. Together they wrote many of the great comedies of director Ernst Lubitsch. Writers of great wit and sophistication, Bracket–Wilder wrote a number of great comedies, adventure, and melodramas for other directors as well, including Howard Hawks. But their arguments about the interpretation of their work with director Mitchell Lersen persuaded them to strike out on their own. Brackett produced while the more gregarious Wilder directed.

Although undeniably important and successful, the two men had a volatile relationship and they often argued about their projects. When Wilder suggested the two adapt James M. Cain's popular novel *Double Indemnity*, Brackett refused to work on what he considered pornographic rubbish and the team temporarily broke up.

The two writers re-teamed in the mid-forties and together they made one of the classics of the genre, *Sunset Boulevard*. It is an unrelentingly angry exposé of Hollywood which definitely shows the strong hand of the cynical Wilder, while tempered by Brackett's somewhat more romantic, sentimental style.

The team again broke up after making this classic, this time permanently, but Brackett contributed another classic to the genre: *Niagara*. Far more conventional than its predecessor, this is still a bitter, dark view of humanity, surprisingly cynical for a man who usually avoided such subjects.

Filmography: *Sunset Boulevard* (Paramount, 1950). *Niagara* (20th Century–Fox, 1952).

Brackett, Leigh (1915–1978)
Screenwriter. Leigh Brackett (no relation to Charles Brackett), was one of the most successful women screen writers from Hollywood's golden age. She is probably best remembered for her long, sporadic collaboration with the great director Howard Hawks. Indeed, it is for this director that she co-wrote her only *film noir*, the brilliant adaption of Raymond Chandler's novel *The Big Sleep*, which retains the plot intact, but adds some piquant, amusing dialog — Brackett's specialty.

Filmography: *The Big Sleep* (Warner Bros., 1946).

Bradley, David (1919–)
Director. David Bradley is one of American film's real enigmas. He originally came to the attention of Hollywood through his self-financed short films and amateur features. He was signed to MGM in 1951 and promptly directed *Talk About a Stranger*, an interesting, if minor film. It is, in fact, his only major production. He directed a few films afterward, but by the early sixties he had completely disappeared.

Filmography: *Talk About a Stranger* (MGM, 1952).

Brady, Scott (Gerald Tierney) (1924–1985)
Actor. Although not as well known as his brother Lawrence Tierney, Scott Brady was also one of the major "B" actors of the late-forties and fifties. Tough-looking and rather menacing, he played violent criminals of various sorts in many films. including a few "A" productions and he was a mainstay in low-budget westerns of the 1950's. He appeared in a few *films noirs*, mostly as villainous henchmen. However, in *Undertow*, he had one of his few lead roles as a returning war veteran who must prove his innocence when unjustly accused of murder.

Filmography: *Canon City* (Eagle-Lion, 1948). *He Walked By Night* (Eagle-Lion, 1948). *Undertow* (Universal, 1949).

Brahm, John (Hans Brahm) (1893–1974)
Director. Brahm has been called one of the most neglected masters of gothic style in American film. He is certainly one of the best directors of "B" movies.

Brahm was born in Germany and first made a name for himself as a leading stage director in Berlin, Vienna and Paris. A commercial director, he brought expressionist elements to his stage productions, a stylistic force that would have a profound influence on his film work.

Brahm first made films in England in the late thirties beginning as an editor and later, briefly as a screenwriter before becoming a director at the age of forty. He directed a few unimportant films in England before moving to the United States.

Brahm's best films were made in Hollywood in the mid and late forties. With only a small budget per film, he managed to create some of the most visually striking films of the era. He made effective use of the studio and made a series of uniquely dark and paranoid melodramas including a harrowing tale of a Victorian London murder, *Hangover Square* (20th Century–Fox, 1945), which is known for its *noir*-like atmosphere and a superior score by Bernard Hermann.

Brahm's three *films noirs* are equally notable. *The Brasher Doubloon* is based on Raymond Chandler's *The High Window*. It is, perhaps, the least known Philip Marlowe film, but it is as stylish as the others. The same is true of *The Locket*. *Singapore*, a *noir* adventure starring the post-*Double Indemnity* Fred MacMurray, is enjoyable, unpretentious entertainment.

As it turned out, *Singapore* was Brahm's last major production. Although he continued to direct films steadily until the mid–fifties, his best later work was as a director of macabre television shows, including episodes of "The Twilight Zone" and "Alfred Hitchcock Presents."

John Brahm's best work awaits rediscovery. In the meantime, his accomplishments entertain a small group of appreciators in the know.

Filmography: *The Brasher Doubloon* (20th Century–Fox, 1947). *The Locket* (RKO, 1947). *Singapore* (Universal, 1947).

Brainstorm (Warner Bros., 1965). 114 min.

Producer and Director: William Conrad. Screenplay: Mann Rubin, story by Larry Marcus. Director of Photography: Sam Leavitt. Music: George Duning. Art Director: Robert Smith. Editor: William Ziegler.

Cast: Jeff Hunter (James Grayan), Anne Francis (Lorrie Benson), Dana Andrews (Cort Benson), Viveca Lindfors (Dr. Elizabeth Larstedt), Stacy Harris (Josh Reynolds). With: Kathie Browne, Phillip Pine, Michael Pate, Joan Swift.

After James Grayan, a brilliant scientist, saves the beautiful Lorrie Benson from suicide, he begins an affair with her. She is the wife of a powerful and sadistic industrialist, Cort Benson, who upon learning of the affair, tries to break it up. Grayan had once had a nervous breakdown and Benson creates an elaborate plan to make it look like Grayan is going insane. Grayan agrees to go to a psychiatrist, Dr. Elizabeth Larstadt, but he has an ulterior motive: by pretending to be insane, he can kill Benson and get away with it. In fact, when he does publicly murder the wealthy industrialist, his defense is "guilt by insanity." He is committed to an institution, but when Lorrie deserts him, he slowly descends into true madness.

Brainstorm is a minor, neglected little masterpiece from the 1960's. Produced and directed with great style by actor William Conrad, its story and strong expressionist style have much in common with certain *films noirs* from the late-forties. The emphasis is on character rather than action. Its screenplay is rich and compelling. It demonstrates further that, while *film noir* had run its course by 1959, the genre was still alive and had an impact well past the 1950's.

Brand, Neville (1921–)

Character actor. In the 1960's, Brand co-starred as Al Capone on the popular television series *The Untouchables*. It was a memorable role for an actor who had played villains and hard-boiled heroes in some two dozen films beginning in the early 1950's. Although he was chiefly a character actor, Brand also played second leads, particularly in the many westerns he appeared in. His *noir* roles were generally small and he almost always played bad guys and henchmen. His most prominent and important *noir* role is in *D.O.A.* in which he played the crazed killer.

Filmography: *D.O.A.* (United Artists, 1950). *Kiss Tomorrow Goodbye* (Warner Bros., 1950). *Where the Sidewalk Ends* (20th Century-Fox, 1950). *Kansas City Confidential* (United Artists, 1952). *The Turning Point* (Paramount, 1952). *Cry Terror* (MGM, 1958).

Brando, Jocelyn (1919–)

Character actress. The elder sister of Marlon Brando, Jocelyn has some of the same intensity of her more famous sibling. Her career has been devoted almost exclusively to the stage. She had small, supporting roles in two *films noirs* in the fifties including Fritz Lang's classic *The Big Heat* , but her parts were insignificant.

Filmography: *The Big Heat* (Columbia, 1953). *Nightfall* (Columbia, 1956).

Brando, Marlon (1924–)

Actor. Brando's early film roles were certainly his least self-indulgent. His role as a disillusioned boxer who sold himself and took a fall on the advice of his mob connected brother in Elia Kazan's *On the Waterfront*, a kind of pseudo-*noir*, is his best performance and deservedly famous.

Filmography: *On the Waterfront* (Columbia, 1953).

The Brasher Doubloon (20th Century-Fox, 1947)

Producer: Robert Brassler. Director: John Brahm. Screenplay: Dorothy Hannah, adapted by Dorothy Bennett and Leonrard Praskins from the novel *The High Window* by Raymond Chandler. Director of Photography: Lloyd Ahern. Music: David Buttolph. Art Director: James Basevi and Richard Irvine. Editor: Harry Reynolds.

Cast: George Montgomery (Philip Marlowe), Nancy Guild (Merle Davis), Conrad Janis (Leslie Murdock), Ray Roberts (Lt. Breeze), Fritz Kortner (Vannier), Florence Bates (Mrs. Murdock). With: Marvin Miller, Housely Stevenson, Bob Adler, Jack Conrad.

Although it is not as well known as other *films noirs* based on Raymond Chandler's novels, *The Brasher Doubloon* has its virtues. Indeed, it is one of the best "B" *noirs* made at 20th Century-Fox in the late forties.

The story is adapted from Chandler's weakest Philip Marlowe novel. A stolen coin brings Marlowe into the employ of a rich, eccentric widow, Mrs. Murdock. He quickly realizes there is more to the case than simple theft and the twisted trail leads from robbery to blackmail and murder. Marlowe's own life is soon endangered and he suffers a savage beating at the hands of unknown criminals. Eventually, through the help of Merle Davis, Mrs. Murdock's secretary, he discovers the culprit behind the complicated plot of fraud is none other than the elderly Mrs. Murdock.

A simplification of Chandler's novel, the screenplay for *The Brasher Doubloon* is quite good. George Montgomery is merely adequate as Philip Marlowe, but the film's virtues really lie with its director, John Brahm. Brahm has been called a neglected master of gothic style and *The Brasher Doubloon* is certainly one of the most extravagantly expressionist of all the Fox *films noirs*. Brahm lets the plot unfold at a leisurely pace so that the paranoid and menacing qualities seem to emerge subversively as the film progresses.

Brasselle, Keefe (1923–1981)

Actor. When he entered films in the mid-fifties, after a brief career on stage, Keefe Brasselle was billed as a new Cary Grant, but although he had a penchant for romantic comedy, he did not live up to his publicity. In fact, he had little screen presence and except for one memorable performance in the title role in *The Eddie Cantor Story* (Universal, 1953), his career is all but irrelevant. He had minor supporting roles in three minor *films noirs*. Interestingly, when he tried to rebuild his career as a television producer in the 1960's, he was equally unsuccessful. He later wrote two bitter Hollywood satires based on his own experiences.

Filmography: *Railroaded* (Producers Releasing Corporation, 1947). *T-Men* (Eagle-Lion, 1948). *The Unknown Man* (MGM, 1951).

The Breaking Point (Warner Bros., 1950). 97 min.

Producer: Jerry Wald. Director: Michael Curtiz. Screenplay: Ranald MacDougall, based on the novel *To Have and Have Not* by Ernest Hemingway. Director of Photography: Ted McCord. Music: Ray Heindorf. Art Director: Edward Carrere. Editor: Alan Crosland, Jr.

Cast: John Garfield (Harry Morgan), Patricia Neal (Leona Charles), Phyllis Thaxter (Lucy Morgan), Juano Hernandez (Wesley Park). With: Wallace Ford, Edmond Ryan, Ralph Dumke, Sherry Jackson.

The Breaking Point is the second adaption of Ernest Hemingway's minor novel *To Have and Have Not*. Its plot sticks reasonably close to the novel. Harry Morgan, owner of a charter boat, agrees to smuggle a group of illegal Chinese immigrants into the United States when he is left stranded in Mexico by another client. The plan backfires, however, and the U. S. Coast Guard impounds the boat. He returns to the U. S. and despondent over the loss of his boat, begins an illicit affair

with Leona. She introduces him to a crooked lawyer who helps him get his boat back in exchange for him carrying a group of thugs to Catalina Island. When they murder his alcoholic first mate, he realizes they intend to kill him, too. Instead, over the course of the day, he manages to kill all of them. Badly wounded after a gun battle with the hoodlums, he returns home to start a new life with his wife, Lucy.

Unlike Howard Hawk's more famous version of the novel, this version retains the fatalism of the novel, making it a true *film noir*. In addition, many of the people who worked on the film were important *noir* figures: John Garfield, who gives one of his best performances in this film; art director, Edward Carrere; screenwriter, Ranald MacDougall and director Michael Curtiz. Curtiz gives the film a strong, expressionist style, combining it with realism to create one of the more unique minor *films noirs*.

Bredell, Woody ( )

Cinematographer. A staff cinematographer for Universal, Bredell worked on a variety of films with little obvious personal style. However, he was an important member of Robert Siodmak's team of collaborators, photographing two of his most important *films noirs*, *Phantom Lady* and *The Killers*. Visually, both can be viewed as archetypal *noirs*: shadowy, fog-shrouded streets; rainy city scapes; dark, threatening bars and shimmering, even flattering close-ups of the actors. Of course, this is a consistent element of Siodmak's style, whomever the cinematographer, and it is debatable how much Bredell contributed, at least creatively, to the look of his Siodmak-directed films. Outside of his work with Siodmak, Bredell only photographed one other *film noir* and, although by no means a bad film, it is not up to the standards achieved with Siodmak.

Filmography: *Christmas Holiday* (Directed by Robert Siodmak)(Universal, 1944). *Phantom Lady* (Directed by

Ava Gardner in *The Killers* (Universal, 1946).

Robert Siodmak) (Universal, 1944). *The Killers* (Directed by Robert Siodmak) (Universal, 1946). *The Unsuspected* (Warner Bros., 1947).

Breen, Richard L. (1919–1967)
Screenwriter. At one time the president of the Screenwriter's Guild, Breen co-wrote many popular films of little distinction. However, of his two *films noirs*, both written in collaboration. *Niagara* (co-written with Charles Brackett) is a notable exception.

Filmography: *Appointment with Danger* (RKO, 1950). *Niagara* (20th Century–Fox, 1952).

Bremer, Lucille (1922–)

Actress and dancer. Pretty and talented, Bremer was groomed for stardom by MGM, but never really caught on. Still, she did co-star in two important musicals, *Yolanda and the Thief* (MGM, 1945) and *Ziegfeld Follies* (MGM, 1945) which marked the beginning of that studio's golden age of musicals. Dropped by MGM, Bremer co-starred in a handful of very minor films. In *Behind Locked Doors*, her last film, she is the only attractive, watchable element in an otherwise very poor film. It is a sad end for a once promising career.

Filmography: *Behind Locked Doors* (Eagle-Lion, 1948).

Brennan, Walter (1894–1974)

Character actor. Brennan is probably one of the best known American character actors. He acted in literally dozens of films and rarely failed to steal the scenes in which he appeared. Although he played a wide variety of parts, he's best known as the craggy sidekick in a number of westerns. His two *film noir* roles are not among his most famous work but his performances are typically memorable.

Filmography: *Fury* (MGM, 1936). *Nobody Lives Forever* (Warner Bros., 1946).

Brent, George (George Nolan) (1904–1979)

Actor. A suave and attractive Irish born leading man, Brent's career was similar to Robert Young and Robert Montgomery's. He was essentially decoration in films dominated by strong females. His personality was best suited to costume epics; but Brent did make one notable *film noir* appearance, as the crazed serial killer in Robert Siodmak's superior thriller, *The Spiral Staircase*.

Filmography: *The Spiral Staircase* (RKO, 1946).

The Bribe (MGM, 1949). 98 min.

Producer: Pandro S. Berman. Director: Robert Z. Leonard. Screenplay: Marguerite Roberts, based on the short story by Frederick Nebel. Director of Photography: Joseph Ruttenberg. Music: Miklos Rozsa. Song: "Situation Wanted" by Nacio Herb Brown and William Katz. Art Director: Cedric Gibbons and Malcolm Brown. Editor: Gene Ruggiero.

Cast: Robert Taylor (Rigby), Ava Gardner (Elizabeth Hintten), Charles Laughton (A.J. Bealer), Vincent Price (Carwood), John Hodiak (Tug Hintten), Samuel S. Hinds (Dr. Warren). With: John Hoyt, Tito Renaldo, Martin Garralaga.

The Bribe is an interesting, minor *film noir* with a deeply sensual performance by Ava Gardner and for a refreshing change of pace, an exotic, foreign setting.

A federal agent, Rigby, is sent to a small South American island to break up a smuggling ring dealing in contraband war surplus. The organization, is headed by Carwood and his two associates, A. J. Bealer and Tug Hintten. Rigby, working undercover, becomes romantically involved with Elizabeth Hintten. Elizabeth, however, double crosses him. Exposed, Rigby confronts Carwood during a spectacular fireworks display. Rigby wins the fight and resigns himself to life without Elizabeth.

While marginal, this film is certainly in the *noir* tradition in its depiction of a pervasive corruption abetted by a romantic setting. Likewise, the film has several *noir* icons in leading and supporting roles including Ava Gardner, Charles Laughton and Vincent Price. There are also some interesting *film noir* visuals: mirrored images and shots of Ava Gardner, as Elizabeth, through rain-streaked windows.

Bridges, Lloyd (1913–)

Actor. Although he never achieved the stardom he seemed destined for early in his career, Lloyd Bridges is still one of the most familiar faces to the public, thanks to his television success.

For much of his early film career, Bridges was typecast as a tough leading man and played occasional heavies in low-budget thrillers in the 1940's and 1950's. Of his two *films noirs*, both minor films, his best role was in *Try and Get Me*, in which he starred as one of two kidnappers whose plot tragically unravels.

Filmography: *Moonrise* (Republic, 1949). *Try and Get Me* (United Artists, 1950).

Brocco, Peter (1918–)

Character actor. Brocco acted in two or three dozen movies, always in small parts that amounted to little more than a walk-on. His *noir* roles include everything from bartenders to small time hoods.

Filmography: *The Reckless Moment* (Columbia, 1949). *The Undercover Man* (Columbia, 1949). *The Breaking Point* (Warner Bros., 1950). *Tension* (MGM, 1950). *The Killer That Stalked New York* (Columbia, 1951). *Roadblock* (RKO, 1951). *Rogue Cop* (MGM, 1954). *Underworld USA* (Columbia, 1961).

Brodie, Steve (1919–)

Actor. Steve Brodie was a character lead in mainly second features. Tough looking and rather menacing, he specialized in villains of various types. He is one of the minor icons of *film noir*, co-starring in a number of good films and one or two classics of the genre. In 1947 he acted in three *noirs*, including the great films *Out of the Past* and *Crossfire*. The latter provided him with one of his more unusual roles as the Jew who is murdered by the violently anti-semitic character played by Robert Ryan. The role he played in *Out of the Past*, however, was more typical: the crooked partner of private investigator Robert Mitchum. He was a memorably sadistic sidekick of the James Cagney gangster character in *Kiss Tomorrow Goodbye*. His role in *M*, on the other hand, was one of his rare good guys, in this case as a good-natured cop.

Filmography: *Crossfire* (RKO, 1947). *Desperate* (RKO, 1947). *Out of the Past* (RKO, 1947). *Bodyguard* (RKO, 1948). *Armored Car Robbery* (RKO, 1950). *Kiss Tomorrow Goodbye* (Warner Bros., 1950). *M* (Columbia, 1951).

Brodine, Norbett (1893–1970)

Cinematographer. Norbett Brodine is one of the great American cinematographers. His career began in the late teens and continued unabated until the early fifties. He was a master of black and white photography, specializing in brightly lit, romantic comedies and brought a sense of style and grace to *film noir*, photographing several outstanding titles of the genre.

Filmography: *Beast of the City* (MGM, 1932). *House on 92nd Street* (20th Century–Fox, 1945). *Somewhere in the Night* (20th Century–Fox, 1946). *Kiss of Death* (20th Century–Fox, 1947). *Thieves' Highway* (20th Century–Fox, 1949).

Bronson, Charles (1922–)

Character actor and leading man. With his rugged features and tough on-screen presence, Charles Bronson might, at first, seem to be a natural for *film noir*. Indeed, many of his later action features have *noir*-like elements but Bronson's attachment to the genre is tenuous at best. Unfortunately, he achieved stardom only after the genre had run its course and he appeared in small character parts in only three minor *films noirs*.

Filmography: *The Mob* (Columbia, 1951). *The People Against O'Hara* (MGM, 1951). *Crime Wave* (Warner Bros., 1954).

Brooks, Geraldine (Geraldine Stroock) (1925–1977)

Actress. Intense and talented, Geraldine Brooks looked for a time in the forties like she was going to be a great star, but she never lived up to her early promise. Still, she left behind a few compelling performances including roles

Paul Valentine, Dickie Moore in *Out of the Past* **(RKO, 1947).**

in two *films noirs*. Of the two, her best performance was as Bea, the impressionable daughter in *The Reckless Moment* whose actions are the catalyst for the tragedy that follows.

Filmography: *Possessed* (Warner Bros., 1947). *The Reckless Moment* (Columbia, 1949).

Brooks, Richard (1912–)

Novelist and screenwriter. Although his *noir* filmography is not as extensive as some of the other *noir* writers, Richard Brooks is certainly one of the important screenwriters of the genre simply by virtue of the quality of his work. He co-wrote *The Killers*, taking the bare bones of an Ernest Hemingway story, expanding it into a tale of deception, greed and murder. It remains one of the classics of the genre. Brooks also wrote *Brute Force*, an equally important early *noir*. His greatest contri-

bution to the genre however, is the novel and subsequent screenplay for the Edward Dmytryk classic, *Crossfire*. In the original novel, the story centered around the murder of a homosexual, but it was Dmytryk and producer Adrian Scott's idea to make the murder victim in the film version a Jew, thus giving the story a special urgency in the post-war era. Brook's screenplay is both poignant and crisp, avoiding many of the cliches of the genre.

Filmography: *The Killers* (Universal, 1946). *Brute Force* (Universal, 1947). *Crossfire* (RKO, 1947). *Key Largo* (Warner Bros., 1948). *Mystery Street* (MGM, 1950). *Storm Warning* (Warner Bros., 1950).

The Brothers Rico (Columbia, 1957). 92 min.

Producer: Lewis J. Rachmil. Director: Phil Karlson. Screenplay: Lewis

Meltzer and Ben Perry, based on the novelette *Les Freres Rico* by George Simenon. Director of Photography: Burnett Guffey. Music: George Duning. Art Director: Robert Boyle. Editor: Charles Nelson.

Cast: Richard Conte (Eddie Rico), Dianne Foster (Alice Rico), Kathryn Grant (Norah), Larry Gates (Sid Kubik), James Darren (Johnny Rico). With Argentina Brunetti, Lamount Johnson, Harry Bellaver, Paul Picerni.

Eddie Rico, an ex-mobster turned successful businessman, is contacted by the mob to help locate his two brothers who have apparently double-crossed their gangland associates. Eddie feels obliged, mainly because he believes he can intervene and save his brothers lives. He discovers, however, that his brothers problems are far more complicated than he realized and that the mob is just using him. Unable to save his brothers, he returns to his wife, mentally and physically scarred by the deadly affair.

The Brothers Rico is adapted from a novel by the great French crime novelist, George Simenon. Phil Karlson and his collaborators, scenarists Lewis Meltzer and Ben Perry, fashioned a violent screenplay from the original material and made it thoroughly American with its action and tough dialog.

In fact, the film marks the final gasp of *film noir* in the late 1950's. It replaced the cool, dark ambiance of classic *noir* style with crude violence and flat, natural lighting. Thematically, the film is clearly *film noir*, with its story of unrelenting paranoia and despair. More importantly, however, the film is one of the first of the new generation of contemporary thrillers that were influenced by *noir* aesthetics and themes, but would become something else.

Brown, Harry (1917–1986)

Screenwriter. Brown specialized in action-pictures, particularly war films. He co-wrote two *films noirs*, including the notably violent James Cagney

vehicle, *Kiss Tomorrow Goodbye. The Sniper*, about a rifleman who terrorizes a city, is one of Edward Dmytryk's lesser *films noirs*.

Filmography: *Kiss Tomorrow Goodbye* (Universal, 1948). *The Sniper* (Columbia, 1952).

Brown, Rowland (1901–1963)

Screenwriter and director. Rowland Brown is an enigma. In the early thirties he began a career as a film director which looked as if it were the beginning of an important new career. He co-wrote and directed one of the best early gangster films, *Quick Millions* (MGM, 1931), but his career as a director came to an abrupt end after only two additional films. His career as a screenwriter was equally sporadic and by far his most important later contributions are the two *films noirs* he co-wrote.

Filmography: *Nocturne* (RKO 1946). *Kansas City Confidential* (United Artists, 1952).

Brute Force (Universal, 1947). 95 min.

Producer: Mark Hellinger. Director: Jules Dassin. Screenplay: Richard Brooks, based on a short story by Robert Patterson. Director of Photographer: William Daniels. Music: Miklos Rozsa. Art Directors: Bernard Herzbrun and John F. DeCuir. Editor: Edward Curtiss.

Cast: Burt Lancaster (Joe Collins), Hume Cronyn (Captain Munsey), Charles Bickford (Gallagher), Yvonne DeCarlo (Gina), Ann Blythe (Ruth), Ella Raines (Cora), Anita Colby (Flossie), Howard Duff (Soldier), Roman Bohnen (Warden Barnes) With: Jeff Corey, Whit Bissell, Ray Teal, Jay C. Flippen, Charles McGraw.

As victims of Captain Munsey,a sadistic head of the prison guards, a group of inmates led by Joe Collins, plan an escape. Munsey is a violent psychotic and he resorts to acts of uncontrollable brutality in order to get information and stop the escape. The subsequent breakout turns into a savage

Burt Lancaster confronting other inmates in *Brute Force* (Universal, 1947).

and incredible eruption of fatal violence that destroys all of the escaping convicts and Captain Munsey.

Brute Force can be seen in two ways. First, on the surface, it is a simple expose of prison violence and the criminal underworld. Second, the plot setting and characters stand as metaphors for the world at large. In fact, this was exactly what screenwriter Richard Brooks and director Jules Dassin had in mind. Both were political liberals who saw popular cinema and literature as a convenient and interesting way of expressing political ideals. Thus, while it is true the film can stand on its own as simple entertainment, it is also a symbolic film in which the prison represents a political, decidedly conservative system, Munsey represents corrupt police and the prisoners repressed citizens.

Indeed, Jules Dassin would become, ironically, one of the major victims of Joseph McCarthy's "anti-communist" witch hunt in the early 1950's. All of Dassin's films were politically symbolic of liberal ideals, an element which got him into trouble in the United States, but allowed his career to flourish in Europe. In any case, Dassin is a vastly under-rated talent who was technically inventive and his *films noirs*, including *Brute Force*, are some of the best of the genre.

The cast of *Brute Force* is equally good. Burt Lancaster and Hume Cronyn stand out and the film is filled with brief appearances by many minor *noir* icons including Yvonne DeCarlo and Ella Raines as wives of convicts and Howard Duff, Whit Bissell and Charles McGraw as inmates.

Despite its fatalism, *Brute Force* was a surprising success and led to a number of "B" movie imitators including the all female prison drama, *Caged* (Warner Bros., 1950).

The Burglar (Columbia, 1957). 90 min. Producer: Louis W. Kellman. Director: Paul Wendkos. Screenwriter: David Goodis, based on his novel. Director of Photography: Don Malkames. Music: Sol Kaplan. Song: "You are Mine" by Bob Marcucchi and Pete Deangelo. Art Director: Jim Leonard. Editor: Herta Horn.

Cast: Dan Duryea (Nat Harbin), Jayne Mansfield (Gladden), Martha Vickers (Della), Peter Capell (Baylock), Mickey Shaughnessy (Dohmer). With: Wendell Phillips, Phoebe Mackay, Stewart Bradley, John Facenda.

Gladden helps her guardian, Nat Harbin and his associates steal a necklace from a spiritualist's mansion. Spotted by the police, the gang goes into hiding. Nat sends Gladden to Atlantic City until things cool down. However, Della, a female associate of Nat's, plans to kidnap Gladden and take the necklace as ransom. Meanwhile, rival criminals begin killing off Nat's gang while trying to steal the necklace for themselves. Nat joins Gladden in Atlantic City, but when they are cornered by the rival crooks, Nat is murdered. Della, in a single act of remorse and guilt, turns in her associates to the police.

David Goodis' novels are concerned more with the feelings of the characters and how they react in dangerous situations, rather than plot or action. *The Burglar* is probably his most exciting novel and it made a perfect *film noir* screenplay. Unfortunately, the movie's director, Paul Wendkos, a disciple of Orson Welles, filled the film with visual pyrotechnics which, at times, overwhelm the individual scenes. There are a number of scenes which echo Welles' more extreme innovations, including a sequence set in a steel pier that resembles the climatic fun house shoot out in *The Lady From Shanghai* (Columbia, 1948).

The performances in *The Burglar* are interesting. Dan Duryea, as Nat Harbin, is very good. Jayne Mansfield is surprisingly subdued and is quite good. Martha Vickers, so memorable as the slutty younger daughter in *The Big Sleep* (Warner Bros., 1946), makes a striking *femme-fatale* as Della.

Although the film suffers from a self-conscious technique, it is an interesting experiment in expressionist style.

Burks, Robert (1910–1968)

Cinematographer. Burks was one of the great cinematographers of his generation. One of Alfred Hitchcock's chief collaborators, he was the director of photography for many of the master's greatest films. Burks was equally at home in black and white or color and his work on Hitchcock's *Vertigo* is a masterpiece of semi-impressionist, color *noir* photography. He demonstrates with his work in this film, that it is not whether the film is shot in black and white or color that determines if a film is *noir* or not, but rather how one uses technique to enhance the story. His more traditional black and white *films noirs* are all excellent, with *Strangers on a Train*, directed by Hitchcock, being particularly outstanding.

Filmography: *Beyond the Forest* (Warner Bros., 1948). *The Enforcer* (Warner Bros., 1951). *Strangers on a Train* (Warner Bros., 1951). *Rear Window* (Paramount, 1954). *Vertigo* (Universal, 1958).

Burnett, W. R. (1899–1982)

Novelist and screenwriter. In the pantheon of great, forgotten American writers, W. R. Burnett began a successful career as a novelist and short story writer that would last for over four decades. His gangster and crime novels were immensely influential, particularly on the generation of crime novelists that would emerge in the thirties and forties.

Burnett's influence on *film noir*, both directly and indirectly, cannot be discounted. While his greatest impact was on the gangster genre of the thirties — he wrote the novel on which *Little*

Caeser (Warner Bros., 1930) was based—a number of his novels and stories were adapted as *noirs*. He also worked on a number of screenplays.

Burnett's work is distinguished by violence and tight, linear plots. He was also a brilliant writer of humorous dialog.

Filmography: *Beast of the City* (based on his novel) (MGM, 1932). *High Sierra* (co-wrote screenplay based on his novel) (Warner Bros., 1941). *This Gun for Hire* (co-wrote) (Paramount, 1942). *Nobody Lives Forever* (original screenplay) (Warner Bros., 1946). *The Asphalt Jungle* (based on his novel) (MGM, 1950). *The Racket* (co-wrote) (RKO, 1951). *I Died a Thousand Times* (wrote screenplay based on his novel *High Sierra*) (Warner Bros., 1955).

Burr, Raymond (1917–1993)

Character actor. Long before he achieved fame as the brilliant trial lawyer Perry Mason on television, Raymond Burr had a long and successful career as a character actor in movies. Unlike the kindly, thoughtful Perry Mason, however, most of the characters played by Burr in his film career were villains and murderers. He was one of the busiest character actors in *film noir*, appearing in nearly a dozen titles of the genre.

Burr's physical appearance—he was bulky, tall and rather menacing—made him a natural "heavy." He played gangsters in *Desperate* and *Raw Deal*, and murderers of various sorts in a number of other *films noirs* including, most spectacularly, Alfred Hitchcock's *Rear Window*. He also seemed to specialize in spectacular deaths: in *Raw Deal*, faced with being burned alive, he leaps to his death out of a window; in *Red Light* he was electrocuted on a neon sign; and in *The Blue Gardenia* he was bludgeoned to death by a woman.

Filmography: *Desperate* (RKO, 1947). *Pitfall* (United Artists, 1948). *Raw Deal* (Eagle-Lion, 1948). *Sleep, My Love* (United Artists, 1948). *Abandoned* (Universal, 1949). *Red Light* (Columbia, 1950). *The Blue Gardenia* (Warner Bros., 1951). *Rear Window* (Paramount, 1954). *Crime of Passion* (United Artists, 1957).

Busch, Niven ( )

Screenwriter. Busch was a studio professional, employed mainly at MGM and he worked on a great variety of films throughout his career. He wrote the western *Pursued* (MGM, 1947), sometimes described as a western-noir. His single contribution to *film noir* is the brilliant adaption of James M. Cain's *The Postman Always Rings Twice*, co-written with Harry Ruskin.

Filmography: *The Postman Always Rings Twice* (MGM, 1946).

Buttolph, David (1902–)

Composer. An extremely prolific composer, David Buttolph is mainly associated with 20th Century-Fox. While he composed scores for a wide variety of films, he particularly excelled at *films noirs*. His music is haunting and sometimes quite beautiful and romantic. All but forgotten today, Buttolph was a major figure in *film noir* and deserves renewed interest.

Filmography: *Street of Chance* (Paramount, 1942). *This Gun for Hire* (Paramount, 1942). *The House on 92nd Street* (20th Century-Fox, 1945). *Shock* (20th Century-Fox, 1946). *The Brasher Doubloon* (20th Century-Fox, 1947). *Kiss of Death* (20th Century-Fox, 1947). *The Enforcer* (Warner Bros., 1951). *Talk About a Stranger* (MGM, 1952). *Crime Wave* (Warner Bros., 1954).

Butts, Dale (1910–)

Composer. Butts was a staff composer for Republic Pictures. He composed and arranged countless scores for Republic in the late forties and the fifties. While a competent composer, few of his scores are memorable.

Filmography: *Too Late for Tears* (United Artists, 1949). *City That Never Sleeps* (Republic, 1953). *Hell's Half Acre* (Republic, 1954).

Cabot, Bruce (Etienne Pelissier de Bujac) (1904–1971)

Actor. In the 1930's, Cabot was most often cast as a tough adventurer in modest-budget action films. He also co-starred in westerns and crime melodramas, almost always cast as a villain. He had important supporting roles in Fritz Lang's pre-*noir* classic *Fury* and Otto Preminger's *Fallen Angel*, his only true *noir* role.

Filmography: *Fury* (MGM, 1936). *Fallen Angel* (20th Century–Fox, 1946).

Cady, Jerome (1917–)

Screenwriter. Cady worked on many films in the late forties and early fifties and later worked extensively for television. He co-wrote two interesting *films noirs*.

Filmography: *Call Northside 777* (20th Century–Fox, 1948). *Cry Danger* (RKO, 1951).

Caged (Warner Bros., 1950). 97 min.

Producer: Jerry Wald. Director: John Cromwell. Screenplay: Virginia Kellogg and Bernard C. Shoenfeld. Director of Photography: Carl Gutherie. Music: Max Steiner. Art Directors: Charles H. Clarke. Editor: Owen Marks.

Cast: Eleanor Parker (Marie Allen), Agnes Moorehead (Ruth Benton), Ellen Corby (Emma), Hope Emerson (Evelyn Harper), Betty Garde (Kitty Stark), Jan Sterling (Smoochie). With: Jane Darnell, Gertrude Michael, Sheila Stevens, Joan Miller.

Marie Allen is arrested after a botched robbery attempt in which her husband was shot and killed. She is sentenced to prison. Over the course of serving her sentence, she is changed from a naive and fundamentally innocent young woman to a hardened, shrewd adult. The corrupting influence of the prison environment and the actions of the sadistic (and lesbian) matron have their effect on the impressionable young woman. Released from prison with no hope for the future except to turn to prostitution, the warden and her assistant watch her leave, knowing she will soon be back.

Caged is certainly the best woman-in-prison film ever. It avoids the more obvious clichés inherent in the setting. Indeed, the film has much in common with the Warner Brother's prison exposés of the 1930's. It is totally unsentimental and pessimistic in its examination of the effects of prison life on inmates.

Caged is shot in an unpretentious, gritty, realistic style by the veteran director John Cromwell. The performances are all very good, with Hope Emerson being particularly notable as the psychotic matron.

Cagney, James (1899–1986)

Actor. Cagney's early film career was devoted tó playing villains and gangsters, but as he achieved stardom in the mid–thirties, his image quickly changed and he became identified with tough heroic characters. However, he continued to occasionally play bad guys as he did in his two *films noirs*.

Indeed, the two Cagney *noir* titles are two of the toughest and most violent of all *films noirs*. His portrayal of Ralph Cotter in *Kiss Tomorrow Goodbye* is one of the most utterly evil villains in *film noir*. Cody Jarrett, the mother-fixated psychopath in *White Heat*, is equally vile. This emotional and psychological cripple is one of the genre's most memorable villains. Who can forget the apocalyptic image of Cagney as Jarrett disappearing in a mass of smoke and flame as he cries out defiantly, "Top of the world, Ma!" It remains one of cinema's most enduring images.

Filmography: *White Heat* (Warner Bros., 1947). *Kiss Tomorrow Goodbye* (Warner Bros., 1950).

Cahiers du Cinéma

French film magazine. A pretentious film monthly co-founded by Andre

Bazin, the magazine served as the critical center of the rise of cinema as a recognized, legitimate art form in the fifties. Bazin and his protégés, including future directors Jean Luc Godard and François Truffaut, first identified a unique genre of American crime films as *film noir* as a unique genre and gave them that name. The term was quickly adapted throughout the world, giving these films a unique identity and establishing the critical foundation for the genre.

Cahn, Edward L. (1907–1963)

Director. "Fast Eddie" Cahn was a prolific director of extremely low-budget programmers and "B" movies of all types. Probably his best known film is the science fiction horror "classic" *It! The Terror from Beyond Space* (United Artists, 1958). His one *film noir* has the usual Cahn characteristics: poor screenplay, bad acting, fast action, sloppy direction. However, it is not really a bad movie; rather, it is typical of many "B" productions, whatever the genre. Despite its great flaws, it remains an entertaining film, if a completely insignificant one.

Filmography: *Destination Murder* (RKO, 1950).

Cain, James M. (1892–1977)

Novelist and screenwriter. James M. Cain is probably the most important popular crime novelist of the forties and his influence can be felt today in the work of contemporary crime writers. He was the first to break with the tradition of gangster and detective novels and add an element of overt sexuality to his stories. Indeed, chiefly because of this Freudian element, his novels were extremely controversial and often declared pornographic. Nevertheless, many of his books were adapted for the screen at the time and made into successful films.

Double Indemnity, *The Postman Always Rings Twice* and *Mildred Pierce*, all masterpieces of the genre, were based on Cain's novels. Interestingly enough, Cain was not successful as a screenwriter. He did, however, contribute to the screenplay of yet another *film noir* masterpiece, *Out of the Past*.

Filmography: *Double Indemnity* (based on his novel) (Paramount, 1944). *Mildred Pierce* (based on his novel) (Warner Bros., 1945). *The Postman Always Rings Twice* (based on his novel) (MGM, 1946). *Out of the Past* (uncredited contribution) (RKO, 1947). *Slightly Scarlet* (based on his novel) (RKO, 1956).

Calcutta (Paramount, 1947). 83 min.

Producer: Seton I. Miller. Director: John Farrow. Screenplay: S.I. Miller. Director of Photography: John F. Seitz. Music: Victor Young. Song: "This Is Madness" by Bernie Wayne and Ben Raleigh. Art Directors: Hans Dreier and Franz Bachelin. Editor: Archie Marshek.

Cast: Alan Ladd (Neale Gordon), Gail Russell (Virginia Moore), William Bendix (Pedro Blake), June Duprez (Marina Tamev), Lowell Gilmore (Eric Lasser). With: Edith King, Paul Singh, Gavin Muir, John Whitney, Benson Fong.

Veterans Neale, Pedro and Bill are commercial pilots living in India. Bill, engaged to the beautiful and exotic Virginia Moore, is murdered under mysterious circumstances. Neale begins investigating the death of his friend. A twisted trail leads through the dark, smoke-filled bars and exotic bazaars of Calcutta to a band of murderous jewel smugglers. Eventually, Virginia is unmasked as one of the gangster's molls. Neale is impervious to her pathetic pleas for mercy as he turns her over to the police.

Calcutta is the most conventional of John Farrow's *films noirs* and while it isn't a major film, it is a highly entertaining one. It was obviously an attempt to cash in on the phenomenal success of *Casablanca*. *Calcutta* does recapture some of the exotic spirit of that film with its recreated Calcutta on Paramount's back lot. Farrow was a master of atmospheric effects and he certainly created a land of languid eroticism with this film and Gail Russell's performance as a dark-haired, doe-eyed *femme-fatale* was an inspired bit of casting. The screenplay by veteran S. I. Miller (who also produced), is cheerful, if a bit misogynist (Neale slaps a confession out of Virginia), with few surprises; but altogether the film survives as an unpretentious entertainment.

Calhern, Louis (Carl Henry Vogt) (1895–1956)

Character actor. Calhern was one of the great character actors of American cinema. He played judges, generals and western heroes in countless films. He appeared in two *films noirs*, most notably as the corrupt lawyer Alonzo D. Emmerich, who finances the jewel thieves in *The Asphalt Jungle*.

Filmography: *Notorious* (RKO, 1946). *The Asphalt Jungle* (MGM, 1950).

Call Northside 777 (20th Century–Fox, 1948). 111 min.

Producer: Otto Lang. Director: Henry Hathaway. Screenplay: Jerome Cady and Jay Dratler, adapted by Leonard Hoffmann and Quentin Reynolds from a series of *Chicago Times* articles by James P. McGuire. Director of Photography: Joe MacDonald. Music Director: Alfred Newman. Art Directors: Lyle Wheeler and Mark-Lee Kirk. Editor: Watson Webb, Jr.

Cast: James Stewart (McNeal), Richard Conte (Frank Wiecek), Lee J. Cobb (Brian Kelly), Helen Walker (Laura McNeal), Betty Garde (Wanda Skutnik). With: Kasia Orzazewski, Howard Smith, John McIntyre, E. G. Marshall.

McNeal is a skeptical, cynical Chicago newspaper reporter investigating the story of a man, Frank Wiecek, falsely accused and convicted of murder. McNeal does not believe in Wiecek's innocence at first, but as he begins to investigate the story, he discovers a number of glaring inconsistencies in the case. Inevitably, he uncovers an official cover-up and a conspiracy involving the police and others to hide the facts. He proves Wiecek's innocence and Wiecek is released from prison.

Call Northside 777 is one of the most prominent *films noirs* to feature a newspaper reporter as the protagonist. It is an unflinching look at official corruption and its far reaching effects. No one in the film is innocent. The police try to stymie the investigation; a witness refuses to change her testimony even when confronted by the truth; the newspaper publisher quits when "pressure from above" becomes too rough.

Furthermore, it is also one of the few *films noirs* based on real events. Director Henry Hathaway uses a semi-documentary style, thus increasing the viewer's alienation. As rendered by cinematographer Joe McDonald, the city in which the film is set — Chicago — is an all pervasive gray and dim, as dirty and depressing as the story itself.

James Stewart is perfectly cast as the reporter. His skepticism erodes slowly over the course of the film until it explodes into disbelief and horror at the helplessness against a powerful, corrupt political machine.

Canon City (Eagle-Lion, 1948). 82 min.

Producer: Robert T. Kane. Director: Crane Wilbur. Screenplay: Crane Wilbur. Director of Photography: John Alton. Music Director: Irving Friedman. Art Director: Frank Durlaf. Editor: Louis H. Sackin.

Cast: Scott Brady (Jim Sherbony), Jeff Corey (Schwartz Miller), Whit Bissell (Heilman), Stanley Clements (New), Charles Russell (Tolley). With De Forest Kelley, Ralph Byrd, Warden Ward Best, Henry Brandon.

A group of vicious convicts escape from Colorado State Penitentiary, taking with them another inmate, Jim Sherbony, against his will. They terrorize the rural citizens, but eventually all are killed except Sherbony. He takes refuge in a poor family's farmhouse, taking them hostage. When the young son has an attack of appendicitis, Sherbony allows the mother to take him to the hospital. Sherbony flees on foot, hoping to escape through the surrounding forest; but the farmer, realizing that Sherbony is not a hardened criminal, picks him up in his car and attempts to help him. They are stopped at a road block, however, and Sherbony is arrested and returned to prison.

Canon City is one of several minor prison *noirs* influenced by and released after *Brute Force* (Universal, 1947). The film opens like a documentary with real footage of the Colorado State Penitentiary and a brief interview with the prison's warden. The story of the escape is interesting, chiefly because of the helplessness of Sherbony as he descends from minor criminal to major criminal, against his own desires. Rarely has a *noir* protagonist been in such a hopeless situation.

The film, despite its excellent premise, is only partially successful. Crane Wilbur's screenplay is passable, his direction perfunctory.

Cape Fear (Universal, 1962). 105 min. Producer: Sy Bartlett. Director: J. Lee Thompson. Screenplay: James R. Webb, based on the novel *The Executioners* by John D. MacDonald. Director of Photography: Samuel Leavitt. Music: Bernard Herrmann. Art Directors: Alexander Golitzen and Robert Boyle. Editor: George Tomasini.

Cast: Gregory Peck (Sam Bowden), Robert Mitchum (Max Cady), Polly Bergen (Peggy), Lori Martin (Nancy), Martin Balsam (Chief Dutton), Telly Savalas (Sievers). With: Barrie Chase, Paul Comi, Page Slatterly.

Cape Fear marks the last successful gasp of *film noir* and is one of the most familiar titles of the genre.

The story is well known. Max Cady, a violent psychopath, terrorizes the family of a District Attorney, Sam Bowden, whom he blames for sending him to prison. At first, Cady torments the wife, Peggy, and daughter Nancy, without breaking any laws, causing Bowden to react in an increasingly irrational manner. The film climaxes on a houseboat on the Cape Fear River when Cady attacks the family. He almost succeeds in killing them, but at last Bowden overpowers him. Bowden finally has the evidence to send Cady to prison for life.

Cape Fear is an interesting film. It takes cliché thriller elements and expands them to cover, chiefly, the theme of a secure family terrorized by dark and violent forces—a subconscious fear of middle class Americans.

The plot itself presents this clash of values and Max Cady, of course, is a metaphor for the uncontrollable, violent forces set loose in a repressed, sedate world. The excellent screenplay adapted from a novel by thriller novelist John D. MacDonald—is rife with tension and suspense. The terror is reinforced by the astringent, swirling music of Bernard Herrmann, and tight, spare direction by J. Lee Thompson. The performances are all first rate, with Robert Mitchum a standout as the maniacal Max Cady.

Martin Scorsese's contemporary remake (1992) replaced much of the spooky atmosphere for cheap effect and typically extravagant style; and, rather annoyingly, he tried to create a religious metaphor out of the relationship between the family members and Max Cady (obviously as the Devil). Thus, the film lost much of the original's *noir* spirit and, ultimately, is a pale imitation of the much less pretentious first film.

Capers or Heists

The planning and execution of a heist is one of *films noirs* most recognizable plot devices. The first caper film in *film noir* is Robert Siodmak's neglected classic *Criss Cross* (Universal, 1949). An otherwise simple plot involving the planned (and doomed) robbery of a payroll is made complicated by romantic and erotic entanglements. More famous is John Huston's classic adaption of the W. R. Burnett novel, *The Asphalt Jungle* (MGM, 1950), a huge box-office hit and still one of *film noir*'s most satisfying films. In fact, the plot is typical of its type: a planned heist collapses thanks, in large part, to the corruption of the thieves. Like *Criss Cross*, however, the plot of *The Asphalt Jungle* is not merely a bad guys get their come-uppance story, but a device used to explore the psychology of its characters and the general malaise and greed of post-war America. This is also true of Stanley Kubrick's *The Killing* (United Artists, 1956) which, of course, also has the same central leading actor as *The Asphalt Jungle*, Sterling Hayden. In addition, both films are also technically innovative with outstanding cinematography by Harold Rosson in *The Asphalt Jungle* and Lucien Ballard in *The Killing*.

The Asphalt Jungle began a run of similar if less metaphorical caper dramas in the fifties. *Armored Car Robbery* (RKO, 1950), a "B" movie directed by Richard Fleischer, was the first to cash in on the new craze. It is a fast-moving, unpretentious film that makes up in action what it lacks in artistic invention. *Appointment with Danger* (Paramount, 1951), centers on a post office investigator (Alan Ladd) as he tangles with a group of violent hoodlums planning a mail robbery. Likewise, *Kansas City Confidential* concerns an ex-con who seeks revenge for being made the patsy in an armored car robbery gone wrong. Although not as well know, *Plunder Road* (20th Century–Fox, 1957) and *Odds Against Tomorrow* (United Artists, 1959) are two particularly fatalistic caper films; the latter, directed with great visual flair by Robert Wise, is usually considered the last *film noir* of the initial cycle.

The Captive City (United Artists, 1952). 90 min.
Producer: Theron Webb. Director: Robert Wise. Screenplay: Karl Lamb and Alvin M. Josephy, Jr., story by Alvin M. Josephy. Director of Photography: Lee Garmes. Music: Jerome Moross. Art Director: Maurice Zuberano. Editor: Ralph Swink.
Cast: John Forsythe (Jim Austin), Joan Camden (Marge Austin), Harold J. Kennedy (Don Carey), Ray Teal (Chief Gillette), Marjorie Crossland (Mrs. Sirak). With: Victor Sutherland, Halk Dawson, Geraldine Hall, Martin Milner.

Jim Austin, editor for the *Kennington Journal*, discovers his town is run by the mob. The corruption reaches all levels of society, including the Mayor's office and even the police Chief Gillette. Austin flees Kennington with his wife after the murder of an associate. He testifies before a Senate Committee investigating organized crime. When offered money by a syndicate representative at the hearing, Austin refuses.

An important, transitional film, *The Captive City* is an uneasy synthesis between excessive *noir* style and standard exposé. In fact, the film was part of a new trend just beginning that would develop into other genres in the 1960's and 1970's.

Technically, Robert Wise and cinematographer Lee Garmes capture the expressionist style of early *film noir*: deserted streets lit by dim lamp light, dark alleyways, and frightened faces emerging from shadows. But the high style of the body of the film is in conflict with the opening and closing documentary footage of real-life Senator Estes Kefauver speaking directly to the audience about the evils of organized crime.

The Capture (RKO, 1950). 81 min.
Producer: Edward Siaga. Director: John Sturges. Screenplay: Niven Busch.

Director of Photography: Edward Cronjager. Music: Daniele Amfitheotrof. Art Directors: Albert S. D'Agostino and Carroll Clark. Editor: James Ballard.

Cast: Lew Ayres (Vanner), Teresa Wright (Ellen), Victor Jory (Father Gomez), Jacqueline White (Lanna), Jimmy Hunt (Mike). With: Duncan Renaldo, William Bakewell, Barry Kelley, Milton Parsons.

Vanner is the field boss of a small American oil company who shoots a man suspected of having stolen the company payroll. Vanner falls in love with Ellen, his victim's beautiful widow and when he discovers that the man was probably innocent, his conscience moves him to clear up the mystery. The decision leads to a second accidental killing and makes him a fugitive, just as his first victim was.

The Capture is one of John Sturges' early films as a director. While it lacks some of the stylized violence of his later films, it is tightly directed and maintains the existential themes of the screenplay. Nevertheless, it is a minor *film noir* with its chief assets being an excellent score by Daniele Amfitheotrof and a good performance by Lew Ayres as the man doomed by coincidence and his own rash behavior to forever run from the police.

Carey, Timothy (1925–)
Character actor. Carey was a memorably loathsome villain of westerns and action films in the 1950's. He generally played second leads and sidekicks. His most famous *film noir* role is in *The Killing* in which he played the sharpshooter.

Filmography: *Crime Wave* (Warner Bros., 1954). *The Killing* (United Artists, 1956). *The Outfit* (MGM, 1973).

Carfagno, Edward C. (1903–1981)
Art director. A busy production designer, Carfagno worked on a variety of motion-pictures and television from the forties. He was serviceable but not particularly inventive. He designed sets for one *film noir*, a low-budget movie directed by Joseph H. Lewis.

Filmography: *A Lady Without Passport* (MGM, 1950).

Carlson, Richard (1912–1977)
Producer, director, and actor. Carlson is best known as an actor in 1950's sci-fi films including *It Came from Outer Space* (Universal, 1953). He also produced and directed a few "B" movies during that same decade including a rather insignificant *film noir*, *Appointment with a Shadow*. He also had small supporting roles in two other *films noirs*.

Filmography: *Behind Locked Doors* (Eagle-Lion, 1948). *Try and Get Me* (United Artists, 1950). *Appointment with a Shadow* (Universal, 1958).

Carne, Marcel (1903–)
A great French director, Marcel Carne was one of the leading filmmakers of his native country 1937–1945. Like many of his contemporaries, particularly Jean Renoir, Carne was interested in the lower classes and criminal pathology. Many of his early, best films have *noir*-like qualities and, indeed, the term *film noir* seems to have been used by French critics in the late thirties to describe his dark, tragic crime drama *Le Jour Se Leve* (1939), the story of the last days of a small time criminal, not unlike the *noir* classic *High Sierra* (Warner Bros., 1941).

Carr, Marion (1933–)
Actress. Sensual and strong, Marion Carr was briefly popular in the mid–fifties. She appeared in four excellent *films noirs*, including two directed by Robert Aldrich (*Kiss Me Deadly* and *World for Ramson*), but she disappeared from the screen after 1956, leaving behind several intriguing performances.

Filmography: *World for Ransom* (Allied Artists, 1954). *Kiss Me Deadly* (United Artists, 1955). *The Harder*

They Fall (Columbia, 1956). *Nightmare* (United Artists, 1956).

Carrere, Edward (1911–)

Art director. Carrere worked on a number of important *films noirs* including Raoul Walsh's *White Heat*. Although he is not a particularly important art director, the work he did was always professional, if rarely outstanding.

Filmography: *White Heat* (Warner Bros., 1949). *The Breaking Point* (Warner Bros., 1950). *I Died a Thousand Times* (Warner Bros., 1955). *Sweet Smell of Success* (United Artists, 1957).

Carter, Janis (Janis Dremann) (1921–)

Actress. A star of radio in the early forties, Carter became a leading lady of routine and "B" movies of the forties and fifties. One of her best roles was in the good "B" *noir, Framed*, as a memorably corrosive *femme-fatale*.

Filmography: *Framed* (Columbia, 1947).

Caspary, Vera (1899–1989)

Novelist and screenwriter. Vera Caspary was a well-liked novelist who also worked sporadically in Hollywood as a screenwriter. She wrote or co-wrote several popular films, and two of her novels were adapted by others to become classic *films noirs*. Both are distinguished by their concentration on female characters and their complicated psychologies.

Filmography: *Laura* (20th Century–Fox, 1944). *The Blue Gardenia* (Warner Bros., 1953).

Castle, Peggie (1927–1973)

Actress. Peggie Castle was a star of "B" movies in the 1950's, and made many appearances on television. She never became a full-fledged star despite some memorable performances. Two of her best performances were as *femme-fatales* in the "B" *noirs, The Long Wait*, in which she played Venus, a particularly deadly variation of the character type and in *I, the Jury*.

Filmography: *I, the Jury* (United Artists, 1953). *99 River Street* (United Artists, 1953). *The Long Wait* (United Artists, 1954).

Castle, William (1914–1977)

Producer and director. Castle is best known for the gimmicky promotions of his low-budget horror films in the 1950's and 1960's. Castle's film career began in the early forties. He was immediately established as a leading director of "B" movies, making films like the *film noir, When Strangers Marry*, a decent version of the wife-in-distress story that served Alfred Hitchcock so well in *Suspicion* (RKO, 1941). Despite its low budget, *Undertow* also has its virtues. In addition, Castle was also an associate producer for Orson Welles' *noir* masterpiece, *The Lady from Shanghai* (Columbia, 1948).

Filmography: *When Strangers Marry* (Monogram, 1944). *Undertow* (Universal, 1949).

Caught (MGM, 1949). 88 min.

Producer: Wolfgang Reinhardt. Director: Max Ophuls (with uncredited contributions by John Berry). Screenplay: Arthur Laurents, based on the novel *Wild Calender* by Libbie Block. Director of Photography: Lee Garmes. Music: Frederick Hollander. Art Director: F. Paul Sylos. Editor: Robert Parrish

Cast: James Mason (Larry Quinada), Barbara Bel Geddes (Leonora Eames), Robert Ryan (Smith Ohlrig), Ruth Brady (Maxine), Curt Bois (Franzi). With: Frank Fergusson, Natalie Schaefer, Art Smith, Sonia Darren.

Leonora Eames is an impressionable, naive young department store model. Influenced by the media into believing that the road to happiness is with a rich man, she marries Smith Ohlrig, a neurotic, reclusive millionaire she meets at the store. Lonely in his huge mansion where she is left while he is constantly away on business, her only companion is Ohlrig's slimy assistant

Barbara Bel Geddes, James Mason in *Caught* **(MGM, 1949).**

Franzi, who takes special delight in tormenting her.

Leonora runs away to a small town where she goes to work as an assistant for the kindly Doctor Larry Quinada. She falls in love with him, but when Ohlrig finds her, she returns to live with him. She is pregnant, and wants a secure home for her child. Once back in the mansion, however, Ohlrig returns to his old ways, despite promises to stay with her and, once again, she is left alone with Franzi. When she has a miscarriage, however, brought on in part by the pressure caused by Franzi's constant torments, she at last feels free to return to Quinada who has asked her to marry him.

In many ways, *Caught* is a traditional romantic melodrama, but with the hopelessness and horror of the relationships heightened to almost operatic proportions, and a sense of extravagant style rendered by director Max

Ophuls, cinematographer Lee Garmes (here temporarily abandoning his newly developed realist style for the extremes of his thirties films), and art director F. Paul Sylos.

Leonora is a true female *noir* protagonist. She finds herself in a desperate, inescapable situation that is, in part, of her own creation. It is only through outside forces—the unfortunate loss of her unborn child—which ultimately allows her to escape. Barbara Bel Geddes, in one of her few leading roles, is extremely good as Leonora, bringing a palpable pathos to the character.

Robert Ryan is also excellent as the neurotic millionaire, a character obviously based on Howard Hughes. The character is unsympathetic and cruel, yet Ryan manages to create some compassion for him.

Curt Bois, however, almost steals the film as Franzi, the slightly effeminate, obsessively jealous personal assistant to Ohlrig.

With his collaborators, Max Ophuls creates a duplicitous world of reality and dream. He never ceases to exploit the differences between Leonora's shabby apartment and careless romanticism with Ohlrig's opulent mansion and overwhelming greed: for him, Leonora is just another beautiful possession. It is not an accident that Leonora finds herself so alone in the huge mansion, but an irony created by Ophuls and screenwriter Arthur Laurents.

More than anything, this elegant, extraordinary film is Ophuls' profound attack against greed and the ridiculous, destructive ideals behind the American Dream.

Cause for Alarm (MGM, 1951). 74 min.
Producer: Tom Lewis. Director: Tay Garnett. Screenplay: Mel Dinelli and Tom Lewis, story by Larry Marcus. Director of Photography: Joseph Ruttenberg. Music: Andre Previn. Art Director: Cedric Gibbons and Arthur Lonergan. Editor: James E. Newcom.
Cast: Loretta Young (Ellen Jones), Barry Sullivan (George Z. Jones), Bruce Cowing (Dr. Ranney Grahame), Margolo Gillmore (Mrs. Edwards). With: Irving Bacon, George Bakus, Don Haggerty.

While an insanely jealous husband, George Z. Jones, is recovering from an illness which has left him bedridden, he imagines his wife Ellen is having an affair with the family doctor. He informs her he plans to commit suicide and has mailed a letter which would make it look like he was murdered and implicate both her and Dr. Grahame. Much of the film is then concerned with Ellen's desperate search for the incriminating letter. However, when it is surreptitiously returned, she at last has the strength to leave her abusive husband. *Cause for Alarm* is one of those films which is an uneasy balance between real *film noir* and conventional melodrama. While it certainly has some of the technical elements associated with *film noir*, the story is really little more than the sort of woman-in-distress plot of countless thirties and forties melodramas. It is, however, the film's bleak portrait of a trapped marriage, and its overwhelming sense of hopelessness and desperation, at least until the end, which makes it closer to *film noir*, than similar films.

Champion (United Artists, 1949). 90 min.
Producer: Stanley Kramer. Director: Mark Robson. Screenplay: Carl Foreman, based on a story by Ring Lardner. Director of Photography: Franz Planer. Music: Dimitri Tiomkin. Editor: John Morgan.
Cast: Kirk Douglas (Midge Kelly), Marilyn Maxwell (Grace Diamond), Arthur Kennedy (Connie Kelly), Paul Stewart (Tommy Haley), Ruth Roman (Emma Bryce), Lola Albright (Mrs. Harris).

The third in the trilogy of classic boxing *films noirs* — the other two were *Body and Soul* (United Artists, 1947) and *The Set-Up* (RKO, 1949) — *Champion* is in some ways a less satisfying film than the others. The story is very similar to *Body and Soul*, although the main character, boxer Midge Kelly, is more thoroughly nasty and greedy than the boxer in the other film, and *Champion's* ending is decidedly more bleak.

Kirk Douglas was a successful character lead before *Champion*, but this film propelled him into a superstar. Although Midge Kelly is an extremely unpleasant character, Douglas manages to make the role almost sympathetic.

Mark Robson's direction is rather flat, and uninspired, particularly in the fight scenes which are improbably spectacular. Although it pales in comparison to *Body and Soul* and *The Set-Up*, *Champion* still survives as one of *film noir's* acknowledged classics, however minor, held together largely by its central performance.

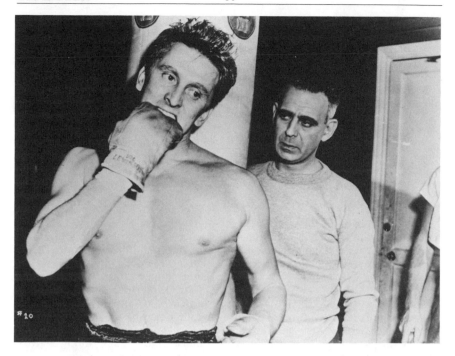

Kirk Douglas, Paul Stewart in *Champion* **(United Artists, 1949).**

Chandler, Jeff (Ira Grossel) (1918–1961)
Actor. Chandler is remembered for his shock of prematurely gray hair and his performance as the Indian Chief Cochise in the great western *Broken Arrow* (Universal, 1950). He never really achieved true stardom, however, and except for a handful of films was relegated to low-budget features. He appeared in three *films noirs*.

Filmography: *Johnny O'Clock* (Columbia, 1947). *Female on the Beach* (Universal, 1955). *The Tattered Dress* (Universal, 1957).

Chandler, Raymond (1888–1959)
Novelist and screenwriter. Raymond Chandler was unquestionably one of the great American novelists of the early twentieth century. His sarcastic, cynical, metaphorical detective novels— featuring the famous Philip Marlowe— had a profound influence on a whole generation of writers and, in Europe at least, he is considered the equal of Ernest Hemingway and William Faulkner.

Chandler, like so many others, was attracted to Hollywood because of the easy money. His novels and stories were purchased and adapted successfully for the screen, but Chandler found screenwriting even more lucrative.

Although he found the occupation demoralizing at best, he wrote or co-wrote several brilliant screenplays including at least two classic *films noirs: Double Indemnity* and *The Blue Dahlia.* The former, co-written with director Billy Wilder, is an extraordinary adaption of James M. Cain's novel, an assignment that Chandler took on with disdain: he hated the novel and he hated Wilder. Ever the professional mercenary, however, he worked hard on the project and the result is one of *noir's* greatest masterpieces.

The Blue Dahlia, commissioned by producer John Houseman, was Chandler's only original screenplay. It is essentially a criticism of the post-war American malaise and corruption disguised as a mystery. Despite certain lapses of reason, the screenplay holds up well today, and is particularly notable for its brilliant dialog.

Filmography: *Double Indemnity* (co-wrote), (Paramount, 1944). *Murder, My Sweet* (based on his novel) (RKO, 1944). *The Big Sleep* (based on his novel), (Warner Bros., 1946). *The Blue Dahlia* (Paramount, 1946). *The Brasher Doubloon* (based on his novel *The High Window* (20th Century–Fox, 1947). *Lady in the Lake* (based on his novel) (MGM, 1947). *Strangers on a Train* (co-wrote) (Warner Bros., 1951).

Charisse, Cyd (Tula Ellice Finklea) (1921–)

Actress and dancer. Charisse is certainly one of the most sensual screen performers of the fifties, starring in several memorable musicals. She was one of the last female musical stars promoted by MGM. She also acted in romances and melodramas of various sorts, but her easy going personality was ill-suited to the dark, unsentimental world of *film noir*, and she appeared as second female lead in only one *noir* title.

Filmography: *Tension* (MGM, 1950).

The Chase (United Artists, 1946). 86 min.

Producer: Seymour Nebenzal. Director: Arthur Ripley. Screenplay: Phillip Yordan, based on the novel *The Black Path of Fear* by Cornell Woolrich. Director of Photography: Franz Planer. Music: Michel Michelet. Art Director: Robert Usher. Editor: Edward Mann.

Cast: Michele Morgan (Lorna), Robert Cummings (Chuck Scott), Steve Cochran (Eddie Roman), Lloyd Corrigan (Emmerick Johnson), Jack Holt (Commander Davidson). With: Don Wilson, Alexis Minotis, Nina Koschetz, Peter Lorre.

Chuck Scott, a veteran down on his luck, takes a job as a chauffeur for a millionaire, Eddie Roman, after he returns a wallet lost by the wealthy man. Scott discovers that Roman is a dangerously ruthless man who is not above murdering his rivals. Scott falls in love with Lorna, Roman's beautiful wife, and they plan to run away to Havana together. However, a recurrence of malaria, a condition contracted during the war, confines Scott to bed. He falls into a deep sleep, dreams that Lorna is murdered and that he is the suspect, but Gino, Roman's sadistic assistant, is the real killer. When he finally awakens, he and Lorna carry out their escape plans. Roman, discovering the plan, chases the couple in his car with Gino at his side, but they wreck and are killed and Lorna and Chuck arrive safely in Havana.

Although it is not a major *film noir*, *The Chase* captures the dream-like, almost surreal elements of Cornell Woolrich's fiction. The film is full of *noir* themes and characters (the disillusioned war veteran, for example), and expressionist style. A long dream sequence is very effective. Franz Planer, one of the great German born cinematographers, fills the film with rich visual textures and a languid eroticism.

Chicago Deadline (Paramount, 1949). 87 min.

Producer: Robert Fellows. Director: Lewis Allen. Screenplay: Warren Duff, based on the novel *One Woman* by Tiffany Thayer. Director of Photography: John F. Seitz. Music: Victor Young. Art Directors: Hans Dreier and Franz Bachelin. Editor: LeRoy Stone.

Cast: Alan Ladd (Ed Adams), Donna Reed (Rosita Jean D'Ur/Ellen Rainer), June Havoc (Leona), Irene Harvey (Belle Dorset), Arthur Kennedy (Tommy Ditman), Berry Kroeger (Solly). With: Harold Vermilyea, Sheppart Strudwick, John Beal.

Alan Ladd stars as a journalist, Ed Adams, who discovers the body of a young girl, Ellen Rainer, dead of tuberculosis in a cheap hotel. He is intrigued by the exquisite corpse and steals her address book before the police arrive. He begins to investigate the girl's past, discovering that her real name is Rosita Jean D'Ur. Her seedy past is recounted in flashback through the memories of people who knew her. Adams uncovers a world of murder and blackmail, with Ellen/Rosita just one link in a twisted deadly chain of crime and violence. Adam's own life is endangered but he tricks the main villain, Solly, during the climactic confrontation and Solly is killed instead. At Ellen's funeral, he burns her address book, but is told by her brother that he, Adams, probably knew her best.

In its flashback technique and the necrophilic fascination of the main character, *Chicago Deadline* is an obvious attempt to recapture the spirit of *Laura* (20th Century-Fox, 1944). While it fails to live up to the genius of its predecessor, *Chicago Deadline* is still a compelling melodrama. Lewis Allen brings a fatalistic romanticism to the film, and Ladd's performance is typically stoic and tough-minded.

Chinatown (Paramount, 1974). 130 min.
Producer: Robert Evans. Director: Roman Polanski. Screenplay: Robert Towne. Director of Photography: John A. Alonzo. Music: Jerry Goldsmith. Art Director: W. Steward Campbell. Editor: Sam O'Steen.
Cast: Jack Nicholson (J. J. Gittes), Faye Dunaway (Evelyn Mulwray), John Huston (Norah Cross), Perry Lopez (Escobar), John Hillerman (Yel Burton), Darrell Zwerling (Hollis Mulwray), Diane Ladd (Ida Sessions). With: Roman Polanski, Joe Mantell, Namdu Hinds, James Hong, Jerry Fugikawa.
Chinatown was a deliberate attempt by screenwriter Robert Towne and director Roman Polanski to create a modern *film noir* and with the possible exception of *Bodyheat* (Warner Bros.,

1981), it is the most successful attempt to date to actually capture the spirit of the genre at its artistic heights.

Los Angeles, 1937: The city is plagued by a terrible drought.

As small time private investigator, J. J. Gittes, is hired by Evelyn Mulwray to see if her husband is faithful. He photographs Hollis Mulwray at a local hotel with a young girl. When the story makes the papers the next day, Gittes learns that he was duped in a plot to discredit Mulwray, a prominent water commissioner. The real Mrs. Mulwray comes forward and threatens to sue Gittes, but when her husband is murdered, she hires Gittes to investigate. He uncovers a complicated plot involving water rights and, ultimately, incest. During the violent climax, Evelyn Mulwray shoots her father, Norah Cross. Gittes, unable to intervene, watches helplessly as she is gunned down. Cross, meanwhile, comforts his granddaughter who is also his daughter by Evelyn.

Robert Towne's rich, complex screenplay is full of metaphors of acridness. There is some complicated symbolism involving water and the desert, but it is also a compelling mystery which never ceases to entertain.

Roman Polanski's direction is perfectly restrained and manages to catch the feel of Los Angeles in the late thirties and the complex narratives of Raymond Chandler's novels.

John Alton's photography is also on target. He gives the film a dusty, hot, and claustrophobic ambiance. He also recreated the feel of black and white by heightening the colors, drenching the film in earthy browns and bright, sunlit yellows.

More than anything, *Chinatown* proved that *noir* was still a valuable genre, and it opened the way for such post-*noir* classics as *Body Heat*, *Blue Velvet* (DEG/Lorimar, 1986) and *The Grifters* (Miramax, 1991).

Chodorov, Edward (1904–)
Screenwriter. Chodorov was a typical Hollywood screenwriter: He took

on whatever assignments he was given, undertaking them with professionalism but little invention. He co-wrote many films including *Undercurrent*, a well written film that was badly cast. *Road House* is a better film which builds to a strong, suspenseful climax.

Filmography: *Undercurrent* (MGM, 1946). *Road House* (20th Century–Fox, 1948).

Christmas Holiday (Universal, 1944). 93 min.

Producer: Frank Shaw. Director: Robert Siodmak. Screenplay: Herman J. Mankiewicz, based on the novel by W. Somerset Maugham. Director of Photography: Woody Bredell. Music: Hans J. Salter. Art Directors: John B. Goodman and Robert Chatworthy. Editor: Ted Kent.

Cast: Deanna Durbin (Jackie Lamont/Abigail Mannette), Gene Kelly (Robert Manette), Richard Whorf (Simon Fenimore), Dean Harens (Charles Mason), Gale Sondergaard (Mrs. Manette). With Gladys George, David Bruce, Minor Watson, Cy Kendall, Charles McMurphy.

While en route to San Francisco for Christmas furlough, Naval Lt. Charles Mason meets a local chanteuse, Jackie Lamont, in New Orleans. They attend Mass together where, in tears, she confesses her real name is Abigail Manette and she recounts her miserable life with a criminal, Robert Manette. Manette is the scion of an old New Orleans family. He is a severe neurotic, prone to violence and crime. He murdered a bookie and is serving a sentence in the local penitentiary.

Lt. Mason, unable to offer any help, departs. Abigail Manette walks home in the lonely city night, only to find that her husband has escaped from prison and is hiding out at her apartment. He accuses her of infidelity because she has not visited him in prison. But she claims that she took a job as a nightclub singer — a job she despises — in sympathy with his plight. Robert does not believe her

and, in a violent rage, murders her. Before being gunned down by the police, Robert sarcastically exclaims to Abigail's corpse, "You can let go now, Abby".

Christmas Holiday is Robert Siodmak's most fatalistic *film noir*. Although it is not his best work, it is a compelling character study of doomed lives.

One of the most interesting aspects of the film is its casting. Deanna Durbin was cast against type in the role of Abigail Mannette, and she fought bitterly with Siodmak who was attempting to create a slutty allure for the character. Durbin, of course, was a popular juvenile singer and actress best known for her happy-go-lucky films and good girl personality, and she was afraid that such a drastic change of character would hurt her career. Likewise, Gene Kelly, in the role of the murderous Robert Mannette, was also cast against type and today, seeing him in the role is a bit unnerving, at least in light of the indelible good guy character he created after this film was made.

Finally, Siodmak's use of music in the film is quite inspired. Throughout the film, he uses bits and pieces of the *Liebestod* ("Death Music") from Richard Wagner's opera *Tristan and Isolde* to reiterate the themes of inevitable tragedy and romantic/sexual obsession.

Cianelli, Eduardo (1887–1969)

Italian born character actor. Cianelli, a veteran of Broadway, was one of Hollywood's more debonair villains of the 1930's and 1940's. His European personality, however, was ill-suited to a genre which, after its initial films, was wholly American. Thus, his most memorable *film noir* appearance, of the two such films he acted in, is the European set piece, *The Mask of Dimitrios*. As usual, he played a villain in this splendid espionage thriller.

Filmography: *The Mask of Dimitrios* (Warner Bros., 1944). *The People Against O'Hara* (MGM, 1951).

Cinematography

In no other genre is cinematography as important as it is in *film noir*. For all other genres — comedy, the western, the historical epic — cinematography is generally simple and unobtrusive. But in *film noir*, with its roots in German cinema and expressionism, the photography is metaphorical. Black and white cinematography reached its zenith in *film noir*, and while it is not whether the film is photographed in black and white or color which determines if a film is a *film noir* (but, rather, if the cinematography is used to enhance themes, plot and character), the majority of *films noirs* were photographed in black and white. The qualities of black and white lend themselves naturally to the genre, with its contrasts between light and dark, and its rendering of landscapes in either a pseudo-romantic or realistic fashion, depending on the director and cinematographer.

Of the cinematographers associated mainly with *film noir*, there are several outstanding individuals: Nicholas Musuraca, John Seitz, George Diskant, John Alton, Woody Bredell and John MacDonald. Each had a distinct style, with Musuraca and Woody Bredell being the more experimental and elegantly romantic, while Alton and Diskant preferred a more realistic style. MacDonald also demonstrated how well color can be adapted to *noir* aesthetics in *House of Bamboo* (20th Century–Fox) and *Niagara* (20th Century–Fox).

City of Fear (Columbia, 1959). 81 min.
Producer: Leon Chuoluck. Director: Irving Lerner. Screenplay: Steven Ritch and Robert Dillon. Director of Photography: Lucien Ballard. Music: Jerry Goldsmith. Art Director: F. Paul Sylos. Editor: Benjamin Spencer.
Cast: Vince Edwards (Vince Ryker), Lyle Talbot (Chief Jenson), John Archer (Lt. Mark Richards), Steven Ritch (Dr. Wallace), Patricia Blair (June).
When an escaped convict steals a box he thinks is filled with heroin, but actually contains dangerous radioactive material, a desperate hunt is set in motion by the police.

City of Fear is not a major film, but it is an interesting one for its recapitulation of themes explored in better, earlier films including *Panic in the Streets* (20th Century–Fox, 1950). *City of Fear* is typical of late fifties "B" *noirs*. It is competently made, but with little inventive photography (in fact, it is quite flat and ordinary), or the subtlety of character that is familiar from the great *films noirs*. By the time the film was released the genre had exhausted itself, and was quickly going into decline.

City That Never Sleeps (Republic, 1953). 90 min.
Producer and Director: John H. Auer. Screenplay: Steve Fisher. Director of Photography: John L. Russell, Jr. Music: R. Dale Butts. Art Director: James Sullivan. Editor: Fred Allen.
Cast: Gig Young (Johnny Kelly), Mala Powers (Sally Conners), William Talman (Hayes Stewart), Edward Arnold (Penrod Biddell), Chill Wills (Sgt. Joe), Marie Windsor (Lydia Biddell), Paula Raymond (Kathy Kelly). With: Wally Cassell, James Andelin, Thomas Poston, Bunny Kacher.
City That Never Sleeps is a low budget attempt to recapture the spirit and cash in on the success of *The Naked City* (Universal, 1948). Set in Chicago, the complicated plot involves a young cop, Johnny Kelly, and his mistress Sally, a stripper with whom he plans to run away. They get mixed up with Penrod Biddell, a wealthy lawyer whose wife Lydia is having an affair with Hayes Stewart, a dangerous criminal. Stewart's violent jealousy leads to murder and a confrontation with Kelly. In the end, Sally changes her mind about running away with Kelly, who then returns to his wife and the continued routine of a cop on the beat.
Like *The Naked City*, *City That Never Sleeps* is filmed in a semi-documentary

fashion. The style works quite well with the story's themes of self-doubt, alienation and dehumanization in a big city, but clashes with some of the film's stranger, surreal-like elements. Nevertheless, the movie is fairly successful as entertainment and is also notable for its early appearance of Marie Windsor, one of the most important of all female *noir* icons.

The City vs. the Country/Small Towns

An important, if neglected, theme in *film noir* is the different portrayals of the city and rural environments. In general, the city is a place of danger, repression and corruption, while the country and small towns represent tranquility and safety. This can be seen most explicitly in *Out of the Past* (RKO, 1947), in which the rural scenes are sunlit and serene (even the music is quiet and reserved), while the city scenes, usually night scenes, are dark and menacing. More often than not, when in trouble, the *noir* protagonist flees the city to hide out in the country, as Jeff Bailey (Robert Mitchum) does in this film. There are some notable exceptions, however. In *Beyond the Forest* (Warner Bros., 1949) and *Boomerang* (20th Century–Fox, 1947), small town life is viewed as repressive and destructive as big city life.

Clark, Carroll (1894–1968)

Art director. Carroll Clark was a unit art director at RKO from 1932 to the late 1950's. He often collaborated with Albert S. D'Agostino.

Filmography: *Suspicion* (RKO, 1941). *Experiment Perilous* (RKO, 1944). *Notorious* (RKO, 1946). *The Capture* (RKO, 1950). *Beyond a Reasonable Doubt* (RKO, 1956). *While the City Sleeps* (RKO, 1956).

Clark, Dane (Bernard Zanville) (1913–)

Character actor. The diminutive tough guy actor Dane Clark has often been described as a second string John Garfield. He achieved a degree of stardom in the 1940's, but is all but forgotten today. He starred in the minor *noir*, *Moonrise* which, despite its low budget, is a particularly well written, acted and directed film. Clark's performance is typically intense as the man who fears he is the victim of "bad blood."

Filmography: *Moonrise* (Republic, 1949).

Clark, Fred (1914–1968)

Character actor. An explosive character comedian, Clark played supporting roles in countless comic films. He also played small roles — generally public officials and the like — in dramas including several *films noirs*.

Filmography: *Ride the Pink Horse* (Universal, 1947). *The Unsuspected* (Warner Bros., 1947). *White Heat* (Warner Bros., 1947). *Cry of the City* (20th Century–Fox, 1948). *Sunset Boulevard* (Paramount, 1950).

Clash by Night (RKO, 1952). 104 min.

Producer: Jerry Wald. Director: Fritz Lang. Screenplay: Alfred Hayes and David Dortort, based on a play by Clifford Odets. Director of Photography: Nicholas Musuraca. Music: Roy Webb. Music Director: Constantin Bakaleinikoff. Art Directors: Albert S. D'Agostino and Carroll Clark. Editor: George J. Amy.

Cast: Barbara Stanwyck (Mae Doyle D'Amato), Paul Douglas (Jerry D'Amato), Robert Ryan (Earl Pfeiffer), Marilyn Monroe (Peggy), J. Carroll Naish (Uncle Vince). With: Keith Andes, Silvio Minciotti, Diane and Deborah Stewart.

Disillusioned by big city high life, Mae Doyle returns to her home town of Monterey after a long absence. She rekindles relationships with many old friends including two old boyfriends, Jerry D'Amato, a good natured fisherman and the cynical businessman, Earl Pfeiffer. She is sexually attracted to Earl, but their mutual cynicism keeps them apart. She marries the monotonous Jerry. They have a child and are

personal style, but a great deal of success. He was much in demand by all the major studios until his leftist political ideals and activities got him into trouble during the McCarthy witch hunt of the early fifties and destroyed his career. He co-wrote two minor, but interesting, *films noirs*.

Filmography: *Among the Living* (Paramount, 1941). *The High Wall* (MGM, 1947).

Columbia Pictures

The biggest of the so-called "poverty row" studios, Columbia was the operation of one man, Harry Cohn (1891–1958), who founded it in 1924 after a career as a salesman and movie shorts producer. A gruff, arrogant man, Cohn ran the studio with an iron fist. The company survived by churning out countless low budget westerns and action pictures, but it was also the home of producer/director Frank Capra who made his best films at the studio. The studio also provided a temporary home for other directors including Howard Hawks who made his great romantic-adventure film *Only Angels Have Wings* (1939) and *His Girl Friday* (1940) for the studio.

Although production values were less than perfect, and budgets were generally low, the studio had a fine team of production designers led by Stephen Goosson and including the brilliant Cary Odell and Robert Peterson. They specialized in rain-swept, smoggy sets such as shipping yards, docks, airfields, warehouses, etc. Indeed, in some respects, the studio's production design somewhat resembles a cheaper version of the simple, uncluttered style of Warner Bros.

Typically, Columbia's *films noirs* were made on small budgets. The emphasis is on action and violence, not symbolism or psychology. On the other hand, Fritz Lang, Max Ophuls, and Orson Welles all made symbol-laden films for the studio. Likewise, Joseph H.Lewis, a neglected pictorial stylist,

was a contract director for the studio in the forties and made some of the best *films noirs* for Columbia: *My Name Is Julia Ross; So Dark the Night; and The Undercover Man*. Of course, the studio's best known *film noir* is *Gilda*, directed by contract director Charles Vidor.

The true *noir* classics are rare at Columbia, but the company did release many of the best "B" *noirs*. This tradition continued when, in the 1970's, they released Martin Scorsese's *Taxi Driver*, a low budget production that received instant acclaim as a classic, and has thematic and stylistic characteristics of *films noirs* made at the studio three decades earlier.

Releases: 1945: *My Name Is Julia Ross*. 1946: *Gilda. Johnny O'Clock. Night Editor*. 1947: *Dead Reckoning. Framed*. 1948: *The Dark Past. The Lady from Shanghai*. 1949: *All the King's Men. Knock on Any Door. The Reckless Moment. The Undercover Man*. 1950: *Between Midnight and Dawn. Convicted. In a Lonely Place. 711 Ocean Drive*. 1951: *The Killer That Stalked New York. M. The Mob*. 1952: *Affair in Trinidad. Scandal Sheet. The Sniper*. 1953: *The Big Heat*. 1954: *Drive a Crooked Mile. Human Desire. Pushover. On the Waterfront*. 1955: *The Brothers Rico. The Night Holds Terror. Tight Spot*. 1956: *The Harder They Fall. So Dark the Night*. 1957: *The Burglar. The Garment Jungle. Nightfall*. 1958: *The Line-Up*. 1959: *City of Fear. The Crimson Kimono*. 1961: *Underworld USA*. 1962: *Experiment in Terror*. 1976: *Taxi Driver*.

Conflict (Warner Bros., 1945). 86 min.

Producer: William Jacobs. Director: Curtis Bernhardt. Screenplay: Arthur T. Horman and Dwight Taylor, story by Robert Siodmak and Alfred Neuman. Director of Photography: Merritt Gerstad. Music: Frederick Hollander. Art Director: Ted Smith. Editor: David Weisbart.

Cast: Humphrey Bogart (Richard

Mason), Alexis Smith (Evelyn Turner), Sydney Greenstreet (Dr. Mark Hamilton), Rose Hobart (Katherine Mason), Charles Drake (Prof. Norman Holdsworth). With: Grant Mitchell, Patrick O'Moore, Ann Shoemaker, James Flavin.

Richard and Katherine Mason are having marital problems, which are only exacerbated when Richard confesses that he is in love with Katherine's younger sister, Evelyn. Katherine, however, refuses to believe her husband and sister are having an affair. One night, while returning from a dinner party with their friend, psychiatrist Mark Hamilton, the Masons are involved in a minor automobile accident. Richard's leg is injured. He pretends that the injury is worse than it really is and when, several weeks later, his wife leaves for a skiing vacation, he stays home. She leaves, but Richard, who in fact has healed, intercepts her car on a lonely mountain road, strangles her, and then pushes the car off a cliff. He returns home and reports her missing to both the police and Mark Hamilton.

Shortly thereafter, Richard begins to be haunted by a series of strange events: the reappearance of a piece of his wife's jewelry (which she had been wearing when he murdered her), the odor of her perfume in their house, eerie phone calls, etc. To make matters worse, Evelyn breaks off their relationship. When Richard goes to his friend Hamilton for advice, Hamilton tells him that he believes Mason has not been entirely truthful about his wife's disappearance. To convince himself that he isn't going insane, Richard returns to the scene of the crime. Hamilton and the police arrive right behind him, and Mason is arrested. Dr. Hamilton admits that the hallucinations were a ruse created by himself, and carried out with the help of Evelyn, because of discrepancies in Mason's report of his wife's disappearance.

What ordinarily would have been a standard thriller was heightened by some excellent performances by Warner's stock players, and superb direction by Curtis Bernhardt. Bernhardt fills the film with a *noir* ambiance: shots through rain-streaked windows, and sinister close-ups of Bogart emerging from the shadows as he prepares to murder his wife.

Bogart's performance as a serial killer in the making is one of his best, if least well known, and remains chilling today.

Finally, it must also be noted that the screenplay was based on a story cowritten by director Robert Siodmak, one of *film noir*'s greatest figures, and, like Bernhardt, a veteran of German commercial cinema of the late twenties when it was most influenced by expressionism.

Conrad, William (1920–)

Heavy set character actor. Conrad achieved stardom in the 1970's as Cannon, the private investigator on the television series of the same name. For most of his career prior to the series, however, he played villains in low-budget films. He played villainous henchmen in all of his *films noirs*, except in *Tension*, in which he played a police officer. Although somewhat similar, particularly physically, to Raymond Burr, he did not make the same impact.

Filmography: *The Killers* (Universal, 1946). *Body and Soul* (United Artists, 1947). *Sorry, Wrong Number* (Paramount, 1948). *One Way Street* (Universal, 1950). *Tension* (MGM, 1950). *Cry Danger* (RKO, 1951). *The Racket* (RKO, 1951).

Conte, Richard (Nicholas Conte) (1911–1975)

Actor. For some strange reason, Richard Conte never quite achieved true stardom, despite many excellent performances. He was one of the most popular action heroes of the mid-forties, but he never managed to capitalize on the strong impression he initially made.

Although he did not achieve the sort of fame that several of his contemporaries did — particularly Richard Widmark — he was an important actor in *film noir*, appearing in ten movies.

Unlike many of *noir's* better known icons, Conte specialized in villains, but of a very special type. In *Cry of the City*, for example, he played a criminal who has a great deal more charm than the cop who is tracking him down. This role is typical of the ambiguous qualities that Conte brought to many of his roles.

Another of Conte's outstanding performances is in Nicholas Ray's *Thieves' Highway*. Indeed, it is largely thanks to Conte's strong performance which helps save the film from its almost overwhelming improbable melodrama.

Probably Conte's greatest *film noir* performance is in the neglected classic *The Big Combo*, directed by Joseph H. Lewis. Conte is typically charming as the mob boss Mr. Brown, but he brings to the role a sense of sexual sadism seething just under the surface. His scenes with Jean Wallace, in which he covers her body with kisses, are some of the strangest, and sexiest in fifties' American movies.

While today Conte is usually called a minor *noir* icon, he is also one of the most interesting and talented.

Filmography: *Call Northside 777* (20th Century-Fox, 1948). *Cry of the City* (20th Century-Fox, 1948). *House of Strangers* (20th Century-Fox, 1949). *Thieves' Highway* (20th Century-Fox, 1949). *The Sleeping City* (Universal, 1950). *The Blue Gardenia* (Warner Bros., 1953). *The Big Combo* (United Artists, 1955). *New York Confidential* (Warner Bros., 1955). *The Brothers Rico* (Columbia, 1957).

Convicted (Columbia, 1950). 91 min.
Producer: Jerry Bressler. Director: Henry Levin. Screenplay: William Bowers, Fred Niblo, and S. I. Miller, based on a play *Criminal Code*, by Martin Flavin. Director of Photography: Burnett Guffey. Music: George Duning. Art Director: Carl Anderson. Editor: Al Clark.

Cast: Glenn Ford (Joe Hufford), Broderick Crawford (George Knowland), Millard Mitchell (Malloby), Dorothy Malone (Kay Knowland), Carl Benton Reid (Capt. Douglas), Frank Faylen (Ponti). With: Will Geer, Martha Stewart, Henry O'Neill, Ed Begley.

An innocent man, Joe Hufford, is accused of murdering a member of an important family and is sentenced to prison. George Knowland, a District Attorney, believes that Joe is innocent, but is powerless to help after the defense lawyer assigned to the case messes it up. Joe becomes a model prisoner. The real killer is finally found, thanks to a persistent investigation by Knowland and others. Joe Hufford is released, but has lost the respect of his family and friends.

Convicted is not an important *film noir*, but Glenn Ford does give it some legitimacy by his appearance. He lends the film a typically tough ambiance sorely missed by many minor *noirs*. It is also a rather slow, verbose film, perhaps because of its original material, a moderately successful play.

Cook, Elisha, Jr. (1902–)
Character actor. Elisha Cook Jr. is one of *film noir's* most familiar faces. Short and wiry, he came to epitomize the small-time, cowardly criminal. Like many character actors, he was a scene stealer and it is his performances that often stand out in the films in which he appeared.

Cook's film career began in the early thirties, but did not really hit its stride until the early forties. One of his outstanding early performances in *film noir* was as Wilmer the gunsel in *The Maltese Falcon*. It was the sort of role he repeated in many of his *noir* films. Two of his more interesting *noir* appearances were in *I Wake Up Screaming* and *The Stranger on the Third Floor*. In the former he played an obsessed murderer, typically fidgety and strangely menacing. In *The Stranger on the Third Floor* he was brilliantly cast against type as an innocent suspected of murder.

Cook's best *noir* role was in Stanley Kubrick's late-*noir* classic, *The Killing*. On the surface it was a typical Cook type role (a sniveling, cowardly criminal), but at the mercy of a sexually voracious and greedy *femme-fatale*. Cook brought a sense of pathos to the role which is often all too absent in the genre, and it remains one of *film noir's* great performances.

Filmography: *Stranger on the Third Floor* (RKO, 1940). *The Maltese Falcon* (Warner Bros., 1941). *I Wake Up Screaming* (20th Century-Fox, 1942). *Phantom Lady* (Universal, 1944). *The Big Sleep* (Warner Bros., 1946). *Born to Kill* (RKO, 1947). *Fall Guy* (Monogram, 1947). *The Gangster* (Allied Artists, 1947). *I, the Jury* (United Artists, 1953). *The Killing* (United Artists, 1956). *Baby Face Nelson* (United Artists, 1957). *Plunder Road* (20th Century-Fox, 1957).

Coppel, Alec (1910–1972)

Australian born playwright and screenwriter. Coppel had some success as a playwright in his native country before coming to the United States. He continued to write plays and support his income by occasionally co-writing films. He worked on two late *films noirs*. The first, *Appointment with a Shadow*, is a good, if rather insignificant film. However, he also co-wrote Alfred Hitchcock's masterpiece, *Vertigo*. Although not strictly *film noir*, the film has many *noir*-like elements. It is, arguably, the greatest of all color *films noirs*.

Filmography: *Appointment with a Shadow* (Universal, 1958). *Vertigo* (Universal, 1958).

Corey, Jeff (1914–)

Gaunt character actor. Corey played bits and small supporting roles in several dozen films beginning in the early forties until the mid–eighties. In *film noir*, Corey is most often seen as a henchman of the main villain.

Filmography: *The Killers* (Universal, 1946). *Somewhere in the Night* (20th Century-Fox, 1946). *Brute Force* (Universal, 1947). *The Gangster* (Allied Artists, 1947). *Canon City* (Eagle-Lion, 1948). *Follow Me Quietly* (RKO, 1949).

Corey, Wendell (1914–1968)

Actor. After experience on Broadway in the mid forties, Corey was signed by producer Hal Wallis, and starred in many of his productions. However, he never achieved true stardom, perhaps because of his unconventional appearance.

For the most part, Corey's *film noir* roles were as villains. In *The Killer Is Loose*, he played a myopic killer stalking a city's streets. In Robert Aldrich's *The Big Knife*, he was the second in command to the main villain. Corey's most notable *noir* performance was in *The File on Thelma Jordan* in which he played the adulterous District Attorney whose affair is the catalyst of the destructive action.

Filmography: *The Accused* (Paramount, 1946). *I Walk Alone* (Paramount, 1948) *Sorry, Wrong Number* (Paramount, 1948). *The File on Thelma Jordan* (Paramount, 1950). *Rear Window* (Universal, 1954). *The Big Knife* (United Artists, 1955). *The Killer Is Loose* (United Artists. 1956).

Cormack, Bartlett (1896–1967)

Playwright. Cormack's proletarian melodrama, *The Racket*, was a popular and critical success in the mid twenties. It was first adapted for the screen in 1929. The most famous version of the play, however, is the one made in 1951 starring Robert Mitchum, and generally acknowledged as an important *film noir*. He worked as a screenwriter only briefly in the late thirties, writing, most importantly, Fritz Lang's early *noir* classic, *Fury*.

Filmography: *The Racket* (based on his play) (Paramount, 1929). *Fury* (screenwriter) (MGM, 1936). *The Racket* (based on his play) (RKO, 1951).

Cornered (RKO, 1945). 102 min.
Producer: Adrian Scott. Director: Edward Dmytryk. Screenplay: John Paxton, story by John Wexley. Director of Photography: Harry J. Wild. Music: Roy Webb. Music Director: Constantin Bakaleinikoff. Art Directors: Albert S. D'Agostino and Carroll Clark. Editor: Joseph Noriega.

Cast: Dick Powell (Gerard), Walter Slezak (Incza), Micheline Cheirel (Mme. Jarnac), Nina Vale (Senora Carmago), Morris Carnovsky (Santana), Edgar Barrier (DuBois). With Steven Geray, Jack La Rue, Luther Adler, Jean Del Val.

Gerard, a Canadian pilot recently released from a prisoner of war camp, begins searching for Marcel Jarnac, a Vichy official who was responsible for the death of his French war bride. Jarnac is a man of mystery, and few can remember him. A twisted trail leads through Switzerland to Buenos Aires where Jarnac is allegedly hiding out among the wealthy European expatriots. Gerard meets the wife of Jarnac and a group of her friends including DuBois and Santana; but when DuBois is killed during Gerard's persistent investigation, Santana admits that they belong to an anti-fascist group. Furthermore, Gerard learns that Mme. Jarnac has never met her husband, but married him by proxy in France so that she and her sister could get out of the country. Gerard follows Jarnac to a dark bar, and in the subsequent confrontation, manages to kill him. Santana arrives and helps Gerard with the local authorities.

Dmytryk, Powell, Paxton and Scott, the team that had created the early *film noir* classic, *Murder, My Sweet*, again created one of the finest of all *noirs*. John Paxton's screenplay is typically hard-boiled, as is Powell's performance.

While the style is not as extravagant as its predecessor, it is inventive and rather violent.

The film is also notable for its undisguised attack against fascism and political conservatism, elements which would get its liberal producer and director into a great deal of trouble in several years after the film's release.

Cornfield, Hubert (1929–)
Director. Cornfield directed a handful of films, all "B" productions, in the 1950's. Despite their low budgets, these films are generally of high quality. He directed a little known *film noir* gem, *Plunder Road*, a very good caper drama.

Filmography: *Plunder Road* (20th Century–Fox, 1957).

Cortesa, Valentina (1914–)
Italian born leading lady. Cortesa was an exotic, earthy beauty imported from her native Italy after World War II and given the big push by the powerful Hollywood publicity machine. She never achieved the expected stardom, but she did enliven some Hollywood films with her exotic sensuality, and played supporting roles in two *films noirs* that were dominated by their male leads.

Filmography: *Thieves' Highway* (20th Century–Fox, 1949). *House on Telegraph Hill* (20th Century–Fox, 1951).

Cotten, Joseph (1905–1994)
Actor. Cotten's quiet performances would not seem to make him a natural *film noir* actor, yet he acted in a surprising number of the genre's titles. His on screen persona, however, was adaptable and he could play both unwary innocents hounded by sinister forces (as in *Journey into Fear*) or quiet killers (*Shadow of a Doubt*).

Cotten was originally a member of Orson Welles' Mercury Theatre, and followed Welles to Hollywood in the early 1940's. He acted in the master's greatest films, *Citizen Kane* (RKO, 1941) and *The Magnificent Ambersons* (RKO, 1942), and wrote the screenplay for Welles-produced *Journey into Fear*, one of the most important early *films noirs*.

Two of Cotten's most memorable *noir* performances were as killers—in *Shadow of a Doubt* and *Niagara*. Both performances are very effective and understated.

Filmography: *Journey into Fear* (RKO, 1942). *Shadow of a Doubt* (Universal, 1943). *Beyond the Forest* (Warner Bros., 1949). *Niagara* (20th Century-Fox, 1952). *The Killer Is Loose* (United Artists, 1956). *Touch of Evil* (Universal, 1958).

Coulouris, George (1903–)

British born character actor. Coulouris specialized in debonair, but explosive villains of various types. He appeared in three early *noir* titles. In *Lady on a Train*, he played a menacing killer for hire. In *Nobody Lives Forever*, he played the leader of a gang of murderous gamblers. As *noir* became increasingly Americanized after 1946, European actors were used less and less. After 1950, Coulouris returned to England and continued acting in many films.

Filmography: *Lady on a Train* (Universal, 1945). *Nobody Lives Forever* (Warner Bros.,1946). *Sleep, My Love* (United Artists, 1948).

Crack-Up (RKO, 1946). 93 min.

Producer: Jack J. Gross. Director: Irving Reis. Screenplay: John Paxton, Ben Bengal and Ray Spencer, based on the short story "Madman's Holiday" by Frederic Brown. Director of Photography: Robert de Grasse. Music: Leigh Harline. Music Director: Constantin Bakaleinikoff. Art Directors: Albert S. D'Agostino and Jack Okey. Editor: Frederick Knudtson.

Cast: Pat O'Brien (George Steele), Claire Trevor (Terry Cordeau), Herbert Marshall (Traybin), Ray Collins (Dr. Lowell), Wallace Ford (Cochrane).

With: Dean Harens, Danion O'Flynn, Erskine Sanford, Mary Ware.

When George Steele, a respected expert on art forgeries, appears to be drunk one night while at work, he is fired from his position as lecturer and tour guide at the New York Metropolitan Museum. Steele claims his condition is the result of involvement in a train wreck. However, he cannot remember what happened between the time of the wreck and his appearance at the museum, and the police have no evidence of a train wreck. Retracing his footsteps of the day he was fired, with his girlfriend Terry Cordeau, a reporter, he uncovers a complicated forgery scheme run by the respected Doctor Lowell. Lowell and his associates had kidnapped Steele and put him under a trance to get information and then made him think he was involved in a train wreck. Now Lowell has kidnapped both Steele and Cordeau and plans to put them under sodium pentothal and then kill them in an automobile "accident." They are rescued just in the nick of time by Traybin, a Scotland Yard detective who has been investigating another case involving forgeries and Dr. Lowell.

Crack-Up is a neglected, key *film noir*. It is filled with typical RKO *noir* chiaroscuro, created by cinematographer Robert de Grasse. The screenplay, co-written by the important John Paxton, also contains the usual *noir* themes of alienation and official corruption, as well as amnesia. It is also notable for its attack against conservative art critics while, at the same time, attacking surrealism.

In any case, *Crack-Up* is a major *film noir* and, if not quite a classic of the genre, is an important one in its early development.

Craig, James (John Meador) (1912–1986)

Actor. Craig was a tough leading man of mostly low budget features. He starred in many westerns and several good, minor *films noirs*. He had a prominent role in Joseph H. Lewis' *A Lady Without Passport*, and played a seedy journalist who will stop at nothing to catch a serial killer in Fritz Lang's *While the City Sleeps*.

Filmography: *A Lady Without Passport* (MGM, 1950). *Side Street* (MGM, 1950). *The Strip* (MGM, 1951). *While the City Sleeps* (RKO, 1956).

Crain, Jeanne (1905–)

Actress. A star in the 1940's, Crain was the leading lady and a second female lead in many popular films. Her rather sweet and innocent on screen persona was ill-suited to the hardboiled world of *film noir*, but she appeared as a second female lead in three of the genre's titles.

Filmography: *Leave Her to Heaven* (20th Century–Fox, 1945). *Vicki* (20th Century–Fox, 1953). *The Tattered Dress* (Universal, 1957).

Crawford, Broderick (1911–1986)

Character actor. Crawford came from a theatrical family. His mother Helen Broderick was a popular stage and film actress. Broderick entered films in the late thirties and quickly established a niche for himself as a menacing gangster or criminal of various deranged sorts, but also occasionally played cops. He played both cops and villains in his six *films noirs*. However, probably his best known performance was as Willie Stark in Robert Rossen's *All the King's Men*.

Filmography: *Black Angel* (Universal, 1946) *All the King's Men* (Columbia, 1949). *Convicted* (Columbia, 1950). *The Mob* (Columbia, 1951). *Scandal Sheet* (Columbia, 1952). *Human Desire* (Columbia, 1954). *New York Confidential* (Warner Bros., 1955).

Crawford, Joan (1906–1977)

Actress. A major star of "women's films" in the 1930's, Joan Crawford found her screen image—stoic in the face of adversity—was remarkably well suited to *film noir* in the 1940's. Although she played what were, essentially *femmes-fatales*, in many of her starring vehicles in the thirties, her *noir* roles were generally of a somewhat more heroic type: a heroine who was as cynical as her male counterparts, and just as susceptible to the elements.

Joan Crawford's most famous *noir* performance is in the title role in *Mildred Pierce*. It is a classic performance, and her role as the over protective mother of a psychotic daughter set the standard for the types of roles she was to play in *Possessed* and *The Damned Don't Cry*.

Filmography: *Mildred Pierce* (Warner Bros., 1945). *Possessed* (Warner Bros., 1947). *The Damned Don't Cry* (Warner Bros., 1950). *Sudden Fear* (RKO, 1952). *Female on the Beach* (Universal, 1955).

Cregar, Laird (1916–1944)

Character actor. Cregar was one of the great character actors of the forties. Although a heart attack cut his career tragically short, he left behind an indelible mark on American film in the 1940's. His range was impressively broad, but he is probably best remembered for his hulking, menacing villains, including appearances in two early *films noirs*.

Filmography: *I Wake Up Screaming* (20th Century–Fox, 1942). *This Gun for Hire* (Paramount, 1942).

Crime of Passion (United Artists, 1957). 87 min.

Producer: Herman Cohen. Director: Gerd Oswald. Screenplay: Jo Eisenger. Director of Photography: Joseph La Shelle. Music: Paul Dunlap. Art Director: Leslie Thomas. Editor: Marjorie Fowler.

Cast: Barbara Stanwyck (Kathy Ferguson), Sterling Hayden (Bill Doyle), Raymond Burr (Inspector Tony Pope), Virginia Grey (Sara). With Royal Dano, Robert Griffin, Jay Adler, Brad Trumbell.

Kathy Ferguson is a lovelorn columnist who has made a name for herself by convincing a murderess to turn herself in. She marries Captain Doyle, a Los Angeles policeman and retires from her newspaper job. At first she is happy in her new life as a suburban housewife, but quickly grows restless at her husband's slow rise in the police department. Through a series of misguided manipulations, including an affair with Doyle's friend Tony Pope, Kathy hopes to help influence his career; but when she believes he still is not rising fast enough, she becomes violently angry and murders Pope, whom she believes is not helping. Doyle is assigned to the case and, realizing his wife is the killer, has to arrest her.

While it is not terribly imaginative, and even falls into soap opera at times, *Crime of Passion* is an interesting late-*noir*, notable chiefly for its excellent performances by several important *noir* icons: Barbara Stanwyck, Sterling Hayden, and Raymond Burr. In addition, its screenplay contains several interesting ironies. For example, Kathy Ferguson, at the film's opening, is quite cynical about her reader's melodramatic lives but then finds, in her own life, she is in a far more melodramatic situation than her readers could have ever imagined!

Crime Wave (Warner Bros., 1954). 73 min.

Producer: Bryan Foy. Director: Andre De Toth. Screenplay: Crane Wilbur, adapted by Bernard Gordon and Richard Wormser, from the story "Criminal's Mark" by John and Ward Hawkins. Director of Photography: Bert Glennon. Music: David Buttolph. Art Director: Stanley Fleisher. Editor: Thomas Reilly.

Cast: Gene Nelson (Steve Lacey), Phyllis Kirk (Ellen), Sterling Hayden (Detective Sgt. Sims), James Bell (Daniel O'Keefe), Ted De Corsia (Doc Penny), Charles Bronson (Ben Hastings). With: Jay Novello, Ned Young, Richard Benjamin, Timoth Carey.

Steve Lacey, an ex-convict, is implicated in a hold up by two former inmates of the same prison. Steve, who has gone straight, agrees to help the two crooks, allegedly to save his family and friends the embarrassment of discovering his past. A police detective, Sgt. Sims, believes that Steve is involved with the two crooks, but when Steve foils the two, Sims reluctantly agrees to help straighten matters out.

Crime Wave is an engaging low budget *film noir* that is both visually exciting and semi-comic, a rarity in *noir*. Andre De Toth was a veteran Hollywood director who specialized in handling actors, and gives the characters certain touches which make them endearing and more human. The film also has an excellent score by David Buttolph.

The Crimson Kimono (Columbia, 1959). 82 min.

Producer, Director and Screenwriter: Samuel Fuller. Director of Photography: Samuel Leavitt. Music: Harry Sukman. Art Directors: William E. Flannery and Robert Boyle. Editor: Jerome Thoms.

Cast: Victoria Shaw (Christine Downs), Glenn Corbett (Detective Sgt. Charlie Bancroft), James Shigeta (Detective Joe Kojaku), Anna Lee (Mac), Paul Dubov (Casale), Jaclynne Greene (Roma). With: Neyle Morrow, Gloria Pall, Barbara Hayden, George Yoshimagu.

The Crimson Kimono was one of the last of the *films noirs* during its initial phase, and, with several other films, ushered in a new era of movies influenced by *film noir* but would develop into other genres.

Police detectives Charlie Bancroft and Joe Kajaku are friends assigned to investigate the murder of a stripper, Sugar Torch. They both meet and fall in love with a beautiful artist, Christine Downs. She falls in love with Joe inadvertently causing racial tension between the two friends. Eventually the investigation leads to Roma, who admits she

Yvonne DeCarlo, Burt Lancaster in *Criss Cross* (Universal, 1949).

killed Sugar because she thought the stripper was having an affair with her lover.

The Crimson Kimono is one of Sam Fuller's most consistent films. It is subtle and sensitive, ahead of its time for its treatment of interracial sexual relationships. Fuller makes good use of actual locations in Little Tokyo and metropolitan Los Angeles for juxtaposition of cultural duplicity, the film's key theme.

The film is full of stylized violence, particularly in a martial arts battle between the two detectives which starts out as practice but reveals the undercurrent of racial tension and jealousy between them. It also contains some excellent chase scenes and Sam Leavitt's color photography captures the spirit of black and white *noir* photography.

Unsentimental and uncompromising, *The Crimson Kimono* is one of the best late *films noirs* that also points the way to later classics *The French Connection* (20th Century–Fox, 1973) and *Dirty Harry* (Warner Bros., 1971).

Criss Cross (Universal, 1949). 88 min. Producer: Michael Kraike. Director: Robert Siodmak. Screenplay: Daniel Fuchs, based on the novel by Don Tracy. Director of Photography: Franz Planer. Art Directors: Bernard Herzbrun and Boris Leven. Music: Miklos Rozsa. Editor: Ted J. Kent.

Cast: Burt Lancaster (Steve Thompson), Yvonne De Carlo (Anna), Dan Duryea (Slim Dundee), Stephen McNally (Pete Ramirezz), Richard Long (Slade Thompson), Percy Helton (Frank). With: Esy Morales, Tom Pecli, Alan Napier, Griff Barnett, Joan Miller, Tony Curtis.

Still plagued by the image of his beautiful ex-wife Anna, Steve Thompson, an armored car guard, frequents the bar where they spent much of their time. One night he is surprised to see Anna on the dance floor and when she comes over she tells him she plans to marry Slim Dundee, a local gambler with mob connections. However, she suggests that physical relationships with Steve were better than with Slim. Despite warnings from his friends and family that she is no good, Steve secretly begins seeing Anna; but when Dundee catches them at his house, Thompson improvises an excuse, claiming he has plans to rob the armored car company. Dundee agrees to help, but in fact he is jealous of Anna and Steve and plans to double cross his romantic rival. Unfortunately, the double cross backfires during the robbery and Thompson's partner is killed. Thompson, however, kills Dundee's two henchmen and, ironically, is praised in the press as a hero.

Anna, meanwhile, has disappeared with the money from the robbery. Dundee has Thompson kidnapped to blackmail Anna, but Thompson bribes his abductor into taking him to Anna's hideout. Dundee is not far behind, and in the ensuing confrontation, he kills both Steve and Anna, and then runs out of the house as police sirens approach.

Criss Cross is one of Robert Siodmak's greatest films, and one of the genre's most neglected classics.

The film's fatalism is established from the very opening with an aerial shot of a bleak urban landscape that dips down into the parking lot of a nightclub where, in the shadows between cars, two lovers—Steve and Anna—are entwined in a kiss. The *noir* themes of dangerous sex, unconquerable fear and romantic tragedy, are reinforced through point-of-view technique and lazy, languorous photography.

The film contains several excellent performances, but Yvonne De Carlo, as the deadly, alluring Anna, is absolutely stunning. Her performance in the role might well be one of *noir*'s best female performances.

The artistic success of *Criss Cross*, however, can be attributed to Robert Siodmak. The tense robbery scenes are brilliantly contrasted with slower, quieter moments, and the film moves steadily forward toward its inevitable tragic end.

Cromwell, John (1887–1979)

Director. Cromwell turned to film direction at the relatively late age of forty after many years as a character actor on stage and film. He directed a number of important, renowned films throughout his nearly three decade career including *Of Human Bondage* (RKO, 1934), *The Prisoner of Zenda* (United Artists, 1937), and *The Goddess* (Columbia, 1958). Cromwell's nondescript style was easily adaptable to the different genres he worked in. *Dead Reckoning* is a famous, rather claustrophobic *film noir* that is yet another variation of the war veteran returns to discover corrupt American theme. *The Racket* is an excellent remake of the early sound exposé of big city crime and official corruption and contains several excellent performances.

Filmography: *Dead Reckoning* (Columbia, 1947). *Caged* (Warner Bros., 1950). *The Racket* (RKO, 1951).

Cronyn, Hume (1911–)

Character actor. Hume Cronyn is the husband of Jessica Tandy and, like her, has divided his career between the stage and film. He played supporting roles in many important films in the 1940's and 1950's. He was an effective villain and in one of his best *noir* roles, in *Brute Force*, played the epitome of sadistic cruelty as Captain Munsey, the head of the prison guards. The performance remains one of *film noir*'s most indelible villains.

Filmography: *Shadow of a Doubt* (Universal, 1943). *The Postman Always Rings Twice* (MGM, 1946). *Brute Force* (Universal, 1947).

The Crooked Way (United Artists, 1949). 87 min.

Producer: Benedict Bogeaus. Director: Robert Florey. Screenplay: Richard H. Landau, based on the radio play "No Blade Too Sharp" by Robert Monroe. Director of Photography: John Alton. Music: Louis Forbes. Production Designer: Van Nest Polglase. Editor: Frank Sullivan.

Cast: John Payne (Eddie Rice), Sonny Tufts (Vince Alexander), Ellen Drew (Nina), Rhys Williams (Lt. Williams). Percy Helton (Petey), John Doucette (Sgt. Barrett). With: Charles Evans, Greta Granstadt, Harry Bronson, Crane Whitley.

Eddie Rice is finally released from the veteran's hospital after recovering from a war injury that has left him an amnesiac. All he knows is that he is originally from Los Angeles. He returns there to see if he can piece together his former life and by coincidence meets Lt. Williams at the train station. Williams, skeptical about Rice's condition, informs him that he was the partner of a local racketeer Vince Alexander, and that his real name is Eddie Ricardi.

Eddie meets his ex-wife, Nina Martin, and decides to rekindle his relationship with her. Meanwhile, Vince Alexander has Eddie beaten up, believing he had joined the military leaving Vince alone to face charges for a previous crime. Vince sets up Eddie in the murder of Lt. Williams, but Nina, realizing he had changed, helps Eddie get away. She takes him to his old, loyal friend Petey, who also agrees to help. In the following confrontation with Vince, a gun battle erupts and Vince is killed. Eddie hopes his old personality will not return.

The Crooked Way is a decidedly minor *film noir*. It is rather static and verbose, perhaps because it was based on a radio play. The performances are generally very good, and director Robert Florey fills the film with his characteristic expressionist visuals.

Crossfire (RKO, 1947). 85 min.

Producer: Adrian Scott. Director: Edward Dmytryk. Screenplay: John Paxton, based on the novel *The Brick Foxhole* by Richard Brooks. Director of Photography: J. Roy Hunt. Music: Roy Webb. Art Directors: Albert S. D'Agostino and Alfred Herman. Editor: Harry Gerstad.

Cast: Robert Young (Finlay), Robert Mitchum (Keeley), Robert Ryan (Montgomery), Gloria Grahame (Ginny), Paul Kelly (the Man), Sam Levene (Samuels), George Cooper (Mitchell), Steve Brodie (Floyd), William Phipps (Leroy). With: Marlo Dwyer, Richard Powers, Lex Barker, Jacqueline White.

Crossfire is one of the great *films noirs* of the forties, both an artistic and commercial success, and helped kick off the flood of similar films in the last part of the decade.

While on leave, four army buddies—Leroy, Montgomery, Floyd and Mitchell—get into an argument with Samuels, a Jew. Montgomery, a psychotic anti-semite, murders Samuels. Detectives Keeley and Finlay investigate the murder. Montgomery murders Floyd who was a witness to the crime. In a state of confusion caused by a trick by the police to convince him that Floyd is still alive, Montgomery returns to the scene of his crimes and is arrested.

Crossfire is a *film noir* that also works as a message film. It was one of the earliest Hollywood films to deal with racial injustice and prejudice, and it does so quite effectively.

The direction by Edward Dmytryk is rather flat, with a few flourishes of brilliance and inventiveness, but there is not real consistent style. It is John Paxton's screenplay (adapted from a novel by Richard Brooks) that holds the film together.

The film is populated with many of *film noir*'s most significant icons. The film is generally noted for its intense performance by Robert Ryan as the racist-murderer. Robert Mitchum's role is less pivotal than his other *noir* performances and Gloria Grahame has a small part as a bar girl.

Interestingly, Paxton changed the victim of the crime in the original novel from a homosexual to a Jew, in light of the horror of Auschwitz (then so prevalent in the news). It was a timely, clever change.

Cry Danger (RKO, 1951). 79 min.

Producer: Sam Weisenthal and W. R. Frank. Director: Robert Parrish. Screenplay: William Bowers, story by Jerome Cady. Director of Photography: Joseph F. Biroc. Music: Emil Newman and Paul Dunlap. Song: "Cry Danger" by Hugo Friedhofer and Leon Pober. Art Director: Richard Day. Editor: Bernard W. Burton.

Cast: Dick Powell (Rocky), Rhonda Fleming (Nancy), Richard Erdman (De Long), William Conrad (Castro), Regis Toomey (Cobb), Jay Adler (Williams). With Jean Porter, Joan Banks, Gloria Saunders, Hy Averback.

Rocky has spent five years in prison for a murder and robbery he did not commit. Released, after a review by the parole board, his best friend Danny remains behind, supposedly framed for the same crime. Rocky begins his own investigation of the events that got him into trouble, and quickly realizes the real culprit is Castro, an acquaintance. As his investigation continues, he discovers that Nancy, Danny's wife, has kept hush money because Danny, in fact, really was Castro's accomplice in the robbery-murder. Unable to do

anything about it, he decides to go on with his life.

Robert Parrish's first film as a director (he was previously a successful editor who had worked on several *films noirs*, *Cry Danger* is an energetic low budget *noir* that moves at a good pace. It is generally unpretentious, with a strong existential theme. Dick Powell is typically hard-boiled as Rocky, accepting the inevitability of the events which have trapped him with characteristic stoicism. Rhonda Fleming is also very good as the *femme-fatale* Nancy and the film provided her with one of her best *noir* roles.

Cry Danger is an admirable debut and, although not particularly distinguished, it is not bad either.

Cry of the City (20th Century–Fox, 1948). 96 min.

Producer: Sol Siegel. Director: Robert Siodmak. Screenplay: Richard Murphy, based on the novel *The Chair for Martin Rome* by Henry E. Helseth. Director of Photography: Lloyd Ahern. Music: Alfred Newman. Art Directors: Lyle Wheeler and Albert Hogsett. Editor: Harmon Jones.

Cast: Victor Mature (Lt. Candella), Richard Conte (Martin Rome), Fred Clark (Lt. Collins), Shelley Winters (Brenda), Betty Garde (Mrs. Pruett), Barry Kroeger (Niles). With: Tommy Cook, Debra Paget, Hope Emerson, Roland Winters.

Martin Rome is recuperating in a hospital after being wounded in a gun battle with the police during a botched robbery. He refuses to reveal the identity of a girl who visited him the night before. Lt. Candella, convinced that Rome had a part in an infamous, unsolved jewel robbery, believes the girl might be involved. In fact she is, and when Rome escapes from the prison ward, he joins the girl, Teena, and goes after the jewels for himself. Through a series of intrigues and double crosses, he plans to steal the jewels from the main crook and leave the country with

Teena. But Candella is right behind, and eventually all comes to a head at Martin's hideout. In the inevitable shootout, Candella is wounded but he also kills Rome.

Cry of the City marks Robert Siodmak's break with the studio, and his attempt at semi-documentary style, location shooting. The film was shot largely in New York City and, in some ways, is more satisfying than the similar *Naked City* (Universal, 1948), although its complex narrative distracts somewhat from the overall quality. Still, Siodmak manages to translate his usual studio/expressionist style to location filming, creating an almost surreal vision of New York and its criminal underworld. Alfred Newman's score is also well above average.

Cry Terror (MGM, 1958). 96 min.
Producers: Virginia and Andrew Stone. Director: Andrew Stone. Screenplay: Andrew Stone. Music: Howard Jackson. Art Directors: William A. Horning and Addison Hehr. Editor: Ben Lewis.
Cast: James Mason (Jim Molnar), Rod Steiger (Paul Hoplin), Inger Stevens (Joan Molnar), Neville Brand (Steve), Angie Dickinson (Kelly), Jack Klugman (Vince). With: Kenneth Tobey, Carleton Young, Barney Phillips, Mae Marsh.

A little known late-*noir*, *Cry Terror* once again explores the theme of a family held captive by a dangerous criminal. In this case, an airline bomber holds the Molnars captive as security for ransom money. Although it is not as well known as certain similarly themed *noirs*, it is quite suspenseful, with some strong direction by Andrew L. Stone, and a good performance by James Mason as the stoic patriarch of the terrorized family.

Cry Vengeance (Allied Artists, 1954). 83 min.
Producer and Director: Mark Stevens. Screenplay: Warren Douglas and George Bricker. Director of Photogra-

phy: William Sickner. Music: Paul Dunlap. Editor: Phil England.
Cast: Mark Stevens (Vic Barron), Martha Hyer (Peggy Hides), Skip Homeier (Roxy), Joan Vohs (Lilly Arnold). With: Douglas Kennedy, Don Haggerty, Cheryl Calloway.

When an ex-con is released from prison, he seeks revenge against those who framed him.

The plot for *Cry Vengeance* is simple and direct, but then again the film is also a straightforward action *noir*. It is notable chiefly for its director Mark Stevens, who also has the leading role. Stevens was a "B" actor of the forties and fifties who acted in a few minor *films noirs*. Here, he manages to create a bleak, dark vision of a character's single minded desire for revenge.

Cukor, George (1899–1983)
Director. Cukor was a specialist of elegant comedies and dramas. He was a "woman's director," an expert handler of female talent and drawing room type scenes. *A Double Like*, his only *film noir*, is more typical Cukor than conventional *film noir*. Its back stage scenes and debonair, central male character (played by the always elegant Ronald Colman) are Cukor standards. However, even for this material, Cukor's touch is a little too light and the film, despite some good moments, falls short of being a true classic.
Filmography: *A Double Life* (Universal, 1948).

Cummings, Irving (1888–1959)
Producer. From the silent era until 1944, Cummings was a successful director of light films, particularly musicals. He retired from directing in the mid-forties but continued to occasionally produce films. He produced John Farrow's *Where Danger Lives* at RKO.
Filmography: *Where Danger Lives* (RKO, 1949).

Cummings, Robert (1908–1991)
Actor. Cummings was a leading man

of the sort Hollywood found so useful in the thirties and forties. Like Robert Taylor and Robert Montgomery, he was generally cast opposite a strong leading lady in "women's films." He achieved real stardom via television. His *noir* roles are typical of his film career: in all three he was the male lead in movies dominated by female leads.

Filmography: *The Accused* (Paramount, 1946). *The Chase* (United Artists, 1946). *Sleep, My Love* (United Artists, 1948).

Cummins, Peggy (1925-)
Actress. The British born Cummins had a successful career in her native country as a child actress. In her late teens, she moved to the United States, perhaps hoping to repeat the success of Elizabeth Taylor, another British emigree who had become, in the mid forties, one of the biggest film stars in the world. Cummins, of course, did not repeat the success of Taylor, but she did enliven a handful of "B" movies with her extraordinarily voluptuous image. A striking, tall blonde, Cummins brings to mind Marilyn Monroe and Jayne Mansfield, and, like them, her strong sexuality was both up front and self-parodying.

Cummins' single *film noir* performance was in *Gun Crazy*. As Annie Star, she is one of the genre's most memorable *femme-fatales*; an irresistible mixture of sensuality with beguiling evil.

Filmography: *Gun Crazy* (United Artists, 1950).

Curtis, Tony (Bernard Schwartz) (1925-)
Actor and leading man. Curtis was a bit too young to establish himself as a viable *noir* protagonist before the genre waned. He had a small part early in his career in the great Robert Siodmak *noir*, *Criss Cross*. He starred in the minor adventure *noir*, *Forbidden*, opposite his wife Janet Leigh. Later, however, he gave a memorable performance

as a corrupt publicity agent in the late-*noir* classic, *Sweet Smell of Success*.

Filmography: *Criss Cross* (Universal, 1949). *Forbidden* (Universal, 1954). *Sweet Smell of Success* (United Artists, 1957).

Curtiz, Michael (Mihaly Kertesz) (1888–1962)
Director. One of the best known Hollywood "characters." A ruthless director on the set, and one of the most prolific directors in film history, Michael Curtiz's eccentricities and excesses have been well documented. Yet, his very considerable talents and achievements have often been overlooked. After all, this was the man who directed *Casablanca* (Warner Bros., 1943). He was a technical genius who knew how to use a camera better than just about any other director.

Curtiz was born Mihaly Kertesz in Hungary in 1888. In 1912, he began acting on stage and in film, and began directing sometime afterward. From the very beginning he proved to be an efficient and inspired director, churning out over two dozen features in the next decade — one of these films, *Moon Over Israel* (1924) impressed Jack Warner who brought him to Hollywood in 1926. He quickly became Warner Brother's leading director and in a sense it would not be an exaggeration to say that this Hungarian who spoke broken English *was* Warner Bros., the most "American" of the Hollywood studios. He took whatever assignments came his way with fervor, and directed many classics.

Curtiz's greatest achievements were with romantic action films. He directed nearly all of the great Errol Flynn pictures including *Captain Blood* (Warner Bros., 1936), *The Charge of the Light Brigade* (Warner Bros., 1936), *The Adventures of Robin Hood* (Warner Bros., 1938), and *The Sea Hawk* (Warner Bros., 1940).

Surprisingly, few of Curtiz's films show the influence of *expressionism*, the predominate influence on European cinema in the twenties and thirties and an equally important influence on the look of *film noir*. Yet, he brought the unique Germanic visuals to several of his important films, particularly the black and white ones. This is true of *Casablanca* as well as his three *noir* titles. They are all distinguished by smooth and brilliant camera movements, exotic, distorted angles, and expressive lighting.

Mildred Pierce is Curtiz's *noir* masterpiece. The thoroughly rotten and nasty world of James M. Cain is Curtiz's type of material. He seemed to take such perverse delight in Joan Crawford's performance and ultimate martyrdom in the title role, that one gets little satisfaction from Mildred's exoneration at the end of the film.

For this single classic, Curtiz holds a special place among the *film noir* directors.

Filmography: *Mildred Pierce* (Warner Bros., 1945). *The Unsuspected* (Warner Bros., 1947). *The Breaking Point* (Warner Bros., 1950).

D'Agostino, Albert S. (1893–1970)

Art Director. Although probably not as well known as his chief rivals, Cedric Gibbons and Hans Dreier, Albert D'Agostino is certainly one of the most important art directors of Hollywood's golden age. As RKO's chief art director from 1936 to the studio's demise in 1958, D'Agostino was responsible for that studio's influential, gothic expressionist style of the 1940's. Indeed, D'Agostino is one of *film noir*'s unsung heroes. It is often his set designs one remembers from the RKO *noirs*, many of which are acknowledged classics.

D'Agostino began his career at Universal in the twenties. There he developed the so-called American Gothic style, so epitomized by the designs for the studio's horror films. Later, at RKO, D'Agostino, often in collaboration, designed the intimate, low budget horror thrillers produced by Val Lewton. These films were particularly influential on the set designs for the seminal *films noirs* at all the major studios. In addition, D'Agostino, most often with Walter Keller, co-designed the sets for many of the great RKO *films noirs*. In one year alone, 1952, D'Agostino worked on *noirs* directed by the following great filmmakers: Joseph Von Sternberg, Fritz Lang, Otto Preminger and Howard Hawks. D'Agostino is clearly one of the most important art directors in *film noir*.

Filmography: *Stranger on the Third Floor* (RKO, 1940). *Journey into Fear* (RKO, 1943). *Experiment Perilous* (RKO, 1944). *Murder, My Sweet* (RKO, 1944). *Cornered* (RKO, 1945). *Johnny Angel* (RKO, 1945). *Crack-up* (RKO, 1946). *Deadline at Dawn* (RKO, 1946). *Nocturne* (RKO, 1946). *Notorious* (RKO, 1946). *The Spiral Staircase* (RKO, 1946). *Born to Kill* (RKO, 1947). *Crossfire* (RKO, 1947). *Desperate* (RKO, 1947). *The Locket* (RKO, 1947). *Out of the Past* (RKO, 1947). *They Won't Believe Me* (RKO, 1947). *Berlin Express* (RKO, 1948). *Race Street* (RKO, 1948). *They Live by Night* (RKO, 1948). *The Dangerous Profession* (RKO, 1949). *Follow Me Quietly* (RKO, 1949). *The Set-Up* (RKO, 1949). *Armored Car Robbery* (RKO, 1950). *The Capture* (RKO, 1950). *Where Danger Lives* (RKO, 1950). *Gambling House* (RKO, 1951). *His Kind of Woman* (RKO, 1951). *The Racket* (RKO, 1951). *Roadblock* (RKO, 1951). *Beware, My Lovely* (RKO, 1952). *Clash by Night* (RKO, 1952). *Macao* (RKO, 1952). *The Narrow Margin* (RKO, 1952). *On Dangerous Ground* (RKO, 1952). *Angel Face* (RKO, 1952). *The Hitch-Hiker* (RKO, 1952).

Dahl, Arlene (1924–)

Actress. The red-haired Arlene Dahl enjoyed a brief taste of fame in the late forties and early fifties, mainly as a star of comedies and innocuous dramas. She co-starred in two rather insignificant *films noirs*.

Joseph Cotten, Everett Sloane, Ruth Warwick in *Journey into Fear* (RKO, 1943).

Filmography: *Scene of the Crime* (MGM, 1949). *Slightly Scarlet* (RKO, 1956).

Dall, John (1924–).

Actor. Dall is a tall, lanky actor, similar in some respects to Gregory Peck, but without the same charm or talent. He appeared exclusively in "B" movies and co-starred in one of the great "B" *noirs, Gun Crazy*, directed by Joseph H. Lewis. Dall's performance in this film is crass and sleazy, but it is his co-star, Peggy Cummings, who is really impressive in the film. Dall also co-starred in another, less memorable *film noir*.

Filmography: *Gun Crazy* (United Artists, 1950). *The Man Who Cheated Himself* (20th Century–Fox, 1951).

The Damned Don't Cry (Warner Bros., 1950). 103 min.

Producer: Jerry Wald. Director:

Vincent Sherman. Screenplay: Harold Medford and Jerome Weidman, story by Gertrude Walker. Director of Photography: Ted McCord. Music: Daniele Amfitheatrof. Art Director: Robert Haas. Editor: Rudi Fehr.

Cast: Joan Crawford (Ethel Whitehead/Lorna Hansen Forbes), David Brian (George Castleman), Steve Cochran (Nick Prenta), Kent Smith (Martin Blackford), Hugh Sanders (Grady), Selena Royle, (Patricia), With: Jacqueline de Wit, Morris Ankrum, Sara Perry.

When Elizabeth Whitehead's son dies, she leaves her husband and moves to the big city. She capitalizes on her beauty, becoming a fashion model in a department store. She is encouraged by one of the models to accept dates with wealthy businessmen, and she soon finds herself the mistress of a mobster, George Castleman. He promotes her as a false Texas Heiress, "Lorna Hansen

Forbes." When she is sent by Castleman to help trap a rebel member of his gang, Nick Prenta, she falls in love with her intended victim. She tries to sabotage Castleman's plans, but when he kills Nick, Ethel flees to her parent's home. Castleman and his second in command follow her and, in the inevitable confrontation, Ethel is wounded. However, seeing his chance to seize power, the second in command shoots and kills Castleman, freeing Ethel from her criminal life.

The Damned Don't Cry is a "woman's problem" *noir* with a strong performance by Joan Crawford in the leading role. At once romantic and desperate, Ethel is a victim of her own greed, a need for success and fame. Her narcissism traps her the way it traps all *noir* protagonists.

In a sense, a romantic tragedy, Ethel is debased by the criminal underworld, cheap sex, and her own personal deception.

Vincent Sherman's direction is perfunctory, and the film is saved solely by Crawford's performance.

Danger Signal (Warner Bros., 1945). 78 min.
Producer: William Jacobs. Director: Robert Florey. Screenplay: Adele Commandini and Graham Baker, based on the novel by Phyliss Bottome. Director of Photography: James Wong Howe. Music: Adolph Deutsch. Art Director: Stanley Fleischer. Editor: Frank Magee.
Cast: Faye Emerson (Hilda Fenchurch), Zachary Scott (Ronnie Mason/ Marsh), Dick Erdman (Bunkie Taylor), Rosemary De Camp (Dr. Silla), Bruce Bennett (Dr. Andrew Lang). With: John Ridgely, Mary Servoss, Joyce Compton, Virginia Sale.

Ronnie Mason, a smooth scoundrel, makes his living by preying on vulnerable women. In a hotel room, he discovers a young woman that he was having an affair with dead, so he steals a wedding ring and some money. The next day, the newspaper reports that the girl committed suicide, but her husband, Dr. Andrew Lang, suspects that she was murdered. He knows she was having an affair with an artist called Marsh.

Mason flees to Los Angeles where he hides out in a boarding house, pretending to be a war veteran, Ron Marsh. He soon seduces a resident of the house, Hilda, who has a teenage daughter, Anne. When he learns that Anne has a substantial inheritance coming from a recently dead relative, he turns his affections to her. Hilda is broken hearted and sees him for what he is, but cannot convince her daughter.

Meanwhile, the husband of the dead girl, Dr. Lang, has tracked Mason down. When Mason tries to flee, he falls off a cliff to his death.

Danger Signal is vaguely similar to Alfred Hitchcock's *Shadow of a Doubt*. However, it fails in comparison to Hitchcock's masterpiece. Its plot is overly complicated, and Florey's direction is typically extravagant. A minor *noir*, *Danger Signal* is still an interesting, worthy film.

A Dangerous Profession (RKO, 1949). 79 min.
Producer: Robert Sparks. Director: Ted Tetzlaff. Screenplay: Martin Rackin and Warren Duff. Director of Photography: Robert de Grasse. Music: Frederick Hollander. Art Directors: Albert S. D'Agostino and Jack Okey. Editor: Sherman Todd.
Cast: George Raft (Vince Kane), Ella Raines (Lucy Brackett), Pat O'Brien (Joe Farley), Bill Williams (Brackett), Jim Backus (Ferrone), With: Ralph Peters, Jane Hazzard, Don Porter.

Vince Kane and Joe Farley are partners in a bail bond firm. Kane is a former police officer and, when a robbery suspect, Brackett, whom he has bailed out, is killed under peculiar circumstances, Kane begins his own investigation. He discovers that Brackett was framed by a gang, and eventually he helps break it up.

A Dangerous Profession is a modest film noir, with a confusing and vague screenplay. It was directed by Ted Tetzlaff in the same year he directed his minor masterpiece, *The Window*, but it has none of the inventive flair of that film. George Raft typically plays a variation of the well groomed tough guy he would perfect in countless action films and thrillers. The film's one redeeming feature is Ella Raines, as the vulnerable widow of the murdered man. Raines is a neglected performer from the era, starring in mostly "B" productions, but always very good in whatever she appeared.

Daniels, Harold (1903–1971)

Director. Daniels directed a few "B" movies that are known now for their sloppiness and air of improvisation. However, his *Roadblock* is one of the best RKO "B" *noirs* as well as one of the most fatalistic.

Filmography: *Roadblock* (RKO, 1951).

Daniels, William (1895–1970)

Cinematographer. William Daniels is, without question, one of Hollywood's greatest cinematographers. His career began in the early twenties as the director of photography for Erich Von Stroheim. In the late twenties he became Greta Garbo's hand-picked cinematographer, and was particularly adept at capturing the exotic, glossy, romantic mood of Garbo's films. However, Daniels was an adaptable, inventive artist. He encouraged the move toward more location shooting in the late forties. He photographed two of the most important *films noirs* during this period, both of which exploited their exterior locations. Indeed, both *Brute Force* and *The Naked City*,, were shot in pseudo-documentary style, the very antithesis of the artificial style developed by Daniels fifteen years before.

Filmography: *Brute Force* (Universal, 1947). *Lured* (United Artists, 1947). *The Naked City* (Academy Award for Best Cinematography) (Universal, 1948). *Forbidden* (Universal, 1954).

Danson, Ted (1947–)

Actor. Danson is probably most famous as Sam on the Emmy award winning television show *Cheers*. Before that, he had a prominent supporting role in the modern *noir*, *Body Heat*, as the friend of Ned Racine (William Hurt) who must, in the end, bring Racine to justice. It is a role similar to that played by Edward G. Robinson in *Double Indemnity* (Paramount, 1944).

Filmography: *Body Heat* (Warner Bros., 1981).

Danton, Ray (1931–)

Actor. Tall, dark leading man, Ray Danton starred or co-starred in a number of features in the 1950's. He was an action hero, but also played second leads in dramas and the occasional epic. He co-starred in two late, minor *films noirs*.

Filmography: *Night Runner* (Universal, 1957). *The Beat Generation* (MGM, 1959).

Dark City (Paramount, 1950). 98 min.

Producer: Hal Wallis. Director: William Dieterle. Screenplay: John Meredyth Lucas and Larry Marcus, with contributions from Leonardo Bercovici, adapted by Ketti Frings from a story by Larry Marcus. Director of Photography: Victor Milner. Music: Franz Waxman. Songs by Harold Arlen and Johnny Mercer, Frank Loesser and Jimmy McHugh, and Dorothy Fields. Art Directors: Hans Dreier and Franz Bachelin. Editor: Warren Low.

Cast: Charlton Heston (Danny Haley), Lizabeth Scott (Fran), Viveca Lindfors (Victoria Winant), Dean Jagger (Capt. Garvey), Don De Fore (Arthur Winant), Jack Webb (Augie), Henry Morgan (Soldier), Mike Mazurki (Sid). With: Ed Begley, Walter Sande, Mark Kevning, Stanley Prager.

After losing a considerable sum of

money to Danny Haley in a rigged poker game, Arthur Wimant kills himself. When another gambler is murdered, all of the other gambling racketeers are cautious about cashing Winant's other checks. Danny Haley begins to investigate and learns that Winant's brother, Sid, is a psychopath who is murdering gamblers as a kind of revenge. With the help of Vicky Winant, Arthur's widow, he captures Sid.

Dark City is an interesting *film noir*, filled with archetypal grotesques: snarling two-bit gangsters (Ed Begley), small time hoods (Jack Webb) and psychopaths (Mike Mazurki in a manic performance). Danny Haley is not exactly a sympathetic character at the beginning of the film, but through his relationship with Vicky Winent, he gradually grows more human and sensitive. These were unusual roles for the two stars of this movie. Heston almost always played dynamic heroes and Lizabeth Scott is probably most famous as the *femme-fatale* in *Dead Reckoning* (Warner Bros., 1948). Heston's character has more depth, however, and Scott is ill used, spending most of her time on screen singing dull songs.

The most interesting elements of the film, however is William Dieterle's expressionist direction. The sets, designed by the great art director Hans Dreier, are shrouded in fog and the streets are rain streaked, throwing back glittering, neon light.

Unfortunately, the story is rather weak and the film does not quite qualify as a true classic.

The Dark Corner (20th Century–Fox, 1946). 99 min.

Producer: Fred Kohlmar. Director: Henry Hathaway. Screenplay: Jay Dratler and Bernard Schoenfeld, based on a short story by Leo Rosten. Director of Photography: Joe MacDonald. Music: Cyril Mockridge. Art Directors: James Basevi and Leland Fuller. Editor: J. Watson Webb.

Cast: Mark Stevens (Bradford Galt), Lucille Ball (Kathleen), Clifton Webb (Hardy Cathcart), William Bendix (White Suit), Kurt Kreuger (Tony Jardine), Cathy Downs (Mari Cathcart). With: Reed Hadley, Constance Collier, Molly Laumonst.

Bradford Galt, a private investigator, is released from prison after being framed by his ex-partner Tony Jardine and he finds himself followed by a man in a white suit. Galt suspects Jardine has hired him, but White Suit is really an employee of an art dealer, Hardy Cathcart. Cathcart is hoping to provoke Galt into killing Jardine because the latter is having an affair with Cathcart's wife. When Galt does not react, White Suit kills Jardine and hides the body in Galt's apartment. Cathcart then pushes White Suit out of the window of a tall building to keep him from talking. Keeping just ahead of the cops, Galt and his secretary, Kathleen, discover Cathcart is behind the scheme, but in the final confrontation, Mari Cathcart shoots her husband, freeing Galt from trouble.

Although it is a minor *film noir*, *The Dark Corner* is still an interesting film, distinguished largely by Mark Stevens as the sullen private detective.

Henry Hathaway's direction is typically tight and effective. The film is enveloped in darkness, a metaphor for Galt's claustrophobic situation. Hathaway and his cinematographer, Joe MacDonald, created a beautiful *noir*, with figures stepping in and out of shadows and shafts of light cascading into blackness.

Clifton Webb's performance as Hardy Cathcart is typically shrill and garish, and Lucille Ball is surprisingly effective as Galt's faithful Girl Friday.

The Dark Mirror (Universal, 1946). 85 min.

Producer: Nunnally Johnson. Director: Robert Siodmak. Screenplay: Nunnally Johnson, story by Vladimir Pozner. Director of Photography:

Milton Krasner. Music: Dimitri Tiomkin. Production Design: Duncan Cramer. Editor: Ernest Nims.

Cast: Olivia De Havilland (Terry Collins/Ruth Collins), Lew Ayers (Dr. Scott Elliot), Thomas Mitchell (Detective Stevenson), Dick Long (Rusty). With: Charles Evans, Garry Owen, Lester Allen, Lela Bliss.

Twin sisters are put under scrutiny when a gentleman caller of one of them is murdered. Although physically identical, the twins are mentally very different. Ruth is sweet and kind, while Terry is ruthless, aggressive and spiteful. A psychiatrist, Dr. Scott Elliot tries to find a clue to the murder through intense interviews of the twins. Finding the scrutiny too great, Terry plans to kill her good sister and take her place. But at the last moment, Dr. Elliot realizes this and Terry is arrested as the killer.

The doppelganger theme is a classic one in expressionist drama and thrillers, and the mirror image is one that occurs throughout *film noir*.

In *The Dark Mirror*, both sisters are at the mercy of their environment. They are lost and confused in a world beyond their comprehension and the good sister does not seem to perceive how truly evil her sister is. They spin inexorably out of control, toward inevitable violence and betrayal.

Dark Passage (Warner Bros., 1947). 106 min.

Producer: Jerry Wald. Director: Delmer Daves. Screenplay: Delmer Daves, based on the novel by David Goodis. Director of Photography: Sid Hickox. Music: Franz Waxman. Art Director: Charles H. Clarke. Editor: David Weisbart.

Cast: Humphrey Bogart (Vincent Parry), Lauren Bacall (Irene Jenson), Bruce Bennett (Bob), Agnes Moorehead (Madge Rapf), Tom D'Andrea (Sam, the taxi driver), Clifton Young (Baker). With: Douglas Kennedy, Rory Mallinson, Houseley Stevenson.

Vincent Parry escapes from Sam Quentin intent on clearing his name of a crime he did not commit. He is picked up by a young punk, Baker, who, on hearing a radio report, realizes he is the escapee. Parry knocks Baker unconscious and fleeing on foot, is picked up next by Irene Jenson, a beautiful, kind woman, who inexplicably at first, hides him at her apartment.

The following day, while Irene is out of the apartment, there is a knock on the door. The voice at the door is familiar, and Parry immediately recognizes it as the voice of Madge Rapf, the widow of the man he is accused of murdering and who perjured herself during his trial, resulting in his conviction. When Irene returns, she confesses that she knew his identity and was interested in helping him because her father was falsely executed for killing her stepmother. Not entirely convinced, Parry agrees to stay with her because he has no other place to go.

Since his face is well known, Parry has plastic surgery which allows him freedom on the streets. However, Baker has followed Parry and tries to blackmail him, but is killed. A friend who has agreed to help is also killed, in such a way that it looks like Parry is his killer.

However, Parry learns that Madge Rapf is the perpetrator of the crimes and when he confronts her, she leaps out of a window to her death, rather than confess to the police. With his only witness dead, Parry and Irene flee to Peru.

Dark Passage is certainly one of the most existential of all *films noirs*, like *Detour* (PRC, 1945), the characters find themselves in circumstances beyond their control, at the mercy of their own inept bad timing as any other outside force. At the end, the protagonists in both films, facing certain blame for the activities of others, have no choice but to flee for their lives. In *Dark Passage*, however, the ending is somewhat more hopeful as it dissolves to a seaside

Humphrey Bogart sees his new face for the first time as Lauren Bacall looks on in *Dark Passage* (Warner Bros., 1947).

restaurant in Peru where Irene and Vince dance.

The most famous element of the film, however, is its use of subjective technique. The first third of the film is told through Vince Parry's "eyes" and it isn't until he undergoes the plastic surgery that the film changes to third person narrative. Unlike Robert Montgomery's *Lady in the Lake* (MGM, 1949), however, the subjective style is more appropriate, creating in the viewer a sense of alienation in sympathy with the main character.

Dark Passage was the first film for director Delmer Daves, until then a successful screenwriter. An extremely talented writer and director, Daves never developed a personal style or set of themes, but he was a good commercial filmmaker. In this film he not only made creative use of subjective technique, but also of low-key lighting, location shooting in San Francisco and its famous fog and rain swept streets.

Humphrey Bogart created one of his most effective *film noir* roles in *Dark Passage*. His is a unique *noir* protagonist in that he is mostly a victim of a *femme-fatale* without his own subconscious participation. Of course, it was also his third teaming with his wife Lauren Bacall which helped make the film a box-office success, one of the biggest of the 1940's *films noirs*.

The Dark Past (Columbia, 1948). 74 min.

Producer: Barry Adler. Director: Rudolph Maté. Screenplay: Philip MacDonald, Michael Blankfort and Albert Duffy, adapted by Malvin Wald and Oscar Saul from the play "Blind Alley" by James Warrick. Director of Photography: Joseph Walker. Music: George Duning. Art Director: Carey Odell. Editor: Viola Lawrence.

Cast: William Holden (Al Walker), Nina Foch (Betty), Lee J. Cobb (Dr. Andrew Collins), Adele Jergens (Laura Stevens), Lois Maxwell (Ruth Collins). With: Barry Kroeger, Steven Geray, Kathryn Card, Bobby Hyatt, Ellen Corby.

While giving a lecture to a group of police officers, Dr. Andrew Collins explains why he believes criminals should be rehabilitated through careful psychiatric treatment by relating a personal experience. He and his wife Ruth were spending a weekend at a lake side cabin with their son Bobby and two friends, Frank and Laura Stevens. A murderer, Al Walker, escaped from a nearby prison with two henchmen and his girl friend, and held the Collins' and the Stevens' hostage at the cabin. Dr. Collins manages to slowly unravel the motivation behind Al's violent behavior: as a teenager he had allowed his father's death when he had betrayed him to the police. At this revelation, Al cannot fire at the police when the cabin is surrounded, and he and his gang surrender.

The Dark Past is the remake of the 1939 film *Blind Alley*, which was based on the play. Despite some compelling performances, particularly by William Holden and Nina Foch as his girl friend Betty, the film is decidedly minor. Part of the film's problems lies with its oversimplification of Freudian psychology. There are also several good dream sequences, but overall the film is a disappointing exposé of criminal psychology.

Darnell, Linda (Moretta Eloyse Darnell) (1921–1965)

Actress. A wide-eyed, dark haired beauty, Darnell was a major star of the 1940's. She appeared mainly in lighthearted entertainments, in mostly forgettable motion-pictures. Her two *films noirs* were both directed by Otto Preminger, and she proved to be a compelling performer, particularly in *Fallen Angel* as the romantically promiscuous Stella whose affections lead to murder.

Filmography: *Fallen Angel* (20th Century–Fox, 1946). *The Thirteenth Letter* (20th Century–Fox, 1951).

Da Silva, Howard (1909–1978)

Character actor. Da Silva is a familiar *noir* character actor, thanks to a handful of notable performances. He almost always played villains. In *The Border Incident*, he is the seedy smuggler of Mexican migrant workers. In *They Live by Night*, he stars as a small time criminal killed by police during a botched robbery. In *M*, however, he was cast against type as the police chief searching for a serial killer.

Filmography: *The Blue Dahlia* (Paramount, 1946). *They Live by Night* (RKO, 1948). *Border Incident* (MGM, 1949). *M* (Columbia, 1950).

Dassin, Jules (1911–1989)

Director. Jules Dassin is one of the great *film noir* directors — all of his *noir* titles are classics — and certainly one of the most talented American film directors of his generation. Unfortunately his film career was cut short by the McCarthy anti-communist witch hunt and he retreated to Europe where he continued to make provocative and occasionally brilliant films. It is tempting to speculate what Dassin could have achieved if his remarkable career hadn't been forced to take a different path just as he was reaching his artistic heights. In any case, he left behind four of the best *films noirs* and for that he will be remembered as one of the most important directors of the genre.

Dassin was first invited to Hollywood by RKO in 1940 on the basis of his acting. After appearing in a few films, MGM hired him as a director of short films. He made a successful adaption of Edgar Allan Poe's *Tell-Tale Heart* (MGM, 1941). Elevated to features, he directed a few undistinguished dramas before joining Universal in 1946.

Dassin was clearly attracted to strong dramatic stories with a social theme, not unlike Richard Brooks, the screenwriter of Dassin's *Brute Force*. One of the most violent of the early *noirs*, the film is set in a prison and starred Burt Lancaster, Charles Bickford and Hume Cronyn. It is also one of the most fatalistic of all *films noirs*, with all the major characters dead at the end of the movie.

The Naked City is a low-key, documentary style treatment of a police murder investigation in New York City. It was shot entirely on location, a new innovation in 1949. The film was photographed in appropriately gritty style by William Daniels, and had a profound influence on American films in the late forties.

Thieves' Highway is probably Dassin's least known *film noir*. It is also, at least in terms of its story, his least conventional. In style and subject, it clearly anticipates *On the Waterfront* (Columbia, 1954), sometimes described as a *film noir*.

In 1949, Dassin's love of location shooting took him to London with Richard Widmark for *Night and the City*, the last of his *films noirs*. His stylized use of London as a background was quite effective and unique. It also contains one of Richard Widmark's best performances as a small time crook on an inevitable road to tragedy.

Shortly after the release of this film, Dassin was named by Edward Dmytryk as a member of the "communist faction" in Hollywood. He was immediately blacklisted and fled to Europe where he spent the rest of his life. He directed several other important films over the next several decades including *Rififi* (United Artists, 1954), a great caper drama.

Jules Dassin's greatest achievement is the four remarkable *films noirs* he directed and they remain classics of the genre.

Filmography: *Brute Force* (Universal, 1947). *The Naked City* (Universal, 1948). *Thieves' Highway* (20th Century-Fox, 1949). *Night and the City* (20th Century-Fox, 1950).

Davis, Bette (1908–1990)

Actress. The legendary Bette Davis was the perpetual strong willed feminist or victim of romantic tragedy in at least twenty melodramas in the thirties and forties. Her acting style was rather abrasive and lacked the psychological subtlety required for *film noir*. She dominated her three *films noirs* in her typical, inimitable style. All are balanced uneasily between tragic melodrama and *film noir*. Of the three, *Beyond the Forest* might well be the best, although *The Letter* was a box-office hit and generally considered an important seminal *noir*.

Filmography: *The Letter* (Warner Bros., 1940). *Beyond the Forest* (Warner Bros., 1949). *Another Man's Poison* (United Artists, 1952).

Davis, George W. (1914–)

Art director. Davis was one of 20th Century–Fox's most important art directors. He worked mainly on conventional films, but collaborated on one *film noir* and several post-*noir* films.

Filmography: *House of Strangers* (20th Century–Fox, 1949). *Point Blank* (MGM, 1967). *The Split* (MGM, 1968). *Marlowe* (MGM, 1969).

Day, Doris (Doris Kappelhoff) (1924–)

Singer and actress. Day is best known for her wildly popular romantic comedies of the fifties and sixties, particularly those co-starring Rock Hudson. In *Julie* she typically plays a nightclub singer. In this case, however, the theme is not comical but melodramatic. She suspects her newlywed husband, an elegant concert pianist (Louis Jordan), is trying to kill her. This movie is her only *film noir*.

Filmography: *Julie* (MGM, 1956).

Day, Laraine (Laraine Johnson) (1917–)

Actress. The beautiful, dark haired Laraine Day was a popular leading lady of the forties, mainly in "good girl" roles. She co-starred in several important films including Alfred Hitchcock's classic espionage thriller, *Foreign Correspondent* (United Artists, 1940). She played a variation of her good girl persona in two *films noirs*, but her on screen character was too conventional for the dark world of *film noir*.

Filmography: *The Locket* (20th Century–Fox, 1946). *Woman on Pier 13* (aka *I Married a Communist for the F.B.I.*, 1949).

Day, Richard (1895–1972)

Art director. One of the most versatile art directors, Day's name is attached to many classic films. He designed the productions for everything from glossy musicals to gritty melodramas, and excelled at all the genres. Of the four *films noirs* he worked on, *Force of Evil* (RKO, 1949), remains the epitome of great production design on a low budget.

Filmography: *I Wake Up Screaming* (20th Century–Fox, 1942). *Force of Evil* (MGM, 1948). *Edge of Doom* (RKO, 1950). *Cry Danger* (RKO, 1951).

Dead Reckoning (Columbia, 1947). 100 min.

Producer: Sidney Biddell. Director: John Cromwell. Screenplay: Oliver H. P. Garrett and Steve Fisher, adapted by Allen Rivkin from a story by Gerald Drayson Adams and Sidney Biddell. Director of Photography; Leo Tover. Music: Marlin Skiles. Art Directors: Stephen Goosson and Rudolph Sternard. Editor: Gene Havlick.

Cast: Humphrey Bogart (Rip Murdock), Lizabeth Scott (Coral Chandler), Morris Carnovsky (Martinelli), Charles Cane (Lt. Kincaid), William Prince (Johnny Drake), Marvin Miller (Krause). With: Wallace Ford, James Bell, George Chandler, Ruby Dandridge.

The disappearance of an old Army buddy leads Rip Murdock to investigate. When he contacts his friend's old girl friend, Coral Chandler, she begins leading him on a wild goose chase. In fact, she is the wife of a local gangster, Martinelli, and he learns that both were responsible for the death of his friend. After a series of violent, complicated events, Rip kills Martinelli. He returns to confront Coral, and almost falls into her seductive trap; but he is jolted back to reality when they are involved in a car wreck that kills the corrupted Coral.

Dead Reckoning provided Humphrey Bogart with a departure from his tough guy roles and gave him one of his best *noir* parts. Although Rip Murdock resorts to tough guy tactics when necessary, he is still a typical vulnerable *noir* protagonist. He is easy prey for the dangerous *femme-fatale* Coral Chandler – Lizabeth Scott in one of her more erotically charged roles.

The director of the film, John Cromwell, was a veteran director whose career stretched back to the silent era. He was an expert handler of hard-boiled material and here combined techniques of the usual Warner Bros. style of no nonsense raw energy, with the expressionist lighting of *noir* to create one of the genre's best neglected classics.

Deadline at Dawn (RKO, 1946). 83 min.

Producer: Adrian Scott. Director: Harold Clurman. Screenplay: Clifford Odets, from a novel by William Irish (Cornell Woolrich). Director of Photography: Nicholas Musuraca. Music: Hanns Eisler. Art Directors: Albert S. D'Agostino and Jack Okey. Editor: Roland Gross.

Cast: Susan Hayward (June Goth), Paul Lukas (Gus), Bill Williams (Alex Winkley), Joseph Calleia (Bartelli), Osa Masson (Helen Robinson), Lola Lane (Edna Bartelli). With Jerome Cowan, Marvin Miller, Roman Bohnen, Steven Geray, Joe Sawyer.

Another of the *films noirs* based on Cornell Woolrich's fiction, *Deadline at Dawn* does not quite live up to its promise, although in the long run it is a worthy addition to the genre.

While on leave, a sailor, Alex Winkley, inadvertently takes money from a girl he spent the night with while drunk. When he tries to return it, he finds her dead in her apartment. He cannot remember the details of what happened that night, but he is convinced that he did not kill her. With the aid of a friendly dancer, June Goth, he begins to investigate the events of the night in question. They enlist the assistance of an oddly friendly taxi driver, who agrees to take them everywhere for free. They encounter a number of likely suspects, but the real killer turns out to be the taxi driver, a psychopath who murdered the girl because she was a tramp.

Taking time off from his collaborations with Edward Dmytryk, Adrian Scott produced this gem. He assembled an excellent group of craftsmen and artists including playwright/screenwriter Clifford Odets and cinematographer Nicholas Musuraca. Odets simplified Woolrich's novel somewhat, although it retained its widely improbable plot twists. Musuraca translated the dreamy, surreal qualities of the story in typical brilliant style.

De Carlo, Yvonne (Yvonne Middleton) (1922–)

Actress. Yvonne De Carlo is probably best known as Lillian Munster on the cult television series *The Munsters*. However, for two decades before that, she had a thriving career as a film actress. She had roles in three *films noirs*. Her appearance in *This Gun for Hire* was brief, and, as the female lead in *Brute Force* was subverted by its male cast. Her most important *noir* role is in Robert Siodmak's neglected classic *Criss Cross*. She plays Anna, neither stereotypical *femme-fatale* nor helpless victim. She brings to the character a wonderful duplicitous nature with subtle hints of both corruption and innocence, a dichotomy which is both compelling and alluring.

Filmography: *This Gun for Hire* (Paramount, 1942). *Brute Force* (Universal, 1947). *Criss Cross* (Universal, 1949).

De Corsia, Ted (1904–1973)

Character actor. De Corsia played surly, violent criminals in a variety of films. He appeared in eight *films noirs*, usually as a villain. One of his best *noir* performances is as a particularly violent criminal in *The Naked City*.

Filmography: *The Lady from Shanghai* (Columbia, 1948). *The Naked City* (Universal, 1948). *The Enforcer* (Warner Bros., 1951). *Crime Wave* (Warner Bros., 1954). *The Big Combo* (Allied Artists, 1955). *The Killing* (United Artists, 1956). *Slightly Scarlet* (RKO, 1956). *Baby Face Nelson* (United Artists, 1957).

Decoy (Monogram, 1946). 76 min.

Producer: Jack Bernhard and Bernard Brandt. Director: Jack Bernhard. Screenplay: Ned Young, story by Stanley Rubin. Director of Photography: L. W. O'Connell. Music: Edward J. Kay. Art Director: Dave Milton. Editor: Jason Bernie.

Cast: Jean Gillie (Margot Shelby), Edward Norris (Jim Vincent), Herbert Rudley (Dr. Lloyd Craig), Robert Armstrong (Frank Olins), Sheldon Leonard (Sgt. Joseph Portugal). With: Marjorie Woodsworth, Philip Van Zant, John Shay.

When she is fatally shot, Margot Shelby, the pretty head of a gang, recounts her sordid life of crime to a police officer just before she dies.

Decoy is a typical, low budget production of Monogram Pictures. The script was obviously written quickly and is full of improbabilities and inconsistencies. The production values are poor at best. However, the film does contain an excellent performance by the British-born actress Gillie as the degenerate, sadistic Margot Shelby.

De Cuir, John (1918–)

Art director. With a long and distinguished career as a production designer, particularly for 20th Century–Fox, De Cuir left an indelible mark on American film in the late forties. He designed the productions for three tough *films noirs*, successfully recreating the dark, depressing hell of prison life in *Brute Force*, the best of his three *noirs*.

Filmography: *Brute Force* (Universal, 1947). *The Naked City* (Universal, 1948). *The House on Telegraph Hill* (20th Century–Fox, 1951).

Deep Valley (Warner Bros., 1947). 104 min.

Producer and Director: Jean Negulesco. Screenplay: Salka Viertel and Stephen Morehouse Avery, based on the novel by Dan Totheroh. Director of Photography: Ted McCord. Music:

Max Steiner. Art Director: Ted Smith. Editor: David Weisbart.

Cast: Ida Lupino (Libby), Dane Clark (Barry), Wayne Morris (Barker), Fay Bainter (Mrs. Saul), Henry Hull (Mr. Saul). With: Frank Wilcox, James Flavin, Ray Hansen.

Barry, a young convict, escapes from prison. He is sheltered by Libby, a vulnerable, unhappy mountain girl who dreams of escape. When he is killed, she returns, disillusioned to her miserable life.

Deep Valley is a modest, minor *film noir* that also works as a romantic melodrama. Its rural setting is unique in *film noir*, again bringing up the differences between rural and urban life, so commonly contrasted in the genre.

The director, Jean Negulesco was an expert director of nostalgic romances, but he was also capable of more hardboiled material, as he did with this film and *Road House* (20th Century–Fox, 1948), an even better film.

The film's strongest asset, however, is Ida Lupino as the cheerless mountain girl. Although the film is not as well known as some of the others in which she appeared, it does contain one of her best performances.

De Fore, Don (1917–)

Actor. De Fore was a lead or second lead in dozens of low budget films of the 1940's and 1950's. He appeared mainly as a hero of westerns, but also a few modern urban melodramas. He co-starred in three *films noirs* only one of which, *Dark City*, is of any importance. He was, typically, a second "heroic" lead in the film.

Filmography: *Too Late for Tears* (United Artists, 1949). *Dark City* (Paramount, 1950). *Southside 1–1000* (Allied Artists, 1950).

De Grasse, Robert (1900–1971)

Cinematographer. De Grasse was a staff cinematographer at RKO from 1934. A competent, if not particularly inventive cinematographer, De Grasse worked on several of the less important *noir* titles made at RKO in the late forties.

Filmography: *Crack-Up* (RKO, 1946). *Born to Kill* (RKO, 1947). *Bodyguard* (RKO, 1948). *A Dangerous Profession* (RKO, 1949). *Follow Me Quietly* (RKO, 1949).

Dekker, Albert (Albert Van Dekker) (1904–1968)

Star character actor. Dekker is considered by some enthusiasts to be one of the greatest American stage actors of the 1930's. He is unquestionably one of the most memorable villains of *film noir*, appearing as a hired killer in *The Killers* and *Kiss Me Deadly*. In *Among the Living* he played two roles, twin brothers, one of which is a psychotic murderer. It is a *tour-de-force*, one of *film noir*'s truly brilliant performances.

Filmography: *Among the Living* (Paramount, 1941). *The Killers* (Universal, 1946). *Suspense* (Monogram, 1946). *Destination Murder* (RKO, 1950). *Kiss Me Deadly* (United Artists, 1955).

De Niro, Robert (1943–)

Actor. De Niro's unusual intensity and extraordinary talent first came to the attention of the public at large in the post-*noir* classic, *Taxi Driver*. His portrayal of Travis Bickle, the frustrated would-be political assassin who vents his anger against a pimp in an explosion of violence is frighteningly realistic.

Filmography: *Taxi Driver* (Columbia, 1976).

Derek, John (Derek Harris) (1926–)

Actor. In the 1950's, Derek was one of the most popular "beef cake" stars, as well known for his dark good looks and well-toned body as for his acting ability, which was minimal in any case. He appeared as a second male lead in three good *films noirs*, giving surprisingly adequate performances in these movies.

Filmography: *All the King's Men* (Columbia, 1949). *Knock on Any Door* (Columbia, 1949). *Scandal Sheet* (Columbia, 1952).

Desperate (RKO, 1947). 73 min.

Producer: Michael Kraike. Director: Anthony Mann. Screenplay: Harry Essex, with additional dialog by Martin Rackin, story by Dorothy Atlas and Anthony Mann. Director of Photography: George Diskant. Music: Paul Sawtell. Art Directors: Albert S. D'Agostino and Walter E. Keller. Editor: Marston Fay.

Cast: Steve Brodie (Steve Randall), Audrey Long (Anne Randall), Raymond Burr (Walt Radak), Douglas Fowley (Pete), William Challee (Reynolds), Jason Robards, Sr. (Ferrari). With: Freddie Steele, Lee Frederick, Paul E. Burns, Ilka Gruning.

When the brother of a gang leader is convicted of murder and robbery and sentenced to die, the leader of the gang, Walt Radak, attempts to blackmail an innocent warehouse man, Steve Randall, into confessing the crime to help the convicted man get off. The gang also threatens the life of his wife, Anne. They hide out in a house in the country and for a brief time they are safe; but it does not take Radak and his gang long to find them. However, the police are right behind them, and the couple is saved just in the nick of time.

Desperate was the first *film noir* directed by Anthony Mann. It is a cynical and brutal tale of relentless paranoia and vengeance, told in typically hard-boiled style by Mann. Its story contrasts the values of the middle class with the criminal underworld. It is also one of the most explicit examples of the *noir* theme of safe rural settings versus dangerous urban settings. Altogether, it is one of the most thoughtful, well made RKO "B" *films noirs*.

The Desperate Hours (Paramount, 1955). 112 min.

Producer and Director: William

Fredric March, Martha Scott, Humphrey Bogart in *The Desperate Hours* **(Paramount, 1955).**

Wyler. Screenplay: Joseph Hayes, based on his play and novel. Director of Photography: Lee Garmes. Music: Gail Kubik. Art Directors: Hal Pereira and Hans Dreier. Editor: Robert Golden.

Cast: Humphrey Bogart (Glenn), Frederic March (Dan Hilliard), Arthur Kennedy (Jesse Bard), Martha Scott (Eleanor Hilliard), Dewey Martin (Hal), Gig Young (Chuck), Robert Middleton (Ray).

A well made thriller, *The Desperate Hours* is chiefly notable as Humphrey Bogart's last appearance as a gangster.

The story is simple: Three violent criminals, recently escaped from prison, hold a family hostage in their own house. Two of the criminals, Glen and Hal, are brothers, while the other, Ray, is a psychopath. They terrorize the family until the police close in and, in the violent confrontation, either captures or kills the escapees.

This is certainly William Wyler's best

film noir, directing with his usual meticulous care. The film, despite its simple setup, is surprisingly suspenseful. Its screenplay is equally good, unusual in that it probed beneath the surface tension to show unexpected strengths and weaknesses of the characters involved. The strong performances were highlighted by Bogart as the deceptively brave criminal, and by Frederic March's brave patriarch of the family who is not ashamed to admit his fear to his impressionable young son.

Destination Murder (RKO, 1950). 72 min.

Producer: Edward L. Cahn and Maurice M. Suess. Director: Edward L. Cahn. Screenplay: Don Martin. Director of Photography: Jackson L. Rose. Music: Irving Gertz. Art Director: Boris Leven. Editor: Philip Cahn.

Cast: Joyce Mackenzie (Laura Mansfield), Stanley Clements (Jackie Wales),

Hurd Hatfield (Stretch Norton), Albert Dekker (Armitage), Myrna Dell (Alice Wentworth). With: James Flavin, John Dehmer, Norma Vance, Suzette Harbin.

Laura Mansfield witnesses the murder of her father, a local big shot, by a youth wearing a messenger uniform. Later, she recognizes Jackie Wales as the messenger boy and agrees to date him in hopes of finding out more about her father's murder. Jackie takes her to the Vogue Nightclub, a seedy joint owned by Armitage and run by Stretch Norton. Stretch is really the man behind a complicated scheme to take over the city rackets and had Laura's father killed because he stood in the way. The police, however, are closing in on him and in a shoot out with them, Stretch is killed.

Destination Murder was another in the long line of "B" thrillers in the RKO *noir* style. Unfortunately, the screenplay is far too complicated and contains too many coincidences. Nevertheless, the film provided Albert Dekker another familiar role as a criminal aesthete and there are some bizarre homosexual implications between his character, Armitage, and Stretch Norton. The film is of very little interest and remains one of RKO's more minor contributions to the genre.

DeSylva, B. G. (Buddy) (1895–1950)

Producer, studio executive and lyricist. One of the most fascinating, if forgotten, figures of his time, B. G. DeSylva had a long, successful career as a lyricist for Broadway and Hollywood musicals and as a film producer and executive. A ruthless businessman, he managed to become head of production at Paramount in the late thirties and ran it successfully throughout the forties. Although he took credit as executive producer on dozens of Paramount's productions in this era, he was essentially a businessman and had little creative influence on his productions. Nevertheless, it was through his

influence that a number of important directors got their start, among them Preston Sturges and Billy Wilder.

Filmography: *The Glass Key* (Paramount, 1942). *Double Indemnity* (Paramount, 1944). *Ministry of Fear* (Paramount, 1944).

Detective Story (Paramount, 1951). 103 min.

Producer and Director: William Wyler. Screenplay: Philip Yordan and Robert Wyler, based on the play by Sidney Kingsley. Director of Photography: Lee Garmes. Art Directors: Hal Pereira and Earl Hedrick. Editor: Robert Smith.

Cast: Kirk Douglas (Jim McLeod), Eleanor Parker (Mary McLeod), William Bendix (Lou Brody), Cathy O'Donnell (Susan), George Macready (Karl Schneider). With: Horace McMahon, Gladys George, Joseph Wiseman, Lee Grant, Gerald Mohr.

Jim McLeod, a New York detective, is unsympathetic and combative to the people who come into the precinct station. His superior grows suspicious when McLeod is particularly tough on an abortionist who has been arrested. He discovers that McLeod's wife had an abortion by the same doctor many years before, and McLeod, who wanted children, had not been able to forgive her. McLeod's confusion, blinded by anger, grows so great, he deliberately steps into the line of fire from a criminal who has grabbed a gun and is attempting to escape. As he dies in his wife's arms, he recites the Act of Contrition.

Detective Story is an extremely pretentious melodrama based on a play by the moderately respectable playwright Sidney Kingsley. As in most films based on plays, this one is verbose and static, with a single location. However, the latter works to the film's advantage, creating a sense of claustrophobia, in sympathy with the character.

William Wyler directed two *films noirs*. Unfortunately, despite his tight direction, and a powerful performance by Kirk Douglas, the film remains one of the most marginal of the genre's "A" productions.

De Toth, Andre (Endre Toth) (1910–)
Director. De Toth was born in Hungary. After a brief stint studying law, he changed his name to Andre De Toth and became a stage actor, He was not successful, however, and he soon got a production job in Hungarian film industry. Eventually he joined the group of Hungarian filmmakers living and working in Great Britain lead by the producer and director Alexander Korda. He worked briefly in England before moving to the United States in the mid forties where he was quickly established as a director.

Although he is not a major talent, and his accomplishments are modest, they are genuinely well made. He directed the first major studio 3-D film, *House of Wax* (Warner Bros., 1953). He was a fine studio craftsman, strongly influenced by European technique. He directed two good, if minor *films noirs*, both distinguished by tight direction and inventive action sequences.

Filmography: *Pitfall* (United Artists, 1948). *Crime Wave* (Warner Bros., 1954).

Detour (Producers Releasing Corporation, 1945). 68 min.

Producer: Leon Fromkess. Director: Edgar G. Ulmer. Screenplay: Martin Mooney. Director of Photography: Benjamin H. Kline. Music: Leo Erody. Art Director: Edward C. Jewell. Editor: George McGuire.

Cast: Tom Neal (Al Roberts), Ann Savage (Vera), Claudia Drake (Sue), Edmund MacDonald (Charles Haskell, Jr.) Tim Ryan (Diner Proprietor), Roger Clark and Pat Gleason (men).

Al Roberts, a New York piano player, leaves the city to join his girl friend Sue in California. Hitchhiking, he is picked up by Charles Haskell. Haskell tells him a weird tale about a strange and violent girl he picked up some time before. She had physically attacked him when he made a sexual advance.

When Haskell goes to sleep, Al drives. The next morning, Al tries to wake up Haskell, but he has apparently died. As he opens the passenger door, Haskell falls out, striking his head on a rock. Al panics and pulls the body behind some rocks.

Continuing on in Haskell's convertible, Al picks up another hitchhiker, Vera. He does not know that she was the girl Haskell had told him about and recognizing the car, she confronts Al. He confesses about the accident, and she promises to remain silent, if he follows her plans.

Once in Los Angeles, they take a room together in a cheap hotel. Initially, she plans only to sell the car, convincing Al to use Haskell's identification. But when she learns via a radio report that Haskell is the heir to a fortune left by a dying relative, she concocts another plan. The millionaire's family had not seen Haskell in many years and she convinces Al to pretend he is Haskell. Al, of course, is reluctant, but he is helpless to refuse.

On the eve of carrying out their plans, however, Vera begins drinking. The two have a violent argument, and Vera stomps off drunkenly into the bedroom and slams the door shut. She collapses onto the bed, with a long phone cord wrapped around her neck. Al angrily pulls on the cord on the other side of the door, not realizing he is strangling her to death.

Later, knowing what he has done, Al Roberts flees the city, having never seen his girl friend. Sitting in a seedy bar, he reflects on what a strange detour his life has taken.

Detour is the most existential of all *films noirs*, which probably accounts for the movie's cult in Europe. It is a film full of unrelenting paranoia and, despite its low budget and poor production values, it is one of the genre's most memorable films. Edgar G. Ulmer created a superior work of minimalist art that is brisk and darkly irresistible.

While Tom Neal is the star of the movie, and is very good in the role of the hapless Al Roberts, the film really belongs to Ann Savage as the predatory Vera. Savage, a "B" actress, was a dark-haired beauty, with some of the same allure as Faith Domergue. She was also a surprisingly good actress who makes Vera both tawdry and complex, not merely a stereotypical *femme-fatale*.

The film's theme is summed up in the final words of Al Roberts: "Fate or some mysterious force can put the finger on you or me for no good reason at all."

Deutsch, Adolph (1897–1980)

Composer. A prolific film composer, Adolph Deutsch composed the music for dozens of mostly routine films for Warner Bros. and, later, MGM. Deutsch's Warner Bros. scores are particularly outstanding and include several acknowledged *film noir* classics.

Filmography: *High Sierra* (Warner Bros., 1941). *The Maltese Falcon* (Warner Bros., 1941). *The Mask of Dimitrios* (Warner Bros., 1945). *Nobody Lives Forever* (Warner Bros., 1946).

The Devil Thumbs a Ride (RKO, 1947). 63 min.

Producer: Herman Schlom. Director: Felix Feist. Screenplay: Felix Feist, based on the novel by Robert C. De Soe. Director of Photography: J. Roy Hunt. Music: Paul Sawtell. Art Director: Charles E. Pyke. Editor: Phil Warren.

Cast: Lawrence Tierney (Eddie), Ted North (Johnny), Nan Leslie (Ann), Betty Lawford (Nancy), Andrew Tombes (Lt. Davidson). With: Harry Shannon, Glenn Vernon, William Gould, Josephine Whittel, Phil Warren.

Lawrence Tierney stars in this obscure RKO "B" *noir* as a hitch-hiking psychopath who terrorizes the businessman who picks him up and the two women they meet in a small town. The film is a typical "B" movie of the era: brisk, sloppy and silly. However, Tierney gives one of his best performances as the homicidal maniac and the film remains of interest simply because of his appearance.

De Vol, Frank (1916–1984)

Composer. De Vol worked intermittently in both film and television since the mid fifties. He is mainly associated with the films of director Robert Aldrich, for whom he composed scores for several important films including three *noirs*, and one notable post-*noir*.

Filmography: *World for Ransom* (Allied Artists, 1954). *The Big Knife* (United Artists, 1955). *Kiss Me Deadly* (United Artists, 1955).

Diana Productions

A production company formed by director Fritz Lang, actress Joan Bennett and producer Walter Wanger (Bennett's husband). The trio produced two important *films noirs* under this banner: *Scarlet Street* (Universal, 1945) and *Secret Beyond the Door* (Universal, 1948).

Dickinson, Angie (Angeline Brown) (1931–)

Actress. A star of film and television, Angie Dickinson was given the big buildup in the mid fifties. Although she did not achieve real screen stardom, she was a welcome diversion in mostly routine films in the fifties and sixties. She co-starred in the weak, violent remake of *The Killers* (United Artists, 1964), and later, a great post-*noir* thriller *Point Blank*.

Filmography: *Cry Terror* (MGM, 1958). *The Killers* (United Artists, 1964). *Point Blank* (MGM, 1967).

Dieterle, William (Wilhem) (1893–1972)

Director. Dieterle was certainly one of the most expressionist of the German bred Hollywood commercial directors. He was an expert handler of crowd scenes and expansive melo-dramas, and he directed one of the greatest gothic horror films, *The Hunchback of Notre Dame* (Warner Bros., 1939).

Dieterle's career began in Germany as both a stage and film actor in the early silent era. Among the films he acted in is Paul Lewis' masterful ex-pressionist horror film, *Waxworks* (UFA, 1919). When he became a direc-tor in the late twenties, Dieterle applied expressionist techniques to his com-mercial films. This was a great era in German cinema, led by Fritz Lang. Dieterle was also one of the leading filmmakers working in Germany and developed his own style in these early films. All of his films, German and American, are characterized by ex-travagant lighting schemes, mobile camera movements and bizarre angles and certain thematic elements that would become familiar in *film noir*, not the least of which is a central character who is alienated for some reason.

Dieterle directed three *films noirs*, each a unique, interesting contribution to the genre if not true classics. Of the three, *Dark City* is the best known, with an unusually strong performance by Charlton Heston. *The Turning Point*, a less well known exposé of big city corruption, also contains a very good performance by its male lead, William Holden.

If Dieterle is not a major *noir* direc-tor, he certainly is not worthy of neglect either. Hopefully, in the future, his career will be reevaluated and he will be acknowledged as one of the best com-mercial directors of his time.

Filmography: *The Accused* (Para-mount, 1946). *Dark City* (Paramount, 1950). *The Turning Point* (Paramount, 1950).

Dietrich, Marlene (Maria Magdalena Von Losch) (1901–1992)

Actress and singer. The legendary Marlene Dietrich was an alluring, sen-sual star of early thirties romantic epics directed by her mentor, Joseph Von Sternberg. The films, and, to a lesser extent, her performances and roles, had a profound influence on *film noir*. She was an exotic and occasionally deadly *femme-fatale* in Sterberg's melodramas. She only appeared in one true *film noir*, *Touch of Evil*, directed by another strong director, Orson Welles. The role was a unique variation of her early roles, a combination of the *femme-fatale* and victim of romantic obsession.

Filmography: *Touch of Evil* (Uni-versal, 1958).

Dillon, Robert (1937–)

Screenwriter. Dillon had some suc-cess in the 1970's mainly as a writer of pretentious commercial films. He also worked on the sequel to *The French Connection*; the film retained the ori-ginal's fatalistic, *noir* elements, but not much of its brilliance.

Filmography: *French Connection II* (20th Century–Fox, 1975).

Dinelli, Mel (1917–1988)

Screenwriter. Dinelli was a moder-ately successful playwright and short story writer who was attracted to the more lucrative career of screenwriting in the mid forties. He wrote or co-wrote a number of minor *films noirs* begin-ning in the late forties, and at least three major films of the genre, *The Spiral Staircase*, *The Window*, and *The Reckless Moment*. His screenplay for *Beware, My Lovely* is based on his play, *The Man*.

Filmography: *The Spiral Staircase* (RKO, 1946). *The Reckless Moment* (Columbia, 1949). *The Window* (RKO, 1949). *House by the River* (Republic, 1950). *Cause for Alarm* (MGM, 1951). *Beware, My Lovely* (RKO, 1952). *Jeopardy* (MGM, 1953.

Directors

Unquestionably, *film noir*'s greatest directors are Fritz Lang and Robert Siodmak. Lang and Siodmak were the most Germanic of the great *noir* directors, preferring to work in the studio where they had more control over the look of their films. Their styles, although different in many ways, were similarly characterized by dark shadows, dizzy camera angles, and distorting close ups.

Lang's superb silent films are profoundly expressionist and extroverted; his American films are introspective and more personal, but no less brilliant. In fact, they are the most consistently exceptional films of the genre and Lang was the only director whose best work spans the entire movement: from the early *noir* masterpiece, *Woman in the Window* (RKO, 1944), to such fifties classics as *The Big Heat* (Columbia, 1953), and *While the City Sleeps* (RKO, 1955).

Like Lang, Robert Siodmak had roots in 1920's German cinema. A more commercially oriented director than the often didactic and independent Lang (Siodmak was an employee of Universal for most of his American career), Siodmak's films could also be tougher and more tragically romantic. He made a series of classic *films noirs* beginning in the mid forties: *Phantom Lady* (Universal, 1944), *The Killers* (Universal, 1946), *The Spiral Staircase* (RKO, 1946), and *Criss Cross* (Universal, 1949).

Several other directors achieved their greatest success in the genre: Edward Dmytryk, Jules Dassin, John Farrow, John Brahm and Curtis Bernhardt.

Edward Dmytryk was one of the most important directors of early *film noir*, developing a gritty, hard-boiled style at RKO. His classics include *Murder, My Sweet* (RKO, 1944), *Cornered* (RKO, 1945), and *Crossfire* (RKO, 1946). Each is distinguished by a politically liberal sub text and anti-fascist message which dates them somewhat.

Jules Dassin was also a political liberal whose ideas influenced his films. *Brute Force* (Universal, 1947), *The Naked City* (Universal, 1948), *Thieves' Highway* (20th Century–Fox, 1949), and

Night and the City (20th Century–Fox, 1950), are characterized by sympathy for the repressed protagonists, and a great command of technique.

John Farrow's *films noirs* for Paramount and RKO, although not as well known as other classic *noirs*, are characterized by inventive style and attention to detail. *The Big Clock* (Paramount, 1948), and *Night Has a Thousand Eyes* (Paramount, 1948), are his best films, although *Where Danger Lives* (RKO, 1950) is also outstanding.

Working with modest budgets, John Brahm also managed to create several interesting films including the minor *noir* classic, *The Brasher Doubloon* (20th Century–Fox, 1947), yet another adaption of a novel by Raymond Chandler.

Curtis Bernhardt's classic *noir* is *Conflict* (Warner Bros., 1945), a psychological complex story of a serial killer in the making.

Farrow, Brahm and Bernhardt were masters of the "gothic," meaning they were heavily influenced by expressionism with dark, moody lighting, fog-shrouded sets and psychological perversion.

Alfred Hitchcock also brought a sense of expressionist style and interest in psychological deviation to his *films noirs: Shadow of a Doubt* (Universal, 1943), *Strangers on a Train* (Warner Bros., 1951), and the great color *noir*, *Vertigo* (Universal, 1958). Each is typically brimming with Catholic guilt and an overwhelming fear of sex.

John Huston preferred a more realistic approach, both in style and theme, in his *films noirs. The Maltese Falcon* (Warner Bros., 1941) was an important seminal *film noir*, but his greatest classic of the genre is *The Asphalt Jungle* (MGM, 1950).

Michael Curtiz, the director of *Casablanca* (Warner Bros., 1942), was also a veteran of European, expressionist film although much more commercial than many of his contemporaries. He directed several *films noirs* including the classic *Mildred Pierce* (Warner Bros., 1945), one of the most important early films of the genre.

Henry Hathaway created a series of violent, visceral *films noirs* in which overt style was less important than the story and performances. Among these is *Kiss of Death* (20th Century–Fox, 1947), *Call Northside 777* (20th Century–Fox, 1948), and the color *noir* classic, *Niagara* (20th Century–Fox, 1952).

Finally, of the "A" *noir* directors, Billy Wilder combined technical expertise with psychological insight and social satire to create three classics of the genre: *Double Indemnity* (Paramount, 1944), *Sunset Boulevard* (Paramount, 1950), and *The Big Carnival* (Paramount, 1951).

Several "B" directors created a number of low budget classics of the genre. Richard Fleischer, for example, directed the wonderful *The Narrow Margin* (RKO, 1952), one of the most exciting of all *films noirs*. Phil Karlson directed a series of extremely violent *noirs* in the 1950's: *Kansas City Confidential* (United Artists, 1952), and *The Phenix City Story* (Allied Artists, 1955). The greatest of the "B" *noir* directors, however, is Joseph H. Lewis, whose baroque style is best demonstrated in *The Big Combo* (Allied Artists, 1955) and *Gun Crazy* (United Artists, 1950).

In the 1950's, a new generation emerged. In the popular style of the new age, these directors had a simpler, more violent approach. The three leading figures of the age are Robert Aldrich, Sam Fuller, and Stanley Kubrick. Of these, Kubrick had the most extravagant style, being both self-conscious and strangely unobtrusive.

Several other, generally minor, directors created at least one masterpiece of the genre: Jacques Tourneur directed *Out of the Past* (RKO, 1947), Mark Robson directed *Champion* (United Artists, 1949), and Robert Rossen directed *Body and Soul* (United Artists, 1947).

All of these artists had their own style and approach, demonstrating further that *film noir* was not merely a style, but a true genre.

Dirty Harry (Warner Bros., 1971). 103 min.

Producer and Director: Don Siegel. Screenplay: Harry Julian Fink, R. M. Fink and Dean Riesner, story by Julian and R. M. Fink. Director of Photography: Bruce Surtees. Music: Lalo Schifrin. Art Director: Dale Hennesy. Editor: Carl Pingitore.

Cast: Clint Eastwood (Harry Callaghan), Reni Santoni (Chico), Harry Gaurdino (Bressler), Andy Robinson (Scorpio Killer), John Mitchum (De-Georgia), John Larch (Chief), John Vernon (Mayor). With Mae Mercer, Lyn Edington, Craig G. Kelly, James Nolan, Joe De Winter.

Dirty Harry is the most prominent post-*noir* police thriller, recapturing themes found in the genre proper and, with its director, Don Siegel, a direct link to the genre.

"Dirty" Harry Callaghan is aptly named for his unscrupulous and unethical treatment of criminals. When San Francisco, is threatened by a kidnapper/killer who calls himself "Scorpio," Harry is assigned to the case.

Scorpio has kidnapped a young girl and is holding her in an underground well. Harry quickly identifies the suspect, but without any proof is unable to do anything but follow him. Eventually overcome by frustration and desperation, Harry corners the suspect in an empty stadium and tortures him until he confesses where he is keeping the girl, but unfortunately she is already dead.

The suspect is arrested and then released, but Harry is not about to allow him to get away that easy. He follows the suspect relentlessly. Eventually, the psychopath hijacks a bus load of school children. After a long

Perhaps the most famous post-*noir* cop, Harry Callahan (Clint Eastwood) in *Dirty Harry* (Warner Bros., 1971).

chase, Harry again corners the killer and this time shoots him.

Contrary to certain criticisms, *Dirty Harry* is not really a celebration of violence or a call to fascist techniques. *Dirty Harry* is clearly a *noir* protagonist, unable to deal with uncontrollable violence other than resorting to it himself. Furthermore, he is just as much a victim of violence as any other in the film — in his case, the cruelty and alienation of the city has caused his callousness.

This was a theme which first appeared in some late *noirs*, in particular, Fritz Lang's *The Big Heat* (Columbia, 1953).

Don Siegel manages to capture the overwhelming fear and paranoia of the screenplay in a near perfect film, aided by Clint Eastwood's strong performance and Bruce Surtees' excellent color cinematography.

Finally, the film's location, San Francisco, is also the location of several notable *films noirs*, including *Dark Passage* (Warner Bros., 1948). The mysterious qualities of the city, here made even more sinister by a modern, sleazy landscape, only add to the film's feel of paranoia and lurking danger.

Diskant, George (1903–1965)

Cinematographer. Diskant is associated mainly with RKO's "B" movies. A competent, occasionally brilliant and inventive craftsman, Diskant worked on a number of visually striking films. Among these is the extraordinary and unfairly neglected adventure drama *Riff-Raff* (RKO, 1947), interestingly enough, directed by ex-cinematographer Ted Tetzlaff. He was the director of photography for an excellent *film noir* directed by Nicholas Ray — *They Live by Night* — as well as the high quality, low budget *The Narrow Margin*. His style was simple and naturalistic, with intermittent expressionist flourishes.

Filmography: *Desperate* (RKO, 1947). *They Live by Night* (RKO, 1949). *Between Midnight and Dawn* (Columbia, 1950). *The Racket* (RKO, 1951). *Beware, My Lovely* (RKO, 1952). *Kansas City Confidential* (United Artists, 1952). *The Narrow Margin* (RKO, 1952).

Dixon, Joan (1928–)

Actress. A dark haired beauty, Dixon starred in a few "B" movies in the late forties and early fifties. She was a memorable *femme-fatale* in *Roadblock* — indeed, one of the genre's deadliest.

Filmography: *Roadblock* (RKO, 1951).

Dmytryk, Edward (1908–)

Director. A talented filmmaker, Edward Dmytryk might well be one of the 1940's most neglected, underrated directors. Nevertheless, there can be little question about his importance to *film noir*. He displayed a crisp, efficient style which perfectly suited his modest budgets and reflected his training as an editor. Indeed, he was the first of three leading editors — Robert Wise and Mark Robson were the others — to move to film direction, all creating substantial careers at RKO.

Dmytryk's film career began in the late twenties and he worked his way through the usual production jobs before becoming a top editor in the mid thirties. He was hired by Paramount and worked on many of their top films during this era. Paramount's relatively liberal practice of promoting certain loyal and efficient writers and editors to positions as producers or directors, worked to Dmytryk's advantage when he decided to try his hand at directing in the late thirties. He proved successful in his new profession and directed several popular films for the studio including the neglected slapstick-political satire *Million Dollar Legs* (Paramount, 1939).

In 1940, Dmytryk joined Columbia Pictures for whom he directed seven features including a superior Boris Karloff horror-thriller, *The Devil Commands* (Columbia, 1941), in which he first experimented with expressionist lighting.

Dmytryk joined RKO in 1942 when the studio was undergoing a transformation which attracted many soon-to-be important talents including Orson Welles. Dmytryk immediately established himself as one of the more commercial (but still inventive) filmmakers. His first film for RKO, *Hitler's Children* (RKO, 1942), generally considered one of the best "B" movies ever. The enormous success of the film elevated its director above "B" movie status, although all of his RKO films would remain essentially low budget productions.

The first of the Adrian Scott produced/Edward Dmytryk directed *films noirs* was *Murder, My Sweet*, based on Raymond's Chandler's novel, *Farewell, My Lovely*. In fact, it was the first important adaption of a Chandler novel, and provided an important part for Dick Powell as Chandler's hero, the private investigator Philip Marlowe. Claire Trevor, an important female *noir* icon, also had an important role in the film, but it is Dmytryk's direction which is particularly outstanding. Its effective mixture of muted photography, fast paced editing and staccato, Chandleresque dialog added up to one of *film noir*'s most striking early classics. Its box office success was also spectacular and it can be fairly said that this film, more than any of its contemporaries, kicked off the *noir* cycle.

Dmytryk, Scott, and writer John Paxton, were reunited for a second collaboration with actor Dick Powell for the revenge-*noir*, *Cornered*. Although considered the least important of the team's three collaborations, it is notable for its anti-fascist message and gritty recreation of exotic locales on RKO's back lot.

The Dmytryk, Scott, Paxton collaboration reached its peak with *Crossfire*, based on a novel by Richard Brooks. Visually, it might be Dmytryk's least consistent *film noir*, but he created a fast-paced story of a racial murder with a fine cast of *noir* icons in major and minor roles: Robert Mitchum, Robert Ryan and Gloria Grahame among others.

Unfortunately, Dmytryk, with Adrian Scott and many others, became a target of the House Unamerican Activities Committee, headed by the rabidly anti-liberal Senator Joseph McCarthy. Like several others, Dmytryk went into exile for several years, directing a couple of minor films in Great Britain before returning to the United States and agreeing to name names for McCarthy's committee. Some critics cannot forgive Dmytryk for this admittedly questionable act, (which might account for his relative neglect), it did result in his name being removed from the Blacklist. He returned to Hollywood, but his later films lack the spirit of his early classics. However, he did direct an unpretentious *noir* thriller, *The Sniper*, one of the few high spots of his later career.

Without question, Edward Dmytryk was one of the most important early directors of *film noir*, and his classics of the genre have withstood the test of time.

Filmography: *Murder, My Sweet* (RKO, 1944). *Cornered* (RKO, 1945). *Crossfire* (RKO, 1947). *The Sniper* (Columbia, 1952).

D.O.A. (United Artists, 1950). 83 min.

Producer: Leo C. Popkin. Director: Rudolph Maté. Screenplay: Russell Rouse and Clarence Green. Director of Photography: Ernest Laslo. Music: Dimitri Tiomkin. Art Director: Duncan Cramer. Editor: Arthus H. Nadel.

Cast: Edmond O'Brien (Frank Bigelow), Pamela Britton (Paula Gibson), Luther Adler (Majak), Beverly Campbell (Miss Foster), Lynn Baggett (Mrs. Phillips). With: William Ching, Henry Hart, Neville Brand, Laurette Luez.

Frank Bigelow is on vacation in San Francisco. After enjoying a night on the town, he feels ill the following day and undergoes a medical examination. The doctor informs him that he has only days to live. Retracing his footsteps with his fiancée Paula, Bigelow discovers a plot to steal and resell iridium that he, as an accountant, had checked and notarized. Confronting the leader of the group, Majak, Bigelow chases his assassin through the streets of the city, eventually killing him. He then explains his story to the police just before collapsing and dying.

D.O.A. is an unusually cynical *film noir*, with a unique concept in which a murder victim explains his own murder. As the doomed Frank Bigelow, Edmond O'Brien is transformed from an ordinary man to an obsessed avenger bent on discovering the reason behind his imminent death. His chaos and paranoia is reinforced by the swirling jazz that haunts the film.

In fact, the inspiration for *D.O.A.* comes from a 1931 German film directed by Robert Siodmak and co-scripted by Billy Wilder. Utilizing this basic story, *D.O.A.* is a prime example of a thriller accentuated by factors of cynicism, alienation, chaos, etc., to convey the corrupt, dark nature of contemporary America.

D.O.A.'s production values are minimalist, but Ernest Laslo's cinematography captured the dark, moody spirit of the film which is reinforced by the fog-shrouded, rain-slicked streets of San Francisco. The film is rightly considered one of the genre's masterpieces.

Domergue, Faith (1925–)

Actress. In the late forties, the dark, mysterious Faith Domergue was given

Edward G. Robinsin, Fred MacMurray in *Double Indemnity* (Paramount, 1944).

the big push by RKO. She appeared on magazine covers, at various public functions, the usual sort of publicity that starlets get. Unfortunately, despite some talent, Domergue never achieved the expected stardom. Still, she gave some good performances in a handful of films, including the minor *noir* classic, *Where Danger Lives*. Domergue's character, Margo Lannington, a murderous *femme-fatale*, is one of the most corrosive and sinister in all of *film* noir.

Filmography: *Where Danger Lives* (RKO, 1950).

Donlevy, Brian (Grossen Brian Donlevy) (1889–1972)

Character actor. Donlevy was a major leading character actor of the thirties, forties and fifties, specializing in villains. He acted in several *films noirs*, almost always in villainous roles. In *The Big Combo*, for example, he is a mobster attempting to stay on top. In *The Glass Key* he played Paul Madvig, a corrupt

political boss. He could also effectively play morally ambiguous protagonists as in *Kiss of Death* and *Impact*.

Filmography: *The Glass Key* (Paramount, 1942). *Kiss of Death* (20th Century-Fox, 1947). *Impact* (United Artists, 1949). *The Big Combo* (Allied Artists, 1950). *Shakedown* (Universal, 1950).

Dorn, Dolores (Dolores Dorn-Heft) (1935–)

Actress. A popular stage actress, Dorn has appeared in a few movies. She co-starred in the late-*noir*, *Underworld U.S.A.*, directed by Sam Fuller, as the prostitute/mob associate Cuddles—a typical Fuller female character with her sexual forthrightness, dyed blonde hair and ultimately, her heart of gold.

Filmography: *Underworld U.S.A.* (Columbia, 1961).

Double Indemnity (Paramount, 1944). 106 min.

Executive Producer: B. G. De Sylva.

Producer: Joseph Sistrom. Director: Billy Wilder. Screenplay: Raymond Chandler and Billy Wilder, based on the novel by James M. Cain. Director of Photography: John F. Seitz. Music: Miklos Rozsa (with additional music adapted from works composed by Cesar Frank). Art Directors: Hal Pereira and Hans Dreier. Editor: Doane Harrison.

Cast: Fred MacMurray (Walter Neff), Barbara Stanwyck (Phyllis Dietrichson), Edward G. Robinson (Barton Keyes), Porter Hall (Mr. Jackson), Jean Heather (Lolo Dietrichson), Tom Peters (Mr. Dietrichson). With: Byron Barr, Richard Gaines, Fortunio Bonanova, Joh Philliber.

An insurance agent, Walter Neff, is seduced by trampy Phyllis Dietrichson, the wife of a client. She convinces Neff to murder her husband for his insurance, but after he commits the crime Neff's passion for her dies.

Barton Keyes, Neff's friend and associate, investigates Mr. Dietrichson's death, and begins to realize it was not an accident. Meanwhile, Neff plans to kill Phyllis and put the blame for both murders on one of her other lovers, the seedy gigolo Nino Zachette. When Phyllis realizes what's going on, she confronts Walter and in the subsequent shootout, both are fatally wounded. Phyllis tells Neff that she loves him just before she dies.

Neff manages to make it back to his office, where he confesses on his dictating recorder. He plans to make it to Mexico, but he collapses and dies in the hallway.

Based on James M. Cain's novel, the screenplay for *Double Indemnity*, by Raymond Chandler and Billy Wilder retained the details of the plot, while adding touches of their own. The hard-boiled dialog is certainly influenced by Chandler who, in fact, was a reluctant participant in the project: he and Wilder hated each other, and the problems were exacerbated by Chandler's dislike of Cain's work, which he considered near pornography. However, the perverse sense of humor which tells the grim story certainly belongs to the cynical, witty co-writer and director, Billy Wilder.

Interestingly, Fred MacMurray was also a reluctant participant, fearing that playing such a thoroughly corrupt character as Walter Neff would ruin his career, but, of course, as he later admitted, it was the one film he is remembered for.

Although MacMurray was very good in the film, it is really Barbara Stanwyck that remains most striking. She revelled in her role as the wicked Phyllis Dietrichson, even loving the change of hair color suggested by Wilder. Her blonde, demonical alluring Phyllis is *film noir*'s archetypal *femme-fatale*.

Wilder and his collaborators—including cinematographer John F. Seitz and Paramount's perennial art director Hans Dreier (here with collaborator Hal Pereira) created a dark, moody world of paranoia and sleazy allure. Although the direction is not extravagant or showy, the film remains an archetype of *film noir*'s expressionist technique at its best.

The film was an enormous success in a year of huge box office successes for *films noirs*, and in league with them, helped kick off the run of such films which would not begin to fade until more than a decade later. Such was the film's impact, it can be felt in contemporary cinema, and *Body Heat* (Warner Bros., 1981) was a virtual remake and a minor classic in its own right.

A Double Life (Universal, 1948). 103 min.

Producer: Michael Kanin. Director: George Cukor. Screenplay: Ruth Gordon and Garson Kanin. Director of Photography: Milton Krasner. Music: Miklos Rozsa. Production Design: Harry Horner. Art Directors: Bernard Herzbrun and Harvey Gillett. Editor: Robert Parrish.

Cast: Ronald Colman (Anthony John), Signe Hasso (Brita), Edmond

O'Brien (Bill Friend), Shelley Winters (Pat Kroll), Ray Collins (Victor Donlan), Phillip Loeb (Max Lasker). With: Millard Mitchell, Joe Sawyer, Whit Bissell, Peter Thompson, Elizabeth Dunne.

Anthony John, an egomaniacal stage actor is obsessed with his latest role as Othello. Overwhelmed by anger during an argument, he strangles his lover, Pat, as he recites lines from the play. Although the police believe he is the killer, they cannot prove it until they get another girl to imitate Pat in a confrontation with him. Sensing he has been found out, he plunges a dagger into his heart, ironically dying as Othello does in the play.

George Cukor's only *film noir*, *A Double Life* is not entirely satisfying. Cukor manages to capture the backstage intrigue of stage life, but did not seem to appreciate the seediness of the story. Likewise, the screenwriters, Ruth Gordon and Garson Kanin (veterans of Broadway), seem ill at ease with such sordid material.

Nevertheless, the film succeeds in other areas, particularly on its superior cinematography by Milton Krasner. He creates a landscape of glittering, shifting surfaces of rain swept streets throwing back reflections of street lights and flashing neon signs.

The doppelganger, of course, is one of *noir*'s themes, and Ronald Colman manages to capture the duplicity of his character with a splendid over the top performance that ranks as one of *film noir*'s hammiest performances.

Doucette, John (1901–)
Character actor. Doucette was the ultimate small parts actor, appearing in literally dozens of films. His parts rarely amounted to little more than a walk on: waiters, gas station attendants, mobsters, etc. His *film noir* roles are all bit parts and cameos, covering his usual range of supporting parts.

Filmography: *Ride the Pink Horse* (Universal, 1947). *I Wouldn't Be in Your Shoes* (Monogram, 1948). *Criss Cross* (Universal, 1949). *The Crooked Ways* (United Artists, 1949). *The Breaking Point* (Warner Bros., 1950). *Convicted* (Columbia, 1950). *Strangers on a Train* (Warner Bros., 1951). *House of Bamboo* (20th Century–Fox, 1955). *New York Confidential* (Warner Bros., 1955).

Doud, Gil (1923–)
Screenwriter. Doud was briefly employed at Universal in the early fifties, and co-wrote several undistinguished "B" movies. He co-wrote one minor *film noir*.

Filmography: *Forbidden* (Universal, 1954).

Douglas, Gordon (1909–)
Director. Douglas was a prolific director of generally undistinguished "B" movies. He worked in all the genres, even directing Laurel and Hardy in *Saps at Sea* (United Artists, 1940), one of their last good films. However, Douglas really excelled at action films and westerns.

Among Gordon Douglas' three *films noirs*, probably the best known is the "A" production, *Kiss Tomorrow Goodbye*. It is typically action oriented, with a memorable hard-boiled performance by James Cagney. Of his other two *noir* films, *Between Midnight and Dawn* is equally solid, another action oriented *film noir* with some fine performances.

Had he made more films of this type, Gordon Douglas might today rank as one of the best directors of "B" *noirs*. As it is, his *noirs* are all excellent and worthy of renewed interest.

Filmography: *Between Midnight and Dawn* (Columbia, 1950). *Kiss Tomorrow Goodbye* (Warner Bros., 1950). *I Was a Communist for the FBI* (Warner Bros., 1951).

Douglas, Kirk (Issur Danielovitch Demsky) (1916–)
Actor. Kirk Douglas is one of *film*

noir's greatest icons, as much identified with the style as any other actor. He is particularly well known for his villainous roles in the genre.

After a brief successful career as a stage actor in New York, Douglas went to Hollywood where he made his film debut at the age of twenty nine in the *noir* classic, *The Strange Love of Martha Ivers*. As the ambitious, amoral lover of a murderess, it was an auspicious debut and set the pattern of his early film career.

Douglas was particularly memorable as the witty but dangerous gangster Whit Sterling in another *noir* classic, *Out of the Past*. Sterling is one of *noir's* most memorable villains, both charming and sadistic. Douglas played a similar, but less memorable character in *I Walk Alone*. Variations of Douglas' *noir* villains include the unstable police detective in *Detective Story*, and a corrupt, alcoholic reporter in Billy Wilder's supremely cynical *The Big Carnival*.

Perhaps Douglas' most famous *noir* role, however, was as the hapless boxer Midge Kelly in *Champion*, one of the best noir studies of the corrupt underworld of sports and boxing, and its occasionally destructive effects on the athletes.

Kirk Douglas appeared in fewer *films noirs* than most other *noir* icons, yet he was memorable in every film. For those extraordinary performances, he will be forever identified with the genre.

Filmography: *Strange Love of Martha Ivers* (Paramount, 1946). *Out of the Past* (RKO, 1947). *I Walk Alone* (Paramount, 1948). *Champion* (United Artists, 1949). *The Big Carnival* (Paramount, 1951). *Detective Story* (Paramount, 1951).

Douglas, Paul (1907–1959)

Character actor. An ex-football player, Paul Douglas is probably best known for his bombastic comic performances in *Born Yesterday* (Columbia, 1954) and *The Solid Gold Cadillac* (Columbia, 1956). His two *film noir*

roles are variations of his comic characters, which is probably why he never developed into an important *noir* villain, despite some physical characteristics similar to Raymond Burr, one of *noir's* most memorable villains.

Filmography: *Panic in the Streets* (20th Century–Fox, 1950). *Clash by Night* (RKO, 1952).

Douglas, Warren (1921–)

Screenwriter. A minor screenwriter active in the early fifties, Douglas co-wrote several low budget films including one minor *film noir*. He later worked extensively in television.

Filmography: *Loophole* (Allied Artists, 1954).

Dow, Peggy (Peggy Varnadon) (1928–)

Actress. Peggy Dow was a brief, bright star in Hollywood in the early fifties. She gave several impressive performances in a handful of films before suddenly retiring from the profession. She had a supporting role in William Castle's *Undertow*.

Filmography: *Undertow* (Universal, 1949).

Dowling, Constance (1923–1969)

Actress. The pretty dark-haired Constance Dowling enjoyed a brief burst of fame in the mid forties. By the fifties she was starring in inferior "B' movies. However, one of those films, *Black Angel*, is unjustly neglected. In this interesting, little known *film noir*, Dowling made an impression as the wife of a man unjustly accused of murder who helps another man prove his innocence. Constance was the younger sister of character actress Doris Dowling.

Filmography: *Black Angel* (Universal, 1946).

Dowling, Doris (1921–)

Character actress. Although Doris' career never achieved the heights of her young sister's brief burst of fame, it was more long lived and, in some ways, more interesting. She had a small supporting role in the *film noir* classic *The Blue Dahlia*. She went to Italy in the late forties and had bigger roles in several important neo-realist dramas, before returning to the United States in the 1960's.

Filmography: *The Blue Dahlia* (Paramount, 1946).

Dratler, Jay (1908–1979)

Novelist and screenwriter. By virtue of a handful of excellent screenplays — all written in the mid to late forties, Dratler is an important figure of *film noir*. He co-wrote the adaption of Vera Caspary's novel for the *noir* classic, *Laura*. Although *The Dark Corner* and *Call Northside 777* are not true classics, each is distinguished by strong dialog, concise plots and a lack of clichés. Dratler also co-wrote a superior "B" *noir*, *Impact*.

Filmography: *Laura* (co-wrote) (20th Century–Fox, 1944). *The Dark Corner* (co-wrote) (20th Century–Fox, 1946). *Call Northside 777* (co-wrote) (20th Century–Fox, 1948). *The Pitfall* (co-wrote) (United Artists, 1948). *Impact* (co-wrote) (United Artists, 1949).

Dreier, Hans (1885–1966)

Art director. Like so many of his fellow production designers, Hans Dreier began his career as an architect before entering films in 1919. Dreier was employed at UFA, the film company that was responsible for many of the classic German films including those of Fritz Lang. It was while at UFA that Dreier developed his heavily expressionist style which had a profound influence on *film noir* style.

In 1923, Dreier moved to the United States and joined Paramount as their supervising art director. He quickly became one of the most influential art directors in American film history. Dreier, deeply influenced by European artifact, brought a sense of elegant, witty style to American films. He designed the extravagant art deco sets

for Ernst Lubitsch's comedies, as well as the more gritty, two-toned sets for Joseph Von Sterberg's melodramas of the 1930's.

Under Dreier's control, Paramount's *films noirs* achieved an opulence never equalled. MGM's *noirs* may have had more polish, Paramount's films had an incomparable glow that was also integrated into the film. With collaborators, Dreier worked on nearly all of the great Paramount *films noirs*, including films directed by Fritz Lang, John Farrow and Billy Wilder.

Filmography: *Underworld* (Paramount, 1927). *Thunderbolt* (Paramount, 1929). *The Glass Key* (Paramount, 1942). *Street of Chance* (Paramount, 1942). *Double Indemnity* (Paramount, 1944). *Ministry of Fear* (Paramount, 1945). *The Blue Dahlia* (Paramount, 1946). *The Strange Love of Martha Ivers* (Paramount, 1946). *Calcutta* (Paramount, 1947). *The Big Clock* (Paramount, 1948). *I Walk Alone* (Paramount, 1948). *The Night Has a Thousand Eyes* (Paramount, 1948). *Sorry, Wrong Number* (Paramount, 1948). *The Accused* (Paramount, 1949). *Chicago Deadline* (Paramount, 1949). *The File on Thelma Jordan* (Paramount, 1950). *Sunset Boulevard* (Paramount, 1950). *Union Station* (Paramount, 1950). *Appointment with Danger* (Paramount, 1951). *The Desperate Hours* (Paramount, 1955).

Drive a Crooked Road (Columbia, 1954). 83 min.

Producer: Jonie Taps. Director: Richard Quine. Screenplay: Blake Edwards, adapted by Richard Quine from a story by James Benson. Director of Photography: Charles Lawton, Jr. Music: Ross Demaggio. Editor: Jerome Thoms.

Cast: Mickey Rooney (Eddie Shannon), Dianne Foster (Barbara Mathews), Kevin McCarthy (Steve Norris), Jack Kelly (Harold Baker), Harry Landers (Ralph). With: Jerry Paris, Paul Picerni,

Dick Crockett, Mort Mills, Peggy Maley.

Eddie Shannon, a mechanic and amateur auto racer, leads a lonely existence until he meets the beautiful Barbara Mathews. Unknown to him, she is the mistress of a local crook who has convinced her to lead Eddie on so that they can use him as a getaway driver in a bank robbery they have planned. Spurred on by Barbara, Eddie reluctantly agrees. The robbery is a success, but Eddie then discovers Barbara's real intentions. Steve convinces his partner Harold to kill Eddie, but Eddie purposely crashes the car they are riding in, and Harold is killed instead. Returning to Steve's house, he discovers Steve beating Barbara. In a fit of rage, Eddie kills Steve and then consoles Barbara as they await the arrival of the cops.

The modest style of *Drive a Crooked Road* typifies *film noir* in the 1950's. Much of the film was shot on location in and around Los Angeles, making effective use of locales.

The screenplay, co-written by Blake Edwards, concentrates on the dark nature and easy virtue of the characters. The film also creates sympathy for the characters, a quality missing in much of *film noir*. Thus, Dianne Foster's *femme-fatale* is more modest and vulnerable than similar roles in the 1940's.

Mickey Rooney is excellent as the hapless, lonely auto racer. He makes his character's loneliness almost palpable as he tosses and turns in bed, lusting after the object of his desire.

While *Drive a Crooked Road* is not a major film, it demonstrates how passion for a subject can over-ride the modest intentions and create a viable work.

Dru, Joanne (Joanne LaCoque) (1923–)

Actress. Although she is all but forgotten today, Joanne Dru was a major star of the late forties and early fifties, giving impressive performances in a number of interesting films including several classic westerns. Beautiful and talented, Dru never became the true mega-star she seemed destined for. Nevertheless, she left behind several memorable performances. Unfortunately, her single *film noir* is not one of the best films of the genre, but Dru is the standout in an otherwise rather uninteresting movie.

Filmography: *Forbidden* (Universal, 1954).

Duff, Howard (1917–)

Actor. Duff first achieved fame as a radio actor, playing private investigator Sam Spade in a popular radio series. His film career was devoted largely to playing a variety of tough heroes and the occasional bad guy. Indeed, his *noir* roles tend to be unscrupulous characters and crooked cops. In *Naked City*, his most famous *film noir*, he played the spoiled, rich kid killer of a young woman.

Filmography: *Brute Force* (Universal, 1947). *Naked City* (Universal, 1948). *Shakedown* (Universal, 1950). *Private Hell, 36* (Filmmakers, 1954).

Duning, George (1908–)

Staff composer and music director for Columbia, 1941-1955. Duning was a prolific composer who worked on a variety of movies. As a staff composer, he took whatever assignments he was given. Few of his scores are really distinguished, but always appropriate to the material. His *noir* scores are typical of the genre: melancholy and romantic. Three of his *noir* scores are outstanding: *Between Midnight and Dawn*, *The Dark Past*, and *Nightfall*.

Filmography: *Johnny O'Clock* (Columbia, 1947). *The Dark Past* (Columbia, 1948). *The Undercover Man* (Columbia, 1949). *Shockproof* (Columbia, 1949). *Between Midnight and Dawn* (Columbia, 1950). *Convicted* (Columbia, 1950). *Affair in Trinidad* (Columbia, 1952). *Tight Spot* (Columbia, 1955). *Nightfall* (Columbia, 1957).

Dunlap, Paul ( )

Composer. Dunlap composed music for many "B" movies in the 1950's and 1960's. Probably the most famous *film noir* on which he worked is Sam Fuller's *The Naked Kiss*.

Filmography: *Cry Danger* (RKO, 1951). *Loophole* (Allied Artists, 1954). *Shield for Murder* (United Artists, 1954). *Crime of Passion* (United Artists, 1957). *The Naked Kiss* (United Artists, 1966).

DuPar, Edwin (1913–)

Cinematographer. DuPar is an undistinguished director of photography on mostly "B" movies, many of them for Warner Bros. However, his single *noir* is distinguished for its gritty expressionist photography.

Filmography: *I Was a Communist for the FBI* (Warner Bros., 1951).

Durbin, Deanna (Edna Mae Durbin) (1921–)

Singer and actress. With an extraordinary and beautiful voice, the talented Deanna Durbin was one of the biggest film star's of the 1940's. Precocious and very attractive, Durbin was the sweet-tempered girl next door of many classic Universal comedy-musicals. By the mid forties, with her popularity waning, she attempted to change her image somewhat. However, when cast in Robert Siodmak's production of *Christmas Holiday*, she fought bitterly with the great director who wanted to change her image dramatically: as the doomed chanteuse, he imagined a tawdry, but alluring character. Durbin disagreed and the compromise is less than satisfying. Still, as her one *film noir* appearance, it created a tantalizing glimpse at a career which might have developed in an interesting direction.

Filmography: *Christmas Holiday* (Universal, 1944).

Duryea, Dan (1907–1968)

Actor. Dan Duryea is one of *film noir*'s most important actors, appearing in more films of the genre than almost any other leading man. His slightly offbeat good looks and air of decadent charm made him perfect as a rakish con man and was strangely attractive to women.

Duryea played a variety of charming villains in several *films noirs* including *Criss Cross* and *Ministry of Fear*. However, he also played heroes, as in Robert Aldrich's *World for Ransom*.

Two of Duryea's more unusual *noir* roles include a law abiding brother of a criminal on the run in *Storm Fear*, and as a sympathetic alcoholic/murderer in *Black Angel*.

Duryea brought to all of his performances a quiet intensity that was always compelling. Generally the second male lead, he was also a scene stealer, and it is often his performances one remembers from the movies he appeared in.

Filmography: *Lady on a Train* (Universal, 1945). *Ministry of Fear* Paramount, 1945). *Scarlet Street* (Universal, 1945). *Black Angel* (Universal, 1946). *Criss Cross* (Universal, 1949). *Manhandled* (Paramount, 1949). *Too Late for Tears* (United Artists, 1949). *One Way Street* (Universal, 1950). *Storm Fear* (United Artists, 1956). *The Burglar* (Columbia, 1957).

Dvorak, Ann (Ann Mckim) (1912–1979)

Actress. The remarkable and beautiful Ann Dvorak was one of the 1930's most intelligent actresses. Strangely, despite appearing in several classics of the era, she never achieved real stardom. In the early forties she spent several years in Great Britain where she appeared in a few insignificant films. She returned to Hollywood in 1944 and continued to act in American films until the mid fifties. She had a supporting role in one minor *film noir*.

Filmography: *The Long Night* (RKO, 1947).

Dwan, Allan (Joseph Aloysius Dwan) (1885–1981)

Director. Dwan's career began in the silent era and continued unabated until

the late fifties. The consumate Hollywood professional, Dwan directed a
variety of movies with competence, but
he was particularly adept at action
films. His color *noir, Slightly Scarlet* is
a study of big city corruption reminiscent of *The Big Heat* (Columbia, 1953).
    Filmography: *Slightly Scarlet* (RKO,
1956).

Eagle-Lion

Eagle-Lion was the latter version of
Producers Releasing Corporation after
being renamed in 1948. The company
continued production under this name
until the mid fifties. Despite the new
name, the production values remained
the same: rarely more than merely adequate at best. In its first year with its
new name, the company released a
handful of *films noirs* including two
directed by Anthony Mann*.
    Releases: 1948: *Behind Locked Doors.
Canon City. He Walked by Night. Hollow Triumph. Raw Deal*. T-Men*.*

Edeson, Arthur (1891-1970)

Director. Arthur Edeson was an
expert at gloomy, foggy photography.
Although his name is less well known
than many of his contemporaries,
Edeson was certainly an important
cinematographer. After all, this was
the man who photographed some of
the most important, expressionist influenced films of the early thirties: *All
Quiet on the Western Front* (Universal,
1930), *Frankenstein* (Universal, 1931),
and *The Invisible Man* (Universal,
1933). Edeson moved to Warner Bros.
in the forties, where he was the cinematographer on three important *films
noirs. The Mask of Dimitrios* is particularly outstanding, in which Edeson
created a foggy, sinister ambiance,
appropriate for this moody espionage
thriller.
    Filmography: *The Maltese Falcon*
(Warner Bros., 1941). *The Mask of
Dimitrios* (Warner Bros., 1944). *Nobody Lives Forever* (Warner Bros.,
1946).

Edge of Doom (RKO, 1950). 99 min.
    Producer: Samuel Goldwyn. Direc-
tor: Mark Robson (with uncredited
scenes by Charles Vidor). Screenplay:
Philip Yordan, with additional scenes
by Ben Hecht, based on the novel by
Leo Brody. Director of Photography:
Harry Strandling. Music: Hugo Fried-
hofer. Art Director: Richard Day.
Editor: Daniel Mandell.
    Cast: Dana Andrews (Father Roth),
Farley Granger (Martin Lynn), Joan
Evans (Rita Conroy), Robert Keith
(Mandel), Paul Stewart (Craig), Mala
Powers (Julie), Adele Jergens (Irene).
With: Harold Vermilyea, John Ridgeley, Douglas Fowley, Mabel Paige,
Howland Chamberlain.
    Martin Lynn is a frustrated, poor
young man from the ghettos. When his
devout mother dies from cancer, a
neighbor suggests he go to the local
catholic church and ask Father Kirkman for a "proper burial." However,
he asks for an elaborate funeral and
when Father Kirkman turns him down
because his parish is poor and they
could not afford such an expense, Martin, in a blind rage, stabs the Father
with a crucifix. By coincidence, while
fleeing, Martin is arrested for a petty
theft he did not commit. The new
parish priest, Father Roth, unaware
that Martin is the killer of Father
Kirkman, has Martin released into his
custody. Slowly he comes to realize
that Martin is guilty of the murder.
Eventually, Father Roth convinces
Martin to surrender in exchange for his
mother's elaborate funeral.
    Edge of Doom is, in many ways,
similar to the Warner Bros. films of the
1930's. Its Roman Catholic setting and
moral are, in fact, counter to *film noir*,
but this film's *mise-en-scène* subverts
that outlook; and ultimately the film's
ending is as bleak and uncompromising
as any other *film noir*.
    Despite its pretentions, the film is a
minor one. Its strongest virtues are its
performances by Farley Granger as the
deranged youth and Dana Andrews as

the kindly Father Roth, although Andrews is a little too worldly to be entirely convincing in the role.

Edwards, Blake (William B. Edwards) 1922–)
Writer and director. Before he became a great director of comedies, Blake Edwards had a rich and varied career as a screenwriter. Early in his career he was known for his tough-minded melodramas, even creating the *noir*-influenced television series *Peter Gunn*. While it is not a really important film, *Drive a Crooked Mile* is distinguished by Edwards' excellent screenplay. The film is surprisingly bitter and its female characters about as vile and dangerous as one is likely to encounter even in *film noir*. He also directed a superior late-*noir*, *Experiment in Terror*, which is best known for its suspense and well-staged climax in a crowded stadium.
Filmography: *Drive a Crooked Road* (screenplay) (Columbia, 1954). *Experiment in Terror* (Columbia, 1962).

Edwards, Vince (Vincent Edward Zointe) (1928–)
Actor. A leading man of modest-budget action films, Edwards enjoyed a brief bit of stardom in the 1950's. After a brief run of box-office success, he turned to television, and his film roles grew few and far between in the sixties. He played supporting leads in three *films noirs*. His most significant role in the genre was in the "B" *noir*, *The Night Holds Terror*, in which he starred as a small time hood who kidnaps a family.
Filmography: *Rogue Cop* (MGM, 1954). *The Night Holds Terror* (Columbia, 1955). *The Killing* (United Artists, 1956).

Eisenger, Jo (1916–)
Screenwriter. Eisenger co-wrote several screenplays including a number of *films noirs* beginning in the late forties. By far the most important screenplay she worked on was the *noir* classic, *Gilda*, best known for its romantic fatalism, but *Night and the City* is also a major film and one of the genre's most cynical movies.
Filmography: *Gilda* (Columbia, 1946). *Night and the City* (20th Century-Fox, 1950). *The Sleeping City* (Universal, 1950). *Crime of Passion* (United Artists, 1957).

Elam, Jack (1916–)
Character actor. Elam was a laconic character actor who played everything from western villains to comic supporting roles. He had major supporting parts in several Robert Aldrich's films in the 1950's, including the *film noir* classic, *Kiss Me Deadly*. Generally, his *noir* roles were small and not as significant as his roles in other films.
Filmography: *Kansas City Confidential* (United Artists, 1952). *Kiss Me Deadly* (United Artists, 1955). *Baby Face Nelson* (United Artists, 1957).

Elliot, Biff (1929–)
Actor. Elliot appeared in a handful of "B" movies in the early fifties. However, his one shot at stardom, as Mike Hammer in *I, the Jury*, was not successful or convincing, and he quickly disappeared.
Filmography: *I, the Jury* (United Artists, 1953).

Ellis, Don (1933–1978)
Composer. A former jazz trumpeter, Don Ellis became active as a film composer in the mid seventies, excelling at a provocative jazz-influenced style. His scores for the two *French Connection* films are masterpieces of modern film music, and are evocative of the jazzy *film noir* scores.
Filmography: *The French Connection* (20th Century–Fox, 1971). *French Connection II* (20th Century–Fox, 1974).

Emerson, Faye (1917–1983)
Actress. Her cool beauty made Emerson a natural for "uppercrust" socialites

and classy ladies. She starred in two minor, but interesting *films noirs*. In *Danger Signal* she plays the target of a smooth con man (Zachary Scott) who plans to marry her teenage daughter for an inheritence. In *Nobody Lives Forever*, an atypical role, she has a supporting part as a slutty gangster moll.

Filmography: *Danger Signal* (Warner Bros., 1945). *Nobody Lives Forever* (Warner Bros., 1946).

The Enforcer (Warner Bros., 1951). 88 min.

Producer: Milton Sperling. Director: Bretaigne Windust (with uncredited scenes by Raoul Walsh). Screenplay: Martin Rackin. Director of Photography: Robert Burks. Music: David Buttolph. Art Director: Charles H. Clarke. Editor: Fred Allen.

Cast: Humphrey Bogart (Martin Fergusson), Zero Mostel (Big Babe Lazich), Ted De Corsia (Joseph Rico), Everett Sloane (Albert Mendoza), Roy Roberts (Captain Frank Nelson), Lawrence Tolan (Duke Malloy). With: King Donavan, Robert Steele, Patricia Joiner, Tito Vuolo, John Kellogg.

Martin Fergusson, an assistant D.A. is ready to prosecute Albert Mendoza, a local mobster, for a series of crimes including homicide. However, his key witness, Big Babe Lazich, is killed. Fergusson and Police Captain Frank Nelson spend a night going through their records and documents on the case, putting together a grisly record of Mendoza's criminal history. At the last moment, Fergusson finds a clue that leads to another witness and secures his case.

One of Bogart's least important *films noirs*, *The Enforcer* is still interesting mainly because of its semi-documentary style, and its realistic portrait of mobster life. It also contains an excellent, all too brief performance by Zero Mostel as the small time hood/informant murdered near the beginning of the film.

Erskine, Chester (1905–1986)

Writer, producer and director. Erskine had a varied career, mainly as a screenwriter, beginning in the thirties. He wrote and produced a number of popular and rather pretentious melodramas including a version of Arthur Miller's play, *All My Sons* (Universal, 1949), and *The Egg and I* (Columbia, 1947) which he directed. He also had a hand in writing two *films noirs* including Otto Preminger's neglected classic, *Angel Face*, for which he contributed the story.

Filmography: *Angel Face* (RKO, 1953). *Witness to Murder* (United Artists, 1954).

Essex, Harry (1910–)

Screenwriter in the 1940's and 1950's, almost exclusively of low budget thrillers and action pictures. However, despite their modest budgets, many of these films are well above average. All of his *films noirs* are commendable. He also wrote and directed a notoriously violent and mean-spirited version of Mickey Spillane's *I, the Jury*. Indeed, all of Essex's screenplays tend to substitute subtle and psychological insight with violence and swift action.

Filmography: *Desperate* (RKO, 1947). *Bodyguard* (RKO, 1948). *He Walked By Night* (Eagle-Lion, 1949). *The Killer That Stalked New York* (Columbia, 1950). *Kansas City Confidential* (United Artists, 1952). *I, the Jury* (wrote/directed) (United Artists, 1952).

Evans, Gene (1922–)

Actor. Gene Evans was a busy actor in the late forties and the fifties, appearing in many films and a number of popular television series. He played second male leads in all of his *films noirs*. One of his finest performances was in the excellent "B" noir, *Armored Car Robbery*, as one of the doomed criminals.

Filmography: *Berlin Express* (RKO, 1948). *Criss Cross* (Universal, 1949).

Armored Car Robbery (RKO, 1950).
The Big Carnival (Paramount, 1951).
The Long Wait (United Artists, 1954).

Experiment in Terror (Columbia, 1962).
    123 min.
Producer and Director: Blake Edwards. Screenplay: Gordon Gordon and Michael Gordon, based on their novel *Operation Terror* . Director of Photography. Philip Lathrop. Music: Henry Mancini. Art Director: Robert Peterson. Editor: Patrick McCormack.
Cast: Glenn Ford (John "Rip" Ripley), Lee Remick (Kelly Sherwood), Stefanie Powers (Toby), Roy Poole (Brad), Ned Glass (Popcorn), Ross Martin (Red Lynch). With Patricia Huston, Gilbert Green, Clifton Jones, William Bryant, Dick Crockett.

Kelly Sherwood, a pretty young bank teller, is accosted in her garage late one night by a strange man who knows more than he should about her life. Hidden in the dark, with a raspy, asthmatic voice, he threatens Kelly and her younger sister Toby with harm if Kelly will not comply with his wish to steal $100,000 from her bank. She calls the F.B.I. and agent John Ripley is assigned to the case. He posts guards around Kelly and her sister. The investigators discover that Red Lynch is behind the extortion scheme, but before he can be caught, he manages to elude the body guards and kidnap Toby Sherwood. Kelly is then allowed to take the money from the bank, and arranges to meet Lynch at Candlestick Park during a baseball game. Lynch is cornered and killed in the climatic shootout and Toby is released unharmed.

Much of Blake Edward's early career as a director was devoted to a variety of genres, and he brought a rare degree of professionalism (if not much invention) to each of his productions. *Experiment in Terror* might well be one of his best films, if not as well known as his later comedies.

Experiment in Terror is a superior late-*noir*. It creates an enormous amount of tension. It has some classic *noir* style, particularly in the scenes with the killer/extortionist, Red Lynch, whose face is always hidden in shadows.

Experiment Perilous (RKO, 1944). 91
    min.
Producer: Warren Duff. Director: Jacques Tourneur. Screenplay: Warren Duff, based on the novel by Margaret Carpenter. Director of Photography: Tony Gaudio. Music: Roy Webb. Art Directors: Albert S. D'Agostino and Carroll Clark. Editor: Robert Golden.
Cast: Hedy Lamarr (Allida Bedereaux), George Brent (Dr. Huntington Bailey), Paul Lukas (Nick Bedereaux), Albert Dekker (Claghorne), Carl Esmond (John Maitlant), Olive Blakeney (Cissie Bedereaux).

Allida Bedereaux is married to Nick Bedereaux, a jealous maniac who has terrorized her to the brink of insanity and turned their young son into an emotional wreck. Dr. Huntington Bailey, Allida's psychiatrist frustrates the madman and in the process wins the love of his beautiful patient.

Experiment Perilous is an important, seminal *film noir*, notable chiefly for the superb direction of Jacques Tourneur, who managed to create a psychological thriller of absorbing quality. The screenplay, adapted by Warren Duff from the popular novel by Margaret Carpenter, is excessively verbose, complicated by some confusing flashback, but the film's style is undeniably elegant and expressionist, pointing the way to Tourneur's greatest *noir*, *Out of the Past* (RKO, 1947).

Expressionism

An artistic movement founded in Germany in the early nineteenth century. It has broad appeal and influence on all the arts. In cinema, the leading expressionist filmmakers in the 1920's were F. W. Murnau, Robert Weine and Fritz Lang. Their aim was to convey inner subjective experience through external, objective means. The style, which was quickly adapted by both commercial and serious filmmakers, is characterized by highly stylized sets and deliberately exaggerated, dramatic lighting and camera angles to emphasize a particular effect—fear, horror, confusion, insanity. Both Murnau and Lang came to the United States, as did many of their compatriots and expressionist techniques made their way into American commercial films. It is most apparent in Universal's horror films in the 1930's—particularly the *Frankenstein* sagas—and in early *film noir* over a decade later.

Fall Guy (Monogram, 1947). 64 min.

Producer: Walter Mirisch. Director: Reginald LeBorg. Screenplay: Jerry Warner, additional dialog by John O'Dea, based on the short story "Cocaine" by Cornell Woolrich. Director of Photography: Mack Stenger. Music: Edward J. Kay. Art Director: Dave Milton. Editor: William Austin.

Cast: Clifford Penn (Tom Cochrane), Teala Loring (Lois Walter), Robert Armstrong (MacLaine), Virginia Dale (Marie), Elisha Cook, Jr. (Joe). With: Douglas Fowley, Charles Arnt, Harry Strong.

When Tom Cochrane, a nice young man, is arrested for the murder of a woman, he cannot remember the night in question although all clues seem to lead to him. Luckily he has a friend, McLaine, on the police force. MacLaine pulls some strings and gets Tom out on bail. Tom begins his own investigation and discovers that the victim was the mistress of his uncle who was blackmailing her and was also jealous of Tom's relationship with his beautiful girl friend. His uncle had drugged Tom, murdered the woman and set it up to look like Tom was guilty.

A Monogram cheapie, *Fall Guy* has a typically uneven story and eclectic visual style. Adapted from a story by Cornell Woolrich, the film brings the hallucinatory qualities of his fiction to

the screen with several interesting "flashback" sequences.

Fallen Angel (20th Century-Fox, 1946). 98 min.

Producer and Director: Otto Preminger. Screenplay: Harry Kleiner, based on the novel by Marty Holland. Director of Photography: Joseph La Shelle. Music: David Raksin. Song: "Slowly" by David Raksin and Kermit Goell. Art Directors: Lyle Wheeler and Leland Fuller. Editor: Harry Reynolds.

Cast: Alice Faye (June Mills), Dana Andrews (Eric Stanton), Linda Darnell (Stella), Charles Bickford (Mark Judd), Ann Revere (Clara Mills), Bruce Cabot (Dave Atkins). With: John Carradine, Percy Kilbride, Olin Hawkin, Hal Taliaferro.

The impecunious Eric Stanton arrives by bus in a small, Northern California town, and immediately becomes interested in Stella, a pretty café waitress. Pretending to be a medium, he succeeds in impressing one of the town's most respected woman citizens June Mills. He plans on romancing and wooing the impressionable Miss Mills, so that he can impress the aloof Stella.

In fact, many men lust after the beautiful café waitress, including a former New York police detective, Mark Judd. When Stella is murdered, the pushy Eric is the main suspect, and he flees to San Francisco with June (who believes in his innocence), and there he falls in love with her. She gives the encouragement he needs to return and defend himself. He proves that Judd is Stella's real killer.

Otto Preminger's immediate follow up to *Laura* (20th Century-Fox, 1944), *Fallen Angel* reminds one of Jim Thompson's novels: it has some of the same lethargic qualities of the author's fiction. Likewise, its characters—cheap con men, lonely women, murderous psychopaths—are all common to Thompson's novels, as well as James M. Cain's.

Fallen Angel is not as immediately

endearing as *Laura*. It is a much subtler film, working on innuendo and suggestion. Its study of female characters is typical of Preminger's early work. There are some similarities to Preminger's earlier *noir* classic, *Laura*, particularly with its central male character's erotic obsession with an unattainable female.

Linda Darnell, as the temptress Stella, is the representation of destructive female sexuality (although not quite a true *femme-fatale*). Her dark hair and dreamy, doe eyes are in perfect contrast to Alice Faye's blonde, wholesome sexuality, as the nurturing, good-girl figure.

While it is not in the same league as *Laura*, *Fallen Angel* is a well made thriller, and its virtues lie both with its strong performances and excellent location photography. Alfred Hitchcock would exploit the same, dreamy qualities of northern California in his color *noir* masterpiece, *Vertigo* (Universal, 1958).

Farewell, My Lovely (Avco-Embassy, 1975). 97 min.

Producers: George Pappas and Jerry Bruckheimer. Director: Dick Richards. Screenplay: David Zelag Goodman, based on the novel by Raymond Chandler. Director of Photography: John A. Alonzo. Music: David Shire. Art Director: Angelo Graham. Editors: Walter Thompson and Joel Cos.

Cast: Robert Mitchum (Philip Marlowe), Charlotte Rampling (Mrs. Grayle, Velma), John Ireland (Nulty), Sylvia Miles (Mrs. Florian), Anthony Zerbe (Brunette), Jack O'Halloran (Moose Malloy). With: Harry Dean Stanton, Sylvester Stallone, Kate Murtagh.

Philip Marlowe is hired by the mysterious, beautiful and wealthy Mrs. Grayle to search for a valuable stolen necklace. At the same time, he is hired by Moose Malloy, a murderous gangster, to search for his missing girl friend, Velma. They are, in fact, one and the same. Marlowe's investigation uncovers a sinister gambling ring involving Malloy and Mrs. Grayle. In the end, Malloy kills Mrs. Grayle and Marlow kills Malloy.

A splendid update of Raymond Chandler's novel *Farewell, My Lovely* is more faithful to the novel than Edward Dmytryk's *Murder, My Sweet* (RKO, 1944). It is further proof how artistically viable *film noir* can still be. Of course, with its star, Robert Mitchum, and a small supporting role by John Ireland, the film also had a direct connection with *noir* of two decades before.

The film is also an interesting and successful attempt to recapture the classic look of *film noir* in color. Shot on location in Los Angeles, with many night scenes, it is a neon-drenched, eerie film. The ambiance is enhanced by an excellent jazz score by David Shire.

Robert Mitchum is typically hard-boiled as Chandler's famous private investigator, if a little too old for the part.

However, despite its virtues, the film was too old fashioned and slow to appeal to a mass audience and it was a box-office failure.

Farrow, John (1904–1963)

Director. John Farrow is one of American cinema's more overlooked artists. He was neglected by the studio, Paramount, for whom he worked for, most of his career. Neglected much in the same way that John Brahm was ignored by 20th Century–Fox. Despite both men's considerable and obvious talents, they were rarely given assignments that suited those talents, but when they were, they excelled. Like Brahm, Farrow was a "gothic" filmmaker, steeped in the traditions of expressionist cinema: baroque camera angles; endless, complicated dollies; dark, foreboding lighting; and ambitiously complex narrative structures full of metaphors.

Farrow, Australian born and an expert

Faith Domergue, Robert Mitchum in *Where Danger Lives* (RKO, 1950).

on marine biology, thanks to his training while in the Royal Navy, came to the United States originally as a marine biologist. He worked briefly as a technical adviser for various film studios in the mid twenties before trying his hand at screenwriting. He was a success and by the late thirties he began directing. Unlike many writers turned directors, Farrow proved to have a rich visual imagination. He enjoyed complicated camera work, as in the memorable opening aerial/crane dolly scene, on the miniature of the Janoth Publications building in *The Big Clock*.

Besides *The Big Clock*, an underrated masterpiece, Farrow made at least one other acknowledged *noir* masterpiece—*Night Has a Thousand Eyes*—and three other minor classics. Both *Night Has a Thousand Eyes* and the little known *Where Danger Lives* are distinguished by their despairing views of humanity. All of his *noirs* are characterized by moody lighting, eerie music and brilliant dialog.

Farrow may have been a systematic and rather inflexible disciplinarian (as has often been claimed), but he managed to get strong, memorable performances out of notoriously undisciplined actors such as Charles Laughton. Laughton was one of *film noir*'s best remembered villains in Farrow's *The Big Clock*. He was also a classic *auteur*, collaborating on all aspects of his films including the writing and directing.

There can be little question of John Farrow's technical brilliance and he is worthy of renewed critical attention, even for his minor films. Several of his *films noirs* remain classics of the genre.

Filmography: *Calcutta* (Paramount, 1947). *The Big Clock* (Paramount, 1948). *Night Has a Thousand Eyes* (Paramount, 1948). *Where Danger Lives* (RKO, 1950). *His Kind of Woman* (RKO, 1951).

Fear (Monogram, 1946). 68 min.
Producer: Lindsley Parsons. Director: Alfred Zeisler. Screenplay: Alfred

Zeisler and Dennis Cooper. Director of Photography: Jackson Rose. Art Director: Dave Milton. Editor: Ace Herman.

Cast: Warren Williams (Capt. Burke), Anne Gwynne (Eileen), Peter Cookson (Larry Crain), James Cardwell (Ben), Nestor Paiva (Schaefer). With: Francis Pierlot, Johnny Strong, William Moss, Darren McGavin.

When a college student kills his professor, a detective taunts him to the point of confession. In the end, however, it turns out to be a nightmare.

Fear is the most consistent of Monogram's *films noirs*, with some inventive direction and a curious screenplay derived from Dostoevsky's *Crime and Punishment*. An interesting, if very minor, "B" *noir*.

Fear in the Night (Paramount, 1947). 71 min.

Producers: William H. Pine and William C. Thomas. Director: Maxwell Shane. Screenplay: Maxwell Shane, based on the short story "Nightmare" by William Irish (Cornell Woolrich). Director of Photography: Jack Greenhalgh. Music: Rudy Schrager. Art Director: F. Paul Sylos. Editor: Howard Smith.

Cast: Paul Kelly (Cliff Herlihy), DeForrest Kelly (Vince Grayson), Ann Doran (Lil Herlihy), Kay Scott (Betty Winters), Robert Emmett Keane (Lewis Belnap). With Jeff York, Charles Victor, Janet Warren, Michael Harvey, Gladys Blake.

The film opens in the middle of Vince Grayson's dream. There is a room composed entirely of mirrors. A pretty young girl stands over a man cutting into a safe with a torch. Vince enters, struggles with the thief and stabs the man with the torch. The girl disappears through one of the mirrored doors.

When Vince awakens the next morning, he is clutching a button from the man's jacket and a key to one of the room's closets. He is convinced it was not a dream, but when he tells his

brother-in-law Cliff, a police detective, Cliff convinces him that it was only a nightmare.

However, when Cliff and his wife and Vince and his girl friend Lil are on a picnic several days later, they take refuge in an abandoned mansion during a rainstorm. Exploring the old house, Cliff discovers a room exactly as Vince described from his dream. Cliff is convinced that Vince is a murderer. He begins his own investigation and discovers some bizarre, coincidental links between Vince and his middle aged neighbor Belnap and that the woman described in Vince's dream matches Belnap's wife who apparently died in a car crash on the night of Vince's dream.

Cliff believes Belnap hypnotized Vince to make him believe that he had committed murder. Confronting Belnap, the suspect admits that he did in fact hypnotize Vince. He convinces Cliff to allow him to hypnotize Vince again to erase the false memory, but he actually gets Vince to confess to murder and then attempt suicide. Luckily, Vince is saved just in time and Belnap is, ironically, killed in a car crash while trying to escape.

Despite its wildly improbable and complicated plot (based on a Cornell Woolrich short story), *Fear in the Night* is an interesting low budget *film noir*. Writer/director Maxwell Shane manages to capture the hallucinatory aspects of the story with some interesting dream sequences. Shane later remade the film on a higher budget, as *Nightmare*, but it is not nearly as interesting as this early version.

Feist, Felix (1906–1965)

Director. After many years of writing, producing and directing short films, Felix Feist graduated to directing features in the mid forties. He directed mainly "B" movies of various types— specializing in horror films—with an agreeable, visceral style. His two *films noirs* are minor movies.

Filmography: *The Devil Thumbs a Ride* (RKO, 1947). *The Man Who Cheated Himself* (20th Century–Fox, 1950).

Felton, Earl (1905–1969)

Screenwriter. Felton was a staff writer for RKO in the thirties and forties and later had a substantial career as a television writer. At RKO, Felton wrote many of the best "B" productions in the early fifties, including two superior *films noirs*. *Armored Car Robbery* is an exhilarating caper film, while *The Narrow Margin* is a classic adventure *noir*.

Filmography: *Armored Car Robbery* (RKO, 1950). *The Narrow Margin* (RKO, 1952).

Female on the Beach (Universal, 1955). 97 min.

Producer: Albert Zugsmith. Director: Joseph Pevney. Screenplay: Robert Hill and Richard Alan Simmons. Director of Photography: Charles Lang. Music: Joseph Gershenson. Art Director: Alexander Golitzen. Editor: Edward Curtiss.

Cast: Joan Crawford, (Lynn Markham), Jeff Chandler (Drummond Hall), Jan Sterling (Amy Rawlinson), Cecil Kellaway (Osbert Sorenson). With: Charles Drake, Stuart Randall, Romo Vincent.

Lynn Markham is the widow of a Las Vegas gambler. She has just moved to Balboa Beach to take up residence in a beach house formerly occupied by a wealthy widow who was killed in a bizzare accident. Lynn meets Drummond Hall, a handsome neighbor and after a brief romance, the couple is married. She soon discovers that she is marked for murder, but in the end the killer turns out to be Amy Rawlinson, a pretty real estate lady who wants Drummond for herself.

Female on the Beach is a little known late-*noir* starring Joan Crawford. Although the film has some interesting moments, it suffers from Crawford's histrionics which, by this time, had deteriorated to self-parody.

Femme-fatale

The fatal female who leads men to their moral destruction and sometimes death is not an invention of or exclusive to *film noir*, but the character reached its artistic maturity in the genre. Certain reactionary feminist critics have attacked the character type (and the genre in general) as misogynist; the opposite, however, is probably more to the point. Indeed, it was a real attempt to deal with women by American filmmakers in an honest (if somewhat brutal) way: as in real life, just as sexually voracious and as potentially murderous as any man, and just as susceptible to corruption and greed. Indeed, the feminist criticism is in fact a misinterpretation of the themes of the genre, for the truth of the matter is that *film noir* was essentially *misanthropic*: male and female characters are equally corrupt.

The roots of the *film noir femme-fatale* lay in silent film's vamps — Theda Bara, et al. — as well as the Marlene Dietrich characters in the influential Josef Von Sternberg melodramas of the thirties. The *noir femme-fatale* is a departure essentially in the overall moral degeneracy of the character; and, although less exotic than the Bara/Dietrich variety, they were also more overtly sexual: voluptuous; tight, revealing clothes; heavy make-up; and dyed hair are traits of the *noir* character.

The *femme-fatale* role was used by some actresses to enhance fading careers and by others to carve out new careers. Interestingly, some of the actresses who took the role of *noir*'s spider women had previously played "good girls," homemakers, virgins and the like. Dorothy Malone and Gail Russell are the most striking examples of these actresses, while Barbara Stanwyck and Joan Crawford were known as strong-willed working women who always

Lana Turner, John Garfield in *The Postman Always Rings Twice* **(MGM, 1946).**

triumphed over adversity in their melodramas in the 1930's. On the other
hand, Jan Sterling, Claire Trevor,
Audrey Totter and Marie Windsor
were brassy actresses who had previously played "the other woman" in
romantic melodramas. Finally, a whole
new group, on the surface attractive
"girls-next-door," emerged as if created
specifically for the genre: Gloria
Grahame, Veronica Lake, Evelyn
Keyes and Jane Greer.

The *film noir femme-fatale* made
striking early appearances, played by
the dark, sensual Joan Bennett in Fritz
Lang's *Woman in the Window* (RKO,

1944) and Barbara Stanwyck's trashy Phyllis Dietrichson in Billy Wilder's *Double Indemnity* (Paramount, 1944). Both roles set the standards for all of *noir*'s female villains to follow and, of course, both actresses would play variations on these early roles in later films: Bennett in *Scarlet Street* (Universal, 1945) and Barbara Stanwyck in *The Strange Love of Martha Ivers* (Paramount, 1946). Equally important was Lana Turner's performance in *The Postman Always Rings Twice* (MGM, 1946), which, like *Double Indemnity* was based on a novel by James M. Cain.

Other famous *femme-fatales* include Rita Hayworth in the title role in *Gilda* (Columbia, 1946) and as Elsa Bannister in *The Lady from Shanghai* (Columbia, 1948), Marie Windsor in *The Killing* (United Artists, 1956), Veronica Lake in *This Gun for Hire* (Paramount, 1942), Gloria Grahame in *Human Desire* (Columbia, 1954) and Jane Greer in *Out of the Past* (RKO, 1947). Less well known, but no less lethal than the characters performed by the actresses above, was Faith Domergue's particularly corrupt Margo Lannington in John Farrow's neglected minor classic, *Where Danger Lives* (RKO, 1950).

The *femme-fatale* is also a major character in many "B" *noirs:* Loretta Young in *The Accused* (Paramount, 1949), Bette Davis in *Another Man's Poison* (United Artists, 1952), Jean Gillie in *Decoy* (Monogram, 1946), Helen Walker in *Impact* (United Artists, 1949) and Joan Dixon in *Roadblock* (RKO, 1951).

The character is still an important one in post-*noir* American crime films. Kathleen Turner played a striking variation of the type in *Body Heat* (Warner Bros., 1981).

American cinema has too often been the domain of men. *Film noir* is one of the few exceptions and the genre provided women with roles in which they were able to make a substantial contribution through strength of character, ambition, and through the *femme-*

fatale, a compelling ability to exploit the power of their sexuality.

Fenton, Frank (1906–1957)

Screenwriter. Fenton was a staff writer at RKO. He co-wrote two *films noirs* including John Farrow's *His Kind of Woman*, one of the most entertaining films of the genre.

Filmography: *Nocturne* (co-wrote) (RKO, 1946). *His Kind of Woman* (co-wrote) (RKO, 1946).

Ferguson, Perry (1901–1979)

Art director. Perry Ferguson might well be one of the most neglected American art directors of Hollywood's golden age. There is some dispute about his contribution to *Citizen Kane* (RKO, 1941) for which he is listed as associate art director under Van Nest Polglase as art director. The cinematographer of that masterpiece, Gregg Toland, argued that it was Ferguson, not Polglase who deserved full credit. In any case, he is given major credit for a number of other important productions and his contributions to the look of *film noir* in the late forties and early fifties is indisputably important.

Filmography: *The Stranger* (RKO, 1946). *Follow Me Quietly* (RKO, 1949). *711 Ocean Drive* (Columbia, 1950). *Try and Get Me* (United Artists, 1950).

The File on Thelma Jordan (Paramount, 1950). 100 min.

Producer: Hal B. Wallis. Director: Robert Siodmak. Screenplay: Ketti Frings, story by Marty Holland. Director of Photography: George Barnes. Music Victor Young. Art Directors: Hans Dreier and Earl Hedrick. Editor: Warren Low

Cast: Barbara Stanwyck (Thelma Jordan), Wendell Corey (Cleve Marshall), Paul Kelly (Miles Scott), Joan Tetzel (Pamela Marshall), Stanley Ridges (Kingsley Willis), Richard Rober (Tony Loredo). With: Minor Watson, Barry Kelley, Laura Elliott, Basil Ruysdael, Jane Novak.

Late one evening, Thelma Jordan walks into the D.A.'s office in a small town to discuss burglaries at her aunt's mansion where she also resides. Soon, a love affair develops between her and the Assistant D.A., Cleve Marshall. Thelma's affections appear confused when she is met one evening by Tony Loredo, a sinister man who seems to know a great deal about her. She admits to Cleve that she is married to Tony, but they are estranged and she never wants to see him again.

Thelma's aunt is killed and her safe broken into during a burglary. Before the police are called, Thelma calls Cleve and implicates Tony. Cleve tells Thelma to pretend she is asleep while he sets up things to make absolutely sure Tony is arrested; but she is seen by a butler and the police are called. Tony, it turns out has an alibi—he is in Chicago—and Thelma is arrested as the suspect in her aunt's murder.

Cleve, in love with Thelma, is determined to get her off. He begins to investigate her background and uncovers a seedy past. Regardless, he lies at her trial and she is released.

When Cleve confronts Thelma, she admits that the burglary was all a ruse and that, indeed, Tony was guilty of the murder. In the subsequent confrontation, Tony knocks Cleve unconscious. Thelma flees with Tony but overcome by remorse and her love for Cleve, deliberately wrecks the car, killing Tony instantly and fatally injuring herself. Thelma confesses her sins to the police and Cleve who has, by this time, caught up with them. Realizing his career is ruined for helping her get out of prison, Cleve walks off into the shadows.

As Thelma Jordan, Barbara Stanwyck is a different sort of *femme-fatale* than her earlier role as Phyllis Dietrichson in *Double Indemnity* (Paramount, 1944) because, in this case, she actually does love her victim. Cleve's actions are equally impulsive because he too loves Thelma, the primary cause for his

actions. They are an unusual *film noir* couple, being both guilt ridden and obsessively romantic.

As the catalyst of the tragedy, Richard Rober, as Tony Loredo, represents animalistic sexuality—a man of the city who invades the peaceful rural life that Cleve represents.

The File on Thelma Jordan is not quite a major *film noir*, despite all of the talent involved, including director Robert Siodmak. Except for Stanwyck's performance, the other performances are not particularly strong and the script is weak in spots. Yet, it is not a bad film either, and is a must see for any fan of the genre.

Fisher, Steve (1911–)

Novelist and screenwriter. Fisher's best selling novel *I Wake Up Screaming* was twice adapted for the screen, the second version of which is known simply as *Vicki*. He also wrote or co-wrote a variety of *films noirs*, all of which are above average. He specialized in complex narratives, dream sequences and was an expert handler of dialog.

Filmography: *I Wake Up Screaming* (based on his novel) (20th Century-Fox, 1942). *Johnny Angel* (RKO, 1945). *Dead Reckoning* (co-wrote) (Columbia, 1947). *Lady in the Lake* (MGM, 1947). *I Wouldn't Be in Your Shoes* (Monogram, 1948). *Roadblock* (co-wrote) (RKO, 1951). *City That Never Sleeps* (Republic, 1953). *Vicki* (based on his novel *I Wake Up Screaming*) (20th Century–Fox, 1953).

Fitzgerald, Barry (William Joseph Shields) (1888–1961)

Irish-born character actor. Fitzgerald's heavy Irish accent typecast him as a good natured Irishman in dozens of Hollywood films. He is one of American cinema's best known character actors, often sharing billing with the nominal stars of the films he appeared in. He had prominent supporting roles in two *films noirs*. He played cops in both, with his role as a disillusioned, grizzled veteran in *The Naked City* being particularly outstanding. It is one of the finest performances in the genre.

Filmography: *The Naked City* (Universal, 1948). *Union Station* (Paramount, 1950).

Fitzgerald, Geraldine (1914–1990)

Irish-born actress. Fitzgerald was discovered in Ireland by Orson Welles. She appeared in a number of mostly indifferent films, but her performances were always intense and interesting. She was the female lead in two minor *films noirs*, the former directed by Robert Siodmak.

Filmography: *Uncle Harry* (Universal, 1945). *Nobody Lives Forever* (Warner Bros., 1946).

Fleischer, Richard (1916–)

Director. Richard Fleischer is the son of the great animator Max Fleischer (1889–1972), the creator of Popeye, Betty Boop, etc. Richard became a major talent in his own right, chiefly as a director of expansive entertainments. Early in his career, as a contract director at RKO, he directed several notable "B" movies including four *films noirs*. All are above average, with *Armored Car Robbery* and *The Narrow Margin* being particularly good. The former is a little known, but excellent, fast-paced caper film. The latter is equally fast-paced and is generally considered one of the best "B" *noirs*.

Filmography: *Bodyguard* (RKO, 1948). *Follow Me Quietly* (RKO, 1949). *Armored Car Robbery* (RKO, 1950). *The Narrow Margin* (RKO, 1952).

Fleming, Rhonda (Marilyn Louis) (1923–)

Actress and leading lady. A beautiful, very photogenic redhead, Rhonda Fleming was one of the early stars of technicolor productions. She co-starred in many costume epics in the late forties and early fifties, and was one of the most popular stars of her time. She also appeared as a variety of bad girls in

several *films noirs*. One of her most important appearances in the genre was in a supporting role as a *femme-fatale* in *Out of the Past*, in which she makes as great an impression in her small role as Jane Greer did as the leading *femme-fatale* in the *noir* classic.

Filmography: *The Spiral Staircase* (RKO, 1946). *Out of the Past* (RKO, 1947). *Cry Danger* (RKO, 1951). *The Killer Is Loose* (United Artists, 1956). *Slightly Scarlet* (RKO, 1956). *While The City Sleeps* (RKO, 1956).

Flippen, Jay C. (1898–1971)

Character actor. Large and bulky, Flippen played the usual range of small parts and supporting roles — cops, villainous sidekicks, sheriffs and politicians. He appeared in four *films noirs*, with a prominent role in *The Killing* as one of the doomed race-track robbers.

Filmography: *Brute Force* (Universal, 1947). *They Live by Night* (RKO, 1948). *The People Against O'Hara* (MGM, 1951). *The Killing* (United Artists, 1956).

Florey, Robert (1900–1979)

Director. Florey has been called the greatest of the French-gothic film directors and with good reason. He directed a handful of superior, low budget horror films including *Murders in the Rue Morgue* (Universal, 1932) and *The Beast with Five Fingers* (Warner Bros., 1946). Indeed, the French born Florey was certainly one of Hollywood's great "B" movie directors with many excellent films to his credit. Whatever the project, he brought to it a great sense of expressionist style and fluid camera movements. Although his two *films noirs* are minor, they are typical of Florey: dark, moody, and visually striking.

Filmography: *Danger Signal* (Warner Bros., 1945). *The Crooked Way* (United Artists, 1949).

Follow Me Quietly (RKO, 1949). 59 min.

Producer: Herman Schlom. Director:

Richard Fleischer. Screenplay: Lillie Hayward, story by Francis Rosenwald and Anthony Mann. Director of Photography: Robert De Grasse. Music: Leonid Raab. Art Directors: Albert S. D'Agostino and Walter E. Keller. Editor: Elmo Williams.

Cast: William Lundigan (Grant), Dorothy Patrick (Ann), Jeff Corey (Collins), Nestor Paiva (Benny), Charles D. Brown (Mulvaney). With: Paul Guilfoyle, Edwin Max, Frank Fergusson, Marlo Dwyer, Michael Brandon.

A detective, Grant, searches for a serial killer known as "the Judge." From scraps of evidence and a partial description of the murderer, Grant constructs a mannequin resembling the criminal to use as an aid in his painstaking hunt for the killer. More emblematic than convincing, the dummy nevertheless leads the police investigator to his quarry.

Follow Me Quietly is a typical "second feature"—the short feature that was shown before the main feature in an age of double bills. It is brisk and unpretentious, moving quickly and inevitably toward its predictable end. Richard Fleischer's direction manages to hold the film together, despite its ridiculous plot twists and brings to it a cold, dark look at city life and the criminal underworld.

Fonda, Henry (1905–1983)

Actor. Fonda's amiable personality was too good natured for the cynical, dark world of *film noir*. Yet, it was the very "innocent" qualities which Alfred Hitchcock was able to exploit in the marginally *noir*, *The Wrong Man*. Likewise, in Fritz Lang's *You Only Live Once*, a seminal *noir*, Fonda played an innocent man caught up in tragic circumstances. In the post-noir cop thriller *Madigan*, on the other hand, Fonda played a heroic police detective. He also starred in one minor, but interesting early RKO *noir*, *The Long Night*.

Filmography: *You Only Live Once* (United Artists, 1937). *The Long Night* (RKO, 1947). *The Wrong Man* (Warner Bros., 1956). *Madigan* (Universal, 1968).

Fontaine, Joan (Joan De Havilland) (1917–).

Actress. The younger sister of Olivia De Havilland, Joan Fontaine was typecast as the shy innocent in romantic melodramas of the late thirties and early forties. Probably her most convincing such role is in Alfred Hitchcock's *Suspicion*, as the wife who suspects her husband of being a murderer. However, her wholesome qualities did not make her a natural *noir* heroine (and certainly not a *femme-fatale*), but she did act in two other of the genre's titles. In *Kiss the Blood Off My Hands*, she plays a shy nurse who gets mixed up with a small time hood and ends up killing his black mailer. She also co-starred in Fritz Lang's last American film, *Beyond a Reasonable Doubt*.

Filmography: *Suspicion* (RKO, 1941). *Kiss the Blood Off My Hands* (Universal, 1948). *Beyond a Reasonable Doubt* (RKO, 1956).

Forbidden (Universal, 1954). 85 min.

Producer: Ted Richmond. Director: Rudolph Maté. Screenplay: William Sackheim and Gil Doud. Director of Photography: William Daniels. Music: Frank Skinner. Art Directors: Alexander Golitzen and Robert Boyle. Editor: Al Joseph.

Cast: Tony Curtis (Eddie Darrow), Joanne Dru (Christine Lawrence), Lyle Bettger (Justin Keit), Marvin Miller (Cliff Chalmer), Victor Sen Young (Allan). With: Peter J. Mamakos, Charles J. Conrad, Helen Marshall.

Eddie Darrow, down on his luck, takes on the assignment given to him by his boss, Justin Keit: go to Macao and bring back to the United States Christine Lawrence, the errant, runaway girlfriend of Keit, who also has incriminating evidence against the mobsters.

However, Darrow falls in love with his quarry and together, after much double crossing and violent confrontations, they manage to defeat the mobsters and end up in each other's arms.

Forbidden is a would-be hard-boiled *film noir* which does not live up to its pretentions. Its problems are two fold: the screenplay relies too heavily on clichés, and its performances are generally lackluster. Nevertheless, its exotic, foreign setting gives it some value as entertainment, and its direction, by *D.O.A.* director Rudolph Maté, is brisk and tight. Interestingly, its plot resembles Maté's *Second Chance* (RKO, 1952), a much more satisfying thriller.

Force of Evil (MGM, 1948). 88 min.
Producer: Bob Roberts. Director: Abraham Polonsky. Screenplay: Abraham Polonsky and Ira Wolfert, based on the novel *Tucker's People* by Ira Wolfert. Director of Photography: George Barnes. Music: David Raksin. Art Director: Richard Day. Editor: Art Seid.

Cast: John Garfield (Joe Morse), Beatrice Pearson (Doris Lowry), Thomas Gomez (Leo Morse), Howland Chamberlain (Freddy Baver), Roy Roberts (Ben Tucker), Marie Windsor (Edna Tucker). With: Paul McVey, Tim Ryan, Sid Tomak, Georgia Backus, Sheldon Leonard.

Joe Morse, a lawyer for a gambling syndicate, is inextricably bound to a set of ethics he does not fully understand. His fear of failure and overwhelming greed allow him to justify his defense of the rackets. His brother Leo runs a small bookie joint and will not relinquish his business to the mob. Joe tries to convince his brother to change his mind, but he stubbornly refuses. Eventually the situation is taken out of Joe's hands when Leo is murdered by the mob. Realizing what he has done, Joe tries to break up the syndicate and, although he partially succeeds, he too is destroyed in the process.

Force of Evil is one of *film noir*'s acknowledged masterpieces. It is, in fact, a political manifesto disguised by *noir* iconography and it works both as social criticism and serious drama.

Abraham Polonsky, the creative force behind the movie, was a Marxist who tried to combine political idealogy with entertainment and he was partially successful. He also was one of the most prominent victims of the McCarthy witch hunt and *Force of Evil* would prove to be his last film as a director for nearly thirty years.

The political message of the film is not overbearing. Indeed, the virtues of the film really lay with its excellent combination of direction, photography, music and performances.

While John Garfield is at his best in the film, Marie Windsor almost steals it in her pivotal role as a *femme-fatale* used by the mob to manipulate Garfield's character, Joe Morse, into accepting the destruction of his brother's organization. It is one of Windsor's early appearances in *film noir*, helping to establish her as one of the genre's greatest female icons.

Ford, Glenn (Gwylln Ford) (1916–)
Actor. Glenn Ford is certainly one of *film noir*'s most important actors. His gruff ordinariness was in contrast to the more glamorous stars of the era, helping to inject a sense of realism into the unreal world of Hollywood cinema in the forties and fifties.

After nearly a decade working as an actor at Columbia (mainly in "B" movies and as a second male lead in "A" productions), Ford shot to stardom in 1946 in the classic *film noir*, *Gilda*. Ford starred as Johnny Farrell, a gambler who works for the brilliant criminal Ballin Mundson. The role was injected with a strange sense of sexual ambiguity. The homosexual undertones of the two men's relationship has often been discussed by certain critics, but it is the overtly sexual attraction between Farrell and Rita Hayworth's *Gilda* which remains the most important theme of the film.

Ford's role in *Gilda*, as an essentially ordinary guy sucked into a maelstrom of conflicting emotions and loyalties by a *femme-fatale*, is also central to his roles in three other *noirs: Framed, Affair in Trinidad* and *The Big Heat.*

The Big Heat is one of the genre's greatest and best known films. Its influence on later police dramas was profound, as was Ford's role as an independent cop working on a case against all odds, including his own department's corruption. His role in *Gilda* and *The Big Heat* remain Ford's most important *noir* performances.

Glenn Ford was the right man at the right time, presenting the perfect image for the new genre, and he is one of *films noirs* greatest male icons.

Filmography: *Gilda* (Columbia, 1946). *Framed* (Columbia, 1947). *The Undercover Man* (Columbia, 1949). *Convicted* (Columbia, 1950). *Affair in Trinidad* (Columbia, 1952). *The Big Heat* (Columbia, 1953). *Human Desire* (Columbia, 1954). *Experiment in Terror* (Columbia, 1961).

Ford, Wallace (Samuel Grundy) (1897–1966)

Character actor. Ford was one of the most prominent American movie character actors for over three decades. He played both good and bad guys in dozens of films of various types. His *film noir* roles tend to be villainous roles in mostly "B" titles.

Filmography: *Beast of the City* (MGM, 1932). *Shadow of a Doubt* (Universal, 1943). *Crack-Up* (RKO, 1946). *Dead Reckoning* (Columbia, 1947). *T-Men* (Eagle-Lion, 1948). *The Set-Up* (RKO, 1949). *The Breaking Point* (Warner Bros., 1950). *He Ran All the Way* (United Artists, 1951).

Foreman, Carl (1914–1984)

Screenwriter. Foreman was one of the most consistently brilliant American screenwriters, writing many first rate films. He wrote the most cynical of the three great *noir* boxing films, *Champion*. Several of his other screenplays have *noir*-like elements.

Filmography: *Champion* (United Artists, 1949).

Foster, Dianne (Dianne Laruska) (1928–)

Actress. A sultry and dark haired beauty, the Canadian-born actress had a rather erratic film career, starring in a few unmemorable films beginning in the late forties. She was a memorable *femme-fatale* in the late *noir*, *Drive a Crooked Road*. Sadly, it was her only *noir* performance.

Filmography: *Drive a Crooked Road* (Columbia, 1954).

Foster, Jodie (1962–)

Actress. Foster's role as a kind of pre-pubescent *femme-fatale* in Martin Scorcese's film, *Taxi Driver* was shocking even in the contemporary American cinema. As the child prostitute whose mere existence leads a confused Vietnam veteran to take on the New York underworld made her into a star. Her performance still has the power to move the viewer.

Filmography: *Taxi Driver* (Universal, 1976).

Foster, Norman (1900–1976)

Director. Foster was originally an actor, starring on Broadway in the mid–twenties and many early sound features. He turned to film direction in 1936. Foster was essentially a "B" movie director working on only a handful of "A" productions. Among these is the early *film noir* classic, *Journey into Fear*. However, the film's virtues must be credited to its producer/co-writer/co-star, Orson Welles, who "ghost directed" many scenes. His two additional *films noirs* are minor.

Filmography: *Journey into Fear* (RKO, 1943). *Kiss the Blood Off My Hands* (Universal, 1948). *Woman on the Run* (Universal, 1950).

Foster, Preston (1901–1990)

Actor. The big, square-jawed Foster was one of the big movie stars of the 1930's, comparable in many ways to today's Arnold Schwarzenegger. He was a star of unpretentious action films. In his middle age, Foster settled easily into character roles, generally playing villains or big city bosses. He appeared in a handful of *film noirs*. In the low budget version of Mickey Spillane's *I, the Jury*, he played Pat Chambers, Mike Hammer's perennial cop friend. His best *noir* role, however, was in Phil Karlson's *Kansas City Confidential*, as an embittered retired cop who arranges an armored car robbery.

Filmography: *I Am a Fugitive from a Chain Gang* (Warner Bros., 1932). *Inside Job* (Universal, 1946). *Strange Triangle* (20th Century–Fox, 1946). *Kansas City Confidential* (United Artists, 1952). *I, the Jury* (United Artists, 1953).

Fourteen Hours (20th Century–Fox, 1951). 92 min.

Producer: Sol C. Siegel. Director: Henry Hathaway. Screenplay: John Paxton, based on an article by Joel Sayre. Director of Photography: Joe MacDonald. Music: Alfred Newman. Art Directors: Lyle Wheeler and Leland Fuller. Editor: Weldon Duncan.

Cast: Paul Douglas (Dunnigan), Richard Basehart (Robert Cosick), Barbara Bel Geddes (Virginia), Debra Paget (Ruth), Agnes Moorehead (Mrs. Cosick), Howard Da Silva (Lt. Moksar). With: Grace Kelly, Robert Keith, Jeffrey Hunter, Martin Gabel.

One of the best *films noirs* to use semi-documentary effects, *Fourteen Hours* is simply the story of a desperate, confused man, Robert Cosick, who stands on the ledge of a tall building threatening suicide, and the individuals who eventually convince him not to jump.

Screenwriter John Paxton—one of *film noir's* unsung heroes—based his taut, suspenseful screenplay on a real story giving it a typically happy Hollywood ending (the real story ended tragically). The performances are convincing and Henry Hathaway's direction manages to capture the paranoia inherent in the potential suicide victim's warped psychology.

Foy, Brian (1895–1977)

Producer. Foy was the eldest of the "seven little Foys" of vaudeville fame. Later, Foy ran the "B" unit at Warner Bros., and brought a sense of style and panache to the studio's low budget features. Few of the films he produced have stood the test of time, but many are quite memorable. His crime films are notable for their cynicism and extreme violence, as well as their rather campy wit.

Filmography: *Hollow Triumph* (Eagle-Lion, 1948). *I Was a Communist for the F.B.I.* (Warner Bros., 1951). *Crime Wave* (Warner Bros., 1954).

Framed (Columbia, 1947). 82 min.

Producer: Jules Schermer. Director: Richard Wallace. Screenplay: Ben Maddow, story by Jack Patrick. Director of Photography: Burnett Guffey. Music: Marlin Skiles. Art Director: Stephen Gooson. Editor: Richard Fantl.

Cast: Glenn Ford (Mike Lambert), Janis Carter (Paula Craig), Barry Sullivan (Stephen Price), Edgar Buchanan (Jeff Cunningham), Karen Morley (Mrs. Price). With: Jim Bannon, Sid Tomack, Barbara Woodell, Paul Burns.

Mike Lambert, a mining engineer down on his luck, takes work as a truck driver. He is seduced by Paula Craig to be used by her and her lover, Stephen Price, in a scheme to embezzle money from the local bank. Price, an employee of the bank, needs someone who looks something like him, to frame for the crime, and Lambert is that man. Unfortunately, the plan begins to unravel when Paula falls in love with Lambert.

After the theft is successfully carried out, Paula murders Price. However, realizing that Paula is a murderess, he traps her into incriminating herself.

Framed has some of the same qualities of James M. Cain's fiction, but without the substance. Janis Carter is a cheap imitation of Barbara Stanwyck's Phyllis Dietrichson, but she is appropriately alluring in a trashy way. Unfortunately, despite the appearance of Glenn Ford and Carter's performance, the film is rather flat.

Frankenheimer, John (1930–)

Director. Frankenheimer was a once promising director who never quite lived up to his early acclaim. He directed the superior late-*noir* classic, *The Manchurian Candidate*. His other significant contribution to the genre is *French Connection II*, a surprisingly bleak, despairing cop film.

Filmography: *The Manchurian Candidate* (United Artists, 1962). *French Connection II* (20th Century–Fox, 1975).

Fregonese, Hugo (1908–)

Director. Fregonese is probably the only Argentine director to achieve international success. Originally a journalist, he turned to film direction, making several successful films in Argentina before settling in the United States in the early fifties. He was a prominent director of "B" movies, including two *films noirs*.

Filmography: *One Way Street* (Universal, 1950). *Black Tuesday* (United Artists, 1954).

The French Connection (20th Century–Fox, 1971). 104 min.

Producer: Philip D'Antoni. Director: William Friedkin. Screenplay: Ernest Tidyman, based on a book by Robin Moore. Director of Photography: Owen Roizman. Music: Don Ellis. Art Director: Ben Kazaskon. Editor: Jerry Greenberg.

Cast: Gene Hackman (James "Popeye" Doyle), Fernando Rey (Alain Charnier), Roy Scheider (Buddy Russo), Tony Lo Bianco (Sal Boca), Marcel Bozzuffi (Pierre Nocoli), Frederic De Pasquale (Devereaux). With Bill Hickman, Ann Rebbot, Harold Gray, Arlene Farber, Eddie Egan.

New York narcotics detectives Popeye Doyle and Buddy Russo are investigating a narcotics shipment from France. The archcriminal, Charnier, personally undertakes the smuggling operation and targets Doyle and his partner. However, in the final confrontation, at Charnier's New York hideout, Doyle mistakenly shoots a fellow officer and Charnier gets away.

Although it is not a particularly striking film visually, *The French Connection* is important because of its updating of *noir* themes: the cop who, against all odds, fights against an ubiquitous, powerful syndicate. Furthermore, that he does not ultimately succeed is also in the *noir* tradition. With its sequel, *The French Connection*, is one of the most powerful examples of *film noir's* influence on contemporary film two decades after its artistic zenith.

French Connection II (20th Century–Fox, 1975). 113 min.

Producer: Robert L. Rosen. Director: John Frankenheimer. Screenplay: Alexander Jacobs, Robert Dillon and Lauri Dillon, story by Robert and Lauri Dillon. Director of Photography: Claude Renoir. Music: Don Ellis. Art Directors: Gerard Viard and Georges Clon. Editor: Tom Rolf.

Cast: Gene Hackman (James "Popeye" Doyle) Fernando Rey (Alain Charnier), Bernard Fresson (Barthelemy), Jean Pierre Castaldi (Raoul Diron), Charles Millot (Miletto). With: Cathleen Nesbitt, Pierre Collet, Alexandre Fabre.

Popeye Doyle takes his fight with the archcriminal/drug smuggler Charnier to France. With the help of the French police, he breaks up the Marseilles mob and succeeds in killing Charnier.

Unlike the original, which was based on real events, *French Connection II* is wholly imaginary. Its characterizations, however, are richer and Doyle emerges as a tougher, more impassioned revenge seeker. Likewise, Charnier is more like the typical *noir* "gentleman" criminal.

John Frankenheimer, the director of the late-*noir* classic, *The Manchurian Candidate* (United Artists, 1962), here creates a dark and compelling hard-boiled drama in the tradition of Phil Karlson and Sam Fuller. The film is *film noir*, but of a particularly modern type.

Freund, Karl (1890–1969)

Cinematographer. There is little question that the Czech-born Karl Freund is one of the most important cinematographers of his generation. Before he came to the United States in the early thirties, Freund made a name for himself in the thriving German film industry during the 1920's. He worked on a number of great German silent films including Fritz Lang's *Metropolis* (1926). Freund was instrumental in the development of expressionist techniques to popular German cinema and he brought those elements—dark, moody lighting, shadowy effects—to his American films. Interestingly, Freund was the director of photography on only two *films noirs*, both of which are excellent examples of his technique.

Filmography: *Undercurrent* (MGM, 1946). *Key Largo* (Warner Bros., 1949).

Friedhofer, Hugo (1902–1981)

Composer. A distinguished film composer, Friedhofer won an Academy Award for the William Wyler classic, *The Best Years of Our Lives* (Warner Bros., 1946). He also composed the music for a number of *films noirs* including the classic boxing *noir*, *Body and Soul*. His music is always appropriately dramatic, although rarely outstanding.

Filmography: *So Dark the Night* (Columbia, 1946). *Body and Soul* (United Artists, 1947). *Edge of Doom* (RKO, 1950). *Try and Get Me* (United Artists, 1950). *The Harder They Fall* (Columbia, 1956).

Friedkin, William (1939–)

Director. Like John Frankenheimer, William Friedkin is a director who never lived up to his early promise. He has proven to be little more than a commercial director with pretentions. However, one of his early successes, *The French Connection*, is one of the best films of its era, and it is generally considered to be one of the major crime films of the 1970's to carry on the traditions of *film noir*.

Filmography: *The French Connection* (20th Century-Fox, 1971).

Friedman, Seymour (1917–)

Director. Friedman was a contract director for Columbia. He was one of the studio's prolific "B" directors and few of his films rise above the merely mediocre. He also directed a single *film noir* for Lippert, one of the cheapest Hollywood studios operating in the 1950's.

Filmography: *Loan Shark* (Lippert, 1952).

The Friends of Eddie Coyle (Paramount, 1973). 102 min.

Producer: Charles McGuire. Director: Peter Yates. Screenplay: Paul Monash, based on the novel by George V. Higgins. Director of Photography: Victor J. Kemper. Music: Dave Gruson. Production Design: Gene Callaghan. Editor: Pat Jaffe.

Cast: Robert Mitchum (Eddie Coyle), Peter Boyle (Dillon), Richard Jordan (Dave Foley), Steven Keats (Jackie), Alex Rocco (Scalise), Joe Santos (Artie Van). With: Mitchell Ryan, Peter Maclean, Kevin O'Morrison, Marvin Litchterman, Carolyn Pickman.

Eddie Coyle is out on bail, facing life in prison as a three time loser if convicted on the latest charges against him.

While continuing to transport stolen goods for the mob, Coyle also begins to inform to the police, hoping to plea bargain. Both sides manipulate him. Eventually the mob puts a contract out on Coyle. His assassin treats him to one last night on the town before killing him and leaving his body in an abandoned car.

This movie is another important post-*noir*. *The Friends of Eddie Coyle* is known chiefly for its *noir* characterizations and it also has a link with the past because of Robert Mitchum's inclusion; but like many contemporary *noirs*, it suffers from self awareness and thus comes off as pretentious.

Frings, Ketti (1909-1981)

Novelist and screenwriter. Besides two excellent *noir* screenplays, Frings wrote the original novel, *Hold Back the Dawn* which was adapted by Charles Brackett and Billy Wilder and turned into one of the classic films of the early forties. Both *The Accused* and *The File on Thelma Jordan* are written from a woman's perspective, a unique approach for *film noir*.

Filmography: *The Accused* (Paramount, 1949). *Dark City* (Paramount, 1950). *The File on Thelma Jordan* (Paramount, 1950).

Fuchs, Daniel (   )

Screenwriter. Fuchs was mainly a writer of low budget thrillers. He worked on a number of *films noirs* which vary in quality, but at their best are very innovative and surprisingly mature. *Criss Cross* and *Panic in the Streets* are his best *noir* screenplays. The latter, with its story about the search for a group of criminals unknowingly carrying bubonic plague, is one of *noir's* unique plot devices. All of Fuch's screenplays are distinguished by hardboiled dialog and strong characterizations.

Filmography: *The Gangster* (Allied Artists, 1947). *Hollow Triumph* (Eagle-Lion, 1948). *Criss Cross* (Universal,

1949). *Panic in the Streets* (20th Century-Fox, 1950). *Storm Warning* (Warner Bros., 1950). *The Human Jungle* (Allied Artists, 1954).

Fuller, Leland (1899-1967)

Art director. Like so many of cinema's great art directors, Leland Fuller began his career as an architect. One of 20th Century-Fox's major talents, he worked closely with Otto Preminger on several of the director's important films of the forties. He designed the sets for *Laura*, Preminger's most important *film noir*. He was particularly adept at transforming small sets and obvious studio settings into interesting visual metaphors.

Filmography: *Laura* (20th Century-Fox, 1944) *Fallen Angel* (20th Century-Fox, 1946). *The Dark Corner* (20th Century-Fox, 1946). *Shock* (20th Century-Fox, 1946). *Whirlpool* (20th Century-Fox, 1950). *Fourteen Hours* (20th Century-Fox, 1951).

Fuller, Samuel (1911-   )

Director. Fuller might well be the greatest "B" movie director. He made a conscious decision early in his career to work in low budget features because of the relative freedom it provided him. He used that freedom to create some of the most inventive and personal of all American commercial films. He excelled at the crime genres and his *films noirs* are visceral, violent and unsentimental.

Fuller's characters are driven by subconscious motives and obsessions with wealth, success and sex. They do not do things because they want to or have given much thought to them, they do them because they simply have to.

Fuller's first *film noir* was *Pickup on South Street*, a relatively big budget thriller about communist spies and the search for valuable classified microfilm. The movie is brilliantly written and directed by Fuller (who almost always wrote or co-wrote his own scenarios) in his typically brisk, hard-boiled style. Its cinematography, by Joe MacDonald,

Richard Widmark, Thelma Ritter in *Pickup on South Street* **(20th Century-Fox, 1953).**

is inventive and it contains excellent performances by Richard Widmark and Jean Peters.

Fuller's color *noir, House of Bamboo*, is an unpretentious, violent mystery full of action and staccato, campy dialog in the usual Fuller style.

In the early 1960's, Fuller made three unique *films noirs* which have undergone considerable critical analysis. All three display the psychological depths of his stories and characters (an element generally overlooked in Fuller's other films), and despite their modest budgets, each is characterized by a flamboyant visual style.

The single thematic element which seems to link all of Fuller's *film noir* characters is their unabashed sexuality.

Beginning with Jean Peters in *Pickup on South Street* to Constance Cummings in *The Naked Kiss*, the females in Fuller's *noirs* are tramps, but tramps with intelligence. However, Fuller does not resort to the clichés of the genre and his male characters are not only rarely smart, but the women often treat them as manipulatable fools.

Sam Fuller is a unique artist, vastly underrated by American critics. He is one of late-*noirs* greatest talents and his films remain powerful, evocative testaments of the American underworld.

Filmography: *Pickup on South Street* (wrote and directed) (20th Century-Fox, 1953). *House of Bamboo* (co-wrote and directed) (20th Century-Fox,

1955). *The Crimson Kimono* (wrote, directed, produced (Columbia, 1959). *Underworld U.S.A.* (wrote, directed, produced) (Columbia, 1961). *Shock Corridor* (wrote, directed, produced) (Allied Artists, 1963). *The Naked Kiss* (wrote, directed, produced) (Allied Artists, 1964).

Furthman, Charles (1891–1972)

Screenwriter. The younger brother of the important screenwriter Jules Furthman, Charles worked intermittently in Hollywood from the late twenties. He contributed to a number of gangster films in the late twenties and early thirties, the most important being Josef Von Sterberg's *Underworld*, a film that showed the way to the gangster genre and *film noir*.

Filmography: *Underworld* (Paramount, 1927).

Furthman, Jules (1888–1966)

Screenwriter. Jules Furthman was one of the great screenwriters of Hollywood's golden age. He specialized in romantic melodramas and action-adventures set in exotic locales. He co-wrote most of Josef Von Sternberg's great films including *Morocco* (Paramount, 1930), *Shanghai Express* (Paramount, 1932) and *Blonde Venus* (Paramount, 1932). His uncredited collaborator was often Howard Hawks and it was for Hawks that Furthman wrote the majority of his important screenplays. Two of three *films noirs* were directed by these two notable directors: Hawks directed *The Big Sleep* and Von Sternberg directed *The Shanghai Gesture*.

Filmography: *The Shanghai Gesture* (United Artists, 1941). *The Big Sleep* (Warner Bros., 1946). *Nightmare Alley* (20th Century-Fox, 1947).

Fury (MGM, 1936). 90 min.

Producer: Joseph L. Mankiewicz. Director: Fritz Lang. Screenplay: Bartlett Cormack and Fritz Lang, based on the short story "Mob Rule" by Norman Krasna. Director of Photography: Joseph Ruttenberg. Music: Franz Waxman. Art Directors: Cedric Gibbons, William A. Horning and Edwin B. Willis. Editor: Frank Sullivan.

Cast: Spencer Tracy (Joe Wheeler), Sylvia Sydney (Catherine Grant), Walter Abel (District Attorney), Edward Ellis (Sheriff), Walter Brennan (Buggs Myers), Bruce Cabot (Bubbles Dawson). With: George Walcott, Frank Albertson, Arthur Stone, Morgan Wallace.

Fritz Lang's existential thriller about a man falsely accused of kidnapping is one of the most important early *films noirs*. Spencer Tracy stars as Joe Wheeler, a man who, while travelling to meet his girl friend, stops in a small town and is instantly accused of being a notorious kidnapper. Housed in the local jail and protected by the sheriff, Wheeler nevertheless becomes the target of the town's mindless rage. The jailhouse is burned down, but Wheeler secretly escapes. Violently angry, he allows over twenty of the town's citizens to be sentenced to long jail terms for his vigilante "murder" before stepping forward.

Fury was Fritz Lang's first American film, and it set the standard he would follow for the rest of his career. The social criticism is more obvious in this film than his later *films noirs* and Lang's liberal political ideals were always an important ingredient of his subsequent melodramas. More importantly, one first encounters the true *noir* protagonist in this film in the guise of Joe Wheeler. Likewise, the expressionist visual influences are more evident here than in any other 1930's crime film.

Fury, however, was too "hot" for a studio like MGM (who had wooed and signed the great director) and despite some enormous critical praise and box-office success, Lang's contract was terminated. From then on he was an independent filmmaker, making his films at whatever studio would finance the project at hand and there were many more classics to come from this director.

Gambling House (RKO, 1951). 80 min.
Producer: Warren Duff. Director: Ted Tetzlaff. Screenplay: Marvin Borowsky and Allen Rivkin. Director of Photography: Harry J. Wild. Music: Roy Webb. Art Directors: Albert S. D'Agostino and Jack Okey. Editor: Sherman Todd.

Cast: Victor Mature (Marc Fury), Terry Moore (Lynn Warren), William Bendix (Joe Farrow), Cleo Moore (Sally), Zachary Charles (Willie). With: Ann Doran, Basil Ruysdale, Donald Randolph, Damian O'Flynn.

Marc Fury, a foreign born gambler, has never bothered to take out naturalization papers and finds himself facing deportation when his status is revealed during a murder trial. Lynn Warren, a pretty social worker who falls in love with him, convinces Marc to fight a big time underworld boss, Joe Farrow, thus allowing him to remain in the country.

Gambling House is a variation on the old "reformation of the gangster" plot that dates back to the silent era. It is a minor *film noir* notable chiefly for its director, Ted Tetzlaff, and star, *noir* icon Victor Mature. However, it suffers from an improbable screenplay.

The Gangster (Allied Artists, 1947). 84 min.
Producers: Maurice and Frank King. Director: Gordon Wiles. Screenplay: Daniel Fuchs, based on his novel *Low Company*. Director of Photography: Paul Ivano. Music: Louis Gruenberg. Song: "Paradise" by Gordon Clifford and Nacio Herb Brown. Art Director: F. Paul Sylos. Editor: Walter Thompson.

Cast: Barry Sullivan (Shubunka), Belita (Nancy Starr), Joan Loring (Dorothy), Akim Tamiroff (Nick Jammey), Henry Morgan (Shorty), John Ireland (Karty). With: Fifi D'Orsay, Virginia Christine, Sheldon Leonard, Leif Erickson, Charles McGraw, Elisha Cook, Jr.

Shubunka, a neurotic gangster, is at a crossroads in his life. He is fighting a series of losing battles, chiefly with his main rival, Cornell. Shubunka is giving all of his attention to his mistress, Nancy, about who he is intensely jealous. A gambler who owes him money sells him out to Cornell, setting the stage for his demise. After alienating Nancy in an argument, Shubunka is shot down by Cornell's paid assassins on a rainy street.

An excellent low budget *film noir*, with little thematic connection to the gangster genre of the 1930's. This film is not an exposé of the criminal underworld, but rather the study of a gangster and his failure as a man. Indeed, the film is morally neutral. Shubunka succumbs to his own corruption, and he is replaced by a man who is equally corrupt.

Technically, the film seems like a cheap art film, with some flamboyant moments. Its style is typical of the era: smoky, claustrophobic rooms and rainy streets.

Gardner, Ava (1922-1989)
Actress. Ava Gardner was often described as one of the world's most beautiful women and she was certainly one of the most photogenic women in American film after World War II. Her dark black hair, ivory skin, and big expressive eyes made her one of the most exotic and sensual stars of her time. Whatever her abilities as an actress, she was always the focus of attention in whatever scene she appeared in.

Interestingly, Gardner appeared in only three *films noirs*. Although she was adequate in *Singapore* and *The Bribe*, adding an exotic allure to dull films, she was one of *noir's* most striking *femme-fatales* in *The Killers*. As the sultry, corrupt Kitty Collins, she helps lead the Swede (Burt Lancaster) to his death.

Filmography: *The Killers* (Universal, 1946). *Singapore* (Universal, 1947). *The Bribe* (MGM, 1949).

Garfield, John (Julius Garfinkle) (1913–1952)

Actor. Garfield was one of the most extraordinary, visceral actors of his time. He was one of the first Method actors to achieve success in film, opening the way for the more self-conscious styles of Marlon Brando and James Dean.

Off camera, Garfield was a proletarian radical, a member of communist-related organizations and a defiant loner. After making an impression as a member of New York's Group Theatre (which also promoted the career of playwright Clifford Odets among others), Garfield was lured to Hollywood in the late thirties. He spent the first several years of his film career playing juvenile roles and second leads before his strong, individual personality struck a chord with audiences in the 1940's. With Glenn Ford, Robert Mitchum, Burt Lancaster and Kirk Douglas, Garfield became one of *film noir*'s greatest icons and, like them, is identified almost exclusively with the genre.

Garfield's first appearance in *film noir* was in the classic, *The Postman Always Rings Twice*. His powerful and unsentimental performance as drifter Frank Chambers brought life to the character and his scenes with Lana Turner, although not explicit by contemporary standards, are some of the most erotic of that era.

Garfield's performance as the doomed boxer Charlie Davis in the archetypal boxing *noir*, *Body and Soul* is equally compelling.

Probably one of Garfield's best performances, in *film noir* and otherwise, was in Abraham Polonsky's *Force of Evil*. The theme of exploited working people and people who sell out their ideals must have been close to Garfield's heart and he is particularly memorable

as the mob's lawyer who allows the destruction of his brother.

Garfield's last *noir* showing was also his last film, *He Ran All the Way*. Garfield stars as a psychotic criminal who takes refuge with a sympathetic family.

Unfortunately, John Garfield died of a heart attack shortly thereafter, brought on, in part, by the pressures of the House Unamerican Activities Commission's investigation of "communist infiltration" of Hollywood. At thirty-nine he was at the height of his creative talents and it is tempting to think of what he might have achieved if he had continued to live and work. As it is, he remains one of *film noir*'s most important actors.

Filmography: *Nobody Lives Forever* (Warner Bros., 1946). *The Postman Always Rings Twice* (MGM, 1946). *Body and Soul* (United Artists, 1947). *Force of Evil* (MGM, 1948). *The Breaking Point* (Warner Bros., 1950). *He Ran All the Way* (United Artists, 1951).

The Garment Jungle (Columbia, 1957). 88 min.

Producer: Henry Kleiner. Director: Vincent Sherman (uncredited co-director, Robert Aldrich). Screenplay: Harry Kleiner, based on a series of articles by Lester Velie. Director of Photography: Joseph Biroc. Music: Leith Stevens. Art Director: Robert A. Peterson. Editor: William Lyon.

Cast: Lee J. Cobb (Walter Mitchell), Kerwin Matthews (Alan Mitchell), Gia Scala (Theresa Renata), Richard Boone (Artie Ravidge), Valerie French (Lee Hackett). With: Robert Loggia, Joseph Wiseman, Adam Williams, Harold J. Stone, Wesley Addy.

When Korean war veteran Alan Mitchell returns to the United States, he joins his father's New York garment business. His father Walter does not want his shop organized by the union, but Alan supports the union. Alan learns that his father is paying off a local racketeer, Artie Ravidge, to help keep out the union. Alan secretly infiltrates the mob, but his interference results in his father's murder by the racketeers. With the help of Lee Hackett, an associate with whom he is having an affair and who has mob connections, Alan eventually manages to break up the anti-union racket.

Director Robert Aldrich was fired midway through the production of the film, and it was completed by Vincent Sherman who received sole credit. However, the film has the feel of a Robert Aldrich *film noir*, with its strong social theme and hard-boiled, unsentimental style. Indeed, it is Vincent Sherman's best *film noir*, but obviously much of the credit for the film's aesthetic success must be given to Aldrich.

Made near the end of the *noir* cycle, *The Garment Jungle* contains many of the genre's key themes. Among these is the returning, disillusioned war veteran. He is back from the conflict in Korea only to discover a wholly corrupt system, the system he was sent to fight to protect!

In the end, in typical *noir* fashion, Alan Mitchell succumbs to the corruption in a subtle way. The final scenes of him busily at work in his father's office suggest that he has inherited his father's workaholic, callous ways, and like his father, is headed irrevocably on the road to his own self destruction.

Garmes, Lee (1897–1978)

Cinematographer. Garmes is one of cinema's greatest cinematographers. A veteran of silent movies, Garmes was a master of low-key, highly dramatic lighting. He is probably best remembered for his collaborations with director Josef Von Sternberg in the early thirties. Their films reached new heights in black and white cinematography and had a profound influence on world cinema, particularly *film noir* a decade and a half later.

Of his *films noirs*, probably the best is the Max Ophuls directed *Caught*,

which demonstrated his talents at their extravagant best, but all of his *noir* titles are worthy of acclaim. In each, his photography and complicated, expressionist lighting schemes perfectly captured the claustrophobic, brooding tales.

Filmography: *Nightmare Alley* (20th Century–Fox, 1947). *Caught* (MGM, 1949). *The Detective Story* (Paramount, 1951). *Captive City* (United Artists, 1952). *The Desperate Hours* (Paramount, 1955).

Garnett, Tay (1894–1977)

Director. Although almost completely forgotten today, Tay Garnett was one of the must successful American film directors of the 1930's and 1940's. He specialized in low budget, high quality action pictures, many with exotic settings. Many of these films, while enjoyable, are not particularly memorable, but his war film, *Bataan* (MGM, 1943) is an underrated classic.

However, Garnett's masterpiece is unquestionably *The Postman Always Rings Twice*. His work is superb, despite his bouts with debilitating alcoholism which often hampered production.

Unfortunately, Garnett's career went into a rapid decline a few short years later. One of his last major productions was the *film noir*, *Cause for Alarm*, a minor title.

Whatever his other achievements, Tay Garnett will be forever remembered as the director of *The Postman Always Rings Twice*, one of the genre's greatest films.

Filmography: *The Postman Always Rings Twice* (MGM, 1946). *Cause for Alarm* (MGM, 1951).

Garrett, Oliver H. P. (1897–1952)

Screenwriter. Garrett co-wrote many popular dramas beginning in the mid thirties. He contributed to a single *film noir*, *Dead Reckoning*, which provided Humphrey Bogart and Lizabeth Scott with their best *noir* roles.

Filmography: *Dead Reckoning* (Columbia, 1947).

Gershenson, Joseph (1904–)

Composer. Gershenson was head of Universal's music department from 1941. He contributed scores to many movies including three *films noirs*, but he did not have a particularly distinctive style.

Filmography: *Shakedown* (Universal, 1950). *Appointment with a Shadow* (Universal, 1951). *The Naked Alibi* (Universal, 1954).

Gibbons, Cedric (1893–1960)

Art director. One of the legendary figures from Hollywood's golden age, Cedric Gibbons was the arbiter of style and extravagant taste as the head of production design for MGM from 1924 to 1956. He was one of the major influences of MGM's glittering, art deco style. Nominated for thirty-seven Academy Awards, he won eleven.

Like most of the heads of the art departments of the major studios, Gibbons actually delegated his responsibilities to his associates. Although it is debatable how much work he did on each of the over one thousand films he received credit on, there is no question about his influence on the look of MGM's productions, while head of design for the studio. He worked on nearly twenty *films noirs* and each is a reflection of his style at its best. Although at first it might seem alien to the gritty milieu of *film noir*, his style was surprisingly adaptable.

Filmography: *Fury* (MGM, 1936). *Johnny Eager* (MGM, 1942). *Bewitched* (MGM, 1945). *The Postman Always Rings Twice* (MGM, 1946). *Undercurrent* (MGM, 1946). *The High Wall* (MGM, 1947). *Lady in the Lake* (MGM, 1947). *The Bribe* (MGM, 1949). *Scene of the Crime* (MGM, 1949). *The Asphalt Jungle* (MGM, 1950). *Jeopardy* (MGM, 1950). *A Lady Without Passport* (MGM, 1950). *Mystery Street* (MGM, 1950). *Side Street* (MGM, 1950).

Tension (MGM, 1950). *The People Against O'Hara* (MGM, 1951). *The Strip* (MGM, 1951). *The Unknown Man* (MGM, 1951). *Talk About a Stranger* (MGM, 1952). *Rogue Cop* (MGM, 1954).

Gilbert, Herschel Burke ( )

Composer. Gilbert was particularly active in the 1950's, mainly as a composer for independent productions. He composed the scores for Fritz Lang's last two American films, *Beyond a Reasonable Doubt* and *While the City Sleeps*, as well as three other *films noirs*.

Filmography: *The Thief* (United Artists, 1952). *Witness to Murder* (United Artists, 1952). *Beyond a Reasonable Doubt* (RKO, 1956). *Nightmare* (United Artists, 1956). *While the City Sleeps* (RKO, 1956).

Gilda (Columbia, 1946). 110 min.

Producer: Virginia Van Upp. Director: Charles Vidor. Screenplay: Marion Parsonnet, adapted by Jo Eisenger from a story by E. A. Ellington. Director of Photography: Rudolph Maté. Music: Morris Stoloff. Songs: "Put the Blame on Mame" and "Amado Mio" by Doris Fisher and Allan Roberts. Art Directors: Stephen Goosson and Van Nest Polglase. Editor: Charles Nelson.

Cast: Rita Hayworth (Gilda), Glenn Ford (Johnny Farrell), George Macready (Ballin Mundsen), Joseph Calleia (Obregon), Steven Geray (Uncle Rio), Joe Sawyer (Casey), Gerald Mohr (Captain Delgado). With: Robert Scott, Lionel Royce, S. Z. Martel.

One of *film noir*'s best known titles, *Gilda* certainly contains some of the genre's most familiar scenes: Rita Hayworth's sensual strip tease in a slinky, black dress for example.

The film opens at night when Johnny Farrell, an American gambling hustler, is attacked on a Buenos Aires waterfront by a group of toughs who have discovered his loaded dice. He is rescued by the debonair Ballin Mundsen.

Gilda (Rita Hayworth) strips to the sultry strains of "Put the Blame on Mame" in *Gilda* (Columbia, 1946).

Mundsen is impressed by Farrell's daring and insouciant manner and hires him to manage his nightclub and casino establishment.

Everything is okay until Gilda, Mundsen's new wife, arrives. Unknown to Mundsen, Gilda and Johnny were once lovers. Mundsen makes Farrell

follow the amoral, sexually flirtatious Gilda to make sure she does not stray. Gilda teases Farrell by doing a strip tease to the sensual jazz tune, "Put the Blame on Mame."

Mundsen, meanwhile, is fronting for a Nazi-controlled cartel. When he kills a man in an argument, he rushes home only to find Gilda and Johnny in an embrace and although they are fighting, Mundsen believes they are having an affair. He rushes to his private plane, but crashes into the ocean on take off.

Gilda, upset, leaves Buenos Aires, and Johnny inherits the nightclub. With his newly acquired wealth, he woos Gilda back. However, Ballin Mundsen suddenly reappears, having faked his death. He wants to go back to the way things were, but neither Gilda nor Johnny is willing to change. In the final confrontation, Ballin is shot by the nightclub janitor who prefers Johnny Farrell as his boss, and Johnny and Gilda are permanently reunited.

Gilda was a fortuitous combination of talents — a case of literally being in the right place at the right time. The seemingly disparate elements came together to create one of Hollywood's best remembered films. It is certainly Charles Vidor's best film and arguably it contains the best work of Rita Hayworth, Glenn Ford, George Macready and of cinematographer Rudolph Maté (who, as a director, would make several notable *films noirs*), as well as production designer Stephen Goosson.

Gilda is certainly one of the most sensual films of the genre. While some critics have pointed out the homosexual undercurrents of the relationship between Ballin Mundsen and Johnny Farrell, the film remains sexless until Gilda's arrival. Gilda's presence gives an extra charge to the film and Rita Hayworth is constantly shown in revealing dresses and lingerie.

Gilda is one of the most interesting *femme-fatales* in *film noir*. Her affairs lead to death and destruction, but ultimately she is a "good girl" and her love redeems Johnny Farrell.

George Macready and Glenn Ford played more conventional *noir* roles. Macready's Ballin Mundsen, the elegant, but decadent man of corruption, is a familiar character from early *film noir*.

Gilda demonstrates the height of studio film making. It remains Charles

Vidor's masterpiece and one of the great films of the genre.

Gillie, Jean (1915–1949)

Actress. The British born Jean Gillie was a very attractive, talented actress and in the thirties, a major light leading lady in her native country. She moved to the United States in the late forties, but her promising career was cut short by a fatal illness. She made a striking appearance as a particularly deadly *femme-fatale* in the low budget *Decoy*, her single *film noir*.

Filmography: *Decoy* (Monogram, 1946).

Glasgow, William (1906–1972)

Art director. One of Robert Aldrich's right-hand men in the early fifties, Glasgow worked on several of the great director's early films, including three *films noirs*.

Filmography: *World for Ransom* (Allied Artists, 1954). *Kiss Me Deadly* (Allied Artists, 1955). *The Big Knife* (United Artists, 1956).

The Glass Key (Paramount, 1942). 85 min.

Executive Producer: B. G. DeSylva. Director: Stuart Heisler. Screenplay: Jonathan Latimer, based on the novel by Dashiell Hammett. Director of Photography: Theodore Sparkuhl. Music: Victor Young. Art Directors: Hans Dreier and Haldane Douglas. Editor: Archie Marshek.

Cast: Brian Donlevy (Paul Madvig), Veronica Lake (Janet Henry), Alan Ladd (Ed Beaumont), Bonita Granville (Opal Madvig), Joseph Calleia (Nick Varna), Moroni Olsen (Senator Henry). With: Richard Denning, William Bendix, Margaret Heyes, George Meador.

Ed Beaumont is the loyal lieutenant of political boss Paul Madvig. He is upset when Madvig supports Senator Henry, a "reform candidate." Ed believes that the Senator and his beautiful daughter, Janet, are using Madvig for their own gains.

Senator Henry's son is having an affair with Paul's sister, Opal Madvig, and when the son is murdered, Paul Madvig is naturally implicated. Believing it is a frame-up by Paul's enemies, Beaumont infiltrates Nick Varna's gang, but is beaten up when discovered.

Meanwhile, Janet Henry, mistress and fiancée of Madvig, has fallen for Beaumont. Even though Ed Beaumont is interested in her, he is loyal to his boss and does not return her affections. Eventually, he comes to believe that Senator Henry is the real killer. He has Janet arrested, hoping to force a confession out of the Senator, and it works. The Senator admits that he killed his son after an argument and in fact, Paul Madvig, who was a witness to the crime, helped cover it up.

Ed and Janet are at last free to pursue their mutual fascination with one another.

A seminal *film noir*, *The Glass Key* is important chiefly because it was the film which first teamed Alan Ladd and Veronica Lake, catapulting them to stardom. They would become *noir*'s most famous romantic team in the next several years.

The film is based on a novel by Dashiell Hammett, one of the key American novelists whose work helped establish *noir* themes and characters. Indeed, in many ways, the character's interrelations resemble those in *Gilda*, and as in the later classic, the film is full of sexual ambiguities and masochistic characters.

Although not as extravagant or as inventive as the cinematography in later *noir*, Theodore Sparkuhl's photography for *The Glass Key* is also important as a break with the "natural," flat lighting of 1930's thrillers.

Glennon, Bert (1893–1967)

Cinematographer. A distinguished cinematographer, Glennon's career began in 1916. He is associated mainly with large scale epics and his collaborations with John Ford. His style was generally straight forward and unobtrusive and thus best suited to conventional dramas. However, he was the cinematographer for Josef Von Sternberg's *Underworld*, a seminal film which had a profound influence on both the emerging gangster genre, and the later *film noir*.

Filmography: *Underworld* (Paramount, 1927). *Red Light* (United Artists, 1941). *Crimewave* (Warner Bros., 1954).

Godfrey, Peter (1899–1970)

Director. Godfrey was a successful British stage actor and producer who began directing movies in the late 1930's. He worked mostly in Hollywood and directed a single *film noir*, *The Two Mrs. Carrolls* which provided Humphrey Bogart and Barbara Stanwyck with two good roles. Most of Godfrey's other films are routine "B" productions.

Filmography: *The Two Mrs. Carrolls* (Warner Bros., 1947).

Goldsmith, Martin M. (1917–1984)

Screenwriter. Goldsmith was a writer of low budget melodramas. He co-wrote four *films noirs*, including the legendary *Detour* and *The Narrow Margin*. The former is known for its relentless pessimism, while the latter is an action oriented *noir* with a well conceived plot and brilliant dialog.

Filmography: *Detour* (co-wrote) (PRC, 1945). *Blindspot* (co-wrote) (Columbia, 1947). *Shakedown* (co-wrote) (Universal, 1950). *The Narrow Margin* (co-wrote) (RKO, 1952).

Golitzen, Alexander (1907–)

Art director. The Russian born Alexander Golitzen is one of the most important, if neglected, art directors in American film history. He began his film career at MGM in the mid thirties after immigrating to the United States. Originally an illustrator, he soon graduated to production design, but he achieved his greatest success after moving to Universal in the forties. He was

Tom Neal in *Detour* (PRC, 1945).

the art director for many important productions during and after this decade, including several memorable late *noirs*, and the important post-*noir* police thriller, *Madigan*, directed by Don Siegel.

Filmography: *Scarlet Street* (Universal, 1945). *Forbidden* (Universal, 1954). *Female on the Beach* (Universal, 1955). *The Night Runner* (Universal, 1957). *The Tattered Dress* (Universal, 1957). *Touch of Evil* (Universal, 1958). *Cape Fear* (Universal, 1962). *Madigan* (Universal, 1968).

Gomez, Thomas (1905–1971)

Character actor. Gomez was a familiar face in American films in the forties and fifties. Bulky, balding and with a thick moustache, Gomez could play either menacing villains or average businessmen. He performed the usual range of supporting roles, and a few somewhat bigger parts. He appeared in six *films noirs*. His most prominent role in the genre was in the classic *Force of Evil*, as a small time bookie betrayed by his younger brother.

Filmography: *Phantom Lady* (Universal, 1944). *Johnny O'Clock* (Columbia, 1947). *Ride the Pink Horse* (Universal, 1947). *Force of Evil* (MGM, 1948). *The Breaking Point* (Warner Bros., 1950). *He Ran All the Way* (United Artists, 1951).

Goodis, David (1923–1974)

Novelist and screenwriter. Goodis was a mysterious figure with a reclusive personality not unlike Cornell Woolrich. His novels were successful and he wrote a number of screenplays, yet he rarely left his home in New England where he lived with his elderly mother. Goodis is best known for his influential crime novels which eschewed action and linear plot for character development and existential themes. His most important novel was *Dark Passage*, made into a memorable film by Delmer Daves. The film is a faithful adaption of Goodis' novel and is typical of his work.

Filmography: *Dark Passage* (based on his novel) (Warner Bros., 1947). *The Unfaithful* (screenplay) (Warner Bros., 1947). *The Burglar* (based on his novel) (Columbia, 1957). *Nightfall* (based on his novel) (Columbia, 1957).

Goodman, John B. (1901–1976)

Art director. Goodman worked at Universal in the 1940's, where he often collaborated with Alexander Golitzen. He worked on a single *film noir*.

Filmography: *Shadow of a Doubt* (Universal, 1943).

Goosson, Stephen (1889–1973)

Art director. After a short apprenticeship as a free lance designer, Goosson joined Columbia in the early thirties where he remained for the rest of his career. Despite restricted budgets, Goosson managed to create an interesting style based on expressionist theatre effects and art deco. He is associated mainly with the films of Frank Capra, but he excelled at whatever genre he worked in. His three prominent *films noirs* are all masterpieces of film production design: *Gilda*, *Dead Reckoning*, and *The Lady from Shanghai*. The former is famous for its nightclub interiors and recreations of an exotic semi-tropical locale. The latter is famous mainly for its final sequences, set in a deserted amusement park and house of mirrors.

Filmography: *Gilda* (Columbia, 1946). *Dead Reckoning* (Columbia, 1947). *Framed* (Columbia, 1947). *Johnny O'Clock* (Columbia, 1947). *The Lady from Shanghai* (Columbia, 1948).

Gordon, Michael (1909–)

Director. Gordon was an adaptable commercial director who cheerfully took on whatever assignment came his way. His single *film noir*, *The Web*, is an excellent low budget thriller which contains one of Edmond O'Brien's best performances.

Filmography: *The Web* (Universal, 1947).

Goulding, Edmund (1891–1959)

Director. For two decades, Edmund Goulding was one of Hollywood's top directors, making a series of excellent, entertaining films with great style. Several of his films are acknowledged classics — *Grand Hotel* (MGM, 1932) and *Dark Victory* (Warner Bros., 1939) — but Goulding is probably the least appreciated of the major directors of Hollywood's golden age. Like George Cukor, Goulding was an expert at "women's pictures," films dominated by their female stars, but he was also an expert handler of male dominated action pictures. His single *film noir* is very well made, a minor classic of the genre.

Filmography: *Nightmare Alley* (20th Century–Fox, 1947).

Grahame, Gloria (Gloria Hallward) (1925–1981)

Actress. Gloria Grahame is one of the most unusual of *film noir*'s great female icons. Unconventionally sensual, with fair hair, wide-eyes and distinctive bee-stung lips, Grahame specialized in ambiguous characters: her characters might well be dangerous, but they were also vulnerable. Her single *femme-fatale* was in Fritz Lang's *Human Desire*, but she inhabited the character with such ferocity that it remains one of *noir*'s truly great performances, although the film is somewhat disappointing. Even though she appeared in a variety of genres, she is identified almost exclusively with *film noir*, such was her impact in these films.

Gloria Grahame's *noir* career began with a small, but prominent role in *Crossfire*. Although her screen time was minimal, she made an impact with the critics and somehow manages to hold her own in a film dominated by strong male leads.

She was equally impressive as a second female lead in *Macao*, and opposite Humphrey Bogart in the Nicholas Ray classic, *In a Lonely Place*.

Grahame's greatest performances were in the two films directed by Fritz Lang: *The Big Heat* and *Human Desire*. In both, she displayed a strong masochistic quality. In *The Big Heat*, for example, she plays Debby Marsh, an amoral, scatterbrained woman who is the mistress of a mobster and his sadistic underling. The latter throws scalding coffee into her face resulting in one of *noir*'s indelible images of Grahame's face half-swathed in bandages. In *Human Desire*, she plays a promiscuous woman who provokes her husband to kill her.

Grahame also starred in one of the last films of the genre *Odds Against Tomorrow*. An over-looked classic directed by Robert Wise, the film contains yet another brilliant performance by Grahame. As Helen, the lover of a violent criminal, she is the very ideal of female perversity as she is aroused by her lover's vivid description of a brutal murder.

Grahame's peculiar qualities made her a natural for *film noir*. She remains one of the genre's most memorable females.

Filmography: *Crossfire* (RKO, 1947). *In a Lonely Place* (Columbia, 1950). *Macao* (RKO, 1952). *Sudden Fear* (RKO, 1952). *The Big Heat* (Columbia, 1953). *Human Desire* (Columbia, 1954). *The Naked Alibi* (Universal, 1954). *Odds Against Tomorrow* (United Artists, 1959).

Granger, Farley (1925–)

Actor. Granger was a popular leading man of the forties and fifties. He was not a major *noir* personality but he did co-star in two of the genre's best films. In Alfred Hitchcock's *Strangers on a Train*, he was the tennis pro

hounded by a psychotic fan. His best *noir* performance was in Nicholas Ray's *They Live by Night* as a small time bank robber patterned after Clyde Barrow of Bonnie and Clyde infamy. His three other *films noirs* are minor.

Filmography: *They Live by Night* (RKO, 1948). *Edge of Doom* (RKO, 1950). *Side Street* (MGM, 1950). *Strangers on a Train* (Warner Bros., 1951). *The Naked Street* (United Artists, 1955).

Grant, Cary (Archibald Leach) (1904– 1986)

Actor. Grant occasionally varied his well-groomed, gentlemanly image with tougher roles, as in the arrogant, hard-boiled pilot in Howard Hawks' *Only Angels Have Wings* (Columbia, 1939). He starred in Alfred Hitchcock's great espionage *noir*, *Notorious*, but his upper class, British personality was unsuitable to the American middle class milieu of *film noir*.

Filmography: *Notorious* (RKO, 1946).

Grant, Kathryn (Olive Grandstaff) (1933–)

Actress. Kathryn Grant enjoyed a brief bit of stardom in the early fifties before retiring to marry Bing Crosby. She was the female lead in Phil Karlson's *The Phenix City Story*, but the action oriented film is dominated by its male stars.

Filmography: *The Phenix City Story* (Allied Artists, 1955).

Graves, Peter (Peter Arness) (1925–)

Actor. The younger brother of television star James Arness of "Gunsmoke," Graves was the star of low budget action films in the fifties before becoming a television star in his own right in the sixties. He had a supporting role in a single *film noir*, as one of several hostages held by an escaped convict played by Edward G. Robinson.

Filmography: *Black Tuesday* (United Artists, 1954).

Gray, Colleen (Doris Jensen) (1922–).

Actress. Although the beautiful Colleen Gray never became a full-fledged star, she had a thriving career as a film actress in the late forties and the fifties. She starred in "B" movies and played second female leads in major productions. She co-starred in several *films noirs*.

Filmography: *Kiss of Death* (20th Century–Fox, 1947). *Nightmare Alley* (20th Century–Fox, 1947). *The Sleeping City* (Universal, 1950). *Kansas City Confidential* (United Artists, 1952). *The Killing* (United Artists, 1956).

Greene, Clarence (1918–)

Screenwriter. Greene co-wrote a number of interesting films with Russell Rouse including three *films noirs*. Among these is *D.O.A.*, one of the genre's acknowledged classics. The other two titles, both somewhat experimental were directed by Rouse.

Filmography: *D.O.A.* (United Artists, 1950). *The Thief* (United Artists, 1952). *New York Confidential* (Warner Bros., 1955).

Greene, Graham (1904–1991)

British novelist and screenwriter. Greene divided his work into "entertainments" and "serious works." The latter were generally crime novels influenced by American genre fiction. He stands with Eric Ambler as Great Britain's best espionage novelist. Several of his novels were made into *films noirs*. This *Gun for Hire*, set in America, is typical of Greene's early novels and is obviously influenced by Dashiell Hammett and Raymond Chandler.

Ministry of Fear, on the other hand, is in the tradition of British espionage thrillers, but was given the full *noir* treatment by Fritz Lang. These are his major contributions to the genre. *Short Cut to Hell* is a minor film.

Filmography: *This Gun for Hire* (Paramount, 1942). *Ministry of Fear* (Paramount, 1944). *Short Cut to Hell* (Paramount, 1957).

Greene, Harold ( )

Screenwriter and scenarist. Among the many films Greene contributed to were two *films noirs*. He also worked occasionally as an associate producer and worked in this capacity on one minor *noir*, *Sleep, My Love*.

Filmography: *Sleep, My Love* (United Artists, 1948). *Kansas City Confidential* (United Artists, 1952). *Vicki* (20th Century–Fox, 1953).

Greenstreet, Sydney (1879–1954)

Character actor. For many years, Sydney Greenstreet was a successful stage actor before making his film debut at the age of sixty-one. His first film appearance, as Kaspar Gutman (the Fatman) in *The Maltese Falcon*, made him into an instant star. He became one of Warner Brother's key personalities in the 1940's. He is probably best remembered as Humphrey Bogart's foil in several films from this period including *Casablanca* (Warner Bros., 1943). In *Conflict*, he plays a psychiatrist who proves his friend, played by Humphrey Bogart, is a murderer. He played a villain in Fritz Lang's espionage *noir*, *The Mask of Dimitrios*.

Filmography: *The Maltese Falcon* (Warner Bros., 1941). *The Mask of Dimitrios* (Warner Bros., 1944). *Conflict* (Warner Bros., 1945).

Greer, Jane (Bettyjane Greer) (1924–)

Actress and leading lady. If for only a single performance, Jane Greer, will be forever identified with *film noir*. As Kathie Moffet in the classic, *Out of the Past*, she was one of the genre's most lethal *femme-fatales*. A deeply sensual performance, she manages to be at once beguiling and evil. Greer also co-starred in two other minor classics, *They Won't Believe Me* and *The Big Steal*. Unfortunately, when she did not return the romantic advances of millionaire Howard Hughes, who had purchased RKO in 1949, he had her unofficially blackballed. She married and retired shortly afterwards, appearing in a handful of films over the decades including brief parts in the post-*noir*, *The Outfit* and *Against All Odds* (Paramount, 1984), the abysmal remake of *Out of the Past*.

Filmography: *Out of the Past* (RKO, 1947). *They Won't Believe Me* (RKO, 1947). *The Big Steal* (RKO, 1949). *The Outfit* (MGM, 1973).

The Grifters (Miramax, 1991). 114 min.

Producer: Martin Scorsese. Director: Stephen Frears. Screenplay: Donald Westlake, based on the novel by Jim Thompson. Director of Photography: Oliver Stapleton. Music: Elmer Bernstein. Production Design: Dennis Gassner. Editor: Michael Audsley.

Cast: Angelica Huston (Lilly Dillon), John Cusak (Roy Dillon), Annette Bening (Myra Langtry). With: Pat Hinkle, Jan Munroe, Robert Weems, Stephen Toblowsky, Jimmy Noonan, Richard Holden.

A group of small time confidence tricksters, known as "grifters," are at the crossroads of their lives. Through a series of doublecrosses and violent confrontations with mobsters, all three plunge into tragedy, betrayal and death.

The Grifters is the most prominent contemporary *film noir*. Produced by Martin Scorsese, the film was directed in high style by British director Stephen Frears. The screenplay was adapted from a novel by Jim Thompson and is typically saturated with the trials and tribulations of small time criminals and overtones of incest. However, like many recent attempts to revive the feel of *film noir*, it suffers from self-conscious artiness.

Grot, Anton (Antocz, Franziszek Groszewski) (1884–1974)

Art director. The Polish born Anton Grot might well be one of the most neglected of the great Hollywood art directors. As Warner Brother's chief art director, 1927–1948, he was largely responsible for that studio's Germanic influenced, hard-boiled style. Grot was an active art director in Europe (where he absorbed the influence of expressionism), and in America during the late silent era, however, he did not achieve importance until he worked on *Svengali* (Warner Bros., 1931) directed by Archie Mayo. The bizarre, foreshortened set designs of the film were obviously influenced by German models and the style would be refined by Grot throughout the thirties. He worked on six *films noirs* and his influence on the entire genre cannot be discounted. Almost all of his *noir* titles are important, with a strong, gothic style, perfectly matched to the extravagant direction of Michael Curtiz (who made *Mildred Pierce* and *The Unsuspected*), and the inventive lighting schemes of the various cinematographers who worked on them.

Filmography: *Mildred Pierce* (Warner Bros., 1945). *Deception* (Warner Bros., 1946). *Nora Prentiss* (Warner Bros., 1947). *Possessed* (Warner Bros., 1947). *The Two Mrs. Carrolls* (Warner Bros., 1947). *The Unsuspected* (Warner Bros., 1947).

Gruber, Frank (1904–1969)

Screenwriter. Gruber is almost exclusively associated with a series of violent westerns. He also co-wrote two *films noirs*, both of very high quality and one of them, *The Mask of Dimitrios* (adapted from Eric Ambler's novel), is a neglected early classic of the genre.

Filmography: *The Mask of Dimitrios* (Warner Bros., 1944). *Johnny Angel* (RKO, 1945).

Guest, Val (Valmond Guest) (1911–)

Writer, producer and director. As a screenwriter, Val Guest was one of the leading figures of the golden age of British film comedy of the thirties and forties. He also wrote a number of other films including a single *film noir*, *Another Man's Poison*. Adapted from

Ann Blyth, Zachary Scott, Joan Crawford in *Mildred Pierce* **(Warner Bros., 1945).**

a play and set in London (with an American cast that included Bette Davis), the film is an interesting, if failed, attempt to capture the spirit of contemporary American crime films.

Filmography: *Another Man's Poison* (United Artists, 1952).

Guffey, Burnett (1905–1983)

Director of Photography. An extremely prolific *film noir* cinematographer, Guffey had a more conventional approach to the photographic elements than John Alton and Nicholas Musuraca. He worked on a variety of classic films beginning in the forties, including *All the King's Men* (Columbia, 1949), sometimes mistakenly identified as a *film noir*, *From Here to Eternity* (20th Century–Fox, 1953) and the later color masterpiece, *Bonnie and Clyde* (Warner Bros., 1967). He worked on several *films noirs* which demonstrated a more extravagant style than was usual (and was probably more influenced by the films' directors): *My Name Is Julia Ross*, *Knock on Any Door*, *The Reckless Moment* and *Human Desire*. All of his work is above average.

Filmography: *My Name Is Julia Ross* (Columbia, 1945). *Night Editor* (Columbia, 1946). *So Dark the Night* (Columbia, 1946). *Framed* (Columbia, 1947). *Johnny O'Clock* (Columbia, 1947). *All the King's Men* (Columbia, 1949). *Knock on Any Door* (Columbia, 1949). *The Reckless Moment* (Columbia, 1949). *The Undercover Man* (Columbia, 1949). *Convicted* (Columbia, 1950). *Scandal Sheet* (Columbia, 1952). *The Sniper* (Columbia, 1952). *Human Desire* (Columbia, 1954). *Private Hell, 36* (Filmmakers, 1954). *Tightspot* (Columbia, 1955). *The Harder They Fall* (Columbia, 1956). *Nightfall* (Columbia, 1957).

The Guilty (Monogram, 1947). 71 min.

Producer: Jack Wrather. Director: John Reinhardt. Screenplay: Robert E.

Presnell, Sr. based on the story "Two Men in a Furnished House" by Cornell Woolrich. Director of Photography: Henry Sharp. Music: Rudy Schrager. Art Director: Oscar Yerge. Editor: Jodie Caplan.

Cast: Bonita Granville (Estelle Mitchell/Linda Mitchell), Don Castle (Mike Carr), Wally Carsell (Johnny Dixon), Regis Toomey (Detective Heller), John Litel (Alex Tremholt). With Ruth Robinson, Thomas Jackson, Olive Blake, Caroline Andrews.

Attracted by the memory of Estelle Mitchell, a beautiful girl he knew in his youth, Mike Carr returns to his old neighborhood. In a bar, he tells the story of the tragic events of his youth. When Estelle's younger sister Linda was brutally murdered, Mike helped the police discover the killer was Alex Tremholt, like Mike, one of Estelle's many boy friends. In the dark of night, Alex had apparently mistaken Linda for Estelle, whom he was violently jealous of.

As his story comes to an end, Estelle enters the bar. Kissing her in greeting, Mike discerns that she no longer holds the charm for him she once did.

Upon leaving the bar, Mike returns to the scene of the crime where Linda's body was discovered. The police, by coincidence, are also there and Mike is arrested. New evidence has surfaced which implicates Mike. He confesses that he was Linda's killer. He had killed her by mistake, believing she was Estelle, who had threatened to break up their relationship.

The Guilty contains a typical convoluted, contrived plot by Cornell Woolrich. As in many of Woolrich's stories, coincidence plays a major part in the proceedings. The film is replete with *noir* themes: chiefly the "mirror image"/doppelganger. There are also some interesting flashback sequences, but as a whole the film fails to rise above the merely mediocre.

Guilty Bystander (Film Classics, 1950). 92 min.

Producer: Rex Carlton. Director: Joseph Lerner. Screenplay: Don Ettlinger, based on the novel by Wade Miller. Director of Photography: Gerald Hirschfeld. Music: Dimitri Tiomkin. Editor: Geraldine Lerner.

Cast: Zachary Scott (Max Thursday), Faye Emerson (Georgia), Mary Bolan (Smitty), Sam Levene (Capt. Tonetti), J. Edward Bromberg (Varkas), Kay Medford (Angel). With: Jed Prouty, Harry Landers, Dennis Harrison, Elliot Sullivan, Garney Wilson.

Max Thursday, an alcoholic ex-police detective, is reduced to being a house detective in the boarding house he lives in with his wife and young son. When his son is kidnapped, Max begins investigating, uncovering a complicated plot involving jewel smugglers, of which the leader of the gang is supposed to be the kind, old concierge, Smitty. He turns her over to the police after rescuing his son. He decides to give up alcohol and start his life over.

Guilty Bystander is a minor, low budget *film noir* with a good cast. Zachary Scott was a hard-boiled action star of modest adventures and westerns and he was appropriately cast as the over-the-hill detective who gets a chance to start his life anew. Unfortunately, like the Monogram *noirs*, the film suffers from its poor production values and sloppy direction.

Gun Crazy (United Artists, 1950). 87 min.

Producer: Frank and Maurice King. Director: Joseph H. Lewis. Screenplay: MacKinlay Kantor and Millard Kaufman, based on the short story by Mackinlay Kantor. Director of Photography: Russell Harlan. Music: Victor Young. Art Director: Arthur Gardner. Editor: Harry Gerstad.

Cast: Peggy Cummins (Annie Laurie Starr), John Dall (Bart Tare), Berry Kroeger (Packett), Morris Carnovsky (Judge Willoughby), Anabel Shaw (Ruby Tare). With: Harry Lewis,

Medrick Young, Trevor Bardette, Rusty (Russ) Tamblyn.

Bart Tare's fascination and expertise with guns has led him to a life time of trouble. As a teenager, he spent time in a home for wayward boys after stealing a gun from a downtown shop.

When he returns to his hometown, Bart attends a travelling carnival that is in town. Proving he is an expert marksman and trick shooter, he is asked to join and seems to have, at last, found a real home. However, he has fallen for his fellow trick shooter, the beautiful, but avaricious and amoral Annie Starr. They quit the carnival and become outlaws, graduating from robbing filling stations to liquor stores. They decide to flee to Mexico after one last job. Despite good planning, however, the trigger happy Annie kills two men. Unable to find refuge in his hometown with his family, they flee on foot into the hills. In frustration when surrounded by the local cops (including several childhood friends), Bart shoots Annie at the exact moment that he is shot by the police. Bart and Annie fall into a lifeless embrace.

Despite its modest budget, *Gun Crazy* is one of *film noir*'s classic films, thanks largely to Joseph H. Lewis' brilliant direction, and the heightened performances of John Dall and Peggy Cummins.

Like all of Lewis' films, *Gun Crazy* is extremely erotic, but in a subversive way. Cummins' voluptuous, trashy sexuality is used to heighten the tension between the two characters. *Gun Crazy* is certainly one of the most inventive low budget *films noirs*, with a famous robbery sequence shot entirely from the back seat of a car, through the front windshield. The sequence reiterates the overpowering sense of alienation that haunts the film.

Gun Crazy is the forerunner of *Bonnie and Clyde*. The final scene of the two lovers being pursued in the countryside brings up images of the latter film. However, being chased by Bart's childhood friends adds an element of ironic expressionism to the film.

Gun Crazy, with *The Big Combo* (Allied Artists, 1955), confirms John H. Lewis' place as one of the great, neglected American filmmakers of his generation.

Haas, Hugo (1901–1968)

Actor, producer, writer and director. Haas was for many years a successful character actor, generally comparable to both Elisha Cook, Jr. and Peter Lorre. The Czech born actor was popular in European cinema before fleeing the war ravaged continent in the mid–forties. He acted in many different productions, including films directed by Jacques Tourneur and Douglas Sirk, but amazingly he did not appear in any *films noirs* until the fifties.

In the 1950's, Haas began directing a series of strange, masochistic melodramas in which he also starred. The first of these low budget movies, *The Other Woman*, is the most important of the series. Haas, who also wrote the film, starred as the victim of a nasty, young *femme-fatale*.

Filmography: *The Other Woman* (20th Century–Fox, 1954).

Haas, Robert (1887–1962)

Art director. Haas, one of Anton Grot's chief collaborators, helped create the classic Warner Bros. image: gritty, dark and angular. A trained architect, Haas entered the movies in the mid–twenties and joined Warner Bros. in 1929. He remained there until 1950. Haas contributed to the films of several notoriously hard-boiled directors including Henry King, John Huston, Raoul Walsh and Michael Curtiz. He collaborated on the production designs for a handful of *films noirs*.

Filmography: *The Maltese Falcon* (Warner Bros., 1941). *Beyond the Forest* (Warner Bros., 1949). *The Damned Don't Cry* (Warner Bros., 1950).

Hackman, Gene (1930–)

Actor. Hackman is one of the most prominent of the new breed of leading men who emerged in the 1960's: a character actor who was neither handsome nor particularly charismatic, but who added a sense of realism to his roles. He starred in several important post-*noirs*, always in agreeable hard-boiled roles.

Filmography: *The Split* (MGM, 1968). *The French Connection* (20th Century-Fox, 1971). *French Connection II* (20th Century-Fox, 1975). *Night Moves* (Warner Bros., 1975).

Haller, Ernest (1896–1970)

Cinematographer. Haller was a distinguished cinematographer who excelled at both color and black and white photography. His color photography on *Gone with the Wind* (MGM, 1939) is superb. His three *films noirs* are all of superior quality.

Filmography: *Mildred Pierce* (Warner Bros., 1945). *The Unfaithful* (Warner Bros., 1947). *Plunder Road* (20th Century-Fox, 1957).

Mike Hammer

Mickey Spillane's private detective represented the new, more violent generation of crime fiction heroes. Although clearly in the tradition of Sam Spade and Philip Marlowe, Hammer was a break with the past essentially in his violent methods and extreme misogyny. Hammer is often downright cruel and reactionary. Unlike Spade or Marlowe, Hammer would never try to talk his way out of a tight spot, but would rather fight his way out. Hammer was portrayed in two *films noirs: I, the Jury* (United Artists, 1953) and *Kiss Me Deadly* (United Artists, 1955). The former was badly miscast (the innocuous Buff Elliot was not strong enough to carry the role) and poorly directed. Ralph Meeker played the role in the latter film, giving the character the appropriate callousness.

Hammett, Dashiell (1894–1961)

Novelist and screenwriter. Hammett was the first of the great modern American detective novelists. His minimalist, hard-boiled style had a profound influence on crime fiction in the decades immediately following the publication of his popular novels beginning in the late twenties and his characters set the standard for the familiar types in both fiction and film. His Sam Spade, for example, was the prototype of Philip Marlowe, Mike Hammer and others in novels and in *film noir* of Jeff Bailey in *Out of the Past* (RKO, 1947), among many others.

Hammett spent several years in Hollywood, writing or co-writing a number of screenplays, but his greatest contribution were his novels which were adapted into several classic films including two seminal *noirs*.

Filmography: *The Maltese Falcon* (Warner Bros., 1941). *The Glass Key* (Paramount, 1942).

Hardcore (Columbia, 1978). 108 min.

Producer: Buzz Feitshans. Director: Paul Schrader. Screenplay: Paul Schrader. Director of Photography: Michael Chapman. Music: Jack Nitzsche. Production Design: Paul Sylbert. Editor: Tom Rolf.

Cast: George C. Scott (John Van Dorn), Peter Boyle (Andy Mast), Season Hubley (Niki), Dick Sargent (Wes DeJong), David Nichols (Kurt), Gary Rand (Tod). With: Larry Block, Marc Alaimo, Leslie Ackerman.

When his young daughter runs away from home while on a school trip in California and takes up with pornographers, a deeply religious man from Michigan travels to Los Angeles in search of her. John Van Dorn's trip leads him into the nightmare world of hardcore pornography, professional sadists and strip joints. With the aid of Andy Mast, a sleazy private detective, he eventually finds and rescues his daughter and Mast shoots and kills her pimp/kidnapper.

Written and directed by the author of *Taxi Driver* (Columbia, 1976), Paul Schrader, *Hardcore* is a dark and solemn treatment of modern big city corruption. Its themes are typical of Schrader and of *film noir*: moral ambiguity, social decay, the loner in a world of corruption and lies. Like *Taxi Driver*, the story moves inevitably forward toward a violent conclusion. Although it received mixed critical notices on release, the film is a fine update of *noir* style and themes.

The Harder They Fall (Columbia, 1956). 108 min.

Producer: Philip Yordan. Director: Mark Robson. Screenplay: Philip Yordan, based on the novel by Budd Schulberg. Director of Photography: Burnett Guffey. Music: Hugo Friedhofer. Art Director: William Flannery. Editor: Jerome Thoms.

Cast: Humphrey Bogart (Eddie Willis), Rod Steiger (Nick Benko), Jan Sterling (Beth Willis), Mike Lane (Toro Moreno), Max Baer, Sr. (Buddy Brannen), Jersey Joe Wolcott (George). With: Harold J. Stone, Carlos Montalban, Nehemiah Persoff, Felice Orlandi.

Nick Benko, the head of a fight promotion syndicate, hires Eddie Willis, an alcoholic ex-reporter, to promote a new acquisition, a bumbling South American boxer, Toro Moreno. Moreno wins a series of fixed fights in preparation for the championship. In a fight against the ex-champ, Moreno succeeds in knocking him out; but when the fighter dies of a brain hemorrhage shortly afterwards, Moreno blames himself. Willis then confesses that Toro has been fighting fixed matches. Toro is at once embarrassed and angry, but, against the advice of Willis, he decides to go through with his fight for the championship against Buddy Brannen. Toro is severely beaten by his opponent and he decides to leave America to return to his country with his earnings from the fight. Willis gives Moreno

his $26,000 take and then sets out to write a series of newspaper articles exposing the boxing rackets.

Unlike *On the Waterfront*, a diatribe against social injustice, *The Harder They Fall*, also based on a Budd Schulberg novel, is a real *film noir* with themes common to the genre: the boxer fighting his way to the top, only to fall all the way back down, and an overwhelming sense of corruption that pervades the story and characters. Thus, it is not merely an exposé, but a link with similar films of the genre.

Likewise, Bogart's character, as central to the story, is a typical *noir* protagonist: a loner who, partially by his own moral weakness, finds himself a party to events he would normally condemn.

The director, Mark Robson, had made the even more cynical boxing *noir*, *Champion* (United Artists, 1949). This film is not as distinguished as its predecessor but it does have the same unsentimental, hard-edged style of the former.

The film is also notable as Humphrey Bogart's last.

Harlan, Russell (1903–1974)
Cinematographer. Harlan, as a former stuntman, had one of the strangest backgrounds of all cinematographers. As a cinematographer, he worked mainly on routine, low budget productions, but his work is often of superior quality.

Filmography: *The Shanghai Gesture* (United Artists, 1941). *Gun Crazy* (United Artists, 1950). *Southside 1-1000* (Allied Artists, 1950). *The Man Who Cheated Himself* (20th Century–Fox, 1951).

Harline, Leigh (1907–1969)
Composer. Harline first achieved fame as a song composer. He co-wrote the songs for two Disney classics, *Snow White and the Seven Dwarfs* (United Artists, 1937), and *Pinocchio* (United Artists, 1939). He became one of the

most prolific and brilliant film composers of the forties and fifties. Among his many excellent scores, are several important *films noirs*.

Filmography: *Johnny Angel* (RKO, 1945). *Crack-Up* (RKO, 1946). *Nocturne* (RKO, 1946). *The Woman on Pier 13* (RKO, 1949). *They Live by Night* (RKO, 1949). *His Kind of Woman* (RKO, 1951). *Vicki* (20th Century-Fox, 1953). *House of Bamboo* (20th Century-Fox, 1955).

Harrison, Joan (1911–)

Screenwriter and producer. The British born Joan Harrison was one of Alfred Hitchcock's closest collaborators. Beginning in the late thirties, she co-wrote many of his best films including *Jamaica Inn* (Mayflower/ United Artists, 1939), *Rebecca* (United Artists, 1940), *Foreign Correspondent* (United Artists, 1940), an important early *film noir*, *Suspicion* (RKO, 1941) and *Saboteur* (Universal, 1942). In the mid-forties she moved to film production becoming one of the few successful women producers of the era. Among the films she produced were five *films noirs* including two directed by Robert Siodmak: *Phantom Lady* and *Uncle Harry*.

Filmography: As producer unless otherwise noted. *Suspicion* (co-wrote screenplay only) (RKO, 1941). *Phantom Lady* (Universal, 1944). *Uncle Harry* (Universal, 1945). *Nocturne* (RKO, 1946). *Ride the Pink Horse* (Universal, 1947). *They Won't Believe Me* (RKO, 1947).

Hart, Dorothy (1923–)

Actress. Hart was mainly a second female lead, briefly popular in the late forties. She appeared in three *films noirs*, always in supportive roles, usually as the wife.

Filmography: *Naked City* (Universal, 1948). *Undertow* (Universal, 1949). *I Was a Communist for the F.B.I.* (Warner Bros., 1951).

Haskin, Byron (1899–1984)

Director. Haskin had a varied career in film production before becoming a cinematographer in the late twenties. An expert at special effects, he worked on a number of prominent films over the next twenty years. When he moved to film direction in the late forties, he quickly became known for his films, laden with special effects, although he directed many different films.

He directed two *films noirs* including the hard-boiled *I Walk Alone*, an underrated Paramount *noir* with excellent performances by Burt Lancaster and Kirk Douglas.

Filmography: *I Walk Alone* (Paramount, 1948). *Too Late for Tears* (United Artists, 1949).

Hasso, Signe (Signe Lars) (1910–)

Actress. The beautiful Swedish born Signe Hasso was an exotic presence in Hollywood films of the forties and fifties. Although she did not achieve the expected stardom that her compatriot Ingrid Bergman did, she did appear in a number of notable films. She had an important role in the little known *film noir*, *Strange Triangle* as a *femme-fatale* who, with her husband, is planning a bank heist.

Filmography: *Strange Triangle* (20th Century-Fox, 1946).

Hathaway, Henry (1898–1985)

Director. Hathaway was one of the great Hollywood action directors whose best work can be favorably compared to the best work of Alfred Hitchcock, John Ford, Howard Hawks and John Huston. His *films noirs* are characterized by violent action and the dichotomy of innocence versus corruption usually expressed through perverse sexuality. It has been claimed by certain critics that Hathaway never made any real masterpieces and while this is certainly not true, many of his films do usually fall short of expectations. Of his six *noirs*, only *Niagara* and *Kiss of Death* can be said to be true classics, but all of his *noirs* are entertaining and complex melodramas.

The Dark Corner is a studio bound film with an interesting, if somewhat contrived plot. It is directed in typically straight forward style by Hathaway and contains good performances by Mark Stevens as a private detective mixed up in a plot to kill the lover of a wealthy art dealer's wife.

The House on 92nd Street was loosely based on real espionage stories from the files of the F.B.I. Shot on location, it initiated a new phase for Hathaway's thrillers. *Call Northside 777* is also based on a real story and makes good use of the Chicago locations.

One of Hathaway's best *films noirs* is a tense thriller, *Fourteen Hours* about a potential suicide standing on a thin ledge and threatening to jump. The film is one of Hathaway's few to eschew physical action for psychological explorations, and the entire action centers around the desperate attempts to talk the potential suicide out of leaping.

On the other hand, *Kiss of Death* is one of the most violent of the major *films noirs*. It is remembered chiefly for Richard Widmark's graphic portrayal of a vicious, maniacal hired killer.

Niagara might well be his best color *film noir*. It is directed in high style by Hathaway and contains a strikingly demonic performance by Marilyn Monroe as a murderous, cruel *femme-fatale*.

It might be said that Henry Hathaway was the least pretentious of the major *film noir* directors. Because of their visceral style, many of his films are still wildly entertaining. They are certainly not burdened with complex themes or metaphors, which probably accounts for his neglect by many critics.

Filmography: *The Dark Corner* (20th Century–Fox, 1946). *House on 92nd Street* (20th Century–Fox, 1947). *Kiss of Death* (20th Century–Fox, 1947). *Call Northside 777* (20th

Century–Fox, 1948). *Fourteen Hours* (20th Century–Fox, 1951). *Niagara* (20th Century–Fox, 1952).

Haworth, Ted (1917–)

Art director. Haworth was an adaptable art director with little personal style. He worked for many of the major studios on a variety of films, including a single *film noir*, Alfred Hitchcock's *Strangers on a Train*. Nonetheless, the production design shows the strong influence of its director.

Filmography: *Strangers on a Train* (Warner Bros., 1951).

Hayden, Sterling (Sterling Walter Relyea) (1916–1986)

Actor and leading man. Although he is not generally considered one of the important *film noir* actors, Sterling Hayden might, in fact, be more important than some critics are willing to give him credit for. Indeed, one glance at his filmography should convince otherwise.

Hayden was known for his stoic heroes in action pictures of various types. Tall, rangy and stalwart, he was a natural hero of the hard-boiled school. In his *films noirs*, Hayden almost always played cynical heroes and a few tight lipped villains.

Sterling Hayden's best two *noir* performances were, in fact, variations of the same type of character. In *The Asphalt Jungle* he played Dix Handley, the toughest if not the brightest member of a gang planning a jewel robbery. In *The Killing*, on the other hand, he stars as Johnny Clay, the tough, smart leader of a makeshift group of thieves planning a race track robbery.

Filmography: *Manhandled* (Paramount, 1949). *The Asphalt Jungle* (MGM, 1950). *Crime Wave* (Warner Bros., 1954). *The Naked Street* (Universal, 1954). *Suddenly* (United Artists, 1954). *The Killing* (United Artists, 1956). *Crime of Passion* (United Artists, 1957). *The Long Goodbye* (United Artists, 1973).

Hayes, Alfred (1903–1985)

Screenwriter. Hayes was a successful screenwriter in the 1950's. He co-wrote many popular films of various genres. All three of his *films noirs* are commendable, with both Fritz Lang's *Human Desire* and Alfred Hitchcock's *Vertigo* being two of the genre's most pessimistic films.

Filmography: *Clash by Night* (RKO, 1952). *Human Desire* (Columbia, 1954). *Vertigo* (Universal, 1958).

Hayes, Joseph (1913–1987)

Playwright and screenwriter. Hayes' single contribution to *film noir* is the screenplay for *The Desperate Hours*. Based on his novel and play of the same title, the film is one of the most prominent "hostage" *noirs*, in which a group of vicious criminals hold a family of innocents, terrorizing them in their own home.

Filmography: *The Desperate Hours* (Paramount, 1955).

Hayward, Louis (Seafield Grant) (1909–1985)

Actor. A South African native, Louis Hayward was a popular leading man of mostly mild, family oriented American films in the late thirties and early forties. He co-starred in several interesting low budget melodramas in the late forties including two pseudo-films *noirs* directed by Edgar J. Ulmer: *The Strange Woman* (United Artists, 1946) and *Ruthless* (Eagle-Lion, 1948). The latter is known as one of the best "B" films of the era, a poor man's *Citizen Kane* (RKO, 1941). His single true *noir* appearance was in the little known Fritz Lang film, *House by the River*. He starred as a writer desperately trying to cover up an accidental killing.

Filmography: *House by the River* (20th Century–Fox, 1945).

Hayward, Susan (Edythe Marrener) (1918–1975)

Actress. The vivacious redhead, Susan Hayward was one of the biggest stars of the forties. She was mainly a star of "women's pictures," a kind of forties version of the sort of characters that Barbara Stanwyck and Joan Crawford had played a decade before. Unlike the harsher working women of those stars, Hayward's characters were generally more vulnerable, less astringent. She appeared in four strong *films noirs*, but never developed into one of the genre's female icons. Her best *noir* performance was in *Deadline at Dawn* as a night club dancer who helps prove the innocence of a sailor who believes he might have killed a girl.

Filmography: *Among the Living* (Paramount, 1941). *Deadline at Dawn* (RKO, 1946). *They Won't Believe Me* (RKO, 1947). *House of Strangers* (20th Century–Fox, 1949.

Hayworth, Rita (Margarita Carmen Cansino) (1918–1987)

Actress and dancer. Although Rita Hayworth starred in only three *films noirs*, she will be forever identified with the genre because of her single, extraordinary performance in the title role in *Gilda*. Her character, the tempestuous nightclub performer, is one of the most sensual performances in all of American film, and has beguiled generations of film buffs.

Hayworth also co-starred in another legendary *film noir*, *The Lady from Shanghai*, directed by her then husband Orson Welles. Her legion of fans derided her hair change for the role, but Hayworth did some of her best work in the movie.

Affair in Trinidad re-teamed her with *Gilda* co-star Glenn Ford. Unfortunately, this rather lame attempt to recapture the spirit of its predecessor was artistically and commercially indifferent.

Filmography: *Gilda* (Columbia, 1946). *Lady from Shanghai* (Columbia, 1948). *Affair in Trinidad* (Columbia, 1952).

He Ran All the Way (United Artists, 1951). 77 min.

Producer: Bob Roberts. Director:

John Berry. Screenplay: Guy Endore and Hugo Butler, based on the novel by Sam Ross. Director of Photography: James Wong Howe. Music: Franz Waxman. Art Director: Harry Horner. Editor: Francis Lyon.

Cast: John Garfield (Nick Robey), Shelley Winters (Peg Dobbs), Wallace Ford (Mr. Dobbs), Selena Royle (Mrs. Dobbs), Bobby Hyatt (Tommy Dobbs), Gladys George (Mrs. Robey), Norman Lloyd (Al Molin).

Nick and Al are small time holdup men. When they are involved in a botched hold up and subsequent shoot-out, Al is critically wounded. Nick flees the scene, taking temporary refuge at a public pool. There, he meets and be-friends Peg Dobbs. Peg invites Nick to her house for dinner. Her family likes him, but when they return from a movie, he thinks they have found out about him.

Nick panics and holds Peg's family hostage. His mood alternates between violent anger and calmness, but mat-ters grow worse when a guard wounded in the holdup dies and the story makes the front page of the paper. Nick orders Peg's father to call for a car to be sent. When the car arrives and Nick is leav-ing, Peg gets the gun and shoots him. Nick dies in the streets.

He Ran All the Way is the first of the small group of *films noirs* in which a family is held by a violent outside force: a prominent example of the metaphor of middle class values under attack represented by some *noir* themes.

John Garfield gave one of his best performances as the vulnerable, fright-ened criminal. Shelley Winters is equally good as the lonely girl who thinks at least she has found her perfect mate, only to have to kill him when her fath-er's life is at stake.

Much of the last part of the film takes place during a rain storm, a common environmental metaphor that also recurs throughout *film noir*, especially during this film, when there is height-ened emotional conflicts.

Like Garfield, the film's co-writer, Hugo Butler and its director John Berry were targets of the McCarthy witch hunt and their careers were ruined. Sadly, *He Ran All the Way* marked the apex of their film ca-reers.

He Walked by Night (Eagle-Lion. 1949). 79 min.

Producer: Robert Kane. Director: Alfred Werker. Screenplay: John C. Higgins and Crane Wilbur, with addi-tional dialog by Harry Essex, story by Crane Wilbur. Music: Leonid Raab. Art Director: Edward Ilou. Editor: Alfred De Gaetano.

Cast: Richard Basehart (Ray Mor-gan/Martin), Scott Brady (Sgt. Marty Brennan), Roy Roberts (Capt. Breen), Whit Bissell (Reeves), Jimmy Cardwell (Chuck Jones), Jack Webb (Lee). With: Bob Rice, Reed Hadley, Chief Bradlee, John McQuine.

Ray Morgan is a brilliant thief who is an electronics expert and a master of disguise. While trying to burglarize an electronics store, he kills a cop. He changes his last name to Martin and alters his appearance. A composite drawing culled from witnesses of previous crimes, leads to an electronics firm run by Paul Reeves where Ray has rented out equipment he has stolen and modified. With Reeves' aid, the police set a trap, but he discovers the ruse and manages to get away. He flees through the flood control district channels beneath Los Angeles, but he is hunted down by the police and in the inevitable shootout, is killed.

He Walked by Night is not a terribly inventive film. Its use of semi-docu-mentary effects were already common in *film noir*, but better utilized in other films. The director, Alfred Werker (with some uncredited work by Anthony Mann), does create an interesting visual montage of a big city and cata-logs in detail the routines of police in-vestigations. Otherwise, it is a very minor film of little interest.

Hecht, Ben (1894–1964)

Screenwriter, novelist, playwright and poet. Hecht, a former Chicago newspaperman, first achieved fame as a novelist and short story writer in the mid-twenties. With Charles McArthur, another veteran of the tough school of Chicago journalism, Hecht co-wrote two of the legendary Broadway satires: *The Front Page* (1929) and *The Twentieth Century* (1930).

As a screenwriter, Hecht was flexible and brilliant. He specialized in hard-boiled melodramas and comedies, but he also worked on westerns, romantic dramas, fantasies and epics. He co-wrote many films without screen credit, preferring money rather than credit. Like much of his best work, his *noir* scripts are notable for their wicked humor and pessimistic view of humanity and political corruption.

Filmography: *Underworld* (Paramount, 1927). *Notorious* (RKO, 1946). *Kiss of Death* (20th Century-Fox, 1947). *Ride the Pink Horse* (Universal, 1947). *Edge of Doom* (RKO, 1950). *Where the Sidewalk Ends* (20th Century-Fox, 1950).

Hedrick, Earl (1896–1979)

Art director. One of Paramount's in-house production designers, Hedrick collaborated closely with Hans Dreier and Hal Pereira. He worked on a few *films noirs*, all of which are distinguished by a somewhat more American approach than Dreier's strong expressionism.

Filmography: *Sorry, Wrong Number* (Paramount, 1948). *The File on Thelma Jordan* (Paramount, 1950). *Union Station* (Paramount, 1950). *The Big Carnival* (Paramount, 1951). *Detective Story* (Paramount, 1951).

Heflin, Van (Emmett Evan Heflin) (1910–1971)

Actor. Van Heflin was a new kind of film star when he emerged in the forties. Neither handsome nor glamorous, he embodied the average American in countless dramas over the next two decades and was a convincing anti-hero in a handful of excellent *films noirs*.

Without a doubt, Heflin's best known *noir* appearance was in *The Strange Love of Martha Ivers*. He co-starred with Barbara Stanwyck and Kirk Douglas, as Sam Masterson whose rekindled romance with a long lost flame (Stanwyck) exposes her as a murderess.

Less well known is Heflin's strong performance in Fred Zinnemann's *Act of Violence* in which he starred as a war veteran responsible for the deaths of fellow inmates in a prison camp during the war, whose past has come back to haunt him.

Filmography: *Johnny Eager* (MGM, 1942). *The Strange Love of Martha Ivers* (Paramount, 1946). *Possessed* (Warner Bros., 1947). *Act of Violence* (MGM, 1949). *The Prowler* (United Artists, 1951).

Heisler, Stuart (1894–1979)

Director. Born in Los Angeles, Stuart Heisler worked his way up through the film industry beginning as a prop man for Mack Sennett in 1914. By the 1930's he was a leading editor at Paramount and he began directing in 1940. Heisler was not a major artist, but rather a skilled craftsman. He directed two important early *films noirs*, *Among the Living* and *The Glass Key*. The latter is famous as the second teaming of Alan Ladd and Veronica Lake, confirming their popularity. *I Died a Thousand Times*, unfortunately, is a perfunctory remake of *High Sierra* (Warner Bros., 1941) and pales in comparison to the original.

Filmography: *Among the Living* (Paramount, 1941). *The Glass Key* (Paramount, 1942). *I Died a Thousand Times* (Warner Bros., 1955).

Hellinger, Mark (1903–1947)

Producer. A respected New York based journalist, Mark Hellinger was recruited as a screenwriter in the early

Burt Lancaster, Ava Gardner in *The Killers* **(Universal, 1946).**

days of sound. He quickly proved himself a competent, if not particularly brilliant, screenwriter. He co-wrote many popular, unpretentious films in the thirties.

In the forties, Hellinger joined Universal as a producer and quickly proved himself a genius at bringing together talented writers, directors and actors for top projects. He supervised many top films including four great *films noirs*.

Filmography: *High Sierra* (Warner Bros., 1941). *The Killers* (Universal, 1946). *Brute Force* (Universal, 1947). *The Naked City* (Universal, 1948).

Hell's Half Acre (Republic, 1954). 91 min.

Producer and Director: John H. Auer. Screenplay: Steve Fisher. Director of

Photography: John L. Russell, Jr. Music: R. Dale Butts. Art Director: James Sullivan. Editor: Fred Allen.

Cast: Wendell Corey (Chet Chester), Evelyn Keyes (Donna Williams), Elsa Lanchester (Lida O'Reilly), Marie Windsor (Rose), Nancy Gates (Sally Lee).

The second of two John H. Auer directed and Steve Fisher scripted Republic *films noirs*. The *Hell's Half Acre* story concerns Donna Williams' search for her husband, a soldier who disappeared after Pearl Harbor and has turned up in Hawaii years later under a different identity and involved with mobsters. The story is typically convoluted and full of some wild improbabilities, but it is notable for its rather mature approach to the material and some strong performances. Otherwise, it is one of the genre's more insignificant titles.

Hell's Island (Paramount, 1955). 83 min.

Producers: William H. Pine and William C. Thomas. Director: Phil Karlson. Screenplay: Maxwell Shane, based on a story by Jack Leonard and Martin M. Goldsmith. Director of Photography: Lionel Lindon. Music: Irving Talbot. Art Directors: Hal Periera and Al Y. Roelofs. Editor: Archie Marshek.

Cast: John Payne (Mike Cormack), Mary Murphy (Janet Martin), Francis L. Sullivan (Barzland), Arnold Moss (Paul Armand), Paul Picerni (Eduardo Marin). With: Eduardo Noriega, Walter Reed, Sandor Szabo, Robert Cabal.

One of several powerful action oriented *films noirs* directed by Phil Karlson in the 1950's, *Hell's Island* is also unique because it was filmed in color.

The plot is simple. Mike Cormack, an ex–District Attorney down on his luck, gets involved with murderous smugglers and his former fiancée, Janet Martin, who caused a plane crash for insurance money.

Hell's Island came near the end of the *noir* cycle when color was becoming more common, even for "B" productions. Likewise, this film's gratuitous violence was becoming more common in films of the era.

Yet, the film is clearly a true *film noir*. Its theme is common to the genre (the loner against a world of corruption) as are its characters including a *femme-fatale*.

Although not as well known as certain other "B" *noirs*, *Hell's Island* is worth renewed interest.

Helton, Percy (1894–1971)

Character actor. Helton specialized in small comic roles and appeared in dozens of films usually as a hayseed or big city dope. He played small supporting roles in four *films noirs*.

Filmography: *Criss Cross* (Universal, 1949). *The Crooked Way* (United Artists, 1949). *Thieves' Highway* (20th Century-Fox, 1949). *Kiss Me Deadly* (United Artists, 1955).

Hemingway, Ernest (1899–1961)

Writer. In style and certain themes, Hemingway had a profound influence on hard-boiled crime literature and through them, an indirect influence on *film noir*. His short story *The Killers* provided the set up for Anthony Veiler's brilliant screenplay. *The Breaking Point* is a *noir* version of his novel, *To Have and Have Not*.

Filmography: *The Killers* (Universal, 1946). *The Breaking Point* (Warner Bros., 1950).

Hendrix, Wanda (1928–1981)

Actress. Briefly popular in the late forties, Hendrix had a sporadic film career and completely disappeared after the early fifties. She co-starred in two modest *films noirs*, but did not make much of an impression in either.

Filmography: *Nora Prentiss* (Warner Bros., 1947). *Ride the Pink Horse* (Universal, 1947).

Hepburn, Katherine (1907–)

Actress and leading lady. Hepburn's upper crust personality was too grating for the middle class urban milieu of *film noir*. She appeared in a single *film noir*, *Undercurrent*, an interesting failure.

Filmography: *Undercurrent* (MGM, 1946).

Herman, Alfred ( )

Art director. As a unit art director for RKO in the thirties and forties, Herman worked on many important films, always in collaboration. Among these are three *films noirs* which are distinctive for their studio style and inventive set designs.

Filmography: *Crossfire* (RKO, 1947).

Berlin Express (RKO, 1948). *Beware, My Lovely* (RKO, 1952).

Herrmann, Bernard (1911–1975)

Composer. Arguably the greatest of American film composers, Bernard Herrmann was discovered and brought to Hollywood in the early forties by Orson Welles. He composed the music for Welles' first two masterpieces, *Citizen Kane* (RKO, 1941) and *The Magnificent Ambersons* (RKO, 1942). Both scores are masterpieces and important integral elements of the films. His swirling mass of sound, alternating between major and minor keys, influenced generations of composers for movie thrillers. In many ways, Herrmann's music resembled a cross between the late romanticism of Richard Wagner and the early work of Igor Stravinsky. He composed the scores for a handful of late *films noirs*, all of which are excellent.

Filmography: *Vertigo* (Universal, 1958). *Odds Against Tomorrow* (United Artists, 1959). *Cape Fear* (Universal, 1961). *Taxi Driver* (Columbia, 1976).

Herzbrun, Bernard (1891–1976)

Art director. Herzbrun, a veteran of the American film industry as an art director for several studios, was promoted to supervising art director at Universal in 1947. He worked on a number of *films noirs* in the next three years. They are distinctive for their distillation of expressionist style into a new, distinctive, minimalist style, largely dictated by the films' modest budgets.

Filmography: *Brute Force* (Universal, 1947). *Ride the Pink Horse* (Universal, 1947). *A Double Life* (Universal, 1948). *Kiss the Blood Off My Hands* (Universal, 1948). *Abandoned* (Universal, 1949). *Criss Cross* (Universal, 1949). *Undertow* (Universal, 1949). *One Way Street* (Universal, 1950). *Shakedown* (Universal, 1950). *The Sleeping City* (Universal, 1950). *The Naked Alibi* (Universal, 1954).

Heston, Charlton (John Charlton Carter) (1923–)

Actor and leading man. Heston's heroic screen image is best suited to grandiose gestures in historic epics. However, he also played stoic protagonists in a handful of contemporary dramas including two *films noirs*. In *Dark City*, a minor classic of the genre, Heston starred as a gambler who enters a dark, dangerous world of corruption to find a psychotic killer. In *Touch of Evil* he starred opposite director Orson Welles as an honest cop thrown into a dangerous game of double cross and murder. Although he is convincing in both films, Heston did not develop into a *noir* icon.

Filmography: *Dark City* (Paramount, 1950). *Touch of Evil* (Universal, 1958).

Hickox, Sid (1895–1989)

Cinematographer. A staff cinematographer for Warner Bros., Hickox worked on many of the studio's prestige action pictures and melodramas. However, his style was rather conventional and he worked on only three *films noirs*. They are among his best films, with *Dark Passage* being particularly inventive.

Filmography: *The Big Sleep* (Warner Bros., 1946). *Dark Passage* (Warner Bros., 1947). *White Heat* (Warner Bros., 1949).

Higgins, John C. (1913–)

Screenwriter. Higgins wrote or co-wrote many programmers and "B" movies beginning in the mid forties. He worked on a number of minor *films noirs* which are distinguished by their violence and raw cynicism.

Filmography: *Railroaded* (Producers Releasing Corporation, 1947). *Raw Deal* (Eagle-Lion, 1948). *T-Men* (Eagle-Lion, 1948). *Border Incident* (MGM, 1949). *He Walked by Night* (Eagle-Lion, 1949). *Shield for Murder* (United Artists, 1954).

High Sierra (Warner Bros., 1941). 100 min.

Producer: Hal B. Wallis. Director: Raoul Walsh. Screenplay: John Huston and W. R. Burnett, based on the novel by W. R. Burnett. Director of Photography: Tony Gaudio. Music: Adolph Deutsch. Art Director: Ted Smith. Editor: Jack Killifer.

Cast: Humphrey Bogart (Roy Earl), Ida Lupino (Marie), Alan Curtis (Babe), Arthur Kennedy (Red), Joan Leslie (Velma), Henry Hull (Doc Benton), Barton Maclane (Jack Kranner), Cornel Wilde (Mendoza), Henry Travers (Pa). With: Elisabeth Ridson, Minna Gowbell, Paul Harvey, Donald MacBride.

The notorious criminal "Mad Dog" Roy Earl is broken out of prison by Big Mac, an old associate who wants him to go to California to engineer the hold up of a resort hotel. Along the way, Roy meets the Goodhues and their club-footed daughter, Velma. Roy feels sympathy for the pretty young girl because she is too poor to get the operation that would cure her affliction. He resolves to help her.

Meanwhile, Roy's henchmen have brought along Marie, a dance hall girl. Roy is opposed to her presence at first, but he soon falls for her and she for him.

With the help of Mendoza, a corrupt clerk who works at the resort hotel, the robbery is successfully carried out. Roy gives part of his share to Velma.

The henchmen are killed in a car crash immediately after the robbery and Mendoza is arrested. He talks, naming Roy Earl as the leader of the gang. An all points bulletin is put out on Roy and with Marie at his side, he goes on the run. At last, he abandons his car and tries to escape into the Sierra mountains. The police close in, however, and he is gunned down while Marie watches, horrified.

High Sierra is one of the most important early films noirs. Its screenplay, by John Huston and W. R. Burnett (based on Burnett's novel), was one of the first to explicitly identify the genre's existen-

tial themes. Its misfit characters are trapped in circumstances of their own making and at the end seem to accept, perhaps even welcome, death.

Humphrey Bogart was essentially playing the same kind of character he had played during the 1930's, but his performance in this film was much stronger than his early performances and helped establish him as a major star of the forties.

The film's style is relatively subdued when compared to the extravagances to come. In that respect, it resembles some of the genre's later films. Its director, Raoul Walsh, a master of action, directed in the spare, visceral style that was his trademark.

The Highwall (MGM, 1947). 100 min.

Producer: Robert Lord. Director: Curtis Bernhardt. Screenplay: Sydney Boehm and Lester Cole, based on the novel and play by Alan R. Clarke and Bradbury Foote. Director of Photography: Paul Vogel. Music: Bronislau Kaper. Art Directors: Cedric Gibbons and Leonid Vasian. Editor: Conrad A. Nervig.

Cast: Robert Taylor (Steven Kenet), Audrey Totter (Dr. Ann Lorrison), Herbert Marshall (Dr. Whitcombe), Dorothy Patrick (Helen Kenet), H. B. Warner (Mr. Slocum). With Warner Anderson, Moroni Olsen, John Ridgeley, Morris Ankrum, Elisabeth Risdon.

Steven Kenet, an ex-army pilot, is found unconscious in a wrecked car next to the body of his wife who has been strangled. He is arrested for murder. He suffers from blackouts caused by a war injury, but he refuses an operation because he knows that he cannot be executed if legally insane. He is committed to a mental hospital surrounded by a highwall and, eventually, with the encouragement of a kindly doctor, he agrees to undergo a brain operation. Unfortunately when he recovers, Steven still cannot remember the events surrounding his wife's death.

Under a new, experimental drug

therapy, however, Steven begins to recall certain events. His wife had gone to work for a Dr. Whitcombe. He found her at the doctor's place one evening with her overnight bag and in a fit of jealous rage he began to strangle her before passing out. That is all he can remember.

Meanwhile, Dr. Whitcombe visits the asylum, upsetting Kenet. When Whitcombe taunts him and confesses that *he* killed Steven's wife, Steven knocks him unconscious. When Dr. Whitcombe is given sodium pentothal, he confesses to the murder, at last setting Steven Kenet free.

Curtis Bernhardt, a German refugee, gives this ordinary thriller an expressionist *mise-en-scène*, supported by cinematographer Paul Vogel, and some interesting production design by Cedric Gibbons and Leonid Vasian. Obviously, the title of the film refers to both the physical and psychological barriers that imprison Steven Kenet. The theme is reinforced through the claustrophobic set design, dark lighting, and some beautiful, atmospheric music by Bronizlau Kaper. Bernhardt also makes effective use of dream sequences, flashbacks, etc.

Finally, of course, the theme of the disillusioned returning war veteran suffering from amnesia was a fairly common one of *film noir*, particularly in the years immediately following World War II.

His Kind of Woman (RKO, 1951). 120 min.

Producer: Robert Sparks. Director: John Farrow. Screenplay: Frank Fenton and Jack Leonard, based on a story by Gerald Drayson Adams. Director of Photography: Harry J. Wild. Music: Leigh Harline. Music Director: Constantin Bakaleinikoff. Art Director: Albert S. D'Agostino. Editors: Eda Warren and Frank Knudtsen.

Cast: Robert Mitchum (Dan Milner), Jane Russell (Lenore Brent), Vincent Price (Mark Cardigan), Tim Holt (Bill Lusk), Charles McGraw (Thompson), Marjorie Reynolds (Helen Cardigan), Raymond Burr (Nick Ferraro). With Leslye Banning, Jim Backus, Philip Van Zant, John Mylong.

Dan Milner, just released from prison for a petty theft, is beaten up one night by three mysterious men, and then oddly made an offer he can't refuse: $50,000.00 to leave the United States for a year. Figuring he doesn't have anything better to do, he readily agrees. Unknown to him, Nick Ferraro is behind the scheme. Ferraro is a syndicate boss in exile in Naples. He is planning to have plastic surgery and take Milner's place after killing him so that he can reenter the United States without the authorities knowing.

Milner goes to Mexico. At a seaside resort he meets the beautiful Lenore Brent, a night club singer who is having an affair with film star Mark Cardigan. Cardigan spends most of his time at the resort hunting and fishing, leaving Milner and Lenore time to get to know each other. They, in turn, spend most of their time gambling, until a United States immigration agent arrives and tells Milner of Ferraro's plans. To make matters even more complicated, Cardigan's wife arrives.

The immigration agent is murdered by a Ferraro assassin. A group of his men kidnap Milner, planning to take him to Ferraro's yacht anchored off shore, but Lenore manages to slip him a pistol and then goes to Cardigan for help. Cardigan gathers a hapless posse, and assaults the yacht. In the ensueing battle, Cardigan and his men kill or capture Ferraro's men, and Milner kills Ferraro.

Back at the hotel, Cardigan holds a triumphant press conference.

His Kind of Woman is a wild and brilliant film, unjustly neglected by critics and historians. It is one of the darkest *films noirs* and one of the funniest. Vincent Price's performance, as the vain, fey, but ultimately tough actor Mark Cardigan, is one of his best.

He provides comic relief from the film's unrelenting action and violence of the movie.

Likewise, Robert Mitchum is equally fine as the cynical, self-destructive, vindictive Milner. He is a laconic hero, bent on the destruction of Ferraro. He is arrogant, tough and callous, at one point snuffing out a cigarette on one of Ferraro's henchman's palms.

Raymond Burr, however, almost steals the movie as the rapacious crime boss, Nick Ferraro. Ferraro is a furious killer, bent on his own perverse plans. He is resplendent in his immaculate white suit and his wicked smile.

His Kind of Woman is special on several levels, other than its rich performances. The screenplay is superb, with some great, sarcastic dialog full of innuendo.

John Farrow was at his extravagant best on this film. He manages to create a swift moving, action oriented *film noir* that might well be his best film.

Hitchcock, Alfred (1899–1980)

Director. Not much can be said about Alfred Hitchcock that hasn't been said at least a hundred times before. Even the casual film buff knows about the obsessions and the genius of this British born film director.

Alfred Hitchcock was not a director of conventional *films noirs*. Like all of his movies, his *noirs* were imbued with a sense of Catholic guilt, fear of sex, and the duplicity of character. Many of his *noirs* are essentially about the nature of guilt and innocence.

Suspicion, Hitchcock's first *film noir*, has roots in Victorian suspense novels. Its plot is well known: a woman marries a handsome gentleman only to become increasingly convinced he is a killer. Its themes of marital trust and psychological betrayal are familiar to Hitchcock, and had a profound influence on similar *films noirs. Conflict* (Warner Bros., 1945) and *The Two Mrs. Carrolls* (Warner Bros., 1948) are two of the most prominent examples of the variations of this theme.

Likewise, *Shadow of a Doubt* concerns a young girl's growing suspicions, finally confirmed, that her uncle is a nefarious serial killer.

Notorious, on the other hand, was in the tradition of early espionage-*noir* thrillers. It has a plot vaguely similar to *Gilda* (Columbia, 1946) and might well be Hitchcock's most conventional *film noir*.

Strangers on a Train is Hitchcock's most extravagant *film noir*. Its tale of an obsessed, psychotic fan of a professional tennis player, is one of the most unique in the genre. Its undertone of homosexuality and ambiguous morality, however, are common themes in *film noir*.

The Wrong Man is a minor film, but two of Hitchcock's color films of the fifties are interesting variations of the genre. *Rear Window* (RKO, 1951), with its claustrophobic feel, helplessness of the characters, questions of guilt, etc., are all common to *film noir*. However, *Vertigo* is clearly a *film noir*. A slow moving ethereal melodrama about the moral and psychological degeneration of a police detective obsessed by a *femme-fatale*, it is one of the genre's most haunting, tragic films.

Filmography: *Suspicion* (RKO, 1941). *Shadow of a Doubt* (Universal, 1943). *Notorious* (RKO, 1946). *Strangers on a Train* (Warner Bros., 1951). *The Wrong Man* (Warner Bros., 1956). *Vertigo* (Universal, 1957).

The Hitch-Hiker (RKO, 1953). 71 min.

Producer: Collier Young. Director: Ida Lupino. Screenplay: Collier Young and Ida Lupino, adapted by Robert Joseph from a story by Daniel Mainwaring. Director of Photography: Nicholas Musuraca. Music: Leith Stevens. Music Director: Constantin Bakalieninkoff. Art Directors: Albert S. D'Agostino and Walter E. Keller. Editor: Douglas Stewart.

Cast: Edmund O'Brien (Ray Collins),

Ingrid Bergman, Cary Grant in *Notorious* (RKO, 1946).

Frank Lovejoy (Gilbert Bowen), William Talman (Emmett Myers), José Torvay (Capt. Alvarado), Sam Hayes (Sam). With: Wendell Niles, Jean Del Val, Clark Howat, Natividad Vacio.

Emmett Myers is a psychotic serial killer who gets his victims by hitchhiking. He captures two fishermen on a trip who pick him up. He terrorizes them at gun point, making them take him to Mexico. When one of his hostages leaves his wedding ring on a gas station pump, it tips off the police and Myers is at last captured.

The Hitch-Hiker is one of the most claustrophobic *films noirs* with most of the action concentrated in the car. Its suspense is thus subtle, yet palpable.

The film is the only one of the genre directed by a woman, *noir* icon Ida

Lupino. She does an excellent job with little budget and the film is both spare and terrorizing.

There are some interesting insights to the psychology of serial killers with hints of child abuse having caused his perverse mind set.

Ultimately, *The Hitch-Hiker* is one of the best "B" *noirs*.

Hively, Jack (1907–)

Director. Hively was an above average director of "B" movies, many for RKO. He worked in all genres and made a single *film noir. Street of Chance* is an excellent, little known *noir* thriller with Burgess Meredith in the leading role.

Filmography: *Street of Chance* (Paramount, 1942).

Hodiak, John (1914–1955).

Hodiak was a general purpose leading man. He enjoyed a brief run of success in the forties when most of the former "A" stars were away at war and his career faded after 1950. He starred in several good action pictures, as well as in Alfred Hitchcock's *Lifeboat* (Universal, 1944). Of his *films noirs*, Hodiak's best performance was in *Somewhere in the Night* as an amnesia victim searching for his real identity.

Filmography: *Somewhere in the Night* (20th Century–Fox, 1946). *The Bribe* (MGM, 1949). *A Lady Without Passport* (MGM, 1950). *The People Against O'Hara* (MGM, 1951).

Holden, William (William Franklin Beedle, Jr.) (1918–1981)

Actor. A vastly underrated talent, William Holden had a realistic style which made him an empathetic personality on screen. He specialized in average-Joes caught up in extraordinary circumstances, a role he played in most of his *films noirs*. In *Sunset Boulevard* for example, he starred as the down-on-his-luck screenwriter who stumbles onto a world of madness that ultimately ends in his untimely demise.

In *The Turning Point*, an under appreciated *film noir*, Holden stars as an investigative reporter who accidently uncovers corrupt politicians. In *The Dark Past*, however, Holden appears in one of his few villainous roles as a murderous escaped convict.

Although William Holden never developed into a full-fledged *noir* icon, his appearances were always welcome.

Filmography: *The Dark Past* (Columbia, 1948). *Sunset Boulevard* (Paramount, 1950). *Union Station* (Paramount, 1950). *The Turning Point* (Paramount, 1952).

Hollander, Frederick (1892–1976)

Songwriter and composer. The German born Hollander brought a spare, strongly Germanic feel to his film scores. His *noir* scores are above average, with flashes of brilliance.

Filmography: *Conflict* (Warner Bros., 1945). *Berlin Express* (RKO, 1942). *Caught* (MGM, 1949). *A Dangerous Profession* (RKO, 1949).

Hollow Triumph (Eagle-Lion, 1948). 82 min.

Producer: Paul Henreid. Director: Steve Sekely. Screenplay: Daniel Fuchs, based on the novel by Murray Forbes. Director of Photography: John Alton. Music: Sol Kaplan. Art Directors: Edward Ilou and Frank Durlauf. Editor: Fred Allen.

Cast: Paul Henreid (John Muller/ Dr. Bartok), Joan Bennett (Evelyn Nash), Edward Franz (Frederick Muller), Leslie Brooks (Virginia Taylor), John Qualen (Rocky Swangron). With: Mabel Paige, Herbert Rudley, Paul Burns, Charles Trowbridge.

Johnny Muller, a former medical student turned con artist, is released from jail after serving a brief sentence for payroll theft. His brother helps him get a job with a medical supply firm, but he falls in with his old gang and they rob a gambling club owned by Rocky Swangron. However, the robbery meets with violence, and only Johnny and one of the other gang members get out alive. They divide the $60,000 take and split up. Johnny returns to work at the medical supply firm.

Shortly thereafter, Johnny discovers that a local psychiatrist, Doctor Bartok, is his exact duplicate except for a scar on his cheek. Johnny has a photo of Bartok taken, kills the doctor, and with a scalpel cuts a scar on his face. However, he printed the photo backwards and he cut the scar on the wrong side of his face. Still, no one notices, not even Bartok's beautiful secretary Evelyn Nash whom he attempts to seduce. Eventually, she realizes that she has been tricked and leaves. At that moment, thugs arrive saying that Bartok owes $90,000 to a local gambler/mobster. Johnny tries to convince them that he is not Bartok, but they of course, do not believe him. When he tries to flee, they shoot him.

Despite the contrived plot, *Hollow Triumph* is an interesting *film noir* that takes the doppelganger theme to an unlikely extreme. The production values are poor, but the film does make good use of some low key lighting and real locations around Los Angeles.

While Paul Henreid is quite good as the avaricious, amoral Johnny Muller, Joan Bennett is the film's chief asset as the cynical Evelyn Nash, a woman who enters the relationship with her boss because she is afraid of getting older without a husband.

Holm, Celeste (1919–)

Actress. After experience on Broadway, Celeste Holm entered movies in 1946 and won an Oscar the following year as Best Supporting Actress in *Gentleman's Agreement* (20th Century–Fox, 1947). She often played supporting roles and second female leads as she does in her single *film noir*, *Road House*, in which she plays the young girl competing with Ida Lupino for the affections of Cornel Wilde.

Filmography: *Road House* (20th Century–Fox, 1948).

Holmes, Geoffrey *see* Daniel Mainwaring

Hopper, Jerry (1907–)

Director. Hopper started in show business as a radio writer. He worked in a variety of positions in the film industry before becoming a director in 1952. He directed a series of very minor "B" movies including a single, unremarkable *film noir*.

Filmography: *The Naked Alibi* (Universal, 1954).

Horner, Harry (1910–)

Art director and film director. The Austrian born Harry Horner first achieved success as a stage designer in his native country. He came to the United States in the mid-thirties and quickly established himself as a versatile art director, mainly for Universal. His set designs for *A Double Life* are outstanding.

Horner moved to directing in the early fifties. He was a competent studio craftsman, but his work is rarely outstanding. His two *films noirs* are better than average but fall short of being classics.

Filmography: *A Double Life* (Universal, 1948). *Beware, My Lovely* (RKO, 1952). *Vicki* (20th Century–Fox, 1953).

Horning, William A. ( )

Art director. Horning was Cedric Gibbons' right hand man at MGM during that studio's golden age. He collaborated with Gibbons on many classic films, and continued to work at the studio after Gibbons' retirement in the early fifties. Although excellent, his *noir* designs are not among Horning's best. He preferred the semi-surrealistic designs of musicals and fantasies, and was the chief designer for *The Wizard of Oz* (MGM, 1939), and many of MGM's color productions in the forties.

Filmography: *Fury* (MGM, 1936). *Julie* (MGM, 1956). *Party Girl* (MGM, 1958). *The Beat Generation* (MGM, 1959).

House by the River (Republic, 1949). 88 min.

Producer: Howard Welsch. Director: Fritz Lang. Screenplay: Mel Dinelli, based on the novel by A. P. Herbert. Director of Photography: Edward Cronjager. Music: George Antheil. Art Director: Boris Leven. Editor: Arthur D. Hilton.

Cast: Louis Hayward (Stephen Byrne), Lee Bowman (John Byrne), Jane Wyatt (Majorie Byrne), Dorothy Patrick (Emily Gaunt), Ann Shoemaker (Mrs. Ambrose). With: Jody Gilbert, Peter Brocco, Howland Chamberlain.

Stephen Byrne is a moderately successful writer working on his latest novel, *The River*. While his wife is out of the house, his maid, Emily tries to seduce him, Stephen strangles her while in a fit. His brother John arrives and agrees to help dispose of the girl's body. They wrap her body in a burlap sack and dump her in the nearby river. Stephen tries to steer suspicions toward his brother, and then, when he confronts him, knocks him unconscious, and pushes John's body into the river.

Stephen returns to his wife, Marjorie, who has read his manuscript against his orders. He attacks her, but when John's "ghost"—he was not dead as Stephen thought, and awoke when he hit the cold water—appears, Stephen panics. He becomes entangled in the heavy draperies and ironically, is strangled by them.

House by the River, shot on a low budget, is Fritz Lang's least known *film noir*. Although set in the Victorian age, the film is uniquely modern in its dress and characters' behavior. Only in its themes of marital/familial betrayal and adultery does it resemble Victorian melodrama. The film looks and feels like an art film, with strongly *expressionist* style—heavy shadows, slow, dreamy sequences, etc.; and its ethereal music.

House by the River is a strange, haunting film, sadly neglected. It represents Fritz Lang's most disparaging view of humanity.

House of Bamboo (20th Century–Fox, 1955). 105 min.

Producer: Buddy Adler. Director: Samuel Fuller. Screenplay: Harry Kleiner, with additional dialog by Samuel Fuller. Director of Photography: Joe MacDonald. Music: Leigh Harline. Art Directors: Lyle Wheeler and Addison Hehr. Editor: James B. Clark.

Cast: Robert Ryan (Sandy Dawson), Robert Stack (Eddie Kenner/Spanier), Shirley Yamaguchi (Mariko), Cameron Mitchell (Griff). With Sessue Hayakawa, Biff Elliot, Sandro Giglio, Elko Hanabusa, Harry Carey.

Sandy Dawson has organized a crime ring of ex-G. I.'s in post war Tokyo. Kenner, an Army undercover agent, joins Dawson's gang. He endears himself to the ruthless crime boss and the Japanese woman, Mariko, he is forced to live with, but when Dawson discovers that Kenner is an interloper he tries to have Kenner killed. Kenner pursues Dawson to an amusement part. They have a gun battle on a giant, whirling globe, but Kenner manages to kill Dawson and Kenner is free to pursue his relationship with Mariko whom he has grown to love.

House of Bamboo is a color/cinemascope remake of *Street with No Name*. Fuller transposes the action to Japan, a brilliant, simple innovation that ultimately, creates an element missing from the original: the conflict between cultures and the exploitation of one society by another.

Fuller makes effective use of the exotic locale, giving the film an almost surreal feel, particularly during a scene set during a Kabuki performance.

House of Bamboo is not a typical undercover cop *film noir*. While its plot is basically simple and linear, its characters are quite complex. Sandy Dawson, it is implied, is a homosexual attracted to Kenner. Kenner, likewise, exploits the attraction.

Robert Ryan and Robert Stack from *House of Bamboo* **(20th Century–Fox, 1955).**

House of Bamboo is a superior film compared to its predecessor. It is rich, psychologically complex and violent, showing the way to the great post-noir crime dramas including *Dirty Harry* (Warner Bros., 1971).

House of Strangers (20th Century–Fox, 1949). 101 min.
Producer: Sol C. Siegel. Director: Joseph L. Mankiewicz. Screenplay: Philip Yordan, based on the novel *I'll Never Go There Again* by Jerome Weidman. Director of Photography: Milton Krasner. Music: Daniele Amfitheotrof. Art Directors: Lyle Wheeler and George W. Davis. Editor: Harmon Jones.
Cast: Edward G. Robinson (Gino Monetti), Susan Hayward (Irene Bennett), Richard Conte (Max Monetti), Luther Adler (Joe Monetti), Paul Valentine (Pietro Monetti), Efrem Zimbalist, Jr. (Tony). With: Debra Paget, Hope Emerson, Esther Minciotti, Diana Douglas.

House of Strangers is a family melodrama that works as marginal *noir*. Its story of the crooked patriarch of a family and the problems he causes (and they cause for themselves), is similar to plays like *All My Sons*, but here the element of crime, sexual perversion and overwhelming greed is played to the *noir* style, combining to make it closer to the genre than similar films. It is also deeply cynical, but ultimately the film fails to satisfy as a real *film noir*.

House on 92nd Street (20th Century–Fox, 1945). 89 min.
Producer: Louis de Rochemont. Director: Henry Hathaway. Screenplay: Barre Lyndon, Charles G. Booth and John Monks, Jr., story by Charles G. Booth. Director of Photography: Norbett Brodine. Music: David Buttolph. Art Directors: Lyle Wheeler and Lewis Creber. Editor: Harmon Jones.
Cast: William Eythe (Bill Dietrich), Lloyd Nolan (Inspector Briggs), Signe

Hasso (Elsa Gebhardt), Gene Lockhart (Charles Ogden Roper), Leo G. Carroll (Hammershon), Lydia St.Clair (Johanna Schwartz). With: William Post, Jr., Harry Bellavar, Bruno Wick, Alfred Linder.

A brilliant student, Bill Dietrich, is recruited by the F.B.I. as an undercover agent after he is approached by Nazi spies to join their side. As the United States enters World War II, Dietrich proves to be an excellent contact. He learns that the Germans have information on the American A-bomb, and he sets out to find the traitor who gave the Nazis the secrets. He uncovers the spy ring, but exposes himself. In the subsequent shoot out, the Nazis accidentally kill Elsa Gebhardt, the leader of the traitors.

House on 92nd Street is an espionage thriller with *noir* elements. Its eerie cinematography and ever present sense of danger give it a sinister, dark ambiance. It avoids the cliches of the spy genre, with a somewhat more cynical approach. Its use of semi-documentary technique anticipates this later stylistic experiment in *film noir*.

The House on Telegraph Hill (20th Century-Fox, 1951). 92 min.

Producer: Robert Brassler. Director: Robert Wise. Screenplay: Elick Moll and Frank Partos, based on the novel by Dana Lyon. Director of Photography: Lucien Ballard. Music: Sol Kaplan. Art Directors: Lyle Wheeler and John DeCuir. Editor: Nick Maggio.

Cast: Richard Basehart (Alan Spender), Valentina Cortesa (Victoria Kowelska), William Lundigan (Major Marc Anders), Fay Baker (Margaret), Gordon Gebert (Chris). With Kei Thing Chung, Steve Geray, Herbert Butterfield, John Burton.

In order to gain admission to the United States after World War II, Victoria Kowelska assumes the identity of Karin de Nokova, a woman who died in a concentration camp. Nokova's son, Chris, lives with his wealthy paternal great aunt in San Francisco and Victoria travels there to join them. Soon afterward, the Aunt dies, leaving her estate to "Karin," including her spacious mansion on Telegraph Hill.

Victoria marries Alan Spender, the trustee of the estate, but she soon discovers that Spender is planning with Margaret, the governess, to kill her so that they can get the money left by the aunt. She tricks Alan into drinking poison meant for her. The police arrest Margaret, and Victoria, still posing as Karin de Nokova, is free to raise Chris as her own son.

House on Telegraph Hill is a rather, slow, dreamy *film noir* that substitutes innuendo and psychological insight for violence and action. It is yet another *noir* shot on location in San Francisco, making good use of the mysterious, fog and rain swept locations.

The film is full of paranoia and fear, with hints of sexual aberrations.

Fay Baker stands out among an excellent cast as the glacial, avaricious governess.

Houseman, John (Jacques Haussmann) (1902–1991)

Producer. Raised in England, Houseman moved to the United States in the early twenties. A successful Wall Street investor, he made a small fortune in the stock market, but like so many he was wiped out by the 1929 crash. He turned to the theater and made a precarious living as a playwright and producer until he teamed with Orson Welles. Together they formed the Mercury Theater, a troop of performers that included Joseph Cotten, Everett Sloane, Dorothy Comingore, George Coulouris, and others. The group achieved success on stage and radio. Welles and Houseman collaborated closely on their productions and Houseman contributed to many of the scripts including the infamous radio adaption of H. G. Welles' *War of the Worlds*.

When Orson Welles and company were hired by RKO to create their own production unit, Houseman was still a member of the team. He co-wrote *Citizen Kane* (RKO, 1941), without credit, but his volatile relationship with the young genius saw him depart.

After some stage and radio success in New York, Houseman returned to Hollywood in the mid forties and joined Paramount as a producer. He was a creative producer, choosing projects and guiding them from inception, through writing, actual production and release

Perhaps Houseman's greatest achievement early in his career as a producer was commissioning Raymond Chandler's only original screenplay, *The Blue Dahlia*. He also cultivated the careers of several young directors including Nicholas Ray, and he produced two *films noirs* for that director while at RKO: *They Live by Night* and *On Dangerous Ground*.

Houseman later produced a series of interesting films for MGM before his retirement in the early sixties. Later, however, in his later years, he emerged as a popular actor in movies and television.

Filmography: *The Blue Dahlia* (Paramount, 1946). *They Live by Night* (RKO, 1949). *On Dangerous Ground* (RKO, 1952).

Howe, James Wong (1899–1976)

Cinematographer. Howe was one of the most distinguished American cinematographers of his generation. His work is always outstanding, whatever the project. His visual sensitivity is charming and palatable in every shot. His style was generally straight forward, simple and unobtrusive. His five *films noirs* are not among the most extravagantly inventive, but Howe's work on each is outstanding.

Filmography: *Danger Signal* (Warner Bros., 1945). *Body and Soul* (United Artists, 1947). *Nora Prentiss* (Warner Bros., 1947). *He Ran All the Way* (United Artists, 1951). *Sweet Smell of Success* (United Artists, 1957).

Huggins, Roy (1914–)

Screenwriter. Huggins was a moderately successful screenwriter in the fifties. In the sixties he turned to television production, producing the cult favorite, *The Fugitive*. He wrote two minor *films noirs*. The former is also based on his novel.

Filmography: *Too Late for Tears* (United Artists, 1949). *Pushover* (Columbia, 1954).

Human Desire (Columbia, 1954). 90 min.

Producer: Lewis J. Rachmil. Director: Fritz Lang. Screenplay: Alfred Hayes, based on the novel *La Bete Humaine* by Emile Zola. Director of Photography: Burnett Guffey. Music: Daniele Amfiitheotrof. Art Director: Robert Peterson. Editor: William A. Lyon.

Cast: Glenn Ford (Jeff Warren), Gloria Grahame (Vicki Buckley), Broderick Crawford (Carl Buckley), Edgar Buchanan (Alec Simmons), Kathleen Case (Ellen Simmons). With: Diane DeLaire, Grandon Rhodes, Dan Seymour, John Pickard.

Carl Buckley convinces his wife, Vicki, to meet with his boss in order to help save Carl's job. He only wants her to tease the boss, but later he is convinced that they have slept together. He arranges an elaborate plan with the cold hearted indifferent Vicki, to kill the boss aboard a train. However, an off duty engineer, Jeff Owen, sees Vicki near the compartment where she and her husband kill the boss. He realizes what has taken place, but lies at the post-mortem to save the beautiful Vicki. They begin an adulterous liaison.

Carl descends into alcoholic jealousy. He keeps Vicki from running off with Jeff, by blackmailing her with a letter that implicates her in the murder. She convinces Jeff to kill Carl, but instead Jeff only beats up the pathetic alcoholic, and receives the incriminating letter. Furious at Jeff's supposed cowardice, Vicki returns to her husband.

Gloria Grahame in *Human Desire* **(Columbia, 1954).**

They leave together on the train, planning to start a new life together. Vicki taunts Carl with her sexual exploits, and he loses control, killing her in a jealous rage.

Of all things, *Human Desire* is based on a novel by Emile Zola. An earlier version had been made in France by Jean Renoir and remains the classic version. Its heightened emphasis of sexual perversion was considerably toned down for the more puritanical American audiences, but the Fritz Lang directed version was still one of the most sexually frank American films up to that time.

Gloria Grahame's performance as Vicki Buckley is masterful, the film's saving grace. Vicki is the archetypal *femme-fatale*, sadistic and masochistic at once. Grahame spends much of the film lounging around in lingerie, and Lang's camera seems to linger on her like an irresistible erotic angel of death. It is Gloria Grahame's finest performance.

Glen Ford's character, Jeff Warren, is the most cynical of his *film noir* roles.

Jeff cannot kill Carl (who deserves it) and he seems to accept Vicki's leaving him with little more than quiet resignation.

Fritz Lang's *mise-en-scène* is, of course, more extravagant than Jean Renoir's characterized by dark, moody lighting and close ups of faces half hidden in darkness.

Yet, despite Gloria Grahame's powerful performance and Fritz Lang's strong style, the film cannot overcome the restrictions imposed by the censors and it falls short of being a true classic.

Humberstone, H. Bruce (1903–1984)

Director. Humberstone was one of the great directors of "B" movies. He was an expert handler of thrillers and mysteries, but he also made comedies, dramas and musicals. He directed a single, superb *noir* thriller, *I Wake Up Screaming*. With its gallows humor and generally less than sympathetic view of humanity, the film presages the more famous *noir* classics, *Double Indemnity* (Paramount, 1944) and *The Postman Always Rings Twice* (MGM, 1946).

Filmography: *I Wake Up Screaming* (20th Century–Fox, 1941).

Hurt, William (1950–)

Actor. Hurt's portrayal of a seedy small time lawyer taken in by a *femme-fatale* in *Body Heat*, is roughly the same as Fred MacMurray's Walter Neff in *Double Indemnity*. Hurt's performance creates a surprising amount of sympathy for an otherwise worthless human being.

Filmography: *Body Heat* (Warner Bros., 1981).

Hustle (Paramount, 1975). 120 min.

Producer and Director: Robert Aldrich. Screenplay: Steve Shagan. Director of Photography: Joseph Biroc. Music: Frank De Vol. Art Director: Hilyard Brown. Editor: Michael Luciano.

Cast: Burt Reynolds (Lt. Phil Gaines), Catherine Deneuve (Nicole Britton), Ben Johnson (Marty Hollinger), Paul Winfield (Sgt. Louis Belgrave), Eileen Brennan (Paula Hollinger). With: Eddie Albert, Ernest Borgnine, Jack Carter, James Hampton.

Robert Aldrich's return to *noir* themes two decades after his masterpiece, *Kiss Me Deadly* (United Artists, 1955). It was a welcome return and a box-office success, if not quite an artistic success.

Lt. Phil Gaines, an honest cop, is obliged to cope with the nasty events of the hustle of police work in Los Angeles. He is in love with Nicole Britton, an elegant prostitute, and is investigating the violent death of a streetwalker. While investigating the victim's past, Lt. Gaines becomes embroiled with the girl's insanely vengeful father, her pathetic mother who hides a seedy past and a corrupt lawyer. Although he solves the case, he is killed in the final shoot out.

Aldrich whipped the story along at a brisk pace and Burt Reynolds injects a trenchant cynicism into the character of Lt. Gaines. The style is comparatively subdued, but altogether the film proved how powerful and successful *film noir* could be in contemporary cinema.

Huston, Angelica (1952–)

Actress. Granddaughter of Walter, daughter of John, Angelica carries on the traditions of her family in contemporary cinema. She co-starred in the modern *noir*, *The Grifters* as the incestuous matriarch of a family of "grifters" — con artists.

Filmography: *The Grifters* (Miramax, 1991).

Huston, John (1906–1989)

Director. A professional, craftsman-like director who also wrote many of his own scripts, John Huston is probably best known as a fine adaptor of novels to the screen. It would not be unfair to compare his best work with

Ernest Hemingway's fiction, for like Hemingway, Huston was a keen observer of ordinary men in extraordinary circumstances. In many of Huston's best films, a protagonist must come to terms with his own bravery and moral ambiguity.

Huston, the son of character actor Walter Huston, was a teenage adventurer and world traveler before eventually settling in Hollywood as a screenwriter in the 1930's. He was extremely successful at screenwriting and co-writing such important films as *Murders in the Rue Morgue* (Warner Bros., 1932), *Jezebel* (Warner Bros., 1938) and *Juarez* (Warner Bros., 1938) among others. His most important screenplay, however, was the early *noir* classic, *High Sierra*, adapted from W. R. Burnett's novel.

Huston's first film as a director was *The Maltese Falcon*, a seminal early *noir* which also helped establish Humphrey Bogart's screen image (and popularity) in the 1940's.

Key Largo is based on a play by Maxwell Anderson. It too contains an excellent Bogart performance, but like Huston's first film is a little too static and verbose.

The Asphalt Jungle is John Huston's most important *film noir*, and one of the genre's masterpieces. Like *High Sierra*, the film is adapted from a novel by W. R. Burnett. Superbly atmospheric and largely shot on location, it ushered in a group of caper films in the 1950's.

Huston later returned to *noir* themes in the espionage thriller *The Kremlin Letter* (20th Century–Fox, 1970), and had a supporting role in *Chinatown* as Norah Cross, an incestuous rancher whose plans to capture the water market during a drought leads to deception and murder.

Filmography: *Key Largo* (co-wrote, directed) (Warner Bros., 1948). *The Asphalt Jungle* (co-wrote, directed) (MGM, 1950). *Chinatown* (Paramount, 1974).

Huston, Virginia (1926–)

Actress. Huston, appeared in several important films and looked to be on the verge of stardom in the late forties, to only disappear as quickly as she appeared. By the early fifties she was co-starring in quickies churned out by Monogram, her chance at stardom long behind her. She appeared in four *films noirs*. By far, her most important role was as Ann, the innocent girlfriend of Robert Mitchum's, Jeff Bailey, in *Out of the Past*. However, she also has a prominent role in *Nocturne*.

Filmography: *Nocturne* (RKO, 1946). *Out of the Past* (RKO, 1947). *The Racket* (RKO, 1951). *Sudden Fear* (RKO, 1952).

Huston, Walter (Walter Houghston) (1884–1950)

Character actor. For three decades, Walter Huston was one of cinema's most popular character actors. He is probably best known today as the father of director John Huston, and as the craggy old prospector in John's classic, *The Treasure of the Sierra Madre*. He was one of the stars of *Beast of the City*, an important break with the gangster genre's traditions that presaged *film noir*. In Josef Von Sternberg's seminal *noir*, *The Shanghai Gesture* he starred as Guy Charteris, a British financier who discovers his long lost daughter has become a prostitute in a Shanghai gambling den. Finally, Huston had a brief cameo in his son's film, *The Maltese Falcon*, as one of Sam Spade's clients.

Filmography: *Beast of the City* (MGM, 1932). *The Maltese Falcon* (Warner Bros., 1941). *The Shanghai Gesture* (United Artists, 1941).

Hyer, Martha (1929–)

Actress. Hyer played second female leads in countless "B" movies and minor films in the 1950's and 1960's. She starred in a single, minor *film noir*.

Filmography: *Cry Vengeance* (Allied Artists, 1954).

I Am a Fugitive from a Chain Gang
(Warner Bros., 1932). 93 min.

Producer: Hal Wallis. Director: Mervyn Le Roy. Screenplay: Howard J. Greene and Brown Holmes, based on Robert Burn's autobiography. Director of Photography: Sol Polito. Art Director: Jack Okey. Editor: William Holmes.

Cast: Paul Muni (James Allen), Glenda Farrell (Marie Woods), Helen Vinson (Helen), Preston Foster (Pete), Allen Jenkins (Barney Skyes). With: Edward Ellis, John Wray, Hale Hamilton, Harry Woods.

Based on a true story, *I Am a Fugitive from a Chain Gang* tells the story of a war veteran who returns from World War I, only to find disillusionment and tragedy. After he is convicted for a crime he did not commit, and sentenced to a chain gang, he escapes to the north. He starts life anew, but when a girl friend convinces him to turn himself in (believing he will be vindicated) he is, nevertheless, returned to prison and a Georgia chain gang. After several years, he manages to escape again. He returns to the northern city and encounters the girl friend who had convinced him to turn himself in. She is horrified by his disheveled appearance and terror in his eyes. When she asks him how he survives, he says simply, "I steal," and then melts back into the shadows.

The movie is not true *film noir*, but it was an important break with the traditions of the gangster genre, with its unrelenting realism, desperation and paranoia. It was also one of the first films to introduce a leading character who was a disillusioned war veteran, not a triumphant character. The type would become familiar in *film noir* over a decade later.

I Died a Thousand Times
(Warner Bros., 1955). 109 min.

Producer: Willis Goldbeck. Director: Stuart Heisler. Screenplay: W. R. Burnett, based on the novel *High Sierra*. Director of Photography: Ted McCord. Music: David Buttolph. Art Director: Edward Carrere. Editor: Clarence Kolster.

Cast: Jack Palance (Roy Earle), Shelley Winters (Babe), Earl Holliman (Red), Perry Lopez (Mendoza). With Gonzalez Gonzalez, Lon Chaney, Jr., Howard St. John, Ralph Moodey.

Based on W. R. Burnett's novel *High Sierra*, *I Died a Thousand Times* was the second film version of the book. Although it is not a classic, this later version is notable chiefly for its strong screenplay (by the author) and its more realistic approach to sex. Palance is good as Roy Earle, but he was not Bogart. The film also makes effective use of color photography, translating the black and white *noir* style successfully to technicolor.

I Married a Communist for the F.B.I.
see *Woman on Pier 13*

I, the Jury
(United Artists, 1953). 88 min.

Producer: Victor Saville. Director: Harry Essex. Screenplay: Harry Essex, based on the novel by Mickey Spillane. Director of Photography: John Alton. Music: Franz Waxman. Art Director: Ward Ihnen. Editor: Frederick Y. Smith.

Cast: Biff Elliot (Mike Hammer), Preston Foster (Captain Pat Chambers), Peggie Castle (Charlotte Maning), Margaret Sheridan (Velda), Alan Reed (George Kalecki). With: Frances Osborne, Elisha Cook, Jr., Paul Dubov, Marry Anderson.

Private Investigator Mike Hammer vows revenge against those who killed his friend Jack Williams, an amputee. However, Pat Chambers, one of Hammer's friends on the police force, warns him not to use his usual strong arm tactics. Checking out everyone that attended a party given by Jack before he was killed, Hammer comes up with several suspects: Myrna, an ex-heroin addict who was Jack's girl friend,

Charlotte Maning, a beautiful, strange psychiatrist, two love-starved twins and George Kalecki, a fight promoter turned art collector. Kalecki turns out to be a narcotics dealer and Hammer kills him. He discovers that Charlotte Maning is trying to take over Kalecki's rackets. Hammer confronts Maning at her apartment. She does not answer his interrogation, but instead slowly disrobes. When she reaches for a hidden gun, Hammer kills her.

The first adaptation of a Mickey Spillane novel, *I, the Jury* was also an early attempt to make a conventional commercial film in 3-D. Cinematographer John Alton, a *noir* veteran, managed to avoid the pitfalls of 3-D, using it quite effectively (within the context of the story) in several scenes.

While the film retains the hard edge and misogyny of Spillane's fiction, Biff Elliot had little screen presence and was barely adequate as Spillane's tough anti-hero, Mike Hammer.

I Wake Up Screaming (20th Century–Fox, 1942). 82 min.

Producer: Milton Sperling. Director: H. Bruce Humberstone. Screenplay: Dwight Taylor, based on the novel by Steve Fisher. Director of Photography: Edward Cronjager. Music: Cyril J. Mockridge. Art Directors: Richard Day and Nathan Juran. Editor: Robert Simpson.

Cast: Betty Grable (Jill Lynn), Victor Mature (Frankie Christopher), Carole Landis (Vicky Lynn), Laird Cregar (Ed Cornell), William Gregan (McDonald). With: Alan Mowbray, Allyn Joslyn, Elisha Cook, Jr., Chick Chandler, Morris Ankrum.

Promoter Frankie Christopher is accused of murdering Vicky Lynn, a young actress he discovered with actor Robin Ray and gossip columnist Larry Evans. Christopher hides out with Vicky's sister Jill, whom he loves, but is soon captured by the police.

The police detective, Ed Cornell, is assigned to the case. He senses that Frankie is innocent, but is powerless to help. Frankie escapes from prison, determined to find the real killer. He discovers that an elevator operator in Vicky's building was obsessed with her, and had killed her in a twisted act of "love." He also discovers that Detective Cornell knew who the real killer was, but had suppressed the information because he is jealous of Frankie's success and fame. Frankie turns in the information to the District Attorney and is free to continue his affair with Jill.

I Wake Up Screaming is important for several reasons. It is a prime example of the developing style and themes of *film noir* in the early forties. It contains the shadowy, low-key lighting that would become familiar as the genre developed. It also contained prototypes of alienated *noir* characters, corrupt officials, and obsessive sexuality. All are encountered in this early *noir* classic, but would become more strongly defined over the course of the next several years.

I Walk Alone (Paramount, 1948). 98 min.

Producer: Hal B. Wallis. Director: Byron Haskin. Screenplay: Charles Schnee, adapted by Robert Smith and John Bright from the play *Beggars Are Coming* by Theodore Reeves. Director of Photography: Leo Tover. Music: Victor Young. Art Directors: Hans Dreier and Franz Bachelin. Editor: Arthur Schmidt.

Cast: Burt Lancaster (Frankie Madison), Lizabeth Scott (Kay Lawrence), Kirk Douglas (Noll Turner), Wendell Corey (Dave), Kristine Miller (Mrs. Richardson). With: George Rigaud, Marc Lawrence, Mike Mazurki, Mickey Knox, Roger Neury.

Frankie Madison is released from prison after serving a long sentence for bootlegging. He returns to his home town to discover his old bootlegging partner, Noll Turner, is running a bar and that his younger brother is working as an accountant for Turner.

Lizabeth Scott and Burt Lancaster in *I Walk Alone* (Paramount, 1948).

Turner has sold the small club he owned with Madison and he refuses to split his profits on the new club with him. He gets his girl friend Kay, a singer in the club, to placate Madison but, predictably, she falls for him. Meanwhile, when Madison's younger brother stands up for Madison, Turner has him killed. In the final confrontation, Madison kills Turner and then sets out with Kay to start a new life.

While it is not the classic of many of its contemporaries, *I Walk Alone* is still a compelling, dark tale of unrelenting greed, vengeance, and old-fashioned romance.

Its performances are typical. Burt Lancaster is hard-boiled and stoic. Kirk Douglas is wickedly evil as Noll Turner. Lizabeth Scott is glamorous and sings several good songs.

First time director Byron Haskin captures the mysterious ambiance of the story in typical high grade Paramount style.

The standout element of the film, however, is its excellent dialog, particularly in the sexual banter between Kay and Frankie Madison.

I Was a Communist for the F.B.I.
(Warner Bros., 1951). 84 min.

Producer: Bryan Foy. Director: Gordon Douglas. Screenplay: Crane Wilbur, based on the article "I Posed as a Communist for the F.B.I." from the *Saturday Evening Post* by Matt Cvetic. Director of Photography: Edwin DePar. Art Director: Leo Kuter. Editor: Folmar Blangsted.

Cast: Frank Lovejoy (Matt Cvetic), Dorothy Hart (Eve Merrick), Philip Carey (Mason), Dick Webb (Crowley), James Millican (Jim Blandon), Ron Hagerthy (Dick Cvetic). With Russ Conway, Hope Cramer, Kasia Orzazekski, Eddie Norris.

The film is a low budget, real life exposé of a steel company worker, Matt Cvetic, who has joined the Communist

Party after being recruited by the F.B.I. No one knows he is undercover, not even his family. Eventually, when ordered to "take care of" a female teacher who is a member of the party but has grown disgruntled, he rescues her. In the inevitable gun battle, Matt kills the local communist party leader. When he testifies at a government inquiry, he is at least redeemed in his friend's and family's eyes.

I Was a Communist for the F.B.I. is a prominent example of ultra-conservative *film noir*. It was a typical product of the "red hysteria" of the early fifties. In fact, the film is a taut, suspenseful mystery with a strong *noir* ambiance.

I Wouldn't Be in Your Shoes (Monogram, 1948). 70 min.

Producer: Walter Mirisch. Director: William Nigh. Screenplay: Steve Fisher, based on the novel by Cornell Woolrich. Director of Photography: Mark Stengler. Music: Edward J. Kay. Art Director: Dave Milton. Editor: Otho Lovering.

Cast: Don Castle (Tom), Elyse Knox (Ann), Regis Toomey (Judd), Charles D. Brown (Inspector Stevens), Rory Mallinson (First Detective). With: Robert Lowell, Bill Kennedy, Ray Dolciame, William Ruhl.

Tom and Ann are a down-on-their-luck team of vaudeville dancers. Tom's dance shoes are discarded when the couple inherit some money, but they turn out to be important evidence in a murder case. Tom is arrested and convicted. Ann hires a detective, Judd, to help get her husband out of prison. They uncover a series of clues and, in a surprising twist, Judd turns out to be the killer!

I Wouldn't Be in Your Shoes is based on another improbable story by Cornell Woolrich. Except for Regis Toomey's tongue-in-cheek performance as the detective/killer, the film has little to recommend.

Impact (United Artists, 1949). 111 min.

Producer: Harry Popkin. Director: Arthur Lubin. Screenplay: Jay Dratler and Dorothy Reid, story by Jay Dratler. Director of Photography: Ernest Laszlo. Music: Michel Michelet. Art Director: Rudi Feld. Editor: Arthur H. Nadel.

Cast: Brian Donlevy (Walter Williams), Ella Raines (Marsha Peters), Charles Coburn (Lt. Quincy), Helen Walker (Irene Williams), Anna May Wong (Su Lin), Robert Warwick (Captain Callahan), Clarence Kolb (Darcy). With Art Baker, William Wright, Mae Marsh, Sheilah Graham.

Walter Williams, a wealthy industrialist, is at a crossroads in his life. He suddenly finds his profession less than satisfying, but he does not know what to do, until his wife inadvertently provides a solution. Unknown to him, his wife Irene and her lover Darcy are planning to kill him. One night while driving along a quiet road, Darcy takes advantage of a flat tire and tries to kill Walter with a tire iron, however he only knocks him unconscious.

Walter, however, has survived, and he decides to start his life anew. He wanders into a small town and charming a young female mechanic, Marsha Peters, he is hired by her uncle to work in his garage. His romance with Peters blossoms until Lt. Quincy enters the picture. Quincy has been investigating the wealthy man's disappearance. His arrival forces Walter to confront his wife and her lover and in the end they are sent to prison and Walter is reunited with Marsha.

Impact is "B" movie making at its best. The budget might have been low, but the writing, directing and acting are all first rate. Helen Walker makes a convincing, avaricious *femme-fatale*, while Ella Raines (here at her best) is well cast as the good girl who makes Walter's life worth living. Even the film's music, composed by Michel Michelet, is also above average.

The screenplay for *Impact*, co-written by *noir* veteran Jay Dratler, is surprisingly witty (an element generally missing from *film noir*), and director Arthur Lubin, one of the best "B" directors, keeps the whole thing moving at a brisk pace so that some of the inconsistencies in the story go unnoticed.

In a Lonely Place (Columbia, 1950). 94 min.

Producer: Robert Lord. Director: Nicholas Ray. Screenplay: Andrew Solt, adapted by Edmund H. North, based on the novel by Dorothy B. Hughes. Director of Photography: Burnett Guffey. Music: George Antheil. Art Director: Robert Peterson. Editor: Viola Lawrence.

Cast: Humphrey Bogart (Dixon Steele), Gloria Grahame (Laurel Gray), Frank Lovejoy (Brub Nicolai), Carl Benton Reid (Capt. Lochner), Martha Stewart (Mildred Atkinson), Robert Warwick (Charlie Waterman). With: Morris Ankrum, William Ching, Steven Geray, Hedda Brooks.

Dixon Steel is a once successful writer whose career has hit the skids thanks to his alcoholism and bad temper. He invites an impressionable young hat check girl up to his apartment under the pretense of having her tell him the plot of a novel she is working on that he plans to turn into a screenplay. They flirt, but nothing else happens and he soon sends her on her way. When the girl turns up dead the next day, Steele is the major suspect. However, his next door neighbor Laurel tells the police that she saw the girl leave alone, thus providing Steel with an alibi.

Steele and Laurel fall in love. They plan to get married, but Steele is violently jealous, and his anger is compounded by the continued suspicions of the police. When Laurel and Steele have an argument one night, he attacks her, grabbing her by the throat, he begins to strangle her. At that moment, the telephone rings. It is a police detective, informing Steele that the murder victim's boy friend confessed to the crime. Although he is remorseful, it is too late for Laurel and Steele and she leaves him.

Nicholas Ray's most tragically romantic *film noir*, *In a Lonely Place* reminds one of the contemporary Charles Bukowski's fiction with its alcoholics and marginal characters. It is essentially a bleak portrait of life on the edge of the middle class. It is also an exploration of repressed violence and jealousy in a love affair.

The film is quite suspenseful, and the viewer is not entirely certain that Steele is innocent until the end. This element of tension is enhanced by the subtle performances of Gloria Grahame and Humphrey Bogart.

The ending, although not as explicitly tragic as Alfred Hitchcock's *Vertigo* (Universal, 1958), does give a glimpse of the bleak, lonely future destined for both Steele and Laurel.

Ingster, Boris (1913–1978)

Director. Ingster is best known for his weird early *film noir*, *Stranger on the Third Floor*. The film was made on a very modest budget, but has some striking expressionist visuals. His later *noir*, *Southside 1-1000*, is not as well made as his first film. Indeed, it was his last film as a director. As a producer, however, he was a success, particularly on television.

Filmography: *Stranger on the Third Floor* (RKO, 1940). *Southside 1-1000* (co-wrote/directed) (Allied Artists, 1950).

Inside Job (Universal, 1946). 65 min.

Producer and Director: Jean Yarbrough. Screenplay: George Bricker and Jerry Warner, story by Tod Browning and Garrett Fort. Director of Photography: Maury Gertsman. Music: Frank Skinner. Editor: Otta Ludwig.

Cast: Preston Foster (Bart Madden), Alan Curtis (Eddie Norton), Ann Rutherford (Claire Gray), Jimmy Moss (Skipper). With: Joe Sawyer, Joan Fulton, Milburne Stone.

Eddie and Claire are a couple whose life of crime has grown tiring and they have decided to go straight. However, Bart Madden, a mob associate, is blackmailing them, forcing them to help him burglarize the department store where they work. A series of double crosses leads to Madden's death, at the hands of a cop, and the couple return the stolen money and turn themselves in. *Inside Job* is a typical Universal programmer. Its production values are minimal at best, and its screenplay resorts to clichés at every turn. Only Preston Foster, as the violent Bart Madden, emerges unscathed.

Interestingly, the story for the film was co-written by Tod Browning, the great horror film director of the early thirties. By the mid-forties he was reduced to providing the occasional contribution to films like this.

Ireland, John (1914–1992)

Actor. A craggy character lead, John Ireland specialized in tough and cynical roles in the late forties and early fifties. He is one of *films noir*'s minor icons. Although very talented, he inexplicably fell from favor with audiences in the mid fifties. His *noirs* were made mainly for studios like Producers Releasing Corporation and Allied Artists. Ireland's performances in each is typically intense and compelling. He was particularly memorable in Anthony Mann's *Railroaded* as a hired gunman. He also played a psychotic killer in Mann's *Raw Deal*, and had a small supporting role in the classic, *All the King's Men*.

Filmography: *The Gangster* (Allied Artists, 1947). *Railroaded* (PRC, 1947). *Raw Deal* (Eagle-Lion, 1948). *All the King's Men* (Columbia, 1949). *Party Girl* (MGM, 1958). *Farewell, My Lovely* (Avco-Embassy, 1975).

Irish, William pseudonym for writer **Cornell Woolrich**

Ivano, Paul (1900–1989)

Cinematographer. A cinematographer for mainly routine productions. Ivano worked on several interesting *films noirs*. His best work, however, as on *The Shanghai Gesture* and *Uncle Harry*, were on films dominated by strong, visual oriented directors, and it is difficult to judge Ivano's true contribution on his films.

Filmography: *The Shanghai Gesture* (co-photographed) (United Artists, 1941). *Uncle Harry* (Universal, 1945). *Black Angel* (Universal, 1946). *The Gangster* (Allied Artists, 1947).

Jaffe, Sam (1893–1984)

Character actor. One of the most talented character actors in American film, Sam Jaffe played eccentrics of various types in dozens of films. His *noir* career was sadly limited to two films. In *The Accused* he gave a brief but memorable portrayal of a callous scientist, a catalyst of the action. His most important *noir* role was as the criminal mastermind Doc Riedenschneider in *The Asphalt Jungle*.

Filmography: *The Accused* (Paramount, 1946). *The Asphalt Jungle* (MGM, 1950).

Jagger, Dean (Dean Jeffries) (1903–)

Actor. A star character actor in the thirties, forties and fifties, Jagger specialized in sympathetic heroes. He played honest cops in both *Dark City* and *Private Hell, 36*. In *When Strangers Marry*, an inexpensive variation of Alfred Hitchcock's *Suspicion* (RKO, 1941), he played a role similar to that of Cary Grant in that film: the newlywed husband suspected of being a murderer by his wife.

Filmography: *When Strangers Marry* (Monogram, 1944). *Dark City* (Paramount, 1950). *Private Hell, 36* (Filmmakers, 1954).

Jeopardy (MGM, 1952). 69 min.

Producer: Sol Fielding. Director: John Sturges. Screenplay: Mel Dinelli and Maurice Zimm, story by Maurice Zimm. Director of Photography: Victor

Milner. Music: Dimitri Tiomkin. Art Director: Cedric Gibbons. Editor: Otto Ludwig.

Cast: Barbara Stanwyck (Helen Stilwin), Barry Sullivan (Doug Stilwin), Ralph Meeker (Lawson), Lee Aaker (Bobby Stilwin).

While on a camping trip, a couple and their son become victims of both man and nature. Doug Stilwin gets separated from his wife, Helen and son, Bobby, and is lost in the woods, and they in turn are trapped by a flood. To make matters worse, Mrs. Stilwin becomes the captive of a sadistic, paranoid escaped convict, Lawsen. In the end, however, all turns out okay when she escapes and helps rescue her injured husband.

Jeopardy is wildly improbable, but Maurice Zimm's story was given so much suspense by *noir* veteran Mel Dinelli, fast pace by director John Sturges, and its strong performances by a minimalist cast, one hardly cares that the film is over in a mere 69 minutes! Despite its cast of major stars, (it is Barbara Stanwyck's least important *film noir*), *Jeopardy* was essentially a programmer, but a superior one nevertheless.

Jewell, Edward C. (1909–1983)

Art director. As the production designer for Producer's Releasing Corporation (PRC), the notorious "Poverty Row" studio, Jewell worked on some of the most obscure commercial films of the American film industry. His budgets were rarely more than a few thousand dollars, yet he did manage to create some interesting, minimalist sets for films like Edgar G. Ulmer's *noir* classic, *Detour*, allegedly shot on an entire budget of $20,000.00. Jewell also worked on Anthony Mann's early *T- Man*.

Filmography: *Detour* (PRC, 1945). *T-Men* (Eagle-Lion, 1948).

Johnny Angel (RKO, 1945). 76 min.

Producer: Jack Gross. Director:

Edwin L. Marin. Screenplay: Steve Fisher, adapted by Frank Gruber from the novel *Mr. Angel Comes Aboard* by Charles Gordon Booth. Director of Photography: Harry J. Wild. Music: Leigh Harline. Song: "Memphis in June" by Hoagy Carmichael and Paul Webster. Art Director: Albert S. D'Agostino and John Keller. Editor: Les Millbrook.

Cast: George Raft (Johnny Angel), Claire Trevor (Lilah), Signe Hasso (Paulette), Lowell Gilmore (Sam Jewell), Hoagy Carmichael (Celestial O'Brien), Marvin Miller (Gustofason). With: Margaret Wycherly, J. Farrell McDonald, Mack Gray.

Johnny Angel is a ship captain who discovers his father's ship abandoned and his dad has been killed. He returns to his home town, New Orleans, to find the killer. Aided by his friend, a taxi driver named Celestial O'Brien, they find a girl named Paula, a witness to the crime. She tells them that the elder Mr. Angel had double crossed a group of gold smugglers led by Gusty Gustafason. Johnny finds Gustafason who admits that he killed Johnny's father, but that his wife, Lilah, in fact, is the head of the smugglers. Lilah shoots Gustafason but Johnny overpowers her and then turns her over to the police.

Set in the seedy dives and exotic back streets of New Orleans, *Johnny Angel* is appropriately atmospheric and dark. Cinematographer, Harry J. Wild did some of his best work on the film.

George Raft is serviceable, but Claire Trevor stands out as the dangerous Lilah Gustafason. She is both sensual and deadly, guided by her greed alone.

The film however, is one of RKO's minor "A" *films noirs*, and except for Trevor's performance, is largely forgettable.

Johnny Eager (MGM, 1942). 102 min.

Producer: John W. Considine, Jr. Director: Mervyn LeRoy. Screenplay: John Lee Mahin and James Edward Grant, story by James Edward Grant.

Director of Photography: Harold Rosson. Music: Bronislau Kaper. Art Directors: Cedric Gibbons and Stan Rogers. Editor: Albert Akst.

Cast: Robert Taylor (Johnny Eager), Lana Turner (Lisabeth Bard), Edward Arnold (John Benson Farrell), Van Heflin (Jeff Hartnett), Robert Sterling (Jimmy Lanthrop), Glenda Farrell (Mae Blythe). With Patricia Dane, Barry Nelson, Henry O'Neill, Charles Dingle, Cy Kendall.

Johnny Eager is a "reformed" petty thief. He drives a taxi, but is planning to open a race track by bribing crooked politicians. He is introduced to two sociology students (including the beautiful Lisabeth Bard) by his parole officer who believes Johnny has gone straight. The girls are writing a paper on criminal psychology. Later, when he meets Lisabeth at a fashionable night club, Johnny discovers that she is the daughter of Benson Farrell, the District Attorney who had prosecuted Johnny several years before, resulting in his being sent to prison. When Farrell finds that Lisabeth is seeing Johnny, he is furious and orders Johnny to quit dating her. Johnny, who wants revenge against Farrell, refuses. He knows that Lisabeth inadvertently will help him obtain his revenge.

Johnny invites Lisabeth to his apartment one evening. He stages a fight with a local tough, arranging it so that she will have to shoot his assailant in order to save him. It works, but Lisabeth is shocked she is capable of such a violent act and has a mental breakdown.

Meanwhile, Johnny's arguments with other racketeers are turning violent. His life is in danger. Farrell asks Johnny to tall Lisabeth the truth about the staged incident. He refuses at first, but then relents when a friend asks him to. Lisabeth is clinging, desperately in love with him. She refuses to leave his side, although he warns her that her life is in danger: he knows he has been followed by hoods to Farrell's place.

He knocks her unconscious and as he is leaving he is caught in the crossfire between the police and the hoods, and is accidently shot and killed by an honest cop he had recently befriended.

Johnny Eager is an important early *film noir* that was one of the most tragically romantic films of its epoch. It helped popularize the *noir* character types and the alienation and corruption of a big city.

Lana Turner's character is the most fascinating in the film. Like many *noir* characters to come (both male and female), Lisabeth Bard is an innocent attracted to the violent world of crime, largely because of a warped sexuality. She is charmed and seduced by the brash, handsome Johnny Eager, who then destroys her.

Johnny O'Clock (Columbia, 1947). 95 min.

Producer: Edward G. Nealis. Director: Robert Rossen. Screenplay: Robert Rossen, story by Milton Holmes. Director of Photography: Burnett Guffey. Music: George Duning. Art Directors: Stephen Goosson and Cary Odell. Editors: Warren Low and Al Clark.

Cast: Dick Powell (Johnny O'Clock), Evelyn Keyes (Nancy Hobbs), Lee J. Cobb (Inspector Kock), Thomas Gomez (Pete Marchettis), Ellen Drew (Nelle Marchettis), Nina Foch (Harriet Hobbs), Jim Bannon (Chuck Blayden). With: John Kellogg, Mabel Paige, Phil Brown, Jeff Chandler.

Nancy Hobbs arrives in New York determined to find the killer of her sister, Harriet. Harriet was the girl friend of Chuck Blayden, a cop who was being bribed by two casino owners, Johnny O'Clock and Pete Marchettis. Nancy's investigation unmasks Marchettis as the killer, while a series of double crosses results in Chuck Blayden's murder as well. Johnny O'Clock realizes that Marchettis was cheating him and when he confronts him, a shoot out occurs. Johnny kills Marchettis, but becomes a fugitive wanted by the police. He takes a police inspector hostage, but eventually gives up, partially because he wants to someday get with Nancy, whom he has grown to love.

Johnny O'Clock was Robert Rosson's first film as a director. He was previously a successful screenwriter. While the film is certainly not a classic and utilizes many of the genre's standard conventions, it is still a compelling film. Rosson proves himself a capable, occasionally splendid, filmmaker. Dick Powell continues to capitalize convincingly on his forties' tough guy persona, and Evelyn Keyes emerges as one of the most sensual, under appreciated, actresses of the period.

Johnson, Nunnally (1897–1977)

Screenwriter. Nunnally Johnson was one of the greatest American screenwriters. Johnson first made a name for himself as a columnist and short story writer based in New York. He was attracted to Hollywood after the stock market crash in 1929, and several years later was firmly established as a successful writer of witty, violent melodramas. He became one of director John Ford's chief collaborators, writing the screenplays for many of the director's classic films. He wrote two *films noirs. Woman in the Window*, adapted from a novel by J. H. Wallis and directed by Fritz Lang, is one of the genre's early classics. *The Dark Mirror*, while less successful, is an interesting mystery concerning twin sisters, one of whom is a murderer.

Filmography: *Woman in the Window* (RKO, 1944). *The Dark Mirror* (universal, 1946).

Jones, Carolyn (1929–1983)

Actress. Carolyn Jones will be remembered forever, for better or worse, as Mortisa Addams in the cult-television comedy, *The Addams Family*. She had an active film career for over a decade before that, usually appearing as a second female lead. She had small supporting roles in four *films noirs*.

Filmography: *The Turning Point* (Paramount, 1952). *The Big Heat* (Columbia, 1953). *The Shield for Murder* (United Artists, 1954). *Baby Face Nelson* (United Artists, 1957).

Jory, Victor (1902–1982)

Character actor. The Canadian born Victor Jory almost always played villains in a variety of films. He co-starred in a single, minor *film noir*, typically in a villainous role.

Filmography: *The Capture* (RKO, 1950).

Jourdan, Louis (Louis Gendre) (1919–)

Actor. For over two decades, Louis Jordan was the very ideal of the suave, romantic Frenchman. While he most often played conventional romantic leads, he also played villainous roles as in Max Ophuls' classic, *Letter from an Unknown Woman* (Republic, 1948) and the minor late-*noir*, *Julie*, his single *noir* appearance.

Filmography: *Julie* (MGM, 1956).

Journey into Fear (RKO, 1943). 71 min.

Producer: Orson Welles. Director: Norman Foster. Screenplay: Joseph Cotten and Orson Welles, based on the novel by Eric Ambler. Director of Photography: Karl Struss. Music: Roy Webb. Art Directors: Albert S. D'Agostino and Mark-Lee Kirk. Editor: Mark Robson.

Cast: Joseph Cotten (Howard Graham), Dolores Del Rio (Josette Martel), Orson Welles (Col. Haki), Ruth Warwick (Stephanie Graham), Agnes Moorehead (Mrs. Mathews), Everett Sloane (Kopeikin). With Jack Moss, Jack Durant, Eustace Wyatt, Frank Readick.

When Howard Graham, a naval engineer who lives and works in Turkey, is the target of a failed assassination, he is informed by a local police officer, Colonel Haki that there is a Nazi conspiracy to kill him because he has information vital to the war effort. He is hastily ushered out of Turkey aboard an old freighter. He befriends the beautiful dancer Josette, another of the ship's passengers, and an old man called Kopeinkin. The ancient ship is full of suspicious characters, at least one of whom is trying to kill him. Landing in another part of the country, Graham rejoins his wife, but discovers he is still being pursued. He leads his pursuer on a dangerous chase, finally coming to a confrontation on the ledge of a building three stories above the street in the driving rain. Graham is saved by Haki who shoots his would-be killer.

Journey into Fear, based on a popular novel by Eric Ambler, is one of the most prominent early *films noirs* with an espionage plot.

Although Norman Foster is given credit as the film's director, it shows the strong hand of Orson Welles. Welles did, in fact, direct many scenes, but overall its style is relatively subdued when compared to its predecessors, *Citizen Kane* (RKO, 1941) and *The Magnificent Ambersons* (RKO, 1942).

The claustrophobic sets, dark shadows, fog and rain swept streets and locations (all created in the studio) echo Howard Graham's sense of alienation. These elements would become familiar as the genre developed over the next several years.

Julie (MGM, 1956). 99 min.
Producer: Martin Melcher. Director: Andrew L. Stone. Screenplay: Andrew L. Stone. Director of Photographer: Fred Jackman, Jr. Music: Leith Stevens. Art Directors: William A. Horning and Addison Hehr. Editor: John Markham.

Cast: Doris Day (Julie Benton), Louis Jourdan (Lyle Benton), Barry Sullivan (Cliff Henderson), Frank Lovejoy (Capt. Pringle). With: Jack Kelly, Hank Patterson, Aline towne, Ann Robinson, John Gallaudet.

Julie, a nightclub singer, marries the handsome, debonair Lyle Benton, a successful concert pianist. She soon discovers he murdered his first wife and may be planning to kill her.

Yet another variation of *Suspicion* (RKO, 1941), *Julie* is surprisingly suspenseful despite certain inconsistencies and improbabilities. A minor *noir* that shows how far the sensibilities of the genre infiltrated commercial movies by the mid–fifties.

Juran, Nathan (1907–)
Art director. Juran's career as a junior art director began in the late thirties. He joined 20th Century–Fox in the early thirties and collaborated on many films with Richard Day. He later moved to directing, overseeing a series of excellent 3-D fantasy films that are more famous for their animation, created by Ray Harryhausen. His three *noirs* as art director are all excellent, if not particularly outstanding examples of *film noir* production design in the 1940's.

Filmography: *I Wake Up Screaming* (20th Century–Fox, 1942). *Body and Soul* (United Artists, 1947). *Kiss the Blood Off My Hands* (Universal, 1948).

Kanin, Garson (1912–) and **Gordon, Ruth** (1896–1983)
Screenwriters. Kanin was a veteran of the New York theatre world when he moved to Hollywood in the late-thirties. He quickly became a leading director of intelligent romantic comedies, but he retired at the height of his success in the mid–forties, and returned to New York. He married stage actress Ruth Gordon and together they became leading playwrights. In the late-forties they began collaborating on film scripts. Most of their scripts were satires disguised as romantic comedies. Their single *film noir* is, perhaps predictably, set in the back stage world of New York Theatre. *A Double Life* is an interesting study of insanity with a splendidly over the top performance by Ronald Colman.

Joan Fontaine and Cary Grant in one of the few calm scenes from *Suspicion* (RKO, 1941).

Filmography: *A Double Life* (Universal, 1948).

Kansas City Confidential (United Artists, 1952). 98 min.
Producer: Edward Small. Director: Phil Karlson. Screenplay: George Bruce and Harry Essex, story by Harold R.

Greene and Rowland Brown. Director of Photography: George E. Diskant. Music: Paul Sawtell. Editor: Buddy Small.
Cast: John Payne (Joe Rolfe), Coleen Gray (Helen), Preston Foster (Timothy Foster), Dona Drake (Teresa), Jack Elam (Harris), Neville Brand (Kane).

With Lee Van Cleef, Mario Seletti, Howard Negley, Ted Ryan, George Wallace.

Angered about his meager pension, retired Kansas City policeman Tim Foster puts together a gang of robbers with three ex-convicts. Wearing masks at their meetings so that none of them will know each other (thus, avoiding possible betrayals if caught later), they plan an armored car heist which goes off without a hitch.

Another ex-convict, Rolfe, who had no connection to the crime, is arrested and brutally questioned by the police. Rolfe, who is angered by the episode, decides to investigate the robbery. Through his underworld connections and by using strong arm techniques, Rolfe uncovers Foster's plans: to set up his fellow robbers and turn them in for the reward while, at the same time keeping the money from the heist. However, in the final confrontation, Foster's two partners are killed and Foster mortally wounded in the gun battle. Having gained a certain degree of respect for Foster, Rolfe lies to the police, saying that Foster helped track down the robbers.

Typical of the new era of *film noir*, *Kansas City Confidential* was concerned more with mindless violence. Director Phil Karlson uses his modest budget and simple sets to great advantage and he films the movie in simple, semi-documentary style. The film also has strong performances by John Payne as Rolfe, the ex-con tough guy and Preston Foster as the disillusioned retired cop.

Kaper, Bronislau (1902–1983)

Composer. The Polish born Kaper was a leading Hollywood composer in the forties and fifties. He won an Academy Award for his score for *Lili* (MGM, 1953), and also composed the excellent score for John Huston's *The Red Badge of Courage* (MGM, 1951). He composed the incidental music for several *films noirs*. His music is distin-guished by a strongly dramatic style, typical of many European trained film composers.

Filmography: *Johnny Eager* (MGM, 1942). *Bewitched* (MGM, 1945). *The Stranger* (RKO, 1946). *The High Wall* (MGM, 1947). *Act of Violence* (MGM, 1949).

Kaplan, Sol (1903–1978)

Composer. Kaplan was a prolific composer of adequate but rarely excep-tional film scores. Of his five *noir* scores, the most outstanding is for *Niagara*. The music imitates the swirl-ing, crashing sound of the Niagara Falls and thus, the film's story and characters.

Filmography: *Hollow Triumph* (Eagle-Lion, 1948). *711 Ocean Drive* (Columbia, 1950). *House on Telegraph Hill* (20th Century–Fox, 1951). *Niagara* (20th Century–Fox, 1952). *The Burglar* (Columbia, 1957).

Karloff, Boris (William Henry Pratt) (1897–1969)

Actor. Boris Karloff is best known for his roles in Universal horror films in the 1930's. He also played character roles in many other films usually in sinister parts as in his single *film noir*, Douglas Sirk's *Lured*.

Filmography: *Lured* (United Artists, 1947).

Karlson, Phil (Philip N. Karlstein) (1908–1986)

Director. Karlson was a prolific di-rector of "B" movies. His career began in the mid–forties and for many years he directed very low budget, undistin-guished films for studios like Mono-gram. He hit his creative peak in the 1950's, however, with a series of unpre-tentious, extremely violent *films noirs*.

Phil Karlson is best known for his films *Kansas City Confidential* and *The Phenix City Story*. The former, like all of his best work, is an exposé of big city crime. In this case, the story concerned a cop forced to participate in a heist.

The latter film is a semi-documentary based on real events.

All of Karlson's films are distinguished by a simple, direct style that would become the norm in the fifties. His lighting is generally flat and camera set ups uncomplicated.

All of Karlson's mature *films noirs* are excellent. They were immensely popular and had a direct influence on the early work of Sam Fuller among others.

Filmography: *Scandal Sheet* (Columbia, 1952). *Kansas City Confidential* (United Artists, 1952). *99 River Street* (United Artists, 1953). *Hell's Island* (Paramount, 1955). *The Phenix City Story* (Allied Artists. 1955). *Tightspot* (Columbia, 1955). *The Brothers Rico* (Columbia, 1957).

Kasdan, Lawrence (1943–)

Screenwriter and director. Kasdan was one of the most successful screenwriters of the late-seventies and early eighties. He wrote or co-wrote a number of critical and/or commercial successes including *The Empire Strikes Back* (20th Century–Fox, 1980) and *Raiders of the Lost Ark* (20th Century–Fox, 1981). As a writer and director, Kasdan made a striking debut with *Body Heat*, a contemporary variation of *noir* stories, particularly *Double Indemnity* (Paramount, 1944) and *The Postman Always Rings Twice* (MGM, 1946). The film proved the artistic and commercial viability of *film noir* in modern commercial cinema.

Filmography: *Body Heat* (Warner Bros., 1981).

Kazan, Elia (Elia Kazanjoglous) (1909–)

Director. Kazan was a veteran of New York's Group Theatre with whom he was first an actor and later director. After several major stage successes, he began directing films in 1945. He had a highly developed, self-conscious style, influenced by expressionism and a heightened sensitivity toward the acting elements. He directed two true *films noirs, Panic in the Streets* and *Boomerang*. The former is a superb thriller, shot mostly on location in New York. *Boomerang* is best known for its early use of semi-documentary techniques and its ending in which a murderer goes free. *On the Waterfront*, with its strong political criticism, is only marginally *film noir*, but it is notable for its strong, *noir*-like photography.

Filmography: *Boomerang* (20th Century–Fox, 1947). *Panic in the Streets* (20th Century–Fox, 1950). *On the Waterfront* (Columbia, 1954).

Keith, Brian (Robert Keith, Jr.) (1921–)

Actor. Keith is well known for his laid back, laconic acting style and for his ubiquitous television appearances, almost always in syrupy roles. Early in his career he was a small parts player, and had supporting roles in two minor *films noirs*.

Filmography: *Tightspot* (Columbia, 1955). *Appointment with a Shadow* (Universal, 1958).

Keller, Walter E. (1902–1981)

Art director. In collaboration with Albert S. D'Agostino, Keller was an important production designer at RKO in the forties. He was also a key collaborator in the great series of "B" horror thrillers produced by Val Lewton. Likewise, all of the *films noirs* Keller worked on were "B" productions, but are notable, in part, for their inventive, expressionist influenced style.

Filmography: *Born to Kill* (RKO, 1947). *Desperate* (RKO, 1947). *Race Street* (RKO, 1948). *Follow Me Quietly* (RKO, 1949). *The Window* (RKO, 1949). *Roadblock* (RKO, 1951). *The Hitch-Hiker* (RKO, 1953). *Private Hell, 36* (Filmmakers, 1954).

Kellogg, Virginia ( )

Screenwriter. Kellogg was briefly successful as a screenwriter in the late-forties. She wrote or co-wrote several popular films including three *films noirs*. The most prominent of these is Raoul Walsh's classic *White Heat*.

Filmography: *T-Men* (Eagle-Lion, 1948). *White Heat* (Warner Bros., 1949). *Caged* (Warner Bros., 1950.

Kelly, Gene (Eugene Curran Kelly) (1912–)

Actor and dancer. While it is hard to imagine today, thanks to his powerful image as the last great dancer-star of American film and because of his good-guy image, Kelly's early career was devoted to trying to develop an image with a variety of performances including playing a murderer in Robert Siodmak's *Christmas Holiday*. Likewise, several years later, while at the height of his popularity, he occasionally took roles to vary his usual type. Thus, he starred in a minor *noir, The Black Hand* as a son seeking revenge for the mafia murder of his father. While Kelly was adequate in the films, it was not up to the standards of his musicals, and audiences refused to accept him as a tough guy.

Filmography: *Christmas Holiday* (Universal, 1944). *The Black Hand* (MGM, 1950).

Kelly, Paul (1899–1956)

Actor. Kelly was the star of "B" movies in the forties and a character actor is "A" productions for three decades, beginning in the 1930's. He was the second male lead in four *films noirs*, but did not make much of an impression in any of them.

Filmography: *Crossfire* (RKO, 1947). *Fear in the Night* (Paramount, 1947). *The File on Thelma Jordan* (Paramount, 1950). *Side Street* (MGM, 1950).

Kennedy, Arthur (1914–)

Character actor. After stage experience, Arthur Kennedy entered films in the 1940's. He starred in a few films but quickly developed into one of the best character actors in American film. His

performances, however brief, were always compelling. His most prominent *film noir* role was in *The Window* as the disbelieving father of a young boy who claims to have witnessed a murder.

Filmography: *High Sierra* (Warner Bros., 1941). *Champion* (United Artists, 1949). *Chicago Deadline* (Paramount, 1949). *Too Late for Tears* (United Artists, 1949). *The Window* (RKO, 1949).

Kent, Robert E. (1921–1988)

Screenwriter. Kent co-wrote many screenplays, mostly "B" films. He worked on two *films noirs*, including Max Ophuls' neglected classic *The Reckless Moment*, Kent's most prominent screenplay.

Filmography: *The Reckless Moment* (Columbia, 1949). *Where the Sidewalk Ends* (co-wrote story only) (20th Century-Fox, 1950).

Kern, James V. (1909–1966)

Director. Kern, a former lawyer, was mainly a director of light musicals. He directed a single, minor *film noir*.

Filmography: *The Second Woman* (United Artists, 1951).

Key Largo (Warner Bros., 1948). 100 min.

Producer: Jerry Wald. Director: John Huston. Screenplay: Richard Brooks and John Huston from Maxwell Anderson's play. Director of Photography: Karl Freund. Music: Max Steiner. Art Director: Leo K. Kuter. Editor: Rudi Fehr.

Cast: Humphrey Bogart (Frank McCloud), Edward G. Robinson (Johnny Rocco), Lauren Bacall (Nora Temple), Lionel Barrymore (James Temple), Claire Trevor (Gaye Dawn), Thomas Gomez (Curley). With: Harry Lewis, John Rodney, Marc Lawrence, Dan Seymour, Monte Blue.

Frank McCloud, a veteran of World War II, is staying at a rundown hotel in Key Largo, Florida. The hotel is owned by James Temple, an old man confined to a wheel chair. His widowed daughter-in-law, Nora, also lives there. The hotel is taken over by a notorious gangster, Johnny Rocco, and his henchmen. The gangsters are planning to escape to Cuba. Frank is too disillusioned by the events of his life to get involved, and Nora, who had begun to like him, now accuses him of being a coward. Taken as hostage by Rocco and his gang to their boat, Frank manages to overpower them and kill Rocco. He heads back to the hotel, realizing he is in love with Nora.

Based on a play by the now neglected Maxwell Anderson, *Key Largo* is certainly one of the most prominent *films noirs* in which the central character is a disillusioned war veteran. His apathy is used as a metaphor by Anderson for the general malaise of post-war America, and his character is used to contrast the quasi-fascist Rocco (Edward G. Robinson reminds one of Benito Mussolini in several scenes), and the moral indignation of Nora and James Temple.

While the film was the fourth teaming of Humphrey Bogart and Lauren Bacall, a formidable team, the film is almost stolen by Edward G. Robinson and the brilliant Claire Trevor as Rocco's long suffering girl friend. Trevor won an Academy Award for Best Supporting Actress for her performance in the movie.

Like so many films based on plays, *Key Largo* suffers from its verbose script and lack of a variety of locations. All the talent involved, however, were first rate and the film survives as a classic.

Keyes, Evelyn (1919–)
Actress. Evelyn Keyes first achieved fame when, at twenty, she played Scarlett O'Hara's younger sister in *Gone with the Wind* (MGM, 1939). The diminutive ex-dancer developed into a deeply sensual actress in the late-forties. Although she never became a full-fledged star, she was a compelling actress and remains one of *film noir*'s best female icons.

Of all of *noir*'s females, Keyes did not develop a particular character type. She played an innocent who falls in love with a suspected murderer in *Johnny O'Clock*. In *The Prowler* she was a typical *femme-fatale*. In *The Killer That Stalked New York*, perhaps her best *noir* film, she starred as a jewel smuggler unknowingly carrying smallpox. She is also good in the minor *99 River Street*, in which she plays a stage actress who confuses her stage role (as a *femme-fatale*) with her real life.

Unfortunately, Keyes was relegated to mainly "B" movies of varying quality. Had she been cast in better films there is little question she would now be regarded as one of the major actresses of her time.

Filmography: *Johnny O'Clock* (Columbia, 1947). *The Killer That Stalked New York* (Columbia, 1951). *The Prowler* (United Artists, 1951). *99 River Street* (United Artists, 1953).

Kiley, Richard (1922–)
Character actor. Famous for his rich, sonorous voice, Richard Kiley was a major Broadway star who also played second male leads and character roles in movies. He starred in the "B" *noir*, *The Mob*, as a cop searching for a psychotic criminal. He had secondary character parts in his three other *noirs*.

Filmography: *The Mob* (Columbia, 1951). *The Sniper* (Columbia, 1952). *Pickup on South Street* (20th Century-Fox, 1953). *The Phenix City Story* (Allied Artists, 1955).

The Killer Is Loose (United Artists, 1956). 73 min.
Producer: Robert L. Jacks. Director: Budd Boetticher. Screenplay: Harold Medford, story by John and Ward Hawkins. Director of Photography: Lucien Ballard. Music: Lionel Newman. Art Director: Leslie Thoms. Editor: George Gittens.

Cast: Joseph Cotten (Sam Wagner), Rhonda Fleming (Lila Wagner), Wendell Corey (Leon "Foggy" Poole), Alan Hale, Jr.(Denny) Michael Pate (Chris Gillespie), Virginia Christine (Mary Gillespie). With: John Larch, John Beradino, Paul Bryar, Dee J. Thompson.

Foggy Poole, an extremely myopic bank clerk, assists in a robbery of his bank. When he is named by the other holdup men who were caught, Poole is arrested and in the confrontation, his wife is accidentally killed. Poole vows to get revenge against Sam Wagner, the officer involved in the incident. He targets the officer's wife, Lila, planning to kill her when he gets out of prison. Poole is a model prisoner and is sent to a work farm. He escapes and takes a local family hostage. Eventually, Sam Wagner reluctantly allows his wife Lila to be used as bait. Poole almost succeeds in killing her before he is shot down.

The Killer Is Loose is a superior "B" *noir*. Its performances are all first rate, particularly Wendell Corey as Foggy Poole. His performance is subdued and the character, who wears very thick glasses, gives the impression of normality, which adds tension to the scenes.

The film is typical of late-*noir*, with very little style in common with the genre's early movies. Its director, Budd Boetticher, was a strong director of "B" westerns and he brought the techniques of that genre—crosscutting, colorful antagonists, violent action—to this film.

The Killer That Stalked New York
(Columbia, 1951). 79 min.

Producer: Robert Cohn. Director: Earl McEvey. Screenplay: Harry Essex, based on an article by Milton Lehman, published in *Cosmopolitan*. Director of Photography: Joseph Biroc. Music: Hans J. Salter. Art Director: Walter Holscher. Editor: Jerome Thoms.

Cast: Evelyn Keyes (Sheila Bennet), Charles Korvin (Matt Krane), William Bishop (Dr. Ben Wood), Dorothy Malone (Alice Lorie), Lola Albright (Francie Bennet). With: Barry Kelly, Carl Benton Reid, Ludwig Donath, Peter Brocco.

Sheila Bennet returns to the United States from Cuba where she had gone to mail back to the U. S. some stolen diamonds in a plan concocted by her husband, Matt. She is unaware that she has been infected with small pox while in Cuba. She does know that she is being followed by a Treasury Agent and, on the advice of her husband (who is having an affair with her sister), Sheila stays at a hotel. Feeling ill, she sneaks out of the hotel losing the Treasury Agent. She visits a doctor who tells her she simply has a cold. Later, however, a girl who was in the office at the same time and was infected by small pox, dies of the disease. The Federal authorities are notified, and a desperate search is begun for the carrier of the disease.

When Sheila rejoins her husband, the diamonds have arrived, but he does not tell her because he plans to run away with her sister. Discovering his infidelity, Sheila plans to kill him, but fate intervenes and he is killed in a bizarre accident.

When Sheila is finally located, she is deathly ill. Before she dies, she gives the doctor a list of all the people she can remember coming into contact with.

The Killer That Stalked New York is a compelling low budget thriller with an inventive plot. It is a primary example of the influence of a right wing politics in the early fifties. The plot can be seen as a metaphor for the "foreign disease" (i.e., communism) invading the United States.

The film manages to capture the sinister elements of New York City, but it is Evelyn Keyes' performance that stands out. Sheila Bennet is one of the genre's most unique *femme-fatales*.

The Killers (Universal, 1946). 105 min.

Producer: Mark Hellinger. Director: Robert Siodmak. Screenplay: Anthony

Veiller, based on the short story by Ernest Hemingway. Director of Photography: Woody Bredell. Music: Miklos Rozsa. Art Directors: Jack Otterson and Martin Obzina. Editor: Arthur Hilton.

Cast: Edmund O'Brien (Riordan), Ava Gardner (Kitty Collins), Albert Dekker (Colfax), Sam Levene (Lubinsky), John Miljan (Jake), Virginia Christine (Lilly), Vince Barnett (Charleston), Burt Lancaster (the Swede), Charles McGraw (Al), William Conrad (Max). With: Charles D. Brown, Donald MacBride, Phil Brown, Jeff Corey.

Max and Al, a pair of hired killers enter a small town hunting their target, the Swede. They find him waiting in a darkened room, and he offers no resistance.

Riordan, an insurance investigator on another case, becomes obsessed with the murder of Swede, and why he allowed himself to be killed. He learns that Swede was involved with a group of thieves and that he had been double crossed by a woman he had fallen in love with. Eventually, Riordan helps solve the case and, after setting himself up as a target, helps capture the murderers as well.

The quintessential *film noir*, *The Killers* is one of the genre's best films. Its plot was wholly original, developed by Anthony Veiller from Ernest Hemingway's short story which merely provided the set up for the film. It is filled with *noir* archetypes: the man who waits for his own existential end, the victim of a *femme-fatale*; the killers in shadows; an investigator with little or no connection to the case who helps solve it; etc.

The Killers introduced Burt Lancaster to film audiences in the mid-forties and helped establish his on screen persona. It also helped to identify Albert Dekker and to a lesser degree, William Conrad, with the genre.

The film is also Robert Siodmak's masterpiece. It is filled with dark shadows, claustrophobic interiors and a complicated, rich scenario with a disjointed narrative.

The Killers was an enormous success on its initial release and was generally recognized by contemporary critics as a classic.

In 1964, Don Siegel remade the film for Universal. Originally made for television, its violence and brutality made it necessary for the film to be released theatrically. It starred Ronald Reagan in the role created by Burt Lancaster and Angie Dickinson in the role created by Ava Gardner. Although good, the Siegel version is less than a classic.

Killer's Kiss (United Artists, 1955). 67 min.

Producers: Stanley Kubrick and Morris Bousel. Director: Stanley Kubrick. Screenplay: Stanley Kubrick. Director of Photography: Stanley Kubrick. Music: Gerald Fried. Editor: Stanley Kubrick.

Cast: Frank Silvera (Vincent Rapallo), Jamie Smith (Davy Gordon), Irene Kane (Gloria Price), Jerry Jarrett (Albert), Julius Adelman (owner of Mannequin Factory). With: Mike Dana, Felice Orlandi, Ralph Roberts, Phil Stevenson, David Vaughn, Alec Rubin.

Davy Gordon, a down on his luck boxer, plans to run away with Gloria, a beautiful night club dancer. Their plans are thwarted by Vince, the owner of the night club who wants Gloria for himself. He kidnaps Gloria and holds her in a warehouse full of mannequins. When Davy discovers the hiding place, he goes to rescue Gloria, and in the resulting gun battle he kills Vince. Having been betrayed by Gloria (who was trying to save her own life) during the gun battle, Davy plans to leave by himself. However, just as his train arrives, he is joined at the station by Gloria.

Killer's Kiss, Stanley Kubrick's second film was privately financed and was thus shot on an extremely low budget. It resembles a college art film with all the excess and clumsiness. Yet, it also helped establish Kubrick as a new director. It is an admirable film, with a famous and inspired sequence shot in the mannequin factory.

The Killing (United Artists, 1956). 84 min.
Producer: James B. Harris. Director: Stanley Kubrick. Screenplay: Stanley Kubrick, with additional dialog by Jim Thompson, based on the novel *The Clean Break* by Lionel White. Director of Photography: Lucien Ballard. Art Director: Ruth Sobotka Kubrick. Editor: Betty Steinberg.
Cast: Sterling Hayden (Johnny Clay), Coleen Gray (Fay), Vince Edwards (Val Cannon), Jay C. Flippen (Marvin Unger), Marie Windsor (Sherry Peatty), Ted DeCorsia (Randy Kennan), Elisha Cook, Jr. (George Peatty). With: Joe Sawyer, Timothy Carey, Jay Adler, Kola Kwarian, Joseph Turkell.
A group of makeshift criminals led by Johnny Clay, an ex-con, plan to rob a race track. The gang includes Randy Kennan, a cop on the take; Mike O'Reilly, a bartender at the track; George Peatty, a betting-window teller; and a sharpshooter. The shooting of a race horse during a race serves as a diversion, and the rest of the plan is carried off without a hitch. But Sherry Peatty, George's avaricious wife, has learned of the robbery and with her lover, plans to rob the robbers. Her boy friend arrives at the gang's hide out and is killed in the subsequent shoot out. George is badly wounded, and angry at his wife's betrayal, returns home and kills her.
Meanwhile, Clay is apprehended at the airport, while trying to escape. A money laden suitcase, Clay had fled with, falls off a baggage cart and bills are scattering in the wind.
The Killing is Stanley Kubrick's first professional feature, representing the artistic heights of *film noir* in the mid-fifties. It is an extremely well made film with a cast and crew of first rate talent.

The heist plot was a familiar one, having already been used, in variation, in several notable films. However, Kubrick's screenplay, in collaboration with Jim Thompson, was one of the genre's most misanthropic and fatalistic.
Sterling Hayden is typically stoic as the leader of the gang, but the film's best performances are by Elisha Cook, Jr. and Marie Windsor. Cook specialized in weaklings and pathetic characters of various types, but he was rarely more sympathetic than as George Peatty, a man who only wants to please his beautiful wife. Unfortunately, his wife Sherry is one of the most evil of *femme-fatales*, nagging and belittling her husband until he finally kills her. Marie Windsor's performance as Sherry, is completely unsympathetic and it remains one of the genre's most splendidly wicked performances.

King, Frank (1903–1979) and **King, Maurice** (1901–1967)
Producers. Before the advent of Roger Corman and Samuel Z. Arkoff in the 1950's, the Kings were the dominant independent producers of low budget movies. They made horror films, westerns and crime melodramas for Monogram, Producers Releasing Corporation and other Poverty Row studios. Their *films noirs* are of little aesthetic interest, with the exception of John H. Lewis' *Gun Crazy*. All are notable for their emphasis on extreme violence and psychological perversion.
Filmography: *When Strangers Marry* (Monogram, 1944). *Suspense* (Monogram, 1946). *The Gangster* (Allied Artists, 1947). *Gun Crazy* (United Artists, 1950). *Southside 1–1000* (Allied Artists, 1950).

Kirk, Mark Lee (1903–1969)
Art Director. Kirk was an important art director for RKO in the 1940's. Kirk is noted especially for his collaborations with Orson Welles. He designed the sets for Welles' classic *The Magnificent Ambersons* (RKO, 1942), as well

as the *noir* masterpiece, *Journey Into Fear*. His only other *noir* was *Call Northside 777*, one of his first jobs after joining 20th Century–Fox.

Filmography: *Journey Into Fear* (RKO, 1943). *Call Northside 777* (20th Century–Fox, 1948).

Kiss Me Deadly (United Artists, 1955). 105 min.

Producer and Director: Robert Aldrich. Screenplay: A. I. Bezzerides, based on the novel by Mickey Spillane. Director of Photography: Ernest Laszlo. Art Director: William Glasco. Music: Frank DeVol. Editor: Michael Luciano.

Cast: Ralph Meeker (Mike Hammer), Albert Dekker (Dr. Soberin), Paul Stewart (Carl Evello), Maxine Cooper (Velda), Gaby Rodgers (Gabrielle/Lily Carver), Wesley Addy (Pat), Cloris Leachman (Christina). With: Jack Lambert, Jack Elam, Jerry Zinnemann, Percy Helton, Fortunio Bonanova.

While returning to Los Angeles one night in his new sports car, Mike Hammer is flagged down by a woman wearing only a trenchcoat. She tells him her name is Christina and he concludes, from radio reports, that she is an escapee from a nearby insane asylum. Intrigued by the young woman, he takes her through a road block, but is soon being pursued by a car that runs him off the road. Hammer is knocked unconscious and Christina is tortured and killed.

Hammer awakens in a brightly lit hospital room. His loyal secretary Velda and his friend, police detective Pat, are at his bedside. They inform him that the Feds are investigating the events surrounding his accident.

Released from the hospital, Hammer begins his own investigation. He soon uncovers a conspiracy involving a local mobster, Carl Evello, and radioactive material being sold overseas. Hammer plunges into Evello's nightmare world of deceit and violence. He is aided by Lily Carver, an associate of Evello's, but she is only interested in the radioactive material for herself. At the final confrontation at a beach house, owned by Dr. Soberin, a scientist involved in the scheme, Lily Carver shoots Mike Hammer and retrieves the black box. She opens it and the radioactive material sets off a mini chain reaction and Lily is disintegrated. Hammer and Velda manage to escape the house before it is destroyed in an explosion.

Kiss Me Deadly is a frenetic, fast-moving, elegant motion picture that is also violent, callous and angry.

While retaining the plot and general misogyny of Mickey Spillane, Robert Aldrich and his scenarist, A. I. Bezzerides, added the obsession with gadgets which haunts the film. Not only are Evello, Dr. Soberin, et.al. obsessed with electronic gadgets, but so is Hammer, whose apartment is filled with them. In *Kiss Me Deadly*, science is both liberating and repressive.

The style of the film is extravagant, characterized by high angles, hand held shots, and sweeping camera movements.

Ralph Meeker's performance is, to date, the best interpretation of Mike Hammer and Gaby Rodgers is equally good as the avaricious, deadly Lily Carver.

Kiss Me Deadly marks the apex of *noir* style in the 1950's. and it remains one of the genre's classics.

Kiss of Death (20th Century–Fox, 1947). 98 min.

Producer: Fred Kohlmar. Director: Henry Hathaway. Screenplay: Ben Hecht and Charles Lederer, story by Eleazar Lipsky. Director of Photography: Norbet Brodine. Music: David Buttolph. Art Directors: Lyle Wheeler and Leland Fuller. Editor: J. Watson Webb, Jr.

Cast: Victor Mature (Nick Bianco), Brian Donlevy (D'Angelo), Coleen Gray (Nettie), Richard Widmark (Tom Udo), Karl Malden (Sgt. William Collen).

Victor Mature, Richard Widmark in *Kiss of Death* **(20th Century-Fox, 1947).**

With Taylor Holmes, Howard Smith, Anthony Ross, Mildred Dunnock.

A small time hood, Nick Bianco, robs a jewelry store for money to buy his family christmas gifts, but he is wounded in a shoot out with the police. After recovering, he is sentenced to prison, but he is offered a reduced sentence if he informs on local mobsters.

He refuses at first but when he later learns that his wife was having an affair with a mobster and has subsequently committed suicide, he agrees to cooperate with the District Attorney, D'Angelo. Bianco names Rizzo as an informant and the mob puts out s contract on him. Rizzo is killed,.

Meanwhile, Bianco is released from

prison on the grounds that he testify against a notorious and sadistic killer, Tom Udo. When Udo is acquitted, Bianco sends his children away, knowing that Udo will try to get revenge against him. In the final confrontation, Bianco is wounded and Udo is shot and killed by the police. An ambulance takes Bianco away, leaving the audience to believe that Bianco is on his way to a new life.

Praised at the time of its initial release for its semi-documentary style and hard boiled realism, *Kiss of Death* is best known today for its unrelenting violence and Richard Widmark's sadistic, leering Tom Udo. The scene of Udo pushing a wheelchair bound woman down a flight of stairs while laughing manically, is one of the genre's most famous scenes.

Screenwriters Ben Hecht and Charles Lederer were specialists in sophisticated comedy, but here they created a world of danger and madness at every turn.

Henry Hathaway's direction is typically visceral and he makes good use of real locations in what is one of the bleakest of all the great *films noirs*.

Kiss the Blood Off My Hands (Universal, 1948). 79 min.
Producer: Richard Vernon. Director: Norman Foster. Screenplay: Leonardo Bercovici, with additional dialog by Hugh Gray, adapted by Ben Maddow and Walter Bernstein, based on the novel by Gerald Butler. Director of Photography: Russell Metty. Music: Miklos Rozsa. Art Directors: Bernard Herzbrun and Nathan Juran. Editor: Milton Carruth.
Cast: Joan Fontaine (Jane Wharton), Burt Lancaster (Bill Saunders), Robert Newton (Harry Carter), Lewis L. Russell (Tom Widgery), Aminta Dyne (Landlady). With Grizelda Hervey, Jay Novello, Reginald Sheffield.
When the war veteran Bill Saunders kills a pub owner in a blind rage, he takes refuge in a boarding house where a kindly nurse, Jane, also lives. Harry,

one of Bill's acquaintances and a witness to his crime, attempts to blackmail Bill into joining his criminal activities. Bill refuses, but his uncontrollable rage gets him into further trouble and he spends a short time in jail. When released, Jane gets him a job at the medical supply company she works for. Harry blackmails Bill into stealing supplies to sell on the black market. When Bill refuses to carry out a further theft, Harry threatens Jane and she kills him. Bill and Jane plan to run off together, but Bill realizes that if he confesses to the murder of the pub owner (thus proving that Harry was blackmailing him), Jane will be let off for justifiable homicide.

One of several *films noirs* set in England, a setting generally alien to the *noir* ambiance, *Kiss the Blood Off My Hands* succeeds largely because of its male lead, *noir* icon Burt Lancaster and its unrelentingly dour screenplay. Nevertheless, despite its good performances and adequate direction, it is still only a minor film.

Kiss Tomorrow Goodbye (Warner Bros., 1950). 102 min.
Producer: William Cagney. Director: Gordon Douglas. Screenplay: Harry Brown, based on the novel by Horace McCoy. Director of Photography: J. Peverell Mareley. Music: Carmen Dragon. Editors: Truman K. Wood and Walter Hannemann.
Cast: James Cagney (Ralph Cotter), Barbara Payton (Holiday Carleton), Helena Carter (Margaret Dobson), Ward Bond (Inspector Weber), Luther Adler (Cherokee Mandon), Barton MacLane (Reece). With: Steve Brodie, Rhys Williams, Herbert Heyes, John Litel.
When the life long criminal Ralph Cotter and his friend Jinx Raynor escape from prison, they take refuge in a corrupt small town. Cotter takes a mistress, Holiday, and begins bribing local officials. At the same time, he is stealing from the mob. He is successful,

but his actions catch up with him in an ironic twist: instead of being arrested, or killed by the mob, Holiday shoots him rather than give him up to another woman.

Kiss Tomorrow Goodbye is a deeply cynical *film noir* about small town corruption. It is also an unrelenting portrait of evil nature. There is no compassion between the characters, least of all between Cotter and Holiday.

James Cagney dominates the film with a usual, inimitable performance. Gordon Douglas directs in the typical Warner Bros. style, concentrating on the violent elements of the story. Together, they created one of the most unique of all the major *films noirs*.

Kleiner, Harry (1916–)

Screenwriter. Kleiner is associated almost exclusively with action oriented pictures. He wrote several interesting *films noirs*. The most important are Otto Preminger's little known *Fallen Angel* and Sam Fuller's *House of Bamboo*, but all of his screenplays are well above average.

Filmography: *Fallen Angel* (20th Century–Fox, 1945). *The Street with No Name* (20th Century–Fox, 1948). *House of Bamboo* (20th Century–Fox, 1955). *The Garment Jungle* (Columbia, 1957). *Cry Tough* (United Artists, 1959).

Knight, Patricia (1924–)

Actress. Knight starred in a handful of "B" movies in the early fifties. Although attractive and with some talent, she never quite caught on and disappeared after 1954. She was the female lead in Douglas Sirk's *Shockproof* as a *femme-fatale* who leads an ex-cop into her life of crime.

Filmography: *Shockproof* (Columbia, 1949).

Knock on Any Door (Columbia, 1949). 100 min.

Producer: Robert Lord. Director: Nicholas Ray. Screenplay: Daniel Taradash and John Monks, Jr., based on the novel by Willard Motley. Director of Photography: Burnett Guffey. Music: George Antheil. Art Director: Robert Peterson. Editor: Viola Lawrence.

Cast: Humphrey Bogart (Andrew Morton), John Derek (Nick Romano), George Macready (D.A. Kerman), Allene Roberts (Emma), Susan Perry (Adele), Mickey Knox (Vito). With Barry Kelley, Dooley Wilson, Jimmy Conlin, Sumner Williams.

Andrew Morton, a lawyer who was raised in the slums, feels compelled to defend Nick Romano, a youth from the same neighborhood who is charged in a robbery in which a cop was killed. Morton, in fact, believes in Romano's innocence. As the trial progresses, the misery of Romano's life is exposed, including a history of petty thefts and a wife who committed suicide. Under relentless pressure by the District Attorney, Romano breaks down and confesses to killing the cop. He is sentenced to death. Just before Romano is scheduled to be executed, Morton visits him in his cell.

Knock on Any Door is one of the few courtroom dramas of the genre. It suffers from its static setting, and from its overbearing social criticism. *Film noir* works best when a message is subverted.

John Derek made his film debut in this movie and he would soon develop into a major beef-cake star of the 1950's. However, like any film featuring him, the movie is dominated by Humphrey Bogart's performance.

Nicholas Ray's direction is adequate, but ultimately this is the least important of his *films noirs*.

Koch, Howard (1902–)

Screenwriter. Koch was, for most of his career, a staff writer for Warner Bros. For them he co-wrote many outstanding films including the legendary *Casablanca* (Warner Bros., 1942). He won an Academy Award for his contribution to this film. He co-wrote two important *films noirs*. Both of his works are distinguished by a surprisingly frank approach to sexuality.

Filmography: *The Letter* (Warner Bros., 1940). *The Thirteenth Letter* (20th Century–Fox, 1951).

Koch, Howard W. (1916–)

Producer and director. Koch, not to be confused with Howard Koch, the screenwriter, was for many years a producer of popular, unpretentious films. He also directed a few "B" films including two minor *films noirs*.

Filmography: *The Street with No Name* (20th Century–Fox, 1948). *The Last Mile* (United Artists, 1959). *The Manchurian Candidate* (produced only) (United Artists, 1962).

Kohlmar, Fred (1905–1967)

Producer. A producer who specialized in the sort of family oriented films that Sam Goldwyn made (and for whom Kohlmar worked as an associate producer in the thirties), Kohlmar nevertheless produced some of the toughest, most cynical *films noirs*.

Filmography: *The Glass Key* (Paramount, 1942). *The Dark Corner* (20th Century–Fox, 1946). *Kiss of Death* (20th Century–Fox, 1947).

Krasner, Milton (1901–1984)

Cinematographer. Krasner was an adaptable cinematographer who worked on many notable films. He was an important figure in early *film noir*, developing an extravagant, expressionist influenced style characterized by dark, moody lighting and dramatic camera angles. Whatever the overall quality of his *films noirs*, his work on each is always outstanding.

Filmography: *Scarlet Street* (Universal, 1945). *The Woman in the Window* (RKO, 1945). *The Dark Mirror* (Universal, 1946). *A Double Life* (Universal, 1948). *The Accused* (Paramount, 1949). *House of Stranger* (20th Century–Fox, 1949). *The Set-Up*

(RKO, 1949). *Vicki* (20th Century–Fox, 1953).

Kubrick, Stanley (1928–)

Director. Originally a staff photographer for *Life* magazine in the early fifties, Stanley Kubrick is known for his extravagant style. He is one of the few directors still working to have been influenced by expressionist cinema and photojournalism.

Two of Kubrick's earliest films are *films noirs*. *Killer's Kiss* is an extremely low budget tale of a second-rate boxer who plans to run away with a night club owner's mistress. Only sixty seven minutes long, the film is taut and violent, and displays the embryonic Kubrick style that would become so familiar in years to come.

Kubrick's second *film noir*, *The Killing*, is generally considered one of the great late *noirs*. Kubrick wrote the screenplay (with additional dialog by Jim Thompson) to this remarkable caper film and its success helped establish him as a viable new filmmaker. Unfortunately, Kubrick did not pursue the same themes in subsequent films.

Filmography: *Killer's Kiss* (United Artists, 1955). *The Killing* (United Artists, 1956).

Ladd, Alan (1913–1964)

Actor. After a decade in the movies, mainly in small parts, Alan Ladd shot to stardom as the hired killer in the early *noir* classic, *This Gun for Hire*. Despite his small stature, Ladd projected toughness and independence, and his stone-face was perfectly suited to the developing genre in the mid-forties. *This Gun for Hire* firmly established Ladd as the first of the new *noir* actors to emerge in the decade and he is still identified almost exclusively with the genre.

This Gun for Hire was a seminal film for a number of reasons, not the least of which was its first teaming of Ladd with the equally diminutive Veronica

Lake. They were immediately popular together and reteamed in *The Glass Key*. It is actually in this film that the familiar Ladd on screen persona first appeared. As the loyal assistant of a crooked politician, Ladd's character is stoic in the face of danger, and does not hesitate to use physical violence when he deems necessary.

It is this tough, unromantic role that Alan Ladd would make his own. Although indifferent to women, even cruel in some films, he nevertheless almost always manages to win the girl at the end of the movie. This is certainly true of *The Blue Dahlia*, another Ladd *film noir*. He teamed with director Lewis Allen for two films: *Chicago Deadline* and *Appointment with Danger*. The first is an interesting attempt at a *Laura*-like romantic tragedy, while the latter is a typical action oriented "B" *noir*, with Ladd as a violence prone postal inspector.

Far more interesting is the John Farrow directed *Calcutta*. Although the film is one of Farrow's least important *films noirs*, it does contain one of Ladd's least sentimental characters, typically resorting to violence as a pilot investigating the murder of his friend, a fellow pilot.

Alan Ladd presented the perfect image for audiences in the 1940's and he remains one of the genre's indelible faces from its early years.

Filmography: *This Gun for Hire* (Paramount, 1942). *The Glass Key* (Paramount, 1942). *The Blue Dahlia* (Paramount, 1946). *Calcutta* (Paramount, 1947). *Chicago Deadline* (Paramount, 1949). *Appointment with Danger* (Paramount, 1951).

The Lady from Shanghai (Columbia, 1948). 86 min.

Producer and Director: Orson Welles. Screenplay: Orson Welles, based on the novel *Before I Die* by Sherwood King. Director of Photography: Charles Lawton, Jr. Music: Heinz Roemheld. Song: "Please Don't Kiss Me" by Allan Roberts and Doris Fisher. Art Directors: Stephen Goosson and Sturges Carne. Editor: Viola Lawrence.

Cast: Rita Hayworth (Elsa Bannister), Orson Welles (Michael O'Hara), Everett Sloane (Arthur Bannister), Glenn Anders (George Grisby), Ted de Corsia (Sidney Broome). With: Erskine Sandford, Gus Schilling, Evelyn Ellis, Harry Shannon, Wong Show Chong.

Michael O'Hara, a down-on-his-luck sailor, rescues a beautiful woman one night while she is being mugged. The woman, Elsa Bannister is so grateful she arranges for O'Hara to go to work as a crew member on her husband Arthur's yacht. Arthur is a successful defense lawyer. O'Hara soon finds himself embroiled in a mystery involving murder of Arthur's associate, George Grisby. Michael is arrested as a suspect and Arthur Bannister volunteers as his lawyer. At O'Hara's trial, however, Arthur seems determined to see O'Hara convicted.

O'Hara escapes and hides out in Chinatown, but he is secretly being followed by Elsa. Several of her Oriental associates drug O'Hara and take him to an abandoned amusement part. Awakening from being drugged, O'Hara has a final showdown with the cruel Elsa Bannister, whose affair with George Grisby, was the catalyst for the events which followed. Her husband arrives and in the shoot out in a house of mirrors, Arthur kills his faithless wife.

O'Hara walks away, ambivalent about the whole affair.

The Lady from Shanghai is one of the most famous *films noirs* if only for its final sequence in the house of mirrors. This is the most explicit use of the mirror image, a recurrent metaphor in *film noir*. When the mirrors are shattered in the shoot out between O'Hara and the Bannisters, the whole illusions created by Elsa, and even by O'Hara, come to a crashing final end. For once in *film noir*, a *noir* protagonist has broken through the wall of illusions.

Claire Trevor, Robert Montgomery in *Lady in the Lake* **(MGM, 1947).**

The plot of the film is admittedly rather weak, but individual scenes are impressive and overwhelm the film's weaknesses. The film unfolds at a lethargic, dreamy pace, and the photography and style reinforce the hallucinatory ambiance.

Despite imperfections, *The Lady from Shanghai* is an archetypal *film noir*. Rita Hayworth's performance of Elsa Bannister is yet another impressive *femme-fatale* whose actions permanently affect and destroy those around her. In the end, after shattering her illusion, only Michael O'Hara escapes her trap, but he is changed forever and not necessarily for the better.

Lady in the Lake (MGM, 1947). 105 min.

Producer: George Haight. Director: Robert Montgomery. Screenplay: Steve Fisher, based on the novel by Raymond Chandler. Director of Photography: Paul C. Vogel. Music: David Snell. Art Directors: Cedric Gibbons and Preston Ames. Editor: Gene Ruggiero.

Cast: Robert Montgomery (Philip Marlowe), Lloyd Nolan (Lt. De Garmo), Audrey Totter (Adrienne Fromset), Tom Tully (Capt. Kane), Leon Ames (Derace Kingsby), Jayne Meadows (Mildred Haveland). With: Morris Ankrum, Lila Leeds, Richard Simmons, Ellen Ross.

The private investigator Philip Marlowe is trying to cultivate a new career as a mystery writer. He meets with a publisher, Derace Kingsby, but Kingsby is more interested in hiring Marlowe to follow his estranged wife whom he wants to divorce. Marlowe accepts the case and the trail leads into a complicated plot involving the murderous Mildred Haveland and her boy friend, police Lt. Demargo, who kill Kingsby's wife and plan to extort money from Kingsby. Demargo, however, is not exactly a completely willing participant in his girl friend's schemes, and in the final conflict he kills her to prevent her from killing anyone else. He also plans to kill Marlowe, setting it up to make it look like Marlowe was Mildred's associate, but Captain Kane, Demargo's friend on the police force, arrives just in time and shoots Demargo before he can kill Marlowe.

Lady in the Lake is best known for its unusual technique of being filmed in the first person: all the action is seen through Philip Marlowe's "eyes" and thus the other characters address the camera directly. An interesting experiment, it is not wholly successful and the style was used more effectively a year later for Delmer Daves' *Dark Passage* (Warner Bros., 1947).

Director and actor Robert Montgomery was a conventional Hollywood leading man, and he was not convincing as Raymond Chandler's misanthropic private eye. However, Jayne Meadows, later famous for her television performances, is surprisingly vicious as the cruel *femme-fatale*, Mildred Haveland.

Lady on a Train (Universal, 1945). 94 min.
Producer: Felix Jackson. Director: Charles David. Screenplay: Edmund Beloin and Robert O'Brien, story by Leslie Charteris. Director of Photography: Woody Bredell. Music: Miklos Rozsa. Art Director: John B. Goodman. Editor: Ted Kent.

Cast: Deanna Durbin (Nikki Collins), Ralph Bellamy (Jonathan), Edward Everett Horton (Mr. Haskell), George Coulouris (Mr. Saunders), Allen Jenkins (Danny). With: David Bruce, Patricia Morrison, Dan Duryea.

While en route to meet with her lawyer in New York City, Nikki Collins witnesses a murder in a building across the street from the train station. Enlisting the aid of a mystery writer, their investigation uncovers the associate of a wealthy shipping magnate as the killer.

Sometimes listed as a *film noir*, *Lady on a Train* is really an easy cross between the genre and parody. Comedy is the antithesis of *film noir* and despite some vague stylistic similarities (it is a black and white film) and a mystery plot, the film fails to rise above conventional comic-mystery.

A Lady Without Passport (MGM, 1950). 72 min.
Producer: Samuel Marx. Director: Joseph H. Lewis. Screenplay: Howard Dimsdale, adapted by Cyril Hume from a story by Lawrence Taylor. Director of Photography: Paul C. Vogel. Music: David Raksin. Art Directors: Cedric Gibbons and Edward Carfagno. Editor: Frederick Y. Smith.

Cast: Hedy Lamarr (Marianne Lorress), John Hodiak (Pete Karczag), James Craig (Frank Westlake), George Macready (Palinov), Steven Geray (Frenchman, Bruce Cowling (James). With: Nederick Young, Steven Hill, Robert Osterloh, Trevor Bardette.

Pete Karczag, an undercover agent, is sent to Cuba to work on a case involving an illegal alien smuggling ring. He meets Marianne Lorress, a beautiful Eastern European refugee who wants to come to the United States. Manipulated by Karczag, she infiltrates the smuggling ring, discovering its leader is a man called Palinov. Palinov, learning that someone has infiltrated the gang (although he does not know who the interloper is), takes

Marianne with him as he attempts to escape in his private airplane. Unfortunately he crashes into the Florida swamps. In the final shoot out, Palinov is killed and Marianne narrowly escapes.

One of Joseph H. Lewis' minor *films noirs*, *A Lady Without Passport* uses the conventions of the genre including a *femme-fatale*, a woman working under dangerous conditions undercover, the debonair leader of a gang, etc. It also contains performances by *noir* icons including George Macready as Palinov, a variation on his villainous roles in *films noirs* like *Laura* (Columbia, 1946).

Hedy Lamarr is quite good as the woman who infiltrates the smuggling ring, but her cool, European beauty is atypical of Lewis' usual trashy, brash American beauties.

The film is also an excellent example of Lewis' mannered, studio-bound style, a style that had gone out of style by 1950, but which Lewis would continue to develop into light art.

Lake, Veronica (Constance Ockleman) (1919–1973)

Actress. Veronica Lake was the pure *film noir femme-fatale*. Although she was not the sort of *femme-fatale* who willingly, sadistically leads her victims to destruction purely for her own pleasure or greed, Lake's *femme-fatale* roles did tempt men to take paths they would not ordinarily take. She remains one of the genre's premier female icons.

Lake is famous for her striking looks, accentuated by her "peek-a-boo" hairstyle, the wave of blonde hair that hung over her left eye. Even though she could not act, she was a stunning sensual presence and was always compelling while on screen.

Veronica Lake's *film noir* career consists entirely of her three films teamed with Alan Ladd: *This Gun for Hire*, *The Glass Key* and *The Blue Dahlia*. In each she is typically cool, ethereal even and always ready with a wisecrack. Her

characters in all three are more like benevolent *femme-fatales*, in roles similar to Lauren Bacall's in her *films noirs* with Humphrey Bogart. Indeed, the Lake and Ladd combination is second only to Bogart and Bacall. Both teams are indelible images of forties' American film.

Besides her three *films noirs*, Veronica Lake also starred in two classic Paramount comedies in the forties: *Sullivan's Travels* (Paramount, 1941) and *I Married a Witch* (Paramount, 1942).

Filmography: *This Gun for Hire* (Paramount, 1942). *The Glass Key* (Paramount, 1942). *The Blue Dahlia* (Paramount, 1946).

Lamarr, Hedy (Hedwig Keisler) (1913–)

Actress. Dark haired and exquisitely beautiful, the Austrian born Hedy Lamarr was coldly mysterious on screen , an exotic glamour queen. Her single *film noir* appearance was in Jacques Tourneur's *Experiment Perilous*, as a wife held in a mansion by an insanely jealous, possessive husband.

Filmography: *Experiment Perilous* (RKO, 1944).

Lambert, Jack (1920–)

Character actor. The Scottish born Jack Lambert was a general purpose character actor who appeared in many Hollywood films. His *noir* career is surprisingly extensive. He played the usual run of small parts: hired killers, henchmen, cab drivers, etc.

Filmography: *The Killers* (Universal, 1946). *The Unsuspected* (Warner Bros., 1947). *Border Incident* (MGM, 1949). *The Enforcer* (Warner Bros., 1951). *99 River Street* (United Artists, 1953). *Kiss Me Deadly* (United Artists, 1955).

Lancaster, Burt (1913–)

Actor. From his first appearance in *The Killers*, as The Swede, the catalyst of the film's action, Burt Lancaster was a star to be reckoned with. With Kirk Douglas, Robert Mitchum and Richard Widmark, he represented the new breed of American film actors in the postwar era: more realistic than their predecessors, they were not stereotypical handsome, but rugged and flawed. All of them, Lancaster included, became *film noir's* greatest male icons.

Burt Lancaster's on screen persona is duplicitous. His characters are commanding and regal and also remarkably vulnerable. His roles display the streak of masochism which lies just beneath the surface of many *noir* protagonists.

The Killers immediately established Lancaster. He followed this success with roles in several equally good *films noirs*. In each he was the epitome of the existential anti-hero: doomed by his own actions and weaknesses. In *I Walk Alone* he starred as a recently released convict who barely manages to outsmart his former colleagues. In *Brute Force* he played a convict planning an escape that turns tragic. His greatest *film noir* role, however, might well have been in the neglected classic, *Criss Cross*, directed by Robert Siodmak. Lancaster co-starred with Yvonne De Carlo as a man who unwittingly enters into a plan to rob an armored car and his actions lead to tragedy and death.

After 1950, Lancaster began to vary the types of roles he played and he only returned to the genre in the late-*noir* classic, *Sweet Smell of Success* in one of his only genuinely villainous roles as an egomaniacal gossip columnist who will stop at nothing to get his way.

Filmography: *The Killers* (Universal, 1946). *Brute Force* (Universal, 1947). *I Walk Alone* (Paramount, 1948). *Kiss the Blood Off My Hands* (Universal, 1948). *Sorry, Wrong Number* (Paramount, 1948). *Criss Cross* (Universal, 1949). *Sweet Smell of Success* (United Artists, 1957).

Lanchester, Elsa (Elizabeth Sullivan) (1902–1986)

Character actress. The British born Elsa Lanchester was the wife of Charles Laughton. She appeared in many Hollywood films but will be remembered forever as the female companion of Boris Karloff's monster in the classic horror film, *The Bride of Frankenstein* (Universal, 1935).

Lanchester played small supporting roles in three *films noirs*. She supplied the light moments in *The Big Clock* as an eccentric artist. In the minor *Mystery Street*, as an avaricious, blackmailing landlady, she was one of the genre's most unique *femme-fatales*.

Filmography: *The Spiral Staircase* (RKO, 1946). *The Big Clock* (Paramount, 1948). *Mystery Street* (MGM, 1950).

Lane, Priscilla (Priscilla Morgan) (1917–)

Actress. Priscilla was one of three actress sisters who were all briefly popular in the late-thirties. Priscilla's career was the most long-lived of the sisters. She appeared in a single *film noir*, but her light, cheerful personality was ill suited to the genre.

Filmography: *Bodyguard* (RKO, 1948).

Lang, Arthur (1907–1984)

Composer. Lang co-composed a number of film scores with Emil Newman including two *films noirs*. He also composed some solo scores, including the music for Fritz Lang's *The Woman in the Window*.

Filmography: *The Woman in the Window* (solo score) (RKO, 1944). *Woman on the Run* (w/Emil Newman) (Universal, 1950). *99 River Street* (United Artists, 1953).

Lang, Charles B. (1902–)

Cinematographer. Mainly employed by Paramount, Charles Lang was one of the finest studio craftsmen of his time. He was particularly adept at the glossy art deco style so familiar to fans of Paramount's comedies. His three *film noir* titles are all excellent films typically less gritty or excessive as many of their contemporaries, but still notable for their inventive, clever lighting.

Gordon Oliver, George Brent, Dorothy McGuire in *The Spiral Staircase* (RKO, 1946).

Filmography: *The Big Carnival* (Paramount, 1951). *Sudden Fear* (RKO, 1952). *The Big Heat* (Columbia, 1953).

Lang, Fritz (1890–1976)

Director. Certain critics prefer Fritz Lang's silent films claiming that his later American films were increasingly compromised by their modest budgets and were too "commercial." Yet one is struck how relentlessly commercial his silent films really were, despite their social criticism and they ultimately resemble the impersonal films of a modern director like Steven Spielberg. In fact, despite their low budgets, Lang's American films — his westerns as well as his *films noirs* — are much more personal than his silent films and equally brilliant if more subtle.

Fritz Lang was the best German director of his generation. He combined a sense of strong expressionist style with a commercial sensibility in all of his work. One of the most distinctly modern of the great silent directors, and even his silent films hold up surprisingly well. Through all his films runs a sophisticated core of 20th Century themes: the alienation of the individual in an increasing mechanized and/or desensitized modern world and man's continued struggle against moral, political and social corruption.

Lang's first talkie, *M*, established the style he would pursue in his American films. This movie also had a profound influence on world cinema and was at least fifteen years ahead of its time. It is a real *film noir*, and its story of a child murderer (Peter Lorre) hunted down by his fellow criminals remains a powerful story that is still relevant.

Lang left Germany after the rise of Adolf Hitler. Deeply affected by the rise of the Nazis (he was half-Jewish), he made one of his most personal films, *Fury*, the story of a man who is wrongly accused of a crime and becomes the target of mob violence. Although not strictly *film noir*, *Fury*, with *You Only Live Once*, pointed the way to the new genre.

In the mid-forties, Fritz Lang emerged as the greatest *noir* director making a series of classics beginning with *Woman in the Window*. An archetypal *film noir*, it helped establish the themes and characters of the genre. Joan Bennett stars as a *femme-fatale* who leads an innocent man, played by Edward G. Robinson, down a path of destruction. The film is directed in superior style by Lang and has a witty screenplay by Nunnally Johnson.

Joan Bennett had starred in Lang's espionage thriller *Manhunt* (20th Century-Fox, 1941) and had instantly befriended the great director. Together they made three important *films noirs*, following *Woman in the Window* with the similar *Scarlet Street* and the less well known *The Secret Beyond the Door*. *Scarlet Street* is a classic, one of the most unrelenting and paranoid of all *films noirs*.

Among Lang's important early *films noirs* is the espionage thriller *Ministry of Fear*, based on a novel by Graham Greene.

In the fifties Lang made three films with Gloria Graham, as important a relationship as the early one with Joan Bennett. The series began with *The Big Heat* and was followed by *The Blue Gardenia* and *Human Desire*. The latter is one of the genre's most sensual films.

Lang tailored his flamboyant expressionist style for his American thrillers, yet each, even the minor films, is as visually inventive as his early German films. His ratio of good to bad films is higher than almost any other director and it would be fair to say that he was the greatest of all *film noir* directors.

Filmography: *M* (Germany/UFA, 1930). *Fury* (MGM, 1936). *You Only Live Once* (United Artists, 1937). *Woman in the Window* (RKO, 1944). *Ministry of Fear* (Paramount, 1944). *Scarlet Street* (Universal, 1945). *The Secret Beyond the Door* (Republic, 1949). *House by the River* (Republic, 1950). *Clash by Night* (RKO, 1952). *The Big Heat* (Columbia, 1953). *The Blue Gardenia* (Warner Bros., 1953). *Human Desire* (Columbia, 1954). *While the City Sleeps* (RKO, 1955). *Beyond a Reasonable Doubt* (RKO, 1956).

La Shelle, Joseph (1916–1988)

Cinematographer. La Shelle was mainly employed by 20th Century-Fox where he worked on a variety of routine melodramas until the mid-forties. With *Laura*, however, La Shelle was elevated to major status. He translated the mysterious romance into a world of shadows and fog and rain swept streets. An archetypal *film noir*, *Laura* helped set the standard for the developing genre in the years to come. Indeed, through his collaborations with director Otto Preminger, La Shelle was a major figure of the genre. All of La Shelle's *films noirs* are highlights of the 20th Century-Fox productions and many remain classics.

Filmography: (*Directed by Otto Preminger) *Laura** (20th Century-Fox, 1944). *Fallen Angel** (20th Century-Fox, 1945). *Road House* (20th Century-Fox, 1948). *Where the Sidewalk Ends** (20th Century-Fox, 1950). *The Thirteenth Letter** (20th Century-Fox, 1951). *Storm Fear* (United Artists, 1956). *Crime of Passion* (United Artists, 1957).

Laszlo, Ernest (1905–1984)

Cinematographer. Laszlo's film career began in the 1940's and stretched over three decades. He was the director of photography on many leading productions and in the 1960's was one of the leading proponents of color, wide screen productions. He was also a leader of the more realistic school of *film noir* cinematography in the 1950's and worked on two of Robert Aldrich's best *noirs*, *The Big Knife* and *Kiss Me Deadly*. With *D.O.A.*, these are Laszlo's best films in the genre, but he also worked on *Impact*, a "B" *noir* that is well above average, and one of Fritz Lang's' last American movies, *While the City Sleeps*.

Filmography: *Impact* (United Artists, 1949). *Manhandled* (Paramount, 1949). *D.O.A.* (United Artists, 1950). *M* (Columbia, 1951). *The Big Knife* (United Artists, 1955). *Kiss Me Deadly* (United Artists, 1955). *While the City Sleeps* (RKO, 1956).

Lathrop, Phillip (1916–)

Cinematographer. Lathrop is a prolific cinematographer whose career began in the late-fifties. He has worked on everything from cheap horror films to a neglected late-*noir*, *Experiment in Terror* to the post-*noir* minor classic, *Point Blank*.

Filmography: *Experiment in Terror* (Columbia, 1962). *Point Blank* (MGM, 1967).

Latimer, Jonathan (1906–1984)

Screenwriter. Latimer specialized in entertaining thrillers, including everything from ghost stories to *films noirs*. He worked on several important *noirs* in the 1940's, including two collaborations with John Farrow, *The Big Clock* and *Night Has a Thousand Eyes*. Both are classics of the genre.

Filmography: *The Glass Key* (Paramount, 1942). *The Accused* (Paramount, 1946). *Nocturne* (RKO, 1946). *They Won't Believe Me* (RKO, 1947). *The Big Clock* (Paramount, 1948). *Night Has a Thousand Eyes* (Paramount, 1948).

Laughton, Charles (1899–1962)

Character actor. Laughton was a larger than life character, an oversized actor known for his outsized performances. His performances could be over the top, but under a good director he was incomparably brilliant. He costarred in two *films noirs*. In *The Big Clock*, under the strong willed John Farrow, Laughton gave one of his best film performances as a megalomaniacal, murderous publisher.

Laughton also directed a brilliant thriller, *Night of the Hunter*, a gothic suspense film with strong *noir* elements.

Filmography: *The Big Clock* (Paramount, 1948). *The Bribe* (MGM, 1949). *Night of the Hunter* (director only) (United Artists, 1955).

Laura (20th Century–Fox, 1944). 88 min.

Producer and Director: Otto Preminger. Screenplay: Jay Dratler, Samuel Hoffenstein and Betty Reinhardt, based on the novel by Vera Caspary. Director of Photography: Joseph La Shelle. Music: David Raksin. Song: "Laura" by Johnny Mercer and David Raksin. Art Directors: Lyle Wheeler and Leland Fuller. Editor: Louis Loeffler.

Cast: Gene Tierney (Laura Hunt), Dana Andrews (Mark McPherson), Clifton Webb (Waldo Lydecker), Vincent Price (Shelby Carpenter), Judith Anderson (Ann Treadwell), Dorothy Adams (Bessie Clary). With: James Flavin, Clyde Fillmore, Ralph Dunn, Grant Mitchell, Kathleen Howard.

Investigating the murder of model Laura Hunt, a police detective, Mark McPherson, questions radio personality Waldo Lydecker. Lydecker is an egomaniac with a biting sarcastic wit and he apparently thought of Laura as his greatest creation and as his personal property. McPherson learns that Laura was to be married to Shelby Carpenter, much to the chagrin of Lydecker and Carpenter's former girl friend, Ann Treadwell.

Returning to her apartment to continue his investigation, McPherson becomes mesmerized by Laura's portrait. Suddenly she walks in, breaking the erotic trance. She tells McPherson that she has been in the country contemplating her impending marriage to Shelby. At that moment the phone rings, and the caller informs McPherson that the body found is another girl, Diane Redfern.

Although he has four possible suspects, all evidence seems to lead to Lydecker. This is confirmed when the murder weapon, a knife, is discovered in a clock given to Laura as a present. Lydecker is jealous of her relationship with Shelby Carpenter.

Lydecker goes on the air with his popular radio show, but in fact he is broadcasting a tape to give himself an alibi. He sneaks into Laura's apartment intent on killing her, but McPherson arrives just in time and arrests Lydecker.

Laura is one of the most outstanding of all *films noirs* with many superior elements including its famous, haunting score by David Raksin. It was also Otto Preminger's first important movie, elevating him into the elite rank of Hollywood directors. Preminger creates a world of shifting ambiguities in which all the suspects are possibly guilty. His use of a sinuously gliding camera in a style similar to that used by Michael Curtiz in *Casablanca*, reiterates the character's shifting emotions.

The performances are all first rate. Both Clifton Webb and Shelby Carpenter are typically over the top, but here their extravagances worked to their advantage. Webb's idiosyncratic performance immediately established the long suffering stage actor into a major film star after years of struggle for any kind of success.

Likewise, as the central characters of the story, Gene Tierney and Dana Andrews are perfectly understated. Andrews, with his half-cocked fedora and overcoat, established the image of the *noir* detective. The film also established Tierney and Andrews as major box-office attractions.

Lawton, Charles, Jr. (1904–1965)
Cinematographer. Lawton was a competent cinematographer who worked on many films. His greatest contribution to *film noir, The Lady from Shanghai* is an inventive example of *noir* photography at its best. However, it is questionable if Lawton or the film's director, Orson Welles, was really responsible for the quality of the cinematography on the film. In any case, Lawton did work on two other *films noirs*, but neither is of the same quality as the predecessor.

Filmography: *The Lady from Shanghai* (Columbia, 1948). *Shockproof* (Columbia, 1949). *Drive a Crooked Road* (Columbia, 1954).

Leachman, Cloris (1926–)
Character actress. Leachman is famous for her television stardom in the 1970's. For many years she was a small parts actress with brief roles in many films. She had a small, but important role in Robert Aldrich's *Kiss Me Deadly* as the woman Mike Hammer picks up at the beginning of the movie and who turns out to be the catalyst of the action which follows.

Filmography: *Kiss Me Deadly* (United Artists, 1954).

Leave Her to Heaven (20th Century-Fox, 1945). 110 min.
Producer: William A. Bacher. Director: John M. Stahl. Screenplay: Jo Swerling, based on the novel by Ben Ames Williams. Director of Photographer: Leon Shamroy. Music: Alfred Newman. Art Directors: Lyle Wheeler and Maurice Ransford. Editor: James B. Clark.

Cast: Gene Tierney (Ellen Berent), Cornel Wilde (Richard Harland), Jeanne Crain (Ruth Berent), Vincent Price (Russell Quinton), Mary Phillips (Mrs. Berent), Ray Collins (Glen Robie). With: Gene Lockhart, Chill Wills, Darryl Hickman, Paul Everton, Olive Blakeney.

Ellen Berent is insanely jealous of her husband, Richard Harland, a writer. He resembles her dead father whom she was abnormally devoted to. She commits a series of petty crimes to get back at his friends and associates whom she believes are taking his time away from her. She even throws herself down a flight of stairs to cause a miscarriage. She is particularly jealous of her younger sister, Ruth. When she learns that Richard is going to leave her for Ruth, Ellen commits suicide and sets it up to look like Ruth and Richard are guilty of murder. Although they are eventually acquitted, Richard is sent to prison as an accessory to his wife's crimes. After he is released, he joins Ruth to restart his life.

John Stahl, the director of *Leave Her to Heaven* was the Douglas Sirk of his generation. He specialized in glossy romantic tragedies and indeed, Sirk later remade two of Stahl's best films

Leave Her to Heaven, with its emphasis on crime and psychological perversion, as well as the hopeless trap that Richard Harland finds himself in, are all closer to *noir* themes than the usual trifles of Stahl's other melodramas. As such, *Leave Her to Heaven* is a prominent early color *film noir*.

Gene Tierney, coming off the success of *Laura* (20th Century–Fox, 1944), was a compelling *femme-fatale*, but it is Leon Shamroy's color cinematography that remains the film's most remarkable feature. He captures the story's ominous spirit by drenching the film in orange and various shifting watercolor hues, to enhance the shifting alliances and spirit of bloodletting that dominate.

Leavitt, Samuel (1917–1984)

Cinematographer. An Academy Award winning cinematographer, Leavitt specialized in brightly lit, glossy entertainments. His style is rather conventional, but he did photograph one of Samuel Fuller's gritty late-*noirs*, *The Crimson Kimono* and the excellent *Cape Fear*. Although less well known, *The Thief* and *Brainstorm* are equally good.

Filmography: *The Thief* (United Artists, 1952). *The Crimson Kimono* (Columbia, 1959). *Cape Fear* (Universal, 1962). *Brainstorm* (Warner Bros., 1965).

Le Borg, Reginald (1902–)

Director. Le Borg was a prolific director of "B" movies. He worked mainly for Universal and Monogram, directing everything from musicals to westerns to light comedies, but he is best known for his horror films. He also directed a single *film noir*, *Fall Guy*, which suffers from its minuscule budget but has some interesting scenes.

Filmography: *Fall Guy* (Monogram, 1947).

Lederer, Charles (1906–1976)

Screenwriter. Another neglected figure of Hollywood's Golden Age, Lederer was a splendidly gifted screenwriter who worked on many classic films beginning in the early-thirties. He was one of Howard Hawks' chief collaborators, co-writing several of the master's best films. He co-wrote, with Ben Hecht, two *films noirs*, including the extraordinary *Kiss of Death* and *Ride the Pink Horse*.

Filmography: *Kiss of Death* (20th Century–Fox, 1947). *Ride the Pink Horse* (Universal, 1947).

Leigh, Janet (Jeanette Morrison) (1927–)

Actress. A voluptuous blonde, Leigh decorated many epics and male dominated features in the sixties, but she will probably be forever best remembered as Norman Bate's most striking victim in Alfred Hitchcock's *Psycho* (Universal, 1959). She was the female lead in *Act of Violence*, but her role was rather conventional.

Filmography: *Act of Violence* (MGM, 1949).

Leonard, Robert Z. (1889–1968)

Director. Leonard was a contract director for MGM between 1929–1955.

He was a productive and adaptable craftsman with no real signature of his own. He often produced his films as well and most are typical MGM family fare. He directed a single *film noir*.

Filmography: *The Bribe* (MGM, 1949).

Leonard, Sheldon (Sheldon Bershed) (1907–)

Character actor. Long before he became one of television's most successful producers, Sheldon Leonard had a long and successful career in film and television as a character actor. He specialized in semi-comic, Runyonesque parts (sharpies, con men, small time gangsters), and tough sidekicks. His *film noir* roles are generally small. The exception is the "B" *noir*, *The Gangster* in which he played the rival of the film's central character.

Filmography: *Street of Chance* (Paramount, 1942). *Decoy* (Monogram, 1946). *Somewhere in the Night* (20th Century–Fox, 1946). *The Gangster* (Allied Artists, 1947). *Force of Evil* (MGM, 1948).

Lerner, Irving (1909–1976)

Director. Lerner was one of the least prolific, quality "B" movie directors. He made a grand total of only eight features over some two decades. He had a hard-edged, realistic approach to his material. He made a single *film noir*, *City of Fear*, a surprisingly well made, suspenseful melodrama. One wishes Lerner had made more films of this type.

Filmography: *City of Fear* (Columbia, 1959).

Lerner, Joseph (1911–)

Director. Lerner was a director of low budget "B" movies for one-shot companies and fringe producers. *Guilty Bystander*, an interesting little *film noir*, is compromised by its extremely low budget and bad performances.

Filmography: *Guilty Bystander* (Film Classics, 1950).

Le Roy, Mervyn (1900–1987)

Director. Although not as well known as many of his contemporaries, Le Roy is one of the most important and influential directors of the thirties. A prolific craftsman, Le Roy had a hard-boiled, visceral style which served him best on action films and thrillers, but over the course of thirty years as a top film director, he directed many different kinds of films. He is best known, however, for the remarkable group of gangster dramas he made for Warner Bros. in the early thirties.

Le Roy directed a single true *film noir*, *Johnny Eager* and the important *I Am a Fugitive from a Chain Gang*. The latter is known as a significant break with the traditions of the gangster genre, an early example of an exploration of themes which would become familiar as the genre developed and matured over a decade later.

Filmography: *I Am a Fugitive from a Chain Gang* (Warner Bros., 1930). *Johnny Eager* (MGM, 1942).

The Letter (Warner Bros., 1940). 95 min.

Producer: Hal B. Wallis. Director: William Wyler. Screenplay: Howard Koch, based on the short story by W. Somerset Maugham. Director of Photography: Tony Guadio. Music: Max Steiner. Art Director: Carl Jules Weyl. Editor: George Amy.

Cast: Bette Davis (Leslie Crosbie), Herbert Marshall (Robert Crosbie), James Stephenson (Howard Joyce), Freida Inescort (Dorothy Joyce), Gale Sondergaard (Mrs. Hammond). With: Bruce Lester, Elizabeth Earl, Cecil Kellaway, Sen Young, Willie Fung.

Set on a tropical plantation, the story of *The Letter* centers around the self absorbed Leslie Crosbie. Leslie shoots her lover in a jealous rage. She claims it was self defense and her husband's lawyer, Howard Joyce, defends her. A letter is discovered that implicates Leslie, but Joyce suppresses it and Leslie is acquitted.

Robert Crosbie is shocked at the revelations contained in the letter. When he tells her that he forgives her, however, Leslie tells him that she still loves the man she killed and has no intention of remaining with her husband. As she storms out of the house, Leslie is shot dead by an assassin hired by the native mistress of the man Leslie killed.

The Letter is considered an important, early *film noir* because of the existential fate of the characters and the mysterious, repressive ambiance of its tropical setting. However, William Wyler's influence was a little too light and the film has a simpler style than most 1940's *films noirs*.

Leven, Boris (1900–1986)

Art director. Leven was one of the few journeymen art directors in Hollywood. He specialized in science fiction movies and historical epics, but he also worked on a few *films noirs*. His style was an odd cross between the elegant, shiny art deco style and the dark style of expressionism.

Filmography: *The Shanghai Gesture* (United Artists, 1941). *Criss Cross* (Universal, 1949). *House by the River* (Republic, 1950). *Sudden Fear* (RKO, 1952).

Levin, Henry (1909–1980)

Director. For two decades, beginning in 1944, Levin was one of the best "B" movie directors. He worked mainly for Columbia, specializing in horror films that were distinguished by a rather dark sense of humor: *The Devil's Mask* (Columbia, 1946) and *The Corpse Came C.O.D.* (Columbia, 1947). Likewise, his two *films noirs* are notable for their perverse humor and violent action.

Filmography: *Night Editor* (Columbia, 1946). *Convicted* (Columbia, 1950).

Lewis, Joseph H. (1900–)

Director. Lewis is one of the neglected masters of technique of American cinema. He was certainly one of the greatest directors of "B" movies. Perhaps because his films were "B" productions he was neglected by specific critics; yet his best work can be favorably compared to the best work of many "A" directors.

Lewis's style was similar to that of Michael Curtiz and Max Ophuls. His forte was fluid, often baroque camera movements and complicated lighting schemes. Like Ophuls, Lewis's films often featured a woman as the central character, but Lewis's women were less romantic, more street wise and overtly erotic. He particularly likes blonde trollops, as typified by Peggy Cummins in *Gun Crazy* and Jean Wallace in *The Big Combo*, his two best *films noirs*.

Lewis's *noir* career began in the mid-forties with the excellent *My Name Is Julia Ross*. He made six *noirs*, all of which are well above average. *Gun Crazy* and *The Big Combo* are the outstanding titles, but *A Lady Without Passport* and *So Dark the Night* are nearly as good.

Filmography: *My Name Is Julia Ross* (Columbia, 1945). *Undercover Man* (Columbia, 1949). *Gun Crazy* (United Artists, 1950). *A Lady Without Passport* (MGM, 1950). *So Dark the Night* (Columbia, 1954). *The Big Combo)* (Allied Artists, 1955).

Lewton, Val (Vladimir Leventon) (1904–1951)

Producer. Val Lewton was one of the most influential producers of the early forties. Hired by RKO in 1942 to head up his own "B" production unit (after years as an associate producer and story editor at various studios), Lewton brought the same care and attention to his low budget productions that his former boss, David O. Selznick, brought to his big budget productions. Like Selznick, Lewton was the real *auteur* of his productions. He co-wrote, co-directed, and collaborated on the production design (all without credit) on his films.

Lewton's greatest achievement is the

remarkable series of horror films produced in the early forties: *Cat People* (RKO, 1942), *I Walked with a Zombie* (RKO, 1943), *The Leopard Man* (RKO, 1943), *The Seventh Victim* (RKO, 1943), *Curse of the Cat People* (RKO, 1944), *The Body Snatcher* (RKO, 1945) and *Bedlam* (RKO, 1946). Each is characterized by moody, dark lighting, extravagant angles and existential themes, and emphasized repressed sexuality. Because of their success, they had a profound influence on the emerging genre of *film noir*. Equally important, he promoted the careers of several directors who would learn and develop their craft under him and apply what they learned to the new genre. Jacques Tourneur, Mark Robson, Robert Wise and Robert Rossen all began their careers with Lewton.

Linden, Lionel (1905–1971)

Cinematographer. Linden's extensive filmography includes several *films noirs*. His work is less extravagant and inventive than his greater contemporaries, but well above average.

Filmography: *The Blue Dahlia* (Paramount, 1946). *The Turning Point* (Paramount, 1952). *The Manchurian Candidate* (United Artists, 1962).

The Line Up (Columbia, 1958). 85 min.

Producer: Jamie Del Valle. Director: Don Siegel. Screenplay: Sterling Silliphant. Director of Photography: Hal Mohr. Music: Mischa Bakaleinikoff. Art Director: Ross Bellah. Editor: Al Clark.

Cast: Eli Wallach (Dancer), Robert Keith (Julian), Warner Anderson (Inspector Guthrie), Richard Jaeckel (Sandy McLain), Emile Meyer (Quine). With: Mary La Roche, William Leslie, Marshall Reed, Raymond Bailey.

New York police detectives Guthrie and Quine hunt for the source of heroin shipments while sadistic hired killers Dancer and Julian are sent to the city to retrieve lost parcels of the drug. Their search leads to the deaths of unwitting innocents who get in the way. However, they do not retrieve the heroin and the boss grows tired of their excuses. He threatens to kill Dancer and Julian, but they decide to retaliate. Dancer kills the wheelchair bound head of their gang. In the resulting car chase with Guthrie and Quine, Dancer and Julian are involved in a crash and then killed in the shoot out.

A violent, action-oriented "B" *noir*, *The Line Up* has a simple, linear plot expertly handled by Don Siegel. Criminals are at the core of the film, a remarkable feature at the time, although in typical Hollywood fashion Dancer and Julian are ultimately defeated by the police. The film, of course, is typical of 1950's *noir*, lacking the poetic iconography of the genre's earlier films.

Ling, Eugene ( )

Screenwriter. Ling co-wrote many films in all the usual genres, but few are really outstanding. He worked on four "B" *noirs*, with *Between Midnight and Dawn* and *Scandal Sheet* being the best.

Filmography: *Behind Locked Doors* (Eagle-Lion, 1948). *Between Midnight and Dawn* (Columbia, 1950). *Loan Shark* (Lippert, 1952). *Scandal Sheet* (Columbia, 1952).

Litvak, Anatole (1902–1974)

Director. The Russian born Litvak was a talented director of high quality commercial films. Although his career began in Germany in the early-thirties, he didn't really hit his stride until the mid–forties in Hollywood. Like many European filmmakers of his generation, he was deeply influenced by expressionism, most evident in his case in *The Snake Pit* (Warner Bros., 1948) and the little known, but intriguing *noir*, *The Long Night* (RKO, 1947).

Filmography: *The Long Night* (RKO, 1947).

Loan Shark (Lippert, 1952). 79 min.

Producer: Bernard Luber. Director:

Seymour Friedman. Screenplay: Martin Rackin and Eugene Ling, story by Martin Rackin. Director of Photography: Joseph Biroc. Art Director: Feild Gray. Editor: Al Joseph.

Cast: George Raft (Joe Gargen), Dorothy Hart (Ann Nelson), Paul Stewart (Donelli), Helen Westcott (Martha), John Hoyt (Phillips). With: Russell Johnson, Benny Baker, Larry Dobkin, Charles Meredith.

Joe Gargen, an ex-con, seeks to avenge the murder of his hard working brother-in-law. He infiltrates a loan shark racket that exploits factory workers. He eventually uncovers the shadowy leader of the syndicate, Mr. Phillips and kills him by throwing him into a huge cleaning fire that boils him alive.

A low budget feature, *Loan Shark* is best distinguished by the performances of Paul Stewart and John Hoyt. George Raft had seen better days and his on screen persona was growing tired by the film's appearance.

The Locket (RKO, 1947). 85 min.

Producer: Bert Granet. Director: John Brahm. Screenplay: Sheridan Gibney. Director of Photography: Nicholas Musuraca. Music: Roy Webb. Art Directors: Albert S. D'Agostino and Alfred Herman. Editor: J. R. Whittredge.

Cast: Laraine Day (Nancy Blair), Brian Aherne (Dr. Blair), Robert Mitchum (Norman Clyde), Gene Raymond (John Willis), Sharyn Moffett (Nancy, age 10), Richard Cortez (Mr. Bonner). With: Henry Stephenson, Katherine Emery, Fay Helm, Reginald Denny.

John Willis and Nancy Blair are to be married. On their wedding day, Nancy's ex-husband, Dr. Blair, arrives and tells Willis of her lifelong kleptomania. Blair had likewise been unaware of her problems until informed of them by her former boy friend. Her problems were caused by a childhood event. As a young girl, Nancy was accused of stealing a valuable heirloom, a beautiful locket. Willis, however, refuses to believe the accusation. Just prior to the ceremony, though, Nancy is given the locket as a wedding present. Her childhood flashes before her eyes and she collapses with a mental breakdown. She is institutionalized, hopelessly insane.

The Locket is an unusual *film noir*, relying on compelling psychological insight and almost completely lacking action or violence. Its narrative is more complex than the above scenario might suggest, with a series of flashbacks within flashbacks. Its production design is the typical RKO style and director John Brahm creates an atmospheric, mesmerizing film with a splendid performance by Laraine Day.

Lockhart, Gene (1891–1957)

Writer and character actor. Lockhart wrote stories, novels and the odd screenplay. He acted in some three dozen films, almost always in small supporting roles. Of his four *noir* appearances, his most prominent role was in Robert Aldrich's *World for Ransom*, as a murderous black market dealer.

Filmography: *Leave Her to Heaven* (20th Century–Fox, 1945). *House on 92nd Street* (20th Century–Fox, 1949). *Red Light* (Columbia, 1950). *World for Ransom* (Allied Artists, 1954).

Lom, Herbert (Herbert Charles Angelo Kuchacevich ze Schluderpacheru) (1917–)

Czech born character actor. Lom is a familiar face from his appearances in many popular British films of the fifties. He had a prominent, villainous role in Jules Dassin's London based *Night and the City*, his only *noir* appearance.

Filmography: *Night and the City* (20th Century–Fox, 1950).

Lonergan, Arthur (1906–)

Art Director. Lonergan created the production designs for one of the best science fiction films of the fifties, *Forbidden Planet* (MGM, 1956). He also contributed designs for two minor *films noirs*.

Filmography: *Cause for Alarm* (MGM, 1951).

The Long Night (RKO, 1947). 97 min.

Producer and Director: Anatole Litvak. Screenplay: John Wexley, story by Jacques Viot and a screenplay by Jacques Prevert. Director of Photography: Sol Polito. Music: Dimitri Tiomkin. Art Directors: Albert S. D'Agostino and Carroll Clark. Editor: Elmo Williams.

Cast: Henry Fonda (Joe Adams), Barbara Bel Geddes (Jo Ann), Vincent Price (Maximilian the Great), Ann Dvorak (Charlene). With: Moroni Olsen, Elisha Cook, Jr., Queenie Smith.

Joe Adams, a recently demobilized soldier, is goaded by jealousy into shooting a philandering magician, Maximilian the Great, whom he believes is trying to seduce his girlfriend, Jo Ann. He hides out in the building where Jo Ann lives, surrounded by the police. Eventually, with Jo Ann's pleading, Adams gives himself up.

Although it is a gorgeous looking film, filled with extravagant, expressionist visuals, *The Long Night* is ultimately a bloodless, boring remake of Marcel Carne's masterpiece *Le Jour se Leve* (1939). The performances are generally credible, but the screenplay lacks the unsentimental and bitter exposé effects of environment on psychology. Indeed, audiences found the film excruciatingly boring and it lost $1,000,000, a disaster particularly considering RKO's precarious financial situation at the time.

The Long Wait (United Artists, 1954). 94 min.

Producer: Lesser Samuels. Director: Victor Saville. Screenplay: Alan Greene and Lesser Samuels, based on the novel by Mickey Spillane. Director of Photography: Franz Planer. Music: Mario Castlenuovo-Tedesco. Art Director: Boris Leven. Editor: Ronald Sinclair.

Cast: Anthony Quinn (Johnny McBride), Charles Coburn (Gardiner), Gene Evans (Servo), Peggie Castle (Venus), Mary Ellen Kay (Wendy), Shawn Smith (Carol). With: Dolores Donlon, Barry Kelley, James Millican, Bruno Ve Sota.

Johnny McBride suffers from amnesia, the result of a car wreck. Arrested as a murder suspect, he is released when his burned fingertips, the result of the automobile accident, fail to produce usable finger prints. He then sets out to prove his innocence.

Henchmen working for a local mob leader, Servo, try to put a stop to McBride's private investigation. He kills them, and then visits a woman called Venus, an associate of Servo's. All evidence seems to point to the mobster's involvement and he needs information to put the pieces of the puzzle together. Venus, however, double crosses him and McBride is caught. He is beaten unconscious. When he awakens, he is tied to a chair and blinded by a bright light. Venus suddenly appears, crawling on the ground and carrying a gun. She frees McBride and shoots and kills Servo.

McBride, having discovered in the meantime that his ex-employer Gardiner is the financier behind the mob, goes to confront Gardiner at his house. Gardiner admits that McBride was merely a dupe in a complicated plot. McBride captures Gardiner and turns him in to the police.

Although it is based on a novel which did not feature Mike Hammer, *The Long Wait* still manages to capture the violent, misogynist world of Mickey Spillane. Unlike most of Spillane's Mike Hammer novels, *The Long Wait* is set in a small town.

Peggie Castle is excellent in her brief role as Venus, one of the genre's most corrupt and brutal *femme-fatales*. It is the highlight of Castle's *film noir* career.

Loophole (Allied Artists, 1954). 79 min.

Producer: Lindsley Parsons. Director: Harold Schuster. Screenplay: Warren Douglas, story by George Bricker and Dwight V. Babcock. Director of Photography: William Sickner. Music: Paul Dunlap. Art Director: David Milton. Editor: Ace Herman.

Cast: Barry Sullivan (Mike Donavan), Charles McGraw (Gus Slavin), Dorothy Malone (Ruthie Donavan), Dan Haggerty (Neil Sanford), Mary Beth Hughes (Vera). With: Don Beddoe, Dayton Lummis, Joanne Jordan, John Eldredge, Richard Reeves.

When Herman Tate, a bank teller, absconds with $50,000 from a drawer of fellow teller Mike Donavan after pretending to be an examiner, Donavan is the only suspect. Although the police and bank manager are convinced of his innocence, Gus Slavin, a special investigator for a bonding company, is not entirely sure. He hounds Donavan, making sure he loses a series of jobs by informing his bosses that he is a suspect in the embezzlement.

While driving a cab, Donavan accidentally encounters Tate. Realizing that he is the thief, Donavan tries to force him to share the stolen money because he and his wife's bank account is running low. However, Tate's girl friend, Vera, wants him to kill Donavan. Tate refuses and in the inevitable showdown, Vera shoots both Tate and Donavan. Though wounded, Donavan manages to subdue Vera until the cops arrive.

A typical low budget Allied Artists production, *Loophole* is populated by minor *noir* icons and some fair production values. It has some interesting location scenes from around Los Angeles, but the movie is only of minor interest.

Lord, Robert (1900–1976)
Writer and producer. As a staff writer for Warner Bros., Robert Lord specialized in tough action pictures and melodramas. As a producer, he continued to make the kind of films he wrote. He worked at several studios as a producer in the mid–forties before going independent. With his close friend, Humphrey Bogart, Lord created Santana Productions and he produced many of the actor's later films.

Filmography: *The High Wall* (MGM, 1947). *Knock on Any Door* (Columbia, 1949).

Lorre, Peter (Lazlo Lowenstein) (1904–1964)
Character actor. Probably the most recognizable character actor in film history, Lorre's specialty was playing weasels, scoundrels and cowardly criminals of various types. Off camera, Lorre was one of the legendary "wild men" of Hollywood in the late-thirties and forties and counted among his closest friends such notable rogues as John Barrymore, Erroll Flynn and Humphrey Bogart.

The Hungarian born actor first achieved fame on stage in Berlin in the late forties before making a striking film debut in Fritz Lang's *M*, as the serial killer. The film made him into a star, although his career was hampered somewhat over the next several years due to his addiction to opium.

Lorre moved to the United States in the late-thirties, after several lean years in Great Britain and signed with Warner Bros. He was in many of that studio's top productions throughout the forties, often cast opposite his friend Humphrey Bogart. They appeared together in a single *film noir*, *The Maltese Falcon* in which Lorre played the ratty criminal Joel Cairo.

Indeed, all of Lorre's *noir* roles were villainous. In the early *noir*, *Stranger on the Third Floor* (RKO, 1940), he played a role similar to that in his first triumph, *M*. However, his European personality was ill suited to the American middle class milieu of *film noir* and as the genre matured, sinister foreigners were less in demand. Still, he was one of the most memorable early *noir* villains in a handful of excellent films.

Filmography: *M* (Germany/UFA, 1930). *Stranger on the Third Floor* (RKO, 1940). *The Maltese Falcon* (Warner Bros., 1941). *The Mask of Dimitrios* (Warner Bros., 1944). *Black Angel* (Universal, 1946). *The Chase* (United Artists, 1946).

Los Angeles

With its combination of different ethnicity and variety of urban and rural landscapes within a relatively small area, Los Angeles has proven a perfect location for the American industry. The area has also entered the general mythology of America and has served as a metaphor for many writers since the turn of the century. Raymond Chandler, for example, found the city and its inhabitants corrupt and dangerous—the most common such depiction of the city that appears in *film noir*. Many *noirs* made effective use of the city and surrounding areas, among them: *Between Midnight and Dawn* (Columbia, 1950), *The Big Heat* (Columbia, 1953), *The Big Sleep* (Warner Bros., 1946), *The Blue Dahlia* (Paramount, 1946), *Criss Cross* (Universal, 1949), *Double Indemnity* (Paramount, 1944), *He Walked by Night* (Eagle-Lion, 1948), *The Killing* (United Artists, 1956), *Kiss Me Deadly* (United Artists, 1955), *Mildred Pierce* (Warner Bros., 1945), *Murder, My Sweet* (RKO, 1944), *The Postman Always Rings Twice* (MGM, 1946), *Roadblock* (RKO, 1951), *Sunset Boulevard* (Paramount, 1950), *While the City Sleeps* (RKO, 1956).

Losey, Joseph (1909–1984)

Director. Losey was yet another victim of the McCarthy witch hunt. His promising career was cut short almost before it began, although he later managed to rebuild his career as an exile in Great Britain. Three of Losey's earliest American films were *noirs* and are typically filled with existential themes. Among these is a remake of Fritz Lang's *M* which stuck close to the original script, but made effective use of Los Angeles locales.

Filmography: *The Big Night* (United Artists, 1951). *M* (Columbia, 1951). *The Prowler* (United Artists, 1951).

Lourié, Eugène (1905–)

Art director. The Russian born Lourié worked in Hollywood for many years, generally specializing in glossy art deco style. He worked on two interesting *films noirs*.

Filmography: *Uncle Harry* (Universal, 1945). *The Naked Kiss* (Allied Artists, 1964).

Lovejoy, Frank (1914–1962)

Actor. Frank Lovejoy was a prominent "B" leading man who also played character part in "A" films. He mainly played heroic roles and tough guys in action pictures and was thus a natural for "B" *noirs*. In the "A" film *In a Lonely Place*, Lovejoy played a supporting role but in all of his other *noir* titles, Lovejoy was either the star or second lead. In the jingoistic *I Was a Communist for the F.B.I.*, he played the title role of a steel worker who joins the local Communist Party, but is, in fact, secretly working for the F.B.I.

Probably Lovejoy's most famous *noir* role was in Ida Lupino's *The Hitch-Hiker* as one of two fishermen held captive by a serial killer. In *Try and Get Me*, a little known but surprisingly good "B" *noir*, he co-starred as a down on his luck veteran who reluctantly joins an acquaintance in a doomed kidnapping scheme.

Filmography: *In a Lonely Place* (Columbia, 1950). *Try and Get Me* (United Artists, 1950). *I Was a Communist for the F.B.I.* (Warner Bros., 1951). *The Hitch-Hiker* (RKO, 1953). *Julie* (MGM, 1956).

Lubin, Arthur (1901–)

Director. Lubin was one of the most

Lana Turner in *The Postman Always Rings Twice* **(MGM, 1946).**

Lana Turner, John Garfield in *The Postman Always Rings Twice*.

talented "B" movie directors. Despite their low budgets, many of his films are excellent. Among the better ones is a very good "B" *noir*, *Impact*, with a lively script by Dorothy Reid, several good performances and crisp direction by Lubin.

Filmography: *Impact* (United Artists, 1949).

Lukas, Paul (Paul Luckas) (1887–1971)

Character actor. Hungarian born Lukas, after success in Europe and New York as a stage actor, was a busy character actor in Hollywood beginning in the mid–twenties. Lukas was a suave, handsome actor who specialized in European cads as he did in Jacques Tourneur's early *noir*, *Experiment Perilous*, his single *noir* appearance.

Filmography: *Experiment Perilous* (RKO, 1944).

Lund, John (1913–1992)

Actor. Lund was a successful stage actor, but he never quite caught on with film audiences. He played second leads in a few films in the forties, but did not make much of an impression in his single *noir*, perhaps because his competition was Edward G. Robinson and Gail Russell.

Filmography: *The Night Has a Thousand Eyes* (Paramount, 1948).

Lupino, Ida (1918–)

Actress and director. The diminutive, British born Ida Lupino was an ideal heroine in several Warner Bros. and RKO action pictures and *films noirs* in the 1940's and one who would seem to be more in vogue today, for she seems to sum up that era's and this one's sense of disillusionment, weary toughness and preparedness for heart break. She was *noir's* most intelligent female icon and she directed one of the genre's classic "B" productions.

Lupino was not a *femme-fatale* in the classic sense, but specialized in innocents and stoic females caught up in webs of intrigue and danger, usually

caused by a lover. In *High Sierra*, for example, she is the "fun time" girl who has the bad luck to fall in love with Roy Earle, a doomed thief.

In *Beware, My Lovely*, an interesting, minor *noir*, Lupino starred as a good natured widow who inadvertently hires a psychotic handyman, thus jeopardizing her life.

One of Lupino's best performances was in Nicholas Ray's *On Dangerous Ground*, in which she stars as a blind girl whose gentleness breaks down the shell of a tough city cop.

Although her roles were less significant in her other *noir* films, Lupino is typically excellent in each.

In the early fifties, Lupino began directing films becoming the only successful female director of the era. By far, her most important film as a director was the superior "B" *noir*, *The Hitch-Hiker*. A taunt and claustrophobic thriller, it is one of the best portrayals of madness and impending danger in 1950's American film.

Filmography: *High Sierra* (Warner Bros., 1941). *Road House* (20th Century-Fox, 1948). *Beware, My Lovely* (RKO, 1952). *On Dangerous Ground* (RKO, 1952). *The Hitch-Hiker* (directed only) (RKO, 1953). *Private Hell, 36* (co-wrote/acted) (Filmmakers, 1954). *While the City Sleeps* (RKO, 1956).

Lured (United Artists, 1947). 102 min.

Producer: Hunt Stromberg. Director: Douglas Sirk. Screenplay: Leo Rosten, based on a story by Jacques Campaneez, Ernest Neuville and Simon Gantillon. Director of Photography: William Daniels. Editor: John M. Foley.

Cast: George Sanders (Robert Fleming), Lucille Ball (Sandra Carpenter), Charles Coburn (Inspector Temple), Boris Karloff (Artist), Sir Cedric Hardwicke (Julian Wilde). With: Alan Mowbray, George Zucco, Joseph Calleia.

An interesting cast stars in an early American Douglas Sirk directed *film noir*. The plot is simple and rather contrived: Sandra Carpenter, an American dancer working in London helps Scotland Yard by placing a personal ad in the paper to catch a notorious psycho killer. She then becomes the target of the mysterious killer and is saved in the nick of time by the police.

Although it is a minor film, *Lured* is interesting for its excellent cast and some inventive photography by William Daniels.

Lynch, David (1946–)

Director. Of all the major directors to have emerged in the 1980's, Lynch is the only one who seems to be influenced largely by expressionism and surrealism, rather than more contemporary art movements. His *Blue Velvet*, while not completely successful, is one of the most intriguing contemporary *films noirs*.

Filmography: *Blue Velvet* (Lorimar, 1986).

M (U.F.A., 1931). 89 min.

Producer: Seymour Nebenzal. Director: Fritz Lang. Screenplay: Thea von Harbou, Paul Falkenberg, Adolf Jansen and Kark Vash. Directors of Photography: Fritz Arno Wagner and Gustave Rathje. Art Directors: Carl Volbrecht and Emil Hasler. Editor: Paul Falkenberg.

Cast: Peter Lorre (Franz Becker), Otto Wernicke (Karl Lohmann), Gustave Grundgens (Shraenker), Theo Lingen (Bauren Faenger), Theodor Loos (Commissioner Groeber). With: George John, Ellen Widdman, Inge Landgutt, Rosa Velliti.

A serial murderer of children, Franz Becker, manages to evade the police but is eventually caught, tried and executed by the city's criminals who find his activities have given them a "bad name."

Fritz Lang's first sound feature, *M* is also his most truly expressionist, in theme and style, and had a profound influence on world cinema in decades to come. Entirely filmed in the studio the film is the ultimate example of the high contrast lighting that would characterize *film noir*. Its story, with its existential theme, is also typical of *film noir*. In typical expressionist style, it is also partly satirical, an element generally missing from *noir*. It also introduced Peter Lorre and helped establish his later, sinister persona.

In the years immediately following *M*'s release, Hitler came to power in Germany and Lang was then Germany's leading director. Hitler's propaganda minister, Josef Goebbels, offered Lang the position of heading up the film industry, apparently unaware that Lang was half-Jewish. Lang, of course, refused Goebbels' offer and soon fled the country. His wife, Thea von Harbou (who wrote most of his great silent films) remained behind and became one of the Nazis' most rabid propagandists.

M (Columbia, 1951). 87 min.

Producer: Seymour Nebenzal. Director: Joseph Losey. Screenplay: Norman Reilly Raine and Leo Katcher, additional dialog by Waldo Salt, based on the 1931 screenplay by Thea von Harbou, Paul Falkenberg, Adolf Janses and Kark Vash. Director of Photography: Ernest Laszlo. Music: Michel Michelet. Art Director: Martin Obzina. Editor: Edward Mann.

Cast: David Wayne (M), Howard Da Silva (Carney), Martin Gabel (Marshall), Luther Adler (Langley), Steve Brodie (Lt. Becker). With: Glenn Anders, Norman Lloyd, Walter Burke, Raymond Burr.

A remake of the 1931 movie, reset in Los Angles. Losey added some Americanisms and some clever location shooting qualifies it as legitimate *film noir*, however, it lacks some of the satirical elements of the original and despite a good performance by David Wayne as the child murderer, he is not nearly as convincing as Peter Lorre and the film is ultimately one of the genre's minor titles.

Robert Mitchum, Jane Russell in *Macao* (RKO, 1952).

Macao (RKO, 1952). 81 min.

Producer: Alex Gottlieb. Director: Josef Von Sternberg. Screenplay: Bernard C. Shoenfeld and Stanley Rubin, story by Bob Williams. Director of Photography: Harry J. Wild. Music: Anthony Collins. Music Director: Constantin Bakaleinikoff. Songs: "One More For My Baby" by Johnny Mercer and Harold Arlen, "You Kill Me" by Jule Styne and Leo Robin, "Ocean Breeze" by Lerios-Jenkins. Art Directors: Albert S. D'Agostino and Ralph Berger. Editors: Samuel E. Beetly and Robert Golden.

Cast: Robert Mitchum (Nick Cochran), Jane Russell (Julie Benson), William Bendix (Lawrence Trumbell), Thomas Gomez (Lt. Sebastian), Gloria Grahame (Margie), Brad Dexter (Halloran). With: Edward Ashley, Phillip Ahn, Vladimir Sokoloff, Don Zelaya.

Nick Cochran, a down on his luck ex–G.I. and small time crook arrives in Macao, hoping only to get a job and avoid any kind of trouble. Unfortunately, he soon finds himself embroiled with Julie Benson, a sexy nightclub singer, Halloran, a murderous racketeer and Lawrence Trumbell, an American agent who has come to arrest Halloran. Halloran mistakes Cochran for the agent and kidnaps him. Cochran is held at one of Halloran's safe houses, guarded by Halloran's men. However, Halloran's girl friend, Margie, helps Cochran escape so that he can take Julie out of Macao because she is jealous of the singer. Trumbell is killed by Halloran's men, but eventually, with Julie's help, Cochran captures Halloran and delivers him to the proper authorities.

Macao is a confused but visually dynamic *film noir* that tried to capitalize on the success of *His Kind of Woman*

(RKO, 1951), which also co-starred Robert Mitchum and Jane Russell. In fact, the film was a moderate popular success, but it lacked the quality of its predecessor. The film owed much of its success to Jane Russell's revealing, tight gowns and the film's exotic setting. However, although Josef Von Sternberg received credit as director of the film, most of it was actually directed by Nicholas Ray. Sternberg's methodical style proved too slow for RKO chief Howard Hughes who had a special interest in the film, namely his protégé, Jane Russell. In any case, Ray retained the exotic elements of the story, but kept the pace moving so that one hardly notices the credibility gaps in the story.

Macao remains an interesting film largely because of its performances by its principals. William Bendix brought his usual whimsical qualities to his role and Gloria Grahame almost steals the film with her subversively sensual performance as Halloran's jealous girl friend.

McCarey, Raymond (1904–1948)

Director. Raymond was the younger brother of the famous comedy director Leo McCarey. Like Leo, Raymond worked his way up through the business, beginning as a prop boy, eventually becoming a director in the thirties. Unlike Leo, Raymond never broke out of the ranks of "B" movies, hampered, no doubt, by his severe alcoholism. He directed an interesting "B" *noir*, *Strange Triangle*, a variation of *Double Indemnity* (Paramount, 1944).

Filmography: *Strange Triangle* (20th Century–Fox, 1946).

McCord, Ted (1898–1976)

Cinematographer. McCord was a staff cinematographer for Warner Bros. for nearly three decades. Although his work was adequate and often well above average, he was not a particularly inventive stylist. He worked on three *films noirs*.

Filmography: *Deep Valley* (Warner Bros., 1947). *The Breaking Point* (Warner Bros., 1950). *The Damned Don't Cry* (Warner Bros., 1950).

McCoy, Horace (   )

Novelist. McCoy was a major hardboiled crime novelist of the forties and fifties. Like W. R. Burnett, McCoy's fiction was more concerned with external violence rather than psychological insight. his novel *Kiss Tomorrow Goodbye* was adapted and made into an interesting *noir* vehicle for James Cagney. He also contributed the story for *The Turning Point*, an interesting minor *film noir*.

Filmography: *Kiss Tomorrow Goodbye* (based on his novel) (Warner Bros., 1950). *The Turning Point* (story only) (Paramount, 1952).

MacDonald, Joseph (1906–1968)

Cinematographer. MacDonald was a staff cinematographer for 20th Century–Fox. He was an inventive cinematographer who specialized in glossy entertainments. However, he also worked on a number of important *films noirs*, collaborating with Henry Hathaway and Samuel Fuller on many of their classic *noirs*. He translated black and white *noir* style brilliantly into color in Henry Hathaway's *Niagara*.

Filmography: *The Dark Corner* (20th Century–Fox, 1946). *Shock* (20th Century–Fox, 1946). *Call Northside 777* (20th Century–Fox, 1948). *The Street with No Name* (20th Century–Fox, 1948). *Panic in the Streets* (20th Century–Fox, 1950). *Fourteen Hours* (20th Century–Fox, 1951). *Niagara* (20th Century–Fox, 1952). *Pickup on South Street* (20th Century–Fox, 1953). *House of Bamboo* (20th Century–Fox, 1955).

MacDonald, Philip (1896–   )

Screenwriter. A British born novelist and short story writer, MacDonald was the author of countless short stories. His adventure and horror stories were extremely popular and several of them were successfully adapted to the screen. MacDonald settled in Hollywood in the thirties and he wrote a variety of screenplays including Charlie Chan and Mr. Moto mysteries. He also co-wrote a few minor *films noirs*.

Filmography: *Love from a Stranger* (Eagle-Lion, 1947). *The Dark Past* (Columbia, 1948). *The Man Who Cheated Himself* (20th Century–Fox, 1951).

MacDougall, Ranald (1915–1973)

Screenwriter. MacDougall was a writer of action films. His *film noirs* are distinguished by their strong structure and psychological insight. Three of his four *noir* screenplays were for Michael Curtiz, including the classic *Mildred Pierce*, starring Joan Crawford. *Possessed*, directed by Curtis Bernhardt and *Mildred Pierce*, directed by Michael Curtiz are unjustly neglected films. Indeed, all of MacDougall's *noirs* are well above average.

Filmography: *Mildred Pierce* (Warner Bros., 1945). *Possessed* (Warner Bros., 1947). *The Unsuspected* (Warner Bros., 1947). *The Breaking Point* (Warner Bros., 1950).

McGivern, William P. (1924–1983)

Novelist. McGivern was a popular novelist of crime novels in the fifties. He differed from his contemporaries in that his fiction was concerned mainly with gangsters and conventional law enforcement. His novels are quite violent with an extra element of perverse sexuality. Four of his novels were adapted to the screen, including the Fritz Lang classic *The Big Heat*.

Filmography: *The Big Heat* (Columbia, 1953). *Rogue Cop* (MGM, 1954). *Shield for Murder* (United Artists, 1954). *Odds Against Tomorrow* (United Artists, 1959).

McGraw, Charles (1914–1980)

Actor. McGraw was a busy character actor and occasional lead in countless movies in the forties and fifties. He appeared in more *films noirs* than almost any other actor, usually in small supporting roles. His rugged appearance and gruff manner made him a perfect hard-boiled actor and he played tough guys on both sides of the law.

Probably McGraw's best known leading role in a *film noir* is in the cult favorite, *The Narrow Margin*, as the tough cop assigned to escort a gangster's moll (Marie Windsor), who is set to testify against her ex-lover.

He played an equally tough and cynical cop in *Armored Car Robbery*, a superior "B" *noir* that, like *The Narrow Margin*, was directed by Richard Fleischer.

One of McGraw's least known leading roles in a *film noir* was the little known RKO "B" movie, *Roadblock*. Against type, McGraw was cast as an insurance investigator who plans and executes a heist to please his avaricious girl friend.

McGraw's best villainous performance was in the "A" *noir*, *His Kind of Woman*. McGraw plays the sadistic, cruel nemesis of Robert Mitchum's character in this wildly entertaining, relentlessly violent *film noir* directed by John Farrow.

Even in his small roles, McGraw was always a welcome, compelling performer and he remains one of *film noir's* most consistently interesting minor icons.

Filmography: *The Killers* (Universal, 1946). *Brute Force* (Universal, 1947). *The Gangster* (Allied Artists, 1947). *Berlin Express* (RKO, 1948).

McIntyre, John (1907–)

Actor. McIntyre specialized in tough guys, particularly stoic, quiet lawmen in many "B" westerns. He had a small, rather insignificant role in *The Asphalt Jungle* and starred as an honest cop in Phil Karlson's violent *The Phenix City Story*.

Filmography: *The Asphalt Jungle* (MGM, 1950). *The Phenix City Story* (Allied Artists, 1955).

MacKendrick, Alexander (1912–1993)

Director. An American, MacKendrick found his greatest success in England. There he wrote and directed several classic comedies: *Whiskey Galore* (Ealing, 1949), *The Man in the White Suit* (Ealing, 1951) and *The Ladykillers* (Ealing, 1955). He returned to the United States in the late-fifties where he directed a superior late-*noir*, *Sweet Smell of Success*. Unfortunately, his career went into a decline after this success.

Filmography: *Sweet Smell of Success* (United Artists, 1957).

MacLane, Barton (1902–1969)

Character actor. MacLane, an ex-college football player, was a large, burly man who, as an actor, specialized in heavies. He played sidekicks and villains in many films and played small supporting roles in a few *films noirs*.

Filmography: *You Only Live Once* (MGM, 1937). *High Sierra* (Warner Bros., 1941). *The Maltese Falcon* (Warner Bros., 1941). *Kiss Tomorrow Goodbye* (Warner Bros., 1950). *Red Light* (Columbia, 1950).

MacMurray, Fred (1908–1991)

Actor. A leading man, MacMurray was a contract player for Paramount. He acted in many films, including several great films. He was mainly a light leading man, starring in comedies and musicals, but he also occasionally played heroes and the odd villain.

MacMurray's most famous *noir* role was as Walter Neff in Billy Wilder's classic, *Double Indemnity*. He was at first reluctant to take the part, afraid that such an unsympathetic role would hurt his career, but, it is probably the film role he is mostly remembered for.

MacMurray's other two *noirs* were minor, but *Pushover* is known as a cheap variation of *Double Indemnity*, with MacMurray reprising the role of an immoral man who falls "victim" to a *femme-fatale*.

Without doubt, Fred MacMurray will be forever remembered for that singular great performance in *Double Indemnity*, one of *noir's* most memorable presentations.

Filmography: *Double Indemnity* (Paramount, 1944). *Singapore* (Universal, 1947). *Pushover* (Columbia, 1954).

MacRae, Gordon (1921–1986)

Actor and singer. MacRae was a popular radio personality. A singer, he was known for his rich baritone. His film career never took off, but he starred in a single *film noir* in a notable bit of bizarre miscasting.

Filmography: *Backfire* (Warner Bros., 1950).

Macready, George (1909–1983)

Character actor. Macready had a long, successful career on Broadway before entering films in the early forties. His scarred features and elegant persona typecast him as a criminal aesthete in some sixty films.

Without question, Macready's most famous performance was as Ballin Mundsen, the rather fey and peculiarly menacing criminal in *Gilda*. The film immediately established his onscreen image, and he played variations of this role in his subsequent *films noirs*.

Macready, like Peter Lorre, Elisha Cook, Jr., and Sidney Greenstreet, was a scene stealer and he was always a compelling performer. He remains an important, if minor, figure in *film noir*, thanks to a handful of splendid portrayals of evil.

Filmography: *My Name Is Julia Ross* (Columbia, 1945). *Gilda* (Columbia, 1946). *The Big Clock* (Paramount, 1948). *Knock on Any Door* (Columbia, 1949). *A Lady Without Passport* (MGM, 1950). *Detective Story* (Paramount, 1951).

Maddow, Ben (   )

Screenwriter. Maddow was a screenwriter who worked on a variety of motion pictures in the late-forties. He co-wrote three *films noirs*, including the classic *The Asphalt Jungle*. It is his most important screenplay.

Filmography: *Framed* (Columbia, 1947). *Kiss the Blood Off My Hands* (Universal, 1948). *The Asphalt Jungle* (MGM, 1950).

Madigan (Universal, 1968). 101 min. Producer: Frank P. Rosenberg. Director: Don Siegel. Screenplay: Henri Simoun and Abraham Polonsky, based on the novel by Richard Dougherty. Director of Photography: Russell Metty. Music: Don Costa. Art Directors: Alexander Golitzen and George C. Webb. Editor: Milton Shifman.

Cast: Richard Widmark (Daniel Madigan), Henry Fonda (Commissioner Russell), Inger Stevens (Julia Madigan), Harry Gaurdino (Rocco Bonaro), James Whitmore (Chief Inspector Charles Kane), Susan Clark (Trisha). With: Steve Ihnat, Sheree North, Don Stroud, Michael Dunn, Warren Stevens.

A prominent post-*noir*, *Madigan* is a cop melodrama cast from strength with Richard Widmark, a *noir* icon, as a tough New York police detective who, with Rocco Bonaro is out to apprehend a dangerous criminal. Susan Clark costars as Madigan's intelligent mistress and Henry Fonda as his boss. Director Don Siegel toned down his usual over generous ladlings of sex and violence in favor of an intelligent exposé of the forces of evil, in a script co-written by black listed Abraham Polonsky, the writer/director of the *noir* classic, *Force of Evil* (MGM, 1949). The film points the way to a number of classic post-*noir* police oriented thrillers including Siegel's *Dirty Harry* (Warner Bros., 1971).

Mahin, John Lee (1902–1984)
Screenwriter. Mahin was an immensely successful screenwriter in the early thirties. Among the screenplays he wrote or co-wrote during this prolific period are *Scarface* (United Artists, 1932), *Red Dust* (MGM, 1932) and

Bombshell (MGM, 1933). Although his best work dates from this period, Mahin remained active until the late-sixties, writing everything from biblical epics to slapstick comedies. He wrote the early gangster film *Beast of the City*, considered an important early exploration of *noir* themes and style. His only true *noir* is *Johnny Eager*, one of the genre's earliest films.

Filmography: *Beast of the City* (MGM, 1932). *Johnny Eager* (MGM, 1942).

Mainwaring, Daniel (1907–1977)
Novelist and screenwriter. Under the pseudonym Geoffrey Homes, Mainwaring, a former publicist, wrote the best selling novel, *Build My Gallows High*, which he adapted (with an uncredited Frank Fenton and James M. Cain) as the classic, *Out of the Past*. He subsequently co-wrote *The Big Steal* and contributed the original screen story for *Roadblock* under the Homes pseudonym. With his real name, he co-wrote the original screen story for *The Hitch-Hiker*, and co-wrote the late-*noir*, *Baby Face Nelson*. Also, as Daniel Mainwaring, he wrote the screenplay for the classic science fiction film *The Invasion of the Body Snatchers* (United Artists, 1955) which has many *noir*-like elements.

Filmography: *Out of the Past* (as Geoffrey Homes) (RKO, 1947). *The Big Sleep* (co-wrote, as G. Homes) (RKO, 1949). *Roadblock* (story only, as G. Homes) (RKO, 1951). *The Hitch-Hiker* (co-wrote story only) (RKO, 1953). *Baby Face Nelson* (co-wrote) (United Artists, 1957).

Malden, Karl (Malden Sekulovich) (1913–)
Character actor. After Broadway success in the late forties, Karl Malden began a successful film career, usually playing tough characters of great moral strength. He had small supporting roles in two *films noirs*.

Filmography: *Boomerang* (20th

Humphrey Bogart, Sidney Greenstreet, Peter Lorre, Mary Astor in *The Maltese Falcon*
(Warner Bros., 1941).

Century–Fox, 1947). *Where the Side-walk Ends* (20th Century–Fox, 1950).

Malone, Dorothy (Dorothy Maloney)
(1925–)

Actress. A soulfully attractive woman, Dorothy Malone is one of *film noir*'s most interesting female icons. In her first few films she played stereotypical girls next door, but her roles grew more substantial. She was neither *femme-fatale* nor victim in her *films noirs*, but generally played second leads and female "support" to male leads. In *Pushover*, for example, she played the friendly neighbor of the *femme-fatale* (Kim Novak), while in *Private Hell, 36*, she played the wife of one of the doomed police detectives who find a suitcase of stolen money.

Unfortunately, Malone was woefully misused. Although generally identified with *film noir*, she actually became a full-fledged star in the late-fifties as a sultry lead in several romantic melodramas.

Filmography: *The Big Sleep* (Warner Bros., 1946). *Convicted* (Columbia, 1950). *The Killer That Stalked New York* (Columbia, 1951). *Loophole* (Allied Artists 1954). *Private Hell, 36* (Filmmakers, 1954). *Pushover* (Columbia, 1954).

The Maltese Falcon (Warner Bros., 1941). 100 min.

Producer: Hal B. Wallis. Director: John Huston. Screenplay: John Huston, based on the novel by Dashiell Hammett. Director of Photography: Arthur Edeson. Music: Adolf Deutsch. Art Director: Robert Haas. Editor: Thomas Richards.

Cast: Humphrey Bogart (Sam Spade), Mary Astor (Brigid O'Shaughnessy), Gladys George (Iva Archer), Peter Lorre (Joel Cairo), Sydney Greenstreet (Kasper "The Fatman" Gutman), Elisha Cook, Jr. (Wilmer Cook). With: Ward Bond, Barton MacLane, Murray Alper, Emory Parnell, John Hamilton.

After his partner, Miles Archer, is killed while following a man named Thursby for a mysterious Mrs. Wonderly, Private Investigator Sam Spade is determined to find his killer. He confronts Wonderly who admits that her real name is Brigid O'Shaughnessy and that her life is threatened by the same person who killed Miles. Spade is naturally attracted to her and agrees to help her.

Spade's investigation leads to Kasper "The Fatman" Gutman, "The Fatman's" incompetent gunsel Wilmer and the foppish Joel Cairo. He learns that they are all searching for a valuable sculpture covered with gems, The Maltese Falcon. Gutman and his associates believe that Spade has the Falcon because of his relationship with Brigid.

Eventually, Spade exposes Wilmer as a murderer and he sends the police after Gutman, et al. He also realizes that Brigid is a liar and when he confronts her, she admits to killing Miles. Spade, disillusioned, turns her over to the police.

John Huston's first film as a director turned out to be a success for all involved. It helped build Humphrey Bogart into a superstar, established Sydney Greenstreet into a popular character star helped re-establish Mary Astor after a notorious sex scandal and also firmly established the screen images of Elisha Cook, Jr. and Peter Lorre.

Although the film is rather flat looking and static at times, it was one of the earliest popular successes to deal with the familiar *noir* themes of disillusionment, lurking danger, moral and official corruption. Likewise, Mary Astor's

Brigid O'Shaughnessy was one of the earliest examples of the true *noir femme-fatale*.

Maltz, Albert (1908–1985)
Screenwriter. Maltz was a victim of the anti-communist witch hunt of the late-forties. He co-wrote a number of popular films before his career was cut short by the blacklist. He co-wrote two classic *films noirs*, by far his most important screenplays.

Filmography: *This Gun for Hire* (Paramount, 1942). *The Naked City* (Universal, 1948).

The Man Who Cheated Himself (20th Century–Fox, 1951). 81 min.
Producer: Jack W. Warner. Director: Felix E. Feist. Screenplay: Seton I. Miller and Philip MacDonald, story by Seton I. Miller. Director of Photography: Russell Harlan. Music: Louis Forbes. Art Director: Van Nest Polglase. Editor: David Weisbart.
Cast: Lee J. Cobb (Ed Cullen), John Dall (Andy Cullen), Jane Wyatt (Lois), Lisa Howard (Janet), Alan Wells (Nito Capa), Harlan Warde (Howard Frazer). With: Tito Vuolo, Mimi Aguglia, Charles Arnt, Marjorie Bennett, Bud Wolfe.

The Cullen brothers are both cops. Ed Cullen is a bachelor and playboy while his younger brother, Andy, is happily married. Ed is having an affair with Lois Frazer, a beautiful socialite who is divorcing her husband Howard. When Howard tries to set up a burglary of his wife's residence while supposedly out of town, Lois shoots and kills him with his own gun. Ed helps cover up the crime of his lover, but he makes several mistakes and his brother Andy, who is investigating the crime, begins to believe his beloved elder brother is involved. Eventually, both Ed and Lois are arrested. As they are awaiting trial outside of the courtroom, Ed notices that a successful lawyer has replaced him in Lois' affections.

The Man Who Cheated Himself interweaves two familiar *noir* themes: the bad cop vs. good cop and the callous *femme-fatale* in a compelling way. The familial element heightens the tension in the film and its ambiguous ending is also interesting.

The film's director, Felix E. Feist, makes effective use of real San Francisco locations. Interestingly, John Dall, here coming off the success of *Gun Crazy* (United Artists, 1950), plays a conventional good guy rather than the corruptible young man of the earlier film.

The Manchurian Candidate (United Artists, 1962) 126 min.

Producer: George Axelrod and John Frankenheimer. Director: John Frankenheimer. Screenplay: George Axelrod and John Frankenheimer, based on the novel by Richard Condon. Director of Photography: Lionel Lindon. Music: David Amram. Production Design: Richard Sylbert. Editor: Ferris Webster.

Cast: Frank Sinatra (Bennett Marco), Lawrence Harvey (Raymond Shaw), Janet Leigh (Rosie), Angela Lansbury (Raymond's Mother), Henry Silva (Chunjin), James Gregory (Senator Iselim). With: Leslie Parrish, John McGiver, Khigh Dhiegh, James Edwards, Douglas Henderson.

Bennett Marco, a Major in Army Intelligence, is haunted by a recurring nightmare of the Korean War and seeing his former comrade, Raymond Shaw, murder two fellow soldiers. He reports his dream to his superiors who, believing he is suffering from exhaustion, give him leave.

After suffering an anxiety attack, Marco begins his own investigation. As he uncovers more facts, he slowly begins to remember that as a captor in Korea, he was brainwashed along with Shaw and others. He discovers that Shaw is programmed to kill at the will of a communist agent, Senator Iselin and Shaw's wickedly sadistic mother. When Shaw is assigned to assassinate a presidential candidate, Marco attempts to stop him. In the suspenseful climax Shaw, finally realizing what has happened, kills Iselin, his mother, and finally himself.

The Manchurian Candidate is a cold war update of the espionage *noir*. It is a contemporary nightmare involving the paranoia of communist invasion (a viable fear in the era of the Cuban Missile Crisis).

The atmosphere of the film is oppressive and dark and the film is full of dark shadows and alienating effects. It was also a popular and critical success, establishing John Frankenheimer as a major director. Unfortunately, he did not live up to the promise of this early film, which remains one of the most important late *noirs*.

Mancini, Henry (1924–)

Composer. Probably one of the best known film composers, Mancini is famous for his jazz laden, latin influenced scores. His single *noir* score, while not one of his best known, is very good.

Filmography: *Touch of Evil* (Universal, 1958).

Manhandled (Paramount, 1949). 97 min.

Producers: William H. Pine and William C. Thomas. Director: Lewis Foster. Screenplay: Lewis Foster and Whitman Chambers, based on the story "The Man Who Stole a Dream" by L. S. Goldsmith. Director of Photography: Ernest Laszlo. Music: Darryl Calker. Art Director: Lewis H. Creber. Editor: Howard Smith.

Cast: Dorothy Lamour (Meryl Kramer), Dan Duryea (Karl Benson), Sterling Hayden (Joe Cooper), Irene Hervey (Ruth Bennett), Philip Reed (Guy Bayard). With: Harold Vermilyea, Alan Napier, Art Smith, Irving Bacon.

Taking a sharp detour from the happy-go-lucky "Road" pictures in which she starred with Bob Hope and Bing Crosby, Dorothy Lamour here stars as a secretary to a crooked psychiatrist involved in a jewel robbery and murder. An excellent cast, however, was bogged down by a shoddy script and slow direction. The film is quite predictable, with little suspense and it remains notable for its production values.

Mankiewicz, Herman J. (1897–1953)

Screenwriter. Mankiewicz was the elder brother of the great screenwriter/producer/director Joseph L. Mankiewicz. Herman, a former New York wit and second string journalist/theatre critic, went to Hollywood in the early sound era and quickly established himself as an adaptable writer of comedies and dramas. Few of his screenplays have stood the test of time, however, he did co-write what is thought by many critics to be the greatest film yet made, *Citizen Kane* (RKO, 1943). He wrote a single *film noir*, Robert Siodmak's *Christmas Holiday*, generally considered one of the director's least interesting films.

Filmography: *Christmas Holiday* (Universal, 1944).

Mankiewicz, Joseph L. (1909–)

Writer/Producer/Director. The younger brother of screenwriter Herman Mankiewicz, Joseph was one of the most talented men of Hollywood's Golden Age. He originally was a top screenwriter at RKO and Paramount before becoming one of the top producers for MGM in the late thirties. When his affair with a nineteen year old Judy Garland ended his career at that studio in 1945 Mankiewicz reestablished himself at 20th Century–Fox as a top writer/director. For them, he directed two interesting, if not completely successful *films noirs*.

Filmography: *Fury* (Produced only) (MGM, 1936). *Somewhere in the Night* (co-wrote and directed) (20th Century–Fox, 1946). *House of Strangers* (Directed only) (20th Century–Fox, 1949).

Mann, Anthony (Anton Bundsmann) (1906–1967)

Director. Before becoming a director, Anthony Mann worked for producer David O. Selznick as a casting director and talent scout. In the early forties, he worked at Paramount as an assistant director. There, among several notable films he was the assistant director for Preston Sturges on the great comedy director's Hollywood satire, *Sullivan's Travels* (Paramount, 1941).

For much of his early career as a director, Mann worked at the Poverty Row studio Eagle-Lion. Yet, as Edgar G. Ulmer discovered, there were advantages to working for such companies, the main one being a relatively higher degree of creative freedom. Mann used this freedom to create some of the best "B" *films noirs*. While none of them is a true classic, they are far from insignificant. Each is characterized by a strong visual style and violent action. The best of his *noirs* are *T-Men* and *Border Incident*, although all are much better than average.

Strangely, once Mann was elevated to "A" status in the fifties, he quit making the sort of films that had originally established his reputation. In the fifties, Mann teamed with actor James Stewart for a series of classic westerns: *Winchester '73* (Universal, 1950), *The Tall Target* (MGM, 1951) and *The Man from Laramie* (Columbia, 1955). Although not as well known, Mann's earlier *films noirs* are no less worthy of critical praise.

Filmography: *Desperate* (RKO, 1947). *Railroaded* (PRC, 1947). *Raw Deal* (Eagle-Lion, 1948). *T-Men* (Eagle-Lion, 1948). *Border Incident* (MGM, 1949). *He Walked By Night* (uncredited co-director) (Eagle-Lion, 1949). *Side-Street* (MGM, 1950).

March, Frederick (Frederick McIntyre Bickel) (1897–1975)

Actor. The former Frederick Bickel of Racine, Wisconsin, became one of the most respected actors of his generation. Technically brilliant, he was capable of playing any role, but he lacked the charisma of many of his better known contemporaries, James Cagney and Humphrey Bogart. He starred in a single *film noir*, *The Desperate Hours*, as the patriarch of a family held captive by dangerous criminals, one of whom, of course, is played by Humphrey Bogart.

Filmography: *The Desperate Hours* (Paramount, 1955).

Marcus, Lawrence (Larr) (1919–)

Screenwriter. Marcus co-wrote many popular and interesting films in the early fifties, including four *films noirs*.

Filmography: *Backfire* (Warner Bros., 1950). *Dark City* (Paramount, 1950). *Cause for Alarm* (MGM, 1951). *Brainstorm* (Warner Bros., 1965).

Marin, Edwin L. (1899–1951)

Director. Marin was a prolific, occasionally above average director of "B" movies. For most of the thirties, he worked at MGM, directing many of their modest budget features. After leaving MGM in the early forties, Marin worked variously at RKO and Warner Bros., specializing in unpretentious, violent westerns. He also directed three *films noirs*, all starring George Raft. Although none is a classic, they are among Raft's best films.

Filmography: *Johnny Angel* (RKO, 1945). *Nocturne* (RKO, 1946). *Race Street* (RKO, 1948).

Marlowe (MGM, 1969). 95 min.

Producers: Gabriel Katzka and Sidney Beckerman. Director: Paul Bogart. Screenplay: Stirling Silliphant, based on the novel *The Little Sister* by Raymond Chandler. Directors of Photography: William H. Daniels and Peter Matz. Art Directors: George W. Davis and Addison Hehr. Editor: Gene Ruggiero.

Cast: James Gardner (Philip Marlowe), Gayle Hunnicutt (Maxis Wald),

Carroll O'Connor (Lt. Christy French), Rita Moreno (Dolores Gonzales), Sharon Farrell (Orfamay Quest). With: H. M. Wynant, Jackie Coogan, Kenneth Tobey.

Private Investigator Philip Marlowe is hired by a young girl to find her missing brother. He finds the brother dead with an ice pick in his side. The trail leads to gangster H. M. Wynant. Wynant is the center of a series of blackmailing schemes and, in the end, an ex-lover murders him and then, in turn, is murdered by the man who, with her, was blackmailing the gangster.

Marlowe is an interesting update of Raymond Chandler's novel *The Little Sister*. It sets the action among the "counterculture" of hippies, drugs, rock 'n' roll, etc., with Marlowe standing in as a cynical representative of old values. James Gardner was perfectly cast as the private investigator and the film was a moderate success. However, it is one of the least important post *noirs* working mainly as unpretentious entertainment.

Marlowe, Philip

Raymond Chandler's character is probably the most fully realized private detective in American literature. He is certainly the most human and vulnerable of all such characters. Sloppy, misogynist, brash yet honorable, Marlowe was a completely independent man who viewed the corrupt world around him—the political and economic elite and, above all, the police—with a critical, occasionally bemused eye.

Philip Marlowe was portrayed in three *films noirs* in the 1940's: Humphrey Bogart in *The Big Sleep* (Warner Bros., 1946), Dick Powell in *Murder, My Sweet* (RKO, 1944) and George Montgomery in *The Brasher Doubloon* (20th Century–Fox, 1947). Chandler claimed that Powell's portrayal was closest to his original conception, although Bogart's remains the most endearing (and enduring). In the 1970's,

Robert Mitchum played the character in the remake of *The Big Sleep* (Avco-Embassy, 1976) and *Farewell, My Lovely* (Avco-Embassy), while James Gardner played the character in *Marlowe* (MGM, 1969).

Marshall, George (1891–1975)

Director. Marshall might well be one of the most prolific film directors in the history of American cinema, with some 400 titles to his credit. His career began in the late-teens and continued successfully until the sixties. He is best remembered for a number of stylish comedies, many starring Bob Hope, including *The Ghost Breakers* (Paramount, 1940), *Monsieur Beaucaire* (Paramount, 1946) and *Scared Stiff* (Paramount, 1953) among many others. A superior craftsman, Marshall also directed a few action yarns, romantic dramas and a single *film noir*, *The Blue Dahlia*, an extremely well made early *noir*.

Filmography: *The Blue Dahlia* (Paramount, 1946).

Marshall, Herbert (1890–1966)

Actor. The British born actor Herbert Marshall was, for several decades, the very epitome of old world elegance and charm. He was a popular leading man in the twenties and thirties and later developed into a second lead, usually as a professional: doctors, diplomats, etc. He appeared in three *films noirs*, most notably as a Scotland Yard Detective investigating art forgery in *Crack-Up* and as a murderer in *The High Wall* who uses hypnosis to trick another man into accepting blame for his crime.

Filmography: *The Letter* (Warner Bros., 1940). *Crack-Up* (RKO, 1946). *The High Wall* (MGM, 1947). *Angel Face* (RKO, 1953).

Marvin, Lee (1924–1987)

Actor. Marvin would come to embody tough, heroic roles in the sixties, but was for many years a popular char-

acter actor. In *The Big Heat*, his most important *noir*, he had a famous supporting part as a sadistic henchman who is having an affair with his boss's mistress (Gloria Grahame). He also starred in the important post-*noir*, *Point Blank*, as a gangster seeking bloody revenge against his former employers.

Filmography: *The Big Heat* (Columbia, 1953). *I Died a Thousand Times* (Warner Bros., 1956). *Point Blank* (MGM, 1967).

The Mask of Dimitrios (Warner Bros., 1944). 95 min.

Producer: Henry Blanke. Director: Jean Negulesco. Screenplay: Frank Gruber, based on the novel *A Coffin for Dimitrios* by Eric Ambler. Director of Photography: Arthur Edeson. Music: Adolph Deutsch. Art Director: Ted Smith. Editor: Frederick Richards.

Cast: Sydney Greenstreet (Mr. Peters), Zachary Scott (Dimitrios), Faye Emerson (Irama Preveza), Peter Lorre (Cornelius Latimer Leyden), George Tobias (Fedor Muishkin), Victor Francen (Wladislaw Grodek). With: Steve Geray, Florence Bates, Eduardo Ciannelli, Kurt Katch, Marjorie Hoshell.

Cornelius Latimer Layden, a mystery writer living in Turkey, is intrigued by the life of an internationally known criminal, Dimitrios, whose body he has been shown by a policeman/friend. Layden reconstructs Dimitrios' life. He meets with people from Dimitrios' past who recall his pimping, smuggling, murder, political assassination and espionage.

Layden's investigation is aided by Mr. Peters, a one time associate and victim of Dimitrios. Peters soon reveals that, in fact, Dimitrios is not dead at all, but has faked his death. Peters is using Layden to blackmail Dimitrios. Dimitrios at least shows himself when he tries to kill both Layden and Peters, but Dimitrios and Peters shoot and kill each other.

In both plot and characters, *The*

Mask of Dimitrios, based on a novel by Eric Ambler, resembles the much more famous *The Third Man* (United Artists, 1948), based on Graham Greene's novel. Both use a cynical novelist to expose the life of a notorious criminal who faked his own death. Both are also set in exotic locations, with *The Third Man* set in post-war Vienna and this film's Turkish setting. The difference, of course, is that *The Mask of Dimitrios*, filmed entirely in Hollywood studios, has a stronger *noir* style than the later film.

Indeed, *The Mask of Dimitrios* is an important, if neglected, early *film noir*. Its style is typical Warner Bros. — expressionist, reminding one of *Casablanca* (Warner Bros., 1942) with its spacious bars, palm tree filled sets, rainswept streets, etc. Likewise, Sydney Greenstreet and Peter Lorre were co-stars of that famous film. Here, for once, Lorre was cast in a good guy leading role and he is quite good as the vain novelist who eventually exposes and ultimately is the catalyst in the death of, Dimitrios.

Zachary Scott, As Dimitrios, was an odd choice, but he manages to hold his own against notorious scene stealers Lorre and Greenstreet.

Mason, James (1909–1984)

Actor. An enormously talented actor with a rich voice and rather rugged appearance, the British born Mason first achieved stardom in the mid–forties after many years on the stage and in small film roles. His extraordinary performance in Carol Reed's *Odd Man Out* (Gaumont, 1946) made him into a star. He came to the United States shortly thereafter and starred in *Caught*, the first of two extraordinary *films noirs* directed by Max Ophuls. In *Caught* and the subsequent Ophuls classic, *The Reckless Moment*, he played sympathetic parts. He also co-starred in the less notable *Cry Terror* and *One Way Street*.

Filmography: *Caught* (MGM, 1949). *The Reckless Moment* (Columbia, 1949). *One Way Street* (Universal, 1950). *Cry Terror* (MGM, 1958).

Maté, Rudolph (Rudolf Mathéh) (1898–1964)

Director. Maté was born in Poland and his film career began in Germany as a cinematographer in the 1920's. He worked with directors Fritz Lang and René Clair among others, establishing a reputation as a brilliant, inventive craftsman. He moved to the United States in the mid–thirties and worked on many excellent films before becoming a director in the mid–forties.

As a director, Rudolf Maté's reputation rests with the classic *noir*, *D.O.A.* and the science fiction classic, *When Worlds Collide* (Paramount, 1951). He brought a sense of expressionist style to all of his films, but he was not a particularly inventive director. *D.O.A.* is certainly his best film, but all of his *noirs* are admirable entertainments.

Filmography: *The Dark Past* (Columbia, 1948). *D.O.A.* (United Artists, 1949). *Union Station* (Paramount, 1950). *Second Chance* (RKO, 1951). *Forbidden* (Universal, 1953).

Mature, Victor (1915–)

Actor. Tall, muscular, florid and dark, Victor Mature was known as "the Hunk." Critics attacked his wooden acting style, but he was a popular leading man in the forties and fifties, and is generally acknowledged as one of *noir's* major male icons.

Mature specialized in stoic heroes and the occasional anti-hero. In *Cry of the City*, a little known Robert Siodmak-directed thriller, Mature was the good cop to Richard Conte's bad cop. Likewise, in the early *noir* classic, Mature stars as an innocent suspected of murder who must prove his innocence.

Mature's best *noir* role was in *Kiss of Death* as a petty thief turned police informant who is hunted by an insane hired killer played by Richard Widmark.

Of *film noir*'s major male icons, Victor Mature was the most limited. In addition, he appeared in relatively few of the genre's titles, yet he remains one of the most indelible figures, perhaps due more his choice of film rather than how he performed in them.

Filmography: *The Shanghai Gesture* (United Artists, 1941). *I Wake Up Screaming* (20th Century-Fox, 1942). *Kiss of Death* (20th Century-Fox, 1947). *Cry of the City* (20th Century-Fox, 1948). *Gambling House* (RKO, 1951).

Maugham, W. Somerset (1874–1965)

Writer. Maugham was a successful writer of novels, short stories and plays. Many of his works were adapted for the screen and, although hardly a hard-boiled writer, two of his works were made into *films noirs*. *The Letter* is more typical of his work, with its tropical setting and repressed sexuality turning to violence.

Filmography: *The Letter* (Warner Bros., 1940). *Christmas Holiday* (Universal, 1944).

Maxwell, Marilyn (1922–1972)

Actress. Despite her wide-ranging talents, Maxwell was stereotyped as a dimwitted blonde—a kind of second string Marilyn Monroe. She appeared in the classic *film noir*, *Champion*, as the ideal female beauty whose mere existence is reason enough for the main character, a boxer (Kirk Douglas) to do anything for fame and fortune, and to win her. She also co-starred in the minor *noir*, *Race Street*.

Filmography: *Race Street* (RKO, 1948). *Champion* (United Artists, 1949).

Mayo, Virginia (Virginia Jones) (1920–)

Actress. Mayo was the ideal of the "all American girl next door" in the 1940's. A very attractive blonde, she was teamed with Danny Kaye in a series of popular comedies. However, she tried to break out of the typecast of the perennial good girl in several films most notably *White Heat*, as the evil Verna Jarrett, wife of the sadistic gangster Cody Jarrett (James Cagney). She was also the female lead in the minor *Red Light*, but did not have much to do in a film dominated by its male stars.

Filmography: *White Heat* (Warner Bros., 1947). *Red Light* (Columbia, 1950).

Mazurki, Mike (Mikhail Mazurski) (1901–)

Character actor. Mazurki was a football player and professional wrestler before bringing his blunt features and hefty figure to the screen in the 1940's. He specialized in dimwitted thugs of the sort he played in *Farewell, My Lovely*. He also played "The Strangler," a wrestler, in *Night and the City*. His fight scene in this film is one of the most vivid depictions of sports on film.

Mazurki was one of the busiest character actors in *film noir*, and his brief appearances are always enjoyable and welcome.

Filmography: *The Shanghai Gesture* (United Artists, 1941). *Murder, My Sweet* (RKO, 1944). *Nightmare Alley* (20th Century-Fox, 1947). *I Walk Alone* (Paramount, 1948). *Abandoned* (Universal, 1949). *Dark City* (Paramount, 1950). *Night and the City* (20th Century-Fox, 1950). *New York Confidential* (Warner Bros., 1955).

Meehan, John (1902–1984)

Director. One of Hans Dreier's many collaborators at Paramount, Meehan contributed production designs for two *films noirs*. Both are excellent examples of film production design at its very best.

Filmography: *The Strange Love of Martha Ivers* (Paramount, 1946). *Sunset Boulevard* (Paramount, 1950).

Meeker, Ralph (Ralph Rathgeber) (1920–)

Actor. Meeker was a popular stage actor in the late forties, taking over the

Van Heflin, Kirk Douglas in *The Strange Loves of Martha Ivers* **(Paramount, 1946).**

role of Stanley Kowalski from Marlon Brando in the Broadway production of *A Streetcar Named Desire*. Ruggedly handsome, Meeker specialized in virile heroes. His best known film role was as Mike Hammer in the late-*noir* classic *Kiss Me Deadly*.

Filmography: *Kiss Me Deadly* (United Artists, 1955).

Mellor, William (1904–1963).

Cinematographer. Mellor, a competent professional, was one of director George Stevens' chief collaborators in the fifties. He was the director of photography on two *noirs*, but neither is particularly notable for their cinematography.

Filmography: *Too Late for Tears*

(United Artists, 1949). *The Unknown Man* (MGM, 1951).

Melville, Jean-Pierre (1917–1973).

Director. A French film director, Melville was a well respected filmmaker in his native country. He was the predominant director of crime films in France in the 1950's. The term *film noir* was regularly applied to his movies by French critics in that decade and indeed he was clearly influenced by the parallel American genre.

Merrill, Gary (1914–)

Actor. Merrill, who was married to Bette Davis for many years, was a star of mostly routine action films. He starred in a single *noir* with his wife.

Filmography: *Another Man's Poison* (United Artists, 1952).

Metro-Goldwyn-Mayer

MGM was the leading American motion-picture production company for nearly five decades. The company came together in 1925 from three leading production companies: Metro, Goldwyn and Louis B. Mayer Pictures. The namesake of the latter, Louis Mayer, was named Vice President in charge of the studio. He was not the owner of the new studio, but was allowed to run it as he wished by the financial backers in New York.

Mayer's taste ran to the pedestrian and glossy entertainments, but he was supplemented by Irving Thalberg, "the boy genius" in the thirties. Thalberg's taste helped establish the literary flare of the studio before his death in 1937.

More than any other major studio, MGM was essentially a producer's company. The producer had full creative control of each production. The product was geared toward stars: Greta Garbo, Jeannette MacDonald, Nelson Eddy, Joan Crawford, Spencer Tracy, Jean Harlow and many others.

However, a few directors managed to develop their own style. Still, most of MGM's films were unambitious

family movies and musicals. As a result, the company produced relatively few *films noirs*. The *noirs* that were produced by the company tend to suffer from overproduction, with a few exceptions: John Huston's *The Asphalt Jungle*, Robert Montgomery's *Lady in the Lake*, Fritz Lang's *Fury* and Joseph H. Lewis' *A Lady Without Passport*.

Releases: **1932:** *Beast of the City.* **1936:** *Fury.* **1942:** *Johnny Eager.* **1945:** *Bewitched.* **1946:** *Undercurrent.* **1947:** *The High Wall. Lady in the Lake. Scene of the Crime.* **1948:** *Force of Evil.* **1949:** *Act of Violence. Border Incident. The Bribe. Caught. Side Street.* **1950:** *The Asphalt Jungle. Jeopardy. Mystery Street. Tension.* **1951:** *Cause for Alarm. The People Against O'Hara. The Strip. The Undercover Man. The Unknown Man.* **1952:** *Talk About a Stranger.* **1954:** *Rogue Cop.* **1956:** *Julie.* **1958:** *Cry Terror. Party Girl.* **1959:** *The Beat Generation.* **1967:** *Point Blank.* **1968:** *The Split.* **1969:** *Marlowe.* **1974:** *The Outfit.*

Metty, Russell (1906–1978)

Cinematographer. Metty was a fairly significant cinematographer, working on a variety of films of some note. Of his *noir* titles, the two most important are those directed by Orson Welles, but the cinematography on all of his *noirs* is well above average.

Filmography: (*Directed by Orson Welles). *The Stranger* (RKO, 1946). Ride the Pink Horse* (Universal, 1947). *Kiss the Blood Off My Hands* (Universal, 1948). *The Naked Alibi* (Universal, 1954). *Touch of Evil** (Universal, 1958).

Meyer, Emil (1903–)

Character actor. Meyer played the usual small parts. In three of his seven *noir* appearances—*The Line Up*, *The People Against O'Hara* and *Shield for Murder*—he played cops. His appearances were always brief but enjoyable.

Filmography: *The Big Night* (United

Joan Crawford in *Mildred Pierce* (Warner Bros., 1945).

Artists, 1951). *The Mob* (Columbia, 1951). *The People Against O'Hara* (MGM, 1951). *Shield for Murder* (United Artists, 1954). *Sweet Smell of Success* (United Artists, 1957). *The Line Up* (Columbia, 1958). *The Outfit* (MGM, 1973).

Michelet, Michel (1899–1988)

Composer. Michelet, a French born composer who settled in the United States in the late thirties, is known for his excellent scores for several interesting low budget films including four *films noirs*. His music combines elements of European romanticism and American idioms including jazz.

Filmography: *The Chase* (United Artists, 1946). *Lured* (United Artists, 1947). *Impact* (United Artists, 1949). *M* (Columbia, 1951).

Mildred Pierce (Warner Bros., 1945). 113 min.

Producer: Jerry Wald. Director:

Michael Curtiz. Screenplay: Ranald MacDougall (w/uncredited Michael Curtiz), based on the novel by James M. Cain. Director of Photography: Ernest Haller. Music: Max Steiner. Art Director: Anton Grot. Editor: David Weisbart.

Cast: Joan Crawford (Mildred Pierce), Jack Carson (Wally Fay), Zachary Scott (Monte Beragon), Eve Arden (Ida), Ann Blythe (Veda Pierce), Bruce Bennett (Bert Pierce). With: George Tobias, Lee Patrick, Moroni Olsen, JoAnn Marlowe, Barbara Brown.

The murder of wealthy Monte Beragon unveils the sordid past of Mildred Pierce and her family.

Mildred was a bored middleclass housewife, married to real estate broker Bert Pierce. Mildred is obsessed with providing luxuries for her older daughter Veda, as well as her younger daughter, Kay. She leaves her husband, temporarily taking a job as a waitress.

Partly to placate Veda's snobbery, Mildred plans to open a restaurant with the help of Wally Fay, her ex-husband's old partner, and is sponsored by Monte Beragon, a millionaire speculator/ playboy.

Veda is sexually attracted to the bored, decadent Beragon and breaks her engagement with an heir to a small fortune in order to seduce Beragon. Meanwhile, the restaurant is opened successfully, but success is followed by tragedy when Mildred's younger daughter is killed in an accident.

Mildred eventually marries Beragon as she turns the restaurant's success into an equally successful chain of restaurants. However, she soon discovers that Beragon is squandering her hard earned fortune. He bankrupts the business with his bad investments. When Mildred confronts him, he denounces her and Veda, calling the daughter a "rotten little tramp." Veda, in uncontrollable anger, kills Beragon. Although Mildred tries to cover up for her beloved daughter, she is unsuccessful and Veda is arrested. Mildred, in sorrow, is reunited with her first husband.

James M. Cain was the only hard-boiled novelist of his generation to feature females as main characters and to avoid the cliches of crime fiction, he did not write about private investigators, gangsters, or policemen. Instead, he was almost exclusively concerned with the corrupting aspirations of a complacent middle class, driven to extremes by their own prejudices and greed. The catalyst for his character's actions is, more often than not, sex.

Mildred Pierce is an archetypal *film noir* in style, story and even narrative. The opening murder sets up the flashback that makes up the body of the film. The flashback was a device used in many *films noirs*.

The film, of course, was a vehicle for Joan Crawford who is quite good as the titular anti-heroine. However, Ann Blythe, as the avaricious, slutty Veda

Pierce is equally good and Zachary Scott's decadent millionaire is one of the genre's best depictions of the type.

Director Michael Curtiz was at his best with *Mildred Pierce*. His baroque style has a way of reiterating the boiling passions of the story. Indeed, the film can stand as a textbook example of *noir* style at its extravagant best: a gliding, probing camera, quick cuts in the middle of tracking shorts, shimmering, sensual close-ups, and low-key lighting. The film also has a superb score by Max Steiner.

Milestone, Lewis (Lewis Milstein) (1895–1980)

Director. Milestone is noted for his extraordinary visual style. His early work outshines his later films and he was certainly one of the great American directors of the 1930's. A great technician, Milestone developed in his masterpiece *All Quiet on the Western Front* (Universal, 1930), a fast crabwise tracking shot which has been much imitated since. He directed the original version of *The Racket*. It is not wholly successful, but his later *film noir*, *The Strange Love of Martha Ivers*, is a classic. It is noted for, among other things, its brilliant style.

Filmography: *The Racket* (Paramount, 1928). *The Strange Love of Martha Ivers* (Paramount, 1946).

Milland, Ray (1905–1986)

Actor. The Welsh born Milland was a popular leading man in mostly light films beginning in the thirties. Today, he is probably best known as the alcoholic writer in Billy Wilder's *The Lost Weekend* (Paramount, 1947) and as the haunted co-owner of a house in *The Uninvited* (Paramount, 1944). However, he also starred in three notable *films noirs*. In Fritz Lang's early *noir* classic, *Ministry of Fear*, Milland starred as an ex-convict who finds himself embroiled in a Nazi espionage plot against the British government. In *The Big Clock*, another classic, he plays a brilliant writer caught up in a complicated mystery involving murder and a psychotic publisher. Milland's final *noir* appearance was in *The Thief*, a unique experiment as a film without dialog.

Filmography: *Ministry of Fear* (Paramount, 1945). *The Big Clock* (Paramount, 1948). *The Thief* (United Artists, 1952).

Miller, David (1909–)

Director. Miller was one of the first editors to make the successful transition to directing. He is associated mainly with light dramas of little visual style. However, he also directed an excellent, if minor, *film noir, Sudden Fear*. Unfortunately, Miller did not make another film of this type.

Filmography: *Sudden Fear* (RKO, 1953).

Miller, Seton I. (1902–1974)

Screenwriter. In the twenties, Miller was a popular actor in silent films. Like so many silent stars, Miller found it difficult to make the change to sound, but he was literate and decided to move into screenwriting. In fact, he quickly became one of the most successful and prolific screenwriters of Hollywood's Golden Age. He specialized in fast moving adventures and costume epics and co-wrote two of Erroll Flynn's best films, *The Adventures of Robin Hood* (Warner Bros., 1938) and *The Sea Hawk* (Warner Bros., 1940). His *films noirs* are characterized by swift action and exotic locales. Seton is an overlooked but important *film noir* screenwriter and, indeed, in American cinema in general.

Filmography: *Ministry of Fear* (Paramount, 1944). *Calcutta* (Paramount, 1947). *Singapore* (Universal, 1947). *Convicted* (Columbia, 1950). *The Man Who Cheated Himself* (20th Century-Fox, 1951).

Milner, Victor (1893–1986)

Cinematographer. Milner was a staff cinematographer at Paramount. In the early thirties he worked on many of the classic Paramount films including several significant titles of directors Cecil B. DeMille and Ernet Lubitsch. He was the director on three *noirs*, each of which are visually compelling and in the classic *noir* style: dark shadows, lighting pointed up from the floor to give a sinister look to the faces, rain and fog swept sets, etc.

Filmography: *The Strange Love of Martha Ivers* (Paramount, 1946). *Dark City* (Paramount, 1950). *Jeopardy* (MGM, 1953).

Milton, David ( )

Art Director. Milton has been called the Cedric Gibbons of Monogram. He was one of the busiest art directors in Hollywood in the thirties and forties, often working single handedly on more than twenty productions a year. Monogram's budgets were usually adequate at best and Milton had to use whatever materials were at hand. He developed a style that was spare and angular, enhanced by inventive lighting by cinematographers and inventive camera work of the directors to disguise the minimalism of the sets.

Filmography: *Decoy* (Monogram, 1946). *Fear* (Monogram, 1946). *Fall Guy* (Monogram, 1947). *I Wouldn't Be in Your Shoes* (Monogram, 1948). *Southside 1-1000* (Allied Artists, 1950). *Loophole* (Allied Artists, 1954). *The Phenix City Story* (Allied Artists, 1955). *Baby Face Nelson* (United Artists, 1957).

Ministry of Fear (Paramount, 1945). 86 min.

Executive Producer: B. G. DeSylva. Director: Fritz Lang. Screenplay: Seton I. Miller, based on the novel by Graham Greene. Director of Photography: Henry Sharp. Music: Victor Young. Art Directors: Hal Pereira and Hans Dreier. Editor: Archie Marshek.

Cast: Ray Milland (Stephen Neale), Marjorie Reynolds (Carlo Hilf), Carl Esmond (Willi Hilf), Hillary Brooke (the second Mrs. Bellaire), Percy Waran (Prentice), Dan Duryea (Travers). With: Alan Napier, Erskine Sanford, Thomas Louden, Aminta Dyne, Eustace Wyatt.

Stephen Neale is released from prison after serving time for a mercy killing he did not commit. He returns to his hometown of London. The war is raging and the city is under constant attack by German bombers.

While attending a bazaar, Neale unknowingly utters a secret word and is handed a cake intended for a Nazi spy. The cake contains micro-film of invasion plans. Neale is chased by Nazi spies. He hires a detective to help him, but the man is murdered by the Nazis who make it look like Neale killed him.

Since he can not go to the police, Neale, with the aid of his girl friend Carla, breaks up the ring. When Carla, an Austrian refugee, discovers her brother is one of the Nazi conspirators, she kills him. With Carla's help, Neale proves his innocence.

Ministry of Fear is a perfect example of the developing *noir* sensibilities in the mid–forties. While it is an espionage thriller, it is a decidedly unconventional one, filled with fear, paranoia and lurking danger. Likewise, its character's dilemma is typically existential, beginning really with his previous trouble before the film begins: one has the feeling that Stephen Neale is doomed to a lifetime of trouble.

Fritz Lang took advantage of Paramount's qualities, including its great art directors Hal Pereira and Hans Dreier, to create a glossy, fast moving, exciting *film noir*, filled with the usual images associated with the genre.

Mr. Arkadin (Warner Bros., 1955). 100 min.

Producer: Louis Dolivet. Director: Orson Welles. Screenplay: Orson Welles, based on his novel. Director of Photography: Jean Bourgoin. Music: Paul Misraki. Art Director: Orson Welles. Editor: Renzo Lucid.

Cast: Orson Welles (Gregory Arkadin), Paola Mori (Raina Arkadin), Robert Arden (Guy Van Stratten), Akim Tamiroff (Jacob Zouk), Michael Redgrave (Burgomi Trebitsch). With: Patricia Medina, Mischa Auer, Katina Paxinou, Jack Watling.

Orson Welles' least known *film noir*, *Mr. Arkadin* was largely privately financed and not released in the United States until 1962.

Set in Spain and Italy, the story is complicated, one involving a small time con man, Guy Van Stratten who is hired by Arkadin, one of the world's richest men, to investigate his past because Arkadin claims he can not remember it. In fact, Stratten eventually realizes that Arkadin is using him to find persons from his past who might be able to compromise his success because of what they know about him: his fortune was made largely by trafficking in human flesh, as he sold beautiful women into sexual slavery. Arkadin is killing his old friends and is planning to kill Stratten. Stratten, however, exposes the millionaire's sordid past to Raina Arkadin, the old man's beloved daughter. When she rejects him, Arkadin kills himself.

Mr. Arkadin, despite its many faults (its dialog was tortuously dubbed after it was completed), is a fascinating portrait of a corrupt millionaire. Its style and narrative structure are similar to *Citizen Kane* (RKO, 1942), but the elements of mindless corruption and violence qualify it as a true *film noir*.

Mitchell, Millard (1900–1953)

Character actor. A rangy character actor famous for his nasal delivery, Mitchell played tough guys in many movies, particularly westerns. He had small supporting roles in two *films noirs*.

Filmography: *A Double Life* (Universal, 1948). *Convicted* (Columbia, 1950).

Mitchum, Robert (1917–)

Actor. Robert Mitchum is one of the

great male *noir* icons, perhaps *the* great star of the genre. A strong, durable actor, he was a forceful presence on screen and he remains one of American film's enduring legends. His sleepy eyes, stoic, almost indifferent persona and natural style made him a perfect star for the cynical post war era and more than any other actor he has come to embody those qualities one usually associates with *film noir*.

Mitchum held a variety of jobs, including a brief stint as a journalist before turning to acting in the early forties. He played small parts in mostly forgettable films, including several Hopalong Cassiday westerns. However, his personality did not assert itself until the late forties. Like Robert Ryan, Kirk Douglas and others, the peculiar qualities of his personality found a home in the developing genre and through his appearances in *films noirs*, Mitchum became a full fledged star.

Among his several early, pre-star *noir* appearances, Robert Mitchum was particularly notable in the "B" film *When Strangers Marry*, as the murderous villain. He also had supporting roles in the "A" *noirs*, *The Locket* and *Undercurrent*, but it was not until *Out of the Past* that he achieved real fame.

Out of the Past was a modest "A" production, designed to exploit the talents of its director and two promising RKO contract players, Jane Greer and Robert Mitchum. Despite its modest origins, it quickly developed into one of the studio's most important releases in 1947. It established Mitchum as a viable star and helped form his image in the late forties. He was perfectly cast as the corruptible private investigator Jeff Bailey, and his chemistry with Greer and Kirk Douglas (as Bailey's nemesis) was irresistible.

Mitchum's laconic, witty, self-deprecating style was suddenly in vogue in the late forties and he found himself (much to his surprise) a major box-office attraction. RKO, his studio, immediately exploited his popularity with a series of films in which he played variations of Jeff Bailey: *The Big Steal* (in which he was again teamed with Jane Greer), *Where Danger Lives* (neglected minor classic), and his two films with Jane Russell, *His Kind of Woman* and *Macao*.

While Mitchum's early *noir* career was devoted to tough heroes and doomed cynics, he later played some of the late *noir*'s most vicious villains. In *Cape Fear* he starred as Max Cady, an ex-con trying to avenge his conviction against the family of the District Attorney who had prosecuted him. In the gothic *noir*, *Night of the Hunter*, he was particularly striking as the fake psychotic evangelical minister who terrorizes a southern family.

Mitchum provided a legitimate link with *film noir* later when he starred as Philip Marlowe in two unique post-*noirs*, *The Big Sleep* and *Farewell, My Lovely*.

There are a few indelible images associated with *film noir*, and one of the strongest must be Robert Mitchum in a trenchcoat, from *Out of the Past*. Although he never took himself or his work very seriously, his performances were always excellent and he remains one of the genre's most important actors.

Filmography: *When Strangers Marry* (Monogram, 1944). *Undercurrent* (MGM, 1946). *Crossfire* (RKO, 1947). *The Locket* (RKO, 1947). *Out of the Past* (RKO, 1947). *Where Danger Lives* (RKO, 1950). *His Kind of Woman* (RKO, 1951). *The Racket* (RKO, 1951). *Macao* (RKO, 1952). *Angel Face* (RKO, 1953). *Night of the Hunter* (United Artists, 1955). *Thunder Road* (United Artists, 1958). *Cape Fear* (Universal, 1962). *The Friends of Eddie Coyle* (Paramount, 1973). *Farewell, My Lovely* (Avco-Embassy, 1975). *The Big Sleep* (Avco-Embassy, 1978).

The Mob (Columbia, 1951). 87 min.

Producer: Jerry Bresler. Director: Robert Parrish. Screenplay: William

Bowers, based on the novel *Waterfront* by Ferguson Findley. Director of Photography: Joseph Walker. Music: George Duning. Art Director: Cary Odell. Editor: Charles Nelson.

Cast: Broderick Crawford (Johnny Danico), Betty Buehler (Mary Kierman), Richard Kiley (Thomas Clancy), Otto Hulett (Lt. Banks), Matt Crowley (Smoothie), Neville Brand (Gunner), Ernest Borgnine (Castro). With: Walter Klaven, Lynne Baggett, Jean Alexander, Ralph Dunke.

Johnny Damico, an undercover cop, infiltrates the local mob. He finds that the waterfront is rife with corruption. With Gunner and Joe Castro, mob associates, he works on the fringes of mob activities and is exposed to all of its corrupt elements. With the help of Tom Clancy, another undercover cop, Smoothie, the leader of the mob, is exposed. Smoothie is finally killed in a shootout with the cops.

The Mob is an unpretentious *film noir* with elements of the simpler 1950's style and a concentration on violence. It is a thoroughly unsentimental tale of hard-boiled cops against hard-boiled mobsters. The police, particularly Broderick Crawford's Damico character are not glamorized, but more human than their predecessors: gruff, vulgar, yet determined to get the job done.

Robert Parrish's direction is well above average and *The Mob* remains an eclectic, interesting "B" *noir*.

Mockridge, Cyril (1896–1979)

Composer. A british born composer, Mockridge came to the United States in 1931. He was a staff composer for 20th Century–Fox. He was a prolific composer of film music, but few of his scores are memorable. He composed the scores for several important *films noirs*, but his work is rarely better than adequate.

Filmography: *I Wake Up Screaming* (20th Century–Fox, 1941). *The Dark Corner* (20th Century–Fox, 1946). *Nightmare Alley* (20th Century–Fox,

1947). *Roadhouse* (20th Century–Fox, 1948). *Where the Sidewalk Ends* (20th Century–Fox, 1950).

Mohr, Hal (1894–1974)

Cinematographer. An immensely talented cinematographer, Mohr worked extensively in all the genres. His *films noirs*, however, are not among his most inventive but his work on each is adequate enough.

Filmography: *Woman on the Run* (Universal, 1950). *The Big Night* (United Artists, 1951). *The Second Woman* (United Artists, 1951). *Baby Face Nelson* (United Artists, 1957). *The Line Up* (Columbia, 1958). *Underworld U.S.A.* (Columbia, 1961).

Monks, John Jr. (1912–)

Screenwriter. Monks was a prolific writer of mostly "B" movies and action pictures. He co-wrote three good *films noirs*.

Filmography: *The House on 92nd Street* (20th Century–Fox, 1945). *Knock on Any Door* (Columbia, 1949). *The People Against O'Hara* (MGM, 1951).

Monogram

The subsidiary of Allied Artists, Monogram was the company that was supposed to produce the "routine" films of the corporation, although it is difficult to tell the difference between the Monogram and Allied Artists productions. Monogram's budgets were modest at best and its production values were minimal. Films were generally made in only a few days. Still, there is a certain charm to their best films and the company has a huge cult following today among aficionados. The company released a handful of *films noirs*.

Releases: 1944: *When Strangers Marry*. 1946: *Decoy. Fear. Suspense*. 1947: *Fall Guy. The Guilty*. 1948: *I Wouldn't Be in Your Shoes*.

Monroe, Marilyn (Norma Jean Baker) (1926–1962)

Actress. Before her superstardom,

Monroe played small parts and supporting roles in many films, including several striking *noir* appearances. Her roles in *Clash by Night* and *The Asphalt Jungle* were small, but she was memorable in each, particularly the latter in which she played the mistress of the crooked lawyer (Louis Calhern) who bankrolls a jewel robbery. Her most important *noir* performance, however, was in *Niagara*. She starred as Rose Loomis, a *femme-fatale* planning the murder of her husband. Although the film firmly established her popularity and glamorous image, she would never play an unsympathetic character again. That is unfortunate because she gave one of her best performances in the film.

Filmography: *The Asphalt Jungle* (MGM, 1950). *Clash by Night* (RKO, 1952). *Niagara* (20th Century–Fox, 1953).

Montagne, Edward J. (1917–)
Director. Montagne was a director of a few "B" films in the late forties. He directed a single, interesting *film noir*, demonstrating a baroque style.

Filmography: *The Tattooed Stranger* (RKO, 1950).

Montgomery, George (George Letz) (1916–)
Actor. Montgomery was a boxer before making his way into Republic westerns in the 1930's. He later played tough, stalwart heroes in countless "B" westerns, action pictures and adventures. He starred in *The Brasher Doubloon* as Philip Marlowe.

Filmography: *The Brasher Doubloon* (20th Century–Fox, 1947).

Montgomery, Robert (1904–1981)
Actor and director. Montgomery was a popular leading man of the conventional type. He co-starred in many MGM films, almost always in support of a strong female lead. In the mid-forties he directed and starred in two *films noirs*. In *Lady in the Lake* he played

Philip Marlowe. The film is notable for its first person narrative. Although inventive, it is not wholly successful. *Ride the Pink Horse* is more conventional and like its predecessor, is very well made. However, it too falls short of classic status.

Filmography: *Lady in the Lake* (acted/directed) (MGM, 1946). *Ride the Pink Horse* (acted/directed) (Universal, 1947).

Moonrise (Republic, 1949). 90 min.
Producer: Charles Haas. Director: Frank Borzage. Screenplay: Charles Haas, based on the novel by Theodore Strauss. Director of Photography: John L. Russell. Music: William Lava. Songs: "It Just Dawned On Me" by William Lava and Harry Tobias, "Lonesome" by Theodore Strauss and William Lava. Production Design: Lionel Banks. Editor: Harry Keller.

Cast: Dane Clark (Danny Hawkins), Gail Russell (Gilly Johnson), Ethel Barrymore (Grandma), Allyn Joslyn (Clem Otis), Rex Ingram (Mose), Henry Morgan (Billy Scripture). With: David Street, Selena Royle, Harry Carey, Jr., Lloyd Bridges.

When Danny was a young boy, his father was convicted and hanged for murder. Growing up in a small southern town, Danny is constantly reminded of his heritage, and is exposed to prejudice and harassment. Eventually, his obsessions leads him to kill an enemy in self defense. He leaves his sympathetic girl friend, Gilly, to live in the swamps. However, when he seeks out his beloved grandmother, she helps him work out the past and convinces him to turn himself in.

Director Frank Borzage was a master of romantic melodrama. His films are filled with shimmering images and tragic themes. *Moonrise* is both typical and atypical of his work. It is typical in its expressionist, extravagant style and existential themes, but atypical in its obsessions with psychological perversion and crime. *Moonrise*, while ultimately a minor *film noir*, is an admirable one.

Moore, Joanna (1933–)

Actress. A very attractive woman, Moore co-starred in a few films in the fifties, but never made it out of "B" productions. She was the female lead in a late "B" *noir*.

Filmography: *Appointment with a Shadow* (Universal, 1958).

Moorehead, Agnes (1906–1974)

Character actress. The sharp featured intense Moorehead was a graduate of Orson Welles' Mercury Theatre. She co-starred in several of Welles' productions including *Citizen Kane* (RKO, 1941), *The Magnificient Ambersons* (RKO, 1942) and the early *noir*, *Journey into Fear*. She had second female leads in a number of other *noirs*, her most famous being in *Dark Passage* as the murderess. She later starred for many years on televisions *Bewitched* as Eudora, the haughty witch/mother of Elizabeth Montgomery.

Filmography: *Journey into Fear* (RKO, 1943). *Dark Passage* (Warner Bros., 1947). *Caged* (Warner Bros., 1950). *Fourteen Hours* (20th Century–Fox, 1951).

Morgan, Henry (also known as Harry) (Harry Bratsburg) (1915–)

Character actor. After many years as a character actor in movies, Morgan achieved cult fame via television series *Dragnet* and *M.A.S.H.*. He had small supporting roles in many *films noirs*, generally as a sidekick of the hero or villain.

Filmography: *Somewhere in the Night* (20th Century–Fox, 1946). *The Gangster* (Allied Artists, 1947). *The Big Clock* (Paramount, 1948). *Race Street* (RKO, 1948). *Moonrise* (Republic, 1949). *Dark City* (Paramount, 1950). *Red Light* (Columbia, 1950). *Appointment with Danger* (Paramount, 1951). *Scandal Sheet* (Columbia, 1952).

Morgan, Michele (1920–)

Actress. Morgan, a sultry French brunette with a wicked smile and hypnotic eyes, is a legend in her native country. She was discovered by director Marc Allégret and cast by Marcel Carné in one of his greatest films, *Quai des Brumes* (Rabinovitch, 1938). Her career in America never quite took off although she had memorable roles in several good films including *The Chase*, her only *film noir*. She returned to France in 1946 where she immediately reestablished herself as one of the leading stars of French cinema.

Filmography: *The Chase* (United Artists, 1946).

Murder Is My Beat (Allied Artists, 1955) 77 min.

Producer: Aubrey Wisberg. Director: Edgar G. Ulmer. Screenplay: Aubrey Wisberg, story by Aubrey Wisberg and Martin Field. Director of Photography: Harold E. Wellman. Music: Al Glaser. Art Director: James Sullivan. Editor: Fred R. Feitshaus, Jr.

Cast: Paul Layton (Ray Patrick), Barbara Payton (Eden Lane), Robert Shayne (Bert Rawley), Selena Royle (Mrs. Abbott), Roy Gordon (Abbott). With: Tracey Roberts, Kate McKenna, Henry A. Harvey, Sr., Jay Adler.

The body of Mr. Deane is discovered with his head in the fireplace, burned beyond recognition. Eden Lane, a nightclub singer, is arrested and convicted of his murder. On the way to prison, however, she sees a man on the street who looks exactly like the alleged victim and she manages to escape.

Ray Patrick, a police detective, believes that Eden is innocent and he begins his own investigation. Eventually, he uncovers a complicated plot involving Dean and his wife, romantic doublecrosses and the murder of the wife's suitor, the real body in the fireplace. The couple is arrested and Eden is free to continue her life.

Murder Is My Beat is an interesting "B" *noir* that makes effective use of

Raymond Chandler's favorite "Philip Marlowe," Dick Powell (right) in *Murder, My Sweet* **(RKO, 1944)**

flashbacks and ambiguous characters. Eden Lane, for example, while not the killer, is far from sympathetic.

However, the story lacks the existential quality of Ulmer's *Detour*, and the film's style is much less inventive than the former.

Murder, My Sweet (RKO, 1944) 95 min. Producer: Adrian Scott. Director: Edward Dmytryk. Screenplay: John Paxton, based on the novel *Farewell, My Lovely* by Raymond Chandler. Director of Photography: Harry J. Wild. Music: Roy Webb. Music Director: Constantin Bakaleinikoff. Art Directors: Albert S. D'Agostino and Carroll Clark. Editor: Joseph Noriega.

Cast: Dick Powell (Philip Marlowe), Claire Trevor (Velma/Mrs. Grayle), Anne Shirley (Ann), Otto Krueger (Am Thor), Mike Mazurki (Moose Malloy), Miles Mantor (Mr. Grayle). With: Douglas Walton, Don Douglas, Ralf Harolde, Esther Howard.

Moose Malloy, a thug recently released from jail, hires private detective Philip Marlowe to find his girl friend, Velma. He is simultaneously working on a case for a wealthy woman, Mr. Grayle, whose jewels have been stolen. Marlowe does not have much luck finding Velma, but his search for the missing jewels leads to the seedy underworld of Los Angeles. Marlowe is beaten and drugged by thugs. Eventually, however, as he begins to assemble the facts, he uncovers Mrs. Grayle's seedy past. He realizes that she is Velma.

Marlowe arranges for a meeting of his clients at a beach house. The meeting explodes into an orgy of violence as Moose Malloy, Mrs. Grayle and Mr. Grayle shoot and kill each other.

Murder, My Sweet is one of the great early *films noirs* and it perfectly captured the spirit of Raymond Chandler's fiction.

The film was the first teaming of producer Adrian Scott, director Edward Dmytryk, screenwriter John Paxton and actor Dick Powell. Powell, a popular musical star of the 1930's, rebuilt his career as the tough, cynical Philip Marlowe. Indeed, Raymond Chandler would claim that Powell was the closest embodiment of his character.

Dmytryk broke out of the ranks of "B" directors with *Murder, My Sweet* and, for a time, was the leading American director. The film introduced his mature expressionist style, creating a nightmare world of half-lit landscapes, cloaked in shadows and fog. The feat and paranoia rampant in the story is likewise echoed in the superior score by Roy Webb, one of Hollywood's sadly neglected figures.

Murphy, Richard (1912–)

Screenwriter. Murphy mainly wrote action pictures. His two *films noirs* are among his best work, emphasizing action and violence. Both are classics of the genre.

Filmography: *Cry of the City* (20th Century-Fox, 1948). *Panic in the Streets* (20th Century-Fox, 1950).

Murray, Lyn (1909–)

Composer. A prolific composer of film music, Murray worked mainly on routine productions. He composed the scores for two *noirs* directed by Josef Losey.

Filmography: *The Big Night* (United Artists, 1951). *The Prowler* (United Artists, 1951).

Musuraca, Nocholas (1895–)

Cinematographer. Musuraca, a veteran of the American films industry who entered the movies in 1918, is generally considered one of the great studio craftsmen. A brilliant, inventive cinematographer, Musuraca hit his stride in the early forties when he teamed with producer Val Lewton and director Jacques Tourneur on a series of classic low budget horror films: *Cat People* (RKO, 1942), *The Seventh Victim* (RKO, 1943), *Curse of the Cat People* (RKO, 1944). These gothic, psychosexual thrillers, with their strong expressionist style had a profound influence on *film noir*.

Musuraca was a major figure in the genre, working as the director of photography on several striking classics. Each is characterized by his brooding photography which emphasized the dark foreboding nature of the stories. Equally at home in the studio or on location, he was particularly adept at filling narrow rooms and bars with deeply disconcerting shadows and shafts of light. Nicholas Musuraca's name might not be as well known as some directors and performers, but he is no less important. His work lives on as testament of his true stature as one of *noir's* greatest figures.

Filmography: *The Stranger on the Third Floor* (RKO, 1940). *The Spiral Staircase* (RKO, 1945). *Deadline at Dawn* (RKO, 1946). *The Locket* (RKO, 1946). *Out of the Past* (RKO, 1947). *The Woman on Pier 13* (RKO, 1949). *Where Danger Lives* (RKO, 1950). *Roadblock* (RKO, 1951). *Clash by Night* (RKO, 1952). *The Blue Gardenia* (Warner Bros., 1953). *The Hitch-Hiker* (RKO, 1953).

My Name Is Julia Ross (Columbia, 1945). 64 min.

Producer: Wallace MacDonald. Director: Joseph H. Lewis. Screenplay: Muriel Roy Bolton, based on the novel *The Woman in Red* by Anthony Gilbert. Music: Mischa Bakaleinikoff. Art Director: Jerome Pycha, Jr. Editor: James Sweeney.

Cast: Nina Foch (Julia Ross), Dame May Whitty (Mrs. Williamson Hughes), George Macready (Ralph Hughes), Roland Varno (Dennis Bruce), Anita Bolster (Sparkes). With: Doris Lloyd, Leonard Mudie, Joy Harrington, Queenie Leonard, Harry Hays Morgan.

Julia Ross needs a job and accepts a position as resident secretary to Mrs. Williamson Hughes, a wealthy matron whose son, Ralph, lives with her. Not long thereafter, Julia is drugged. She awakens in a mansion surrounded by a wall. Mrs. Hughes and Ralph tell her that she has been married to Ralph and that she has been recently released from a mental hospital. Later, Julia overhears Mrs. Hughes and Ralph discussing a plan to fake Julia's suicide to cover up Ralph's murder of his real wife. Eventually, though, the plot unravels. Julia is rescued, the old woman arrested and Ralph falls to his death while trying to escape the police by fleeing across a seaside cliff.

John H. Lewis' first *film noir* has, in terms of plot, more in common with gothic thrillers. Its setting is English (recreated in a Hollywood back lot) and most of the action takes place in the old mansion. However, its overwhelming paranoia and sense of impending doom, reinforced by Lewis' baroque style, is clearly *noir*. Indeed, it is the film's style which is most memorable, particularly its many hallucinatory shots through rain splashed windows.

Mystery Street (MGM, 1950) 94 min.
Producer: Frank E. Taylor. Director: John Sturges. Screenplay: Sydney Boehm and Richard Brooks, story by Leonard Spigelgass. Director of Photography: John Alton. Music: Rudolph G. Kopp. Art Directors: Cedric Gibbons and Gabriel Scognamillo. Editor: Ferris Webster.
Cast: Ricardo Montalban (Lt. Peter Moralas), Sally Forrest (Grace Shanway), Bruce Bennett (Dr. McAdoo), Elsa Lanchester (Mrs. Smerrling), Marshall Thompson (Henry Shanway), Jan Sterling (Vivian Heldon), Edmon Ryan (James Harkley). With: Betsy Blair, Wally Maher, Ralph Dumke, Willard Waterman.
Vivian Heldon, a cheap blonde, dupes an impressionable young man,

Henry Shanway, that she meets in a bar and steals his car so that she can meet her boyfriend, James Harkley, to tell him of her pregnancy. Her boyfriend, the descendent of an old Boston family shoots and kills her. After he strips her body and puts it in Shanway's car, he then pushes the car into the river. Shanway, meanwhile, reports his car missing.

Later, when Vivian's skeleton washes up on shore and the river dragged, Shanway's car is discovered and he is arrested for the girl's murder.

Harkley, meanwhile, is being blackmailed by Mrs. Smerrling, Vivian's avaricious landlady. The police, led by Lt. Peter Moralas, are not convinced that Shanway is guilty and they have found a connection between Harkley and the victim. They manage to track him down and arrest him before he can kill Mrs. Smerrling as he had planned to do.

Mystery Street is, in many ways, typical of 1950's *film noir*. It has elements of social consciousness in its murderer being a member of the elite and the main police officer, Lt. Peter Moralas, is a non-caucasian, a first for a major studio release. Its style is also comparatively simple.

A surprisingly tough, cynical thriller, *Mystery Street* also has one of the genre's most unique *femme-fatales* in Elsa Lanchester as Mrs. Smerrling.

Nader, George (1921–)
Actor. Handsome and stalwart, Nader was a leading man in Universal "B" action films in the 1950's. He starred in a single, disappointing late-*noir*.
Filmography: *Appointment with a Shadow* (Universal, 1958).

The Naked Alibi (Universal, 1954) 85 min.
Producer: Ross Hunter. Director: Jerry Hopper. Screenplay: Lawrence Roman, story by J. Robert Bren and Gladys Atwater. Director of Photography: Russell Metty. Music: Joseph

Gershenson. Art Director: Bernard Herzbrun. Editor: Al Clark.

Cast: Sterling Hayden (Joseph Conroy), Gloria Grahame (Marianna), Gene Barry (Al Willis), Marcia Henderson (Helen), Casey Adams (Lt. Parks), Billy Chapin (Petey).

An exercise in violent contrivance, *The Naked Alibi* is the far-fetched story of a cop, Joseph Conroy, discharged of his detective duties for accusing an "innocent" businessman, Al Willis, of the murder of three fellow cops, sets out to prove himself correct in a chase that takes him to a border town where Willis is hiding out with his girl friend, Marianna, a singer in a cheap saloon. Conroy eventually wins Marianna's confidence, paving the way for an all out chase across roof tops in which Marianna is killed and Willis falls to his death.

Despite an excellent cast, *The Naked Alibi* is little more than a cheap chase thriller fleshed out with violence and silly dialog.

The Naked City (Universal, 1948). 96 min.

Producer: Mark Hellinger. Director: Jules Dassin. Screenplay: Albert Maltz and Marvin Wald, story by Marvin Wald. Director of Photography: William Daniels. Music: Miklos Rozsa and Frank Skinner. Art Director: John F. DeCuir. Editor: Paul Weatherway.

Cast: Barry Fitzgerald (Lt. Dan Muldoon), Howard Duff (Frank Niles), Dorothy Hart (Ruth Morrison), Don Taylor (Jimmy Holloran), Ted De Corsia (Garzah). With: House Jameson, Anne Sargent, Adelaide Klein, Grover Burgess, Tom Pedi, Enid Markey, Narrator: Mark Hellinger.

Veteran New York detective Dan Muldoon investigates the unexplained murder of a beautiful young woman. Working with a younger, uninspired detective, Jimmy Halloran, they begin going over their leads. They eventually narrow it down to two suspects: Frank Niles, the decadent son of wealth and Garzah, an unintelligent muscle boy. The two men killed the girl for a sick thrill. The police arrest Niles without incident, but Garzah panics and runs. Cornered on the Brooklyn Bridge, he is gunned down by the police.

The story of *The Naked City* is loosely based on the infamous Leopold and Loeb murders. The two homosexual lovers murdered a young boy merely as a thrill and the case became a sensation in the early thirties. The producer of the film, Mark Hellinger, had been a newspaper reporter at the time and had covered the case and there is little doubt that he influenced the writing of the screenplay.

Police investigations were subjects of many films before *The Naked City*, but this was the earliest to introduce the overall theme of urban malaise and corruption and ineffective police. The police do not solve the murder of the young girl through intuitive brilliance (as was so common before the film), but through hard work and several fortuitous accidents.

The film is also famous for its extensive location filming and semi-documentary style, an innovation at the time. It remains a classic of its type.

The Naked Kiss (Allied Artists, 1964). 92 min.

Producer, Director, and Screenwriter: Sam Fuller. Director of Photography: Stanley Cortez. Music: Paul Dunlap. Art Director: Eugne Lourie. Editor: Jerome Thoms.

Cast: Constance Towers (Kelly), Anthony Eisley (Griff), Michael Dante (Grant), Virginia Grey (Cady), Patsy Jekky (Mac), Betty Bronson (Miss Josephine), Marie Devereaux (Buff). With: Karen Conrad, Linda Francis, Barbara Perry, Walter Matthews, Christopher Barry, George Spell.

Kelly, a warm-hearted prostitute with a violent temper, decides one morning to "go straight." She leaves the big city and gets a job in a small town nursing handicapped children. She establishes a tentative relationship with Griff, a local cop who knows about her past. She also grows fond of Grant, a wealthy intellectual who regales her with romantic stories about Venice. Eventually, she confesses to Grant about her past. He says that he accepts her as she is and asks her to marry him. She eagerly accepts, but something about his kiss disturbs her.

On the eve of their marriage, Kelly witnesses Grant sexually molesting a little girl. Confronting him, Grant tells her that they belong together because of their mutual perversions. However, when she reports the crime, the whole town turns on her, believing Grant is incapable of such a thing. Griff, though, believes Kelly and he helps her track down the little girl. The girl tells what happened and Kelly is suddenly declared a heroine by the townspeople. However, disgusted and disillusioned by the petty prejudices of a small town, she leaves to start a new life elsewhere.

Many *noir* protagonists escape the big city to find refuge in small towns and rural life, but they are rarely successful. Occasionally, as in *The Naked Kiss*, they find that small towns can be just as corrupt and violent as the big city.

As is true of much of Fuller's films, *The Naked Kiss* is filled with exotic sexual images, opening with the voluptuous Constance Towers in her provocative hooker attire. The film begins with a famous fight scene in which Kelly, wrestling with her pimp, has her wig pulled off, revealing her shaved head. This humiliation is partly responsible for her determination to start her life anew.

Constance Towers' performance is tough and cynical. Her disillusionment is the film's main theme and for once in a Fuller film, the violence is more personal, less external than usual and the ending is his most ambiguous.

The Naked Street (United Artists, 1955). 84 min.

Producer: Edward Small. Director:

Maxwell Shane. Screenplay: Maxwell Shane and Leo Katcher. Director of Photography: Floyd Crosby. Music: Emil Newman. Art Director: F. Paul Sylos. Editor: George Gittens.

Cast: Farley Granger (Nicky Brada), Anthony Quinn (Phil Regalzyk), Anne Bancroft (Rosalie Regalzyk), Peter Graves (Joe MacFarland), Else Neft (Mrs. Neft), Jerry Paris (Latzi Franks), Whit Bissell (Blaker).

Rosalie Regalzyk marries a worthless small time gangster, Nicky Brada. Brada is arrested for murder, but his father-in-law, Phil Regalzyk, a successful lawyer, gets him off. Unfortunately, Nicky returns to his old ways, sending himself down the inevitable road to annihilation and breaking his wife's heart in the process.

Maxwell Shane's least important *film noir*. *The Naked Street* is a moderately interesting melodrama shot in semi-documentary style.

The Narrow Margin (RKO, 1952). 71 min.

Producer: Stanley Rubin. Director: Richard Fleischer. Screenplay: Earl Fenton, story by Martin Goldsmith and Jack Leonard. Director of Photography: George E. Diskant. Art Directors: Albert S. D'Agostino and Jack Okey. Editor: Robert Swink.

Cast: Charles McGraw (Walter Brown), Marie Windsor (Mrs. Neil), Jacqueline White (Ann Sinclair), Gordon Gebert (Tommmy Sinclair), Queenie Leonard (Mrs. Trull). With: David Clarke, Peter Virgo, Don Beddoe, Harry Harvey.

One of the great "B" *noirs*, *The Narrow Margin* is a fast paced, cynical, highly entertaining melodrama which deserves its considerable reputation.

The plot centers around Mrs. Neil, the widow of a racketeer, who is being escorted on a train by two police detectives, Walter Brown and Gus Forbes. Forbes is immediately killed by the mobsters and Brown finds himself alone, protecting a woman of dubious character for whom he has nothing but contempt. While on the train, Brown befriends Ann Sinclair, a young woman who is travelling with her son Tommy.

Mrs. Neil is eventually killed by the mobsters, but it is then revealed that she was an undercover cop and that Sinclair is the real Mrs. Neil. Brown was duped by his superiors who were not entirely sure he would not succumb to a bribe. Disillusioned, he nevertheless delivers Sinclair/Neil safely.

Despite its low budget, *The Narrow Margin* is filled with the usual RKO style, thanks to art directors D'Agostino and Okey and cinematographer George E. Diskant. Likewise, the performances by Charles McGraw and Marie Windsor, as the *faux femme-fatale*, are excellent.

Director Richard Fleischer makes effective use of the train as a metaphor for both the hemmed-in situations of the characters and of their ever forward rush into the inevitable.

Neal, Tom (1911–1972)

Actor. Neal was a star of "B" movies who also played small supporting roles in "A" films. He was a tough hero in action films. Off camera, Neal was a notorious womanizer whose amorous exploits led eventually to murder and the end of his film career. Probably his most famous role was as the doomed piano player in Edgar G. Ulmer's *Detour*, his only *film noir*.

Filmography: *Detour* (PRC, 1945).

Negulesco, Jean (1900–1984)

Director. The French born Negulesco was a superior director of commercial films. He had a great command of technique, but his style was not extravagant or showy. He directed four *films noirs*. While *The Mask of Dimitrios* is probably the best known of his *noirs*, *Roadhouse* is equally well made with an excellent performance by Richard Widmark. *Nobody Lives Forever* and *Deep Valley*, while not classics, are also interesting contributions to the genre.

Filmography: *The Mask of Dimitrios* (Warner Bros., 1944). *Nobody Lives Forever* (Warner Bros., 1946). *Deep Valley* (Warner Bros., 1947). *Roadhouse* (20th Century–Fox, 1948).

Neill, Roy William (Roland De Gostire) (1890–1946)

Director. Neill was a prolific director of "B" movies, several of which are quite outstanding. Like John Brahm, Neill's films are meticulously made, with densely layered light and shadows, extravagant dollies, etc. He directed a single, neglected, but generally very good "B" *noir*, *Black Angel*.

Filmography: *Black Angel* (Universal, 1946).

New York City

During much of the early sound era, New York City was recreated on Hollywood backlots, but by the mid forties, as location shooting became increasingly popular, a number of filmmakers began to exploit the unique landscape and ambiance of the city. *The Naked City* (Universal, 1948) was one of the earliest movies shot entirely on location in the city and it opened the way for many other notable *films noirs*: *Union Station* (Paramount, 1950), *Sweet Smell of Success* (United Artists, 1957), *Scandal Sheet* (Columbia, 1952). *Side Street* (MGM, 1950) and the post-*noir*, *Taxi Driver* (Columbia, 1976, among others.

New York Confidential (Warner Bros., 1955). 87 min.

Producer: Clarence Greene. Director: Russell Rouse. Screenplay: Clarence Greene and Russell Rouse, based on a book by Jack Lait and Lee Mortimer. Director of Photography: Edward Fitzgerald. Music: Joseph Mullendore. Production Design: Fernando Carrere. Editor: Grant Whytock.

Cast: Broderick Crawford (Charlie Lupo), Richard Conte (Nick Magellan), Marilyn Maxwell (Iris Palmer), Anne Bancroft (Kathy Lupo), J. Carrol

Naish (Ben Dagajanian), Onslow Stevens (Johnny Achilles). With: Barry Kelley, Mike Mazurki, Celia Lovsky, Herbert Heyes.

The New York syndicate is run by Charlie Lupo. At a board meeting with the country's other mobsters, it is decided to get rid of one of their own who made an unauthorized hit. Lupo gets Nick Magellan from the Chicago boss to carry out the assassination. When Magellan is successful, Lupo hires him as a bodyguard.

Kathy Lupo, Charlie's daughter, is attracted to Magellan, but he is wary of having an affair with the boss's daughter. Meanwhile, the mob decides to get rid of a troublemaking lobbyist, against Lupo's wishes. When Kathy is killed in an automobile accident, Lupo decides to expose the mob to the police. When they learn of his plans, the mob orders Magellan to kill Lupo.

Nick comes to Lupo while the gangster is with his mistress. He kills both and Lupo merely smiles, seemingly welcoming death. Nick is later killed by mob assassins.

New York Confidential is a late-*noir* exposé of the corrupt underworld, a subject that was then very much in the headlines. It is typically violent and visually uninventive, as was common in the fifties. The performances, particularly by Marilyn Maxwell as Charlie Lupo's slutty mistress and Anne Bancroft as his beloved daughter, are all very good.

Newman, Alfred (1901-1970)

Composer. A brilliant, prolific composer of scores for over 250 movies, Newman was a leading American film composer for over three decades. In the forties and fifties he was employed by 20th Century-Fox as a staff composer and it is for them that he composed all of his *noir* scores.

Filmography: *Call Northside 777* (20th Century-Fox, 1948). *Cry of the City* (20th Century-Fox, 1948). *Thieves' Highway* (20th Century-Fox, 1949).

Panic in the Streets (20th Century-Fox, 1950). *Fourteen Hours* (20th Century-Fox, 19510.

Newman, Emil (1914-)

Composer. Newman collaborated with Arthur Lange on many film scores, mainly of "B" films.

Filmography: *Woman on the Run* (w/Lange) (Universal, 1950). *Cry Danger* (solo score) (RKO, 1951). *99 River Street* (United Artists, 1953).

Newman, Joseph M. (1909-)

Director. Newman was an assistant director for George Hill and Ernst Lubitsch in the 1930's before becoming a full fledged director himself in the early forties. He was a competent, successful director of "B" movies. His best film was *This Island Earth* (Universal, 1955), but he also made two decent *films noirs*.

Filmography: *Abandoned* (Universal, 1949). *711 Ocean Drive* (Columbia, 1950).

Niagara (20th Century-Fox, 1953). 92 min.

Producer: Charles Brackett. Director: Henry Hathaway. Screenplay: Charles Brackett, Walter Reisch and Richard Breen. Director of Photography: Joe MacDonald. Music: Sol Kaplan. Song: "Kiss" by Lionel Newman and Haven Gillespie. Art Directors: Lyle Wheeler and Maurice Ransford. Editor: Barbara McLean.

Cast: Marilyn Monroe (Rose Loomis), Joseph Cotten (George Loomis), Jean Peters (Polly Cutler), Casey Adams (Ray Cutler), Dennis O'Day (Inspector Sharkey), Richard Allen (Patrick). With: Don Wilson, Lurene Tuttle, Russell Collins, Will Wright.

Arriving in Niagara Falls for a belated honeymoon, Polly and Ray Cutler meet newlyweds, George and Rose Loomis. The Loomis' are an odd couple. Rose is young, openly sexual and rather vulgar, while George is much older and, recently released from a veteran's hospital, is quiet and reserved. The next day, Polly sees Rose kissing a young man, but of course, she does not know that they are planning to kill George for his insurance money.

Shortly after, when George disappears, Rose is taken by the police to the morgue to identify a body believed to be that of George. However, she is shocked to see her young lover, Patrick, on the slab. Realizing he has failed to kill George and not wanting to let on, she "faints" and is taken to the hospital. However, fearing George, whom she believes will try to seek revenge, she sneaks out of the hospital. George, however, is following her and he strangles her as soon as they are out of sight.

Meanwhile, Polly Cutler has been following the case. She is inadvertently aboard a boat George Loomis steals to get away from the Ontario police. The engine on the boat quits and the boat drifts toward the Niagara Falls. George and Polly fight and he pushes her out. Luckily, she falls to a rocky ledge as the boat careers over the falls, killing George. Polly is rescued by helicopter and reunited with her husband.

Niagara might well be the greatest color *film noir*. Director Henry Hathaway and cinematographer Joe MacDonald, translated the familiar black and white style brilliantly, by not only contrasting light and shadow, but dark and bright colors. Only Alfred Hitchcock's *Vertigo* (Universal, 1958) is as successful in recreating the two tone style into color.

Niagara was the first starring vehicle for Marilyn Monroe as 20th Century-Fox elevated her to leading actress. All the familiar Monroe qualities are present in the film, but here the up front, vulgar sexuality is subversive not liberating. Indeed, she is perfectly suitable as a slutty *femme-fatale* and her performance is a revelation.

Hathaway created an almost operatic melodrama, full of extravagant color and odd, obsessive moments. The scene in which George murders Rose is worthy of Hitchcock as George strangles her at a bell tower, the uncontrollable emotion is almost palpable as bells ring loudly in the sound track and the close ups of George and Rose's eyes seem to reflect the very height of sexual passion.

Niblo, Fred (Frederico Nobile) (1874–1948)

Screenwriter. Niblo is one of the real enigmas of American film. After stage experience, he entered films in the late-teens and became one of the leading silent film directors. With the coming of sound, however, his directing career came to an abrupt end. Most of the rest of his career was devoted to screenwriting, although he was certainly not a prolific screenwriter. He co-wrote one minor *film noir*. His son was also a screenwriter.

Filmography: *Bodyguard* (RKO, 1948).

Niblo, Fred, Jr. ( )

Screenwriter. Niblo, Jr., like his father, was a screenwriter of mostly "B" movie productions. He co-wrote one *film noir*.

Filmography: *Convicted* (Columbia, 1950).

Nicholson, Jack (1937–)

Actor. Nicholson starred in the important post-*noir Chinatown* as the private investigator John Gittes. The performance caught the cynical qualities of true *noir* protagonists. He also directed and starred in an abysmal sequel to the film, but the original remains rightly considered a modern classic. He also starred in the remake of *The Postman Always Rings Twice*.

Filmography: *Chinatown* (Paramount, 1974). *The Postman Always Rings Twice* (Lorimar, 1981).

Nigh, William (1881–1955)

Director. William Nigh was a prolific director of "B" movies, many of them for Monogram. He directed a single *film noir*.

Filmography: *I Wouldn't Be in Your Shoes* (Monogram, 1948).

Night and the City (20th Century–Fox, 1950). 95 min.

Producer: Samuel G. Engel. Director: Jules Dassin. Screenplay: Jo Eisenger, based on the novel by Gerald Kersh. Director of Photography: Max Greene. Music: Franz Waxman. Art Director: C. P. Norman. Editors: Nick DeMaggio and Sidney Stone.

Cast: Richard Widmark (Harry Fabian), Gene Tierney (Mary Bristol), Googie Withers (Helen Nosseross), Hugh Marlowe (Adam Dunn), Herbert Lom (Kristo), Stanislau Zbyszko (Gregorios), Mike Mazurki (Strangler). With: Francis L. Sullivan, Charles Farrell, Ada Reeve, Ken Richmond, Elliot Makeham.

Harry Fabian is a small time hustler and thief living in London. He dreams of becoming a successful wrestling promoter, against the wishes of his girl friend Mary, a nightclub singer. Harry convinces Gregorios, the father of a leading wrestling promoter, Kristo, that they can promote wrestling matches in competition with Kristo. However, his series of doublecrosses and lies to raise the money, gets Harry into trouble on all sides. He betrays Mary. Eventually he is tracked down by Kristo's men. Although he pleads for his life, The Strangler, one of Kristo's wrestlers, kills Harry and dumps his body into the Thames River.

Night and the City, Jules Dassin's last *film noir* before falling victim to the McCarthy witch hunt, is also one of the genre's most unique because of its London Setting. Dassin makes effective use of the gothic architecture and unfamiliar landscape to create empathy in the viewer with Harry's situation. The opening sequence, in which Harry flees in the distance across an empty, immense courtyard, sets the film's theme of alienation and hopelessness.

Richard Widmark once again stars as a villain, although unlike his role in *Kiss of Death* (20th Century–Fox, 1947), Harry Fabian is moderately sympathetic.

Gene Tierney's role, however, was perfunctory—merely decoration.

The film is also notable for its brutal fight scenes, including a well choreographed match with Mike Mazurki as The Strangler, that remains one of cinema's great sports scenes.

Night Editor (Columbia, 1946) 66 min.

Producer: Ted Richmond. Director: Henry Lavin. Screenplay: Hal Smith, based on the radio play by Hal Burnick and the short story "Inside Story" by Scott Littleton. Directors of Photography: Burnett Guffey and Philip Tannura. Music: Mischa Bakaleinikoff. Art Director: Robert Peterson. Editor: Richard Fantl.

Cast: William Gargan (Tony Cochrane), Janis Carter (Jill Merrill), Coulter Irwin (Johnny), Charles D. Brown (Crane Stewart), Paul L. Burns (Ole Strom). With: Jeff Donnell, Robert Stevens, Roy Gordon, Michael Chapin.

Tony Cochrane, a police detective, is having an adulterous affair with Jill. They meet at a secluded lovers lane where, in silence, they witness a brutal beating and murder. After the murderer leaves, Jill insists on seeing the body up close. Tony, meanwhile, realizes he cannot report what he has seen because it would expose his affair with Jill and ultimately cause the breakup of his marriage.

Jill begins her own investigation, eventually discovering the identity of the murderer. She blackmails him and rejects Tony. When they meet at a party later and have an argument, Jill stabs Tony with an ice pick. She is taken to jail and Tony quits the police force.

Night Editor is a disparaging "B" *noir* with a cruel *femme-fatale* at its center. Janis Carter plays Jill as a sexually voracious psychotic, aroused by the violence she has witnessed. Eventually, her arousal manifests itself in her attack against Tony at the party.

The film's style is typical of Columbia's minimalist style, concentrating on low lighting and simple camera set ups to disguise the cheap sets.

The Night Has a Thousand Eyes (Paramount, 1948) 81 min.

Producer: Endre Bohem. Director: John Farrow. Screenplay: Barre Lyndon and Jonathan Latimer, based on the novel by Cornell Woolrich. Director of Photography: John F. Seitz. Music: Victor Young. Art Directors: Hans Dreier and Franz Backelin. Editor: Eda Warren.

Cast: Edward G. Robinson (John Triton), Gail Russell (Jean Courtland), John Lund (Elliot Carson), Virginia Bruce (Jenny), William Demarest (Lt. Shawn), Richard Webb (Peter Vinson). With: Jerome Cowan, Onslow Stevenson, John Alexander, Roman Bohnen.

Elliot Carson saves his girl friend, Jean Courtland, from committing suicide, late one starry night. They go to a bar where they meet John Triton. Triton, a medium, tells of his life of predictions. Indeed, he tells them that he knew Jean's mother and he had predicted her death by childbirth—which had turned out true—and even Jill's attempted suicide. Elliot is incredulous, but Jill believes him. Elliot, in fact, believes that Triton is a con man after Jill's inheritance and he contacts the police.

John is arrested, but is released when his prediction of another inmate's suicide turns out true. He has a further premonition that Jill is in danger. He arrives in time to save her from one of her father's crooked associates, but the police mistake him for her attacker and shoot him. In John's pocket they find a note predicting his own death.

Night Has a Thousand Eyes is a doom laden, eerie *film noir*, extremely well made by John Farrow, and with a great score by Victor Young which reiterates the paranoia and existentialism of the story.

The subject of parapsychology is a unique one in film and the subject is rarely treated as realistically as it was by the screenwriters of this film.

Edward G. Robinson gives one of his best performances as the medium whose predictions always comes true, even his own death.

The Night Holds Terror (Columbia, 1955). 85 min.

Producer, Director and Screenwriter: Andrew Stone. Director of Photography: Fred Jackman, Jr. Music: Lucien Cailliet. Editor: Virginia Stone.

Cast: Jack Kelly (Gene Courtier), Hildy Parks (Doris Courtier), Vince Edwards (Victor Gosset), John Cassavetes (Robert Batsford), David Cross (Luther Logan). With: Edward Marr, Jack Kruschen, Joyce McClusky, Jonathan Hale.

The Courtier's are held by three dangerous criminals led by the sadistic Robert Batsford. At first the crooks plan to sell the family car for money, but when they learn that Gene Courtier is heir to a fortune, Batsford decides to hold him for a big ransom. Their plan slowly unravels, resulting in the deaths of the three criminals.

Based on a true story, *The Night Holds Terror* is one of several 1950's action pictures and thrillers directed by Andrew Stone. On all of them he collaborated with his wife, editor Virginia Stone, whose jump cuts and transitions were important to the overall quality of the films.

This particular Stone production was typically made on a low budget, but its cast of talented newcomers, including John Cassavetes as the sadistic Robert Batsford, and its intensity, make it a highly entertaining, unpretentious *noir* thriller.

Night Moves (Warner Bros., 1975). 99 min.

Edward G. Robinson, John Lund, Gail Russell in *The Night Has a Thousand Eyes* (Paramount, 1948)

Producer: Robert M. Sherman. Director: Arthur Penn. Screenplay: Alan Sharp. Director of Photography: Bruce Surtees. Music: Michael Small. Production Design: George Jenkins. Editor: Dede Allen.

Cast: Gene Hackman (Harry Moseby), Susan Clark (Ellen), Edward Binns (Ziegler), Harris Yulin (Marty Heller), Kenneth Mars (Nick), Janet Ward (Arlene Iverson), Melanie Griffith (Delly Grastner). With: Jennifer Warren, Anthony Costello, James Woods, John Crawford, Ben Archibeck.

A tough private investigator, Harry Moseby, is hired by an actress, Arlene, to find her runaway daughter, Delly. His search leads into the promiscuous Delly's dark and dangerous world. Delly is living in Florida with her stepfather, a small time criminal. Harry has an affair with the mistress of Delly's stepfather, but eventually he convinces Delly to return home to Los Angeles. She resumes her acting career, but soon after is killed in a bizarre accident during a stunt on the set. Reviewing footage of the accident, Harry thinks there was foul play. He discovers that Delly's stepfather and his mistress are murderers and smugglers. When he confronts them on their small boat, they try to kill him, but he manages to kill them instead. They fall overboard when shot. Harry is left critically wounded as the motorboat turns endlessly in circles.

Night Moves is typical of the self-conscious attempts to recapture the spirit and mood of *film noir* in the post-*noir* era. It does, in fact, update the characters and themes in a compelling way, but the film is rather flat and boring looking. However, Gene Hackman's performance as the obsessive private investigator and Melanie Griffith's presentation as the flighty, promiscuous Delly, are both very good.

Night of the Hunter (United Artists, 1955). 93 min.

Producer: Paul Gregory. Director: Charles Laughton. Screenplay: James Agee, based on the novel by Davis Grubb. Director of Photography: Stanley Cortez. Music: Walter Shuman. Art Director: F. Paul Sylos. Editor: John F. Schreyer.

Cast: Robert Mitchum (Preacher Harry Powell), Shelley Winters (Willa Harper), Lillian Gish (Rachel), Evelyn Varden (Icey), Peter Graves (Ben Harper), Billy Chapin (John). With: Sally Jane Bruce, James Gleason, Don Beddoe, Gloria Castillo.

A psychotic Pentecostal minister arives in a small Southern town searching for some stolen money that two children hold the secret of where it is hidden. A family is forced to confront their own prejudices, eventually resorting to violence to eliminate this monsterous intruder.

Night of the Hunter is a great film that proved Charles Laughton had talents other than acting. He creates a strongly expressionist, metaphorical universe that plays as a fight between the forces of light and dark. As the representation of evil, Robert Mitchum gave one of his most manic performances, showing the way to his Max Cady in *Cape Fear* (Columbia, 1962).

Of course, with its poetic metaphors (also provided by screenwriter James Agee, one of America's great poet/novelists) and its rural, southern setting, *Night of the Hunter* is not classic *film noir*, but its style is undeniably *noir*-like.

The Night Runner (Universal, 1957). 79 min.

Producer: Albert J. Cohen. Director: Abner Biberman. Screenplay: Gene Levitt, story by Owen Cameron. Director of Photography: George Robinson. Music: Joseph Gershenson. Art Directors: Alexander Golitzen and Robert Boyle. Editor: Al Joseph.

Cast: Ray Danton (Roy Turner), Colleen Miller (Susan Mayes), Willis Bouchey (Loren Mayes), Merry Anders (Amy Hansen), Harry Jackson (Hank Henson). With: Robert Anderson, Jean Inness, Jane Howard, John Stephenson, Richard Cutting.

A psychopath, Roy Turner, is released from a mental ward before being properly cured. He murders the father of his girl friend, Susan, and then attempts to kill her. However, he recovers his sanity just in time to save her from drowning after pushing her over a cliff and then turns himself into the police.

The Night Runner is a tawdry little "B" *noir* with an agreeable cast, but little else to recommend it. Its style is flat and the Freudian elements are contrived.

Nightfall (Columbia, 1957). 80 min.

Producer: Ted Richmond. Director: Jacques Tourneur. Screenplay: Stirling Silliphant, based on the novel by David Goodis. Director of Photography: Burnett Guffey. Music: George Duning. Art Director: Ross Bellah. Editor: William A. Lyon.

Cast: Aldo Ray (James Vanning), Brian Keith (John), Anne Bancroft (Marie Cardner), Jocelyn Brando (Laura Fraser), James Gregory (Ben Fraser), Rudy Bond (Red). With: Frank Albertson, George Cisar, Eddie McLean, Lillian Culver, Maya Kan Horn.

Jim Vanning is being pursued by two mysterious, sinister men. He ducks into a bar where he meets a beautiful young girl, Marie Gardner. After he leaves the bar, he is kidnapped by his two pursuers, John and Red. The two men plan to torture Jim for information. He escapes, however and goes to Marie's apartment. When he convinces her that her life is in danger, she agrees to accompany him. As they flee in her car, he tells her his story.

While on a fishing trip with a friend, Jim witnessed a car accident involving two criminals who had recently robbed a bank. Of course, Jim and his friend, a doctor, did not know this when they stopped to help, but the two crooks, believing them to be a threat, shoot both Jim and his friend. The doctor is killed and Jim wounded. As they flee, the two criminals take the doctor's black bag, believing it to be their bag of stolen money.

For a number of coincidental reasons, Jim knew that he would probably be blamed for his friend's death. He hid out while recovering from his wounds, but when John and Red discovered their mistake, they came looking for him.

Jim had hidden the bag of stolen money at the fishing cabin. Now, Jim and Marie return to the cabin, but John and Red have just been there and found the hidden money. He chases them to a nearby ghost town. In the ensuing fight, Red kills John, but Jim kills Red by crushing him under a tractor. Jim is reunited with Marie.

Jim Vanning's existential plight in *Nightfall* is similar to that of Vincent Parry's in *Dark Passage* (Warner Bros., 1947), both of which were based on novels by David Goodis. Goodis specialized in such themes, although *Nightfall*'s ending is somewhat more ambiguous than the earlier film.

Coming late in the *noir* cycle, *Nightfall*'s style and structure are similar to *Out of the Past* (RKO, 1947), which should come as no surprise since the director, Jacques Tourneur, made both films. While *Nightfall* is not a classic, it is an admirable late-*noir*, combining some of the earlier expressionist style with the new emphasis on violence.

Nightmare (United Artists, 1956). 89 min.

Producers: William C. Pine and William C. Thomas. Director: Maxwell Shane. Screenplay: Maxwell Shane, based on the short story by William Irish (Cornell Woolrich). Director of Photography: Joe Biroc. Music: Herschel Burke Gilbert. Art Director: Frank Sylos. Editor: George Gittens.

Cast: Edward G. Robinson (Rene Bressard), Kevin McCarthy (Stan Grayson), Connie Russell (Gina), Virginia Christine (Sue). With: Rhys Williams, Gage Clark, Barry Atwater, Marian Carr, Billy May.

A young musician has a strange nightmare which convinces him he may have committed murder. He eventually proves, with the help of his brother-in-law, that he was hypnotized by the real killer to trick him into confessing.

Nightmare is a remake of the ingenious *Fear in the Night* by the same writer/director, Maxwell Shane. Despite better production values and performances, the original was more effective.

Nightmare Alley (20th Century–Fox, 1947). 110 min.

Producer: George Jessel. Director: Edmund Goulding. Screenplay: Jules Furthman, based on the novel by William Gresham. Director of Photography: Lee Garmes. Music: Cyril Mockridge. Art Directors: Lyle Wheeler and Russell Spencer. Editor: Barbara McLean.

Cast: Tyrone Power (Stanton Carlisle), Joan Blondell (Zeena), Colleen Gray (Molly), Helen Walker (Dr. Lillith Ritter), Taylor Holmes (Grindle), Mike Mazurki (Bruno). With: Ian Keith, Julia Dean, James Flavin, Roy Roberts, James Burke.

Stanton Carlisle, a small time carnival operator, obtains secrets of a fake mind reader. He settles in Chicago, setting himself up as a spiritualist with two assistants, including Zeena. His wife, Molly, reluctantly joins his act. He is extremely successful until Molly, partly out of jealousy, exposes him as a fake. His fall is as quick as his sudden rise, and he finally returns to the carnival as a "geek" – a freak who eats live chickens.

William Gresham, the novelist whose original book was adapted for the film was obsessed with the dark side of show business. His novels and stories present unrelenting views of shysters, half-wits, and the madness of carnival life, which Gresham had experienced first hand. He later committed suicide.

Nightmare Alley is certainly one of the most unrelenting depressing *films noirs*. Its director, Edmund Goulding is best known for his glossy MGM entertainments, and this was certainly unusual material for such a director. Nevertheless, he did an admirable job, creating an almost surreal environment for the carnival scenes.

Likewise, Tyrone Power, cast against type, is excellent as the avaricious con man whose eventual fall is lower than anything he could have ever imagined before.

99 River Street (United Artists, 1953). 83 min.

Producer: Edward Small. Director: Phil Karlson. Screenplay: Robert Smith, story by George Zuckerman. Music: Emil Newman and Arthur Lange. Art Director: Frank Syles. Editor: Buddy Small.

Cast: John Payne (Ernie Driscoll), Evelyn Keyes (Linda James), Brad Dexter (Victor Rawlins), Frank Faylen (Stan Hogan), Peggie Castle (Pauline Driscoll). With: Jay Adler, Jack Lambert, Eddy Waller, Glen Langan, John Day.

Ernie Driscoll was once a promising fighter, but an eye injury cut his career short. He now drives a taxi. His wife Pauline constantly berates him for his failure to make as much money as he once did as a boxer and his only solace is in his friendships with Stan Hogan, his dispatcher and Linda James, an aspiring actress with whom he drinks coffee in a local restaurant. Pauline plans to run off with Victor Rawlins, a jewel thief.

One night, Linda confesses to Ernie, that she killed a man and asks for his help. He agrees, but it is revealed as a hoax on the part of Linda and her producer as an acting "test." Ernie is not amused and he strikes the producer before angrily stomping out.

Meanwhile, Rawlins kills Pauline in a rage, and the police hunt for Ernie whom they believe to be the killer. Linda, remorseful about the trick she played on him, helps Ernie find the real killer, Rawlins. Having done so, they begin their new life together.

99 River Street is an unusual *film noir* with an overly complicated plot, but it is redeemed by its excellent performances and some inventive direction. Perhaps its most interesting twist is Evelyn Keyes' portrayal of a *faux femme-fatale*. Like *A Double Life* (Universal, 1948), it is essentially about the duplicity of reality versus illusion in the theatre.

Nobody Lives Forever (Warner Bros., 1946). 100 min.

Producer: Robert Buckner. Director: Jean Negulesco. Screenplay: W. R. Burnett. Director of Photography: Arthur Edeson. Music: Adolf Deutsch. Art Director: Hugh Reticker. Editor: Rudi Fehr.

Cast: John Garfield (Nick Blake), Geraldine Fitzgerald (Gladys Halvorsen), Walter Brennan (Pop Gruber), Faye Emerson (Toni), George Coulouris (Doc Ganson). With: George Tobias, Robert Shayne, Richard Gaines, Dick Erdman, James Flavin.

Nick Blake, a former New York gambler and ex–G.I. returns to the United States after the war. He settles in California, disillusioned after his experiences in the war, and hoping to start a new life. However, he is approached by a makeshift gang led by Doc Ganson who wants him to finance a scheme to defraud a lonely rich widow, Gladys Haovorsen. He agrees, but when he meets her, he begins to fall in love with her. He offers to pull out of the deal, but his ex-lover, Toni, convinces Ganson that Nick is trying to doublecross the gang. Ganson kidnaps Gladys. Pop, another of Nick's ex-cronies, takes him to where Ganson is holding Gladys and in the subsequent shoot out, both Pop and Ganson are killed. Nick is reunited with Gladys.

Nobody Lives Forever combines two familiar *noir* themes: the disillusioned war veteran and the heist/caper that goes wrong. Although it is not as well known as John Garfield's other *films noirs*, it is a very compelling, suspenseful film with several good performances including Garfield's and Faye Emerson's brief appearance as the *femme-fatale*, Toni. It also has some interesting visuals, particularly in the scenes at the pier where Ganson holds Gladys. The water in the background is blacker than black and pounds relentlessly against the wood of the dock as if echoing the plight of the characters.

Nocturne (RKO, 1946). 87 min.
Producer: Joan Harrison. Director: Edwin L. Marin. Screenplay: Jonathan Latimer, story by Frank Fenton and Rowland Brown. Director of Photography: Harry J. Wild. Music: Leigh Harline. Music Director: Constantin Bakaleinikoff. Songs: "Nocturne" by Leigh Harline and Mort Greene, "Why Pretend" and "A Little Bit Is Better Than None" by Eleanor Rudolph. Art Directors: Albert S. D'Agostino and Robert Boyle. Editor: Elmo Williams.

Cast: George Raft (Joe Warne), Lynn Bari (Frances Ransom), Virginia Huston (Carol Page), Joseph Pevney (Fingers), Myrna Dell (Susan). With: Edward Ashley, Walter Sande, Mabel Paige, Bernard Hoffman, Queenie Smith.

Police detective Joe Warne is assigned to investigate the murder of a songwriter. Although the case is ruled a suicide, Warne is convinced that one of the composer's many lovers killed him. He searches for a woman referred in one of the victim's songs as "Dolores". His persistance causes several suspects to complain and Warne is suspended from the force, but he continues to investigate on his own. He concentrates

on Francis Ransom, to whom he is reluctantly attracted. Ultimately, he discovers that Ransom's sister, Carol Page, is the "Dolores" referred to in the song. When he confronts Page, a nightclub singer, at the club where she works, her accompanist, Fingers, appears and admits he killed the philandering composer because he was jealous of the man's affair with the beautiful young singer.

Nocturne is an interesting early RKO *noir*, shot in a rich, expressionist style. It opens with a brilliant long travelling shot across a landscaped model of the Hollywood Hills, into the window of an isolated house, toward a man sitting at a piano. The camera continues to move into a tight close up of the back of his head when a hand holding a pistol suddenly appears out of shadows. The gun fires in close up as the composer softly plays the piano. The shot is inventive and surprising.

Nocturne is not quite a major *noir*, but it does contain one of George Raft's strongest performances and co-stars the luminiscent Virginia Huston, who would play the "good girl" in the following year's classic, *Out of the Past* (RKO, 1947).

The Noir Protagonist

In general, the *film noir* protagonist is a representative of an existential persona caught up in a corrupt, immoral world. The *noir* protagonist is also usually aware, indeed complicit, in the events he is caught in, but unable to do anything about them. Once ensnared, the *noir* protagonist is unable to escape and he almost always faces his destruction stoically, unafraid.

Nolan, Lloyd (1902–1985)

Character actor. A star character actor for over four decades, Nolan enlivened a number of *films noirs* with his brief, but always compelling performances. His most important role was in *Brute Force*, as a sadistic prison guard obsessed with the music of the anti-semitic Richard Wagner. In *Street with No Name* and its sequel *House on 92nd Street* he had a recurring role as an F.B.I. agent, Inspector Brigs.

Filmography: *Brute Force* (Universal, 1946). *Somewhere in the Night* (20th Century-Fox, 1946). *Lady in the Lake* (MGM, 1947). *Street with No Name* (20th Century-Fox, 1948). *House on 92nd Street* (20th Century-Fox, 1949).

Nora Prentiss (Warner Bros., 1947) 111 min

Producer: William Jacobs. Director: Vincent Sherman. Screenplay: Richard Nash (w/uncredited Philip MacDonald), story by Paul Webster and Jack Sobell. Director of Photography: James Wong Howe. Music: Franz Waxman. Art Director: Anton Grot. Editor: Owen Marks.

Cast: Ann Sheridan (Nora Prentiss), Kent Smith (Dr. Richard Talbot), Bruce Bennett (Dr. Joel Merrian), Robert Alda (Philip McDade), Rosemary De Camp (Lucy Talbot). With: John Ridgely, Robert Arthur, Wanda Hendrix, Helen Brown, Rory Mallinson.

Richard Talbot is bored with his safe life, his wife and his children. He has an affair with a beautiful nightclub singer, Nora Prentiss. When he reneges on his promise to ask his wife for a divorce, Nora leaves him and moves to New York City to work in a new nightclub. Talbot fakes his death and joins Nora in New York. The police, meanwhile, investigate his alleged death as a murder.

Talbot stays with Nora, afraid to leave her apartment. He descends into alcoholism. Her career as a singer takes off. After a drunken fight with the manager of the nightclub where Nora works, Talbot is in a bad car wreck and horribly burned. After plastic surgery, with a new face, he is temporarily happy. The police have tracked him down, however, as Talbot's "murderer." He tells Nora not to disclose his real identity to spare his family embarrassment. Later, she visits him on death row shortly before he is executed.

The wildly improbable plot of *Nora Prentiss* is closer to soap opera cliches rather than *film noir*. It qualifies as a *noir* because of its obsessions with the corruption of its characters and its strong, extravagant expressionist style.

North, Alex (1910-)

Composer. North is generally acknowledged as one of the most important film composers of his generation. He was particularly active in the fifties when he composed many famous scores. His score for Otto Preminger's *The Thirteenth Letter*, his second movie score, is excellent.

Filmography: *The Thirteenth Letter* (20th Century-Fox, 1951).

Notorious (RKO, 1946). 101 min.

Producer and Director: Alfred Hitchcock. Screenplay: Ben Hecht. Director of Photography: Ted Tetzlaff. Music: Roy Webb. Music Director: Constantin Bakaleinikoff. Art Directors: Albert S. D'Agostino and Carroll Clark. Editor: Theron Warth.

Cast: Cary Grant (Devlin), Ingrid Bergman (Alicia Huberman), Claude Rains (Alexander Sebastian), Louis Calhern (Paul Prescott), Madame Konstantin (Mme. Sebastian), Reinhold Schunzel (Dr. Anderson). With: Moroni Olsen, Ivan Treiscoult, Alex Minotis, Wally Brown, Gavin Gordon.

At the end of World War II, a Nazi agent is sent to prison. His daughter, Alicia Huberman, never involved in his activities, led the profligate life of the international playgirl. She feels guilty about her father's crimes and when approached by F.B.I. agent Devlin to help in an undercover operation against neo-Nazis in South America, she readily agrees.

Alicia's job is to establish contact with Alexander Sebastian, one of her father's former associates. Eventually she is forced to marry him. Devlin, meanwhile, has fallen in love with the beautiful Alicia, but her past reputation and current assignment keeps him at a distance.

Alicia learns of Sebastian's covert activities. At a large party the Sebastians hold, Alicia and Devlin explore the wine cellar of the big house. They discover that some of them contain uranium ore.

When Sebastian learns that Alicia is an American agent, he and his mother begin to slowly poison her with arsenic. Eventually, when he has not heard from Alicia, Devlin breaks into Sebastian's house and rescues her. Sebastian is left facing the consequences of his angry co-conspirators.

One of Alfred Hitchcock's greatest films *Notorious* is famous for several extravagant choreographed scenes in typical Hitchcock style. It is a lush, romantic thriller with Hollywood's most glamorous stars and it was also one of the espionage *noirs*. It remains one of the genre's most entertaining classics.

Novak, Kim (Marilyn Novak) (1933–)

Actress. A cool, beautiful blonde, Novak was one of the 1950's major sex goddesses. Her sexuality was not as overt as Marilyn Monroe's and she was not nearly as talented, but she was an entertaining presence in harmless comedies and romantic dramas. In *Pushover*, her first starring film she played a typical *femme-fatale*. Her peculiarly ethereal qualities were better exploited by Alfred Hitchcock in his masterpiece, *Vertigo*. A deeply sensual performance, it is also her best.

Filmography: *Pushover* (Columbia, 1954). *Vertigo* (Universal, 1958).

Oberon, Merle (Estelle O'Brien Merle Thompson) (1911–1979).

Actress. Born in India to a British father and Indian mother, Oberon was a darkhaired, exotic beauty, best known for her romantic roles in films like *Wuthering Heights* (Goldwyn/United Artists, 1939). She starred in a single *film noir*. Although her exotic qualities were subdued in *Berlin Express*, her performance as a secretary desperately searching for her kidnapped boss, is very good.

Filmography: *Berlin Express* (RKO, 1948).

Oboler, Arch (1909–)

Director. Oboler was a successful radio writer in the 1940's who, like Orson Welles before him, became known because of his popularity in that medium. He wrote and directed a number of curious "B" movies including his *noir, Bewitched*. However, he is probably best known as the writer-producer-director of *Bwana Devil* (United Artists, 1952), the first theatrical feature in 3-D.

Filmography: *Bewitched* (MGM, 1945).

O'Brien, Edmond (1915–1985)

Actor. One of the most neglected *noir* icons, Edmond O'Brien starred in several of the genre's classics, and many of its best "B" titles.

As a young man, O'Brien was a romantic lead. In maturity however, he grew heavier and his angular face with its strong jaw, scowled easily. He specialized in tough, unromantic roles, starring in "B" movies and playing second leads in "A" films.

O'Brien had pivotal supporting roles in several important and interesting *films noirs*. In *The Killers* he played the insurance investigator whose morbid fascination with the Swede's death, slowly unravels the story. He also had important roles in *White Heat*, as an undercover cop and *The Turning Point*, as a crusading politician.

O'Brien's most important *noir* roles were in *The Hitch-Hiker* and *D.O.A.*. In the former he co-starred with Frank Lovejoy as one of the fishermen held captive by a serial killer. In the latter, O'Brien stars as Frank Bigelow, a man who is slowly dying from poison, searching for his killer before he dies.

Famous climax scene from *Vertigo* as Judy Barton (Novak) and Scottie (Stewart) struggle in the bell tower — moments later Judy Barton falls to her death (Universal, 1958).

Although not as well known as many of the other major *noir* icons, O'Brien is no less important and he left behind several of the genre's most memorable performances.

Filmography: *The Killers* (Universal, 1946). *The Web* (Universal, 1947). *White Heat* (Warner Bros., 1947). *A Double Life* (Universal, 1948). *Backfire* (Warner Bros., 1950). *Between Midnight and Dawn* (Columbia, 1950). *D.O.A.* (United Artists, 1950). *711 Ocean Drive* (Columbia, 1950). *The Turning Point* (Paramount, 1952). *The Hitch-Hiker* (RKO, 1953). *The Shield for Murder* (United Artists, 1954).

Obzina, Martin (   )

Art director. Obzina was a staff production designer for Universal beginning in the late thirties. He worked on many important films, but his designs for *The Killers*, echoing the style of director Robert Siodmak, are among his best.

Filmography: *Black Angel* (Universal, 1946). *The Killers* (Universal, 1946). *M* (Columbia, 1951).

Odds Against Tomorrow (United Artists, 1959). 96 min.

Producer and Director: Robert Wise. Screenplay: John O. Killens and Nelson Gidding, based on the novel by William P. McGivern. Director of Photography: Joseph Brun. Music: John Lewis. Art Director: Leo Kerz. Editor: Dede Allen.

Cast: Harry Belafonte (Johnny Ingram), Robert Ryan (Earl Slater), Gloria Grahame (Helen), Shelley Winters (Lorry), Ed Begley (Dave Burke), Will Kuluva (Bacco), Mae Barnes (Annie). With: Carmen De Lavallade, Richard Bright, Lou Gallo, Fred J. Scollary, Lois Rarne.

Dave Burke, an ex-cop, was unjustly dismissed from the force. He gathers a team to rob a bank in a small upstate New York town: Earl Slater, a violent racist; Johnny Ingram, a black man who joins only because Bacco, a thug, has threatened his ex-wife if he does not join in; and Bacco. They carry out the robbery, but afterwards, through a series of coincidences and their own stupidities, their getaway fails. Burke and Bacco are caught without incident. Slater and Ingram, chased by the cops, try to hideout in an oil refinery. However, their hatred of each other explodes — literally — into violence. As they run across the tops of oil tanks, shooting at each other, a bullet pierces one of the drums, causing a huge explosion.

When they are going through the wreckage of the oil refinery later, the bodies of the two men are discovered by a cleaning crew. "Which is which?" one of the crew asks about the charred corpses. "Take your pick," is the answer.

Odds Against Tomorrow is sometimes considered the last film of the initial *noir* cycle. It was the last *noir* caper film and the story was heightened with elements of racial tension.

Robert Wise created a superior thriller in the typical flat style of 1950's *film noir*. The screenplay is taut and unsentimental and the performances are all first rate. Gloria Grahame stands out as a psychotic *femme-fatale* who is sexually aroused by the graphic descriptions of a grisly murder told to her by her boyfriend, Earl Slater.

Odell, Cary (1912–)

Art director. From the mid forties to the early sixties, Cary Odell was a top art director for Columbia Pictures. The quality of his production designs are often superior, particularly for *The Reckless Moment*, the *noir* classic, directed by Max Ophuls. He also was the art director of several other notable *films noirs*.

Filmography: *Johnny O'Clock* (Columbia, 1947). *The Dark Past* (Columbia, 1948). *The Reckless Moment* (Columbia, 1949). *The Mob* (Columbia, 1951).

Odets, Clifford (Odette Goimbault) (1903–1963)

Playwright and screenwriter. Odets' proletarian dramas about the hard lives of working people were both popular and controversial. Several of his plays were adapted successfully to the screen. He also worked sporadically in Hollywood as a screenwriter. He brought some of the same concerns of his plays to his films, although his screenplays are less polemical than his stage plays.

Filmography: *Deadline at Dawn* (screenplay) (RKO, 1946). *Clash by Night* (based on his play) (RKO, 1952). *The Big Knife* (based on his play) (United Artists, 1955). *Sweet Smell of Success* (screenplay) (United Artists, 1957).

O'Donnell, Cathy (Ann Steely) (1923–1970)

Actress. O'Donnell had a sporadic career in film. Her most famous role was in the William Wyler classic *The Best Years of Our Lives* (Warner Bros., 1946), as the understanding girl friend of an injured war veteran. She also co-starred in three *films noirs*. Her most important *noir* role was in Nicholas Ray's *They Live by Night*, as the Bonnie to Farley Granger's Clyde.

Filmography: *They Live by Night* (RKO, 1948). *Side Street* (MGM, 1950). *Detective Story* (Paramount, 1951).

Okey, Jack ( )

Art director. Okey was an important art director, first at Warner Bros. and later at RKO. He was one of the major talents at RKO during the 1940's, helping to establish the famous semi-expressionist style of the studio in that decade. Among the films he worked on was the *noir* classic, *Out of the Past*, the height of early *noir* style. He had a talent for claustrophobic interiors, particularly bars and exotic decorated houses, apartments and offices.

Filmography: *I Am a Fugitive from a Chain Gang* (Warner Bros., 1932). *Johnny Angel* (RKO, 1945). *Crack-Up* (RKO, 1946). *Deadline at Dawn* (RKO, 1946). *The Spiral Staircase* (RKO, 1946). *Out of the Past* (RKO, 1947). *A Dangerous Profession* (RKO, 1949). *The Set-Up* (RKO, 1949). *Gambling House* (RKO, 1951). *The Racket* (RKO, 1951).

On Dangerous Ground (RKO, 1952) 82 min.

Producer: John Houseman. Director: Nicholas Ray. Screenplay: A. I. Bezzerides, based on the novel *Mad with Much Heart* by Gerald Butler. Director of Photography: George Diskant. Music: Bernard Herrmann. Art Directors: Albert S. D'Agostino and Ralph Berger. Editor: Roland Gross.

Cast: Ida Lupino (Mary Malden), Robert Ryan (Jim Wilson), Ward Bond (Walter Brent), Charles Kemper (Bill Daly), Anthony Ross (Pete Santos). With: Ed Begley, Ian Wolfe, Sumner Williams, Gus Schilling.

Jim Wilson, a bitter, lonely New York cop who is prone to violence, is sent out of town on a case involving a teenager who has molested and killed a young girl. He must first placate the young girl's father who wants to kill the youth. Mary, the blind sister of the murderer, pleads for Wilson to find her brother and bring him in alive. While chasing the young man across high rocks, the youth loses his footing and falls to his death.

Wilson consoles Mary. He returns to New York City, but realizing the city offers him nothing, he returns to Mary.

On Dangerous Ground is one of the most moving *films noirs*, a story of despair and salvation with a delicate screenplay, superior direction, and talented performers at their very best.

The film is also one of the most explicit examples of the *noir* theme of a violent city and serene rural life in conflict. The theme is reinforced by style. The city scenes are dark, fast-paced, angry and violent. The country scenes are slower and brighter. Furthermore, Bernard Herrmann's score—one of his best—echoes the theme with violent, swirling music in the city scenes and beautiful, romantic music for the country locales.

On Dangerous Ground is a neglected classic. It stands as one of its director's best films and awaits rediscovery.

On the Waterfront (Columbia, 1954). 108 min.

Producer: Sam Spiegel. Director: Elia Kazan. Screenplay: Budd Schulberg, based on his novel. Director of Photography: Boris Kaufman. Music: Leonard Bernstein. Art Director: Walter Holscher. Editor: Jerome Thoms.

Cast: Marlon Brando (Terry Malloy), Karl Malden (Father Barry), Lee J. Cobb (Johnny Friendly), Rod Steiger (Charles Malloy), Eva Marie Saint

(Edie Doyle). With: Pat Henning, James Westerfield, Leif Erikson, Tony Galento, John Heldabrand.

Elia Kazan's tale of political corruption and its effects on working class, is famous for its great performance by Marlon Brando as the boxer who was betrayed by his brother and took a fall for money. Yet, it is also a thriller and its strong expressionist elements qualify it as a pseudo-*noir*. Like *All the King's Men*, its strong polemical qualities are alien to the genre, however, its author, Budd Schulberg also wrote the original novel that *The Harder They Fall* (Columbia, 1956) is based upon. Despite similarities, *On the Waterfront* is rarely included in lists of *films noirs* while the weaker later film is.

One Way Street (Universal, 1950). 79 min.

Producer: Leonard Goldstein. Director: Hugo Fregonese. Screenplay: Lawrence Kimble. Director of Photography: Maury Gertsman. Music: Frank Skinner. Art Director: Bernard Herzbrun. Editor: Milton Carruth.

Cast: James Mason (Doc Matson), Marta Toren (Laura), Dan Duryea (Wheeler), William Conrad (Ollie), Jack Elam (Arnie). With: King Donavan, Pedra Almendez.

Doc Matson is the head of a gang which has just robbed a bank of $200,000. Running off to Mexico with Laura, the beautiful girl friend of Wheeler, Matson's rival, Matson settles down to a quiet life. He opens a clinic for the locals. Eventually, overwhelmed by guilt, he returns the money to the other crooks so that they can do with it what they will. As he is leaving town, he steps in front of a car and is struck and killed.

One Way Street is a silly minor *film noir* that tries too hard to make a point about the nature of guilt with its existential plot. Despite a good cast, it does not rise above the merely mediocre.

Ophuls, Max (Max Oppenheimer) (1902–1957)

Director. The Austrian born Ophuls was one of the great stylists in cinema. He was an elegant craftsman with a fluid technique, characterized by extravagant dollies and crane shots. However, his opulent style was always subservient to the story. He was also a great romantic whose films were always dominated by female characters and this is certainly true of his two *films noirs*. *Caught* is a romantic tragedy, similar to his great European films while *The Reckless Moment* is a variation of *Mildred Pierce* (Warner Bros., 1945). The former has a strong performance by Barbara Bel Geddes as an impressionable young girl who falls in love and marries an egomaniacal millionaire played by Robert Ryan. The latter provided Joan Bennett with one of her best roles as a woman desperately trying to protect her family from scandal. Both films are classics of the genre.

Filmography: *Caught* (MGM, 1949). *The Reckless Moment* (Columbia, 1949).

Oswald, Gerald (1916–)

Director. Oswald was a director of mostly "B" films, few of which have any merit. He directed a single late-*noir*.

Filmography: *Crime of Passion* (United Artists, 1957).

The Other Woman (20th Century-Fox, 1954). 81 min.

Producer, Director and Screenplay: Hugo Haas. Director of Photography: Eddie Fitzgerald. Music: Ernest Gold. Art Director: Rudi Fehr. Editor: Robert S. Eisen.

Cast: Hugo Haas (Darmen), Cleo Moore (Sherry), Lance Fuller (Ronnie), Lucille Barkley (Mrs. Darmen), Jack Musey (Lester). With: John Qualen, Jan Arven, Carollee Kelly, Mark Lowell, Melinda Markey.

A low budget *film noir*, *The Other*

Robert Mitchum, Jane Greer in *Out of the Past* **(RKO, 1947).**

Woman was the first in a series of bizarre movies written, directed and starring Hugo Haas. All are characterized by sadomasochistic overtones with Haas always the victim of a young, amoral girl.

In this film Haas stars as Darmen, an emigree Hollywood director whose career is largely due to his marriage to the daughter of the production chief for a movie studio. When he refuses to hire a young girl for his next film, she schemes to blackmail him as revenge. She drugs him and makes it look like they had sex. She later tells him she is pregnant and demands money to avoid her going to the press. Instead, he murders her, but when a police detective sees through his alibi and confronts him, Darmen admits his guilt.

Of the series of Haas melodramas, *The Other Woman* comes closest in style and themes to *film noir*. It is,

literally and figuratively, a very dark film and remains one of the strangest "B" *noirs*.

Otterson, Jack (1881–1962)
Art director. Otterson, like so many of his fellow art directors, began his career as an architect. In fact, he was one of several architects who worked on decorations for the Empire State Building. He entered films in the early thirties. He worked on three *films noirs*.

Filmography: *Black Angel* (RKO, 1946). *The Killers* (RKO, 1946). *The Web* (Universal, 1947).

Out of the Past (RKO, 1947). 96 min.
Producer: Warren Duff. Director: Jacques Tourneur. Screenplay: Geoffrey Homes (Daniel Mainwaring) (with uncredited James M. Cain and Frank Fenton), based on the novel *Build My Gallows High* by Geoffrey Homes.

Director of Photography: Nicholas Musuraca. Music: Roy Webb. Music Director: Constantin Bakaleinikoff. Art Directors: Albert S. D'Agostino and Jack Okey. Editor: Samuel E. Beetley.

Cast: Robert Mitchum (Jeff Bailey), Jane Greer (Kathie Moffett), Kirk Douglas (Whit Sterling), Rhonda Fleming (Meta Carson), Richard Webb (Jim), Steve Brodie (Fisher), Virginia Huston (Ann), Paul Valentine (Joe), Dickie Moore (Jimmy, "the kid"). With: Ken Niles, Lee Elson, Frank Wilcox, Mary Field.

In a small northern California town, Jeff Bailey runs a gas station, assisted by a deaf mute teenager, Jimmy. One day, Joe arrives in town and tells Jeff that Whit Sterling wants to see him. On the way to Sterling's house, Bailey tells his girl friend Ann the story of his involvement with Sterling, a racketeer.

Bailey, a private detective, was hired by Sterling to find Sterling's lover, Kathie Moffett, who had shot Sterling, left him for dead and disappeared with $40,000 of his money. Bailey traced her to Mexico where they began having an affair. Kathie denies stealing the money and Jeff decides not to return her to Whit, and he and Kathie move to San Francisco to start a new life together. However, Jeff's crooked partner, Fisher, finds them and attempts to blackmail the couple. During a fight between the two men, Kathie shoots and kills Fisher. She flees, leaving her bank book behind and Jeff discovers that she really did steal Whit's money. Disillusioned, Jeff moved to the small town to open the gas station and start his life over.

Presently, meeting Sterling at his house, he is not entirely surprised to find Kathie living with him again. Jeff is used by Whit as a dupe in a complicated series of doublecrosses involving another racketeer's attempts to blackmail Sterling and Sterling's attempt to frame Bailey for a murder. When Jeff confronts Whit, Whit readily agrees to turn Kathie over to the police as the killer, but instead, when she learns of the plan, she shoots Whit, killing him

Kathie tells Jeff that they belong together and should flee to Mexico. Realizing he will be arrested and probably executed for the murder that Whit framed him for, Jeff agrees to her plan. However, he secretly calls the police. As they try to crash through a roadblock, the police shoot and kill them.

Back in the small town, Jimmy conveys to Ann that Jeff actually loved Kathie, so that Ann will not mourn him and will be able to start her life over.

Out of the Past is the archetypal *film noir*, with all the genre's familiar elements: the destructive *femme-fatale*, the corruptible protagonist, the existential plot moving the characters inexorably toward their doom and the expressionist style.

The screenplay, adapted from Homes/Mainwaring's novel, is subtle and witty and the film is beautifully acted by its principles.

Director Jacques Tourneur created an ethereal, dream-like film, aided by Nicholas Musuraca's shadowy, dark lighting and a wonderful, haunting score by Roy Webb.

Despite its plot complications and occasional lapses in logic, *Out of the Past* remains one of the genre's greatest masterpieces.

The Outfit (MGM, 1973). 103 min.

Producer: Carter De Haven. Director and Screenplay: John Flynn, based on the novel by Richard Stark (Donald Westlake). Director of Photography: Bruce Surtees. Music: Jerry Fielding. Art Director: Tambi Larsen. Editor: Ralph E. Winters.

Cast: Robert Duvall (Earl Macklin), Karen Black (Bett Jarrow), Joe Don Baker (Cody), Robert Ryan (Mailer), Timothy Carey (Jake). With: Richard Jaeckel, Sheree North, Marie Windsor, Jane Greer, Henry Jones.

A racketeer just released from prison

seeks revenge against his fellow mobsters to avenge his brother's murder.

The Outfit is a typically self-conscious post-*noir*, but attempts to update the genre with gratuitous violence. In fact, the film is essentially a cheaper version of *Point Blank* (MGM, 1967), based on a novel by the same writer whose *The Hunter* was the source for that film. However, the film contains an interesting performance by Robert Ryan in his next-to-last film and brief cameos by *noir* icons, Jane Greer and Marie Windsor.

Palance, Jack (Walter Palanchik) (1920–)

Character actor. Palance, who was disfigured during World War II, was typecast as a villain because of his hard etched features. He starred in many classics in the 1950's, including *Shane* (Paramount, 1953). He appeared in a handful of *films noirs* in the fifties, including the classic *Panic in the Streets* as a criminal infected with a deadly contagion. His best *noir* performance, however, was in *The Big Knife* as a drunken film star who finds his fame a prison. In *I Died a Thousand Times*, a remake of *High Sierra* (Warner Bros., 1941), Palance starred as Roy Earle. In *Second Chance*, Palance had a conventional villainous role, but in *Sudden Fear*, his villain is an actor planning to kill his wife, an heiress/playwright who had once turned him down for a part in one of her plays.

Filmography: *Panic in the Streets* (20th Century–Fox, 1950). *Second Chance* (RKO, 1951). *Sudden Fear* (RKO, 1952). *The Big Knife* (United Artists, 1955). *I Died a Thousand Times* (Warner Bros., 1955).

Panic in the Streets (20th Century–Fox, 1950). 96 min.

Producer: Sol C. Siegel. Director: Elia Kazan. Screenplay: Richard Murphy, adapted by Daniel Fuchs from an original screen story by Edna and Edward Anhalt. Director of Photography: Joe MacDonald. Music: Alfred Newman. Art Directors: Lyle Wheeler and Maurice Ransford. Editor: Harmon Jones.

Cast: Richard Widmark (Dr. Clinton Reed), Paul Douglas (Captain Warren), Barbara Bel Geddes (Nancy Reed), Walter (Jack) Palance (Blackie), Zero Mostel (Fitch), Dan Riss (Neff). With Alex Minotis, Guy Thomajan, Tommy Cook, Edward Kennedy, H. T. Tsiang.

When a murder victim is discovered to be infected with a deadly communicable disease, Dr. Clinton Reed of the Public Health service realizes he has forty eight hours to track down the murderers who have been exposed to the disease. He has to find them before they cause an epidemic. Without much police support, he searches through the run-down New Orleans waterfront. He arouses the suspicions and anger of the seedy denizens of the area. Eventually, he does locate the killers and after a chase through the waterfront they are apprehended.

Panic in the Streets is an interesting *film noir* which is partly an exposé of the daily routines of a public health official. As Dr. Reed, Richard Widmark here broke out of being typecast as a villain. Jack Palance, in one of his earliest film roles and still billed as Walter, co-starred with Zero Mostel and Barbara Bel Geddes as the infected criminals.

The screenwriters created an interesting metaphor with the idea of criminals infected with a deadly disease, thus heightening the fear of the underclass as a menace to society at large. However, the film is the least polemic of Elia Kazan's early films

Kazan makes particularly effective use of New Orleans' waterfront, creating a misty, dark world of lurking danger.

Paramount Pictures Corporation

For many years, Paramount was the chief competition of MGM, and ranked with it as second only to that company during Hollywood's golden age, although many prefer the more artistically adventurous and mature films of Paramount. Certainly, under its benevolent founder, Adolph Zucker, the studio provided an atmosphere which encouraged more artistic experimentation and individual creativity than any other major American film studio. It wa also the most "European" of the American studios, in terms of production design, cinematography, writers and directors. Many of its leading artists were European emigres: art directors Hans Dreier and Ernst Fegte, and writers and directors Ernst Lubitsch, William Dieterle, Billy Wilder, etc.

The Paramount *noirs* are characterized by inventive pictorial values (deeply influenced by expressionism), and a thoroughly cynical approach to its romantic themes.

Stars like Veronica Lake, Alan Ladd, Barbara Stanwyck, Ray Milland, Fred MacMurray and Lizabeth Scott provided the requisite glamour.

Among films, Paramount's leading *noir* directors were William Dieterle, John Farrow and Billy Wilder. Robert Siodmak came over from Universal for one film, *The File on Thelma Jordan* and the ubiquitous Fritz Lang made his early *noir* classic *Ministry of Fear* at the studio.

Releases: **1927:** *Underworld.* **1928:** *The Racket.* **1929:** *Thunderbolt.* **1941:** *Among the Living.* **1942:** *The Glass Key. Street of Chance. This Gun for Hire.* **1944:** *Double Indemnity. Ministry of Fear.* **1946:** *The Blue Dahlia.* **1947:** *Calcutta. Fear in the Night.* **1948:** *The Big Clock. I Walk Alone. Night Has a Thousand Eyes. The Strange Love of Martha Ivers.* **1949:** *The Accused. Chicago Deadline. The File on Thelma Jordan. Manhandled.* **1950:** *Dark City. Sunset Boulevard. Union Station.* **1951:** *Appointment With Danger. The Big Carnival. Detective Story.* **1952:** *The Turning Point.* **1955:** *The Desperate Hours.*

Parker, Jean (Lois Mae Greene) (1912–)
Actress. Briefly popular in the 1930's, Parker played character roles in "B" movies in the 1940's and 1950's. She co-starred in *Black Tuesday* as one of several hostages held by a vicious escaped convict, played by Edward G. Robinson.

Filmography: *Black Tuesday* (United Artists, 1954).

Parrish, Robert (1916–)
Director. Parrish was a child actor who appeared in Charlie Chaplin's *City Lights* (United Artists, 1931) before becoming a top editor in the 1940's. As an editor he worked on several *films noirs*. He graduated to directing in the early fifties, mainly making high grade "B" films including two *films noirs*.

Filmography: *Cry Danger* (RKO, 1951). *The Mob* (Columbia, 1951).

Party Girl (MGM, 1958). 99 min.
Producer: Joe Pasternak. Director: Nicholas Ray. Screenplay: George Wells, story by Leo Katcher. Director of Photography: Robert Bronner. Music: Jeff Alexander. Title Song by Nicholas Brodsky and Sammy Cahn. Art Directors: William A. Horning and Randall Duell. Editor: John McSweeny.

Cast: Robert Taylor (Thomas Farrell), Cyd Charisse (Vicki Gaye), Lee J. Cobb (Rico Angelo), John Ireland (Louis Canetto), Ken Smith (Jeffrey Stewart). With: Claire Kelly, Corey Allen, Lewis Charles, Ken Dobbs.

Nicholas Ray's most pretentious film has been described as a satire and a color *noir*. Set in 1920's Chicago, the story concerns a lawyer's fight with a top gangster to win a nightclub dancer/singer (Cyd Charise). It does have some *noir*-like elements, but it is really nothing more than a rather heavy handed, violent version of 1930's gangster sagas.

Patrick, John (aka **Jack**) (1905–)
Screenwriter. Patrick was an immensely successful playwright who also

co-wrote many popular films. He contributed the original stories for two *films noirs*, including the classic *The Strange Love of Martha Ivers*.

Filmography: *The Strange Love of Martha Ivers* (Paramount, 1946). *Framed* (Columbia, 1947).

Paxton, John (1911–1985)

Screenwriter. Paxton was a talented screenwriter. Slow and methodical, he worked on relatively few screenplays for such a major talent, receiving credit for only sixteen in a career that stretched over three decades. He was a major *film noir* screenwriter. Indeed, his career began with the legendary *Murder, My Sweet*, an adaptation of Raymond Chandler's novel, *Farewell, My Lovely*. He collaborated with that film's director, Edward Dmytryk and producer Adrian Scott on two additional classics: *Cornered* and *Crossfire*. He also co-wrote the neglected classic, *Crack-Up* and wrote the screenplay for Henry Hathaway's suspenseful *noir* thriller, *Fourteen Hours*.

Filmography: *Murder, My Sweet* (RKO, 1944). *Cornered* (RKO, 1945). *Crack-Up* (co-wrote) (RKO, 1946). *Crossfire* (RKO, 1947). *Fourteen Hours* (20th Century–Fox, 1951).

Payne, John (1912–)

Actor. Early in his career, Payne was a singer and dancer in musicals. Like Dick Powell, his appearance took on harder characteristics in maturity and he became a popular hard-boiled action hero, mainly of "B" movies. He was a leading minor *noir* icon, starring in five "B" titles. He was cast by director Phil Karlson in two of his best 1950's *noirs*, *Kansas City Confidential* and the less well known, *Hell's Island*.

Filmography: *The Crooked Way* (United Artists, 1949). *Kansas City Confidential* (United Artists, 1952). *99 River Street* (United Artists, 1953). *Hell's Island* (Paramount, 1955). *Slightly Scarlet* (RKO, 1956).

The People Against O'Hara (MGM, 1951). 102 min.

Producer: William H. Wright. Director: John Sturges. Screenplay: John Monks, Jr., based on the novel by Eleazar Lipsky. Director of Photography: John Alton. Music: Carmen Dragon. Art Directors: Cedric Gibbons and James Basevi. Editor: Gene Ruggiero.

Cast: Spencer Tracy (James Curtayne), Pat O'Brien (Vincent Ricks), Diana Lynn (Ginny Curtayne), John Hodiak (Louis Barra), Eduardo Cianeli (Knuckles Lanzetta), James Arness (Johnny O'Hara). With: Yvette Dugvay, Jay C. Flippen, William Campbell, Richard Anderson.

James Curtayne, an ex–district attorney forced into retirement because of his alcoholism, is looking for a way to make a successful comeback as a lawyer. He agrees to take the case of an acquaintance, Johnny O'Hara, who is accused of gunning a man down in the streets. Although he finds evidence proving that O'Hara is innocent, for a number of reasons he does not believe he can win the case. He pays a man to testify in O'Hara's favor. However, the bribe is discovered and in order to redeem himself, he uses a concealed microphone and records a conversation with gangsters who have framed O'Hara. Although he succeeds, the gangsters find out about his plan and kill him before the police arrive.

The People Against O'Hara is a well made, minor *film noir* that is notable for Spencer Tracy's excellent performance and John Alton's location photography: the film is set in New York City. However, as a courtroom drama, the film suffers somewhat from its static plot. The director of the film John Sturges, would later become a leading director of action films.

Pereira, Hal (1905–1983)

Art director. After many years as a theatre designer, Pereira entered films as a unit art director at Paramount in

1942, often collaborating with Hans Dreier. When Dreier retired in 1950, Pereira was promoted to supervising art director at Paramount. Pereira worked on several important *noir* productions.

Filmography: *Double Indemnity* (Paramount, 1944). *Ministry of Fear* (Paramount, 1944). *Detective Story* (Paramount, 1950). *The Turning Point* (Paramount, 1952). *Rear Window* (Paramount, 1954). *The Desperate Hours* (Paramount, 1955). *Vertigo* (Universal, 1958).

Peters, Hans (   )

Art director. One of the industry's most tasteful craftsmen, MGM's Hans Peters was more adept at the typical glossy style of the studio, but he also worked on three *films noirs*.

Filmography: *Act of Violence* (MGM, 1949). *Border Incident* (MGM, 1949). *Rogue Cop* (MGM, 1954).

Peters, Jean (Elizabeth Jean Peters) (1926–)

Actress. Peter's career was at its zenith in 1955 when she retired to marry billionaire Howard Hughes. Pert and attractive, she was also a good actress. She starred in three *films noirs*. In *Niagara*, her voyeuristic heroine exposes a murderous couple's plans to kill each other. She appeared in the title role in *Vicki*, a rather conventional *noir*, but her best *noir* performance was in Sam Fuller's *Pickup on South Street*. In heavy, exaggerated make up and tight, revealing dresses, Peters plays a cheap prostitute caught up in espionage.

Filmography: *Niagara* (20th Century-Fox, 1953). *Pickup on South Street* (20th Century-Fox, 1953). *Vicki* (20th Century-Fox, 1953).

Peterson, Robert (1913–)

Art director. In his long, distinguished career as an art director, Robert Peterson worked with an impressive number of top directors: Samuel Fuller, Fritz Lang, Don Siegel,

Nicholas Ray. He worked on several important *films noirs*, including two collaborations with Fritz Lang and two with Nicholas Ray. He had a sophisticated sense of style, with dark furniture, tropical plants and contrasting areas of light and shade.

Filmography: *Night Editor* (Columbia, 1946). *Knock on Any Door* (Columbia, 1949). *In a Lonely Place* (Columbia, 1950). *Scandal Sheet* (Columbia, 1952). *The Big Heat* (Columbia, 1953). *Human Desire* (Columbia, 1954). *The Garment Jungle* (Columbia, 1957). *Underworld U.S.A.* (Columbia, 1960). *Experiment in Terror* (Columbia, 1962).

Pevney, Joseph (1920–)

Director. Pevney was a prolific, but indifferent director of commercial movies.. He directed a single *film noir*, but his talents were not suited to the material.

Filmography: *Female on the Beach* (Universal, 1955).

Phantom Lady (Universal, 1944). 87 min.

Executive Producer: Milton Feld. Director: Robert Siodmak. Screenplay: Bernard C. Shoenfeld, based on the novel by William Irish (Cornell Woolrich). Director of Photography: Woody Bredell. Music: Hans J.Salter. Song: "Chick-ee-Chick" by Jacques Press and Eddie Cherkose. Art Directors: John B. Goodman and Robert Clatworthy. Editor: Arthur Hilton.

Cast: Franchot Tone (Jack Marlowe), Ella Raines (Carol Richman), Alan Curtis (Scott Henderson), Aurora (Estela Montiero), Thomas Gomez (Inspector Burgess), Fay Helm (Ann Terry), Elisha Cook, Jr. (Cliff March). With: Andrew Tombes, Jr., Regis Toomey, Joseph Crehan, Doris Lloyd.

Scott Henderson, a successful young businessman is arrested for allegedly strangling his wife with his tie. On the night in question, he had met a girl in a bar, but did not know her name. He remembers only that she wore a hat exactly like the singer in the bar. Henderson is convicted and sentenced to die in 18 days, but his faithful secretary, Carol, believes he is innocent and begins searching for the woman he claims he met in the bar to establish his alibi. She is aided by a police detective, Inspector Burgess, who also believes Henderson is innocent.

Carol haunts the bar where Henderson met his "phantom lady." Pretending to be a prostitute, she seduces the band drummer, Cliff March. He tells her that he has been paid off to "forget" the woman, and later Cliff is strangled with a tie, and Carol's purse is stolen from his place,

Later, while visiting Henderson in prison, Carol meets one of his friends Jack Marlowe, who is also visiting Henderson.

Marlowe agrees to help her in her search for the phantom lady. They eventually find the girl, Ann Terry, and Marlowe sets up a meeting at his apartment. When she gets there, Carol sees her purse and realizes that Marlowe is the killer.

He confesses that he killed Henderson's wife out of jealousy. At that moment, Inspector Burgess arrives and Marlowe leaps out of the widow to his death. Henderson is freed.

Phantom Lady was Robert Siodmak's first American success. Essentially a "B" movie, it was made with such energy and inventiveness, that it surpasses the limitation of low budget films and survives as one of the earliest classics of the genre. Siodmak brilliantly mixed expressionist style with an American idiom.

Phantom Lady has several famous scenes. The most inventive, indeed one of *noir's* greatest scenes, is the one where Elisha Cook, Jr. reaches an orgasmic fury during a drum solo.

It is Raines who dominates the film. Her charged performance is the highlight of her career.

Despite being based on one of Cornell Woolrich's weaker novels, *Phantom Lady* manages to avoid the pitfalls of adaptations of his novels. It remains a classic.

The Phenix City Story (Allied Artists, 1955). 100 min.

Producers: Samuel Bischoff and David Diamond. Director: Phil Karlson. Screenplay: Crane Wilbur and Daniel Mainwaring. Director of Photographer: Harry Neumann. Music: Harry Sukman. Art Director: David Milton. Editor: John Conroy.

Cast: John McIntyre (Albert Patterson), Richard Kiley (John Patterson, Kathryn Grant (Edie Rhodes), Edward Andrews (Rhett Turner), Lenka Peterson (Mary Jo Patterson). With: Biff McGuire, Truman Smith, Jean Carson, Katherine Marlowe.

Albert Patterson returns to his hometown after serving in Korea to find gangsters have taken over. Against all odds, he fights back against the racketeers, eventually destroying them, but not before they have seriously affected his family.

The Phenix City Story was based on real events in Phenix City, Alabama, which for much of the forties and early fifties was controlled by racketeers. Nearly every corner of every street in the small town had a house of prostitution and liquor, and drug sales were rampant.

Karlson's film concentrates on violent action rather than the sordid facts of the story. He makes effective use of semi-documentary style, but ultimately the film is unusually disappointing for this director.

Pichel, Irving (1891–1954)

Director. Pichel worked as an actor and screenwriter before becoming a director in the early thirties. He mainly directed unpretentious adventure films. One of his best films is the "B" *noir*, *They Won't Believe Me*.

Filmography: *They Won't Believe Me* (RKO, 1947).

Jean Peters, Richard Widmark in *Pickup on South Street* **(20th Century-Fox, 1953).**

Pickup on South Street (20th Century-Fox, 1953). 83 min.

Producer: Jules Schermer. Director: Samuel Fuller. Screenplay: Samuel Fuller, story by Dwight Taylor. Director of Photography: Joe MacDonald. Music: Leigh Harline. Art Directors: Lyle Wheeler and George Patrick. Editor: Nick DeMaggio.

Cast: Richard Widmark (Skip McCoy), Jean Peters (Candy), Thelma Ritter (Moe), Murvyn Vye (Capt. Dan Tiger), Richard Kiley (Joey), Willis B. Bouchey (Zara). With: Milburn Stone, Henry Slate, Jerry O'Sullivan, Harry Carter.

When a small time New York pickpocket, Skip McCoy, inadvertently steals some microfilm from Candy, the mistress of a communist agent, he becomes the target of an intense search by both the communists and the F.B.I., assisted by the police. The police even-

tually find him, with the aid of Moe, a con artist and informant. However, McCoy denies having the microfilm, even in the face of a strong patriotic appeal by the police.

Moe also helps Candy locate McCoy. She is responsible for retrieving the film but finds herself sexually attracted to McCoy. They begin having an affair.

Candy's ex-boyfriend, Joey, kills Moe when she refuses to sell him McCoy's address after she learns Joey is a communist agent. Candy, however, having retrieved the microfilm from McCoy, is planning to cooperate with the police because she did not like being the dupe of communist agents. Joey beats her savagely, but when she relents and gives him the microfilm, he discovers a vital piece is missing.

Joey goes to McCoy's apartment and a chase ensues through the New York subway system. Eventually, McCoy is cornered and he at last fights back. He beats up Joey for his treatment of Candy and murder of Moe. The police arrest Joey, and McCoy is reunited with Candy.

Pickup on South Street is a typical brutal Samuel Fuller film. It is also brilliantly made, an inspired *film noir* with political overtones. While clearly anti-communist (even the thieves of New York are politically aware), it also celebrates the criminal anti-establishment. This duplicity is also typical of Fuller who, although a political conservative, enjoyed thumbing his nose at the elite.

The film provided Richard Widmark and Jean Peters — as well as its superior supporting cast including Thelma Ritter as Moe — with two of their best roles. Peters is particularly memorable as Candy, the ex-prostitute who is in many ways the calm, human center of this great drama.

Pine, William H. (1896–1955) and **Thomas, William C.** (1892–1988)

Producers. The so-called "Dollar Bills" because of their low budget productions, Pain and Thomas made dozens of second features for Paramount. They produced four *films noirs*, all of which are decidedly "B" movies, but are also of considerable interest.

Filmography: *Fear in the Night* (Paramount, 1947). *Manhandled* (Paramount, 1949). *Hell's Island* (Paramount, 1955). *Nightmare* (Paramount, 1956).

The Pitfall (United Artists, 1948). 86 min.

Producer: Samuel Bishoff. Director: Andre DeToth. Screenplay: Karl Kamb, based on the novel by Jay Dratler. Director of Photography: Harry J. Wild. Music: Louis Forbes. Art Director: Arthur Lonergan. Editor: Walter Thompson.

Cast: Dick Powell (John Forbes), Lizabeth Scott (Mona Stevens), Jane Wyatt (Sue Forbes), Raymond Burr (MacDonald), John Litel (District Attorney). With: Byron Barr, Jimmy Hunt, Ann Doran, Selmer Jackson.

John Forbes is a successful insurance agent. He is married to his high school sweetheart and they have a young son. Unfortunately, he is also bored with his life. His insurance firm has paid off on a robbery pulled by a man who was subsequently convicted and Forbes is assigned to help a private investigator, MacDonald, recover some of the goods purchased with the stolen money. The items are traced to a beautiful blonde model, Mona Stevens, who was the girl friend of the thief.

Forbes begins an affair with Mona. He eventually breaks off the relationship but MacDonald, who is jealous and wants Mona for himself, convinces the just released ex-boyfriend to attack Forbes. Forbes shoots and kills the intruder when he tries to break into the house. Forbes then confesses the affair to his wife who says she will not leave him, but their relationship has permanently changed.

The Pitfall is yet another, rather innocuous tale of a relatively innocent man whose life has been irrevocably changed by a *femme-fatale*. Forbes' reckless affair, however, does not lead to his moral or physical destruction. In a way it ultimately leads to his redemption.

In any case, despite excellent performances by *noir* icons Dick Powell, Lizabeth Scott and Raymond Burr, the film is disappointing and rarely rises above its mediocre, melancholy script.

Planer, Franz F. (1894–1963)

Cinematographer. Planer was a great German born cinematographer. He established himself as a leading cinematographer in Germany in the 1920's, where he absorbed expressionist technique which he would later use in his American productions. He moved to the United States in 1937 and worked on many top productions. He worked on six *films noirs*. Of those, the best is Robert Siodmak's classic, *Criss Cross* which has scenes of breathtaking beauty.

Filmography: *The Chase* (United Artists, 1946). *Champion* (United Artists, 1949). *Criss Cross* (Universal, 1949). *711 Ocean Drive* (Columbia, 1950). *99 River Street* (United Artists, 1953). *The Long Wait* (United Artists, 1954).

Plunder Road (20th Century–Fox, 1957). 82 min.

Producers: Leon Chooluck and Lawrence Stewart. Director: Hubert Cornfield. Screenplay: Steven Ritch and Jack Charney, story by Steven Ritch. Director of Photography: Ernest Haller. Music: Irving Gertz. Art Director: Robert Gill. Editors: Warren Adams and Jerry S. Young.

Cast: Gene Raymond (Eddie), Jeanne Cooper (Fran), Wayne Morris (Commando), Elisha Cook, Jr. (Skeets), Stafford Repp (Roly Adams), Steven Ritch (Frankie), Nora Hayden (Hazel).

After stealing gold ingots from a train, the booty is split three ways and the various members of the group go their separate ways. Only Eddie and Frankie get away long enough to reach their goal, Los Angeles. They unload the gold at a foundry where, with the help of Eddie's girl friend Fran, they cast the gold into a bumper, paint it, and put it on their getaway car. But the following day, as they are attempting to leave the city, they are involved in an auto accident. Their bumper gets locked with another car's bumper and when the police arrive they see the gold under the scratched paint. In the subsequent gun battle, Frankie is shot, Fran runs for it, and Eddie tries to escape by jumping off a bridge onto a truck. Unfortunately he loses his grip on the truck and falls off into traffic where he is crushed to death.

Plunder Road, one of the least known caper *noirs*, is an excellent, unpretentious film made on a low budget.

Its plot is linear and uncomplicated and its style, typical of *noir* in the 1950's, is simple.

Poe, James (1918–1980)

Screenwriter. Poe was a successful writer for film, radio and television. He worked in all the genres and achieved his greatest success in the 1950's. He worked on two *films noirs* including a fine adaptation of Clifford Odet's play *The Big Knife*.

Filmography: *Scandal Sheet* (cowrote) (Columbia, 1952). *The Big Knife* (United Artists, 1955).

Point Blank (MGM, 1967). 92 min.

Producers: Judd Bernard and Robert Chartoff. Director: John Boorman. Screenplay: Alexander Jacobs, David Newhouse and Rafe Newhouse, based on the novel *The Hunter* by Richard Stark (Donald Westlake). Director of Photography: Phillip H. Lathrop. Music: John Mandel. Art Directors: George W. Davis and Albert Brenner. Editor: Henry Berman.

Cast: Lee Marvin (Walker), Angie Dickinson (Chris), Kennan Wynn (Yost), Carroll O'Connor (Brewster), Lloyd Bochner (Frederick Carter). With Michael Strong, John Vernon, Sharon Acker, James Sikking.

A gangster, after recovering from an attempted assassination in Alcatraz, is released from prison. He immediately begins carrying out his vow of revenge against those who betrayed him, including his ex-partner and his wife.

A prominent post-*noir*, *Point Blank*, is at times, a powerful tale of mindless vengeance and betrayal. Its action is visceral and its location shooting, in San Francisco, is effective. However, its screenplay is pretentious and the film is not quite a classic despite its cult status.

Polansky, Roman (1932–)

Director. The polish born Polansky's work shows the influence of expressionism and existentialist philosophy.

His *Chinatown* perfectly captures the spirit and style of classic *film noir* and is, itself, an acknowledged classic.

Filmography: *Chinatown* (Paramount, 1974).

Polglase, Van Nest (1894–1968)

Art director. After experience at MGM and Paramount, Polglase was hired by then RKO production chief David O. Selznick in 1932 as supervising art director for that studio. Although a severe alcoholic, Polglase worked for the studio until 1943 and freelanced for many years after that. He was largely responsible for the art-deco style of RKO in the 1930's. However, by the 1940's he exhibited a stronger expressionist style, best characterized by his set designs for *The Stranger on the Third Floor* and *Gilda*. He worked on only a handful of *films noirs*, but his work on each is well above average.

Filmography: *Stranger on the Third Floor* (RKO, 1940). *Suspicion* (RKO, 1941). *Gilda* (Columbia, 1946). *The Crooked Way* (United Artists, 1949). *The Man Who Cheated Himself* (20th Century–Fox, 1951). *Slightly Scarlet* (RKO, 1956).

Polito, Sol (1892–1960)

Cinematographer. Polito was a leading staff cinematographer for Warner Bros. in the 1930's, before becoming a freelance in the late forties. He worked on two *films noirs* and the influential pre-*noir*, *I Am a Fugitive from a Chain Gang*.

Filmography: *I Am a Fugitive from a Chain Gang* (Warner Bros., 1932). *The Long Night* (RKO, 1947). *Sorry, Wrong Number* (Paramount, 1948).

Polonsky, Abraham (1910–)

Screenwriter and director. Polonsky was one of the most prominent victims of the McCarthy witch hunt in the early fifties. Before his career was ruined, Polonsky wrote and/or directed two classic *films noirs*. He wrote the screenplay for the boxing *noir*, *Body and Soul* and wrote and directed *Force of Evil*. Both demonstrate an unfortunate tendency toward didactic. However, *Force of Evil* shows a great sense of style. After writing several screenplays under various pseudonyms from 1951, Polonsky resumed his career in the late sixties when the blacklist was finally lifted. He continued to write important screenplays, including Don Siegel's post-*noir*, *Madigan*.

Filmography: *Body and Soul* (screenplay) (United Artists, 1947). *Force of Evil* (screenplay/director) (MGM, 1949). *Madigan* (co-wrote only) (Universal, 1968).

Possessed (Warner Bros., 1947) 108 min.

Producer: Jerry Wald. Director: Curtis Bernhardt. Screenplay: Sylvia Richards and Ranald MacDougall, based on the novelette *One Man's Secret* by Rita Weiman. Director of Photography: Joseph Valentine. Music: Franz Waxman. Art Director: Anton Grot. Editor: Rudi Fehr.

Cast: Joan Crawford (Louise Howell Graham), Van Heflin (David Sutton), Raymond Massey (Dean Graham), Geraldine Brooks (Carol Graham), Stanley Ridges (Dr. Harvey Williard), John Ridgely (Harker). With: Moroni Olsen, Erskine Sanford, Gerald Perreau, Isabel Withers.

Wealthy Mrs. Louise Graham is found wandering the streets of downtown Los Angeles as if in a trance, asking for "David." Taken to the hospital, the authorities slowly learn of her story.

As Louise Howell, she was a nurse employed by an industrialist, Dean Graham, to take care of his mentally ill wife. Louise's lover, David, rejects her and takes a job in Canada. Mrs. Graham accuses Louise of having an affair with her husband and kills herself. Later, Graham proposes to Louise and partly out of frustration and loneliness, she accepts. David returns

Cecil Kellaway, John Garfield, Lana Turner in *The Postman Always Rings Twice* **(MGM, 1946).**

from Canada and begins courting Carol, Graham's daughter. She begins to have a nervous breakdown. When she goes to David to ask him to quit seeing Carol, he refuses and she murders him, her mental state completely collapses.

The director of *Possessed*, Curtis Bernhardt, was drawn to psychological subjects and he excelled at capturing the confused, warped mental state of the insane. His style was heavily expressionist, characterized by dark, evocative lighting and rain streaked exteriors. He was also an expert at dream sequences and he uses all of these elements to create a dreamlike tale of madness in *Possessed*.

The Postman Always Rings Twice
(MGM, 1946). 113 min.
Producer: Carey Wilson. Director: Tay Garnett. Screenplay: Harry Ruskin

and Niven Busch, based on the novel by James M. Cain. Director of Photography: Sidney Wagner. Music: George Bassman. Art Directors: Cedric Gibbons and Randall Duell. Editor: George White.

Cast: Lana Turner (Cora Smith), John Garfield (Frank Chambers), Cecil Kellaway (Nick Smith), Hume Cronyn (Arthur Keats), Leon Ames (Kyle Sackett), Audrey Totter (Madge Gorland). With: Alan Reed, Jeff York, Charles Williams, Cameron Grant, Wally Cassell.

Frank Chambers, a drifter, arrives at a small roadside café and is immediately attracted to Cora Smith whose elderly husband, Nick, owns the place. Frank is hired as a handyman for the café, and he begins an affair with the sensual Cora. Cora convinces him that the only way they can stay together is to kill her husband and make it appear like an accident. However, after killing Nick and driving the car off a cliff, Frank cannot get out fast enough and he is severely injured.

While recovering in the hospital, Frank is informed by the district attorney that he plans to prosecute Cora for the murder and Frank is forced to sign a complaint against her. However, the case never goes to court for lack of evidence.

Frank and Cora get married. Their relationship is complicated by an unscrupulous lawyer's blackmail and various other problems, but eventually they get all that behind them. They purchase a new car, but Cora is killed in a bizarre accident in the vehicle. Frank is falsely convicted of her murder and is condemned to die in the electric chair.

James M. Cain's novel of treachery and murder became a film classic and one of the most famous of all *films noirs*. Like *Gilda*, *The Postman Always Rings Twice* was directed by a contract director with little recognizable personal style, yet Tay Garnett managed here to create a film which is both entertaining and a work of art.

Unlike Phyllis Dietrichson, the *femme-fatale* of Cain's *Double Indemnity*, Cora Smith is not merely an avaricious murderess. Cora is trapped in an existential world partly of her own making. We learn that she was poor and married Nick Smith merely to escape poverty. Unfortunately, her life with the older man is both boring and sexually frustrating. Killing Nick, she believes, will take her out of the trap she has created for herself, but in fact it leads only to a deeper trap.

Frank Chambers enters this web of deception, basically an honest man; but he accepts Cora's plans without question or, apparently, moral conflict. He is, like Cora, a victim of himself.

John Garfield and Lana Turner have considerable chemistry as the murderous lovers and their scenes together have an almost palpable sexual spark.

Indeed, the film is one of the most sexually forthright of any 1940 American movie.

Like *Double Indemnity*, *The Postman Always Rings Twice* is narrated by the male protagonist and much of it told in flashback. Both are fatalistic visions of the "American Dream" gone wrong.

The Postman Always Rings Twice (Lorimar, 1981), a remake written by David Mamet, directed by Bob Rafelson and starring Jack Nicholson and Jessica Lang, is notable mainly for its more explicit sexuality and typically intense performance by Nicholson.

Post-noir

The *noir* cycle came to an end roughly in 1959, although a few films followed in the years immediately thereafter, most notably *Cape Fear* (Universal, 1962). The critical analysis and identification of the genre came in the mid sixties. For this book, the term "post-*noir*" is used to identify the group of films after the early sixties which showed strong *noir* influences in theme and/or style. *Dirty Harry* (Warner Bros., 1971) is a good example of this type. The term also encompasses those rare films which are purposeful attempts to create a modern *noir*: *Body Heat* (Warner Bros., 1981) is the most prominent example.

Powell, Dick (1904–1963)

Actor. In the 1930's, Powell was the very representation of the American boy next door in a dozen or so popular musical comedies made at Warner Bros.. When that genre began to loose popularity at the end of the decade, Powell became expendable and he was let go. For several years after that his career went into decline — he starred in a variety of "B" movies — before the unexpected success of *Murder, My Sweet*.

Based on Raymond Chandler's *Farewell, My Lovely*, *Murder, My Sweet* was a modest budgeted film, but its style and performances transcended its relatively small budget. Powell's surprisingly hard-boiled portrayal of Philip Marlowe immediately reestablished his career and screen image. Indeed, Chandler later claimed that Powell's portrayal was the closest to the character.

Powell reiterated his success in *Murder, My Sweet* with several other hard-boiled anti-heroes. In *Cornered* he was again teamed with director Edward Dmytryk in one of the more cynical *noir* tales of vengeance. Likewise, in the excellent *Cry Danger*, Powell stars as an ex-con seeking revenge against those who framed him for robbery.

Although Powell starred in only four *films noirs*, his performance in each was powerful enough to establish him as one of the genre's key male icons.

Filmography: *Murder, My Sweet* (RKO, 1944). *Cornered* (RKO, 1945). *Johnny O'Clock* (Columbia, 1947). *Cry Danger* (RKO, 1951).

Power, Tyrone (1913–1958)

Actor. Power was a legendary star of the 1940's, known for his swashbuckling roles. A romantic lead, typecast by his appearance, he rarely got the chance to prove he could really act as he did in his single *film noir*, *Nightmare Alley*. Power stars as a con artist who achieves temporary success as a false medium, only to find fame fleeting. His performance is great, although the film is flawed.

Filmography: *Nightmare Alley* (20th Century-Fox, 1947).

Preminger, Otto (1906–1986)

Director. One of a select group of Jewish-Viennese directors who brought a European sensibility to Hollywood — the others were Billy Wilder and Ernst Lubitsch — Preminger is also one of the most important *film noir* directors.

Preminger was born to a wealthy family and studied law as a young man before deciding on a career in the theatre. He was a successful stage director in the early thirties before moving to the United States in 1935. He was contracted by 20th Century-Fox as a director and made two "B" movies before a dispute with the studio head, Darryl F. Zanuck, caused him to be fired from the studio.

Preminger was rehired by 20th Century-Fox during one of Zanuck's European travels, but this time Zanuck could ignore his dislike of the director because Preminger immediately made the wildly successful *Laura*. The film established the now familiar Preminger style — a love of long takes and fluid camera work and an obsession with romantic melodrama.

Although *Laura* is certainly Preminger's best *film noir* (and arguably, his best film ever), there is considerable merit in all of his *noirs*. *Fallen Angel* and *Where the Sidewalk Ends* are particularly dark, cynical *noirs*, and both are replete with the requisite *noir* characters, the *femme-fatale* and the bad cop.

While Preminger later directed a variety of ambitious films several of which are excellent, his best work remains his *films noirs*, a group of extraordinary explorations of the decadent and perverse side of humanity.

Filmography: *Laura* (20th Century-Fox, 1944). *Fallen Angel* (20th Century-Fox, 1946). *Where the Sidewalk Ends* (20th Century-Fox, 1950). *The Thirteenth Letter* (20th Century-Fox, 1951). *Angel Face* (RKO, 1953).

The Pretender (Republic, 1947). 69 min.

Producer and Director: W. Lee Wilder. Screenplay: Don Martin, with additional dialog by Doris Miller. Director of Photography: John Alton. Music: Paul Dessau. Art Director: F. Paul Sylos. Editor: Asa Boyd Clark.

Cast: Albert Dekker (Kenneth Holden), Catherine Craig (Claire Worthington), Charles Drake (Dr. Leonard Koster), Alan Carney (Victor

Korrin), Linda Stirling (Flo Ronson). With: Tom Kennedy, Selmer Jackson, Charles Middleton, Ernie Adams, Ben Weldon.

Kenneth Holden, a handsome middle aged investment broker, embezzles money from an estate and then marries the estate's heiress, Claire Worthington to cover up the crime. Unfortunately, he has hired a hit man to kill her ex-fiance and the hit man, in turn has contracted the job to another hit man. Holden becomes paranoid that he will be the target of the killer because of mistaken identity. His paranoia runs his life until, afraid that he is being followed by his potential killer, he is killed in an automobile accident trying to flee. Ironically, the two men who were following him were a bodyguard hired by his wife, and the hired killer who, having learned that the "hit" has been called off, was attempting to return Holden's money.

W. Lee Wilder, Billy Wilder's older brother, had a fitful Hollywood career, mainly as a director of "B" movies. *The Pretender* is typical of his work. All of his films were cynical exposés of psychological perversion. Despite flaws (particularly with the screenplay), this is one of his better films thanks to a fine performance by Albert Dekker, and the work of cinematographer John Alton and art director F. Paul Sylos. It is one of the strangest "B" *noirs*.

Previn, Andre (1929–)
Composer. Before he settled in Britain to become a conductor of "serious" music, Andre Previn was a successful, respected composer of film scores. He won three Academy Awards for his arrangements of Broadway musicals for their film adaptions and another for an original score. Previn was a staff composer for MGM and his scores have all the surface gleam and emotional shallowness of that studio's productions. He has since disavowed his film work and indeed, of film music in general. Interestingly, none of his sub-

sequent compositions have received the same acclaim as his film scores. His four *noir* scores are among his best.

Filmography: *Border Incident* (MGM, 1949). *Scene of the Crime* (MGM. 1949). *Tension* (MGM, 1949). *Cause for Alarm* (MGM, 1951).

Price, Vincent (1911–1994)
Character actor. Price was born in Missouri and educated as an art historian at Yale, but he turned to acting while living in London for a brief time in the 1930's. Price continued his stage career long after his film career began in the late thirties.

As a film actor, Price specialized in aesthetes, usually criminals and murderers. *Laura* provided him with a typical early role as a vain actor in love with the title character. However, probably his best *noir* performance was in John Farrow's *His Kind of Woman* in which he again played a vain actor caught in the middle of a deadly plot by a smuggler to kill another man. Price's performance is at once witty and surprisingly hard-boiled.

Filmography: *Laura* (20th Century-Fox, 1944). *Leave Her to Heaven* (20th Century-Fox, 1945). *Shock* (20th Century-Fox, 1946). *The Bribe* (MGM, 1949). *His Kind of Woman* (RKO, 1951). *While the City Sleeps* (RKO, 1956).

Private Hell, 36 (Filmmakers, 1954). 81 min.
Producer: Collier Young. Director: Don Siegel. Screenplay: Collier Young and Ida Lupino. Director of Photography: Burnett Guffey. Music: Leith Stevens. Art Director: Walter Keller. Editor: Stanford Tischler.

Cast: Ida Lupino (Lilli Marlowe), Steve Cochran (Cal Bruner), Howard Duff (Jack Farnham), Dean Jagger (Capt. Michaels), Dorothy Malone (Francey Farnham), Bridget Duff (Baby Farnham).

After a daring robbery, two bitter Los Angeles police detectives Cal

Bruner and Jack Farnham are assigned to the case. Their investigation leads to a beautiful, nightclub singer, Lilli Marlowe, who was given a tip with marked money. She helps them search for the robbers and an affair begins between her and Bruner. However, she sees no future in the relationship because of his small pay. When they do finally spot and chase the robber, he crashes and is killed. Bruner pockets a large portion of the stolen money found in the car and convinces Farnham to go along with him. The money slowly begins to destroy the two men's lives by their conflicting feelings of guilt. Eventually, the pent up emotions explode into violence and in the resulting gun battle, Farnham is wounded and Bruner is killed.

Private Hell, 36, in many ways, points the way to Don Siegel's later police detective thrillers. This early film differs from the later films essentially in its unrelenting paranoia and unfavorable portrayal of the police. The film's characters belong to the world of *film noir* by the corruptibility. Ida Lupino's *femme-fatale*, however, is not one dimensional, but a fully realized character who feels guilty that her desire for a wealthy husband has led her lover down a road to inevitable destruction.

Producers Releasing Corporation (PRC)

The ultimate poverty row studio, PRC was the temporary home for those on their way up or down, or for those stuck in the world of no budget commercial film production. However, PRC also allowed its directors the freedom to make the kind of films they wanted to, as long as they stayed within their narrow budgets. Legend has it that Edgar G. Ulmer shot his film, *Detour*, in less than three days on a budget of $20,000. In the late forties, after it was purchased by a British corporation, the company changed its name to Eagle-Lion. The titles listed below were released under the PRC banner.

Releases: **1945:** *Detour. Strange Illusion.* **1947:** *Railroaded.*

The Prowler (United Artists, 1951). 92 min.
Producer: S. P. Eagle. Director: Joseph Losey. Screenplay: Hugo Butler, story by Robert Thoeren and Hans Wilhelm. Director of Photography: Arthur Miller. Music: Lyn Murray. Art Director: Boris Leven. Editor: Paul Weatherwax.
Cast: Van Heflin (Webb Garwood), Evelyn Keyes (Susan Gilvray), John Maxwell (Bud Crocker), Katherine Warren (Mrs. Crocker), Emerson Tracy (William Gilvray). With: Madge Blake, Wheaton Chambers, Louise Lorimer, Robert Osterloh, Sherry Hall.
One night, patrolmen Webb Garwood and Bud Crocker respond to a report of a prowler at the home of Susan Gilvray, the wife of a prominent disc jockey. Although they do not find a prowler, Webb falls for Susan and he seduces her. When he discovers that her husband has put her in his will, Webb sets Mr. Gilvray up as a "prowler" and shoots and kills him.
Although Susan suspects Webb, she does not report their affair to the inquest. Webb convinces Susan that it was all an accident and they get married. They use her inheritance to buy a small motel in Las Vegas. However, when he discovers that she is pregnant, Webb panics – Mr. Gilvray was sterile and her pregnancy would, he believes, prove they were having an affair and thus planned the murder of her husband. When she is ready to deliver, Webb calls in a doctor, but Susan, finally realizes the true nature of her husband. She believes that Webb plans to kill the doctor, and she helps him escape. The doctor calls the police. When they arrive, Webb attempts to flee and the police shoot him.
The Prowler, like all of Joseph Losey's early films, suffers from its social criticism. Nevertheless, the film

does have power as it reveals the dark side of the American dream of status and success. As always, Evelyn Keyes' performance is excellent.

Pushover (Columbia, 1954). 88 min.
Producer: Jules Schermer. Director: Richard Quine. Screenplay: Roy Huggins, based on the novels *The Night Watch* by Thomas Walsh and *Rafferty* by William S. Ballinger. Director of Photography: Lester H. White. Music: Arthur Morton. Art Director: Walter Holscher. Editor: Jerome Thoms.

Cast: Fred MacMurray (Paul Sheridan), Kim Novak (Leona McLane), Phil Carey (Rick McAllister), Dorothy Malone (Ann), E. G. Marshall (Lt. Carl Eckstrom), Paul Richard (Harry Wheeler). With: Allen Mourse, Phil Chambers, Alan Dexter, Robert Forrest.

Paul Sheridan, a police detective, infiltrates a robbery gang by seducing Leona, the mistress of Harry Wheeler, the gang's leader. Although she discovers that Paul is a cop, Leona falls in love with him. She convinces Paul to kill Wheeler and together they will run off with the $200,000 he recently stole from a bank. Paul carries out the murder, but the plan begins to unravel immediately. Eventually, Paul's partners realize what has happened, and Paul is critically wounded when he tries to escape.

Pushover is a more brutal version of the *Double Indemnity* type story. Like the early film, Fred MacMurray once again plays a basically honest man whose sexual obsessions with a beautiful, amoral woman led him to murder. Although the performances are quite strong (Kim Novak is very good as the *femme-fatale*), the film has a mechanical, "seen it all before" feel to it.

Quine, Richard (1920–)
Director. Quine, a juvenile actor and supporting lead in several popular films in the thirties and forties, turned to film direction in the fifties. He directed "B"

films and a few "A" films of varying quality. Of his two *films noirs*, *Drive a Crooked Mile* is certainly the best, although *Pushover* is not a bad film. Both, however, demonstrate the unfortunate tendency of *film noir* directors in that decade to display a flat, uninventive style.

Filmography: *Drive a Crooked Mile* (Columbia, 1954). *Pushover* (Columbia, 1954).

Quinn, Anthony (1915–)
Actor. One of the most famous character leads in American film, Quinn co-starred in a single, minor *film noir*.

Filmography: *The Naked Street* (United Artists, 1955).

Raab, Leonid (1911–1989)
Composer. The Russian born Raab composed the music for many "B" movies including two *films noirs*. His scores are not particularly outstanding.

Filmography: *He Walked By Night* (Eagle-Lion, 1948). *Follow Me Quietly* (RKO, 1949).

Race Street (RKO, 1948). 78 min.
Producer: Nat Holt. Director: Edwin L. Marin. Screenplay: Martin Rackin, Story by Maurice Davis. Director of Photography: J. Roy Hunt. Music: Roy Webb. Art Directors: Albert S. D'Agostino and Walter E. Keller. Editor: Elmo Williams.

Cast: George Raft (Ganin), William Bendix (Runson), Marilyn Maxwell (Robbie), Frank Faylen (Phil Dickson), Henry Morgan (Towers). With: Gale Robbins, Calley Richards, Mack Gray, Russell Hicks.

George Raft plays yet another imaculately dressed tough guy in this tale of a big time bookie who avenges a friend's murder and resists a group of Eastern crooks who try to muscle in on his business.

Race Street is typical of "B" movies in general with its sloppy production values and concentration on action. However, it does contain an interesting

Left to right: Robert Mitchum, William Talman and William Conrad from *The Racket* (RKO, 1951).

performance by Marilyn Maxwell as a *femme-fatale* secretly working for the mob.

The Racket (Paramount, 1928). 85 min.
Producer: The Caddo Company. Howard Hughes. Director: Lewis Milestone. Screenplay: Harry Behn and Del Andrews, adapted by Barlett Cormack from his play. Director of Photography: Tony Gaudio. Editor: Tom Mirando.
Cast: Thomas Meighan (Capt. McQuigg), Marie Provost (Helen Hayes), Louis Wolheim (Nick Scarsi), Richard "Skeets" Gallagher (Miller). With: Lee Moran, Lucien Prival, Tony Marlowe, Henry Sedley.
The original version of the film, *The Racket* demonstrates the early appearance of *noir* themes in American literature and drama: the source material

was a successful Broadway play. The part played by Marie Provost, "Helen Hayes," a nightclub singer, was later changed to "Irene" to avoid confusion with the stage and screen actress Helen Hayes.

The Racket (RKO, 1951). 88 min.
Producer: Edmund Grainger. Director: John Cromwell. Screenplay: William Wister Haines and W. R. Burnett, based on Bartlett Cormack's play. Director of Photography: George E. Diskant. Music: Constantin Bakaleinikoff. Song: "A Lovely Way to Spend an Evening" by Jimmy McHugh and Harold Adamson. Art Directors: Albert S. D'Agostino and Jack Okey. Editor: Sherman Todd.
Cast: Robert Mitchum (Capt. McQuigg) Lizabeth Scott (Irene), Robert Ryan (Scanlon), William Talman (Johnson), Ray Collins (Welch),

Joyce MacKenzie (Mary McQuigg). With: Robert Hutton, Virginia Huston, William Conrad, William Sande, Don Porter.

Captain McQuigg, an incorruptible police officer, goes after Nick Scanlon, a gangster in a small midwestern city that he has corrupted through bribes. McQuigg struggles against the corrupt city officials and his own department; Scanlon, in turn, struggles against his superiors who want him to become a more modern, less violent criminal. Scanlon assassinates witnesses. Scanlon is eventually killed by his superiors and McQuigg frustrated by his powerlessness to control the mob resorts to his own form of gangsterism, even betraying his own ethics. Ultimately, however, the mob is never fully defeated.

Howard Hughes produced the original 1928 version of Barlett Cormack's disparaging view of political corruption and gangsters. For this version, which he oversaw as the owner of RKO, he hired W. R. Burnett, the great crime novelist, to heighten the violent elements. Likewise, Hughes, who never missed a chance to heighten the sexual elements of a film, provided plenty of excuses for Lizabeth Scott to wear tight, slinky dresses as nightclub singer Irene, the mutual girl friend of Scanlon and McQuigg.

As is usual of adaptions of stage plays, *The Racket* suffers somewhat from a verbose script and lack of action. Robert Mitchum, in a rare good guy *noir* role, is strangely lackluster as McQuigg. Robert Ryan, however, is absolutely ferocious as the sadistic Scanlon.

Rackin, Martin (1918-1976)

Screenwriter. Rackin specialized in action adventures. One of his best screenplays, *Riff Raff* (RKO, 1947), was directed by Ted Tatzlaff and is an extraordinary neglected adventure film. Rackin also co-wrote four *films noirs*. Filmography: *A Dangerous Profes-*

sion (RKO, 1944). *Race Street* (RKO, 1948). *The Enforcer* (Warner Bros., 1951). *Loan Shark* (Lippert, 1952).

Racksin, David (1912-)

Composer. Racksin achieved lasting fame for his lyrical, romantic score for *Laura* and the film's theme song, co-written with lyricist Johnny Mercer. While this is his most famous score, all of his film music is characterized by strong memorable themes and a great sense of drama. Filmography: *Laura* (20th Century-Fox, 1944). *Fallen Angel* (20th Century-Fox, 1945). *Force of Evil* (MGM, 1948). *A Lady Without Passport* (MGM, 1950). *Suddenly* (United Artists, 1954). *The Big Combo* (Allied Artists, 1955).

Raft, George (1895-1980)

Actor. Raft was a major star in the thirties, specializing in gangster sagas. Always immaculately dressed, Raft most often played gangster aesthetes, but also heroes of various types. His image however, did not survive well, and in the forties his career went into a decline. Still, he did star in several *films noirs*, including two major RKO productions. His performances, whatever the overall quality of the films, are always stiff and adequate at best. Filmography: *Johnny Angel* (RKO,, 1945). *Nocturne* (RKO, 1946). *Race Street* (RKO, 1948). *Red Light* (Columbia, 1950). *Loan Shark* (Lippert, 1952). *Rogue Cop* (MGM, 1954).

Railroaded (PRC, 1947). 71 min.

Producer: Charles F. Reisner. Director: Anthony Mann. Screenplay: John C. Higgins, story by Gertrude Walker. Director of Photography: Guy Roe. Music: Alvin Levin. Art Director: Perry Smith. Editor: Louis H. Sackin.

Cast: John Ireland (Duke Martin), Sheila Ryan (Rosa Ryan), Hugh Beaumont (Mickey Ferguson), Jane Randolph (Clara Calhoun), Ed Kelly (Steve Ryan), Charles D. Brown (Capt. Mac

Taggart). With: Clancy Cooper, Peggy Converse, Hermine Sterler, Keefe Brasselle, Roy Gordon.

The robbery of a beauty shop that served as a front for a gambling racket results in the death of a cop and the capture of one of the robbers who is critically wounded. On his death bed, the robber implicates an innocent friend, Steve Ryan, and Ryan is arrested. Ryan's sister, Rosa, convinces a police detective, Mickey Ferguson, that her brother is innocent and that he should investigate other suspects. The case centers on Duke Martin, a gunman. As Rosa and Ferguson look for witnesses, Duke stays ahead of them, killing potential witnesses. His ritual of perfuming his bullets eventually gives Martin away. In the final shoot out, he is killed by Ferguson.

Railroaded is a crisp, well made "B" *noir* that concentrates on action and violence. Anthony Mann uses the techniques of low budget westerns — jump cuts, mobile camera, cutting back and forth between scenes — to excellent effect, creating a visceral, exciting thriller.

The film also benefits from good performances, particularly by John Ireland as the sadistic, eccentric gunman.

Raines, Ella (Ella Raubes) (1921–)

Actress. Dark and exotically beautiful, Raines was discovered by director Howard Hughes and cast in his film, *Corvette K-225* (Universal, 1943). Although she was a talented actress, she never achieved true stardom. Still, she did appear in a few important films and is a minor icon of *film noir*.

Of the five *noirs* in which she appeared, Raines' most important performance was in Robert Siodmak's early classic, *Phantom Lady*. Raines stars as a secretary of a man convicted of murder who desperately tries to prove his innocence before he is executed. Her performance is both sexy and witty. She also had an important role in Siodmak's *Uncle Harry*, but her roles in

Brute Force and *The Web* were less important. In the little known "B" *noir*, *Impact*, Raines co-starred as the "good" girl opposite Helen Waler's *femme-fatale*. Once again her performance is sexy and witty and quite endearing. unfortunately, after 1949, Raines' film appearances became sparse and she did not appear in any other *films noirs*.

Filmography: *Phantom Lady* (Universal, 1944). *Uncle Harry* (Universal, 1945). *Brute Force* (Universal, 1947). *The Web* (Universal, 1947). *Impact* (United Artists, 1949).

Rains, Claude (1889–1967)

Character actor. Rains was a diminutive, but suave and debonair actor whose witty, self deprecating style endeared him to countless movie fans throughout the world thanks to several excellent performances including his role as the corrupt prefect of police in *Casablanca* (Warner Bros., 1941). He had prominent roles in three *film noirs*. In both *The Unsuspected* and Alfred Hitchcock's classic, *Notorious*, he was the chief villain. In John Farrow's neglected *film noir*, *Where Danger Lives*, he co-starred as the victim of an avaricious *femme-fatale* and is killed off early in the film.

Filmography: *Notorious* (RKO, 1946). *The Unsuspected* (Warner Bros., 1947). *Where Danger Lives* (RKO, 1950).

Ransford, Maurice (1896–1978)

Art Director. As a unit art director at 20th Century–Fox, Ransford worked on a number of big budget *films noirs*. He had a great sense of style and had a feel for the milieu of *film noir* as evidenced by his work on the two color *noirs*, *Leave Her to Heaven* and *Niagara*, and indeed on all of his *noirs*. He was the art director on an Otto Preminger *film noir*, *The Thirteenth Letter*, one of the director's least known movies.

Filmography: *Leave Her to Heaven*

(20th Century–Fox, 1945). *Somewhere in the Night* (20th Century–Fox, 1946). *Strange Triangle* (20th Century– Fox, 1946). *Road House* (20th Century– Fox, 1948). *Panic in the Streets* (20th Century–Fox, 1950). *The Thirteenth Letter* (20th Century–Fox, 1951). *Niagara* (20th Century–Fox, 1953).

Rapper, Irving (1898–)

Director. Rapper was a moderately successful director in the forties and fifties. He did not have a readily discernable personal style. He directed a single undistinguished *film noir*.

Filmography: *Another Man's Poison* (United Artists, 1952).

Raw Deal (Eagle-Lion, 1948) 79 min.

Producer: Edward Small. Director: Anthony Mann. Screenplay: Leopold Atlas and John C. Higgins, story by Arnold Armstrong and Audrey Ashley. Director of Photography: John Alton. Music: Paul Sawtell. Art Director: Edward L. Ilou. Editor: Alfred DeGaetano.

Cast: Dennis O'Keefe (Joe Sullivan), Claire Trevor (Pat), Marsha Hunt (Ann Martin), John Ireland (Fantail), Raymond Burr (Rick Coyle). With: Curt Conway, Chili Williams, Richard Frazer, Whit Bissell, Cliff Clark.

Intent on getting revenge against the men who framed him, gangster Joe Sullivan breaks out of prison with the help of his girlfriend, Pat. The gangsters who framed him kidnap a girl named Ann Martin, who Sullivan corresponded with while in prison. When Joe rescues Ann, she grabs a gun and shoots her kidnapper. Joe and Ann fall in love. Joe discovers that a man named Rick Coyle was behind the scheme to frame him. Joe goes to kill Rick and in the subsequent shoot out, Rick inadvertently starts a fire. He jumps out of a window to his death. Joe, critically wounded, stumbles into the street. Ann cradles him while he dies. Pat, back at her apartment, is resigned to a life of loneliness.

Yet another action oriented "B" *noir*, *Raw Deal* is directed in freewielding, visceral style by Anthony Mann. Vengeance is a theme explored in a few *films noirs*, and here is used as an excuse for the extravagant violence. Unlike Mann's *Railroaded* (PRC, 1947), the action and violence of *Raw Deal* is leavened somewhat by its romantic subplot.

Raymond Burr was particularly striking as the menacing Rick Coyle, one of his best roles as a villain.

Ray, Aldo (1926–1992)

Actor. A beefy character actor, Aldo Ray specialized in playing brawny but lovable tough guys. Although he never achieved real stardom, his performances were almost always good. He starred in Jacques Tourneur's *Nightfall* as a man hunted by police for a murder he didn't commmit and two crooks for stealing their money. Sadly, it is Ray's only *film noir*.

Filmography: *Nightfall* (Columbia, 1957).

Ray, Nicholas (1911–1979)

Director. One of the most original American directors who flourished in the fifties, Nicholas Ray has achieved cult status with many auteur critics. He is noted for his sharply developed visual sense and, thematically, for his concern for society's misfits whom he often portrayed as bitter, troubled and dangerous.

Nicholas Ray directed six *films noirs*. The best are *They Live by Night* and *In a Lonely Place*. The former is a variation of the Bonnie and Clyde story. The latter is one of a handful of *films noirs* set in the Hollywood film industry. Indeed, with its story of a borderline psychotic screenwriter involved in a murder, *In a Lonely Place* is one of the most disparaging views of Hollywood.

Of Ray's six *noirs*, he did not receive credit for *Macao*, originally a Josef Von Sternberg production. When Sterberg proved too slow for RKO's production chief, Howard Hughes, Ray was brought in. He finished the film as well as reshot much of Sternberg's footage. Sterberg, however, was the contracted director and thus received credit for the film.

Ray's last major *noir* is a neglected classic, *On Dangerous Ground*. It is one of the genre's most unusual films, with a tender story that is both romantic and poignant, and like all of Ray's movies, is characterized by strong performances and a great sense of style.

Filmography: *They Live by Night* (RKO, 1949). *Knock on Any Door* (Columbia, 1949). *In a Lonely Place* (Columbia, 1950). *Macao* (uncredited) (RKO, 1952). *On Dangerous Ground* (RKO, 1952). *Party Girl* (MGM, 1958).

Rear Window (Paramount, 1954). 112 min.

Producer and Director: Alfred Hitchcock. Screenplay: John Michael Hayes, based on a novelette by Cornell Woolrich. Director of Photography: Robert Burks. Music: Franz Waxman. Art Director: Hal Pereira. Editor: George Tomasini.

Cast: Jimmy Steward (L. B. "Jeff" Jeffries), Grace Kelly (Lisa Fremont), Wendell Corey (Thomas J. Doyle), Thelma Ritter (Stella), Raymond Burr (Lars Tharwald). With: Judith Evelyn, Ross Bagdasarian, Georgine Darcy, Jesslyn Fax, Irene Winston.

L. B. Jeffries, nicknamed Jeff, is a newspaper photographer who has been confined to a wheelchair because of a broken leg. To counter his boredom, he takes to watching the behavior of his neighbors of his Greenwich village apartment building. He begins to realize that one of his neighbors, Lars Tharwald, has murdered his wife. Lisa Fremont, Jeff's elegant model girl friend, does not at first believe him, but slowly she too begins to believe Tharwald is a killer. Neither Lisa nor Jeff can convince Jeff's old friend, Tom Doyle, a cop, of Tharwald's guilt. Eventually Tharwald discovers that he

is being watched and comes to Jeff's apartment to kill him. Jeff is saved just in the nick of time by Doyle, but not before his other leg is broken in a fall.

Rear Window qualifies as a *film noir* for several reasons. First, it is based on a story by Cornell Woolrich, many of whose stories became *films noirs* including the similar *The Window* (RKO, 1949).Second, because its atmosphere is claustrophobic and restrictive, even dreamlike at times. And third, its villain, Lars Tharwald, is played by *noir* icon Raymond Burr.

All of Alfred Hitchcock's films are filled with dark humor, and humor is certainly an element missing from many *films noirs*, but neither this nor its color cinematography excludes it from the genre.

The Reckless Moment (Columbia, 1949). 81 min.

Producer: Walter Wanger. Director: Max Ophuls. Screenplay: Henry Garson and Robert W. Soderberg, adapted by Mel Dinelli and Robert E. Kent from the short story "The Blank Wall" by Elizabeth Suxnay Holding. Director of Photography: Burnett Guffey. Music: Hans J. Salter. Art Director: Cary Odell. Editor: Gene Havlick,

Cast: James Mason (Martin Donnelly), Joan Bennett (Lucia Harper), Geraldine Brooks (Bea Harper), Shepperd Strudwick (Ted Darby), Roy Roberts (Nagle). With: David Blair, Peter Brocco, Frances Williams, Paul Burns.

Bea Harper, an impressionable young girl, has an affair with the unscrupulous Ted Darby. Darby blackmails the family to prevent him from causing a scandal for the well-to-do Harpers. Bea and Ted have an argument at the Harper's boathouse. She hits him over the head with a flashlight and flees. Darby stumbles, falls into the water and drowns.

The police arrest one of Darby's seedy associates for the murder, but another of his crooked friends, Nagle, has some of Bea's incriminating love

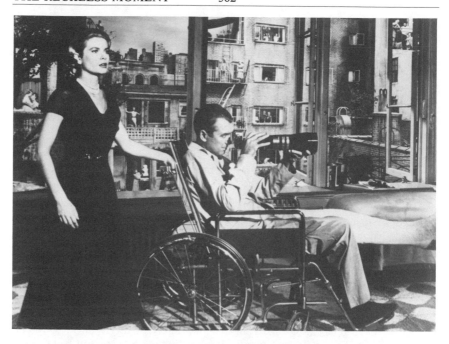

Publicity still from *Rear Window*. Notice all the characters that James Stewart spies on appear in their respective window (Paramount, 1954).

The Great Director Alfred Hitchcock (right) between takes with James Stewart and Grace Kelly.

letters to Darby and he blackmails the family for $5000. Lucia, however, can only raise $800. Donnelly, a family friend who is romantically drawn to Lucia Harper, agrees to help. When he confronts Nagle, the two fight and Donnelly strangles the sleazy blackmailer.

Donnelly puts Nagle's body in the trunk of his car, intent on getting rid of it elsewhere. Lucia follows in her car but Donnelly looses control and crashes. Critically injured, he tells Lucia not to worry, that he will take care of everything. When the police arrive, he confesses to killing both Darby and Nagle, thus freeing Bea and Lucia Harper.

Ironically, Mr. Harper, who has been away on a business trip, returns unaware of the events that nearly destroyed his family.

The Reckless Moment is an interesting *film noir*. It is one of Max Ophuls' best American films. In many ways less extravagant than his other work, it still contains some inventive, extraordinary camera work.

Ophuls preferred female protagonists and here he provided two: Geraldine Brooks as Bea, the catalyst for the story and Joan Bennett as Lucia, the protective matriarch. Bennett's role is similar to Mildred Pierce, a woman who merely wants to protect the reputation of her family that is threatened partly by the actions of her flighty daughter.

James Mason's role as Martin Donnelly, however, is the *noir* center of this tale. Donnelly is a classic *noir* protagonist, caught up in circumstances beyond his control, but partly of his own making and ultimately doomed.

Red Light (United Artists, 1950). 84 min.
Producer and Director: Roy Del Ruth. Screenplay: George Callahan. Director of Photography: Bert Glennon. Music: Dimitri Tiomkin. Art Director: F. Paul Sylos. Editor: Richard Heermance.

Cast: George Raft (John Torno), Virginia Mayo (Carla North), Gene Lockhart (Warni Hazard), Barton MacLane (Sarecker), Henry Morgan (Rocky), Raymond Burr (Nick Cherney). With: Arthur Franz, Arthur Shields, Frank Orth, Philip Pine, Movita Casteneda.

After his brother is killed by gangsters, John Torno searches for his killer. Eventually he finds that Nick Cherney, a sadistic mob gun man is the murderer and in the inevitable confrontation, Torno kills Cherney.

Red Light is a minor *film noir*, notable mainly for a typically great performance by Raymond Burr.

Redgrave, Michael (1908–1985)
Actor. Redgrave, the father of Lynn and Vanessa Redgrave, was a major star of British stage and film. He starred in Fritz Lang's little known *noir*, *Secret Beyond the Door* as an architect who may have killed his first wife. He had a small supporting role in Orson Welles' *Mr. Arkadin*.

Filmography: *Secret Beyond the Door* (Universal, 1948). *Mr. Arkadin* (M.& A. Alexander, 1955).

Reis, Irving (1906–1953)
Screenwriter and Director. Reis was first a successful radio writer and screenwriter. He began directing in the early forties. He had a rather static style, but he directed several notable films including the romantic comedy *The Bachelor and the Bobby Soxer* (RKO, 1947). He also directed a superior *film noir*, *Crack-Up* which demonstrates a more inventive pictorial style.

Filmography: *Crack-Up* (RKO, 1946).

Remisoff, Nicholas (Nicolai) (1887–1963)
Art director. The Russian born Remisoff was one of director Lewis Milestone's chief collaborators in the 1930's. He later worked at several different studios. He was the art director for

Joseph Losey's minor *noir*, *The Big Night*.

Filmography: *The Big Night* (United Artists, 1951).

Renoir, Jean (1894–1979)

Director. Certainly France's greatest director, Renoir is also one of cinema's great humanitarians. All of his films, whether comedies, dramas, or epics, are concerned with the psychology of individuals and how they act in a group and the existential fate of his characters. His classic crime films, *La Chienne* (1931) and *La Bête Humaine* (1938) were immensely successful in Europe and were later adapted by Fritz Lang: *La Chienne* became *Scarlet Street* (Universal, 1945) and *La Bête Humaine* became *Human Desire* (Columbia, 1954).

Republic Pictures Corporation

Founded in 1935 by former tobacco executive Herbert J. Yates, Republic was one of the better "poverty row" studios. It thrived on cheaply produced westerns (particularly the singing cowboy variety — Roy Rogers was one of the studio's biggest stars) and action serials. However, major directors were attracted to the studio because of its relatively relaxed environment and creative freedom. John Ford, Raoul Walsh and Fritz Lang all made films at the studio. Republic's *noirs*, like most of their productions, suffers from their minuscule budgets and a tendency toward exploitation. Of the company's five *noir* releases, Fritz Lang's *House by the River* and Frank Borzage's *Moonrise*, are the best.

Releases: **1947:** *The Pretender*. **1948:** *Moonrise*. **1950:** *House by the River*. **1953:** *City That Never Sleeps*. **1954:** *Hell's Half Acre*.

Richmond, Ted (1912–)

Producer. Originally a screenwriter, Richmond was promoted to producer in the mid thirties. He was employed for many years at Columbia, for whom he produced several films. He produced four interesting *films noirs* including *Nightfall*, Jacques Tourneur's last important film.

Filmography: *The Night Editor* (Columbia, 1946). *So Dark the Night* (Columbia, 1946). *Shakedown* (Universal, 1950). *Nightfall* (Columbia, 1957).

Ride the Pink Horse (Universal, 1947). 101 min.

Producer: Joan Harrison. Director: Robert Montgomery. Screenplay: Ben Hecht and Charles Lederer, based on the novel by Dorothy B. Hughes. Director of Photography: Russell Metty. Music: Frank Skinner. Art Directors: Bernard Herzbrun and Robert Boyle. Editor: Ralph Dawson.

Cast: Robert Montgomery (Gagin), Thomas Gomez, (Pancho), Rita Conde (Carla), Iris Flores (Maria)), Wanda Hendrix (Pila), Grandon Rhodes (Mr. Edison). With: Tito Renaldo, Richard Gaines, Andrea King, Art Smith, Martin Garralaga, Edward Earle.

Ride The Pink Horse is an oddly titled *film noir* in which Robert Montgomery (who also directed), stars as a blackmailer who sets out to track down a war profiteer responsible for the death of a former buddy. He chases the villain to a colorful New Mexico town, at first intent on blackmailing him, but eventually resorts to violence when the villain tries to kill him.

The story line is rather conventional, but Montgomery manages to create a dark, compelling story of desperation.

The screenplay, by veterans Ben Hecht and Charles Lederer, concentrates on violence and action, and Montgomery's performance and direction are assured. Nevertheless, the film doesn't rise above merely interesting.

Ripley, Arthur (1895–1961)

Director. Ripley is an enigmatic figure, described by some as mentally and physically ill. He directed a handful of films in the forties including the strange, eerie thriller *The Chase*. It is a film which almost defies description, with some very odd elements. He also directed Robert Mitchum's production of *Thunder Road*.

Filmography: *The Chase* (United Artists, 1946). *Thunder Road* (United Artists, 1958).

Ritter, Thelma (1905–1969)

Character actress. Born in Brooklyn, New York, Thelma Ritter began acting in her youth and came out of retirement to appear in movies in 1947. For the next two decades she played a succession of sardonic characters who commented on the action with wry humor. Her best *noir* role was in Sam Fuller's *Pickup on South Street* as Moe, the con artist who sells information to the police. In Alfred Hitchcock's color *noir*, *Rear Window*, she played a more typical role: the insurance nurse whose sarcastic disbelief is used to relieve some of the tension.

Filmography: *Pickup on South Street* (20th Century–Fox, 1953). *Rear Window* (Paramount, 1954).

Rivkin, Allen (1909–1978)

Screenwriter. Rivkin was a typical Hollywood screenwriter, working on many different projects, but specializing in none. He worked on four *films noirs*.

Filmography: *Dead Reckoning* (adaption only) (Columbia, 1947). *Tension* (co-wrote) (MGM, 1947). *Gambling House* (RKO, 1951). *The Strip* (co-wrote) (MGM, 1951).

RKO-Radio Pictures

Founded in the late twenties by the young genius behind RCA, David Sarnoff, RKO was the most schizophrenic of the major studios. Underfunded, the studio was always on the verge of bankruptcy despite producing some of the most consistently brilliant Hollywood films for over three decades.

For most of the 1930's, the studio's production was run by Pandro S. Berman, who was largely responsible for the Astaire-Rogers musicals and countless screwball comedies and dramas of various types. The studio's style was then rooted in the popular Art Deco of the era, but after Berman's departure in the late thirties, the studio began to experiment with styles and genres.

Val Lewton was hired in this era to head up his own production unit and he immediately established himself as a top producer. The Lewton "B" horrors were brilliantly made and helped introduce the new, expressionist style of chief art director, Albert S. D'Agostino and a whole group of extraordinarily talented collaborators who would become important in *film noir*: cinematographer Nicholas Musuraca, directors Jacques Tourneur, Robert Wise, Robert Rosson and Mark Robson.

The new era, however, was defined by Orson Welles' classic *Citizen Kane* (RKO, 1942) which firmly established the new style. Welles went on to produce and star in a seminal *noir*, *Journey into Fear* which was successful and helped kick off the genre.

In the forties, a new group of actors emerged at the studio, led by Robert Mitchum and included Robert Ryan, Charles McGraw, Jane Russell, Jane Greer, Faith Domergue and many others.

Leading directors included Edward Dmytryk who, with producer Adrian Scott, suffered from the McCarthy anticommunist witch hunt of the late forties.

Many of the genre's greatest films were produced at RKO before the company finally succumbed to financial pressure in the late fifties. Indeed, RKO is arguably the most important studio in the brief history of *film noir*.

Releases: **1940:** *Strangers on the Third Floor.* **1941:** *Suspicion.* **1943:** *Journey Into Fear.* **1944:** *Experiment Perilous. Murder, My Sweet. Woman in the Window.* **1945:** *Cornered. Johnny Angel.* **1946:** *Crack-Up. Deadline at Dawn. The Locket. Nocturne. Notorious. The Stranger. The Spiral Staircase.*

1947: *Born to Kill. Crossfire. Desperate. The Devil Thumbs a Ride. Out of the Past. They Won't Believe Me. The Long Night.* **1948:** *Berlin Express. Bodyguard. Race Street.* **1949:** *A Dangerous Profession. Follow Me Quietly. The Set-Up. They Live by Night. The Window. The Woman on Pier 13.* **1950:** *Armored Car Robbery. Destination Murder. Edge of Doom. The Tattooed Stranger. The Capture. Where Danger Lives.* **1951:** *Cry Danger. Gambling House. His Kind of Woman. The Racket. Roadblock.* **1952:** *Beware, My Lovely. Clash by Night. Macao. The Narrow Margin. On Dangerous Ground. Sudden Fear.* **1953:** *Angel Face. The Hitch-Hiker.* **1956:** *Beyond a Reasonable Doubt. Slightly Scarlet. While the City Sleeps.*

Road House (20th Century–Fox, 1948) 95 min.

Producer: Edward Chodorov. Director: Jean Negulesco. Screenplay: Edward Chodorov, story by Margaret Given and Oscar Saul. Director of Photography: Joseph LaShelle. Music: Cyril Mockridge. Art Directors: Lyle Wheeler and Maurice Ransford. Editor: James B. Clark.

Cast: Ida Lupino (Lily), Cornel Wilde (Pete), Celeste Holm (Susie), Richard Widmark (Jefty), O. Z. Whitehead (Arthur), Robert Karnes (Mike). With: George Beranger, Ian MacDonald, Grandon Rhodes, Jack Gilee.

Jefty owns a roadhouse near the Canadian border. His friend, Pete, manages the roadhouse. Jefty begins to fall for Lily, while Pete stays aloof despite her friendly disposition. Ann, a girl who works at the roadhouse, is in love with Pete, but he does not reciprocate her affections.

While Jefty is away on a hunting trip, Pete and Lily fall in love. When Jefty returns, he is shocked and his jealousy reveals a psychotic side of his personality. Jefty frames Pete for a theft and then has Pete released into his custody. He takes Pete, Lily and Ann to his cabin near the border. He plans to tempt Pete into trying to escape across the Canadian border and kill him as an escaping fugitive. When Pete and Lily do try to escape, Ann interferes with Jefty's plan and is shot and wounded. Pete returns and kills Jefty in the final, violent confrontation. Pete and Lily return to civilization and safety.

Road House is another neglected *noir* classic. It contains one of Richard Widmark's best villainous performances and the other performances are also quite good.

Jean Negulesco was a very good director, with a great sense of style. He was adaptable, making everything from romantic comedies to hard-boiled *noirs* like this one and indeed this is one of his best movies. The screenplay is superb, with sharp dialog and the characters' emotional isolation is brilliantly echoed in their physical isolation: the roadhouse and claustrophobic hunting cabin are practically the only interiors in the entire film.

Roadblock (RKO, 1951). 73 min.

Producer: Lewis J. Rachmil. Director: Harold Daniels. Screenplay: Steve Fisher and George Bricker, story by Richard Landau and Geoffrey Homes. Director of Photography: Nicholas Musuraca. Music: Paul Sawtell. Music Director: Constantin Bakaleinikoff. Art Directors: Albert S. D'Agostino and Walter E. Keller. Editor: Robert Golden.

Cast: Charles McGraw (Joe Peters), Joan Dixon (Diane), Lowell Gilmore (Kendell Webb), Louis Jean Heydt (Harry Miller), Milburn Stone (Egan), Joseph Crehan (Thompson).

Joe Peters, an insurance investigator, plots a million dollar mail robbery in order to win the love of the beautiful, but cold and avaricious Diane. The robbery is carried out, but their getaway is hampered by police checkpoints. Eventually the cops catch up with the couple and Peters is gunned down while trying to flee through Los Angeles' concrete river beds.

A febrile, unyielding *film noir*, *Roadblock* is one of the most interesting RKO "B" *noirs*. Its story is unrelentingly downbeat, with its characters moving inevitably toward their end.

The story for the film was co-written by Geoffrey Homes (pseudonym for Nicholas Musuraca) who also wrote the *noir* classic *Out of the Past*, and *Roadblock* has some similarities to that film. Not least is its characters: Peters is basically an honest man who falls victim to a completely amoral woman. McGraw's single starring performance in a *film noir* is very good and Joan Dixon, a "B" actress, is also surprisingly good as one of the most unrelentingly evil *femme-fatales* in the genre.

In addition, Nicholas Musuraca, the great cinematographer who worked on *Out of the Past*, also was the cinematographer on *Roadblock*. His work, as always, is masterful, characterized by the usual shadows, fog and rain swept landscapes.

Roberts, Bob (　)

Producer. Roberts produced many films of widely varying quality over three decade. He also produced three classic, enduring *films noirs*.

Filmography: *Body and Soul* (United Artists, 1947). *Force of Evil* (MGM, 1948). *He Ran All the Way* (United Artists, 1951).

Robinson, Edward G. (Emmanuel Goldenberg) (1893-1973)

Actor. More than any of the great thirties stars, except perhaps Humphrey Bogart who did not hit his stride until after 1941, Edward G. Robinson made the transition from gangster melodramas to *film noir* without any noticeable difficulty. There was always an underlying vulnerability to the tough guy roles Robinson played in the 1930's, and he brought that sensibility to his *noir* characters.

Robinson made a striking appearance in two early *films noirs* directed by Fritz Lang: *Woman in the Window* and *Scarlet Street*. In both he starred as the weak victim of a sadistic *femme-fatale*, in both cases played by Joan Bennett. In each, Robinson brought a vulnerability to the character which made him that much more sympathetic.

Robinson played heroic characters in two *films noirs*: Orson Welles' *The Stranger* (as a Federal agent searching for a Nazi war criminal living in the United States), and *Double Indemnity*. In the latter Robinson starred as an insurance investigator who suspects his lifelong friend—played by Fred MacMurray—of insurance fraud and murder.

Robinson reprised his famous gangster characters in two *films noirs*: *Key Largo* and *Black Tuesday*.

However, perhaps Robinson's greatest *noir* performance was in John Farrow's *noir* classic, *Night Has a Thousand Eyes*. Robinson starred as John Triton, a clairvoyant whose predictions, including his own death, always come true.

Edward G. Robinson was always a compelling performer, and he remains one of *noir's* most important male icons.

Filmography: *Woman in the Window* (RKO, 1944). *Scarlet Street* (Universal, 1945). *Double Indemnity* (Paramount, 1946). *The Stranger* (RKO, 1946). *Key Largo* (Warner Bros., 1948). *Night Has a Thousand Eyes* (Paramount, 1948). *House of Strangers* (20th Century-Fox, 1949). *Black Tuesday* (United Artists, 1954). *Tight Spot* (Columbia, 1955).

Robson, Mark (1913-1978)

Director. Robson is another graduate of the Val Lewton produced horror films made at RKO in the early forties. Robson, originally an editor, was promoted to director by Lewton, and directed two Lewton produced horror classics: *The Seventh Victim* (RKO,

1943) and *Bedlam* (RKO, 1946). Robson brought the influence of the expressionist style of the Lewton features to his *films noirs* and he directed two of the genre's classic boxing *noirs*: *Champion* and *The Harder They Fall*. Robson is a neglected filmmaker who made several important films and he deserves renewed interest.

Filmography: *Champion* (United Artists, 1949). *Edge of Doom* (RKO, 1950). *The Harder They Fall* (Columbia, 1956).

Rogers, Ginger (Virginia McMath) (1911–)

Actress. Rogers' career was on the inevitable decline by the mid–fifties when she starred in an indifferent late-*noir*, *Tightspot*, as a tough female convict. It is her single *film noir*.

Filmography: *Tightspot* (Columbia, 1955).

Rogue Cop (MGM, 1954) 87 min.

Producer: Nicholas Nayfack. Director: Roy Rowland. Screenplay: Sydney Boehm, based on the novel by William P. McGivern. Director of Photography: John Seitz. Music: Jeff Alexander. Art Directors: Cedric Gibbons and Hans Peters. Editor: James E. Newcom.

Cast: Robert Taylor (Christopher Kelvaney), Janet Leigh (Karen Stephanson), George Raft (Dan Beaumont), Steve Forrest (Eddie Kelvaney), Anne Francis (Nancy Corlane). With: Robert Ellenstein, Robert F. Simon, Anthony Ross, Alan Hale, Jr., Peter Brocco.

A rookie cop, Eddie Kelvaney is determined to regain his family's honor: his elder brother, Christopher, is a cop on the mob payroll. When Eddie witnesses a mob murder, events are put into motion which ultimately tests the reserve and loyalty of Chris Kelvaney. When Eddie refuses to lie to the police about the killing, the mob has him killed. Chris confronts the mobsters and, in the resulting gun battle, kills Beaumont, the leader of the gang. On the way to the hospital in an ambulance, the critically wounded Chris is told that he has restored the family honor.

MGM released relatively few *films noirs*. The company's production chiefs preferred safer, family fare and MGM's *noirs* are generally compromised by their extravagant production designs.

While it is not a classic, *Rogue Cop* is one of the studio's grittiest *films noirs*. It is an action oriented feature, with some extreme violence. Its characters are absolutely corrupt, with the exception of Eddie Kelvaney who gets killed for refusing to cooperate with the mobsters.

Robert Taylor and George Raft are at their best as the protagonist and antagonist of the film.

The director of *Rogue Cop*, Roy Rowland, also directed *Scene of the Crime*, another surprisingly hardboiled MGM *noir*.

Roman, Ruth (1924–)

Actress. Although she is all but forgotten today, Ruth Roman was a popular star in the 1940's, appearing in several successful films. She co-starred in a handful of *films noirs*, generally in second leads. Her most important *noir* role is as the murderous Mrs. Kellerton in *The Window*.

Filmography: *Beyond the Forest* (Warner Bros., 1949). *Champion* (United Artists, 1949). *The Window* (RKO, 1949). *Strangers on a Train* (Warner Bros., 1951).

Rooney, Mickey (Joe Yule) (1920–)

Actor. Mickey Rooney would, at first, hardly seem like a typical *noir* actor, but in fact, he was one of the most talented movie actors of his time. He could play many different kinds of roles, and appeared in several *films noirs*. In *Drive a Crooked Mile*, for example, he played a race car driver who falls victim to a *femme-fatale* and enters into a life of crime. He also starred in the title role of *Baby Face*

Nelson in which he was surprisingly vicious. Also, as a child he had a small role in the important crime melodrama, *Beast of the City*.

Filmography: *Beast of the City* (MGM, 1932). *The Strip* (MGM, 1951). *Drive a Crooked Mile* (Columbia, 1954). *Baby Face Nelson* (United Artists, 1957).

Rossen, Robert (1908–1966)

Writer, producer and director. Rossen was a man of many talents. As a screenwriter he wrote a number of excellent films including the late thirties gangster film *The Roaring Twenties* (Paramount, 1939); a superior war film, *A Walk in the Sun* (Paramount, 1946); and the classic *film noir*, *The Strange Love of Martha Ivers*. He directed three *films noirs*. *All the Kings Men* is balanced uneasily between social criticism and true *noir*. *Body and Soul*, however, remains one of the genre's classics. *Johnny O'Clock* is less memorable. All of his *noirs* are characterized by a strong visual sense and inventive camera work.

Filmography: *The Strange Love of Martha Ivers* (screenplay only) (Paramount, 1946). *Body and Soul* (Directed only) (United Artists, 1947). *Johnny O'Clock* (wrote/directed) (Columbia, 1947). *All the Kings Men* (wrote/produced, directed) (Columbia, 1949).

Rosson, Harold (1895–1960)

Cinematographer. Rosson, an expert at color cinematography, was the cinematographer on several early classic color films: *The Garden of Allah* (United Artists, 1936), *The Wizard of Oz* (MGM, 1939) and *On the Town* (MGM, 1949). He photographed two black and white *noirs*, including the classic *The Asphalt Jungle*.

Filmography: *Johnny Eager* (MGM, 1942). *The Asphalt Jungle* (MGM, 1951).

Rouse, Russell (1916–)

Screenwriter and director. Rouse, with Clarence Greene co-wrote several

hard-boiled melodramas including the classic *film noir*, *D.O.A.*. He also directed two additional minor *noirs*, both co-written with Greene. *The Thief* is a notable, if not completely successful experiment, a feature without dialog!

Filmography: *D.O.A.* (co-wrote only) (United Artists, 1950). *The Thief* (co-wrote/directed) (United Artists, 1952).

New York Confidential (co-wrote/directed) (Warner Bros., 1955).

Rowland, Roy (1910–)

Director. Rowland was a staff director at MGM in the forties and fifties. He directed many modest budget features for the studio including two minor, but enjoyable *films noirs*. He also directed the independently produced *Witness to Murder*. All three of his *noirs* are characterized by simple style and violent action.

Filmography: *The Scene of the Crime* (MGM, 1949). *Rogue Cop* (MGM, 1954). *Witness to Murder* (United Artists, 1954).

Rozsa, Miklos (1907–)

Composer. The Hungarian born Miklos Rozsa emigrated to the United States in 1940 and quickly became one of the leading film composers. He won three Academy Awards for his lush, neo-romantic scores, including one for a *film noir*, *A Double Life*. He composed the scores for many classic films including many *noirs*. Whatever the overall qualities of the films Rozsa's scores are always brilliant.

Filmography: *Double Indemnity* (Paramount, 1944). *The Killers* (Universal, 1946). *The Strange Love of Martha Ivers* (Paramount, 1946). *Brute Force* (Universal, 1947). *Criss Cross* (Universal, 1948). *A Double Life* (Universal, 1948). *Kiss the Blood Off My Hands* (Universal, 1948). *The Naked City* (Universal, 1948). *Secret Beyond the Door* (Universal, 1948). *The Bribe* (MGM, 1949). *The Asphalt Jungle* (MGM, 1950).

Russell, Gail (1924–1961)

Actress. Dark haired and extremely attractive, Gail Russell is a minor female icon of *film noir*. She had some of the same sensual exotic qualities as Joan Bennett, and like Bennett, played both *femme-fatales* and heroines. In the minor Alan Ladd vehicle, *Calcutta*, Russell co-starred as a particularly evil and avaricious *femme-fatale*. She was the innocent heroine in John Farrow's classic *Night Has a Thousand Eyes*.

Off camera, Russell was something of an enigma. Extremely eccentric, she was painfully shy and often fortified herself before going in front of a camera with large quantities of alcohol. When her fame proved fleeting, alcohol filled the void and she died at the age of thirty-six almost entirely forgotten.

Filmography: *Calcutta* (Paramount, 1947). *Night Has a Thousand Eyes* (Paramount, 1948). *Moonrise* (Republic, 1949). *The Tattered Dress* (Universal, 1957).

Russell, Jane (1921–)

Actress. Jane Russell is probably best known today as the star of Howard Hughes' exploitation-western, *The Outlaw* (United Artists, 1940) and her teaming with Marilyn Monroe in *Gentlemen Prefer Blondes* (20th Century-Fox, 1954). Her dark, voluptuous beauty was exploited in only two *films noirs*, but both are memorable. Her partner in both was Robert Mitchum and her wise-cracking, irreverent style was perfectly suitable to his. In both, which were overseen by her mentor Howard Hughes, she displayed her figure in tight dresses and talent as a singer. Always enjoyable on screen, Russell's roles in both were subordinate to Mitchum's, existing essentially as a Girl Friday.

Filmography: *His Kind of Woman* (RKO, 1951). *Macao* (RKO, 1952).

Rutherford, Ann (1917–)

Actress. Rutherford, like Evelyn Keyes, will be forever remembered as one of the younger sisters of Scarlet O'Hara in *Gone with the Wind* (MGM, 1939). Unlike Keyes, however, Rutherford did not make the transition from juvenile to mature roles well. She co-starred in a single, minor *noir*, with only a small role.

Filmography: *Inside Job* (Universal, 1946).

Ruttenberg, Joseph (1889–1983)

Cinematographer. In the late twenties until the early forties, Ruttenberg was one of the leading Hollywood cinematographers. He had a great sense of style—bright, but moody. He was the director of photography for several *films noirs*, all produced at the studio he was contracted to, MGM.

Filmography: *Fury* (MGM, 1936). *The Bribe* (MGM, 1949). *Side Street* (MGM, 1950). *Cause for Alarm* (MGM, 1951).

Ryan, Robert (1909–1973)

Actor. A versatile leading man and character actor, Robert Ryan's physical qualities were vaguely similar to Burt Lancaster's. Unlike Lancaster, however, Ryan never became a superstar, but he was always a compelling performer and he is one of *film noir*'s most important male icons.

Whether as the leading actor or second lead in his *films noirs*, Ryan's roles always embody the characteristics of the *noir* protagonist: caught up in a dangerous web of intrigue, murder and lust, unable to escape his inevitable doom.

Ryan's craggy, rough good looks and dark, mysterious eyes, meant that he could be cast as either hero or villain. However, his on screen intensity made him a natural villain and his most memorable performances in *film noir* were as psychotic bad guys.

The three outstanding Ryan villain performances are in *Crossfire, Beware, My Lovely* and *The Racket*. The latter is the most conventional role, but his performance in the film is one of *noir's* best. Ryan also played the villain, the oppressive millionaire Ohrlig, in Max Ophuls' neglected classic, *Caught*.

While he specialized in villainous roles, Ryan also played the occasional sympathetic part. Of these, the most memorable is in Nicholas Ray's *On Dangerous Ground*. Ryan starred as a hard-boiled city cop softened by the love of a kindly blind girl, played by Ida Lupino.

However, Ryan's best *noir* performance, indeed the performance of his career, was in the boxing melodrama *The Set-Up*. Ryan stars as Stoker Thompson, a washed up prize fighter who clings desperately to the dying hope that the heavyweight championship is just one punch away, while his private life collapses. Ryan brings considerable warmth and humanity to an unsympathetic part, demonstrating his extraordinary talents as an actor.

Filmography: *Crossfire* (RKO, 1947). *Johnny O'Clock* (Columbia, 1947). *Out of the Past* (RKO, 1947). *Berlin Express* (RKO, 1948). *Act of Violence* (MGM, 1949). *Caught* (MGM, 1949). *The Set-Up* (RKO, 1949). *The Racket* (RKO, 1951). *Beware, My Lovely* (RKO, 1952). *Clash by Night* (RKO, 1952). *On Dangerous Ground* (RKO, 1952). *House of Bamboo* (20th Century-Fox, 1955). *Odds Against Tomorrow* (United Artists, 1959).

Salter, Hans J. (1896–1988)

Composer. Salter composed scores for dozens of modest budget thrillers and melodramas, mainly for Universal. He composed the music for a number of important *films noirs*; his music, however, is rarely more than adequate.

Filmography: *Christmas Holiday* (Universal, 1944). *Phantom Lady* (Universal, 1944). *Scarlet Street* (Universal, 1945). *Uncle Harry* (Universal, 1945). *The Web* (Universal, 1947). *The Reckless Moment* (Columbia, 1949). *The Killer That Stalked New York* (Columbia, 1940).

Samuels, Lesser (1918–)

Screenwriter. Samuels co-wrote a number of films in the fifties. His most important collaboration was with Billy Wilder, with whom he co-wrote *The Big Carnival*. Samuels also co-wrote another *noir*, the little known but surprisingly good *The Long Wait*, adapted from a Mickey Spillane novel.

Filmography: *The Big Carnival* (co-wrote) (Paramount, 1951). *The Long Wait* (co-wrote) (Universal, 1954)

Sanders, George (1906–1972)

Character actor. A suave, well-groomed actor, the British born Sanders specialized in villains and scoundrels, with occasional heroes. He was the most memorable "Falcon", the debonair solver of crimes in a series of low budget comic/thrillers in the early forties. He co-starred in three *films noirs*, most memorable as a murderous villain in *Witness to Murder*.

Filmography: *Uncle Harry* (Universal, 1945). *Lured* (United Artists, 1947). *Witness to Murder* (United Artists, 1955).

Saville, Victor (1897–1979)

Director and producer. Saville made a number of distinguished films in his native Britain in the 1930's before coming to the United States in the forties. He directed only a handful of films after 1940, concentrating instead on production. He directed a minor *film noir*, *The Long Wait*, and produced Robert Aldrich's classic, *Kiss Me Deadly*.

Filmography: *The Long Wait* (directed) (United Artists, 1954). *Kiss Me Deadly* (produced) (United Artists, 1955).

Sawtell, Paul (1906–1971)

Composer. Sawtell was a prolific composer of scores for countless low budget films of all types including many *films noirs*. His music is rarely outstanding, but it is always appropriately dramatic.

Filmography: *Desperate* (RKO, 1947). *Bodyguard* (RKO, 1948). *Raw Deal* (Eagle-Lion, 1948). *T-Men* (Eagle-Lion, 1948). *Born to Kill* (RKO, 1950). *Southside 1–1000* (Allied Artists, 1950). *Another Man's Poison* (United Artists, 1952). *Kansas City Confidential* (United Artists, 1952).

Sawyer, Joe (1901–1982)

Character actor. The burly, gruff Sawyer specialized in policeman and army sergeants. He had small supporting roles in a number of *films noirs*, usually as a sidekick.

Filmography: *Deadline at Dawn* (RKO, 1946). *Gilda* (Columbia, 1946). *A Double Life* (Universal, 1948). *The Killing* (United Artists, 1955).

Scandal Sheet (Columbia, 1952). 82 min.

Producer: Edward Small. Director: Phil Karlson. Screenplay: Ted Sherdeman, Eugene Ling and James Poe, based on the novel *The Dark Page* by Samuel Fuller. Director of Photography: Burnett Guffey. Music: George Duning. Art Director: Robert Peterson. Editor: Jerome Thoms.

Cast: John Derek (Steve McCleary), Donna Reed (Julie Allison), Broderick Crawford (Mark Chapman), Rosemary DeCamp (Charlotte Grant), Henry O'Neill (Charlie Barnes). With: Henry Morgan, James Millican, Griff Barnett, Jonathan Hale, Pierre Watkin.

Steve McCleary is a reporter for the successful tabloid, *New York Express*, edited by Mark Chapman. Chapman has an argument with his estranged wife, strikes her and she falls, killing herself. Chapman sets up things to make it look like she drowned in her tub and escapes unseen. McCleary, with fellow reporter Julie Allison, cover the case. They eventually discover the link between Chapman and the dead woman. When they confront their beloved boss, Chapman holds them hostage with a gun, but is shot and killed by the police. Disillusioned,

McCleary writes Chapman's obituary for the paper's front page.

Phil Karlson's early *noir* is more in the tradition of 1940's *film noir* than his later *noirs* and the story, of course, is reminiscent of John Farrow's *The Big Clock* (Paramount, 1948). The difference lies with the tougher, hard-boiled characterizations familiar to Karlson's films. They are also familiar from Sam Fuller's films and the screenplay for this movie was faithfully adapted from his novel.

Scandal Sheet is a minor *film noir*, but it is well made and an interesting link between forties and fifties *films noirs*.

Scarlet Street (Universal, 1945). 102 min.

Executive Producer: Walter Wanger for Diana Productions. Producer and Director: Fritz Lang. Screenplay: Dudley Nichols, based on the novel *La Chienne* by Georges de la Foucharidiere in collaboration with Mouezy-Eon. Director of Photography: Milton Krasner. Music: Hans J. Salter. Art Director: Alexander Golitzen. Editor: Arthur Hilton.

Cast: Edward G. Robinson (Christopher Cross), Joan Bennett (Kitty March), Dan Duryea (Johnny Prince), Jess Barker (Janeway), Margaret Lindsay (Millie). With: Rosalind Ivan, Samuel S. Hinds, Arthur Loft, Vladimir Sokoloff, Charles Kemper.

Christopher Cross, a lonely man married to a shrewish wife and stuck in a dead end job, finds solace in his hobby as a painter. He becomes infatuated with a young model, Kitty March, and she believes he is a famous, wealthy painter. Egged on by her con man lover, Johnny Prince , Kitty convinces Cross to set her up in an apartment while he paints her portrait. Chris embezzles funds from the company where he works to pay for her apartment. He is happy for a time and his canvases suddenly enjoy some success— under Kitty's name. When he discovers he has been duped, however, he flies

Edward G. Robinson (right) in *Scarlet Street* **(Universal, 1945).**

into a rage and stabs Kitty to death. Johnny is convicted of her murder and is executed. Cross loses his job when the embezzlement is discovered and he slowly goes insane.

Scarlet Street is one of the bleakest of *films noirs*. Its characters are all corrupt and when Christopher Cross, a basically innocent man, succumbs to the corrupting forces of evil, embodied by Kitty March, the result is murder and psychological deterioration.

Joan Bennett's characterization of *noir's* ultimate *femme-fatale* is both seedy and seductive: Kitty is always portrayed in see-through clothes, lingerie, etc., and lounging on exotic furniture. She teases her prey, Christopher Cross, with sex but he never penetrates her body until he finally stabs her with his knife.

Edward G. Robinson's portrayal of Christopher Cross arouses both sympathy and contempt. He is the defini-

tive weakling, driven to his own destruction by his own cowardice.

The film was a remake of Jean Renoir's classic, *La Chienne* (France, 1931), but Lang infused the film with expressionist technique, giving it a different dimension than the earlier film. It is also notable as the first American film in which the murderer is not punished, at least in the conventional sense.

Scene of the Crime (MGM, 1949). 94 min.

Producer: Harry Rapf. Director: Roy Rowland. Screenplay: Charles Schnee, based on the short story "Smashing the Bookie Gang Marauders" by J. B. Martin. Director of Photography: Paul C. Vogel. Music: Andre Previn. Art Directors: Cedric Gibbons and Leonid Vasian. Editor: Robert J. Kern.

Cast: Van Johnson (Mike Conovan),

Gloria DeHaven (Lili), Tom Drake (C. C. Gordon), Arlene Dahl (Gloria Conovan), Leon Ames (Captain Forester), John McIntyre (Fred Piper). With: Norman Lloyd, Donald Woods, Richard Benedict, Anthony Caruso.

When police officer Mike Conovan's ex-partner is killed and $1,000 found on his body, Mike sets out to find his friend's killer and prove he was not taking bribes. With the aid of Lili, a stripper and gangster's moll, he tracks down the killers, a group of extortionists.

Van Johnson was hardly the type of actor one would associate with *film noir* and hard-boiled heroes. He holds his own, but it is Gloria DeHaven as the slutty Lili who stands out in the film.

Typical of Rowland's work, *Scene of the Crime* is simple and violent, surprisingly so for a studio that specialized in family fare. Indeed, the film is an admirable minor *noir* that manages to rise above mediocre by one good performance and an unpretentious approach.

Schaefer, Natalie (1912–1991)

Character actress. Schaefer will probably be forever remembered as Mrs. Lovey Howell on the cult television series, *Gilligan's Island*. She also appeared in a number of films including Anatole Litvak's *The Snake Pit* (Columbia, 1948) and two important *films noirs* and a third minor *noir*.

Filmography: *Secret Beyond the Door* (Universal, 1948). *Caught* (Columbia, 1949). *Female on the Beach* (Universal, 1955).

Schary, Dore (1905–1980)

Producer. Schary, a screenwriter and playwright, was for many years a successful producer and executive. In the late forties he was the production chief at RKO where his liberal political ideals infiltrated a number of the studio's productions in the era. His reign at RKO came to an end when the ultra

conservative Howard Hughes bought the studio in the late forties. He was the executive producer for three *films noirs*.

Filmography: *Crossfire* (RKO, 1947). *Berlin Express* (RKO, 1948). *They Live by Night* (RKO, 1949).

Schnee, Charles (1916–1963)

Screenwriter. Schnee won an Academy Award for his screenplay for the melodrama *The Bad and the Beautiful* (MGM, 1952). He wrote several *noir* screenplays, including Nicholas Ray's *They Live by Night*, a variation of the Bonnie and Clyde myth.

Filmography: *I Walk Alone* (Paramount, 1948). *They Live by Night* (RKO, 1948). *Scene of the Crime* (MGM, 1949).

Schoenfeld, Bernard ( )

Screenwriter. Schoenfeld co-wrote several good *films noirs*, including the early classic, *Phantom Lady*.

Filmography: *Phantom Lady* (Universal, 1944). *The Dark Corner* (20th Century–Fox, 1946). *Caged* (Warner Bros., 1950). *Macao* (RKO, 1952).

Schrader, Paul (1946–)

Screenwriter and director. Schrader is a leading American screenwriter from the mid-west whose screenplays are obsessed with the moral ambiguities and violence of the contemporary urban environment. His masterpiece is *Taxi Driver*, directed by Martin Scorsese. Schrader, who has written critical essays on *film noir*, is deeply influenced by the genre, as demonstrated also by his dark exposé of pornography, *Hardcore*.

Filmography: *Taxi Drive* (Columbia, 1976). *Hardcore* (Columbia, 1978).

Schulberg, Budd (1914–)

Novelist and screenwriter. Budd was the son of producer B. P. Schulberg, and grew up in Hollywood. He developed into a remarkable novelist in the late-forties whose themes of political and moral corruption are told in conventionally commercial stories. His best known novel is *On the Waterfront*, for which he also wrote the screenplay. His similar novel—also centered on boxing personalities—*The Harder They Fall*—was also adapted. The latter is generally considered a true *film noir*, but the former, with its expressionist style, its central character a disillusioned boxer and its theme of political corruption, qualifies it too as *film noir*.

Filmography: *On the Waterfront* (novel/screenplay) (Columbia, 1953). *The Harder They Fall* (original novel only) (Columbia, 1956).

Schuster, Harold (1902–)

Director. Schuster was a prolific director of "B" movies for Universal, 20th Century–Fox and Allied Artists His work is competent if not exceptional. He specialized in violent action pictures. He directed a single *film noir*.

Filmography: *Loophole* (Allied Artists, 1954).

Scorsese, Martin (1942–)

Director. A great technician, Scorsese depends on good screenwriters, but when he collaborates with a talent like Paul Schrader, the result can be extraordinary as it was with their *Taxi Driver*, perhaps the greatest post-*noir*. He also produced the excellent post-*noir*, *The Grifters*.

Filmography: *Taxi Driver* (Columbia, 1976). *The Grifters* (produced only) (Miramax, 1991).

Scott, Adrian (1912–1972)

Producer. As a producer of "B" features at RKO in the mid forties, Scott formed a partnership with director Edward Dmytryk. Together, with screenwriter John Paxton, they made three extraordinary *films noirs*: *Murder, My Sweet*, *Cornered* and *Crossfire*. Scott also produced *Deadline at Dawn*, another notable early *noir*. Like Dmytryk, Scott fell victim of the communist

witch hunt in the late forties and spent time in prison when he refused to testify against his friends.

Filmography: *Murder, My Sweet* (RKO, 1944). *Cornered* (RKO, 1945). *Deadline at Dawn* (RKO, 1946). *Crossfire* (RKO, 1947).

Scott, Lizabeth (Emma Matzo) (1922–)

Actress. Strong and sultry, with a deep, husky voice reminiscent of Lauren Bacall's, Lizabeth Scott was one of the most sensual screen stars of the 1940's. A contract player for Paramount, Scott appeared in several of that studio's major *films noirs*, and she is one of the genre's major female icons.

Lizabeth Scott's *noir* career began with the important *The Strange Love of Martha Ivers*. Scott's role was secondary, but she made a strong impression as a seductress used to entrap a man with whom she subsequently falls in love.

Scott was also a talented torch singer who displayed her abilities in several *films noirs*. In both *Dark City* and *The Racket* she played nightclub singers, and is particularly memorable in the latter as the sultry, elegant *chanteuse* in a romantic triangle with a sadistic mobster and the cop who is trying to bust up his organization.

Scott also played *femme-fatales* in three *films noirs: Pitfall*, *Too Late for Tears* and *Dead Reckoning*. Her *femme-fatale* in *Too Late for Tears* is one of the genre's most sadistic: the film begins after she has committed one murder and over the course of the rest of the movie she murders two other men.

Unfortunately, Lizabeth Scott retired from the screen relatively early. However, she will always be remembered for a handful of extraordinary performances and will remain one of *noir's* most indelible characters.

Filmography: *The Strange Love of Martha Ivers* (Paramount, 1946). *Dead Reckoning* (Columbia, 1947). *I Walk*

Alone (Paramount, 1948). *Pitfall* (United Artists, 1948). *Too Late for Tears* (United Artists, 1949). *Dark City* (Paramount, 1950). *The Racket* (RKO, 1951).

Scott, Martha (1914–)

Character actress. Scott was a Broadway veteran who was lured to Hollywood in the late thirties. She played second female leads in a variety of films with the occasional lead. She co-starred in a single, late *film noir*.

Filmography: *The Desperate Hours* (Paramount, 1955).

Scott, Zachary (1914–1965)

Actor. The Texas born Zachary Scott began his film career in the title role as the ruthless criminal in *The Mask of Dimitrios*. He also co-starred with Joan Crawford in *Mildred Pierce* as the amoral millionaire playboy Monte Beragon. A minor male *noir* icon, Scott also co-starred in two other, less memorable *films noirs*.

Filmography: *The Mask of Dimitrios* (Warner Bros., 1944). *Mildred Pierce* (Warner Bros., 1945). *Danger Signal* (Warner Bros., 1945). *Guilty Bystander* (Film Classics, 1950).

Scourby, Alexander (1913–1985)

Character actor. Scourby, who is best known for his mellifluous, resonant voice, appeared in dozens of films generally in small parts. He was the villain in the minor *noir*, *Affair in Trinidad*.

Filmography: *Affair in Trinidad* (Columbia, 1952).

Second Chance (RKO, 1953). 82 min.

Producer: Sam Wiesenthal. Director: Rudolph Maté. Screenplay: Oscar Millard and Sydney Boehm, story by D. M. Marshman Jr. Director of Photography: William Snyder. Music: Roy Webb. Music Director: Constantin Bakaleinikoff. Art Directors: Albert S. D'Agostino and Carroll Clark. Editor: Robert Ford.

Cast: Robert Mitchum (Russ Lambert), Linda Darnell (Clare Sheppard), Jack Palance (Cappy), Sandro Giglio (Conductor), Rudolofo Hoyos, Jr. (Vasco). With: Reginald Sheffield, Margaret Brewster, Roy Roberts, Salvador Baguez.

A prizefighter, Russ Lambert, embarks on a barnstorming tour of South American to forget an unfortunate ring experience in which his opponent was killed. He meets and falls for Clare, a gangster's moll who, like Russ, is trying for a second chance at life. Unfortunately, their plans are thwarted by Cappy, a hired killer who has been sent to eliminate the moll. The three principles end up on a crippled cable car, along with two tourists and some natives. The cat and mouse games come to an eventual end when the hired killer falls to his death after a fight with the ex-boxer and all are rescued.

In the early fifties, various experiments were introduced by the studios to counteract television's encroachment on their market. Howard Hughes, the then owner of RKO decided that Rudolph Maté's *Second Chance* would be his studio's first 3-D release. Unfortunately, even if it had been shot in black and white, it would have been a minor film, but it is interesting for its *noir* iconography including stars, writers and director. It points out further that black and white photography was a coincidence of time and that *film noir* was not exclusive to the duotone process.

The Second Woman (United Artists, 1951). 91 min.

Producers: Mort Briskin and Robert Smith. Director: James V. Kern. Screenplay: Robert Smith. Director of Photography: Hal Mohr. Music: Nat W. Finston. Editor: Walter Thompson.

Cast: Robert Young (Jeff Cohalan), Betsy Drake (Ellen Foster), John Sutton (Keith Ferris), Florence Bates (Amelia Foster), Morris Carnovsky (Dr. Hartley). With: Henry O'Neill,

Jean Rogers, Raymond Largay, Vici Raaf, Shirley Ballard.

Jeff Cohalan, a successful young architect, has a mental collapse. His girlfriend relates, through flashbacks, how he unnecessarily blames himself for the "accidental" death of his former fiancée, Vivian. Eventually, he confronts his past, realizing he is innocent.

The Second Woman is a low budget *noir*, distinguished largely by its excellent cinematography by the brilliant Hal Mohr. The film's screenplay, however, is rather confusing and the movie moves along at a slow, uninvolving pace.

Secret Beyond the Door (Universal, 1948). 98 min.

Executive Producer: Walter Wanger for Diana Productions. Producer and Director: Fritz Lang. Screenplay: Silvia Richards, based on the story "Museum Piece No. 13" by Rufus King. Director of Photography: Stanley Cortez. Music: Miklos Rosza. Art Director: Max Parker. Editor: Arthur Hilton.

Cast: Joan Bennett (Celia Lamphere), Michael Redgrave (Mark Lamphere), Anne Revere (Caroline Lamphere), Barbara O'Neil (Miss Roobey), Natalie Schaefer (Edith Potter). With: Paul Cavanaugh, Anabel Shaw, Rosa Ray, James Seay.

One of Fritz Lang's minor *films noirs*, *Secret Beyond the Door* is an image-laden version of the *Suspicion* type plot: in this case an heiress, Celia Lamphere, begins to suspect her new husband is a killer. While the plot was not particularly inventive, the style and narrative were extravagantly expressionist and wildly melodramatic. However, it is an interesting experiment, at times extraordinarily inventive and its performances are quite good.

Seitz, John F. (1893–1979)

Cinematographer. John Seitz was the younger brother of George Seitz, a successful director of action serials. John was a staff cinematographer for Paramount. Seitz was one of the great *noir* cinematographers, a master of light and shadow and a specialist of fog shrouded, rainy cityscapes and night photography. He was the director of photography for several classic *films noirs* including two collaborations with director Billy Wilder, *Double Indemnity* and *Sunset Boulevard*.

Filmography: *This Gun for Hire* (Paramount, 1942). *Double Indemnity* (Paramount, 1944). *Calcutta* (Paramount, 1947). *The Big Clock* (Paramount, 1948). *The Night Has a Thousand Eyes* (Paramount, 1948). *Chicago Deadline* (Paramount, 1949). *Sunset Boulevard* (Paramount, 1950). *Appointment with Danger* (Paramount, 1951). *Rogue Cop* (MGM, 1954).

Sekely, Steve (Istvan Szekely) (1899–1979)

Director. The Hungarian born Sekely's career began in Europe in the late twenties and he was still making films a few years before his death. He was a director of mostly "B" movies, his style distinguished by expressionist lighting and a distinctly Germanic sensibility. His single *noir*, *Hollow Triumph*, is a notable "B" *noir* with much in common with Edgar G. Ulmer.

Filmography: *Hollow Triumph* (Eagle-Lion, 1948).

Serial Killers

Far from being a recent phenomenon, serial killers and homicidal psychopaths have been with us from the dawn of civilization. Since the Victorian age and Jack the Ripper, the subject has become increasingly popular with novelists and filmmakers.

Beginning with Fritz Lang's *M* (UFA, 1931) serial murderers have been the subject of a number of *films noirs*. Indeed, the cycle began with *Stranger on the Third Floor* (RKO, 1940). which, like *M*, starred Peter Lorre as an infamous killer.

In Ida Lupino's *The Hitch-Hiker*

(RKO, 1953), two businessmen on a fishing trip find themselves held captive by a notorious serial killer.

In Alfred Hitchcock's *Suspicion* (RKO, 1941) a woman suspects her husband is a wife murderer. This woman in distress plot was reused in several *noirs* including *The Two Mrs. Carrolls* (Warner Bros., 1947) with Humphrey Bogart as the psychopath. In *Among the Living* (Paramount, 1940) and *The Tattooed Stranger* (RKO, 1950), the subject is a police hunt for a serial killer. Uniquely, in Fritz Lang's *While the City Sleeps* (RKO, 1956), the search for a serial killer by journalists is used as a device to criticize the media.

The Set-Up (RKO, 1949). 72 min.

Producer: Richard Goldstone. Director: Robert Wise. Screenplay: Art Cohn. Director of Photography: Milton Krasner. Music: Constantin Bakaleinikoff. Art Directors: Albert S. D'Agostino and Jack Okey. Editor: Roland Gross.

Cast: Robert Ryan (Stoker), Audrey Totter (Julie), George Tobias (Tiny), Alan Baxter (Little Boy), Wallace Ford (Gus), Percy Helton (Red). With: Hal Fieberling, Darryl Hickman, Kenny O. Morrison, James Edwards, David Clarke.

While his wife Julie waits in a shabby hotel room, Stoker, a thirty five year old prizefighter, past his prime, leaves to fight a match. Unknown to him, Stoker's manager Tiny, has arranged with the opposition, Stoker's defeat. Tiny does not believe that Stoker can win the fight against his younger opponent. However, Stoker does well and even looks like he might defeat his opponent. When Tiny tells him of the set-up, the disappointed Stoker fights even harder and wins the match. Afterward, he is cornered by two mob thugs who beat him unmercifully. Battered, his hands broken, Stoker nevertheless has his pride and he stumbles "home" to his wife.

The Set-Up is arguably the best boxing *noir*, with an extraordinary performance by Robert Ryan as the hapless Stoker. The simplicity of the story and the brevity of the film gives the viewer the feeling of getting small glimpse at a real man's life. Robert Wise's direction has rarely been more assured, and the cinematography and art direction are at their very best.

711 Ocean Drive (Columbia, 1950). 102 min.

Producer: Frank N. Seltzer. Director: Joseph M. Newman. Screenplay: Richard English and Francis Swan. Director of Photography: Franz Planer. Music: Sol Kaplan. Production Design: Perry Ferguson. Editor: Bert Jordan.

Cast: Edmond O'Brien (Mal Granger), Joanna Dru (Gail Mason), Donald Porter (Larry Mason), Sammy White (Chippie Evans), Dorothy Patrick (Trudy Maxwell). With: Barry Kelly, Otto Kruger, Howard St. John, Robert Osterloh, Bert Freed.

Mal Granger is a hard working and ingenious telephone repairman. One day he makes a repair call to a bookie joint run by Larry Mason and, impressed with his technical acumen, Mason and his partner persuade Granger to engineer a telephone wire service connecting all the West Coast tracks. Granger eventually takes over Mason's business and wife, but when the big mob bosses feel like he is getting too much power, they decide to freeze him out. Granger is killed and the mob retains power.

711 Ocean Drive is an interesting "B" *noir* about greed and obsession with success, another *noir* exposé of the American dream gone bad. It was made shortly after the release of *D.O.A.* (United Artists, 1949), which also starred Edmund O'Brien. While it is not a classic, *711 Ocean Drive* is distinguished by a straight forward, unsentimental script and a strong performance by O'Brien as the corrupted honest man.

Sex

In *film noir*, sexuality is rarely a liberating force, but rather a subverting, destructive force. The *femmefatale* is certainly the most explicit example of the image of destructive sexuality in *film noir*. While women might often appear in the genre as stereotypical sirens, it must be noted that the male characters are always willing "victims." Walter Neff in *Double Indemnity* (Paramount, 1944) and Jeff Bailey in *Out of the Past* (RKO, 1947), for example, are willing accomplices in their seduction and destruction. Indeed, for a genre whose most outstanding figures were political liberals, *film noir* is incredibly puritanical when it comes to sex.

Shadow of a Doubt (Universal, 1943). 108 min.

Producer: Jack H. Skirball. Director: Alfred Hitchcock. Screenplay: Thorton Wilder, Sally Benson and Alma Reville, story by Gordon McDonnell. Director of Photography: Joseph Valentine. Music: Dimitri Tiomkin. Art Directors: John B. Goodman and Robert Boyle. Editor: Milton Carruth.

Cast: Teresa Wright (Young Charlie), Joseph Cotten (Uncle Charlie), Macdonald Carey (Jack Graham), Henry Travers (Joseph Newton), Patricia Collinge (Emma Newton), Hume Cronyn (Herbie Hawkins). With: Edna Mae Wonacott, Wallace Ford, Irving Bacon, Charles Bates.

Uncle Charlie comes to Santa Rosa to visit his sister's family and elude two detectives on his trail. His sister Emma is married to Joseph Newman and they have a family of precocious children, including a teenage daughter, "Charlie," who idolizes her uncle. However, through a series of incidents, young Charlie begins to suspect Uncle Charlie is the "Merry Widow Killer" hunted by the police. Jack Graham, one of the trailing detectives, further convinces her that Uncle Charlie is probably the notorious serial killer.

Uncle Charlie, realizing his niece suspects him of being the murderer, tries unsuccessfully several times to kill her. The last attempt comes when he boards the train which will take him home. He tries to push her off the platform but in the struggle he himself falls in front of an on-rushing train and he is crushed to death. At the funeral, only young Charlie and the detective know the truth about Uncle Charlie.

Shadow of a Doubt, like all of Hitchcock's films, is a skillfully told story filled with dark humor and poetic ironies. However, its overpowering sense of guilt and betrayal, reinforced by Hitchcock's cool, detached style, qualifies it as an important early *film noir*.

Shakedown (Universal, 1950). 80 min.

Producer: Ted Richmond. Director: Joe Pevney. Screenplay: Alfred Lewis Levitt and Martin Goldsmith, story by Nat Dallinger and Don Martin. Director of Photography: Irving Glassberg. Music: Joseph Gershenson. Art Directors: Bernard Herzbrun and Robert Clatworthy. Editor: Milton Carruth.

Cast: Howard Duff (Jack Early), Brian Donlevy (Nick Palmer), Peggy Dow (Ellen Bennett), Lawrence Tierney (Colton), Bruce Bennett (David Glover). With: Anne Vernon, Stapleton Kent, Peter Virgo, Charles Sherlock, Will Lee.

Newspaper photographer Jack Early will stop at nothing to rise to the top of his profession. He collaborates with a racketeer to photograph and then blackmail another crook into turning over a large portion of some stolen money. The mob sends a killer to take Early out and succeeds in his mission, but Early manages to snap a photograph of his killer, thus ensuring that he too will be caught and punished.

Shakedown is a typical Universal *noir*. Filmed on a low budget, the sets are minimalist, the script corny, the plot improbable, but the violent action keeps the film moving. A minor film,

Joseph Cotten, Teresa Wright in *Shadow of a Doubt* (Universal, 1943).

Shakedown is interesting mainly because of its performances and production values.

Shamroy, Leon (1901–1974)

Cinematographer. Shamroy was a major cinematographer whose work includes a number of important films from the late thirties. He won an Academy Award for his work on the color *film noir*, *Leave Her to Heaven*. He was also the director of photography on Fritz Lang's seminal *noir*, *You Only Live Once*. However, Shamroy was an expert at color photography and worked on many of 20th Century–Fox's musicals and family pictures and the following are his only *films noirs*.

Filmography: *You Only Live Once* (United Artists, 1937). *Leave Her to Heaven* (20th Century-Fox, 1945).

Shane, Maxwell (1905-1983)
Screenwriter and director. Shane was a successful publicist before taking up screenwriting in the forties. As a director, he had a great sense of style, as demonstrated in an extraordinary "B" *noir*, *Fear in the Night* and its remake, *Nightmare*. Unfortunately, he never broke out of "B" productions.

Filmography: *Fear in the Night* (wrote/directed) (Paramount, 1947). *The Naked Street* (co-wrote/directed) (United Artists, 1955). *Nightmare* (wrote/directed) (United Artists, 1956).

The Shanghai Gesture (United Artists, 1941). 106 min.
Producer: Arnold Pressburger. Director: Josef Von Sternberg. Screenplay: Josef Von Sternberg, Karl Vollmoeller, Geza Herczeg and Jules Furthman, based on the play by John Colton. Director of Photography: Paul Ivano. Music: Richard Hageman. Art Director: Boris Leven. Editor: Sam Winston.

Cast: Gene Tierney (Poppy), Walter Huston (Sir Guy Charteris), Victor Mature (Dr. Omar), Ona Mundson (Mother Gin Sling), Phyllis Brooks (Dixie Pomeroy). With: Albert Basserman, Maria Ouspenskaya, Eric Blore, Ivan Lebedeff, Mike Mazurki, Clyde Fillmore.

Mother Gin Sling is the owner of a Shanghai casino which British financier, Sir Guy Charteris, wants closed down—he has his own plans for the property. Gin Sling investigates Charteris's past and learns that as a young man he had married a woman in China and then fled with her money after the birth of a daughter. That daughter, Poppy, is now a habitue of Gin Sling's establishment. Gin Sling and her associates encourage Poppy to run up her gambling debts.

Charteris discovers that Poppy is his daughter. In order to get her out of the corrupt environment of Mother Sling's world, Charteris meets with Gin Sling to hear her blackmail demands. Ultimately, she admits that she, in fact, was the wife he left behind. Charteris is shocked, telling her he believed she had died in an incident after committing adultery with another man. Poppy, however is unable to accept that the cruel Gin Sling is her mother. When she hysterically denounces her, Gin Sling loses control and shoots her.

The Shanghai Gesture is one of the first true *films noirs*. It was adapted from a notorious Broadway play, but lost none of its melodramatic power in translation. Still, it must be noted that a number of important changes were undertaken to skirt the Hays office censorship. In the play, for example, Mother Gin Sling was known as Mother Goddamn. In addition, the establishment was changed from a whorehouse to a casino, although the true nature of the casino is barely disguised.

Josef Von Sternberg created a nightmarish, almost Baroque style which combined elements of expressionism and Art Deco in an exotic, sensual locale.

Gene Tierney made an early *noir* appearance in the film as the pivotal Poppy. Her exotic features typecast her early on as an ethnic, usually oriental, before *Laura* (20th Century-Fox, 1944) helped her break out of the mold.

Sharp, Henry (1892-1966)
Cinematographer. Sharp's career began in the silent era and his filmography includes several major silent movies. His style was rather conventional and he worked on mostly uninventive commercial films—comedies and romantic dramas. However, he was the cinematographer for the early Fritz Lang directed *noir* classic, *Ministry of Fear*. His work on *The Guilty* was less interesting.

Filmography: *Ministry of Fear* (Paramount, 1944). *The Guilty* (Monogram, 1947).

Victor Mature, Gene Tierney in *The Shanghai Gesture* **(United Artists, 1941).**

Sheppard, John (1907–1983)

Actor. Sheppard was usually seen as the cultivated, gentlemanly type in countless films. However, he appeared in only one *film noir*.

Filmography: *Strange Triangle* (20th Century–Fox, 1946).

Sheridan, Ann (Clara Lou Sheridan) (191–1967).

Actress. A native of Denton, Texas, Ann Sheridan was known for her striking red hair, expressive eyes and sense of humor. Although her career in movies began in 1934, she did not achieve real stardom until the 1940's. Although she was particularly adept at comedy, she played all types of parts. She starred in two *films noirs*, the most important of which is *Nora Prentiss* as a nightclub singer who has an affair with a successful doctor that eventually leads to tragedy.

Filmography: *Nora Prentiss* (Warner Bros., 1947). *Woman on the Run* (Universal, 1950).

Sherman, Vincent (Abram Orovitz) (1906–)

Director. Vincent Sherman was an efficient, competent, but generally uninspired director. He worked chiefly for Columbia and Warner Bros., making mostly "B" movies. He directed several modest *films noirs*, including *The Garment Jungle* which was initiated and co-directed, without credit, by Robert Aldrich. However, Sherman's best *noir* is *Nora Prentiss*, a dark, improbable but still fascinating melodrama.

Filmography: *Nora Prentiss* (Warner Bros., 1947). *Backfire* (Warner Bros., 1950). *The Damned Don't Cry* (Warner Bros., 1950). *Affair in Trinidad* (Columbia, 1952). *The Garment Jungle* (Columbia, 1957).

Shield for Murder (United Artists, 1954). 80 min.

Producer: Aubrey Schenk. Directors: Edmond O'Brien and Howard W. Koch. Screenplay: Richard Alan Simmons and John C. Higgins, adapted by Richard Alan Simmons from the novel by William P. McGivern. Director of Photography: Gordon Avil. Music: Paul Dunlap. Editor: John F. Schreyer.

Cast: Edmond O'Brien (Barney Nolan), Marla English (Patty Winters), John Agar (Mark Brewster), Emile Meyer (Capt. Gunnarson), Carolyn Jones (Girl at bar). With: Claude Akins, Larry Ryle, Herbert Butterfield, Hugh Sanders.

Barney Nolan is a corrupt policeman who murders a small time hood and steals $25,000 from him. His justification that the killing was in the line of duty convinces his superiors. However, an elderly man witnessed the crime and Nolan decides he has to be eliminated and then Nolan discovers he is the target of mob revenge. Meanwhile, the police learn that Nolan is the killer and surround the house he is hiding out in. When Nolan tries to escape he is gunned down in the shoot out.

Starring and co-directed by minor *noir* icon Edmond O'Brien, *Shield for Murder* is a typical transitional *noir* that exploits the growing public interest in crooked cops, and the simpler style of *noir* filmmaking. The film concentrates on violence and action, but suffers somewhat from the sketchy characterizations.

Shock (20th Century–Fox, 1946). 70 min.

Producer and Director: Alfred Werker. Screenplay: Eugene Ling, story by Alfred DeMond. Directors of Photography: Glen MacWilliams and Joe MacDonald. Music: David Buttolph. Art Director: Leland Fuller. Editor: Harmon Jones.

Cast: Vincent Price (Dr. Cross), Lynn Bari (Elaine Jordan), Frank Latimer (Lt. Paul Stewart), Anabel Shaw (Janet Street), Reed Hadley (O'Neil). With: Michael Dunne, René Carson, Charles Trobridge.

Elaine Jordan is on vacation when she witnesses a murder and becomes the target of the killers.

Shock is a minor *noir* thriller that suffers mainly from uninspired direction. Vincent Price, however, as the main villain, is typically brilliant.

Shockproof (Columbia, 1949). 79 min.

Producer: S. Sylvan Simon. Director: Douglas Sirk. Screenplay: Helen Deutsch and Samuel Fuller, story by Samuel Fuller. Director of Photography: Charles Lawton. Music: George Duning. Art Director: Walter Holscher. Editor: Harry Gerstad.

Cast: Cornel Wilde (Griff Marat), Patricia Knight (Jenny Marsh), John Baragrey (Harry Wesson), Esther Minciotti (Mrs. Marat), Howard St. John (Sam Brooks).

Griff Marat, an honest parole officer, falls in love with the corrupt but beautiful Jenny Marsh and is slowly pulled into her life of crime until, trapped, he cannot escape.

Predictable and at times silly, *Shockproof* is also a compelling, forceful "B" melodrama. Its low budget does not compromise its drama and Douglas Sirk's direction is assured and occasionally inspired.

Side Street (MGM, 1950). 83 min.

Producer: Sam Zimbalist. Director: Anthony Mann. Screenplay: Sydney Boehm. Director of Photography: Joseph Ruttenberg. Music: Lennie Hayton. Art Directors: Cedric Gibbons and Daniel B. Cathcart. Editor: Conrad A. Nervig.

Cast: Farley Granger (Joe Norson), Cathy O'Donnell (Ellen Norson), James Craig (George Garsell), Paul Kelly (Capt. Walter Anderson), Edmon Ryan (Victor Backett), Jean Hagen (Harriet Sinton). With: Paul Harvey, Charles McGraw, Ed Max,

Adele Jergens, Whit Bissell, Esther Somers.

Joe Norson, a private mail carrier, steals an envelope full of money from an office on his route. Unfortunately, the money is a payoff in a blackmail scheme that involves several murders. At first, Norson is able to use the money to help him construct a dream world for he and his wife. However, several hoodlums eventually find him, force him to reveal where he hid the money and set in motion his desperate attempts to undo his crime. Norson is hunted by the criminals and the police. He is captured by the crooks who plan to kill him, but he is rescued by the police after a high speed chase through New York City. Although wounded, Norson is reunited with his wife and family.

Cathy O'Donnell and Farley Granger were re-teamed after the great success of *They Live by Night* and the result is a taut, unpretentious thriller. O'Donnell has little to do in the film but Granger is good as the basically honest middleclass man whose one dishonest act sends him into a nightmare world of violence and revenge. Although a minor *noir*, *Side Street* is an exciting, effective thriller.

Sidney, Silvia (Sophie Kosow) (1910–)
Actress. A pretty, waif-like actress, Sidney was a major star in the thirties. She was almost always seen as the poor but proud girl, suffering any number of indignities, or the innocent stand-by-your-man roles, exactly the sort she played in the two films directed by Fritz Lang, both seminal *noirs*.

Filmography: *Fury* (MGM, 1936). *You Only Live Once* (United Artists, 1937).

Siegel, Don (1912–1991)
Director. One of the most durable and admirable directors of strong action films, Don Siegel offers a dark vision of American life: the American dream subverted by a contemporary nightmare of urban violence and corruption.

Siegel began his film career as an editor working on, among other things, Orson Welles' classic *Citizen Kane* (RKO, 1942). He began directing in the late forties.

The Big Steal, one of Siegel's early features, was an attempt to cash in on the success of *Out of the Past* (RKO, 1947). Like the early classic, *The Big Steal* stars Robert Mitchum and Jane Greer, but the latter film is an unpretentious chase film, concentrating on action and romance. While it is not a truly great film, *The Big Steal* is an admirable addition to the genre.

In the fifties, Siegel directed three interesting "B" *noirs*: *Private Hell, 36*, *Baby Face Nelson* and *The Line Up*. Each is characterized by a simple, direct style and concentration on swift action. This period also includes Siegel's excellent prison melodrama and sometimes described as a *film noir*, *Riot in Cell Block 11* (Allied Artists, 1954) and the science-fiction classic, *Invasion of the Body Snatchers* (Allied Artists, 1956), written by *Out of the Past* author Daniel Mainwaring.

In the late sixties, Siegel returned to the themes of his earlier films with *Madigan*, a superior post-*noir* police thriller, but it is *Dirty Harry* on which Siegel's reputation rests. Arguably his masterpiece, it is both an entertaining thriller and a dark exposé of contemporary urban America.

Filmography: *The Big Steal* (RKO, 1949). *Private Hell,36* (Filmmakers, 1954). *Baby Face Nelson* (United Artists, 1957). *The Line Up* (RKO, 1958). *Madigan* (Universal, 1968). *Dirty Harry* (Warner Bros., 1971).

Siegel, Sol C. (1903–1982)
Producer. Siegel was one of the most successful producers of his time, producing many high quality movies beginning in 1929. He produced several important *films noirs*.

Filmography: *Among the Living*

(Paramount, 1941). *Cry of the City* (20th Century-Fox, 1948). *House of Strangers* (20th Century-Fox, 1949). *Panic in the Streets* (20th Century-Fox, 1950).

Silliphant, Stirling (1918–)

Screenwriter and producer. In the sixties, Silliphant created several immensely successful television series including *Naked City*, based on the *film noir* classic. A distinguished screenwriter of mostly unpretentious commercial films, Silliphant wrote two *films noirs*.

Filmography: *Nightfall* (Columbia, 1957). *The Line Up* (Columbia, 1958).

Simmons, Jean (1929–)

Actress. Delicately beautiful, the British born Jean Simmons was a major star in her native country in the forties. In 1950 she married Stewart Granger and moved wih him to the United States. In Otto Preminger's *Angel Face*, Simmons stars as Diane Tremayne, the spoiled rich girl with murder in her heart. An extraordinary performance, it was her only *noir* appearance.

Filmography: *Angel Face* (RKO, 1953).

Singapore (Universal, 1947). 79 min.

Producer: Seton I. Miller. Director: John Brahm. Screenplay: Seton I. Miller and Robert Thoeren, story by Seton I. Miller. Director of Photography: Maury Gertsman. Music: Daniele Amfitheotrof. Editor: William Hornbeck.

Cast: Fred MacMurray (Mat Gordon), Ava Gardner (Linda), Roland Culver (Michael Van Leyden), Richard Hadyn (Chief Inspector Hewitt), Spring Byington (Mrs. Bellows), Thomas Gomez (Mr. Mauribus), Porter Hall (Mr. Bellows).

Mat Gordon returns to Singapore, after serving in the Navy during World War II, to resume his career as a pearl smuggler. He discovers that his wife,

Linda, who was presumed to have been killed in a Japanese air raid, is very much alive, but in the grip of amnesia. Mat eventually discovers that Linda's new husband, Michael Van Leyden, is a crook attempting to find out where Mat has allegedly hidden a cache of pearls. In the end, all is resolved to Mat and Linda's favor and they are reunited.

Singapore is a trifle that is notable mainly for its exotic setting, its always gorgeous female lead, and its director John Brahm. Unfortunately, despite some good sequences, the film fails in comparison to Brahm's other *noir* productions. The main problem with the film is its contrived screenplay, but the film remains a must-see for Brahms fans.

Siodmak, Curt (1902–)

Screenwriter. The younger brother of Robert Siodmak, Curt was a master of macabre fiction and his screenplays almost all fall into the horror genre: *Frankenstein Meets the Wolf Man* (Universal, 1942), *Son of Dracula* (Universal, 1943) and *The Beast with Five Fingers* (Universal, 1947). He also contributed original stories that were turned by others into full screenplays, including the original story for Jacques Tourneur's *Berlin Express*.

Filmography: *Berlin Express* (story only) (RKO, 1948).

Siodmak, Robert (1900–1973)

Director. With Fritz Lang, Robert Siodmak was the most prolific of the great *film noir* directors. Although he directed a variety of films, Siodmak was at his best when evoking the dark world of *film noir*, and he made some of the genre's greatest films.

Born in Tennessee, Siodmak was raised in Germany. He entered the German film industry in the early 1920's, but he did not establish himself as a top director until the brilliant satire *People on Sunday* (Filmstudio, 1929), co-written by his brother Carl and Billy

Wilder. His assistant directors on the film were Edgar G. Ulmer and Fred Zinnemann and all except Carl would become important *noir* directors.

After 1933, with the rise of Adolf Hitler, the Jewish Siodmak lived and worked for a time in France where he first demonstrated a talent for cerebral thrillers.

His American career got off to a slow start, but Siodmak eventually established himself with the minor horror classic, *Son of Dracula* (Universal, 1943), written by his brother, Carl.

After directing another horror film, Siodmak made *Phantom Lady*, his first *noir* classic. A box office hit, it helped kick off the genre and firmly established his expressionist-influenced style.

Phantom Lady was followed by several interesting *films noirs* including a superior thriller, *The Spiral Staircase*. However, it is with *The Killers* that Siodmak's reputation rests. One of the genre's great classics, *The Killers*, with all the requisite character types and extravagant style.

Although less well known, Siodmak's *Criss Cross* is equally admirable. Like *The Killers* the film stars Burt Lancaster in yet another *noir* tale of a basically honest man who is tempted into a life of crime by a beautiful, amoral woman.

After 1950, Siodmak's career went into decline. He continued to direct over the next seventeen years, but few of his later films are of more than moderate interest at best. Still, during the five or six years when he was at his best, Robert Siodmak directed his share of classic *films noirs,* and he ranks as one of the genre's great directors.

Filmography: *Christmas Holiday* (Universal, 1944). *Phantom Lady* (Universal, 1944). *Uncle Harry* (Universal, 1945). *The Dark Mirror* (Universal, 1946). *The Killers* (Universal, 1946). *The Spiral Staircase* (RKO, 1946). *Cry of the City* (20th Century-Fox, 1948). *Criss Cross* (Universal,

1949). *The File on Thelma Jordan* (Paramount, 1950).

Sirk, Douglas (Detlef Sierck) (1900–)
Director. Sirk has a huge cult following, particularly in Europe, largely because of his lush color melodramas of the fifties: *Magnificent Obsession* (Universal, 1954), *Written on the Wind* (Universal, 1957) and *Imitation of Life* (Universal, 1959). His earlier low budget *films noirs* are less well known, but are equally well made. Of the three *noirs*, *Shockproof* is probably the best. Like his later films his *noirs* are centered around female characters.

Filmography: *Lured* (United Artists, 1947). *Sleep, My Love* (United Artists, 1949). *Shockproof* (Columbia, 1949).

Skinner, Frank (1898–1968)
Composer. Skinner was a staff composer for Universal where he composed music for mostly routine productions including Abbott and Costello comedies, dramas and some mostly minor *films noirs*.

Filmography: *Black Angel* (Universal, 1946). *Inside Job* (Universal, 1946). *Ride the Pink Horse* (Universal, 1947). *The Naked City* (co-composed) (Universal, 1948). *One Way Street* (Universal, 1950). *The Sleeping City* (Universal, 1950). *Forbidden* (Universal, 1954).

Sleep, My Love (United Artists, 1948). 96 min.

Producer: Charles Buddy Rogers and Ralph Cohn. Director: Douglas Sirk. Screenplay: St. Clair McKelway and Leo Rosten, with contributions from Cyril Endfield and Decla Dunning, based on the novel by Leo Rosten. Director of Photography: Joseph Valentine. Music: Rudy Schrager. Art Director: William Ferrari. Editor: Lynn Harrison.

Cast: Claudette Colbert (Alison Courtland), Robert Cummings (Bruce Elcott), Don Ameche (Richard Courtland), Rita Johnson (Barby), George Coulouris (Charles Verney), Ralph

Colleen Gray and Richard Conte from *The Sleeping City* **(Universal, 1950).**

Morgan (Dr. Rhinehart). With: Hazel Brooks, Queenie Smith, Keye Luke, Fred Nurvey, Raymond Burr.

Alison Courtland is startled when she wakes up aboard a night train to Boston, because she cannot remember leaving her home in New York City. When she returns home to her husband Richard, she sets into motion a series of strange events. Her husband, in fact, has been trying to kill her and through drugs and hypnosis, convince her to kill her psychiatrist, Dr. Rhinehart. She is eventually saved by another man, Elcott, who has fallen in love with her.

Sleep, My Love combines several *noir* elements including hypnosis, hallucinations and the "woman-in-distress" whose husband is secretly planning to kill her. Director Douglas Sirk creates a dark, shadowy film that echoes the female character's dilemma, but unfortunately Claudette Colbert's performance is rather dull and unconvincing.

The Sleeping City (Universal, 1950). 85 min.

Producer: Leonard Goldstein. Director: George Sherman. Screenplay: Jo Eisinger. Director of Photography: William Miller. Music: Frank Skinner. Art Directors: Bernard Herzbrun and Emrich Nicholson. Editor: Frank Gross.

Cast: Richard Conte (Fred Rowan), Coleen Gray (Ann Sebastian), Peggy Dow (Kathy Hall), John Alexander (Inspector Gordon), Alex Nicol (Dr. Bob Anderson). With Richard Taber, James J. Van Dyk, Hugh Reilly, Michael Strong, Frank M. Thomas.

Fred Rowan, an undercover cop, enters Bellevue Hospital as an intern to find out who has murdered another intern and stolen narcotics. He eventually discovers a gang of drug dealers run by an elderly elevator operator and breaks up their operation.

The Sleeping City is a slight film interesting mainly for its semi-documentary style and setting in the real life Bellevue Hospital. Unfortunately, the script often resorts to cliches in its depiction of mental patients. The performances by Richard Conte and Coleen Gray (as a nurse, snared into the illegal drug trafficking) are very good, but do not help the film rise above the mediocre.

Slightly Scarlet (RKO, 1956). 99 min.

Producer: Benedict Bogeaus. Director: Allan Dwan. Screenplay: Robert Blees, based on the novel *Love's Lovely Counterfeit* by James M. Cain. Director of Photography: John Alton. Music: Louis Forbes. Art Director: Van Nest Polglase. Editor: James Leicester.

Cast: John Payne (Ben Grace), Arlene Dahl (Dorothy Lyons), Rhonda Fleming (June Lyons), Kent Taylor (Jansen), Ted DeCorsia (Sol Caspar). With: Lance Fuller, Buddy Baer, Frank Gerstle, Ellen Corby.

Slightly Scarlet was another look at government corruption. John Payne stars as Ben Grace, a mayoral assistant who realizes that the city government is completely corrupt and sets out to depose the gang of racketeers, thus bringing back clean government.

Robert Blees' screenplay was based on one of James M. Cain's least important novels and he was smart enough to add large quantities of violence. John Alton, shooting in technicolor, perfectly translated the characteristics of black and white *noir* cinematography into color, but the film remains a minor one.

Sloane, Everett (1909–1965)

Character actor. Sloane, a protegé of Orson Welles and a member of his Mercury Productions, went to Hollywood with Welles in the early forties and co-starred in *Citizen Kane* (RKO, 1942). He continued to play small supporting roles in major films and co-starred in several *films noirs* including Welles' *Journey Into Fear* and *The Lady from Shanghai*.

Filmography: *Journey Into Fear* (RKO, 1943). *The Lady from Shanghai* (Columbia, 1948). *The Enforcer* (Warner Bros., 1951). *The Big Knife* (United Artists, 1955).

Smith, Robert (1911–)

Screenwriter. Smith co-wrote many films in the late forties and early fifties. He co-wrote several *films noirs*.

Filmography: *I Walk Alone* (co-wrote) (Paramount, 1948). *The Second Woman* (co-wrote) (United Artists, 1951). *Sudden Fear* (co-wrote) (RKO, 1952). *99 River Street* (co-wrote) (United Artists, 1953).

The Sniper (Columbia, 1952). 87 min.

Producer: Stanley Kramer. Director: Edward Dmytryk. Screenplay: Harry Brown, story by Edna and Edward Anhalt. Director of Photography: Burnett Guffey. Music: George Antheil. Art Director: Walter Holscher. Editor: Aaron Stell.

Cast: Adolphe Menjou (Lt. Kafka), Arthur Franz (Eddie Miller), Gerald Mohr (Sgt. Ferris), Marie Windsor (Jean Darr), Frank Faylen (Inspector Anderson), Richard Kiley (Dr. James G. Kent). With: Mabel Paige, Marlo Dwyer, Geraldine Carr, Jay Novello, Ralph Peters, Max Palmer.

Eddie Miller, a mentally unstable young man, feels compelled to kill women. He shoots them from the roof tops of tall buildings around the city. Lt. Kafka is assigned to the case and as his investigation brings him closer to the killer, he begins to realize that the motives of the sniper are psychological. When the police finally track down Miller to a small, seedy hotel, they break into his room. He offers no resistance and a solitary tear of relief falls down his cheek.

Producer Stanley Kramer was interested primarily in addressing social concerns in his films and this is no less true of *The Sniper*. The film was one of the first to probe the psychology of a serial killer. Edward Dmytryk—here returning to American films after being blackballed during the McCarthy witch hunt — gives the film a *noir* ambiance, but its psychological and social concerns almost subverts the *noir* feel. Indeed, the film has much more in common with Elia Kazan's *noirs* than the other more unpretentious films of the genre.

So Dark the Night (Columbia, 1946). 70 min.

Producer: Ted Richmond. Director: Joseph H. Lewis. Screenplay: Martin Berkeley and Dwight V. Babcock, story by Aubrey Wisberg. Director of Photography: Burnett Guffey. Music: Morris W. Stoloff and Hugo Friedhofer. Art Director: Carl Anderson. Editor: Jerome Thoms.

Cast: Steven Geray (Henri Cassin), Micheline Cheirel (Nannette Michand), Eugene Borden (Pierre Michaud), Ann Codee (Mama Michaud), Egon Brecher (Dr. Boncourt). With: Helen Freeman, Theodore Gottlieb, Gregory Gay, Jean Del Val, Paul Marion.

Henri Cassin, a top Paris police detective, takes his first vacation in eleven years. At a small country inn he meets and is immediately attracted to the beautiful Nanette Michaud. Eventually they marry, despite the reservations of her mother and her other boyfriend. When Nanette's body is found floating in the river, it is discovered that she has been strangled. An investigation eventually reveals Henri as a split personality who murdered his wife in an act of jealousy. Just as he is about to kill Mama Michand, the police arrive and shoot Henri through the window.

So Dark the Night was Joseph H. Lewis' second *film noir*. Its European setting is, of course, generally alien to the genre and would completely disappear in a year or so. However, the film's overwhelming cynicism and strong, typically extravagant style qualify it as a unique and fascinating addition to the genre.

Somewhere in the Night (20th Century–Fox, 1946). 110 min.

Producer: Anderson Lawler. Director: Joseph L. Mankiewicz. Screenplay: Howard Dimsdale and Joseph L. Mankiewicz, adapted by Lee Strasberg from a story by Marvin Borowsky. Director of Photography: Norbert Brodine. Music: David Buttolph. Art Directors: James Basevi and Maurice Ransford. Editor: James B. Clark.

Cast: John Hodiak (George Taylor), Nancy Guild (Christy Smith), Lloyd Nolan (Lt. Donald Kendall), Richard Conte (Mel Phillips), Josephine Hutchinson (Elizabeth Conroy). With: Margo Wood, Sheldon Leonard, Lou Nova, John Russell, Houseley Stevenson.

George Taylor, an ex-marine, is a victim of amnesia. He has only two clues to his past: a bitter letter from a girl who hated him and another equally mysterious letter signed "Larry Cravat." Taylor goes to Los Angeles to find Cravat, but his presence seems to attract malevolent attention wherever he goes. With the help of a beautiful nightclub singer, Christy Smith, he discovers that he, in fact, is Cravat and was involved in the robbery of $2,000,000. His old partner, Mel Phillips, has been following him since his arrival in Los Angeles to find the hidden cash. When Taylor/Cravat does find the money, Phillips demands he give it to him; but Taylor leads Phillips into a police trap and Phillips is killed. Taylor and Christy are thus free to start a new life.

Somewhere in the Night is the quintessential amnesia *noir*. The film stars two interesting minor *noir* icons, John Hodiak and Richard Conte and has a strong performance from Lloyd Nolan as the policeman who helps Taylor find his true identity. The improbabilities of the screenplay are overcome by the strong performances and by Joseph L. Mankiewicz's excellent direction.

Sorry, Wrong Number (Paramount, 1948). 89 min.

Producers: Hal B. Wallis and Anatole Litvak. Director: Anatole Litvak. Screenplay: Lucille Fletcher, based on her radio play. Director of Photography: Sol Polito. Music: Gene Merritt and Walter Oberst. Art Directors: Hans Dreier and Earl Hedrick. Editor: Warren Low.

Cast: Barbara Stanwyck (Leona Stevenson), Burt Lancaster (Henry Stevenson), Ann Richards (Sally Lord Dodge), Wendell Corey (Dr. Alexander), Harold Vermilyea (Waldo Evans). With: Leif Erickson, William Conrad, John Bromfield, Jimmy Hunt, Dorothy Neumann.

Leona Stevenson is an invalid heiress who lives alone in her New York apartment. One evening, because of crossed wires, she overhears two men on the telephone planning to kill a woman. She calls the police but they tell her they cannot investigate on the little information she gives them.

In fact, the two men planning the murder is her henpecked husband and a man called Moreno who is blackmailing Henry into helping kill Leona so that Henry can inherit her wealth. Henry, however, tries to call off the plans when he learns that Leona's condition is psychosomatic. Moreno convinces Henry to leave town and sets up the murder to look like a burglary-murder. Henry has a change of heart and calls his wife to warn her. She answers, but it is too late and drops the phone when attacked. Several seconds later the receiver is picked up and a man replies, "wrong number."

As Henry leaves the phone booth, he is arrested by the police who have learned of the murder plot.

Sorry, Wrong Number is a skillful thriller in the style of Alfred Hitchcock. Director Anatole Litvak creates a dark, mysterious atmosphere through expressionist and semi-surrealistic devices. Leona Stevenson, interestingly, is not just a victim of a plot against her, but of her own psychological problems: like all true *noir* protagonists, a victim of her own weakness.

Southside 1-1000 (Allied Artists, 1950). 73 min.

Producers: Maurice and Frank King. Director: Boris Ingster. Screenplay: Leo Townsend and Boris Ingster, story by Milton M. Raison and Bert C. Brown. Director of Photography: Russell Harlan. Music: Paul Sawtell. Art Director: Dave Milton. Editor: Christian Nyby.

Cast: Don DeFore (John Riggs/Nick Starns), Andrea King (Nora Craig), George Tobias (Reggie), Barry Kelley (Evans), Morris Ankrum (Eugene Deane), Robert Osterloh (Albert), Charles Cane (Harris), Kippee Valdez (Singer).

John Riggs, a federal agent, infiltrates a gang of counterfeiters led by Nora Craig and her father, who is serving a life sentence for previous crimes and smuggles counterfeit plates out of prison through Bibles. Riggs takes on the identity of Nick Starns, a gambler wanted by the F.B.I., but Nora eventually discovers his true identity. She locks Riggs in the gang's hideout and sets the house on fire. The police arrive, free him and arrest the gang. Nora, however, gets away. Riggs chases her into the quiet night freight yards where, after a brief fight, she falls to her death on the tracks below.

Unlike his *Stranger on the Third Floor*, Boris Ingster's *Southside 1-1000* is a conventional thriller. However, this film is not less compelling. Its performances by a small group of "B" actors — particularly by the mysterious Andrea King — are all very good, and the action is both violent and suspenseful. One wishes Ingster had made more films because he displays in his two *films noirs* a talent not unlike Anthony Mann's.

Spade, Sam

Dashiell Hammett's independent, well-groomed, intelligent private detective, was the model for all American private detectives to follow his debut in the 1920's. Spade, a rough, hard-boiled, realistic man, was a far cry from the dilettantes who had been featured in most detective fiction before 1929, the year *The Maltese Falcon* was published. Humphrey Bogart's portrayal of the character in John Huston's 1941 version of that novel is the most famous portrayal.

Sparkuhl, Theodore (1894–1945)

Cinematographer. Sparkuhl, a staff cinematographer for Paramount, worked on many important productions beginning in the 1930's. He photographed three early *films noirs* before his untimely death.

Filmography: *Among the Living* (Paramount, 1941). *The Glass Key* (Paramount, 1942). *Street of Chance* (Paramount, 1942).

Spencer, J. Russell (   )

Art director. Spencer was a unit art director for 20th Century-Fox. He specialized in extravagant color productions — usually musicals — but he also worked on two interesting *films noirs*.

Filmography: *Nightmare Alley* (20th Century-Fox, 1947). *Where the Sidewalk Ends* (20th Century-Fox, 1950).

Spiegel, Sam (1901–1985)

Producer. Spiegel was a veteran of many years of producing films as an independent in Hollywood long before independent producers were the norm. Among the many films he produced were two *films noirs*.

Filmography: *The Stranger* (RKO, 1946). *The Prowler* (United Artists, 1951).

Spillane, Mickey (1918–)

Novelist. Spillane, as an inheritor of the traditions of the detective novel in the early fifties, reinvented the genre by adding sex and violence in generous proportions. His chief character, the private detective Mike Hammer, unlike

Raymond Chandler's Philip Marlowe or Dashiell Hammett's Sam Spade, would rather fight than reason his way out of a jam and had no qualms about beating or killing women.

For those reasons, then, it probably is not surprising that Spillane's novels have rarely been adapted for the screen. Mike Hammer appeared in two films: *I, the Jury* and the classic Robert Aldrich film *Kiss Me Deadly*. *The Long Wait* is an adaption of one of Spillane's rare non-Hammer crime novels.

Filmography (all based on his novels): *I, the Jury* (United Artists, 1953). *The Long Wait* (United Artists, 1954). *Kiss Me Deadly* (United Artists, 1955).

The Spiral Staircase (RKO, 1946). 83 min.

Producer: Dore Schary. Director: Robert Siodmak. Screenplay: Mel Dinelli, based on the novel *Some Must Watch* by Ethel Lena White. Director of Photography: Nicholas Musuraca. Music: Roy Webb. Art Directors: Albert S. D'Agostino and Jack Okey. Editor: Samuel Beetley.

Cast: Dorothy McGuire (Helen Chapel), George Brent (Professor Warren), Ethel Barrymore (Mrs. Warren), Kent Smith (Dr. Parry), Rhonda Fleming (Blanche), Gordon Oliver (Steve Warren), Elsa Lanchester (Mrs. Oates).

Helen Chapel is the mute companion servant to the wealthy, bedridden Mrs. Warren. Helen suspects that one of her employer's sons is a maniac who has been murdering young girls. Unaware that she is making a terrible mistake, she locks up the innocent Steve Warren while the real killer, Professor Warren, plots to murder her. Eventually, all is resolved, but not before Chapel is nearly terrified to death.

The Spiral Staircase is a Hitchcock like thriller, that is at once genuinely terrifying and exciting. It is directed with great style by Robert Siodmak, who manages to capture the suspense of the tale.

Ethel Barrymore, Dorothy McGuire in *The Spiral Staircase* **(RKO, 1946).**

In fact, *The Spiral Staircase* is partly in the tradition of Gothic horror. It is set entirely in a huge, spooky mansion, but Siodmak and his collaborators create a strong *noir* ambiance through heavy expressionist lighting (thanks to Nicholas Musuraca), a scary score (Roy Webb) and some very creative production design (Albert S. D'Agostino and Jack Okey).

Dorothy McGuire's performance is sympathetic and George Brent is convincing as the serial killer.

The Spiral Staircase was Robert Siodmak's biggest box-office success and it remains one of the genre's most entertaining psychological thrillers.

The Split (MGM, 1968) 91 min.

Producer: Irwin Winkler and Robert Chartoff. Director: Gordon Flemyng. Screenplay: Robert Sabaroff, based on the novel *The Seventh* by Richard Stark. Director of Photography: Bur-

nett Guffey. Music: Quincy Jones. Art Directors: Urie McCleary and George W. Davis. Editor: Rita Roland.

Cast: Jim Brown (McClain), Diahann Carroll (Ellie), Julie Harris (Gladys), Ernest Borgnine (Bert Clinger), Gene Hackman (Lt. Walter Brill). With: Jack Klugman, Warren Oates, James Whitmore, Donald Sutherland.

McClain, a hardened criminal, plans to rob the Los Angeles Coliseum during a football game. unfortunately, the plot slowly and violently unravels, resulting in the capture of McClain and the deaths of most of his gang.

The Split is in the tradition of the caper *noir*, and several of its behind the scenes talents are familiar *noir* names: art director George W. Davis and cinematographer Burnett Guffey. Typically brutal in the style of Stark/Westlake's crime fiction. An interesting twist is its black leading actors, Jim Brown and Diahann Carroll.

Stanwyck, Barbara (Ruby Stevens) (1907–)

Actress. For three decades Barbara Stanwyck was one of Hollywood's most reliable leading ladies, with an enviable range and longevity. Although she played a wide variety of roles (and was most popular in the thirties in tearjerkers), she was at her best as a wisecracking dame: her New York bred, acid-flavored drawl was perfectly suitable to her playful, forthright sexuality.

Nevertheless, Stanwyck scandalized her faithful female audience in 1944 when she bleached her hair and starred as the *femme-fatale* Phyllis Dietrichson in Billy Wilder's classic *film noir*, *Double Indemnity*. Her glaring sexuality, generally celebrated, was here a subversive force used to tempt a man into committing murder. Like Joan Bennett in *Woman in the Window* (RKO, 1944), the film helped re-establish Stanwyck as a player of unsympathetic parts and, if anything, made her into a bigger star.

Stanwyck played deadly *femme-fatales* in two later *films noirs*. In *The Strange Love of Martha Ivers* she starred as a successful business woman whose murderous past catches up to her. The performance was as memorable as her performance in *Double Indemnity*. Less well known is her role in Robert Siodmak's *The File on Thelma Jordan*, an imperfect movie although Stanwyck is excellent.

In *Sorry, Wrong Number* and *The Two Mrs. Carrolls*, Stanwyck varied her *noir* roles as a "woman in distress" who slowly realizes the man she trusts the most is planning her murder.

Stanwyck's last important *noir* role was in *Clash By Night* as a world weary woman who tries to settle peacefully in a small town.

Barbara Stanwyck is one of the *grand dames* of *film noir*, demonstrating as wide a range in the genre as in her other films and creating several of the genre's indelible female characters.

Filmography: *Double Indemnity* (Paramount, 1944). *The Strange Love of Martha Ivers* (Paramount, 1946). *The Two Mrs. Carrolls* (Warner Bros., 1947). *Sorry, Wrong Number* (Paramount, 1948). *The File on Thelma Jordan* (Paramount, 1950). *Jeopardy* (MGM, 1950). *Clash By Night* (RKO, 1952). *Witness to Murder* (United Artists, 1954).

Stark, Richard *pseudonym for* **Donald Westlake**

Steiger, Rod (1925–)

Character actor. Steiger was one of the foremost Method actors of the 1950's and starred with fellow Method actor Marlon Brando in the Elia Kazan melodrama *On the Waterfront* which has some *noir* elements. He had important supporting roles in two official *films noirs*, *The Big Knife* and *The Harder They Fall*.

Filmography: *On The Waterfront* (Columbia, 1954). *The Big Knife* (United Artists, 1955). *The Harder They Fall* (Columbia, 1956).

Steiner, Max (1888–1971)

Composer. One of Hollywood's most reliable and prolific film composers, the Austrian born Max Steiner was the creator of some of the most famous film scores. His lush, late-romantic style was perfectly suited to Hollywood cinema. The archetypal film composer, Steiner was able to adapt his style to the various genres. Mainly employed at Warner Bros. (for whom all of his *noir* scores were written), he composed the music for several classic films: *King Kong* (RKO, 1933), *The Lost Patrol* (RKO, 1934), *The Informer* (RKO, 1935), *Gone with the Wind* (MGM, 1939) and *Casablanca* (Warner Bros., 1942. His scores for the *films noirs* listed below are all well above average and in several cases the music is more memorable than the movie.

Filmography: *The Letter* (Warner Bros., 1940). *Mildred Pierce* (Warner Bros., 1945). *The Big Sleep* (Warner

Bros., 1946). *Deep Valley* (Warner Bros., 1947). *The Unfaithful* (Warner Bros., 1947). *Key Largo* (Warner Bros., 1948). *Beyond the Forest* (Warner Bros., 1949). *White Heat* (Warner Bros., 1949). *Caged* (Warner Bros., 1950). *Illegal* (Warner Bros., 1955).

Sterling, Jan (Jane Sterling Adriance) (1923–)

Actress. Although her name is not as well known as many of her contemporaries, Jan Sterling is certainly one of *film noir*'s greatest female icons. The daughter of wealthy parents, Sterling specialized in high class floozies. With her heavy make-up, bleached hair and strident, distinctive voice, Sterling brought to life some of *noir's* most interesting and overtly sexual female characters.

Filmography: *Caged* (Warner Bros., 1950). *The Harder They Fall* (Columbia, 1950). *Mystery Street* (MGM, 1950). *Union Station* (Paramount, 1950). *Appointment with Danger* (Paramount, 1951). *The Big Carnival* (Paramount, 1951). *Female on the Beach* (Universal, 1955).

Sternard, Rudolf (1905–)

Art director. Another in the long line of art directors who began as an architect, Sternard worked at both 20th Century-Fox and Columbia. For many years he was one of Stanley Kramer's chief collaborators.

Filmography: *Dead Reckoning* (Columbia, 1947). *The Sniper* (Columbia, 1952).

Stevens, Leith (1909–1970)

Composer. A composer of mainly routine scores, Stevens wrote the music for many films, mostly "B" productions. He also composed extensively for television.

Filmography: *Beware, My Lovely* (RKO, 1952). *The Hitch-Hiker* (RKO, 1953). *Private Hell, 36* (Filmmakers, 1954). *The Garment Jungle* (Columbia, 1957).

Stevens, Mark (Richard Stevens) (1915–)

Actor. Stevens played second leads in many films in the 1940's and 1950's. He also played leads—usually tough heroes—in "B" movies. He co-starred in three *films noirs*. His most famous work is in *The Dark Corner* as a private detective looking for the man who framed him for a crime he did not commit. His performances in the less known *The Street with No Name* and *Between Midnight and Dawn* are equally compelling.

Filmography: *The Dark Corner* (20th Century-Fox, 1946). *The Street with No Name* (20th Century-Fox, 1948). *Between Midnight and Dawn* (Columbia, 1950).

Stevenson, Houseley (1879–1953)

Character actor. Houseley Stevenson was the resident unshaven, usually grumpy old man of Hollywood. He appeared in small supporting roles in a handful of *noirs*.

Filmography: *Somewhere in the Night* (20th Century-Fox, 1946). *The Brasher Doubloon* (20th Century-Fox, 1947). *Dark Passage* (Warner Bros., 1947). *Moonrise* (Republic, 1949). *Edge of Doom* (RKO, 1950).

Stevenson, Robert (1905–1986)

Director. The British born Stevenson was a good director of conventional dramas and family pictures. He directed a single minor *film noir, Woman on Pier 13*. The film is good enough, but Stevenson's talent was for lighter fare.

Filmography: *Woman on Pier 13* (RKO, 1949).

Stewart, James (1908–)

Actor. Stewart's all American image was best suited to Capraesque comedies, but he also played hard-boiled characters in a few films. In Henry Hathaway's *Call Northside 777* he starred as a skeptical reporter who exposes official corruption. He also starred in two Alfred Hitchcock color *noirs, Rear*

Window and, most importantly, *Vertigo*. The latter role, as an ex-police detective tragically obsessed with a beautiful blonde, is both subtle and poignant.

Filmography: *Call Northside 777* (20th Century–Fox, 1948). *Rear Window* (20th Century–Fox, 1953). *Vertigo* (Universal, 1958).

Stewart, Paul (1908–)

Character actor. After stage experience, Paul Stewart made his film debut in Orson Welles' *Citizen Kane* (RKO, 1941). He subsequently appeared in over fifty films including several *films noirs*. Of his *noir* roles, particularly notable is his portrayal of the vicious murderer Joe Kellerton in *The Window* and as Carl Evello, the chief villain in Robert Aldrich's *Kiss Me Deadly*.

Filmography: *Johnny Eager* (MGM, 1942). *Champion* (United Artists, 1949). *The Window* (RKO, 1949). *Edge of Doom* (RKO, 1950). *Appointment with Danger* (Paramount, 1951). *Kiss Me Deadly* (United Artists, 1955).

Stone, Andrew L. (1902–)

Director. Stone is an interesting character. He was a successful director whose career stretched back to the late-thirties and he developed an admirable studio-based style as demonstrated in his great musical, *Stormy Weather* (Universal, 1942). In the mid-forties, with his wife Virginia, he began shooting features on location—one of the first major directors to do so. His *films noirs*, *Cry Terror* and *Julie*, are well made exciting melodramas, if not classics of the genre.

Filmography: *Cry Terror* (also screenplay) (MGM, 1955). *Julie* (also screenplay) (MGM, 1956).

Stone, Milburn (1904–1980)

Character actor. Stone, best remembered as Doc Adams on the long running television series, "Gunsmoke," played the usual run of character parts in dozens of movies. He had small roles in several *films noirs*, most notably as a communist spy in *Pickup on South Street*.

Filmography: *Phantom Lady* (Universal, 1944). *The Racket* (RKO, 1951). *Roadblock* (RKO, 1951). *Pickup on South Street* (20th Century–Fox, 1953).

Storm Fear (United Artists, 1956). 88 min.

Producer and Director: Cornel Wilde. Screenplay: Horton Foote, based on the novel by Clinton Seeley. Director of Photography: Joseph LaShelle. Music: Elmer Bernstein. Art Director: Rudi Feld. Editor: Otto Ludwig.

Cast: Cornel Wilde (Charlie), Jean Wallace (Elizabeth), Dan Duryea (Fred), Lee Grant (Edna), David Stollery (David). With: Dennis Weaver, Steven Hill, Keith Britton.

Charlie and two of his surviving gang members, including Edna, take refuge after a bank robbery in his older brother Fred's New England farmhouse. Charlie tends to his gunshot wounds and plans to cross over the mountains by foot to avoid police roadblocks. At the same time, he attempts to reconcile himself with Fred's wife Elizabeth, with whom he once had an affair and whose son is also actually his child. The tensions eventually erupt into violence when one of the gang members shoots Fred. When they flee across the mountain, the same gang member tries to steal the money for himself, but is killed. Charlie, only yards from safety, is shot by the rifle of the pursuing Fred.

A taut "B" thriller directed by star Cornel Wilde, *Storm Fear* is tense, dark, cynical and ultimately hopeless. Its characters, in classic *noir* fashion, are all susceptible to corruption and self destruction. Wilde does an admirable job, particularly in the outdoor scenes as the crooks try to flee to elusive freedom.

Stradling, Harry (1907–1970).

Cinematographer. Stradling did his best work in the late thirties and early forties on non-*noir* films. His work, however, is always exemplary. He created a dark, claustrophobic world for Otto Preminger's neglected *Angel Face*..

Filmography: *Suspicion* (RKO, 1941). *Tension* (MGM, 1949). *Edge of Doom* (RKO, 1950). *Angel Face* (RKO, 1953).

Strange Illusion (P.R.C., 1945). 84 min.

Producer: Leon Fromkess. Director: Edgar G. Ulmer. Screenplay: Adele Commandini, story by Fritz Rotter. Director of Photography: Philip Tannura. Music: Leo Erody. Art Director: Paul Palmentola. Editor: Carl Pierson.

Cast: James Lydon (Paul Cartwright), Warren Williams (Brett Curtis), Sally Eilers (Virginia Cartwright), Regis Toomey (Dr. Vincent). With: Charles Arnt, George H. Reed, Jayne Hazard, Jimmy Clark.

Paul Cartwright, an adolescent, comes to believe his mother's suitor Brett Curtis, is the murderer of his father. His suspicions are confirmed when he receives a letter from his father written before his death. Feigning insanity in the hopes of catching Brett off guard, the plan nearly backfires when his mother has him committed to a mental institution. Eventually, however, the youth gathers enough evidence to convict Brett of his father's murder.

Strange Illusion is an interesting update of *Hamlet* with its message from beyond the grave and faked insanity in order to catch a killer. The film is Edgar G. Ulmer's most static, slow moving *film noir* but it is by no means a bad movie. It is, in fact, an interesting experiment and one of the most unique of all *films noirs*.

The Strange Love of Martha Ivers (Paramount, 1946). 115 min.

Producer: Hal B. Wallis. Director: Lewis Milestone. Screenplay: Robert Rossen, story by Jack Patrick. Director of Photography: Victor Milner. Music: Miklos Rozsa. Song: "Strange Love" by Haynes and Lyons. Art Directors: Hans Dreier and John Meehan. Editor: Archie Marshek.

Cast: Barbara Stanwyck (Martha Ivers), Van Heflin (Sam Masterson), Lizabeth Scott (Toni Marachek), Kirk Douglas (Walter O'Neil), Judith Anderson (Mrs. Ivers). With: Roman Bohnen, Darryl Hickman, Janis Wilson, Ann Doran, Frank Orth.

As an adolescent Martha Ivers was involved in a bizarre situation in which she killed her aunt. No one is aware of the murder except her. She inherits a huge fortune and for the next twenty years controls a powerful industrial corporation.

An accidental reunion with a childhood friend, Sam Masterson, rekindles old passions and long forgotten guilt in Martha. She tries to force him out of town by using a young girl, Toni Marachek, to seduce him. This annoys Martha's husband, District Attorney Walter O'Neil, an alcoholic weakling.

Masterson has an affair with Martha to discover if, as he has long suspected, she did kill her aunt. He discovers that she did, but it is O'Neil who confronts him. When Martha sees how truly weak and pathetic her husband is, she tries to get Masterson to kill him, but he refuses. Realizing that circumstances will force them to confess to the crime committed years before, both O'Neil and Martha kill themselves.

Masterson leaves town with Toni, whom he has fallen in love with. As the town disappears behind them he remarks casually "I wanted to see if I could be lucky twice."

The Strange Love of Martha Ivers is one of the most psychologically intense of all *films noirs* and Lewis Milestone recreated the oppression and moral corruption of the characters in a particularly dark, shadowy film. The drama is enhanced by a superb score by Miklos Rozsa and a cast of performers at their very best.

The Strange Love of Martha Ivers is a prime example of 1940's *film noir* at its finest. Thematically, with its mixture of sexual temptation, corrupt characters and a long past event coming back to haunt and ultimately destroy the characters, the film is an archetypal *noir*.

While all of its performances are very good, it must be noted that Kirk Douglas's performance in his first movie was so strong, it firmly established both his image and stardom over the next several years.

Strange Triangle (20th Century–Fox, 1946). 65 min.

Producer and Director: Raymond McCarey. Screenplay: Mortimer Braus, adapted by Charles G. Booth from a story by Jack Andrews. Director of Photography: Harry Jackson. Music: David Buttolph. Art Directors: Lyle Wheeler and Maurice Ransford. Editor: Norman Colbert.

Cast: Signe Hassa (Francine Hubber), Preston Foster (Sam Crane), Anabel Shaw (Betty Wilson), John Sheppard (Earl Huber), Roy Roberts (Harry Matthews).

Ray McCarey's little known *noir* character study of an honest bank examiner who gets involved with a crooked couple, embezzlement and eventually murder, is a dark, moody tale. Ray's vision was much more cynical than his famous brother, Leo McCarey's (a leading comedy writer/ director) and *Strange Triangle* is one of the genre's most inevitably tragic "B" movies.

The Stranger (RKO, 1946). 95 min.

Producer: S. P. Eagle (Sam Spiegel). Director: Orson Welles. Screenplay: Anthony Veiller (w/uncredited John Huston and Orson Welles), story by Victor Travis. Director of Photography: Russell Metty. Music: Bronislau Kaper. Production Design: Perry Ferguson. Editor: Ernest Nims.

Cast: Edward G. Robinson (Wilson), Loretta Young (Mary Longstreet), Orson Welles (Franz Kindler/Professor Charles Rankin), Philip Merivale (Judge Longstreet). With: Billy House, Richard Long, Konstantin Shayne, Martha Wentworth.

Franz Kindler is a Nazi war criminal who has escaped the Allied net and taken up residence in a small Connecticut town under the new identity of Professor Charles Rankin. His life is sedate and he meets and marries Mary Longstreet, a local resident. Wilson, an investigator from The Commission for War Crimes, arrives in town intent on forcing a confession out of Rankin/ Kindler. Mary, meanwhile, begins to realize who and what her husband is. Eventually, however, Kindler admits his guilt and tries to escape. Wilson chases him to a clock tower in the town where Kindler slips and is impaled on one of the clock's arms.

The Stranger is Orson Welles' most conventional *film noir*, with a fairly straight forward style and script. In fact, it is a top-notch thriller with a restrained performance by Welles and excellent work by both Loretta Young and Edward G. Robinson.

The subject of escaped war criminals was extremely rare for some odd reason, even in the years immediately following World War II. *The Stranger* is one of the few to deal with the subject in an interesting, unique way.

Unfortunately, Welles' reputation was so damaged by this time that even a success like *The Stranger* could not revive his career as a director and he would direct only a few films after this one.

Stranger on the Third Floor (RKO, 1940). 64 min.

Producer: Lee Marcus. Director: Boris Ingster. Screenplay: Frank Partos. Director of Photography: Nicholas Musuraca. Art Director: Van Nest Polglase. Editor: Harry Marker.

Cast: Peter Lorre (Strangler), John McGuire (Mike Ward), Margaret Tallichet (Jane), Charles Waldron (District

Farley Granger listens bemused to Robert Walker's scheme in *Strangers on a Train* (Warner Bros., 1951).

Attorney), Elisha Cook, Jr. (Joe Briggs). With: Charles Halton, Ethel Griffies, Cliff Clark, Oscar O'Shea, Alec Craig.

Stranger on the Third Floor, an RKO "B" production, has been described as a premature *film noir*. In style and theme it predates the genre by four years.

Set in a claustrophobic urban milieu, the film tells the story of a newspaper reporter, Mike Ward, who gives testimony that sends a young man to the electric chair. Tortured by uncertainty and guilt, Ward suddenly finds himself enmeshed in some bizarre circumstances in which he is accused by a neighbor of being a notorious serial killer. Eventually, however, it is proven that the serial killer, known only as "Strangler" is another resident in the building.

In fact, *Stranger on the Third Floor*

is the first true *film noir* and it represents a distinct break in style and substance with mysteries and thrillers of the previous decade. It is also one of the most truly expressionist of all American films with minimalist sets, heavy extravagant shadows cast on white walls, dream sequences and exaggerated performances, particularly by Peter Lorre as the lurking killer. The film also provided an early *noir* role for Elisha Cook, Jr. as one of the suspects before being proved innocent.

Strangers on a Train (Warner Bros., 1951). 101 min.

Producer and Director: Alfred Hitchcock. Screenplay: Raymond Chandler and Czenzi Ormonde, adapted by Whitfield Cook from the novel by Patricia Highsmith. Director of Photography: Robert Burks. Music: Dimitri Tiomkin.

Art Director: Ted Haworth. Editor: William H. Ziegler.

Cast: Farley Granger (Guy Haines), Ruth Roman (Anne Morton), Robert Walker (Bruno Anthony), Leo G. Carroll (Senator Morton), Patricia Hitchcock (Barbara Morton), Laura Elliott (Miriam). With: Marion Lorne, Jonathan Hale, Howard St. John, John Brown, Norma Varden.

Aboard a Washington-New York train, a brash society playboy, Bruno Anthony, strikes up a conversation with Guy Haines, a tennis champion. Haines is estranged from his wife Miriam and is now in love with Anne Morton. Bruno comments on how much he hates his father and suggests that he will kill Miriam if Guy will kill Bruno's father. Thinking he is joking, Guy laughs and tells Bruno to forget it. Bruno, however, was not joking and several nights later follows Guy's wife and strangles her in an amusement park. When Guy cannot supply an alibi to the police, they keep him under surveillance. Bruno confronts Guy and threatens to frame him if he does not live up to his end of the "bargain." Realizing that Guy could expose him, Bruno sets out to frame him by leaving Guy's cigarette lighter at the amusement park as evidence, while Guy is playing in an important tennis match he cannot miss. After a race against the clock Guy wins his tennis match and then rushes to the amusement park to confront Bruno. While Guy and Bruno are fighting on the merry-go-round it goes out of control and crushes Bruno to death. An observant concessionaire tells the police that Bruno was the man he saw following Miriam the night she was murdered thus freeing Guy of suspicion.

Guilt, real and by association, is a theme which Alfred Hitchcock returned to again and again. In *Strangers on a Train*, Guy Haines is just as guilty as Bruno Anthony, simply because of his extreme self-interest and opportunism. Shocked by Bruno's murder of his wife,

Guy nevertheless welcomes this strange turn of events, for it opens his way to marry Anne Morton.

The corrupt, guilt-ridden world of *Strangers on a Train* is further complicated by the homosexual undertones of Guy and Bruno's relationship. Farley Granger plays Guy as a swaggering, oily athlete who clearly encourages the interest of Bruno, while Bruno sees the supposed agreement with Guy as a shared secret with a lover.

In any case, the film is a well made thriller that, if not quite a masterpiece, is a welcome addition to the genre.

Street of Chance (Paramount, 1942). 74 min.

Producer: Burt Kelly. Director: Jack Hively. Screenplay: Garrett Fort, based on the novel *The Black Curtain* by Cornell Woolrich. Director of Photography: Theodor Sparkuhl. Music: David Buttolph. Art Directors: Hans Dreier and Haldane Douglas. Editor: Arthur Schmidt.

Cast: Burgess Meredith (Frank Thompson), Claire Trevor (Ruth Dillon), Louise Platt (Virginia Thompson), Sheldon Leonard (Joe Marucci), Frieda Inescort (Alma Diedrich). With: Jerome Cowan, Adeline de Walt Reynolds, Arthur Loft, Clancy Cooper.

Frank Thompson "wakes up" in an unfamiliar section of New York City. Returning home, he finds his wife has moved and is using her maiden name. Shocked, she tells him he disappeared over a year before. Attempting to put his life back together, he returns to his job as an accountant and attempts to discover what happened. He eventually learns that after an accident in which he was struck on the head causing him to lose his memory, he met a woman named Ruth. Ruth killed her employee, but Frank is wanted for the murder. However, Ruth is dying from a terminal disease and on her deathbed confesses to both Frank and a police detective who has come to arrest him.

Street of Chance was a minor success

at the time of its release and is still somewhat obscure. However, it is an important early *film noir* for several reasons. It was the first adaption of a Cornell Woolrich work. It was the first *noir* with an amnesia theme. It introduces Claire Trevor as a *noir* icon, here playing a *femme-fatale*, one of the first true portrayals of the type in *film noir*. Finally, its cinematography, by Theodore Sparkuhl, while not as extravagant as later *noirs*, approaches the low-key, shadowy look of the genre's classic films of only two years later.

The Street with No Name (20th Century–Fox, 1948). 91 min.

Producer: Samuel G. Engel. Director: William Keighley. Screenplay: Harry Kleiner. Director of Photography: Joe MacDonald. Music: Lionel Newman. Art Directors: Lyle Wheeler and Chester Gore. Editor: William Reynolds.

Cast: Mark Stevens (Gene Cordell), Richard Widmark (Alec Stiles), Lloyd Nolan (Inspector Briggs), Barbara Lawrence (Judy), Ed Begley (Chief Harmatz), Donald Buka (Shivvy). With: Joseph Penvey, John McIntire, Howard Smith, Walter Greeza.

F.B.I. agent Inspector Briggs investigates the murder of an innocent woman killed in a nightclub holdup. He discovers that the man initially charged with the crime and subsequently released on bail and mysteriously killed, was framed. Another agent, Gene Cordell, is brought in to work undercover. He uses the alias Manley and infiltrates the suspected gang. Within days, he finds himself implicated in a robbery he did not participate in. He is arrested and his bail is arranged, but the leader of the gang, Stiles, has meanwhile learned that Manley is an undercover agent. Stiles devises a plan to kill Manley during a robbery, but when the police arrive, they kill Stiles instead.

Street with No Name was the second of two *films noirs* starring Lloyd Nolan as F.B.I. agent Briggs — the first was *House on 92nd Street*. This later film is essentially a conventional thriller, but its characters' underlying cynicism, overt corruption of a city government and hints of homosexual interest between Stiles and Manley (an element one finds in a few *films noirs*), qualify it as a true *noir*. Its style, however is equally conventional with only brief glimpses of expressionism, particularly in the night scenes.

The Strip (MGM, 1951). 84 min.

Producer: Joe Pasternak. Director: Leslie Kardos. Screenplay: Allen Rivkin. Director of Photography: Robert Surtees. Music: Georgie Stoll. Art Directors: Cedric Gibbons and Leonid Vasian. Editor: Albert Akst.

Cast: Mickey Rooney (Stanley Maxton), Sally Forrest (Jane Tafford), William Demarest (Fluff), James Craig (Delwyn "Sonny" Johnson), Kay Brown (Edna). With: Louis Armstrong and Band, Tommy Rettig, Tom Powers, Jonathan Cott, Tommy Farrell, Myrna Dell.

When an aspiring actress, Jane Tafford is found dying of a gunshot wound and her lover Sonny Johnson dead, Jane's ex-boyfriend Stan Maxton is arrested. He recounts how, after returning from the Korean War, he tried to revive his career as a jazz drummer. He met and fell for Jane and together they entered the dark world of an acquaintance, Sonny, a successful racketeer. Jane and Sonny have an affair, and Sonny's associates beat Stan up to "warn" him against trying to get revenge against Sonny. When Jane protests Sonny's actions, the couple have a violent argument and shoot each other. Jane dies, the police release Stan and he returns unhappily to his musical career.

The Strip is one of several "B" *noirs* starring Mickey Rooney that were made in the fifties. This is a typical example. Dark and moody, it is also tragically romantic. It is a well made movie, held together by Rooney's strong performance and a compelling background in the world of jazz nightclubs.

Stromberg, Hunt (1894–1968)

Producer. Stromberg, a distinguished producer long with MGM, later went independent and produced several interesting, mostly low budget movies including two *films noirs*.

Filmography: *Lured* (United Artists, 1947). *Between Midnight and Dawn* (Columbia, 1950).

Struss, Karl (1891–1981)

Cinematographer. Struss began his career in the mid-twenties. He was the cinematographer for F. W. Murnau's classic late-silent film *Sunrise* (Fox, 1927), an extraordinary expressionist melodrama. Interestingly, he was the cinematographer for only two *films noirs*.

Filmography: *Journey into Fear* (RKO, 1942). *Suspense* (Monogram, 1946).

Sturges, John (1911–)

Director. After many years in the art and editing departments at RKO, Sturges began directing in the late-forties, but did not hit his stride until a decade later with a series of classic action films: *Gunfight at the O.K. Corral* (Paramount, 1957), *The Magnificent Seven* (United Artists, 1960) and *The Great Escape* (United Artists, 1963). All of Sturges' *films noirs* display the same economy of expression and choreographed violence that distinguished his later classics.

Filmography: *The Capture* (RKO, 1950). *Jeopardy* (MGM, 1950). *Mystery Street* (MGM, 1950). *The People Against O'Hara* (MGM, 1951).

Sudden Fear (RKO, 1952). 110 min.

Producer: Joseph Kaufman. Director: David Miller. Screenplay: Lenore Coffee and Robert Smith, based on the novel by Edna Sherry. Director of Photography: Charles Lang, Jr. music: Elmer Berstein. Songs: "Afraid" by Elmer Berstein and Jack Brooks and "Sudden Fear" by Irving Taylor and Arthur Altman. Art Director: Brois Leven. Editor: Leon Barsha.

Cast: Joan Crawford (Myra Hudson), Jack Palance (Lester Blaine), Gloria Grahame (Irene Neves), Bruce Bennett (Steve Kearney), Virginia Huston (Ann), Touch (Mike) Conners (Junior Kearney).

Myra Hudson is a successful playwright and San Francisco heiress. While in New York casting her new play, she vetoes actor Lester Blaine because he does not look like a romantic lead. However, he romances Myra and they soon marry. Lester meets with an ex-girlfriend, telling her that he married Myra for reasons other than love and he warns Irene not to interfere.

By chance, Myra learns of Irene and Lester's plot to kill her. She turns the tables by planning to set up Irene for Lester's murder, but she cannot go through with the plan. Nevertheless, the inevitable has been set in motion and Lester kills Irene by running her down with his car when he mistakes her for Myra. Lester is also killed in the crash.

Sudden Fear, a late RKO *noir* is a stylish thriller with a minimalist cast of *noir* icons at their best. Gloria Grahame, as Irene, displays nuances of masochism as she not only does not even flinch when Lester threatens to beat her, but then asks him to "crush" her with his kiss. Jack Palance is superb as the evil Lester Blaine and with Joan Crawford, brings a strange sense of perverse sexuality to their scenes together.

David Miller, a minor director, does a credible job with his minimalist cast of six actors and few sets. Indeed, in its photography and set design, the film resembles the expressionist influenced early *noirs* rather than the more realistic style of the fifties.

Suddenly (United Artists, 1954). 77 min.

Producer: Robert Bassler. Director:

Lewis Allen. Screenplay: Richard Sale. Director of Photography: Charles Clarke. Music: David Raksin. Art Director: Frank Sylos. Editor: John F. Schreyer.

Cast: Frank Sinatra (John Baron), Sterling Hayden (Tod Shaw), James Gleason (Pop Benson), Nancy Gates (Ellen Benson), Kim Charney (Pidge), Paul Frees (Benny Conklin). With: Christopher Dark, Willis Bouchey, Paul Wexler, Jim Lilburn, Charles Smith.

A peaceful small California town is quietly invaded by a trio of hired assassins who intend to kill the President of the United States. They force their way into a house that overlooks a train depot where the President is secretly scheduled to transfer to a private automobile. John Baron, the leader of the assassins, takes every opportunity he can to humiliate his hostages, the Benson family and a local police officer, Tod Shaw. However, Shaw eventually finds a way to subdue the killers just before the train arrives at the station.

Suddenly is a taut, fast-paced thriller that emphasizes the cruel sadism of the key conspirator, John Baron. Frank Sinatra, in a rare unsympathetic role, was surprisingly effective as the psychopathic assassin.

Beyond the preoccupation with violence, *Suddenly* concentrates on the all pervasive sense of claustrophobia and despair. It is one of the most powerful of that select group of *noirs* in which a family is held hostage by a group of vicious criminals which forces them to confront their own weaknesses.

Sukman, Harry (   )

Composer. Sukman composed the scores for many films and television productions. He composed the music for two of Samuel Fuller's *films noirs*.

Filmography: *The Crimson Kimono* (Columbia, 1959). *Underworld U.S.A.* (Columbia, 1960).

Sullivan, Barry (Patrick Barry) (1912–)

Actor. A forgotten hero of countless forties and fifties action films, Barry Sullivan is a minor *noir* icon. He most often starred in *films noirs* which depended on action, starring in movies made at Monogram (for very little budget) and MGM. One of his most interesting *noir* performances was in the early *Suspense* as a down on his luck carny whose affair with his boss' wife ultimately leads to his death.

Filmography: *Suspense* (Monogram, 1946). *Framed* (Columbia, 1947). *The Gangster* (Allied Artists, 1947). *Jeopardy* (MGM, 1950). *Tension* (MGM, 1950). *Cause for Alarm* (MGM, 1951). *I Was a Communist for the FBI* (bit part) (Warner Bros., 1951). *The Unknown Man* (MGM, 1951). *Julie* (MGM, 1956).

Sunset Boulevard (Paramount, 1950). 115 min.

Producer: Charles Brackett. Director: Billy Wilder. Screenplay: Charles Brackett, Billy Wilder and D. M. Marshman, Jr. Director of Photography: John F. Seitz. Music: Franz Waxman. Song: "The Paramount Don't Want Me Blues" by Jay Livingston and Ray Evans. Art Directors: Hans Dreier and John Meeham. Editor: Arthur Schmidt.

Cast: William Holden (Joe Gillis), Gloria Swanson (Norma Desmond), Erich Von Stroheim (Max Von Mayerling), Nancy Olsen (Betty Schaefer), Fred Clark (Sheldrake). With: Lloyd Gough, Jack Webb, Cecil B. DeMille, Hedda Hopper, Buster Keaton, Anna Q. Nilsson.

Pursued by creditors who want to repossess his car, Joe Gillis, a down and out screenwriter takes refuge in a crumbling garage flanked by a massive, deteriorating old mansion. The mansion is occupied by Norma Desmond, a long forgotten silent film star, and Max, her butler who also used to be her husband and a successful director. Norma is attracted to the virile young Joe and offers him a job writing her comeback film, *Salome*. Joe accepts, if only for the money. He eventually becomes Norma's kept man and enters her world of madness and obsession with past glories.

One night, Joe escapes and goes to a favorite bar where he meets a young studio reader, Betty Schaefer, with whom he falls in love. When he later tries to make a break from Norma, she fakes an attempted suicide, pulling him back into her orbit. She also informs Betty that Joe is no more than her gigolo. When Joe decides to finally leave her, Norma shoots him and he falls dead into the swimming pool. Faced by a barrage of reporters and policemen, Norma goes mad, descending her staircase as if she were in a scene from her beloved movie, *Salome*.

Sunset Boulevard is one of *film noir*'s greatest movies. It begins with a famous shot of Joe Gillis floating face down in the pool as he then tells the story of his own murder in flashback.

The extreme cynicism of the screenplay is leavened somewhat by its director's characteristic black humor. For example, the famous scene of the pet chimp's midnight funeral and the odd card games populated by real silent film personalities: Buster Keaton, Ann Q. Nilsson, Cecil B. DeMille.

Ultimately, however, the movie is a scathing attack against Hollywood told in one of the most tragic, cynical of all American films.

Surtees, Bruce (   )

Cinematographer. Son of the great cinematographer Robert Surtees, Bruce is a competent professional. For Don Siegel's *Dirty Harry*, he did an admirable job of capturing black and white *noir* style in color.

Filmography: *Dirty Harry* (Warner Bros., 1971).

Surtees, Robert (1906–1985)

Cinematographer. A distinguished master of motion-picture photography,

Surtees specialized in brightly-lit entertainments, and he had an affinity for outdoor scenes. Of his two *films noirs*, the most interesting is Fred Zinnemann's *Act of Violence* in which expressionist style is subverted somewhat in favor of a brighter style.

Filmography: *The Street with No Name* (20th Century–Fox, 1948). *Act of Violence* (MGM, 1949).

Suspense (Monogram, 1946). 101 min.

Producers: Maurice and Frank King. Director and Screenplay: Philip Yordan. Director of Photography: Karl Struss. Music: Daniele Amfitheotrof. Art Director: F. Paul Sylos. Editor: Dick Heermance.

Cast: Belita (Roberta Elba), Barry Sullivan (Joe Morgan), Albert Dekker (Frank Leonard), Eugene Pallette (Harry), Bonita Granville (Ronnie). With: Edith Angold, George Stone, Billy Nelson.

Joe Morgan, a down on his luck promoter, joins Frank Leonard's ice show as a peanut seller. When he devises a skating stunt for Roberta Elba, Leonard's wife and the star, Joe is promoted to ringmaster. A romance begins between Joe and Roberta. Later someone takes a shot at Joe with a rifle. They miss, but the shot causes an avalanche. Joe and Roberta believe that it was the jealous Frank who shot at Joe and was buried in the avalanche. They take over the ice show, but Roberta comes to believe that Joe killed Frank, stuffed his body in an old rolltop desk and then burned the desk. Joe decides to kill Roberta by rigging an "accident" during her show, but she discovers it. Walking outside to calm himself, Joe is accosted by Ronnie, a jilted ex-girlfriend, who kills him in anger.

Suspense is typical of the existential, tragic themes of Monogram and P.R.C. *noirs*. With a somewhat higher budget than was usual for Monogram, the studio could afford an excellent craftsman like Frank Tuttle and "A" actors. The result is a visually compelling, well acted melodrama.

Suspicion (RKO, 1941). 99 min.

Producer and Director: Alfred Hitchcock. Screenplay: Samson Raphaelson, Joan Harrison and Alma Reville, based on the novel *Before the Fact* by Francis Iles. Director of Photography: Harry Stradling. Music: Franz Waxman. Art Directors: Van Nest Polglase and Carroll Clark. Editor: William Hamilton.

Cast: Cary Grant (John Aysgarth), Joan Fontaine (Lina MacKinlaw), Sir Cedric Harwicke (General MacKinlaw), Nigel Bruce (Beaky), Dame May Whitty (Mrs. MacKinlaw). With: Isabel Jeans, Auriol Lee, Reginald Sheffield, Leo G. Carroll.

Lina MacKinlaw is a spinsterish wallflower who wants to escape the home of her stuffy parents. She meets Johnny Aysgarth, a reckless playboy and falls in love with him. Disregarding rumors about his supposedly sordid past, she marries Johnny. However, as time passes, through accumulated evidence, Lina begins to suspect her new husband of the murder of a dear friend and believes he plans to kill her too. The crescendo of paranoia reaches a climax as Johnny brings Lina a glass of milk — she is sure the milk is poisoned, but it is not. Later, in a frightening ride along the rocky coast line of England, she almost jumps from the car. He stops the car to save her and the truth of his innocence is established.

Although its ending was changed to please censors at the time (in the original ending, Johnny *is* a murderer), *Suspicion* is one of the most prominent early *films noirs*. Its powerful visuals, influenced by expressionism, had a profound influence on the developing genre, as did its almost overwhelming paranoia. It also set the standard for all the "women-in-distress" *noirs* to follow including perhaps most famous, *The Two Mrs. Carrolls* (Warner Bros., 1947), among many others.

Sweet Smell of Success (United Artists, 1957). 96 min.

Producer: James Hill. Director: Alexander MacKendrick. Screenplay: Clifford Odets, adapted by Ernest Lehman from his novella *Tell Me About It Tomorrow*. Director of Photography: James Wong Howe. Music: Elmer Bernstein. Art Director: Edward Carrere. Editor: Alan Crosland, Jr.

Cast: Burt Lancaster (J.J. Hunsecker), Tony Curtis (Sidney Falco), Susan Harrison (Susan Hunsecker), Martin Milner (Steve Dallas), Sam Levene (Frank D'Angelo). With: Barbara Nichols, Jeff Donnell, Joseph Leon, Edith Atwater, Emile Meyer.

Sidney Falco is a success-starved publicity agent on Broadway who believes he is being ignored by J. J. Hunsecker, a mono-maniacal entertainment columnist. Hunsecker believes that Falco failed to carry out a favor to break up the relationship between his sister Susan and a young guitarist, Steve Dallas. Falco attempts to get back into Hunsecker's good graces by planting a story accusing Dallas of being crazed by marijuana and a "card-carrying" Communist. When Hunsecker confronts his sister and her lover, she reluctantly agrees not to see Dallas again. When she does begin to see him again anyway, Hunsecker has Falco plant some marijuana on Dallas and then has Dallas arrested by a policeman on his payroll.

Joyful about his good fortune, Falco goes to celebrate with Hunsecker, but when he arrives at the columnist's apartment, he finds Susan undressed, about to commit suicide. At that moment, Hunsecker enters and instantly assumes that Falco has sexually assaulted his sister. Hunsecker calls the police to arrest Falco for planting the marijuana on Steve Dallas. Susan packs a suitcase, saying that she will have nothing else to do with her brother.

As Susan crosses the street in front of Hunsecker's apartment building, Falco is beaten by the police and taken into custody.

Cary Grant, Joan Fontaine in *Suspicion* (RKO, 1941).

Sweet Smell of Success is the most cynical of the *noir* depictions of the entertainment business. The main characters are typical leeches who feed off the talents of others and who have become desensitized by the corrupting influences of the big city.

Stylistically, Alexander MacKendrick creates a dark, expressionist view of New York City that reminds one of early *films noirs*.

Sylos, F. Paul (*aka* **Frank Sylos**) (1900–1976)

Art director. A mural painter and designer of covers for *Liberty* magazine before entering films in 1935, Sylos became an adaptable, prolific production designer. He is one of the few art directors to have worked at nearly all the studios, both major and poverty row. His designs are always inventive, making effective use of space and angles.

Filmography: *When Strangers Marry* (Monogram, 1944). *Suspense* (Monogram, 1946). *Fear in the Night* (Paramount, 1947). *The Gangster* (Allied Artists, 1947). *The Pretender* (Republic, 1947). *Caught* (MGM, 1949). *Red Light* (United Artists, 1950). *99 River Street* (United Artists, 1953). *Suddenly* (United Artists, 1954). *The Naked Street* (United Artists, 1955). *City of Fear* (Columbia, 1959).

T-Men (Eagle-Lion), 1948. 92 min.

Producer: Aubrey Schenk. Director: Anthony Mann. Screenplay: John C. Higgins, story by Virginia Kellogg. Director of Photography: John Alton. Music: Paul Sawtell. Art Direction: Edward C. Jewell. Editor: Fred Allen.

Cast: Dennis O'Keefe (Dennis O'Brien), Alfred Ryder (Tony Genaro), Mary Meade (Evangeline), Wallace Ford (Schemer), June Lockhart (Tony's wife), Charles McGraw (Moxie). With: Jane Randolph, Art Smith, Herbert Heyes, Jack Overman.

Two Treasury agents, O'Brien and Genaro, are assigned to investigate the murder of another agent. They infiltrate a gang of counterfeiters. When Genaro's cover is blown, O'Brien is helpless when they kill his partner. O'Brien, however, eventually breaks the counterfeit ring and avenge's Genaro's murder by killing Moxie, the sadistic killer.

Although it was made for a modest sum, *T-Men* immediately established the reputations of Anthony Mann and cinematographer John Alton. It was a surprise success and within a year both men were signed by MGM.

John Alton's inventive photography dominates the movie. Particularly striking is the scene where Genaro is killed while the gang, including O'Brien, watch. The shot is staged so that both O'Brien and Genaro are placed at opposite ends of the frame in deep focus.

The film is basically just a conventional police thriller, but Mann's fast-paced direction and the unrelenting violence of the movie established a new realism that *noir* would continue to explore in the new decade.

Talbot, Lyle (Lyle Henderson) (1904–)

Actor. Talbot was a star of "B" movies, playing parts on both sides of the law in adventures and action films. He starred in the late "B" *noir*, *City of Fear*, his single appearance in the genre.

Filmography: *City of Fear* (Columbia, 1959).

Talk About a Stranger (MGM, 1952). 6 min.

Producer: Richard Goldstone. Director: David Bradley. Screenplay: Margaret Fiits, based on the short story "The Enemy" by Charlotte Armstrong. Director of Photography: John Alton. Music: David Buttolph. Art Directors: Cedric Gibbons and Eddie Imazu. Editor: Newell P. Kimlin.

Cast: George Murphy (Robert Fontaine, Sr.), Nancy Davis (Marge Fontaine), Billy Gray (Robert Fontaine,

Jr.), Lewis Stone (Mr. Wardlaw), Kurt Kaszner (Matlock). With: Anna Glomb, Katherine Warren, Teddy Infuhr.

Matlock, a doctor who is trying to start a new life after his son's death, becomes the target of Robert Fontaine Jr.'s accusations that he killed his dog and the suspicions of his neighbors.

Talk About a Stranger is a unique *film noir* with a juvenile protagonist whose paranoia and prejudice almost destroys an innocent man's life. The film is quite cynical in its depiction of the narrow mindedness of small town people; but, this being an MGM film, the movie ends on an upbeat note when Matlock and the young boy make amends.

Tamiroff, Akim (1899–1972)

Actor and leading man. Tamiroff's film career began in the mid-thirties, but he did not hit his stride until the mid-forties. He was briefly popular while most of the Hollywood superstars were off fighting in World War II. He starred in the "B" noir, *The Gangster* and two late-noirs directed by Orson Welles, most notably in *Touch of Evil* as a vicious racketeer.

Filmography: *The Gangster* (Allied Artists, 1947). *Mr. Arkadin* (Warner Bros., 1955). *Touch of Evil* (Universal, 1958).

The Tattered Dress (Universal, 1957) 93 min.

Producer: Albert Zugsmith. Director: Jack Arnold. Screenplay: George Zuckerman. Director of Photography: Carl E. Guthrie. Music: Frank Skinner. Art Directors: Alexander Golitzen and Bill Newberry. Editor: Edward Curtiss.

Cast: Jeff Chandler (James Gordon Blane), Jeanne Crain (Diane Blane), Jack Carson (Nick Hoak), Gail Russell (Carol Morrow), Elaine Stewart (Charleen Reston), Philip Reed (Michael Reston). With: George Tobias, Edward Andrews, Edward C. Platt, Paul Birch.

James Gordon Blane, a brilliant, amoral lawyer, comes to a desert town in California to defend Michael Reston, a rich misfit who has been charged with murder. Reston is accused of murdering a man who, he claims, assaulted his wife, Charleen. The murdered man was very popular in the town and Blane gets no sympathy from its citizens for defending the unpopular Reston and his trampy wife.

Blane gets Reston off, but he soon finds himself charged by the local sheriff, Nick Hoak, with bribery. He vigorously defends himself with his recently reconciled wife at his side. Eventually he proves that Carol Morron, the woman juror who made the bribery charge, is the sheriff's mistress. As Blane goes free, Carol shoots and kills her husband on the courtroom steps.

The director of *The Tattered Dress*, Jack Arnold, was a competent, occasionally inspired director, of 1950's horror and science fiction films. While this is not one of his best movies, like his classic sci-fi thriller, *It Came from Outer Space* (Universal, 1953), *The Tattered Dress* is set in a remote desert location. The locale works well to create a feeling of alienation and claustrophobia inherent in the screenplay.

The film's best performance is the supporting part by Gail Russell as the mistress of the narrow-minded Nick Hoak. Her performance is both tough and sympathetic.

The Tattooed Stranger (RKO, 1950). 6 min.

Producer: Jay Bonafield. Director: Edward J. Montagne. Screenplay: Phil Reisman, Jr. director of Photography: William Steiner. Music: Alan Schulman. Editor: David Cooper.

Cast: John Miles (Detective Tobin), Patricia White (Mary Mahan), Walter Kinsella (Lt. Corrigan), Frank Twedell (Capt. Lundquist), Rod McLennan (Capt. Gavin). With: Henry Lasko, Arthur Jarrett, Jim Boles, William Gibberson.

The Tattooed Stranger was developed from a two reel documentary produced by Jay Bonafield and directed by Edward J. Montagne. The feature is purely fictional, but it retains the basic realism of the short.

The story concerns two detectives who piece together the mystery of a murdered girl's past, eventually solving the case.

While it is certainly not a major film, *The Tattooed Stranger* is an effective semi-documentary about the day to day grind of police work. Its realistic style and subject would become more familiar in 1950's *films noirs*.

Taxi Driver (Columbia, 1976) 113 min.

Producers: Michael and Julia Phillips. Director: Martin Scorsese. Screenplay: Paul Schrader. Director of Photography: Michael Chapman. Music: Bernard Herrmann. Art Director: Charles Rosen. Editors: Tom Rolf and Melvin Shapiro.

Cast: Robert De Niro (Travis Bickle), Jodie Foster (Iris), Albert Brooks (Tom), Peter Boyle (Wizard), Cybil Sheppard (Betsy), Leonard Harris (Senator Palantine), Harvey Keitel (Sport). With: Murray Mosten, Richard Higgs, Vic Argo, Steven Prince, Martin Scorsese.

Travis Bickle, an ex-Marine and drifter, takes a job as a taxi driver in New York City. He drives through the city at night, finding the city full of filth and degenerates. He meets a pretty young woman, Betsy, who is a campaign worker for Senator Charles Palantine, a presidential candidate. Travis arranges a date with Betsy, but she is disgusted when he takes her to a pornographic movie and refuses to see him again.

Travis' depression increases. He buys guns and begins training himself through rigorous exercise. he meets Iris, a twelve year old prostitute. He watches her until he gets the nerve to approach her and buys her time from her pimp, Sport. However, he does not want to have sex with her, but to convince her to return home and go back to school. She is frightened by his intensity.

Travis is suddenly sure of his "mission" and he goes to a Senator Palantine rally to assassinate the candidate. When he is thwarted by security, he returns to the inner city where he shoots the pimp, Sport, his associate and Iris' customer, "rescuing" the young prostitute. He is wounded in the shoot out but when he recovers he is treated as a hero by the press. He receives a thank you letter from Iris' parents. He returns to work where he picks up a passenger, Betsy, but his passion for her has faded.

Taxi Driver is a modern *noir* which recasts the characters, themes and style in contemporary fashion. Travis Bickle is yet another disillusioned veteran who returns from service to find a city overrun by corruption. Like so many *noir* protagonists before him, he resorts to violence mainly out of frustration. Likewise, the visuals reiterate classic *noir* with hazy, neon photography, much of it at night. Finally, composer Bernard Herrmann provided a physical link to the genre and his score for this, his last film, is a jazz-laden, haunting score which mirrors the alienation and violence of the story.

Taylor, Dwight ( )

Screenwriter. Taylor was a staff writer for 20th Century–Fox in the forties. He co-wrote several *films noirs* and contributed the story for Sam Fuller's *noir* classic *Pickup on South Street*.

Filmography: *I Wake Up Screaming* (20th Century–Fox, 1941). *Conflict* (Warner Bros., 1945). *Pickup on South Street* (story only) (20th Century– Fox, 1953). *Vicki* (20th Century– Fox, 1953).

Taylor, Robert (Spangler Arlington Brugh) (1911–1969).

Actor. A conventional leading man and MGM contract player, Taylor was a star for nearly thirty years. He was married to Barbara Stanwyck for a number of years and starred in several *films noirs*. He is one of the genre's minor male icons.

Of his *noirs*, probably the best is Curtis Bernhardt's *The High Wall* in which Taylor stars as an amnesia victim accused of murdering his wife. He was also very good in *The Bribe*, an action oriented minor *noir* and in the early *Johnny Eager* as an ex-con who gets mixed up with a society girl.

Taylor's personality though was ill suited to a genre which relied on less conventionally handsome, more hard-boiled actors. Still, his performances are always good and he appeared in several of the best MGM *noirs*.

Filmography: *Johnny Eager* (MGM, 1942). *The High Wall* (MGM, 1947). *The Bribe* (MGM, 1949). *Rogue Cop* (MGM, 1954). *Party Girl* (MGM, 1958).

Teal, Ray (1901–1975)

Character actor. Teal was one of the busiest character actors, appearing in literally dozens of movies. He always played small roles, generally cops or corrupt city officials in his *films noirs*.

Filmography: *Brute Force* (Universal, 1947). *I Wouldn't Be in Your Shoes* (bit part) (Monogram, 1948). *Road House* (bit part) (20th Century–Fox, 1948). *Scene of the Crime* (bit part) (MGM, 1949). *The Asphalt Jungle* (bit part) (MGM, 1950). *Convicted* (Columbia, 1950). *Edge of Doom* (RKO, 1950). *Where Danger Lives* (RKO, 1950).

Tension (MGM, 1950). 95 min

Producer: Robert Sisk. Director: John Berry. Screenplay: Allen Rivkin. Director of Photography: Harry Stradling. Music: Andre Previn. Art Directors: Cedric Gibbons and Leonid Vasian. Editor: Albert Akst.

Cast: Richard Basehart (Warren Quimby), Audrey Totter (Claire Quimby), Cyd Charisse (Mary Chanler), Barry Sullivan (Lt. Collier Bonnabel), Lloyd Gough (Barney Deager). With: Tom D'Andrea, William Conrad, Tito Renaldo, Philip Van Zandt.

Warren Quimby, a mild mannered druggist, is shocked when his wife Claire announces that she is leaving him for another man. He begins to develop a new identity to create an alibi for his plan to kill the adulterous pair. In his new identity, he meets and falls in love with Mary Chanler and he decides that killing his wife and her lover would be useless. Still, drawn by curiosity, he goes to his wife's lover's beach house only to find that somebody has already killed him. Quimby is wanted for the murder, but Lt. Bonnabel suspects that Claire actually killed her boyfriend. He traps her into confessing and Quimby is free to continue his new life.

Audrey Totter had the role of her *noir* career in *Tension* as the sullen, cold Claire Quimby. The character is a classic *femme-fatale*, exploiting her weak husband and the cold-hearted murdering of her adulterous lover out of jealousy.

In many ways, *Tension* is a variation of Hitchcock's thrillers as the central character in the film is an innocent man accused of murder. Here, however, he is also the classic *noir* protagonist, trapped also by his own potential corruption—after all, he was planning to kill the man—who is rescued only through the interference of outside forces, in this case, Lt. Bonnabel.

Tension is not a classic *film noir*, but it is an enjoyable, taut thriller with several good performances.

Tetzlaff, Ted (1903–)

Cinematographer and director. Tetzlaff was a respected cinematographer for many years and he was the director of photographer on a number of classic movies including *My Man Godfrey* (Universal, 1936), *I Married a Witch* (United Artists, 1941) and Alfred Hitchcock's *noir*, *Notorious*.

Tetzlaff turned to directing in the late-forties. Although his career as a director was not as distinguished as his career as a cinematographer. He directed a number of good "B" movies including *Riff Raff* (RKO, 1947), a superior action adventure. Of his three *films noirs* as a director, the best is *The Window*, a minor classic based on a Cornell Woolrich short story.

Filmography: *Notorious* (Director of Photography only) (RKO, 1946). *A Dangerous Profession* (Director) (RKO, 1949). *The Window* (Director) (RKO, 1949). *Gambling House* (Director) (RKO, 1951).

They Live by Night (RKO, 1948). 95 min

Producer: John Houseman. Director: Nicholas Ray. Screenplay: Charles Schnee, adapted by Nicholas Ray from the novel *Thieves Like Us* by Edward Anderson. Director of Photography: George E. Diskant. Music: Leigh Harline. Song "Your Red Wagon" by Richard M. Jones, Don Raye and Gene De Paul. Art Directors: Albert S. D'Agostino and Al Herman. Editor: Sherman Todd.

Cast: Cathy O'Donnell (Keechie), Farley Granger (Bowie), Howard Da Silva (Chickamaw), Jay C. Flippen (T-Dub), Helen Craig (Mattie), Will Wright (Mobley). With: Marie Bryant, Ian Wolfe, William Phipps, Harry Harvey.

Two hardened criminals, Chickamaw and T-Dub, are joined in a prison break by a naive youth, Bowie. The three rob a bank, and Bowie is injured in a car accident as they are escaping. Bowie is nursed back to health by Keechie, the daughter of a man who helped in the prison break and the two fall in love. They marry and try to start a new life with their share of the robbery money; but Chickamaw and T-Dub force Bowie into another robbery. T-Dub is killed during the robbery and, after they part, Chickamaw is killed by the police. T-Dub's sister turns Bowie in to help get her own husband out of prison. Bowie is killed by the police when they come to arrest him and the pregnant Keechie is left desolate, but his love is confirmed when she finds a love letter he wrote to her moments before being killed.

Director Nicholas Ray establishes visual and emotional contrasts from the very opening of *They Live by Night*: the pre-credit shot shows the lovers deep in embrace and the shot dissolves to a car full of men speeding toward their night rendezvous with crime and violence.

They Live by Night was Nicholas Ray's first film as a director and it dealt with a familiar theme of first time directors: lovers on the run. His style is both visceral and detached, capturing the fear in the violent scenes and the alienation of the lovers.

The film is also a variation of the Bonnie and Clyde legend of a couple involved in crime and violence— Joseph H. Lewis' *Gun Crazy* (United Artists, 1950) is another version. Unlike the later film, Keechie is not a *femme-fatale* who leads her man into a life of crime, but rather they are a couple trapped by both social and private forces. Ultimately, however, they too succumb to their existential fate.

They Won't Believe Me (RKO, 1947). 95 min.

Producer: Joan Harrison. Director: Irving Pichel. Screenplay: Jonathan Latimer, story by Gordon McDonell. Director of Photography: Harry J. Wild. Music: Roy Webb. Art Director: Albert S. D'Agostino and Robert Boyle. Editor: Elmo Williams.

Cast: Robert Young, (Larry Ballentine), Susan Hayward (Verna Carlson), Jane Greer (Janice Ball), Rita Johnson (Gretta), Tom Powers (Trenton). With: George Tyne, Don Beddoe, Frank Ferguson, Harry Harvey.

Larry Ballentine, on trial for the murder of his girl friend, Verna Carlson, takes the stand in his defense and tells his story. Ballentine admits that he married his wife, Gretta, for her money and, unhappy, had a series of affairs. Eventually he meets a young secretary, Verna, and begins a liaison with her. He runs off to Reno with his lover planning to divorce his wife and marry Verna. However, on the way to Reno, the couple are involved in a terrible auto wreck in which Verna is burned to death. Ballentine allows the police to believe the victim was his wife and when he returns home, he discovers that his wife has committed suicide. He tries to cover up his lies, but eventually Gretta's body is discovered and Ballentine arrested.

When the jury leaves to deliberate, Ballantine kills himself by leaping out of the courtroom window. Ironically, the verdict returned is not guilty.

They Won't Believe Me was one of the early *films noirs* of the RKO cycle. It was released the same year as *Out of the Past*, but did not have the same impact as that classic. Still, it is notable for its typical RKO style, (including a good score by Roy Webb), its producer Joan Harrison, and its co-star, Jane Greer, as one of the women with whom Larry Ballentine has an affair.

The Thief (United Artists, 1952). 8 min.
Producer: Clarence Greene. Director: Russell Rouse. Screenplay: Clarence Greene and Russell Rouse. Music: Herschel Burke Gilbert. Production Design: Joseph St. Amand. Editor: Chester Shaeffer.

Cast; Ray Milland (Allan Fields), Martin Gabel (Mr. Bleek), Rita Gam (the girl), Harry Bronson (Harris), John McKutcheon (Dr. Linstrum), Rita Vale (Miss Philips), Rex O'Malley (Beal), Joe Conlin (Walters).

Dr. Allan Fields, a scientist with the Atomic Energy Commission, sells secrets to the Communists. When a middle man is killed with microfilm in his hand, the F.B.I. begins to investigate. With the heat on him, Fields tries to escape, but when he kills an F.B.I.

agent he realizes the horror of his crimes and waits for the agents to come get him.

The Thief was released with a storm of publicity, partly because of its topical anti-communism, but also because of its unique experiment — the story is told without the benefit of dialog. Director Russell Rouse tells the story through images and sound, creating an odd empathy with the alienated Dr. Fields. Ray Milland's performance is understated, expressed through body language and facial expressions.

Although an interesting experiment, *The Thief* does not rise above being a curiosity.

Thieves' Highway (20th Century–Fox, 1949). 94 min.
Producer: Robert Bassler. Director: Jules Dassin. Screenplay: A. I. Bezzerides, based on his novel *Thieves' Market*. Director of Photography: Norbet Brodine. Music: Alfred Newman. Art Directors: Lyle Wheeler and Chester Gore. Editor: Nich De Maggio.

Cast: Richard Conte (Nick Garcos), Valentina Cortesa (Rica), Lee J. Cobb (Figlia), Barbara Lawrence (Pollu), Jack Oakie (Slob). With: Millard Mitchell, Joseph Pevney, Morris Carnovsky, Tamara Shayne, Kasia Orzazewski.

Nick Garcos, an ex–G.I., invests in a truck to haul produce to San Francisco. With two acquaintances, Slob and Ed, each of whom has their own truck, Nick takes a load of apples to San Francisco. He arrives before the other two at their destination, a distributor run by Figlia. Figlia, a corrupt produce distributor, pays a girl named Rica to entice Nick to her apartment so that he can sell Nick's produce to a wholesaler without having to pay Nick. However, Rica admits to the plan and Nick confronts Figlia, forcing him to pay him his money. Nick, returning to Rica's apartment, is robbed by two of Figlia's henchmen. Ed is killed in a crash, and when Slob and other truckers arrive with the news, Figlia offers to pay them to pick up Ed's load and deliver it to him. When Nick's girlfriend Polly discovers Nick with Rica she angrily tells him she doesn't ever want to see him again.

Enraged by the events, Nick returns to Figlia's warehouse where Slob tells him of Ed's death. When an associate of Figlia's admits that he arranges accidents to steal and resell produce, Nick attacks Figlia, braking his fingers in front of a crooked wholesaler who then returns Nick's money. Nick returns to Rica.

Thieves' Highway is an unrelenting portrait of, literally, highway robbery and the sort of men, like Figlia, who prey on luckless, hard working men like Nick and his friends.

Once again, *Thieves' Highway* demonstrates the *noir* contrasts between city and rural life. The scenes in the country as the truckers load their trucks is shot in bright light, but as they approach the city, the lighting grows darker and Dassin increases his use of odd angles and tight close ups.

Of course, the film is overloaded with political symbolism, with Dassin obviously contrasting the lives of the working class and their exploiters. Interestingly, Nick and Rica's relationship can also be viewed in political terms for it is this exotic, dark-haired, sexually amoral girl that Nick chooses rather than the blonde, but avaricious Polly, who represents the false ambitions of the American middle class.

The Thirteenth Letter (20th Century-Fox, 1951). 88 min.

Producer and Director: Otto Preminger. Screenplay: Howard Koch, from a story and screenplay *Le Corbeau* by Louis Chavance. Director of Photography: Joseph La Shelle. Music: Alex North. Music Director: Lionel Newman. Art Directors: Lyle Wheeler and Maurice Ransford. Editor: Louis Loeffler.

Cast: Linda Darnell (Denise), Charles Boyer (Dr. Laurent), Michael Rennie (Dr. Pearson), Constance Smith (Cora Laurent), Francoise Rosay (Mrs. Sims). With: Judith Evelyn, Guy Sorel, June Hedin, Camille Ducharme.

Dr. Pearson is a young, highly talented doctor who works in a hospital in a small French-Canadian village. He has come to the village to escape the memories of a broken romance. His tranquility, however, is shattered when Cora Laurent, the pretty young wife of the older, revered Dr. Laurent, receives a letter accusing Pearson of having an affair with her. The letter is simply signed "The Raven." Soon, a number of other citizens receive poison-pen letters, all singed by "The Raven." A patient, falsely informed that he has cancer, commits suicide.

When a letter falls from the choir into the congregation in church, Pearson takes control of the investigation. Although he gets samples of all eighteen choir members' handwriting, none of them match the handwriting of the letter. Eventually, Cora admits she wrote the first letter in a moment of weakness because she is sexually attracted to the remote Dr. Pearson. When her husband, Dr. Laurent, discovered what she had done, he forced her to write the other letters to demonstrated his theory of the "insanity of the two": that one person's mad act can inspire a mad act in another.

The mother of the young suicide gets revenge for the tragic death of her child by slitting the throat of Dr. Laurent.

Henri Jacques Clouzot has been called the "French Hitchcock." In the 1940's he made a group of extraordinary suspense films including *Le Corbeau*, a classic. Clouzot's version is much more relentless in its suspense and uncompromising in its view of narrow minded small town people.

While Otto Preminger's version lacks some of the latent sexual perversity of Clouzot's original, Preminger does retain much of the suspense of *Le Corbeau*. Furthermore, his style, here heavily expressionist, makes it one of the most interesting *films noirs*.

This Gun for Hire (Paramount, 1942). 8 min.
Producer: Richard M. Blumenthal. Director: Frank Tuttle. Screenplay: Albert Maltz and W. R. Burnett, based on the novel by Graham Greene. Director of Photography: John Seitz. Music: Frank Loesser and Jacques Press. Art Directors: Hans Dreier and Robert Usher. Editor: Archie Marshek.
Cast: Alan Ladd (Phillip Raven), Veronica Lake (Ellen Graham), Robert Preston (Michael Crane), Laird Cregar (William Gates), Tully Marshall (Alvin Brewster).

Phillip Raven is a psychotic professional assassin and is hired by William Gates to kill a possible police informant. Gates' boss, Alvin Brewster, sells chemicals to the Nazis. Raven carries out his assignment successfully, but is paid by Gates with some "hot cash" and is soon being followed by the police. When he discovers that he was set up, Raven boards a train to return to Los Angeles to get even with Gates for setting him up. On the train he coincidentally meets Ellen Graham, the fiancée of the head detective, Michael Crane, who has been following him.

Raven falls for the beautiful Ellen and she, in turn, sympathizes with him because she believes he has gotten a "tough break" by life. She convinces him that he should use Gates to get to his boss, but, in fact, she is actually a government agent. She has set into motion a series of inevitable events which result in the death of the traitor Alvin Brewster and Raven's death when Crane shoots him. Raven dies without bitterness, realizing he has helped the only person who has ever been kind to him.

This Gun for Hire was one of the most important early *films noirs*, although its propaganda dates it badly.

It is important for its strong Paramount style, particularly John F. Seitz's exotic, atmospheric photography, and of course, the performances of Alan Ladd, Veronica Lake and Laird Cregar. The film's overall theme of self-destruction (in the guise of Ladd's Raven) is here developed to a degree it had not been before, but would become more familiar as *noir* matured.

Thompson, Jim (1906–1977)
Novelist. Thompson's crime novels are in the tradition of James M. Cain: lower middle class con men and people struggling to make it in an indifferent world. He co-wrote Stanley Kubrick's *The Killing*. The modern *noir*, *The Grifters* is based on his novel.
Filmography: *The Killing* (co-wrote) (United Artists, 1956). *The Grifters* (based on his novel) (Miramax, 1991).

Thorpe, Richard (Rollo Smolt Thorpe) (1896–)
Director. An exceptionally prolific director, Thorpe was one of the major staff directors at MGM during the studio's golden age. He directed several of their great epics and a single *film noir*. He was a competent craftsman, but not very inventive and his style was rather conventional.
Filmography: *The Unknown Man* (MGM, 1951).

Thunder Road (United Artists, 1958). 92 min.
Producer: Robert Mitchum. Director: Arthur Ripley. Screenplay: James Arlee Philips and Walter Wise, story by Robert Mitchum. Director of Photography: Alan Stensvold. Music: Jack Marshall. Editor: Margaret Horning.
Cast: Robert Mitchum (Lucas Doolin), Gene Barry (Troy Barrett), Jacques Aubuchon (Carl Kogan), Keely Smith (Francie Wymore), Jim Mitchum (Robin Doolin). With: Trevor Bardette, Sandra Knight, Betsy Holt, Francis Keon, Randy Sparks.

Robert Mitchum's pet project is a downbeat tale of a family of hillbilly bootleggers who defy a Chicago gangster. Action filled and quite violent, the film's rural milieu is alien to *film noir*, but its fatalism and typically strong performance by *noir* icon Mitchum qualify it, at the very least, as marginal *film noir*.

Thunderbolt (Paramount, 1929). 81 min.

Producer and Director: Josef Von Sternberg. Screenplay: Jules Furthman, dialog by Herman J. Mankiewicz, story by Charles and Jules Furthman. Titles: Joseph Mankiewicz. Director of Photography: Henry Gerrard. Art Director: Hans Dreier. Editor: Helen Lewis.

Cast: George Bancroft (Thunderbolt Jim Lang), Fay Wray (Ritzy), Richard Arlen (Bob Morgan), Tully Marshall (Warden), Eugenie Besserer (Mrs. Morgan).

Thunderbolt Jim Lang is a notorious, vicious gangster. When he is caught and convicted in a series of crimes, he has a change of heart and repents.

Thunderbolt is important chiefly because of its extravagant style and its gloomy scenario. Josef Von Sternberg was one of the most influential directors and in this and several other crime movies he directed in this era had a profound effect on the developing gangster genre and later *film noir*.

Tidyman, Ernest (1928–1984)

Novelist and screenwriter. Tidyman wrote the famous *Shaft* series of crime novels. He also wrote a number of screenplays including the post-*noir* classic, *The French Connection*.

Filmography: *The French Connection* (20th Century-Fox, 1971).

Tierney, Gene (1920–1992)

Actress. Tierney was born to a wealthy New York family. When she expressed an interest in acting, her father formed a company to promote her. She had a brief career on Broadway before Hollywood beckoned in the early forties where she signed with 20th Century-Fox.

At first, Tierney's odd, exotic beauty typecast her as an ethnic, and she played Indians, South Americans and Orientals. As the latter, she co-starred in the early *noir*, *The Shanghai Gesture*. Her supporting role as the prostitute/daughter of mother Gin Sling and Sir Guy Charteris, did nothing to change her exotic image, but did confirm her popularity.

It was *Laura*, however, which propelled Tierney to true stardom. As the object of romantic obsession, Laura/Tierney is the very image of ethereal beauty in early *film noir*.

While Laura is not a *femme-fatale*, Tierney's Ellen Berent in *Leave Her to Heaven* is one of the most splendid bitchy villainesses in *film noir*.

Tierney also had important roles in two additional *noirs*, *Night and the City* and *Where the Sidewalk Ends*. Her roles in both movies, while important, were subsidiary to the male leads in each.

It is for her roles in *Leave Her to Heaven* and particularly *Laura* that Gene Tierney remains one of *noir's* most important early female icons.

Filmography: *The Shanghai Gesture* (United Artists, 1941). *Laura* (20th Century-Fox, 1944). *Leave Her to Heaven* (20th Century-Fox, 1945). *Night and the City* (20th Century-Fox, 1950). *Where the Sidewalk Ends* (20th Century-Fox, 19950).

Tierney, Lawrence (1919–)

Actor. Tierney was the older brother of Scott Brady. Tierney's film career began in 1943 and hit its apex two years later with the violent gangster drama, *Dillinger* (Warner Bros., 1945). He starred in many low budget films including several *noirs*. He specialized in violent psychopaths as he played in both *Born to Kill* and *The Devil Thumbs a Ride*.

Filmography: *Born to Kill* (RKO, 1947). *The Devil Thumbs a Ride* (RKO, 1947). *Bodyguard* (RKO, 1948).

Tight Spot (Columbia, 1955). 97 min
Producer: Lewis J. Rachmil. Director: Phil Karlson. Screenplay: William Bowers, based on the novel by Leonard Kantor. Director of Photography: Burnett Guffey. Music: George Duning. Editor: Jerome Thoms.
Cast: Ginger Rogers (Sherry Conley), Edward G. Robinson (Lloyd Hallet), Brian Keith (Vince Striker), Lucy Marlow (Prison Girl), Lorne Greene (Benjamin Costain).
Tight Spot is a kind of "A" version of *The Narrow Margin* (RKO, 1950). In this case a gangster moll, Sherry Conley, is escorted from prison by a tough cop so that she can testify against her former boyfriend. However, this film has none of the suspense of the "B" *noir* classic, and, despite some humor, the performances are perfunctory.

Tiomkin, Dimitri (1894–1979)
Composer. Like Max Steiner, the Russian born Tiomkin was a prolific composer of high quality film scores. He won three Academy Awards in his four decade career and he specialized in grand, sweeping scores that are at once melancholy and epic, but he also adapted his style for smaller scale movies. He composed the music for a number of important *films noirs*.
Filmography: *Shadow of a Doubt* (Universal, 1943). *When Strangers Marry* (Monogram, 1944). *The Dark Mirror* (Universal, 1946). *The Long Night* (RKO, 1947). *Champion* (United Artists, 1949). *Red Light* (United Artists, 1949). *D.O.A.* (United Artists, 1950). *Guilty Bystander* (Film Classics, 1950). *Strangers on a Train* (Warner Bros., 1951). *Angel Face* (RKO, 1953). *Jeopardy* (MGM, 1953).

Tolobuff, Alexander (1881–1940)
Art director. Tolobuff worked at MGM and later for independent producer Walter Wanger. He was the production designer for a single early *noir*, Fritz Lang's *You Only Live Once*.
Filmography: *You Only Live Once* (United Artists, 1937).

Too Late for Tears (United Artists 1949). 98 min.
Producer: Hunt Stromberg. Director: Byron Haskin. Screenplay: Roy Huggins, based on his novel. Director of Photography: William Mellor. Music: Dale Butts. Art Director: James Sullivan. Editor: Harry Keller.
Cast: Lizabeth Scott (Jane Palmer), Don DeFore (Don Blake), Dan Duryea (Danny Fuller), Arthur Kennedy (Alan Palmer), Kristine Miller (Kathy Palmer), Barry Kelly (Lt. Breach).
While driving to a party late one night, Alan Palmer and his wife Jane are arguing. The car swerves off the road and the headlights are accidentally blinked causing the occupants of another car to think they were signalled and a bag of money is thrown into the Palmer's car. Alan wants to turn the $60,000 over to the police, but Jane convinces him to wait a few days before calling them.
While Alan is out, a sleazy private detective calls on Jane, claiming ownership of the money. She agrees to split it with him, but, realizing Alan would not agree to her keeping the money, she murders him when he returns home and disposes of his body.
By coincidence, Don Blake, an old army buddy of Alan's suddenly arrives. He is actually a friend of Jane's first husband whom he suspects Jane murdered. He slowly begins to realize that Jane has killed Alan as well. Eventually, Don calls the police just before Jane departs for Mexico City. As she hurries to elude the police, she falls from a balcony to her death and the money flutters down after her.
Too Late for Tears provided Lizabeth Scott with her most corrosive role as the avaricious Jane Palmer. A minor film it nevertheless is an excellent

example of "B" movie making at its best, particularly in its use of Los Angeles locales.

Toomey, Regis (1902–)

Character actor. Toomey began his film career in the early thirties and for some four decades he played in mostly "B" features. He had small roles in several *films noirs*, playing cops in at least three. One of his best roles was in *Strange Illusion* as an odd psychiatrist in a mental hospital.

Filmography: *Phantom Lady* (Universal, 1944). *Strange Illusion* (P.R.C., 1945). *The Big Sleep* (Warner Bros., 1946). *The Guilty* (Monogram, 1947). *I Wouldn't Be in Your Shoes* (Monogram, 1948). *Beyond the Forest* (Warner Bros., 1949). *Cry Danger* (RKO, 1951). *The People Against O'Hara* (MGM, 1951).

Totter, Audrey (1918–)

Actress. Totter first achieved success as a radio actress. As a film actress, her dyed-blonde hair and voluptuous figure typecast her as a hard-boiled city girl or gangster moll. She is also a minor female *noir* icon.

Totter had small supporting roles in *The Postman Always Rings Twice* and *The Unsuspected*. She had more substantial roles in her other *noir* roles. She specialized in cold professionals, starring in *The High Wall*, for example as a psychiatrist, and in *Lady in the Lake*, as a publishing executive.

Filmography: *The Postman Always Rings Twice* (MGM, 1946). *The High Wall* (MGM, 1947). *Lady in the Lake* (MGM, 1947). *The Unsuspected* (Warner Bros., 1947). *The Set-Up* (RKO, 1949). *Tension* (MGM, 1950).

Touch of Evil (Universal, 1958). 9 min.

Producer; Albert Zugsmith. Director: Orson Welles. Screenplay: Orson Welles, based on the novel *Badge of Evil* by Whit Masterson. Director of Photography: Russell Metty. Music: Henry Mancini. Art Directors: Alex-ander Golitzen and Robert Clatworthy. Editors: Virgil M. Vogel and Aaron Stell.

Cast: Charlton Heston (Ramon Miguel "Mike" Vargas), Janet Leigh (Susan Vargas), Orson Welles (Hank Quinlan), Joseph Calleia (Pete Menzies), Akim Tamiroff (Uncle Joe Brandi), Marlene Dietrich (Tanya), Victor Millan (Sanchez). With: Joanna Moore, Ray Collins, Dennis Weaver.

A millionaire named Linnecker and his blonde companion are blown up in his car on the Mexican border. Two detectives work on the case: Mike Vargas, a Mexican narcotics detective on honeymoon with his American wife, Susan and Hank Quinlan, a brilliant stateside detective. Quinlan believes that a young Mexican, Sanchez, is guilty of the double murder and plants evidence to frame him. Discovering this, Vargas sets out to expose Quinlan. Quinlan sets into motion a series of violent events, beginning with having Susan Vargas kidnapped (to frame her as a drug addict) and ending in his death in a shootout with his associates. Ironically, Sanchez confesses to the original murder.

The reputation of *Touch of Evil* has increased since the mixed reception it received upon initial release. The film displays Orson Welles' extravagant style at its best, but within the framework of a conventional mystery-thriller. Russell Metty's cinematography recalls the expressionist style of early *film noir*, with a heavy reliance on shadows and shafts of light piercing the darkness.

Orson Welles gives one of his best performances as Hank Quinlan. Very obese, the character's physical presence seems to represent his corruption. The sight of Quinlan staggering down an embankment to die in a river full of garbage is one of *noir*'s indelible scenes. As Vargas and his wife leave, the tragedy is underscored by Quinlan's old friend Tanya's epitaph that "he was some kind of man," an understatement which also seems to apply to Welles' career as well—this was his last major film as a director.

Tourneur, Jacques (1904–1977)

Director. Jacques Tourneur was the son of the famous silent film director Maurice Tourneur. Jacques began directing American features in 1939 after many years as a script clerk, editor and director of features and shorts in both the United States and France.

When Tourneur's friend Val Lewton joined RKO as a "B" producer in the early thirties, he immediately hired Tourneur and the director subsequently worked on two of Lewton's greatest films: *Cat People* (RKO, 1942) and *I Walked with a Zombie* (RKO, 1943). These immensely influential films established Tourneur's style; deeply expressionist lighting, fluid camera movements and quick cutaways to environmental metaphors (i.e., leaves blowing in trees, rain pouring down, etc.).

Tourneur's *films noirs* are equally extravagant in their style, but like his best work also strongly humanist. *Experiment Perilous* is a thriller in the *Gaslight* tradition and *Berlin Express* is an excellent, if under appreciated espionage *noir* set in war ravaged Germany.

Out of the Past is Tourneur's masterpiece. It is a quintessential *film noir*. Gloomy, romantic, darkly sensual, the movie is also a textbook case of Hollywood filmmaking at its very best.

Unfortunately, Tourneur never equalled the success of his 1940 movies. Like Lewton, when he was elevated to "A" pictures he seemed to falter. His 1950's films have not stood up well compared to his earlier work. *Nightfall*, an attempt to make a film like *Out of the Past*, while it has some admirable moments, does not have the spirit of its great predecessors.

If, ultimately, Jacques Tourneur is a minor director, he also is undeniably an influential filmmaker whose best movies have withstood the test of time.

Filmography: *Experiment Perilous* (RKO, 1944). *Out of the Past* (RKO, 1947). *Berlin Express* (RKO, 1948). *Nightfall* (Columbia, 1957).

Tover, Leo (1902–1964)

Cinematographer. Tover was a prolific, adaptable craftsman whose work is almost always exemplary if rarely inventive. However, he worked on several striking black and white films including Anatole Litvak's *The Snake Pit* (20th Century-Fox, 1948) and two important *films noirs*.

Filmography: *Dead Reckoning* (Columbia, 1947). *I Walk Alone* (Paramount, 1948).

Towers, Constance (1928–)

Actress. Towers, who has long been married to actor/diplomat John Gavin, starred in a few "B" movies in the fifties and sixties and also appeared for many years on a popular daytime television soap opera. She specialized in hardbitten blondes as in Samuel Fuller's *The Naked Kiss*, in which she played yet another variation of Fuller's whore with a heart of gold. Her performance is excellent.

Filmography: *The Naked Kiss* (Allied Artists, 1964).

Towne, Robert (1936–)

Screenwriter. Towne is one of the leading screenwriters of his generation. His *Chinatown*, one of the great post-*noirs*, is a richly complex, metaphorical script, partly based on real historical events.

Filmography: *Chinatown* (Paramount, 1974).

Trevor, Claire (Claire Wemlinger) (1909–)

Actress. Claire Trevor was a very gifted actress who projected toughness mixed with vulnerability so well that she would be typecast as the whore with the heart of gold or the gangster's moll. While she might not be as well known as several of her contemporaries,

Trevor gave *noir* some of its best per-formances and she is one of the genre's most important female icons.

Trevor played both heroines and *femme-fatales*. As the latter, she was particularly memorable in *Murder, My Sweet*. Her *femme-fatale* in *Street of Chance* was one of the genre's most cruel and vicious.

One of Trevor's best *noir* perfor-mances was in *Born to Kill* as a divorcé who enters the dark world of a homi-cidal maniac with tragic results.

Equally memorable was Trevor's role as the much abused gangster's moll in John Huston's *Key Largo*. Her incredi-ble performance in the film earned her one of *noir's* few Academy Awards.

Filmography: *Street of Chance* (Paramount, 1942). *Murder, My Sweet* (RKO, 1944). *Johnny Angel* (RKO, 1945). *Crack-Up* (RKO, 1946). *Born To Kill* (RKO, 1947). *Key Largo* (Warner Bros., 1948). *Raw Deal* (Eagle-Lion, 1948).

Trivas, Victor (1896–1970)
Screenwriter. Trivas wrote or co-wrote a few successful movies in the forties. He worked on two *films noirs*.
Filmography: *The Stranger* (co-wrote) (RKO, 1946). *Where the Sidewalk Ends* (adaption only) (20th Century–Fox, 1950).

Truffaut, François (1932–1984)
Director and critic. The most talented of the French "new wave" directors who emerged in the late fifties, Truffaut was also a prominent critic in the early part of the decade. He helped establish Alfred Hitchcock's reputation and was one of the earliest critics to identify *film noir* as a genre.

Try and Get Me (United Artists, 1950) 90 min.
Producer: Robert Stillman. Direc-tor: Cyril Endfield. Screenplay: Jo Pagano, based on his novel *The Con-demned*. Director of Photography: Guy Roe. Music: Hugo Friedhofer. Art

Director: Perry Ferguson. Editor: George Amy.
Cast: Frank Lovejoy (Howard Tyler), Kathleen Ryan (Judy Tyler), Richard Carlson (Gil Stanton), Lloyd Bridges (Jerry Slocum), Katherine Locke (Hazel), Adele Jergens (Velma). With: Art Smith, Renzo Cesana, Irene Vernon, Lynn Gray.

Out of desperation, a down on his luck veteran, Howard Tyler, teams up with a casual acquaintance, Jerry Slocum, in a robbery. The robbery backfires into a kidnapping plot, but the victim is accidentally killed. Their plan crumbles and the two men hide out to wait for community anger to cool down. The two men are eventually captured and held in the county jail; but an angry mob gathers, breaks into the jailhouse and beats the two men to death as the police stand by helpless.

Unlike Fritz Lang's *Fury* (MGM, 1936), the first thriller to explore mob violence, *Try and Get Me* does not end on an upbeat note. On the contrary, the mindless violence of the two men is recreated in the violent actions of vigi-lantes—no one is innocent. The direc-tor of the film Cyril Endfield, would shortly be blacklisted for his socialist ideals.

Turner, Kathleen (1954–)
Actress and leading lady. Turner made a striking film debut as Maddy Walker in *Body Heat*, the epitome of the *noir femme-fatale* in a contem-porary setting.
Filmography: *Body Heat* (Warner Bros., 1981).

The Turning Point (Paramount, 1952). 85 min.
Producer: Irving Asher. Director: William Dieterle. Screenplay: Warren Duff, story by Horace McCoy. Direc-tor of Photography: Lionel Lindon. Music: Irving Talbot. Art Directors: Hal Pereira and Joseph McMillan Johnson. Editor: George Tomasini.

Cast: William Holden (Jerry McKibbon), Edmond O'Brien (John Conroy), Alexis Smith (Amanda Waycross), Tom Tully (Matt Conroy), Ed Begley (Eichelberger), Dan Dayton (Ackerman). With: Adele Longmire, Ray Teal, Ted DeCorsia, Don Porter.

John Conroy is an honest lawyer and politician. He is appointed to the head of a special committee investigating organized crime in a large midwestern city. Conroy's friend, Jerry McKibbon, an investigative reporter, covers the activities of Eichelberger, the head of the local mob. Eichelberger targets both men. When Conroy's committee subpoenas some of Eichelberger's records, Eichelberger burns down a building where they are stored, killing many of the people who live there. Eventually a witness to a murder committed by Eichelberger's aide reveals herself to the committee. Unfortunately, McKibbon walks into a trap before Conroy can warn him and is shot and killed by a hired assassin.

Political corruption was a topical subject in the early fifties, a theme that cropped up in a few *films noirs*. Here, it is realistically treated by William Dieterle in semi-documentary style. Indeed, this underrated film is one of Dieterle's best, with a great performance by William Holden as the doomed journalist.

Tuttle, Frank (1892–1963)
Director. Tuttle was born in New York City. A graduate of Yale, he worked for *Vanity Fair* as a journalist before joining Paramount as a screenwriter. He began directing in 1929. Like most staff directors, Tuttle was a competent craftsman, an expert at unpretentious entertainments. He directed two *films noirs*, the best of which is the taut, early *noir* thriller *This Gun for Hire* which first teamed Veronica Lake and Alan Ladd.

Filmography: *This Gun for Hire* (Paramount, 1942). *Suspense* (Monogram, 1946).

20th Century-Fox
A production and distribution corporation founded in 1935 by a merger of Twentieth Century Pictures (a production company founded by Darryl F. Zanuck) and the Fox Film Corporation. Zanuck was named Vice President in charge of Production and he proceeded to turn the studio into a kind of curate MGM: color musicals and nostalgic family dramas were the studio's bread and butter. Art directors Lyle Wheeler, Leland Fuller and their various collaborators supplied the studio with elegant, richly decorated sets and made excellent use of their often modest budgets. The studio had several talented directors under contract including Otto Preminger and Henry Hathaway who made several classic *noirs* each. The studio's *noirs* were often more romantic than the other studios, and with actors like Richard Widmark under contract, seemed to have a corner on violent psychopaths. It would not be unfair to claim 20th Century-Fox as the second most important studio in *film noir* as it produced more *noir* classics than any studio other than RKO.

Releases: **1941:** *I Wake Up Screaming. Laura.* **1945:** *Fallen Angel. House on 92nd Street. Leave Her to Heaven.* **1946:** *The Dark Corner. Somewhere in the Night. Shock. Strange Triangle.* **1947:** *The Brasher Doubloon. Kiss of Death. Nightmare Alley.* **1948:** *Call Northside 777. Cry of the City. Road House. The Street with No Name.* **1949:** *House of Strangers. Thieves' Highway.* **1950:** *Night and the City. Panic in the Streets. Where the Sidewalk Ends.* **1951:** *House on Telegraph Hill. The Man Who Cheated Himself. The Thirteenth Letter. Fourteen Hours.* **1953:** *Niagara.*

The Two Mrs. Carrolls (Warner Bros. 1947). 99 min.
Producer: Mark Hellinger. Director: Peter Godfrey. Screenplay: Thomas Job, based on the play by Martin Vale. Director of Photography: Peverell Marley. Music: Franz Waxman. Art

Director: Anton Grot. Editor: Frederick Richards.

Cast: Humphrey Bogart (Geoffrey Carrolls), Barbara Stanwyck (Sally Carrolls), Alexis Smith (Cecily Latham), Nigel Bruce (Dr. Tuttle), Isobel Elsom (Mrs. Latham). With: Pat O'Moore, Anne Carter, Anita Bolster.

Sally Carrolls, the second wife of the respected portrait painter, Geoffrey Carrolls, begins to suspect that her husband is trying to kill her. Geoffrey, meanwhile, begins painting the portrait of his beautiful blonde neighbor, Cecily Latham. In fact, Geoffrey is a psychopathic murderer who plans to seduce and marry Cecily as his new muse. When Geoffrey discovers that Sally has been throwing out the poisoned milk he has been giving her, he attacks her, strangling her with a curtain cord. The police arrive just in time to save Sally and as they take Geoffrey away, he babbles incoherently.

The Two Mrs. Carrolls is another variation of the *Suspicion* theme of wife suspects husband is trying to kill her. The rural English setting is alien to *film noir*, but it is so well made in its gothic style and great performances by *noir* icons Humphrey Bogart and Barbara Stanwyck, that it qualifies as a true *noir*.

Ulmer, Edgar G. (1904–1972)

Director. Like Billy Wilder, Robert and Curt Siodmak and Fred Zinnemann, Ulmer's career began in Germany in the late twenties. He was an assistant director on Robert Siodmak's *People on Sunday* (UFA, 1929). Ulmer directed a few films in Germany before emigrating to the United States in the early thirties. He subsequently directed a classic horror film, *The Black Cat* (Universal, 1934), but a personal conflict with one of the studio's executives caused him to be blackballed by the major studios.

For about a decade, Ulmer worked on the fringes of the American film industry, making ethnic films until he joined the poverty row studio, Pro-ducers Releasing Corporation (PRC), in the early forties.

Ulmer had enormous creative freedom at PRC. He was allowed to make the kind of films he wanted to make so long as he kept the budgets under $40,000. His best film *Detour*, allegedly cost $20,000 and was shot in only two days.

Detour has an enormous cult following, particularly in Europe, largely because of its tragic theme. Indeed, it is one of the most misanthropic *films noirs*, and Ulmer's dark, expressionist style reiterates the themes.

Although less well known, Ulmer's two additional *films noirs* are worth viewing.

If Ulmer's films look better today, it is probably because he had the freedom to show life in America in the forties as he saw it, not as imposed by imperious studio bosses.

Filmography: *Detour* (PRC), 1945). *Strange Illusion* (PRC, 1945). *Murder Is My Beat* (Allied Artists, 1955).

Uncle Harry (aka The Strange Affair of Uncle Harry) (Universal, 1945). 80 min.

Producer: Joan Harrison. Director: Robert Siodmak. Screenplay: Stephen Longstreet, adapted by Keith Winter from the play by Thomas Job. Director of Photography: Paul Ivano. Music: H. J. Salter. Art Directors: John Goodman and Eugene Lourie. Editor: Arthur Hilton.

Cast: George Sanders (John Quincy), Geraldine Fitzgerald (Lettie Quincy), Ella Raines (Deborah Brown), Sara Allood (Nona), Moyna MacGill (Hester). With: Samuel S. Hinds, Harry Von Zell, Ethel Griffies, Judy Clark, Craig Reynolds.

John Quincy is a lonely bachelor who lives with his two bossy sisters, Lettie and Hester, in Corinth, New Hampshire. He meets Deborah Brown, a visiting fashion expert from New York City. Eventually their friendship develops into love and he asks Deborah to marry him. Although Hester is happy for him, Lettie is jealous of Deborah and sets out to destroy their happiness. Driven to the point of insanity by his sister's action, John plans to poison Lettie, but Hester drinks the poison instead and dies. Lettie is convicted of her sister's murder but she does not implicate John because she knows her execution will prevent him from marrying the hated Deborah.

John suddenly wakes up — all of this has been only a dream.

Uncle Harry is certainly the strangest of Robert Siodmak's *films noirs*. It has hints of an incestuous relationship between John and his sisters. Geraldine Fitzgerald's Lettie Quincy is surely one of the genre's oddest *femme-fatales*.

Despite its strange plot, *Uncle Harry* is extremely well made, displaying the qualities of Robert Siodmak's expressionist style at its best.

Interestingly, the film was previewed with five different endings to appease the Hays Office who objected to the protagonist getting away with murder. When Universal accepted the "dream ending," producer Joan Harrison quit the studio in disgust.

The Undercover Man (Columbia, 1949). 85 min.

Producer: Robert Rossen. Director: Joseph H. Lewis. Screenplay: Sydney Boehm, with additional dialog by Marvin Wald, story by Jack Rubin. Director of Photography: Burnett Guffey. Music: George Duning. Art Director: Walter Holscher. Editor: Al Clark.

Cast: Glenn Ford (Frank Warren), Nina Foch (Judith Warren), James Whitmore (George Pappas), Barry Kelley (Edward O'Rourke), David Wolfe (Stanley Weinberg). With: Frank Tweddell, Howard St. John, John F. Hamilton, Leo Penn.

A group of I.R.S. undercover agents attempt to discover information that would prove a top mobster is guilty of tax evasion. Frank Warren and George Pappas begin the tedious task of locating individuals willing to jeopardize their life to testify against the mobster. Their first witness is murdered, as is their second witness, a bookkeeper. They finally get the information they are looking for from the bookkeeper's widow. Ironically, the mobster's lawyer turns against him, helping set up the mobster for his own death.

The Undercover Man is Joseph H. Lewis' most conventional *film noir*, both in style and themes. However, there are flourishes of his American style expressionism in certain scenes and the film moves at a quick pace, reminding one of the semi-documentary television police dramas of a decade later.

Undercurrent (MGM, 1946). 114 min.

Producer: Pandro S. Berman. Director: Vincente Minnelli. Screenplay: Edward Chodorov, with Marguerite Roberts, based on the novel *You Were There* by Thelma Strabel. Director of Photography: Karl Freund. Music: Herbert Stothart, adapted from Brahms' *Fourth Symphony*. Art Directors: Cedric Gibbons and Randall Duell. Editor: Ferris Webster.

Cast: Katherine Hepburn (Ann Hamilton), Robert Taylor (Alan Garroway), Robert Mitchum (Michael Garroway), Edmund Gwenn (Professor Dink Hamilton), Marjorie Main (Lucy). With: Jayne Cotter, Clinton Sundberg, Dan Tobin, Kathryn Card, Leigh Whipper.

Ann Hamilton is the sheltered daughter of a gentle professor. One day she meets the charming Alan Garroway, an airplane manufacturer and they fall in love. They are married, but Alan is obsessed with his long missing brother, Michael, whom he claims cheated him in business. Ann gradually learns that Michael is actually a gentle, sensitive man who may be missing because Alan, in fact, may have killed him. She begins a secret investigation, eventually finding Michael living in exile on a ranch. He tells her that Alan is insane and killed an inventor who worked for him, assuming credit for his ideas. When Alan learns that he has been betrayed, he attempts to kill Ann, but is himself killed accidentally.

Later, when Ann meets Michael, she tells him that he is the man she has always been looking for.

Director Vincente Minnelli's talents were ill suited to *film noir*. His touch was too light for the genre, but *Undercurrent* does have some interesting moments. Unfortunately, the screenplay is unnecessarily confusing and the performances generally are too self-conscious with the exception of Robert Mitchum.

This film is one of Robert Mitchum's earliest *noir* performances and he plays an uncharacteristic "good guy" in every sense, he is not in the least hard-boiled in portraying Michael Garroway.

Undertow (Universal, 1949). 70 min.
Producer: Ralph Dietrich. Director: William Castle. Screenplay: Arthur T. Horman and Lee Loeb, story by Arthur T. Horman. Director of Photography: Irving Glassberg. Music: Milton Schwarzwald. Art Directors: Bernard Herzbrun and Robert Boyle. Editor: Ralph Dawson.
Cast: Scott Brady (Tony Reagen), John Russell (Danny Morgan), Dorothy Hart (Sally Lee), Peggy Dow (Nancy), Bruce Bennett (John), Rock Hudson (Mark). With: Gregg Martell, Robert Anderson, Ann Pearce.

Tony Reagen, an ex-gambler, plans to manage a mountain lodge when he leaves the military, but on the way to Chicago, after his discharge to pick up his fiancée, Sally Lee, he finds himself framed for murder. Taking refuge in the apartment of Nancy, a girl he met on the plane en route to Chicago, Tony sets out to investigate the crime. Eventually he discovers that his fiancée and her lover, Danny Morgan, are responsible for the frame-up.

Undertow is an inconsequential "B" *noir* that is notable mainly as William Castle's early films.

Underworld (Paramount, 1927). 85 min.
Producer: Hector Turnbull. Director: Josef Von Sternberg. Screenplay: Robert N. Lee, adapted by Charles Furthman from a story by Ben Hecht. Titles: George Marion, Jr. Director of Photography: Bert Glennon. Art Director: Hans Dreier.
Cast: George Bancroft (Bull Weed), Clive Brook (Rolls Royce), Evelyn Brent (Feathers McCoy), Larry Semon (Slippy Lewis), Fred Kohler (Buck Mulligan). With: Helen Lynch, Jerry Mandy, Karl Morse.

A gangster is rescued from prison by his girlfriend and his lieutenant. When he later discovers that they are in love, he allows them to escape as the police close in leaving him to face the law alone.

Mainly because of its extraordinary, lush direction by Josef Von Sternberg *Underworld* qualifies as an early *noir*-like film. Likewise, it was the first gangster movie to be filmed from the criminal's point of view. Finally, its fatalistic plot is reminiscent of the genre's themes. The film's enormous popularity and, thus, influence, can not be discounted.

Underworld U.S.A. (Columbia, 1961). 99 min.
Producer and Director: Samuel Fuller. Screenplay: Samuel Fuller, based on a series of articles by Joseph F. Dinneen. Director of Photography: Hal Mohr. Music: Harry Sukman. Art Director: Robert Peterson. Editor: Jerome Thoms.
Cast: Cliff Robertson (Tolly Devlin), Dolores Dorn (Cuddles), Beatrice Kay (Sandy), Paul Dubov (Gela), Robert Emhardt (Conners), Gerald Milton (Gunther), Allan Gruener (Smith). With: Larry Gates, Richard Rust, Tina Rome, Sally Mills.

As a twelve year old, Tolly Devlin witnessed the murder of his father by four men. Tolly swears revenge. While in prison many years later, Tolly recognizes an inmate as one of his father's killers. The man is dying, but he gives Tolly the names of the three other men: Gela, Smith and Gunther.

Released from prison, Tolly infiltrates the gang responsible for his father's death with the help of Sandy, a friend of his father, and Cuddles, a mob associate. He also works with a government agent to plant information to make it look like Gela and Gunther are working for the government, and the mob boss, Conners, has them killed. Smith is arrested. Feeling his work is not done, Tolly confronts Conners. In the resulting gun battle, Tolly is mortally wounded and dies. Cuddles is determined to avenge his death by testifying against the mob.

Underworld U.S.A. is the most conventional of Samuel Fuller's *films noirs*. It is within the tradition of the vengeance *noir* (a theme of a handful of the genre's titles), concentrating on the hunt for the perpetrators of the crime and the resulting violence. Still, with Dolores Dorn as Cuddles and the character of Sandy, the film is clearly in the tradition of Fuller's work as well. Fuller populated his films with trashy blondes as "whores with the heart of gold" and Dorn, like Constance Towers in *The Naked Kiss* (Allied Artists, 1964), represents the true human values missing from "normal" middle class characters in the film.

Union Station (Paramount, 1950). 80 min.

Producer: Jules Schermer. Director: Rudolph Maté. Screenplay: Sydney Boehm, story by Thomas Walsh. Director of Photography: Daniel L. Fapp. Music: Irving Talbot. Art Directors: Hans Dreier and Earl Hedrick. Editor: Ellsworth Hoagland.

Cast: William Holden (Lt. William Calhoun), Nancy Olson (Joyce Willecombe), Barry Fitzgerald (Inspector Donnelly), Lyle Bettger (Joe Beacom), Jan Sterling (Marge Wrighter). With: Allene Roberts, Herbert Heyes, Don Dunning, Fred Graff, James Seay.

Joe Beacom kidnaps a young blonde girl, setting into motion a frantic search led by Lt. William Calhoun. The kidnapper and victim are cornered in a busy rail terminus where the bustling crowds get in the way of the desperate manhunt. Finally, in the shoot out in the electrified tunnel, Calhoun kills Beacom.

Union Station is a straight forward thriller that succeeds because of its fast paced action and hard-boiled performances. Indeed, in technique and from the quality of its actors, *Union Station* is better than the *noir D.O.A.* (United Artists, 1950), Maté's hit *noir* of the previous year. However, although it was a big box-office hit, *Union Station* has not been recognized as one of the genre's classics by most critics.

United Artists

The company was founded in 1919 by Mary Pickford, Douglas Fairbanks, Charlie Chaplin and D. W. Griffith to make and distribute their and others' product. Unlike the other major American film companies, United Artists was not a real production company with a staff of writers, directors, production designers, etc.; rather, it was an entity which financed independent producers and then released the films. Thus, the studio had no identifiable style.

Many of United Artists *films noirs* were "B" productions, but the studio also released important films directed by, among others, Joseph H. Lewis, Robert Aldrich, Stanley Kubrick and Fritz Lang.

Releases: **1937:** *You Only Live Once.* **1941:** *The Shanghai Gesture.* **1946:** *The Chase.* **1947:** *Body and Soul. Lured.* **1948:** *Pitfall. Sleep, My Love.* **1949:** *The Crooked Way. Red Light. Too Late for Tears. Champion. Impact.* **1950:** *D.O.A.. Gun Crazy. Try and Get Me.* **1951:** *The Big Night. He Ran All the Way. The Prowler. The Second Woman.* **1952:** *The Captive City. Kansas City Confidential. The Thief. Another Man's*

Poison. **1953:** *I, the Jury. 99 River Street.* **1954:** *The Long Wait. The Shield for Murder. Suddenly. Witness to Murder. Black Tuesday.* **1955:** *The Big Knife. Killer's Kiss. Kiss Me Deadly. The Naked Street. Night of the Hunter.* **1956:** *The Killer Is Loose. The Killing. Nightmare. Storm Fear.* **1957:** *Baby Face Nelson. Crime of Passion. Sweet Smell of Success.* **1958:** *Thunder Road.* **1959:** *Odds Against Tomorrow.* **1962:** *The Manchurian Candidate.* **1974:** *The Outfit.*

Universal Pictures, Inc.

The oldest of the Hollwood studios, Universal was founded in 1912 by Carl Laemmle. Like Columbia, Universal was a relatively small studio with little financial resources, yet they managed to compete successfully with the bigger studios by churning out inexpensive action films, westerns and a few modest "A" pictures. The studio's greatest period came in the late twenties and early thirties under the control of boy-wonder producer Carl Laemmle, Jr. who developed the gothic style of the studio in a remarkable series of expressionist influenced horror films: *Dracula* (1930), *Frankenstein* (1931) and *Bride of Frankenstein* (1935).

The heavily Teutonic influence on set design, lighting and themes continued to play a part at Universal well into the forties. The major art director during this decade was John De Cuir, a neglected but innovative designer.

Universal's *films noirs* were generally routine, but there were a few odd classics. The studios's greatest talent was Robert Siodmak, a director with a strong Germanic style who made several classic *noirs* for the studio: *Phantom Lady*, *The Killers* and *Criss Cross*. The latter two co-starred Burt Lancaster, a contract player for the studio who also starred in the classic *Brute Force*. Alfred Hitchcock made his early *noir* classic *Shadow of a Doubt* for the studio, while Fritz Lang made two *noirs* there: *Scarlet Street* and *Secret Beyond the Door*.

Releases: **1943:** *Shadow of a Doubt.* **1944:** *Christmas Holiday. Phantom Lady.* **1945:** *Lady on a Train. Scarlet Street. Uncle Harry.* **1946:** *Black Angel. The Dark Mirror. The Killers. Inside Job.* **1947:** *Brute Force. Ride the Pink Horse. Singapore. The Web.* **1948:** *A Double Life. Kiss the Blood Off My Hands. The Naked City. Secret Beyond the Door.* **1949:** *Abandoned. Criss Cross. Undertow.* **1950:** *Shakedown. The Sleeping City. Woman on the Run. One Way Street.* **1954:** *Forbidden. The Naked Alibi.* **1955:** *Female on the Beach.* **1957:** *The Night Runner. The Tattered Dress.* **1958:** *Appointment with a Shadow. Touch of Evil.* **1961:** *Blast of Silence.* **1962:** *Cape Fear.* **1968:** *Madigan.*

The Unknown Man (MGM, 1951). 88 min.

Producer: Robert Thomsen. Director: Richard Thorpe. Screenplay: Ronald Miller and George Froeschel. Director of Photography: William Mellor. Music: Conrad Salinger. Art Directors: Cedric Gibbons and Randall Duell. Editor: Ben Lewis.

Cast: Walter Pidgeon (Dwight Bradley Mason), Ann Harding (Stella Mason), Barry Sullivan (Joe Buckner), Keefe Brasselle (Rudi Wallchek), Lewis Stone (Judge Hulbrook), Edward Franz, (Layford). With: Richard Anderson, Dawn Adams, Phil Ober, Mari Blanchard.

Joe Buckner, a prominent young District Attorney, tells the story of recently deceased defense attorney Bradley Mason, to a class of graduating law students including Mason's son.

Dwight Mason defended Rudi Wolchek who was accused of murder, winning the young man's acquittal. Later, however, he comes to believe that Rudi was guilty and that a well respected man, Andrew Layford, is head of a gang of racketeers who encouraged Rudi to commit the murder. Enraged, Mason killed Layford when the racketeer laughed in his face about the control over local politics he and his fellow racketeers have. Rudi is again arrested for murder and ironically, is this time convicted and sentenced to death. Feeling guilty, Mason visits Rudi in his cell. Confessing to him, he passes a dagger to the convicted killer hoping, rightly as it turned out, that Rudi would get revenge. Rudi stabs Mason, thus relieving him of his guilt.

The Unknown Man is the most fatalistic of MGM's *noirs*. Typically, however, the studio cast its conventional stars in a film ill suited to their talents, and the production values are also typically glossy. Its view of big city corruption and the psychosis of violence, however, is interesting.

The Unsuspected (Warner Bros., 1947). 103 min.

Producer: Charles Hoffman. Director: Michael Curtiz. Screenplay: Ranald MacDougall, adapted by Bess Meredyth from the novel by Charlotte Armstrong. Director of Photography: Woody Bredell. Music: Franz Waxman. Art Director: Anton Grot. Editor: Frederick Richards.

Cast: Joan Caulfield (Matilda Frazier), Claude Rains (Alexander Grandison), Audrey Totter (Althea Keane), Constance Bennett (Jane Moynihan), Hurd Hatfield (Oliver Keane), Michael North (Steven Howard). With: Fred Clark, Harry Lewis, Jack Lambert.

Alexander Grandison is a psychotic radio personality who has killed a young woman and set it up to make it look like she committed suicide. Grandison's appetite for violence is fed by his radio show, a mystery series that dwells on brutality. However, his world of intellectual evil is invaded by Steven Howard, a veteran who has returned from service set on getting revenge for the murder of his fiancée, Grandison's victim. Howard uses a series of unsavory methods to convince Grandison to confess to the crime. He even tries to convince Grandison's niece, Matilda, that he is her long lost

husband who wants to help her recover from a nervous breakdown. Grandison plans to poison Matilda, but his attempt fails and he is eventually caught.

The Unsuspected is essentially a character study and an exercise in style. In true *noir* fashion, the investigator, Steven Howard, is as corrupt in his own way as the killer, Alexander Grandison, is in his.

Claude Rains' performance is extraordinary as the self absorbed murderer.

The film is slow moving, ethereal and hypnotic and is one of the best looking *noirs*.

Usher, Robert (1901–)

Art director. Usher was an important unit art director at Paramount from the early thirties to 1945. He was the art director for a single *film noir*, the curious *The Chase* for which he created some appropriately odd, almost surreal sets.

Filmography: *The Chase* (United Artists, 1946).

Valentine, Joseph (1900–1949)

Cinematographer. Valentine's long and generally distinguished career as a cinematographer included a number of important films. He was one of Alfred Hitchcock's chief collaborators in the forties, working on *Sabateur* (Universal, 1942), *Rope* (United Artists, 1948) and the *noir* classic, *Shadow of a Doubt*. His style, however, was rather conventional.

Filmography: *Shadow of a Doubt* (Universal, 1943). *Possessed* (Warner Bros., 1947). *Sleep, My Love* (United Artists, 1948).

Van Cleef, Lee (1925–)

Character actor. Van Cleef's sharp features and narrow, steely eyes made him an ideal villain and hard-boiled sidekick.He played villains in his two *films noirs*.

Filmography: *Kansas City Confidential* (United Artists, 1952). *The Big Combo* (Allied Artists, 1955).

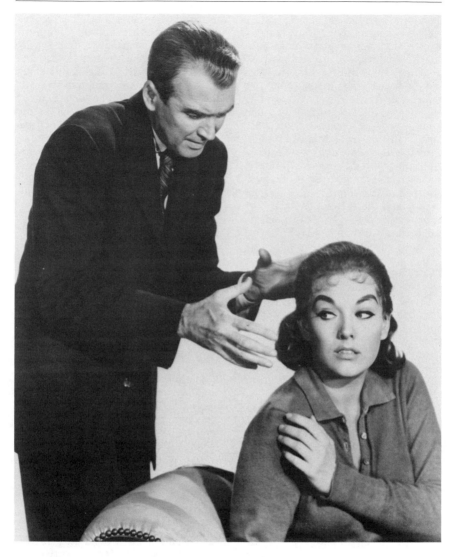

James Stewart, Kim Novak in publicity still from *Vertigo* (Paramount, 1958).

Veiller, Anthony (1903–)

Screenwriter. Veiller was a competent studio craftsman who worked on a number of successful films. His masterpiece, however, is *The Killers*, in which he took Ernest Hemingway's short story and used it as merely a sketch for his expanded screenplay. Veiller also co-wrote Orson Welles' *The Stranger*.

Filmography: *The Killers* (Universal, 1946). *The Stranger* (co-wrote) (RKO, 1946).

Vertigo (Paramount, 1958). 120 min.

Producer and Director: Alfred Hitchcock. Screenplay: Alec Coppel and Samuel Taylor, based on the novel *D'Entre les Morts* by Pierre Boileau and Thomas Narcejac. Director of Photography: Robert Burks. Music: Bernard Herrmann. Art Directors: Hal Pereira and Henry Bumstead. Editor: George Tomasini.

Cast: James Stewart (John "Scottie" Ferguson), Kim Novak (Madeleine Elster/Judy Barton), Barbara Bel Geddes (Midge), Henry Jones (Coroner), Tom Hellmore (Galvin Elster). With: Raymond Bailey, Ellen Corby, Konstantin Shayne, Lee Patrick.

San Francisco: John "Scottie" Ferguson leaves the police force because of his acute acrophobia (a fear of heights which causes extreme dizziness — vertigo). Gavin Elster, an old college buddy, comes to Scottie and hires him to follow his wife Madeleine, who believe she is possessed by the spirit of her great-grandmother Carlotta Valdez, a woman who committed suicide after going insane. Scottie follows Madeleine around San Francisco. When she tries to drown herself in the bay directly beneath the Golden Gate Bridge, Scottie rescues her. He has fallen in love with her and when she has a vision of the Mission at San Juan Batista, he takes her there hoping he can erase her delusion. However, she impulsively climbs to the top of the tower where Scottie is unable to follow because of his phobia. He watches helplessly as she jumps to her death.

Scottie has a nervous breakdown. And his loyal girlfriend Midge helps him recover. Some months later he meets a woman name Judy Barton who resembles the beloved Madeleine. In fact, Judy *is* Madeline, or rather was pretending to be the real Madeleine Elster in a plan by Gavin Elster to kill the real Madeleine. Scottie slowly transforms Judy into looking like Madeleine by buying her clothes and having her hair dyed from red to blonde. When Scottie notices that Judy has an heirloom which originally belonged to Carlotta Valdez, he realizes what has happened. To make Judy confess, he takes her to the San Juan Batista tower.

Startled, she loses her balance and falls to her death.

Vertigo is a masterpiece — quite simply one of cinema's great films. It is a rich and complicated work and to describe it purely on the level of plot is to give no real impression how the film works. It is a film which gets better rather than weaker once one knows the central twist of the plot.

It also brings up the question of whether *film noir* is merely a style or a legitimate genre, for here one encounters all of the thematic elements of classic *film noir*: the mirror images (Judy/Madeleine), the *noir* protagonist who is partly complicit in his own destruction, the hypnotic effects of landscape, and the tragic ending which was actually a rarity in the genre. Furthermore, the color cinematography echoes black and white cinematography of classic *noir*.

With its obsessed, doomed characters, a masterful score by Bernard Herrmann and overall cynical portrait of middle class characters and its extraordinary visual style *Vertigo* is clearly a *film noir*, and one of the genre's undeniable classics.

Vickers, Martha (Martha MacVicar) (1925–1971)

Actress. An attractive, dark-haired actress, Martha Vickers made a striking first appearance in the *noir* classic *The Big Sleep* as the promiscuous Carmen Sternwood. She seemed destined for real stardom but her career never really took off and she was subsequently relegated to mostly minor films. She co-starred in the late "B" *noir*, *The Burglar*, as a woman plotting a jewel theft with a corrupt policeman.

Filmography: *The Big Sleep* (Warner Bros., 1946). *The Burglar* (Columbia, 1957).

Vicki (20th Century–Fox, 1953). 85 min.

Producer: Leonard Goldstein. Director: Harry Horner. Screenplay: Dwight

Taylor, with additional dialog by Harold Greene and Leo Townsend, based on the novel *I Wake Up Screaming* by Steve Fisher. Director of Photography: Milton Krasner. Music: Leigh Harline. Song "Vicki" by Ken Darby and Max Showalter. Art Directors: Lyle Wheeler and Richard Irvine. Editor: Dorothy Spencer.

Cast: Jeanne Crain (Jill), Jean Peters (Vicki Lynn), Elliott Reid (Steve Christopher), Richard Boone (Lt. Ed Cornell), Casey Adams (Larry Evans). With: Alex D'Arby, Carl Betz, Aaron Spelling, Roy Engel.

The murder of Vicki Lynn, a popular New York model, sets off an investigation led by police Lt. Ed Cornell. The investigation is impeded by enormous complications, but eventually Steve Christopher, Vicki's publicity agent, is found to be the killer, while Lt. Cornell's career is ruined for covering up the evidence—he was, himself romantically obsessed with the girl, and his apartment is found with Vicki Lynn's photographs and memorabilia of her career.

Vicki is the second adaption of Steve Fisher's novel *I Wake Up Screaming*. The film uses a complicated flashback structure and is tailored to resemble the immensely popular *Laura* (20th Century-Fox, 1944), nearly a decade before. While it does not quite measure up to the early *noir* class, *Vicki* is by no means a bad film. Its characters are typically *noir* characters (with Lt. Cornell being another variation of the corrupt policeman) and *noir* style. Its performances are good, with the sensual Jean Peters a standout as the doomed title character.

Vidor, King (1894–1982)

Director. Vidor was a great stylist whose best films were made in the late twenties. His *film noir*, *Beyond the Forest*, is notable mainly for its extraordinary style. Two other movies Vidor directed, *Lightning Strikes Twice* (Warner Bros., 1951) and *Ruby Gentry*

(20th Century-Fox, 1952), have been called *films noirs* by some critics, but they are not true *films noirs*. Yet curiously, his *The Fountainhead* (Warner Bros., 1949), one of the most extravagantly expressionist films of its era, is generally ignored by these same critics despite its similarly melodramatic themes compared to the other two. *Beyond the Forest* remains his single *film noir*, but one wishes Vidor had made more movies of this type.

Filmography: *Beyond the Forest* (Warner Bros., 1949).

Viertel, Salka (1909–)

Screenwriter. Viertel was a staff writer at Warner Bros. He co-wrote a single *film noir*.

Filmography: *Deep Valley* (co-wrote) (Warner Bros., 1947).

Vogel, Paul (1899–1975)

Cinematographer. Vogel was an MGM staff cinematographer. A capable, though not particularly inventive craftsman, Vogel was the cinematographer for several of the best MGM *noirs*.

Filmography: *The High Wall* (MGM, 1947). *Lady in the Lake* (MGM, 1947). *Scene of the Crime* (MGM, 1949). *A Lady Without Passport* (MGM, 1950).

Von Sternberg, Josef (1894–1969)

Director. Von Sternberg directed only two true *films noirs*, one of which, *Macao*, was almost entirely reshot by Nicholas Ray. Yet, through force of style and themes (particularly romantic obsession) in his classic early films, Von Sternberg's considerable influence on the genre cannot be denied.

As a cinema stylist, Von Sternberg is without compare. He worked on all the visual aspects of his movies. He was the defacto art director and cinematographer on all of his productions and co-wrote many of his scenarios. His lush, extravagant style; marked by deep contrasts between light and dark areas, diffused lenses, etc; was influenced in part by expressionism. This is most evident in his wildly popular early thirties melodramas (starring his protégée, Marlene Dietrich), but also his silent crime films which, both in style and content, predate *film noir* by nearly two decades. In effect, both *Underworld* and *Thunderbolt* are *films noirs*, bearing a striking resemblance to many classic *noirs*.

The Shanghai Gesture is typical of his work in many ways, with its exotic locale, its style and plot. It is not quite a classic, mainly because of its inconsistent screenplay, but it is an important early film of the cycle.

Macao is also typical of its credited director. Unfortunately, Von Sternberg was removed from the film's production three quarters of the way through by RKO chief Howard Hughes who thought he was moving too slow and did not like the way Von Sternberg was handling Hughes' protégée, Jane Russell. The film was largely reshot by Nicholas Ray, but it still retains much of the exoticism that is familiar to Von Sternberg.

Of course, Von Sternberg was not a major *film noir* director. His sensibilities were too exotic and eccentric. In any case, his great period predated the genre by a decade and his career was in an irreversible decline by the forties. Yet, he remains a compelling and controversial figure, more important because of his influence rather than his own *noirs*.

Filmography: *Underworld* (Paramount, 1927). *Thunderbolt* (Paramount, 1929). *The Shanghai Gesture* (United Artists, 1941). *Macao* (RKO, 1952).

Wald, Jerry (1911–1962)

Producer. Wald was a legendary, hyperactive writer turned producer who is said to be the inspiration for Budd Schulberg's Sammy Glick in his Hollywood *roman-à-clef*, *What Makes Sammy Run?* A former journalist, Wald was lured to Hollywood in the thirties. After spending most of the rest of the decade as a writer of mainly routine dramas, Wald became a producer for Warner Bros. in the early forties, later taking the place of Hal Wallis as production chief. He continued Warner's tradition of hard-boiled, action oriented melodramas. Among these are a number of *films noirs*, almost all of which are of importance.

Filmography: *Mildred Pierce* (Warner Bros., 1945). *Dark Passage* (Warner Bros., 1947). *Possessed* (Warner Bros., 1947). *Key Largo* (Warner Bros., 1948). *The Breaking Point* (Warner Bros., 1950). *Caged* (Warner Bros., 1950). *The Damned Don't Cry* (Warner Bros., 1950).

Wald, Marvin (1906–1982)

Screenwriter. Wald co-wrote four *films noirs*, including two important early titles, *The Dark Past* and *The Naked City*. All of Wald's screenplays are characterized by a strong sense of plot and hard-boiled dialog.

Filmography: *Behind Locked Doors* (Eagle-Lion, 1948). *The Dark Past* (Columbia, 1948). *The Naked City* (Universal, 1948). *The Undercover Man* (Universal, 1949).

Walker, Joseph (1892–1985)

Cinematographer. Walker was a staff cinematographer for Columbia. He was one of Frank Capra's collaborators, working on many of the director's top films: *It Happened One Night* (Columbia, 1934), *Mr. Deeds Goes to Town* (Columbia, 1936), *Lost Horizon* (Columbia, 1937). His *films noirs* are characterized by the same dreamlike qualities of his Capra films.

Filmography: *The Dark Past* (Columbia, 1948). *Affair in Trinidad* (Columbia, 1950).

Walker, Robert (1918–1951)

Actor. Walker was an extremely popular leading man in the forties. He was married to Jennifer Jones, but when she left him for producer David O. Selznick, Walker suffered a series of nervous breakdowns. Repeatedly hospitalized and then released, he turned to alcohol. Still, he managed to give several interesting performances, including a *tour-de-force* as the villain in Alfred Hitchcock's *Strangers on a Train*. He died while working on his following film, a victim of over-sedation and apparently, of a broken heart.

Filmography: *Strangers on a Train* (Warner Bros., 1951).

Wallace, Jean (Jean Wallasek) (1923–)

Actress. A beautiful blonde actress, Wallace starred in many movies in the forties and fifties. In 1951 she married Cornel Wilde and co-starred with him in several movies, including two *films noirs*. She provided just the sort of trashy image that director Joseph H. Lewis preferred in *The Big Combo*. In Cornel Wilde's film, *Storm Fear*, she played a woman who once had an affair with her husband's brother, a wanted criminal.

Filmography: *The Big Combo* (Allied Artists, 1955). *Storm Fear* (United Artists, 1956).

Wallace, Richard (1894–1951)

Director. A leading "B" director, most of Wallace's films are inconsequential. He was at his best with action oriented material. *Framed*, a minor *noir*, is very well made although, ultimately, of little importance.

Filmography: *Framed* (Columbia, 1947).

Wallis, Hal (1898–1986)

Producer. Wallis might well be the most important neglected figure from Hollywood's golden age. A protégé of Darryl F. Zanuck, Wallis was promoted to production chief of Warner Bros. when the dynamic young producer left the company to start his own production company in 1934. Over the next decade, Wallis refined the Warner's style invented by Zanuck. In the mode of producers Zanuck and David O. Selznick, Wallis was a "creative" producer.

He had a hand in all aspects of his productions — from writing to editing — and promoted the careers of Humphrey Bogart, Bette Davis, James Cagney and Edward G. Robinson. The style of the classic Warner Bros.-era (beginning in the mid thirties and ending a decade and half later) owes much to Hal Wallis. He joined Paramount as a producer in 1946, for whom he produced many important films.

Wallis is equally important to *film noir* as the producer with the greatest taste and artistic sensibility.

Filmography: *I Am a Fugitive from a Chain Gang* (Warner Bros., 1932). *The Letter* (Warner Bros., 1940). *High Sierra* (Warner Bros., 1941). *The Maltese Falcon* (Warner Bros., 1941). *The Strange Love of Martha Ivers* (Paramount, 1946). *I Walk Alone* (Paramount, 1948). *Sorry, Wrong Number* (Paramount, 1948). *The Accused* (Paramount, 1949). *The File on Thelma Jordan* (Paramount, 1949). *Dark City* (Paramount, 1950).

Walsh, Raoul (1887–1980)

Director. Walsh was a leading director of action pictures who made many of Warner Bros. classic action films. Over the course of his forty year career, Walsh succeeded in turning out a high number of unpretentious, enjoyable, often brilliant black and white movies, several of which are acknowledged classics including two *films noirs*.

High Sierra is one of the classic early *films noirs*. The film is typical of Walsh's unpretentious style, and it helped confirm Humphrey Bogart's screen image and growing stardom.

White Heat is equally important. It provided James Cagney with one of his most famous roles as the mother-fixated Cody Jarrett. The film's climax, in which Jarrett, surrounded by raging fire, screams "Look ma, top of the world!" is one of *film noir's* most famous scenes.

Unfortunately, Walsh's career was devoted to other genre's, but of his three *films noirs*, two are classics and all are worthy additions to the genre.

Filmography: *High Sierra* (Warner Bros., 1941). *White Heat* (Warner Bros., 1947). *The Enforcer* (Warner Bros., 1951).

Wanger, Walter (1894–1968)

Producer. One of the few truly independent producers of Hollywood's golden age, Walter Wanger's career began in the twenties and ended four decades later. A brilliant organizer, he preferred to work with strong willed directors including Alfred Hitchcock, Max Ophuls and Fritz Lang. In the 1940's he co-founded Diana Production with Fritz Lang and Joan Bennett, a short lived company which produced two *films noirs*. He also produced two additional *noirs*.

Filmography: *You Only Live Once* (United Artists, 1937). *Scarlet Street* (Executive producer for Diana Productions) (Universal, 1945). *Secret Beyond the Door* (Executive Producer for Diana Productions) (Universal, 1948). *The Reckless Moment* (Columbia, 1949).

Warner Bros. Pictures

One of the big five movie companies, the company was founded in 1923 by the four Warner Bros.: Albert, Harry, Sam and Jack. Jack was the only brother to have a hands-on relationship with the company and he was production chief for some four decades. However, the real genius of the early years of the studio was Darryl F. Zanuck. Zanuck, originally a screenwriter, was promoted to vice-president in the late twenties, in which position he personally oversaw the entire studio's output, often ghost writing, editing and directing scenes. It was Zanuck who developed the hard-boiled style that dominated the studio for much of the following four decades.

After the departure of Zanuck in 1934, his assistant Hal B. Wallis was promoted to his position and Wallis refined the studio's style over the next decade. Under Wallis, directors like Michael Curtiz introduced expressionist style, while dialog and character types remained rooted in American pulp literature and culture. This was the age of Erroll Flynn, Bette Davis and finally Humphrey Bogart.

The Warner's *film noirs* are typical of their production: cynical, romantic, strong style, emphasizing action and violence.

Releases: **1932:** *I Am a Fugitive from a Chain Gang.* **1940:** *The Letter.* **1941:** *The Maltese Falcon. High Sierra.* **1944:** *The Mask of Dimitrios.* **1945:** *Conflict. Danger Signal. Mildred Pierce.* **1946:** *The Big Sleep. Nobody Lives Forever.* **1947:** *Dark Passage. Nora Prentiss. Possessed. The Unsuspected. Deep Valley.* **1948:** *Key Largo.* **1949:** *Beyond the Forest. White Heat.* **1950:** *Caged. The Damned Don't Cry. The Breaking Point. Kiss Tomorrow Goodbye. Backfire.* **1951:** *The Enforcer. I Was a Communist for the F.B.I.. Strangers on a Train.* **1953:** *The Blue Gardenia.* **1954:** *Crime Wave.* **1955:** *I Died a Thousand Times. Mr. Arkadin. New York Confidential.* **1956:** *The Wrong Man.* **1965:** *Brainstorm.* **1971:** *Dirty Harry.* **1975:** *Nightmoves* **1981:** *Body Heat.*

War Veterans

A key *noir* theme is the returning war veteran's problems of assimilation after service. This makes sense, considering the very real problems of postwar cities, veteran frustrations, economic difficulties, etc. returning veterans often felt alienated and helpless in this environment and certain *films noirs* echoed this sentiment. *The Blue Dahlia* (Paramount, 1946), *Backfire* (Warner Bros., 1950), *The Crooked Way* (United Artists, 1949), *Somewhere in the Night* (20th Century–Fox, 1946), *Kiss the Blood Off My Hands* (Universal, 1948), *Nobody Lives Forever* (Warner Bros., 1946), *Cornered* (RKO, 1945), *Ride the Pink Horse* (Universal, 1947), and *Act of Violence* (MGM, 1949) are among the most prominent *films noirs* which, each in its own way, deal with this topic.

Waxman, Franz (1906–1967)

Composer. A great, prolific Hollywood composer, the German born Franz Waxman specialized in spooky gothic scores. Indeed, he composed some of the most beloved film scores in Hollywood and much of his music is still respected by critics. He composed many of *noir's* best scores.

Filmography: *Suspicion* (RKO, 1941). *Dark Passage* (Warner Bros., 1947). *Nora Prentiss* (Warner Bros., 1947). *Possessed* (Warner Bros., 1947). *Sorry, Wrong Number* (Paramount, 1948). *Sunset Boulevard* (Paramount, 1949). *Night and the City* (20th Century–Fox, 1950). *He Ran All the Way* (United Artists, 1951). *I, the Jury* (United Artists, 1953).

Wayne, David (1914–)

Actor. A Broadway star in the late thirties and forties, Wayne entered movies in the late forties. He often played second male leads and was particularly adept in comedy as in *How to Marry a Millionaire* (20th Century–Fox, 1953). In Joseph Losey's *M*, Wayne starred as the serial killer, but his performance pales in comparison to Peter Lorre's original.

Filmography: *M* (Columbia, 1951).

The Web (Universal, 1947). 87 min.

Producer: Jerry Bressler. Director: Michael Gordon. Screenplay: William Bowers and Bertram Millhauser, story by Harry Kurnitz. Director of Photography: Irving Glassberg. Music: Hans Salter. Art Director: Jack Otterson. Editor: Russell Schoengarth.

Cast: Edmond O'Brien (Bob Regan), Ella Raines (Noel Faraday), Vincent Price (Andrew Colby), William Bendix (Damico), John Abbott (Murdoch). With: Maria Palmer, Fritz Lieber, Howland Chamberlain.

An incisive screenplay by William Bowers and Bertram Millhauser is the saving grace of *The Web*, an otherwise routine *film noir*. The story centers around a young attorney, Bob Regan, working in tandem with a police lieutenant, Damico, to trap a wealthy industrialist, Andrew Colby, into confessing to two murders and a million-dollar theft.

The Web marked the debut of director Michael Gordon who keeps the pace moving. The performances, by mostly quality "B" actors, are quite good with Vincent Price particularly memorable as yet another *noir* aesthete.

Webb, Clifton (1893–1966)

Actor. Webb came to the movies after many years as a struggling stage actor in 1944. He made a striking first appearance as the fey murderer Waldo Lydecker in *Laura* and his performance made him into a star. He played an equally idiosyncratic villain in the less well known, *The Dark Corner*. However, most of his film career was devoted to comic roles.

Filmography: *Laura* (20th Century–Fox, 1944). *The Dark Corner* (20th Century–Fox, 1946).

Webb, Jack (1920–1982)

Character actor. Long before he achieved immortality as police detective Joe Friday on television's *Dragnet* series, Webb had a successful career as a character actor in films. He had small supporting roles in a number of *films noirs*, generally playing small time criminals, most notably in *Dark City*.

Filmography: *Hollow Triumph* (bit part) (Eagle-Lion, 1948). *He Walked By Night* (Eagle-Lion, 1949). *Dark City* (Paramount, 1950). *Sunset Boulevard* (Paramount, 1950). *Appointment with Danger* (Paramount, 1951).

Webb, Roy (1888–1982)

Composer. Webb was a staff composer for RKO. His piquant and dramatically intense scores were perfectly suited to *film noir*. Extremely prolific, he composed the music for many of the great *films noirs* and his music is an important, intregal part of the movies.

Filmography: *The Stranger on the Third Floor* (RKO, 1940). *Journey into Fear* (RKO, 1943). *Experiment Perilous* (RKO, 1943). *Murder, My Sweet* (RKO, 1944). *Cornered* (RKO, 1945). *The Locket* (RKO, 1946). *Notorious* (RKO, 1946). *The Spiral Staircase* (RKO, 1946). *Crossfire* (RKO, 1947). *Out of the Past* (RKO, 1947). *They Won't Believe Me* (RKO, 1947). *Race Street* (RKO, 1948). *The Window* (RKO, 1949). *Armored Car Robbery* (RKO, 1950). *Gambling House* (RKO, 1951). *Where Danger Lives* (RKO, 1951). *Clash by Night (RKO, 1952).*

Wells, Orson (1915–1985)

Actor, writer, producer, director. Welles' *Citizen Kane* (RKO, 1941), arguably the greatest American film, certainly had a profound influence on American movies in the forties. Welles' use of extravagant camera angles, shadowy lighting, combinations of music and sound, were a revelation when the film was released, although hardly an innovation: Welles certainly was influenced by expressionist cinema, with which he was familiar from his youthful experiences in Europe in the twenties. The influence of the film can be seen particularly in early *noirs*: *The Mask of Dimitrios* (Warner Bros., 1944), *Murder, My Sweet* (RKO, 1944) and *Force of Evil* (MGM, 1948), among many others.

Welles' own *noir* career began with the seminal *Journey into Fear*, which he produced, co-directed (without credit) and co-starred in. The film has some of the visual flair of Welles' best films as a director. His performance as Turkish police officer Colonel Hakim is typically brilliant.

The Stranger is Welles' most conventional film in terms of style. Its script is equally straight forward, and the performances by its three leads — Welles,

Edward G. Robinson and Loretta Young — are understated and realistic.

In *The Stranger* and his two 1950's *noirs*, Welles played villainous roles, but in *The Lady from Shanghai,* Welles provided himself with a rare sympathetic part. The film is one of *noir's* strangest major movies, hampered somewhat by a confusing screenplay, but Welles fills the film with powerful images including a legendary sequence set in a mirrored fun house.

Of his 1950's *noirs*, *Mr. Arkadin* suffers mainly from its poor production values, although it is a compelling experiment. *Touch of Evil*, on the other hand, has become an acknowledged classic with a number of extraordinary, inventive sequences and one of Welles' best performances as a corrupt policeman.

As an actor and director, Orson Welles is one of the most important figures of the *film noir* genre and his legacy lives on through his extraordinary movies.

Filmography: *Journey into Fear* (RKO, 1943). *The Stranger* (RKO, 1946). *The Lady from Shanghai* (Columbia, 1948). *Mr. Arkadin* (Warner Bros., 1955). *Touch of Evil* (Universal, 1958).

Wendkos, Paul (1922–)

Director. Wendkos was a prolific director of "B" movies in the 1950's. He directed a single *film noir*, *The Burglar* which showed the strong influence of Orson Welles in its extravagant style.

Filmography: *The Burglar* (Columbia, 1957).

Werker, Alfred (1896–1975)

Director. Werker was a prolific "B" director, mainly associated with 20th Century–Fox for whom he made a single *film noir*.

Filmography: *Shock* (20th Century–Fox, 1946).

Westlake, Donald (*aka* **Richard Stark**) (1934–)

Novelist and screenwriter. Westlake

was one of the new breed of crime novelists who emerged in the 1960's. His work is characterized by extreme violence and pretentious style. His novels *Point Blank*, *The Split* and *The Outfit* were published under his pseudonym, Richard Stark. Under his real name, he wrote the screen adaption of Jim Thompson's *The Grifters*.

Filmography: *Point Blank* (based on his novel) (MGM, 1967). *The Split* (based on his novel) (MGM, 1968). *The Outfit* (based on his novel) (MGM, 1973). *The Grifters* (screenplay) (Miramax, 1991).

Wheeler, Lyle (1905–)

Art director. Wheeler had one of the longest and most distinguished careers in American film history. After several years as an industrial designer and magazine illustrator, he entered films in the mid thirties as art director for David O. Selznick's independent production company. He worked on all of Selznick's late thirties films including *The Garden of Allah* (United Artists, 1936), *A Star Is Born* (United Artists, 1937), *Nothing Sacred* (United Artists, 1937) and *Gone with the Wind* (MGM, 1939).

Wheeler joined 20th Century–Fox in 1944, where he was the supervising art director. In collaboration, he worked on nearly all of the important *films noirs* produced at the studio.

Filmography: *Laura* (20th Century–Fox, 1944). *House on 92nd Street* (20th Century–Fox, 1945). *Leave Her to Heaven* (20th Century–Fox, 1945). *Fallen Angel* (20th Century–Fox, 1946). *Strange Triangle* (20th Century–Fox, 1946). *Kiss of Death* (20th Century–Fox, 1947). *Nightmare Alley* (20th Century–Fox, 1947). *Road House* (20th Century–Fox, 1948). *Cry of the City* (20th Century–Fox, 1948). *The Street with No Name* (20th Century–Fox, 1948). *Thieves' Highway* (20th Century–Fox, 1949). *Caged* (20th Century–Fox, 1950). *Where the Sidewalk Ends* (20th Century–Fox, 1950). *Fourteen Hours* (20th Century–Fox, 1951). *The House on Telegraph Hill* (20th Century–Fox, 1951). *The Thirteenth Letter* (20th Century–Fox, 1951). *Niagara* (20th Century–Fox, 1953). *Pickup on South Street* (20th Century–Fox, 1953). *Vicki* (20th Century–Fox, 1953). *House of Bamboo* (20th Century–Fox, 1955).

When Strangers Marry (Monogram, 1944). 67 min.

Producers: Maurice and Frank King. Director: William Castle. Screenplay: Philip Yordan and Dennis J. Cooper, story by George V. Moxcov. Director of Photography: Ira Morgan. Music: Dimitri Tiomkin. Art Director: F. Paul Sylos. Editor: Martin G. Cohn.

Cast: Dean Jagger (Paul), Kim Hunter (Millie), Robert Mitchum (Fred Graham), Neil Hamilton (Blake), Lou Lubin (Houser), Milt Kibbee (Charlie). With: Dewey Robinson, Claire Whitney, Edward Keane, Virginia Sale.

A drunk conventioneer meets a man in a hotel bar late one night in New York City and is found strangled to death the next morning, his cash stolen. Later that day, Millie arrives at the hotel to meet her new husband, Paul. By coincidence, she meets an old flame, Fred Graham, in the hotel lobby. He tells her about the murder, warning her to be careful and also wishes her good luck with her new husband. When Paul does not show up that night, Fred urges Millie to report her husband missing to the police.

Later, Millie receives a call from Paul who arranges to meet her secretly. She begins to suspect he is the killer because of his odd behavior; but, although he admits he was the man who met the conventioneer in the bar. When last he saw the man, he was alive. The police soon catch Paul and Millie, but evidence has also led to Fred Graham. As they arrest Graham, he attempts to slip the stolen money from the conventioneer into a mail slot. Paul and Millie are free to begin their life together.

When Strangers Marry is a good early

"B" *noir*, notable chiefly for two reasons. First, it was directed by William Castle, soon to be the master of exploitation movies in the fifties and sixties. Castle combines the elements of Hitchcockian suspense, with Val Lewton–like production values (shadowy bars, neon lights, jazz played in the background, etc.). Second, it also marks the first *noir* appearance of Robert Mitchum, here playing a rather conventional villain. However, his fine performance reveals the perverse insanity that would later reappear in his villainous portrayals in *Night of the Hunter* (United Artists, 1955) and *Cape Fear* (Universal, 1962).

Where Danger Lives (RKO, 1950). 82 min.
Producer: Irving Cummings, Jr. Director: John Farrow. Screenplay: Charles Bennett, story by Leo Rosten. Director of Photography: Nicholas Musuraca. Music: Roy Webb. Music Director: Constantin Bekaleinikoff. Art Directors: Albert S. D'Agostino and Ralph Berger. Editor: Eda Warren.
Cast: Robert Mitchum (Jeff Cameron), Faith Domergue (Margo Lannington), Claude Rains (Frederick Lannington), Maureen O'Sullivan (Julie), Charles Kemper (Police Chief). With: Ralph Dumke, Billy House, Harry Shannon, Phillip Van Zandt.
Margo Lannington, the beautiful young wife of the wealthy Frederick Lannington, is mentally ill and promiscuous. After attempting suicide, she is treated by a young doctor, Jeff Cameron. Cameron, unaware of her mental state, is romantically attracted to her. When he is later warned of her condition by Lannington, Jeff fails to heed the warning. The two men argue and have a brief fight during which Lannington is knocked unconscious. When Jeff leaves the room for a moment, Margo smothers her husband with a pillow. Jeff believes he has killed Lannington and Margo convinces him that they must try to escape to Mexico.

They suspect the police are chasing them and make expensive arrangements to secretly cross the border. However, Jeff has begun to realize that Margo is a psychopath. When she attempts to kill him and enter Mexico alone, Jeff follows and at the border confronts her. She shoots him but is, in turn, shot by the police. Before she dies she admits to killing her husband, freeing Jeff, who will recover from his wounds, to return to his original girlfriend.

Where Danger Lives is probably the least known of Robert Mitchum's mature *films noirs*. It is directed in typically meticulous style by John Farrow who, with the great cinematographer Nicholas Musuraca, creates a particularly dark *mise-en-scène*. The sloe-eyed, laconic Mitchum once again stars as the victim of a murderous *femme-fatale*, but it is the dark haired beauty Faith Domergue—a protégée of Howard Hughes—who stands out as the nymphomaniacal murderess. Interestingly, the film's protagonist, Jeff Cameron, is not completely destroyed at the end of the movie, but, a rarity in RKO *noirs* of the period, is free to start his life over.

Where the Sidewalk Ends (20th Century–Fox, 1950). 95 min.
Producer and Director: Otto Preminger. Screenplay: Ben Hecht, adapted by Frank P. Rosenberg and Robert E. Kent based on the novel *Night Cry* by William L. Stuart. Director of Photography: Joseph LaShelle. Music: Cyril Mockridge. Art Directors: Lyle Wheeler and J. Russell Spencer. Editor: Louis Loeffler.
Cast: Dana Andrews (Mark Dixon), Gene Tierney (Morgan Taylor), Gary Merrill (Scalise), Bert Freed (Klein), Tom Tully (Jiggs Taylor). With: Karl Malden, Ruth Donnelly, Craig Stevens, Robert Simon, Don Appell.
Mark Dixon is a police detective with a history of brutality. He inadvertently kills a robbery suspect while questioning him. Dixon covers up his crime by

making it look like a mob murder. However, evidence leads to Jiggs Taylor, a cab driver whose daughter Morgan was involved with the murdered man. In the course of the investigation, Morgan falls in love with Dixon, who tries to steer the investigation away from Morgan's father and pin the murder on Scalise, a ruthless mobster. A shoot out at the mobster's hideout kills Scalise and wounds Dixon. However, Dixon has a change of heart and confesses to the original killing. He goes to jail knowing that Morgan will be waiting for his release.

Where the Sidewalk Ends is a typical *film noir* cop movie with its hero, a man of questionable morality. Dixon's treatment of suspects gives a strangely distorted and easily corruptible quality to the image of authority he projects, and this corrupt authority combined with urban violence, is an important *noir* theme.

The screenplay is written by Ben Hecht, one of the truly great American screenwriters, whose work is often concerned with big city and official corruption, generally in a humorous vain. There is nothing humorous in this film however.

Otto Preminger directs in his usual elegant, gliding style, with much of the action concentrated in neon-lit exteriors. Like *Laura* (20th Century–Fox, 1944), Preminger's early *noir* classic, *Where the Sidewalk Ends* originated with Vera Caspary and starred Gene Tierney. However, in this film, Tierney's role was one of conventional romantic support.

While the City Sleeps (RKO, 1956). 99 min.

Producer: Bert Friedlob. Director: Fritz Lang. Screenplay: Casey Robinson, based on the novel *The Bloody Spur* by Charles Einstein. Director of Photography: Ernest Laszlo. Music: Herschel Burke Gilbert. Art Director: Carroll Clark. Editor: Gene Fowler, Jr.

Cast: Dana Andrews (Edward Mobley), Rhonda Fleming (Dorothy Kyne), George Sanders (Mark Loving), Howard Duff (Lt. Burt Kaufman), Thomas Mitchell (John Griffith), Vincent Price (Walter Kyne, Jr.). With: Sally Forrest, James Craig, John Barrymore, Jr.

A series of brutal sex murders committed by the "lipstick killer" terrifies the city. Walter Kyne, Jr., who has just inherited one of the city's major newspapers, announces a competition among his staff editors to catch the serial killer and the winner will be promoted to editor-in-chief. The various editors compromise their principles to catch the killer, including Edward Mobley whose girlfriend is almost killed when he uses her as "bait." Eventually, the killer, a delivery boy, is caught in part by Mobley who is given the promotion.

Fritz Lang's penultimate American film, is both a conventional mystery and a criticism of corrupt journalists. It is one of the earliest explorations of the psychology of a serial murderer in modern Freudian terms: he is a pitiable character who lives with a nagging mother and leaves messages at his crime scenes including "Catch me before I kill again." Interestingly, in true *noir* fashion, the serial killer is more sympathetic than the journalists hunting for him.

Lang's style had become very refined by this point and the film generally avoids the extravagant expressionist style of his early *noirs* — except for its use of black and white film stock its style has almost nothing in common with Lang's 1940's *noirs*.

While the City Sleeps is a compelling, neglected thriller that deserves re-evaluation. It is one of Fritz Lang's least sentimental and most lucid of his late-*noirs*.

White Heat (Warner Bros., 1949). 114 min.

Producer: Lou Edelman. Director: Raoul Walsh. Screenplay: Ivan Goff and Ben Roberts, story by Virginia Kellogg. Director of Photography: Sid Hickox. Music: Max Steiner. Art Director: Edward Carrere. Editor: Owen Marks.

Cast: James Cagney (Cody Jarrett), Virginia Mayo (Verna Jarrett), Edmond O'Brien (Hank Fallon/Vic Pardo), Margaret Wycherly (Ma Jarrett), Steve Cochran (Big Ed Somers). With: John Archer, Wally Cassell, Fred Clark, Ford Rainey, Fred Coby.

After robbing a train, Cody Jarrett and his gang, including his mother, take refuge in a mountain cabin. Cody suffers from blinding headaches which are only relieved by his mother's attentions. When Cody is caught, he confesses to a lesser crime to avoid prosecution on the robbery charge. Big Ed takes charge of the gang and seduces Cody's wife, Verna.

While in prison, Cody is befriended by Vic Pardo, who is really an undercover agent, Hank Fallon. When he finds out that Big Ed and Verna killed his mother, Cody breaks out with the help of Fallon and kills Big Ed. Verna persuades Cody she is innocent of Ma's murder and he believes her. Cody then plans another robbery, but it backfires and his gang is wiped out in the shoot out, with the police.

Mortally wounded, Cody shoots it out on top of a tank full of explosive gas. As it bursts into flames, he shouts out to his dead mother, "Look Ma, top of the world!"

Raoul Walsh, a Warner Bros. director who previously directed the early *noir*, *High Sierra*, here made one of the most unrelentingly cynical of all *films noirs*. Walsh's style was simple and direct, realistic rather than experimental and he preferred simple, linear plots as in the case of *White Heat*. Thus, the film is one of the least pretentious of all the major *noirs*.

Besides its excellent direction, *White Heat* is notable for its psychologically crippled characters, particularly the mother-fixated Cody Jarrett. As portrayed by James Cagney, Jarrett is a bundle of nerves, always on the verge of violence. Cagney's performance is one of the genre's best.

Interestingly, the pretty Virginia Mayo, previously known for her girl-next-door roles, brings a dark, barely contained sexuality to her *femme-fatale*, Verna.

Whitmore, James (1921–)

Character actor. After a brief career on Broadway, Whitmore entered films in the late-forties. He was immediately established as a leading character actor. His youthful intensity and palpable intelligence served him well and he played a variety of supporting parts. He had a prominent role as one of the jewel thieves in *The Asphalt Jungle*. He played an undercover cop in Joseph H. Lewis' *The Undercover Man*. Later, he co-starred in Don Siegel's important post-*noir*, *Madigan* and the less well known *The Split*.

Filmography: *The Undercover Man* (Columbia, 1949). *The Asphalt Jungle* (MGM, 1950). *Madigan* (Universal, 1968). *The Split* (MGM, 1968).

Widmark, Richard (1914–)

Actor. Widmark is one of *films noirs* greatest male icons. Blonde and high strung, he was an atypical *noir* leading man and was a particularly memorable villain.

Widmark made a striking movie debut in the *noir* classic *Kiss of Death*. He played Tommy Udo, the sadistic, giggling hitman who gleefully pushes an old woman in a wheelchair down a flight of stairs. The role typecast Widmark as a villain and he played memorable bad guys in the subsequent *Road House*, *The Street with No Name* and *Night and the City*.

Two of Widmark's most unique *noir* roles were in *Panic in the Streets* and *Pickup on South Street*. In the former he plays one of his few *noir* heroes as a Public Health official hunting for some criminals infected with a dangerous contagious disease. In the latter he starred as a pickpocket who inadvertently steals some microfilm and sets in motion a series of violent events.

In the post-*noir Madigan*, Widmark starred as the tough title character, a hard-boiled cop, providing a physical link to the genre.

By virtue of the number of classic *films noirs* in which Richard Widmark appeared and his extraordinary performances, he remains one of the genre's most important male icons.

Filmography: *Kiss of Death* (20th Century-Fox, 1947). *Road House* (20th Century-Fox, 1948). *The Street with No Name* (20th Century-Fox, 1948). *Night and the City* (20th Century-Fox, 1950). *Panic in the Streets* (20th Century-Fox, 1950). *Pickup on South Street* (20th Century-Fox, 1953). *Madigan* (Universal, 1968).

Wilbur, Crane (1887-1973)

Screenwriter and director. Wilbur was a prolific screenwriter of almost exclusively program, "B" features, His work is often above average. His screenplays emphasize violence and actions.

Filmography: *Canon City* (co-wrote/directed) (Eagle-Lion, 1948). *He Walked By Night* (co-wrote) (Eagle-Lion, 1948). *I Was a Communist for the F.B.I.* (wrote) (Warner Bros., 1951). *Crime Wave* (co-wrote) (Warner Bros., 1954). *The Phenix City Story* (co-wrote) (Allied Artists, 1955).

Wild, Harry J. (   )

Cinematographer. A staff cinematographer for RKO, Wild worked on many important movies. With director Edward Dmytryk, Wild helped develop the shadowy, slightly experimental style familiar to RKO. He worked on several of the best *films noirs* released by the studio.

Filmography: *Murder, My Sweet* (RKO, 1944). *Cornered* (RKO, 1945). *Johnny Angel* (RKO, 1945). *Nocturne* (RKO, 1946). *They Won't Believe Me*

(RKO, 1947). *The Pitfall* (United Artists, 1948). *Gambling House* (RKO, 1951). *His Kind of Woman* (RKO, 1951). *Macao* (RKO, 1952).

Wilde, Cornel (1915-   )

Actor. Wilde spent many years struggling as a stage actor in New York before entering films in 1940. Dark and handsome, Wilde played both heroes and heavys in both "A" and "B" movies. His most famous role was as composer Frederic Chopin in *A Night to Remember* (Warner Bros., 1945), but he also had a substantial *noir* career.

Wilde had a small part in the early *noir* classic *High Sierra*. He starred in *Leave Her to Heaven* as a writer married to a murderously jealous woman and *Road House* as Richard Widmark's nemesis.

One of Wilde's best performances was in Joseph H. Lewis' *The Big Combo*, as a tough, cynical cop in love with the mistress of the gangster he is trying to bring down.

Although it is not well known, Wilde starred in and directed a good "B" *noir*, *Storm Fear*. His performance and direction are well above average.

Cornel Wilde is a minor *noir* icon, but an important one, thanks to a handful of strong performances.

Filmography: *High Sierra* (Warner Bros., 1941). *Leave Her to Heaven* (20th Century-Fox, 1945). *Road House* (20th Century-Fox, 1948). *Shockproof* (Columbia, 1949). *The Big Combo* (Allied Artists, 1955). *Storm Fear* (directed/acted) (United Artists, 1956).

Wilder, Billy (1906-   )

Writer and director. Wilder is one of cinema's true geniuses. Although he was not the most prolific of the *noir* directors, there is little question he is one of the genre's most important figures.

After a brief career as a journalist in Berlin in the late twenties, the Austrian born Wilder made an auspicious debut as a screenwriter with *People on Sunday* (U.F.A., 1929), co-written with Curt Siodmak and directed by Robert Siodmak. Wilder was a successful screenwriter in Germany for several years before the rise of Adolf Hitler. After a brief period in France, Wilder moved to Hollywood in 1934.

For a year or so, Wilder languished on the fringes of Hollywood before teaming with Charles Brackett in 1936. The two became the leading screenwriting team of the time — an odd pairing when one considers their completely different personalities.

Brackett and Wilder began making their own films in 1943 with Brackett producing and Wilder directing. Their partnership came to a temporary end when Wilder decided to make a version of James M. Cain's *Double Indemnity*, which Brackett considered pornographic.

Double Indemnity helped kick off the *noir* cycle. Wilder and Raymond Chandler's screenplay improved upon the original novel. The film's sordid tale of betrayal and murder gave Fred MacMurray and Barbara Stanwyck two of their best roles and confirmed Wilder as a leading filmmaker. His Germanic sensibilities and dark humor was perfectly suitable to the genre.

Wilder's second *film noir*, *Sunset Boulevard*, was co-written with Charles Brackett. The abrasive, satirical screenplay gave no quarter to the Hollywood dream factory it criticized. It is most famous for its performance by Gloria Swanson and its expressionist style.

The harshness of *Sunset Boulevard* looked mild, however, when compared to *The Big Carnival*. Wilder's vitriolic view of opportunistic journalists was not leavened by his usual dark humor and it remains one of the genre's most corrosive movies.

Billy Wilder's three *films noirs* are all extraordinary works of art that combine brilliant writing, strong performances and inventive direction. They are three of the genre's most important films.

Filmography: *Double Indemnity* (Paramount, 1944). *Sunset Boulevard* (Paramount, 1949). *The Big Carnival* (Paramount, 1951).

Wilder, W. Lee (1904–)
Director and producer. Elder brother of Billy Wilder, W. Lee Wilder was a director and producer of "B" movies. His world view was even darker than his brother's, if such a thing is possible. His movies have some of the same expressionist qualities as Billy's, but are much more cynical. *The Pretender* is his only true *noir*, although both *The Glass Alibi* (Republic, 1946) and *The Vicious Circle* (United Artists, 1948) have been described as *noirs*.

Filmography: *The Pretender* (Republic, 1947).

Wiles, Gordon (1902–1950)
Director. For most of his film career, Wiles was an art director. He began directing in the mid forties and made a few "B" movies before his death, including a single *film noir*.

Filmography: *The Gangster* (Allied Artists, 1947).

The Window (RKO, 1949). 73 min.
Producer: Frederic Ullman, Jr. Director: Ted Tetzlaff. Screenplay: Mel Dinelli, based on the story "The Boy Cried Murder" by Cornell Woolrich. Director of Photography: William Steiner. Music: Roy Webb. Music Director: Constantin Bakaleinikoff. Art Directors: Walter Keller and Sam Corso. Editor: Frederic Knudtson.

Cast: Barbara Hale (Mrs. Woodry), Bobby Driscoll (Tommy), Arthur Kennedy (Mrs. Woodry), Paul Stewart (Joe Kellerton), Ruth Roman (Mrs. Kellerton).

Tommy Woodry and his parents are working class people who live in a New York tenement building. Tommy is prone to telling lies. One hot summer night, Tommy goes out onto the fire escape to sleep in the cooler night air. There through their window, he observes his neighbors rob and kill a drunken sailor.

Frightened, Tommy runs back to his apartment, but his parents believe it is another of his lies. He sneaks out and reports the incident to the police who send an investigator. When he finds nothing, Mrs. Woodry forces Tommy to apologize to Mrs. Kellerton.

Leaving the boy alone the following night, Mr. Kellerton kidnaps him, but when Tommy is knocked unconscious, Mr. Kellerton puts him on a precarious fire escape, hoping the child will fall to his death. Tommy, however, does not fall and escapes to an abandoned building next door. He is pursued by the Kellertons. Tommy runs up a flight of stairs as the old building begins to collapse. He climbs out on a bare rafter, followed closely by Mr. Kellerton, but Tommy causes him to fall to his death. The police, alerted by Mr. Woodry, arrive and arrest Mrs. Kellerton and persuade Tommy to jump into a safety net. The young boy promises his mother and father that he will never tell another lie.

Although it is not well known today, *The Window* was a huge box office success upon its initial release. The director of the film, Ted Tetzlaff, had been a cinematographer on a few Alfred Hitchcock films and had learned how to direct a thriller from the master. Indeed, the film is tightly constructed by Mel Dinelli from a long story by Cornell Woolrich into a taut, suspense filled thriller. The element of constant danger and paranoia are reiterated by Tetzlaff's *misè-en-scene* which relies heavily on the expressionist play of light and dark.

Cornell Woolrich had a habit of reusing his best plots and the source material for *The Window* would reappear in a variation which would later be adapted as *Rear Window* (Paramount, 1953).

Windsor, Marie (Emily Marie Bertelson) (1923–)

Actress. The blonde Marie Windsor's brassy, vulgar sexuality was exploited in several key *films noirs*. She had a prominent role in *Force of Evil* as a woman used by a gang boss to seduce the character played by John Garfield. She had an important role as an adulteress in *The City That Never Sleeps* and in Edward Dmytryk's last *noir*, *The Sniper*.

Windsor's most important *noir* roles were in *The Narrow Margin* and *The Killing*. In the first she plays an undercover policewoman pretending to be a gangster's moll. In Stanley Kubrick's *The Killing* she starred as one of the genre's most corrosive *femme-fatales*.

For those two performances alone, Marie Windsor deserves to be remembered as one of *noir's* most memorable female icons.

Filmography: *Force of Evil* (MGM, 1948). *The Narrow Margin* (RKO, 1952). *The Sniper* (Columbia, 1952). *The City That Never Sleeps* (Republic, 1953). *The Killing* (United Artists, 1956). *The Outfit* (MGM, 1973).

Windust, Bretaigne (1906–1960)

Director. Windust was mainly a stage director, directing only six movies. Of these, the most important is *The Enforcer*, a minor classic with a typically strong performance by Humphrey Bogart.

Filmography: *The Enforcer* (Warner Bros., 1951).

Winters, Shelley (Shelley Schrift) (1922–)

Actress. Winters first achieved fame as a stage actress on Broadway in the early forties. Blonde and voluptuous, she was typecast early on as a sexpot, but she often chose roles which stretched her abilities.

Winters appeared in a surprising number of *films noirs*, more often than not as the innocent victim of disingenuous male characters as in *He Ran All the Way*. She also co-starred opposite Jack Palance in *I Died a Thousand*

Times, the remake of *High Sierra* (Warner Bros., 1941), in the role of Marie. She was the female lead in Robert Wise's *Odds Against Tomorrow*, but the film was dominated by its male characters.

Filmography: *The Gangster* (Allied Artists, 1947). *Cry of the City* (20th Century-Fox, 1948). *A Double Life* (Universal, 1948). *He Ran All the Way* (United Artists, 1951). *The Big Knife* (United Artists, 1955). *I Died a Thousand Times* (Warner Bros., 1955). *Night of the Hunter* (United Artists, 1955). *Odds Against Tomorrow* (United Artists, 1959).

Wise, Robert (1914–1991)

Director. Wise is yet another graduate of the Val Lewton unit that flourished at RKO in the early forties. An important editor, he worked on the Orson Welles masterpiece, *Citizen Kane* (RKO, 1941). Wise was promoted by Lewton to director and subsequently directed the Lewton-produced classic, *The Body Snatcher* (RKO, 1945). It was an enormous success and immediately established Wise as a major director.

A solid craftsman-like director, Wise was not as inventive as most of the other major *noir* directors, but he brought a great sense of professionalism to his *films noirs*.

Wise directed five *films noirs*. The first, *Born to Kill* is a vastly underrated study of insanity. His boxing *noir*, *The Set-Up*, is arguably the best of the genre. *House on Telegraph Hill* and *The Captive City*, while not quite classics, are very well made. *Odds Against Tomorrow* — sometimes called the last film of the genre — is one of the most fatalistic of all *films noirs*.

Wise's style was simpler than many of his contemporaries. His lighting schemes were not particularly extravagant — with the exception of *The Set-Up* — and camera movement is kept at a minimum. Yet, through force of vision, Wise is undeniably one of *films noirs* major directors.

Filmography: *Born to Kill* (RKO, 1947). *The Set-Up* (RKO, 1949). *House on Telegraph Hill* (20th Century-Fox, 1951). *The Captive City* (United Artists, 1952). *Odds Against Tomorrow* (United Artists, 1959).

Witness to Murder (United Artists, 1954). 81 min.

Producer: Chester Erskine. Director: Roy Rowland. Screenplay: Chester Erskine. Director of Photography: John Alton. Music: Herschel Burke Gilbert. Art Director: William Ferrari. Editor: Robert Swink.

Cast: Barbara Stanwyck (Cheryl Draper), George Sanders (Albert Richter), Gary Merrill (Lawrence Mathews), Jesse White (Eddie Vincent), Harry Shannon (Capt. Donnelly). With: Claire Carleton, Lewis Martin, Dick Elliott, Harry Tyler.

Late one night, Cheryl Draper is closing her bedroom window when she sees a man murder a young woman in the apartment across the way. She calls the police, but the murderer, Albert Richter, hides the body. Richter later breaks into her apartment and using her typewriter, writes himself a series of threatening letters. He convinces the police she is trying to harass him. Convinced that she is insane, the police have her temporarily committed to a mental hospital for "observation." She escapes, but is pursued by Richter. She runs into a building under construction and climbs onto the wooden scaffolding. The police arrive and Richter falls to his death in a fight with one of the cops. Cheryl is saved before the scaffolding collapses.

Witness to Murder immediately brings to mind *The Window* (RKO, 1949) and *Rear Window* (Paramount, 1953), with its witnessed murder through an apartment window, the subsequent disbelief of those informed of the crime and the hairraising ending. However, it also adds the element of "insanity" as Cheryl Draper is confined in a mental institution.

George Sanders gives an excellent performance in this otherwise minor *film noir* as the murderous historical writer Albert Richter, whose neo–Nazi beliefs compel him to think of himself as morally superior to others.

The Woman in the Window (RKO, 1944). 99 min.

Producer: Nunnally Johnson. Director: Fritz Lang. Screenplay: Nunnally Johnson, based on the novel *Once Off Guard* by J. H. Wallis. Director of Photography: Milton Krasner. Music: Arthur Lange. Art Director: Duncan Cramer. Editors: Marjorie Johnson and Gene Fowler, Jr.

Cast: Edward G. Robinson (Richard Wanley), Joan Bennett (Alice Reed), Raymond Massey (Frank Lalor), Edmond Breon (Dr. Barkstone), Dan Duryea (Heidt). With: Thomas E. Jackson, Arthur Loft, Dorothy Peterson, Frank Dawson.

Richard Wanley is a middle aged college professor whose life is quiet and uneventful. After seeing his wife and family off on vacation, he sets out to meet his friends at a club. There, he tells them about the extraordinary beautiful woman he saw in a portrait in a window. The friends tease each other about having a wild night on the town.

On his way home, Wanley stops to admire the portrait and is surprised when the real woman's face appears reflected in the glass. She introduces herself as Alice Reed, and after buying her a drink, Wanley is invited back to her place for an innocent night cap. However, the jealous boyfriend breaks in. The two men fight and Alice hands Wanley a pair of scissors. He stabs her hulking boyfriend to death. Alice and Wanley agree to dispose of the body, which Wanley does by dumping it in a remote forest.

Although they think their problem is behind them, the body is discovered and Wanley's friend, a police inspector, is assigned to the case. Wanley is forced to listen to his friend discuss the investigation. To make matters worse, a friend of the victim, Heidt, contacts Alice, claiming he knows what happened and demands a ransom. When Alice informs Wanley of the blackmail scheme, he decides to commit suicide by taking poison rather than face scandal and disgrace. However, Heidt is killed in a gun battle with police who suspect he murdered Alice's boyfriend.

Alice calls Wanley to tell him that they are off the hook, but Wanley has apparently already swallowed the poison. The camera travels back from a close up of the phone ringing to reveal Wanley slumped in an arm chair. He is suddenly jarred from a deep sleep—he had fallen asleep at the club and it had all been a dream. On his way home a sexy woman approaches him as he passes the portrait gallery. Professor Wanley shuns her and hurries home, his desire for adventure dissipated by his nightmare.

The Woman in the Window is one of the most important early *noirs*. It is one of the earliest examples of the *noir* theme of the doppelganger, here in the interplay of reality versus dream, evil versus good, sordidness versus morality. Wanley is presented as a typical *noir* protagonist, an honest man susceptible to corruption and tempted by a *femme-fatale*. However, unlike the subsequent *Scarlet Street* (Universal, 1945), the characterizations are less harsh and cynical. Alice Reed is not the classic *femme-fatale* that *Scarlet Street*'s Kitty March is and the murder here is an accident. Furthermore, the seediness of the story is leavened by humor and the cliché nightmare twist.

Nevertheless, Fritz Lang's imaginative filmmaking overcame some of the inadequacies of the screenplay. He fills the movie with countless mirror images to reiterate the theme and his usual expressionist characteristics in the cinematography.

The Woman on Pier 13 (*aka I Married a Communist*) (RKO, 1949). 73 min.

Producer: Jack J. Gross. Director: Robert Stevenson. Screenplay: Charles Grayson and Robert Hardy Andrews, story by George W. George and George P. Salvin. Director of Photography: Nicholas Musuraca. Music: Leigh Harline. Music Director: Constantin Bakaleinikoff. Art Directors: Albert S. D'Agostino and Walter E. Keller. Editor: Roland Gross.

Cast: Laraine Day (Nan Collins), Robert Ryan (Brad Collins), John Agar (Don Lowry), Thomas Gomez (Vanning), Janis Carter (Christine), Richard Rober (Jim Travis). With: William Talman, Paul E. Burns, Paul Guilfoyle, G. Pat Collins.

Brad Collins, a shipping executive, was once involved with the Communist Party and a party related murder, but has long since abandoned the past affiliation. He is surprised when a man blackmails him into helping tie up shipping in the Bay area. The situation is complicated by the party's effort to "convert" Brad's impressionable brother-in-law, Don Lowry, to their ideals, and Brad's own inabilities to tell his wife the truth about his past. Trapped, after Lowry is murdered, Brad sacrifices his own life to halt the subversive plot.

The Woman on Pier 13 is an interesting example of the rightwing backlash in the early fifties and of Howard Hughes' nefarious influence on his recently purchased studio, RKO. Hughes often oversaw pet projects, of which this was one. However, despite some interesting scenes, the film suffers from its ridiculous red-baiting dialog and cliché political melodrama. Indeed, it was a huge box office failure at the time of its release and remains little more than a curiosity of its time.

Woman on the Run (Universal, 1950). 77 min.

Producer: Howard Welsch. Director: Norman Foster. Screenplay: Alan Campbell and Norman Foster, from a story by Sylvia Tate. Director of Photography: Hal Mohr. Music: Emil Newman and Arthur Lange. Art Director: Boris Leven. Editor: Otto Ludwig.

Cast: Ann Sheridan (Eleanor Johnson), Dennis O'Keefe (Danny Leggett), Robert Keith (Inspector Ferris), Frank Jenks (Detective Shaw), Ross Elliott (Fran Johnson). With: John Qualen, J. Farrell MacDonald, Thomas P. Dillon.

When her husband, Fran Johnson, an artist, witnesses a gangland slaying, he goes into hiding, leaving his wife Eleanor to track him down. She is aided by a newspaperman, Danny Leggett and the search becomes more desperate when Eleanor learns that her husband maybe suffering from a heart ailment. Eventually Eleanor discovers that Leggett is the murderer and is using her to get to her husband, but the police arrive just in time to save the Johnsons and Leggett is arrested.

Woman on the Run is another *noir* to make effective use of the mysterious qualities of San Francisco. The screenplay for this minor, but enjoyable "B" *noir*, is tightly constructed by Alan Campbell and Norman Foster and well directed by the latter. A deglamorized Ann Sheridan heads up a second string, but talented cast.

Woolrich, Cornell (*aka* **William Irish**) (1903–1968)

Writer. Woolrich was a prolific writer of short stories and novels. Under his real name and various pseudonyms, including William Irish, he wrote a series of odd suspense and mystery tales that were ready made for the screen and many of his works were adapted. Woolrich was a recluse who rarely left his apartment and remains something of an enigma. A number of classic *films noirs* were based on his works, as were many good "B" *noirs*.

Filmography: *Street of Chance* (based on his novel) (Paramount, 1942).

Phantom Lady (based on his novel) (Universal, 1944). *Black Angel* (based on his novel) (Universal, 1946). *The Chase* (based on his novel) (United Artists, 1946). *Deadline at Dawn* (based on his novel) (RKO, 1946). *Fall Guy* (based on his short story) (Monogram, 1947). *Fear in the Night* (based on his short story) (Paramount, 1947). *The Guilty* (based on his short story) (Monogram, 1947). *I Wouldn't Be in Your Shoes* (based on his novel) (Monogram, 1948). *The Night Has a Thousand Eyes* (based on his novel) (Paramount, 1948). *The Window* (based on his short story) (RKO, 1949). *Rear Window* (based on his short story) (Universal, 1953). *Nightmare* (based on his short story) (United Artists, 1956).

World for Ransom (Allied Artists, 1954). 82 min.

Producers: Robert Aldrich and Bernard Tabakin. Director: Robert Aldrich. Screenplay: Lindsay Hardy. Director of Photography: Joseph Biroc. Music: Frank De Vol. Art Director: William Glascow. Editor: Michael Luciano.

Cast: Dan Duryea (Mike Callahan), Gene Lockhart (Alexis Pederas), Patric Knowles (Julian March), Reginald Denny (Major Bone), Nigel Bruce (Governor Coutts), Marian Carr (Frennessey). With: Douglas Dumbrille, Keye Luke, Clarence Lung, Lou Nova.

Mike Callahan, an Irish émigré and war veteran, lives and works in Singapore as a private investigator. One day he is summoned to a club by Frennessey, an old flame from the war, whose husband Julian, the owner of the club, is mixed up in some illegal activities. She wants Mike to help extricate him, if he can. Mike learns that Julian has been recruited by a black marketeer named Alexis Pederas in a scheme. Julian has kidnapped a British nuclear physicist who is being offered to the highest bidder.

Callahan is framed by Pederas and his men. With a British Intelligence officer secretly following him, he slips out of town, heading for a deserted jungle village where he believes the scientist is being held. Indeed, he finds Pederas' hideout. In the resulting shootout, all are killed except Callahan and the scientist.

Returning to Frennessey, Mike reports the death of her husband. When he tries to comfort her, she rejects him, telling him that men are physically repellent to her. Julian was the only man she loved because he was not sexually attracted to her. Dejected, Mike leaves her and returns to his lonely life.

Robert Aldrich's espionage *noir*, *World for Ransom* is a neglected classic of cold war cinema. The topical plot of the kidnapped nuclear scientist, however, serves merely as the framework for *noir* tale of violence, corruption and ultimately, rejection. More than anything, it is a mediation on violence, represented by the reaction of Frennessey when Mike Callahan tries to comfort her at the end: she reacts by viciously slapping him and verbally assaulting him. In the modern world, tenderness and love has been corrupted by repression and greed.

Aldrich, would return to a similar theme in his classic, *Kiss Me Deadly* (United Artists, 1955), an equally ambitious variation on *noir* themes and style.

Wray, Fay (1907–)

Actress. Fay Wray will be forever remembered as the object of King Kong's amorous interest in *King Kong* (RKO, 1933). She was a major star of the early thirties and she continued to play supporting roles right up into the 1960's. She had a small supporting role in a single late *film noir*.

Filmography: *Crime of Passion* (United Artists, 1957).

Wright, Will (1894–1962)

Character actor. Wright played seedy characters, country bumpkins and lugubrious old men in countless movies. His single *noir* appearance is his best: as Dad Newell, the murderer in *The Blue Dahlia*.

Filmography: *The Blue Dahlia* (Paramount, 1946).

The Wrong Man (Warner Bros., 1956). 105 min.

Producer and Director: Alfred Hitchcock. Screenplay: Maxwell Anderson and Angus Mac Phail, based on "The True Story of Christopher Emmanuel Balestero" by Maxwell Anderson. Director of Photography: Robert Burks. Music: Bernard Herrmann. Art Directors: Paul Sylbert and William L. Kuehl. Editor: George Tomasini.

Cast: Henry Fonda (Manny Balestero), Anthony Quayle (O'Connor), Vera Miles (Rose Balestero), Harold J. Stone (Lt. Bowers), Esther Minciotti (Manny's Mother), Charles Cooper (Detective Matthews). With: Nehemiah Persoff, Laurinda Barrett, Norma Connolly, Doreen Lang.

Manny Balestero, a nightclub musician and family man, is accused of an armed robbery he did not commit. The real criminal looks exactly like him, which further condemns him. His wife, Rose, slowly loses her sanity while they wait for the trial to begin. From his arrest to his fingerprinting, handcuffing and jailing, Manny is humiliated by the process of justice. Eventually, however, the real culprit is caught and Manny is freed. When he visits his wife in the sanitarium, all she can do is repeat "Good for you, Manny...."

Alfred Hitchcock is known for his extreme dislike of the police and mistrust of the justice system and he found, with this story, based on real events and people, the perfect vehicle for his criticisms. Yet, *The Wrong Man* is also one of his dullest movies. Its performances are first rate and there are some inspired moments, but overall the film fails to achieve greatness.

Wyatt, Jane (1912–)

Actress. Wyatt's film career began in the early thirties and hit its stride toward the end of the decade. She starred in mostly routine movies, but had major roles in two *films noirs*, *Boomerang* and *House by the River* but she did not develop into a major *noir* actress.

Filmography: *Boomerang* (20th Century–Fox, 1947). *House by the River* (Republic, 1950).

Wyler, William (1902–1981)

Director. Wyler was an important director of great style and variety. His talents were not really suitable to *film noir*, but he still directed three such films. *The Letter* is an important early *noir*. *Detective Story* suffers from its static setting (it was based on a play). *The Desperate Hours* though, is an interesting late *noir* that stars Humphrey Bogart in his last criminal role. A taut thriller, it is Wyler's best *film noir*.

Filmography: *The Letter* (Warner Bros., 1940). *Detective Story* (Paramount, 1951).

Yarbrough, Jean (1900–1975)

Director. Yarbrough, a graduate of the Hal Roach studio, was a prolific "B" director. He alternated between Universal and Monogram, also working at other studios for a few films. He directed a single "B" *noir*, but his talents were better suited to more conventional fare.

Filmography: *Inside Job* (Universal, 1946).

Yordan, Phillip (1913–)

Screenwriter. A prolific screenwriter, Yordan specialized in action and crime movies. He worked at virtually all the major and minor studios and produced a few films as well. He was an inventive craftsman with an agreeable hard-boiled style. He worked on a number of excellent *films noirs* including Joseph H. Lewis' great "B" *noir*, *The Big Combo*.

Filmography: *When Strangers Marry* (Monogram, 1944). *The Chase* (United Artists, 1946). *Suspense* (Monogram,

1946). *House of Strangers* (20th Century–Fox, 1949). *Edge of Doom* (RKO, 1950). *Detective Story* (also produced) (Paramount, 1951). *The Big Combo* (Allied Artists, 1955). *The Harder They Fall* (Columbia, 1956).

You Only Live Once (United Artists 1937). 87 min.
Producer: Walter Wanger. Director: Fritz Lang. Screenplay: Gene Towne and Graham Baker. Director of Photography: Leon Shamroy. Music: Louis Alter and Paul Webster. Art Director: Alexander Tolubuff. Editor: Daniel Mandell.
Cast: Sylvia Sidney (Joan "Jo" Graham), Henry Fonda (Eddie Taylor), Barton MacLane (Stephen Whitney), Jean Dixon (Bonnie Graham), William Gargan (Father Dolan). With: Charles "Chic" Sale, Margaret Hamilton, Guinn Williams, Jerome Cowan.
After Eddie Taylor is released from prison, all he wants is to get on with his life with fiancée Jo Graham. He promises her his life of crime is over. However, when a local bank robbery is committed and a guard killed, Eddie is the prime suspect. Although innocent, he is arrested, convicted and sentenced to death. He slits his wrists in an escape plan and at the prison infirmary, he is slipped a pistol. At that moment, word reaches the warden that the real culprit has been captured and has confessed. Eddie does not believe it when informed — thinking it a ruse — and shoots the prison chaplain as he gets away.
Eddie joins Jo. After their baby is born and given to Jo's sister, the couple try to escape across the border. After a shootout at a roadblock, they abandon the car and flee on foot. A few yards from freedom, both are shot.
Like the earlier *Fury* (MGM, 1936), *You Only Live Once* is a polemical movie about the outrage of the unjustly punished and a corrupt justice system. Like the previous film this one is also an exercise in style and theme. The expres-sionist visuals and the existential fate of the characters are *noir* elements, here in their infancy. In general, the film fore-shadows the obsessions of the genre to come and Fritz Lang's mature *noirs* in particular.

Young, Collier (1908–1980)
Screenwriter. Collier Young co-wrote many movies. A typical Holly-wood professional, his work is always competent but rarely outstanding and he did not specialize in a particular genre or style. He worked on two *films noirs*.
Filmography: *Act of Violence* (story only) (MGM, 1949). *Private Hell, 36* (co-wrote) (Filmmakers, 1954).

Young, Gig (Byron Barr) (1913–1978)
Actor. Young was a popular charac-ter actor and light leading man of romantic comedies in the fifties and six-ties. He also played tougher parts as in *The City That Never Sleeps* as a cor-rupt newspaper editor.
Filmography: *The City That Never Sleeps* (RKO, 1954).

Young, Loretta (Gretchen Young) (1913–)
Actress. A dark haired beauty of the girl-next-door type, Loretta Young was a major star of the thirties and forties. Her movies were generally routine romantic comedies and dramas and she always played innocents as she did in her most prominent *film noir*, *The Stranger*. *The Accused* gave her a different type of role as a sexually repressed psychology professor who kills a student. Her role in *Cause for Alarm* was a routine woman-in-distress part.
Filmography: *The Accused* (Para-mount, 1946). *The Stranger* (RKO, 1946). *Cause for Alarm* (MGM, 1951).

Young, Robert (1907–)
Actor. Young is probably most famous as the star of the television series *Father Knows Best* and *Marcus*

Welby, M.D. For two decades before the first series, Young was a successful leading man with MGM. In the late forties he starred in two RKO *noirs*, including Edward Dmytryk's classic, *Crossfire.* He also starred in an independently produced "B" *noir, The Second Woman.* His image, however, was too debonair and well-kempt for the genre.

Filmography: *Crossfire* (RKO, 1947). *They Won't Believe Me* (RKO, 1947). *The Second Woman* (United Artists, 1951).

Young, Victor (1900–1956)
Composer. Probably the most prolific composer of film scores, Victor Young composed the music for over three hundred movies. He has much in common with his better known contemporary, Max Steiner. Both were competent craftsmen whose work was never less than adequate, but rarely outstanding. However, like Steiner, Young composed a number of classic scores in his usual romantic, lyrical style including *The Quiet Man* (Republic, 1952), *Shane* (Paramount, 1953 and *Around the World in Eighty Days* (MGM, 1956) among others. He also composed the music for many *films noirs.* These are among his best scores.

Filmography: *The Glass Key* (Paramount, 1942). *Ministry of Fear* (Paramount, 1944). *The Blue Dahlia* (Paramount, 1946). *Calcutta* (Paramount, 1947). *The Big Clock* (Paramount, 1948). *I Walk Alone* (Paramount, 1948). *The Night Has a Thousand Eyes* (Paramount, 1948). *The Accused* (Paramount, 1949). *Chicago Deadline* (Paramount, 1949). *Gun Crazy* (United Artists, 1950). *Appointment with Danger* (Paramount, 1951).

Zeisler, Alfred (1892–1988)
Director. The American born Zeisler had his greatest success as a director in Germany in the late twenties through the mid thirties. After the rise of Hitler, Zeisler moved to Great Britain where he continued to direct. After a decade in London, he returned to the United States where he directed a number of interesting "B" movies including *Fear,* an update of Dostoevsky's *Crime and Punishment.*

Filmography: *Fear* (Monogram, 1946).

Zinnemann, Fred (1907–)
Director. Zinnemann had a long apprenticeship before he began directing features in the early forties. The Austrian born director's career began in Berlin in the late-twenties as an assistant director on such films as the Robert Siodmak directed classic, *People on Sunday* (U.F.A., 1929). He moved to the United States in the early thirties and over the next decade, worked as an extra, script clerk and director of shorts before he moved to features in 1942. He brought a strong expressionist oriented style to his classics, *From Here to Eternity* (MGM, 1953), *High Noon* (MGM, 1952) and *Act of Violence,* an underrated *film noir.* Zinnemann is an underrated artist and deserves reevaluation.

Filmography: *Act of Violence* (MGM, 1949).

Zucco, George (1886–1960)
Character actor. Zucco, a British stage actor, was a major figure in cheap Hollywood horror epics in the thirties and forties. He had a small, typically malignant role in Douglas Sirk's *Lured,* his only *film noir.*

Filmography: *Lured* (United Artists, 1947).

Zugsmith, Albert (1910–)
Producer. A specialist in exploitation movies, Zugsmith also occasionally produced low budget films for talented artists. He produced three *films noirs* in the fifties including Orson Welles' *Touch of Evil,* the great director's last important production.

Filmography: *The Tattered Dress* (Universal, 1957). *Touch of Evil* (Universal, 1958). *The Beat Generation* (MGM, 1959).

Selected Bibliography

Books

Agee, James. *Agee on Film* 2 vols. (New York: Grosset and Dunlap, 1969).

Alloway, Lawrence. *Violence in America: The Movies 1946-1964* (New York: The Museum of Modern Art, 1971).

Anderson, Clinton H. *Beverly Hills Is My Beat* (Englewood Cliffs, N.J.: Prentice-Hall, 1960).

Antheil, George. *Bad Boy of Music* (Garden City, N.J.: Doubleday, 1945).

Aros, D. Richard, ed. *A Title Guide to the Talkies, 1914-1974* (Metuchen, N.J.: Scarecrow Press, 1977).

Aylesworth, Thomas G. and Bowman, John S. *The World Almanac Who's Who of Film* (New York: Crown Publishers, 1988).

Bartlett, Donald L. and Steele, James B. *Empire: The Life, Legend, and Madness of Howard Hughes* (New York: Norton, 1979).

Baxter, John. *The Hollywood Exiles* (New York: Taplinger, 1976).

Bazin, Andre. *The Cinema of Cruelty, from Bunuel to Hitchcock* (Translated by Sabine d'Estree and Tifanny Fliss. New York: Scaner, 1972).

————. *Orson Welles: A Critical View* (Translated by Jonathan Rosenbaum. New York: Harper and Row, 1978).

Behlmer, Rudy. *Inside Warner Brothers, 1925-1951* (New York: Viking, 1985).

Berman, Susan. *Easy Street* (New York: Dial, 1981).

Bishop, Jim. *The Mark Hellinger Story.* (New York: Appleton-Century-Crofts, 1952).

Brady, Frank. *Citizen Welles* (New York: Charles Scribner's Sons, 1989).

Cagney, James. *Cagney by Cagney* (Garden City, N.Y.: Doubleday, 1976).

Cameron, Ian *A Pictorial History of Crime Films* (London: Hamlyn, 1975).

Carey, Gary. *All the Stars in Heaven: Louis B. Mayer's M-G-M* (New York: Dutton, 1981).

Ceplair, Larry and Englund, Steve. *The Inquisition in Hollywood: Politics in the Film Colony, 1930-1960* (Garden City, N.Y.: Doubleday/Anchor, 1980).

Ciment, Michel. *Kubrick* (New York: Rinehart & Winston, 1980).

Clarens, Carlos. *Crime Movies: An Illustrated History* (New York: Norton, 1980).

Coffey, Thomas M. *The Long Thirst* (New York: Norton, 1975).

Corlis, Richard, ed. *The Hollywood Screenwriters* (New York: Avon, 1972).

Corlis, Richard. *Talking Pictures* (New York: Overlook Press, 1974).

Cowie, Peter, ed. *International Film Guide* (Cranbury, N.J.: A. S. Barnes, 1964).

Cross, Robin. *The Big Book of B Movies* (New York: St. Martin's Press, 1981).

Crowther, Bruce. *Film Noir: Reflections in a Dark Mirror* (New York: Continuum, 1989).

Davis, Bette. *The Lonely Life: An Autobiography* (New York: Putnam, 1962).

Dickens, Homer. *The Films of Marlene Dietrich* (Secaucus, N.J.: Citadel, 1968).

Dixon, Wheeler W. *The "B" Directors: A Biographical Directory* (Metuchen, N.J.: Scarecrow Press, 1985).

Dmytryk, Edward. *It's a Hell of a Life But Not a Bad Living: A Hollywood Memoir* (New York: Time Books, 1978).

Eames, John Douglas. *The MGM Story* (New York: Crown Publishers, 1979).

————. *The Paramount Story* (New York: Crown Publishers, 1985).

Eisner, Lotte. *Fritz Lang* (New York: Da Capo Press, 1976).

Evans, Mark. *Soundtrack: The Music of the Movies* (New York: Hopkinson and Blake, 1975).

Flynn, Charles, ed. *Kings of the Bs* (New York: E. P. Dutton and Company, 1975).

Friedrich, Otto. *City of Nets* (New York: Harper & Row Publishers, 1986).

Frischauer, Willi. *Behind the Scenes of Otto Preminger* (New York: Morrow, 1973).

Geist, Kenneth. *Pictures Will Talk: The Life and Films of Joseph L. Mankiewicz* (New York: Scribner, 1978).

Goodman, Walter. *The Committee: The Extraordinary Career of the House Committee on Un-American Activities* (New York: Farrar, Straus, and Giroux, 1968).

Halliwell, Leslie. *Halliwell's Film Guide, 7th Edition* (New York: Charles Scribner's Sons, 1989).

————. *Halliwell's Filmgoer's & Video Viewer's Companion, 9th Edition* (New York: Charles Scribner's Sons, 1988).

Hardy, Phil. *Samuel Fuller* (New York: Praeger, 1970).

Harris, Robert A. and Lasky, Michael S. *The Films of Alfred Hitchcock* (Secaucus, N.J.: Citadel, 1976).

Hecht, Ben. *A Child of the Century* (New York: Simon and Schuster, 1954).

Hirshhorn, Clive. *The Universal Story* (New York: Crown Publishers, 1983).

Hyams, Joe. *Bogie: The Biography of Humphrey Bogart* (New York: Signet, 1967).

Jewell, Richard B. and Harbin, Vernon. *The RKO Story* (New Rochelle, N. Y.: Arlington House, 1982).

Jobes, Gertrude. *Motion Picture Empire* (Hamden, Connecticut: Archon Books, 1966).

Kaminsky, Stuart M. *Don Siegel, Director* (New York: Curtis, 1974).

Kaplan, E. Ann (ed.). *Women in Film Noir* (London: British Film Institute Press, 1989).

Katz, Ephraim. *The Film Encyclopedia* (New York: Thomas Y. Gowell, 1979).

Keyes, Evelyn. *Scarlet O'Hara's Younger Sister* (New York: Lyle Stuart, 1977).

Kinnard, Roy & Vitone, R. J. *The American Films of Michael Curtiz* (Metuchen, N. J.: Scarecrow Press, 1986).

Kobal, John. *Rita Hayworth: The Time, the Place, and the Woman* (New York: Norton, 1977).

Kracauer, Sigfried. *From Caligari to Hitler: A Psychological History of German Film* (Princeton, N.J.: Princeton University Press, 1947 — reprinted in 1967).

Krasur, Richard, ed. *American Film Institute Catalog of Motion Pictures: Feature Films, 1961-1970* (2 vols. New York: R. R. Bowler, 1976).

Lake, Veronica. *Veronica* with Donald Bain (New York: Citadel, 1971).

Lasky, Betty. *RKO: The Biggest Little Major of Them All* (Santa Monica, California: Roundtable Publishing, 1989).

LeRoy, Mervyn. *Take One* as told to Dick Kleiner (New York: Hawthorn, 1974).

Linet, Beverly. *Ladd: The Life, the Legend, and the Legacy of Alan Ladd* (New York: Arbor House, 1979).

Lloyd, Ann (ed.). *Movies of the Fifties* (London: Orbis, 1982).

_____. *Movies of the Forties* (London: Orbis, 1982).

McBride, Joseph. *Hawks on Hawks* (Los Angeles: University of California Press, 1982).

MacShane, Frank. *The Life of Raymond Chandler* (New York: Dutton, 1976).

Madsen, Axel. *Billy Wilder* (Bloomington: Indiana University Press, 1969).

Mast, Gerald. *Howard Hawks: Storyteller* (New York: Oxford University Press, 1982).

Miller, Don. *B Movies* (New York: Curtis Books, 1973).

Mordden, Ethan. *The Hollywood Studios: House Style in the Golden Age of the Movies* (New York: Alfred A. Knopf, 1988).

Mosley, Leonard. *Zanuck: The Rise and Fall of Hollywood's Last Tycoon* (New York: McGraw-Hill Book Co., 1984).

Nash, Jay Robert. *Bloodletters and Badmen* (New York: Warner, 1977).

New York Times Films Reviews, 1913–1980 12 vols. (New York: Arno Press, 1982).

Parish, James R. and Pitts, Michael R. *Film Directors: A Guide to Their American Films* (Metuchen, N.J.: Scarecrow Press, 1974).

_____ and _____. *The Great Spy Pictures* (Metuchen, N.J.: Scarecrow Press, 1974).

Phillips, Cabell. *The 1940s: A Decade of Triumph and Trouble* (New York: Mac-Millan, 1975).

Pratley, Gerald. *The Cinema of Otto Preminger* (New York: A. E. Barnes, 1973).

Rand, Christopher. *Los Angeles: The Ultimate City* (New York: Oxford University Press, 1967).

Robinson, Edward G. *All My Yesterdays: An Autobiography* with Leonard Spiegelglass (New York: Hawthorn, 1973).

Rozsa, Miklos. *Double Life: The Autobiography of Miklos Rozsa* (New York: Hippocrene, 1983).

Sarris, Andrew. *The American Cinema: Directors and Directions* (New York: E. P. Dutton, 1968).

Schary, Dore. *Heyday* (Boston: Little, Brown, 1979).

Schumach, Murray. *The Face on the Cutting Room Floor* (New York: William Morrow, 1964).

Schindler, Colin. *Hollywood Goes to War: Films and American Society, 1939–1952* (Boston: Routledge and Kegan Paul, 1979).

Selby, Spencer. *Dark City: The Film Noir* (Jefferson, N. C.: McFarland, 1984).

Sennett, Ted. *Great Movie Directors* (New York: Harry N. Abrams, 1986).

Shatz, Thomas. *The Genius of the System* (New York: Pantheon Books, 1988).

Silver, Alain and Ward, Elizabeth (eds.). *Film Noir: An Encyclopedic Reference to the American Style* (New York: Overlook Press, 1979).

Sklar, Robert. *Movie-Made America: A Cultural History of American Movies* (New York: Random House, 1975).

Spoto, Donald. *The Dark Side of Genius: The Life of Alfred Hitchcock* (New York: Ballantine, 1984).

Stempel, Tom. *Nunnally Johnson: Screenwriter* (New York: Pantheon Books, 1988).

Swindell, Larry. *Body and Soul: The Story of John Garfield* (New York: Morrow, 1975).

Taylor, John Russell. *Strangers in Paradise: The Hollywood Emigres, 1937–1950* (New York: Hold, Rinehart, and Winston, 1983).

Thomas, Bob. *King Cohn: The Life and Times of Harry Cohn* (New York: Putnam, 1967).
Tierney, Gene. *Self-Portrait* with Mickey Herskowitz (New York: Wyden, 1979).
Tuska, John. *The Detective in Hollywood* (Garden City, N. J.: Doubleday, 1978).
Wallis, Hal and Higham, Charles. *Starmaker: The Autobiography of Hal Wallis* (New York: Macmillan, 1980).
Warner, Jack. *My First Hundred Years in Hollywood: An Autobiography* with Dean Jennings (New York: Random House, 1965).
Whitehead, Don. *The FBI Story* (New York: Random House, 1958).
Yablonsky, Lewis. *George Raft* (New York: McGraw-Hill, 1974).
Zierold, Norman. *The Moguls* (New York: Coward, McCann, 1969).

Periodicals

Brody, Merideth. "Missing Persons: David Goodis." *Film Comment* (August, 1984).
Denby, David. "On the Outside Looking In." *Premier* (August, 1989).
_____. "Rear Window: John Huston and *The Asphalt Jungle.*" *Premier* (July, 1990).
_____. "Rear Window: Robert Towne." *Premier* (December, 1988).
Dunne, Philip. "*Zanuck: The Rise and Fall of Hollywood's Last Tycoon*: A Review." *American Film* (July-August, 1984).
Elaesser, Thomas. "The Classic Hollywood Cinema: Film Style and Mode of Production to 1960." *American Film* (May, 1985).
Farber, Stephen. "Violence and the Bitch Goddess." *Film Comment* (Nov.-Dec., 1974).
_____ and Green, Mark. "The Mankiewicz Clan." *Film Comment* (July-August, 1984).
Fox, Terry and Gehr, Richard. "City Knights." *Film Comment* (October, 1984).
Frankenheimer, John. "Dialogue on Film (Interview)." *American Film* (March, 1989).
Goodell, Jeffery. "Unfriendly Witnesses." *Premier Special Issue* (Winter, 1991).
Hodenfield, Chris. "The Art of Noncompromise." *American Film* (March, 1989).
Hogue, Peter. "Fritz Lang Our Contemporary." *Film Comment* (Nov.-Dec., 1990).
Hoopes, Roy. "Hack Slays Movie Colony: James M. Cain in Hollywood." *American Film* (October, 1981).
Jameson, Richard T. "Son of Noir." *Film Comment* (Sept.-Oct., 1974).
Kehr, Dave. "Hitchcock Is Guilty." *Film Comment* (June, 1984).
Kelley, Bill. "This Pen for Hire." *American Film* (December, 1984).
Kennedy, Harlan and Peary, Gerald. "Mitchum and Russell." *Film Comment* (May, 1992).
McDonagh, Maitland. "Straight to Hell." *Film Comment* (Nov.-Dec. 1990).
MacPherson, Malcom. "Kathleen Turner: The Single-Minded Cinderella." *Premier* (November, 1989).
Murphy,Kathleen. "Farewell My Lovelies: Stanwyck and Gardner." *Film Comment* (July-Aug., 1990).
Sarris, Andrew. "Don Siegel." *Film Comment* (Sept.-Oct., 1991).
_____. "Why Billy Wilder Belongs in the Pantheon." *Film Comment* (July-August, 1991).
Schickel, Richard. "Bette." *Film Comment* (March-April, 1989).
_____. "Midsection: Humphrey Bogart." *Film Comment* (May-June, 1986).
_____. "What a Dump." *Film Comment* (March-April, 1989).

Schwager, Jeff. "'The Past' Rewritten." *Film Comment* (Jan.–Feb., 1991).
Silliphant, Stirling. "Dialogue on Film (Interview)." *American Film* (March, 1988).
Thomson, David. "Cary Grant at 80: A Tribute." *Film Comment* (January-February, 1984).
_____. "A Cottage at Palos Verdes." *Film Comment* (May-June, 1990).
_____. "Lana Turner: A Life of Imitation." *Film Comment* (June, 1988).
Turner, George. "*D.O.A.*: Classic Revisited." *American Cinematographer* (August, 1988).
Walker, Beverly. "Huston & Co." *Film Comment* (Sept.–Oct., 1987).

Index

Numbers in **boldface** refer to pages with photographs.